ANALYSIS OF ARITHMETIC
FOR MATHEMATICS TEACHING

ANALYSIS OF ARITHMETIC FOR MATHEMATICS TEACHING

Edited by

Gaea Leinhardt
University of Pittsburgh

Ralph Putnam
Michigan State University

Rosemary A. Hattrup
University of Pittsburgh

LEA LAWRENCE ERLBAUM ASSOCIATES, PUBLISHERS
1992   Hillsdale, New Jersey   Hove and London

Lawrence Erlbaum Associates, Inc., Publishers
365 Broadway
Hillsdale, New Jersey 07642

Library of Congress Cataloging-in-Publication Data

Analysis of arithmetic for mathematics teaching / edited by Gaea
    Leinhardt, Ralph Putnam, Rosemary A. Hattrup.
        p. cm.
    Includes bibliographical references and index.
    ISBN 0-8058-0929-5
    1. Arithmetic—Study and teaching. I. Leinhardt, Gaea.
    II. Putnam, Ralph. III. Hattrup, Rosemary A.
    QA135.5.A54 1992
513'.07—dc20   91-13053
                                                        CIP

Printed in the United States of America
10 9 8 7 6 5 4 3 2 1

CONTENTS

7   FROM PROTOQUANTITIES TO OPERATORS:
     BUILDING MATHEMATICAL COMPETENCE ON A
     FOUNDATION OF EVERYDAY KNOWLEDGE   373
     Lauren B. Resnick

Acknowledgments

This enterprise between a research institute and a teaching organization was a social and intellectual experiment. One result of the experiment is this volume; the other result is a set of volumes authored principally by the teachers who participated in the 3-year effort (*Thinking Mathematics, Volume 1: Foundations, Thinking Mathematics, Volume 1T: Training Modules, Thinking Mathematics, Volume 2: Extensions,* and *Thinking Mathematics, Volume 2T: Training Modules,* Bodenhausen et al., in preparation). Because of the experimental nature of the effort, more people and agencies than usual were involved, and the demands on the reviewers, teachers, researchers, and publishers were heavier than normal.

The editors wish to acknowledge the patience, insights, and good humor of all the authors who contributed to this volume. Several of them had to wait a very long time to see their text in print. We wish to acknowledge the tremendous and very important help of the reviewers of specific chapters: Merlyn Behr, Michael Cole, Vicky Kouba, Stellan Ohlsson, and John P. Smith, III. Their thoughtful comments enhanced the quality of the final product.

The combined teams of teachers that read, interpreted, and critiqued each chapter were also a very important and vocal audience that have influenced the shape of this document: Louise Eggert, Angela Silva, and Carole Tuccy, 1988 Visiting Practitioners; and Nancy Denhart, Judy Bodenhausen, Alice Gill, Meg Kaduce, and Marcy Miller, 1989/1990/1991 Visiting Practitioners. We wish to especially thank Judy Bodenhausen for her careful reading of the chapter by Pearla Nesher.

In addition to the editors who helped assemble this volume, many researchers were present during the summer workshops and contributed much to the effort. Two of the most significant are Barbara Grover and William Bickel, both of whom carried major burdens of the social and intellectual experiment part of this enterprise. Other members of our research community also played important roles. Among these we wish to thank Lauren Resnick, Ed Silver, and Orit Zaslavsky, who reviewed and commented on the chapters with great care and led as well as participated in discussions around the research with the Visiting Practitioners. Gina Beavers, Peg Emmerling, Joyce Fienberg, Sister Madeliene Gregg, Susan Honacki, Diana Jeske, Leda Mance, Judith McQuaide, Swapna Mukhopadhyay, Elizabeth Odoroff, and Kate Stainton were central members of the support team that facilitated the work of all.

We want to thank the American Federation of Teachers, especially Lovely Billups and Marilyn Rauth, for without their leadership this collaboration would not have occurred. We also wish to acknowledge the University of Pittsburgh and the Learning Research and Development Center, which provided not only the concrete home where many of these chapters were worked on, but also the intellectual environment that permitted and encouraged the occurrence of activities that enabled this volume. Finally, the editors thank the National Science Foundation for having the vision and faith to believe that real dialogue between teachers and researchers was desirable and achievable and supporting the workshops, the reviewers, and the authors through grant number TPE-8751494.

REFERENCES

Bodenhausen, J., Denhart, N., Gill, A., Kaduce, M., Miller, M., Grover, B., Resnick, L., Leinhardt, G., Bill, V., Rauth, M., & Billups, L. (in preparation). *Thinking mathematics: Vol. 1. Foundations.* Washington, DC: American Federation of Teachers.

Bodenhausen, J., Denhart, N., Gill, A., Kaduce, M., Miller, M., Grover, B., Hojnacki, S., Resnick, L., Leinhardt, G., Bill, V., & Billups, L. (in preparation). *Thinking mathematics: Vol. 2. Extensions.* Washington, DC: American Federation of Teachers.

PREFACE

This book emerges from a partnership between a teaching organization (American Federation of Teachers) and a research institute (Learning Research and Development Center at the University of Pittsburgh) and represents another step in taking mathematics research through the door of the classroom and taking classroom experience through the door of academe. This partnership has brought researchers together with expert teachers for intensive dialogue sessions focusing on what is known in each community about effective mathematical learning and instruction. The dialogue has been predicated on the belief that both the research and teaching communities bring critically important perspectives to thinking about mathematics learning and instruction and that special attention needs to be paid to increasing communication between and within these communities if teaching is to be informed by current research. This book represents one side of an attempt to openly share our dialogue with the research and teaching communities. A second side is represented in another product of the partnership, *Thinking Mathematics*—a synthesis of the central ideas of this mathematics research written by teachers for teachers.

Analysis of Arithmetic for Mathematics Teaching is intended to serve as a tool for researchers, particularly educational researchers who are interested in research advances in subject matters directly connected to schooling and cognitive scientists who are interested in a broad but embedded view of school subjects. The syntheses presented in this volume represent current research that will be of use to researchers who have an interest in both classroom learning and instruction. It is our hope that the chapters in this book will also be used by teachers and teacher educators who, like the teachers of this partnership, are willing to explore the research base upon which many of the current recommendations for restructuring mathematics education are being made. This book is not intended to be used as a "How to Teach" handbook, but it will no doubt be useful for elementary, middle school, and perhaps even high school teachers who are interested in modifying and improving their teaching and expanding their knowledge base.

It is important to understand that it was never our intent to "water down" the research for the teaching community; such a version would not enable teachers to develop the tools needed to be critical thinkers in the classroom. Thus, this book does not tell a simple story. Rather, it serves as a "language book" for teachers as well as researchers; it provides a strong knowledge base of the mathematics that elementary school teachers teach—addition and subtraction, multiplication and division, fractions, and decimals—of how it is taught and learned, and of the kinds of understandings and misunderstandings students encounter as they learn mathematics. The list of topics under investigation is not exhaustive, nor is it meant to be. The book expands on the themes that are embedded in the curriculum standards established by the National Council of Teachers of Mathematics and current restructuring reform agendas that address the need for a change in the mathematics curriculum; teaching practices; and the knowledge and beliefs held by teachers, other school personnel, and the general public.

One goal of the partnership was to synthesize recent research on mathematical learning and instruction. The early drafts of the chapters presented in this volume served as a part of the initial basis for the collaborative dialogue between teachers and researchers and the intellectual development of *Thinking Mathematics.* In many cases, the chapter authors discussed their papers with the teachers in person. This interaction provided the opportunity for teachers to give feedback to the chapter authors on the relevance of their research syntheses for classroom practice and for the chapter authors to have a voice in the nature of the educational materials being developed by the teachers. Thus, the chapters that appear in this volume have been informed by the authors' interactions with teachers working with the research constructs they consider.

A second goal of this partnership was the transformation of the body of knowledge contained in this volume into materials useful for disseminating these understandings to the professional teaching community. *Thinking Mathematics,* authored by several of the teachers in our partnership, represents a major part of this transformation. These materials will be disseminated through the AFT's Educational Research & Dissemination (ER&D) Program and will support continuing interaction between the research and teaching communities. In transforming this body of knowledge, the teachers came to own the research—they tested the research ideas, accepted some ideas and rejected others, and customized many of the ideas to their own classroom needs. It is our hope that other teachers and teacher educators who come into contact with this research will take on the same challenge of transforming and integrating the research in classroom lessons.

The chapters that follow deal either with the research on and conceptual analysis of specific arithmetic topics, namely addition and subtraction, multiplication, division, decimals, and fractions, or with overarching themes that pervade the early curriculum and constitute the links with the more advanced topics of mathematics, specifically intuition and number sense and estimation. Serving as a link between the communities of cognitive researchers and mathematics educators, the book capitalizes on the recent research successes of cognitive science and reviews the literature of the math education community as well. Three of the chapters constitute comprehensive reviews of large bodies of work, namely Karen C. Fuson's chapter on addition and subtraction, Judith Sowder's chapter on estimation, and Thomas Kieren's chapter on fractions. The chapters by James Hiebert and Magdalene Lampert deal with more personal expositions surrounding the topics of decimals and multiplication, respectively. Pearla Nesher, on the other hand, presents a broad analysis of approaches surrounding multiplication word problems. Lauren Resnick connects to these discussions by reviewing ways her research suggests to capture and extend mathematical intuitions in the classroom.

The book opens with a chapter by Sowder promoting number sense as a way of thinking that should encompass all number learning. She examines the many dimensions of number sense and the ways in which number sense is developed and is exhibited. She then examines current textbook series in light of these dimensions.

Next, Fuson summarizes the current research that is relevant to the learning and teaching of addition and subtraction of whole numbers. Focusing on both research in children's thinking and research on instruction, she begins with a discussion of very simple addition and subtraction as comprehended by preschool children and gradually moves on to more difficult problems contained within the elementary school mathematics curriculum.

Moving into the middle grade mathematics curriculum, Nesher examines a variety of aspects involved in solving multiplication word problems —a process that is more than a simple translation from one language into another. She details three approaches for explaining multiplicative word problems: the implicit model, dimensional analysis, and propositional analysis.

Lampert's chapter examines the important connections between the concepts involved in long division and proportional reasoning and how those ideas are related to the broader concept of multiplicative structures. She provides descriptions of several lessons as a means of demonstrating the type of teaching that might go on in a school classroom to engage students in understanding long division, including the development of discourse in the classroom and the use of everyday school math as occasions for deep mathematical thinking.

Hiebert advocates a shift in current thinking on decimal instruction: Teachers should move from developing symbol manipulation proficiency with decimals and move toward competency with all facets of decimal use and thought. He examines three sites where students experience difficulty with decimals: connecting individual with meaningful referents, connecting rules with actions on referents, and connecting answers with real-world solutions.

Kieren examines the various aspects involved in the knowledge of fractions, particularly the complexity of fractional number concepts and their potential meaning for children. He provides a model of an idealized structure for rational number knowledge and an intuitive model of the process of knowing fractional or rational numbers. Kieren urges that teachers and students go beyond focusing on fractions as part of a whole through experiences with other subconstructs, namely measure, ratio, operator and quotient.

Resnick closes the loop by inviting us to consider a paradox: Mathematical knowledge and arithmetic performance are documented among the "unschooled," while mathematical understanding and arithmetical performance frequently are absent among school students. Resnick then spins out a discussion of how a series of case level anecdotes suggest a way of connecting what students know and understand intuitively about mathematics to what schools hope they will learn. She supports this position with the detailed report of its success with one teacher who has become a teacher educator as well.

Taken together, these chapters are designed to provide a sketch of the depth and the richness of current knowledge of mature mathematics. They are also designed to contribute in a deeper way to the grounding and vision expressed by the recent mathematical reforms in curriculum, teaching, and assessment.

Marilyn Rauth and Lovely Billups of the AFT close the book by highlighting what has been learned by the practitioners who have collaborated with researchers as a result of the partnership between the LRDC and the AFT, and the implications these lessons have for future collaborative efforts between researchers and practitioners. Additionally, they comment on the role teacher professionalism can play in efforts to reform mathematics teaching.

Gaea Leinhardt[1]
Ralph Putnam
Rosemary A. Hattrup

---

[1]The book was completed while the senior editor was a Spencer fellow at the Center for Advanced Studies in the Behavioral Sciences, Stanford, CA.

1

MAKING SENSE OF NUMBERS
IN SCHOOL MATHEMATICS

Judith T. Sowder
San Diego State University

Contents

NUMBER SENSE AND ITS COMPONENTS

The *Curriculum and Evaluation Standards for School Mathematics* (National Council of Teachers of Mathematics, 1989) is a response to the call for reform of school mathematics. The curriculum standards attempt to provide a guide to what mathematics students need to know. The *Standards* has been well received by the education, scientific, and business communities, and has already begun to influence school curricula at the local and state levels and text planning by all major publishers of school mathematics texts.

1

This preamble on the *Standards* is intended to show that its recommendations are being taken quite seriously by the people who decide what is included in school curricula at the state and local levels. Among its recommendations are that the K–4 curriculum should include whole number concepts and skills so that children can develop number sense, and that the 5–8 curriculum should include continued development of number and number relationships so that students can develop number sense for whole numbers, fractions, decimals, integers, and rational numbers. The conscious integration of number sense into the elementary school mathematics curriculum is quite a recent phenomenon. I say conscious, because I believe insightful teachers of mathematics have always taught in a manner that encourages the development of number sense, even though they may not consciously have had number sense as an instructional goal. "Instruction that promotes number sense is no doubt the same kind of instruction that promotes meaningful mathematics learning across the board" (Hiebert, 1989, p. 83). As I show later in this chapter, some text series, through the philosophy of teaching mathematics that they impart to teachers, are likely to lead students to develop better number sense than other texts, even though it is not yet possible to find number sense specifically addressed in the texts' program descriptions, lists of objectives, or scope-and-sequence charts. A text program's philosophy can be discerned through the manner and extent to which it focuses on conceptual development and encourages teachers to discuss and explore diverse problems, and through the types of exercises it provides for students.

As textbook companies take upon themselves the responsibility consciously to include number sense in their respective curricula, there is concern on the part of many (see Sowder & Schappelle, 1989) that number sense will be treated in a piecemeal fashion, with activities designed to promote number sense strategically placed on student pages and listed in scope-and-sequence charts, rather than promoted as a way of thinking about numbers that should encompass all of number learning. Textbooks cannot teach number sense, even though they can help the teacher to do so through many reminders and examples.

> Number sense . . . develops gradually as a result of exploring numbers, visualizing them in a variety of contexts, and relating them in ways that are not limited by traditional algorithms. [T]extbooks . . . can only suggest ideas to be investigated, they cannot replace the "doing of mathematics" that is essential for the development of number sense. No substitute exists for a skillful teacher and an environment that fosters curiosity and exploration at all grade levels. (Howden, 1989, p. 11)

The purpose of this chapter is to attempt to clarify the many dimensions of number sense, and to examine the ways in which number sense develops and is exhibited. In this first section, I explore four curricular topics that are closely related to number sense: numeration, number magnitude, mental computation, and computational estimation. Understanding our numeration system, according to the *Standards,* requires relating counting, grouping, and place value. Understanding of number magnitude, exhibited by the ability to order and compare numbers, is a defining characteristic of number sense. Acquiring skill at mental computation and computational estimation calls on number sense and at the same time provides opportunities for expanding one's number sense. Acquisition of skills with these alternate types of computation is also a focus of the K–4 and 5–8 *Standards.* Sowder and Markovits (1991) argued that instruction in each of the four areas, when the approach used is one that encourages discussion and exploration of alternative strategies, will help students develop number sense. Certainly, proficiency within these four skill areas is indicative of the possession of a high-degree of number sense. Although these four areas of mathematical learning are admittedly interrelated, it should be noted that all have distinct and unique characteristics that justify their treatment as curriculum topics and arenas for research apart from number sense (R. Reys, 1989).

In this section, I also examine some other areas of learning that should be addressed when considering the role of instruction in developing number sense. Finally, I briefly describe some current, innovative programs where number sense happily appears to be a byproduct of the instruction. Against this backdrop, the second section contains a survey of two current elementary mathematics textbook programs and contrasts their approaches to the topics discussed in the first part of the chapter. To provide perspective to the discussion of these programs, the approaches taken by an older, out-of-print-series, and by the state-mandated Soviet elementary school mathematics programs also are considered.

Dimensions of Number Sense

Attempting to define number sense is in many ways analogous to attempting to define problem solving. We have not reached consensus on a definition of problem solving, although most teachers and scholars believe they have an understanding of what problem solving encompasses. This lack of a uniformly accepted definition has not dampened enthusiasm for teaching or for studying problem solving. Another way that number sense is like problem solving is that both represent a certain way of thinking rather than a body of knowledge that can be transmitted to others. Trafton (conference notes, in Sowder & Schappelle, 1989) spoke of number sense as something that "unfolds" rather than something that is taught "directly."

Resnick (conference notes, in Sowder & Schappelle, 1989) has suggested that perhaps we need a different type of definition for number sense, more like Rosch's (1973) idea of central prototypes that one carries around and uses to judge particular cases as being closer to or farther away from the prototype. One way to begin to formulate a central prototype, or an understanding of the various dimensions of number sense, is to consider the attempts of others to define and characterize number sense. The *Standards* (NCTM, 1989) claims that "children with good number sense (1) have well-understood number meanings, (2) have developed multiple relationships among numbers, (3) recognize the relative magnitudes of numbers, (4) know the relative effect of operating on numbers, and (5) develop referents for measures of common objects and situations in their environment" (p. 38). Many of these same components appear in a characterization of number sense that I have frequently used: Number sense (a) is a well-organized conceptual network that enables a person to relate number and operation properties; (b) can be recognized in the ability to use number magnitude, relative and absolute, to make qualitative and quantitative judgments necessary for (but not restricted to) number comparison, the recognition of unreasonable results for calculations, and the use of nonstandard algorithmic forms for mental computation and estimation; (c) can be demonstrated by flexible and creative ways to solve problems involving numbers; and (d) is neither easily taught nor easily measured. This characterization hints at some assessable aspects of number sense while at the same time indicating that any assessment items we might develop could never fully measure number sense.

From these attempts to define numbers sense, and from the characteristics of number sense noted by others (Behr, 1989; Greeno, 1989; Hiebert, 1989; Howden, 1989; Markovits, 1989; Resnick, 1989a; Silver, 1989; Trafton, 1989), it is possible to compile a list of behaviors that demonstrate some presence of number sense. These behaviors are, admittedly, not without some overlap.

1. Ability to compose and decompose numbers; to move flexibly among different representations; to recognize when one representation is more useful than another. Examples would include the case of a second grader noting that sharing 24¢ among four children is easy if 24¢ is thought of as four nickels and four pennies, or the sixth grader thinking of 25 as 100/4 before mentally multiplying 12×25. The ability to decompose and recompose numbers is closely related to understanding place value concepts because most compositions and decompositions are place value related,

such as when thinking of 53 as four tens and 13 ones in order to subtract 28 from 53.

2. Ability to recognize the relative magnitude of numbers. This includes the abilities both to compare and to order numbers, such as recognizing that 89 is smaller than 91, and that $\frac{1}{3}$ is larger than $\frac{1}{4}$ which in turn is larger than $\frac{1}{8}$; the ability to understand and use the density property of rational numbers (without the terminology), such as in finding a number between $\frac{1}{3}$ and $\frac{1}{4}$; and the ability to compare differences relatively, such as in noting that the difference between 3 and 5 and the difference between 123 and 125 are absolutely the same but relatively very different.

3. Ability to deal with the absolute magnitude of numbers; for example, to realize that I cannot hold 200 pennies in my hand at one time, or that 1 million people cannot attend a rock concert.

4. Ability to use benchmarks. For example, using 1 as a benchmark, the sum of $\frac{7}{8}$ and $\frac{9}{10}$ should be a little under 2, because each fraction is a little under 1. Resnick (1989a) rephrased this as using well-known number facts to figure out facts of which one is not so sure.

5. Ability to link numeration, operation, and relation symbols in meaningful ways. Hiebert (1989) noted that written symbols function both as records of things already known and as tools for thinking, and that number sense requires symbols to function in both ways. Symbols that act as records can produce anchors of reasonableness that can then be used to monitor actions on symbols. Trafton (1989) made a distinction between manipulation of quantities and the manipulation of symbols. Children with number sense often think of symbols as quantities, as shown in their use of expressions such as "knocking off" and "tacking a little on here." He gave as an example a boy asked to find $6.00 − $2.85 mentally: "If you take away the two dollars, that only leaves four dollars, and you knock off eighty-five cents, and that leaves $3.15" (p. 16). Similarly, Greeno (1989) noted that operations on quantities have counterparts in operations on numbers.

6. Understanding the effects of operations on numbers. Behr (1989) noted two aspects of this characteristic: (a) Recognizing how to compensate (if necessary) when one or more operands are changed in a computational problem; for example, if 348 − 289 is 59, then what is 358 − 289? (b) Recognizing when a result of a computation remains the same after changing the original numbers operated upon; for example, how can knowing 350 − 291 = 59 be used to find 348 − 289?

7. The ability to perform mental computation through "invented" strategies that take advantage of numerical and operational properties. A student faced with finding 1,000 − 784 might try counting up, 16 to 800, 200 more to 1,000, making the problem much easier than it would be if the

student attempted to mentally apply the standard paper-and-pencil algorithm.

8. Being able to use numbers flexibly to estimate numerical answers to computations, and to recognize when an estimate is appropriate. The level of resolution with which estimation can be performed will vary with age. Young children may only be able to say whether the sum of two-digit numbers is more than or less than 100. An older student may be able to estimate the sum of four six-digit numbers to different levels of accuracy, depending on how the estimate is going to be used. The student who estimates $1,487 \div 33$ by changing the problem to $1,400 \div 35$ because 7 divides both 1,400 and 35 is demonstrating flexibility with numbers.

9. A disposition toward making sense of numbers. Students must believe that mathematics makes sense and that they are capable of finding sense in numerical activity. This disposition will lead the individual to make judgments concerning the reasonableness of answers.

There are some caveats to be made. First, we cannot always accept the exhibition of one of these characteristics as evidence of number sense. A student who has been taught a rule of always using an adding-on procedure for mental subtraction and who has been given ample opportunity to practice that procedure does not show real flexibility of thought when finding $1,000 - 784$ by adding on. Second, there are levels of number sense, and there is always the potential for number sense to expand to reflect new experiences (B. Reys, 1989). Third, number sense is dependent on the number system within which one is working. It is possible to have good number sense for whole numbers, but not for fractions, for example.

Rather than discussing each of these nine areas separately, the first eight will be subsumed under the four major headings of numeration, number magnitude, mental computation, and computational estimation, in order to discuss the available research on these topics more easily. The abilities listed in (1), namely composing and decomposing numbers, moving flexibly among representations, recognizing when one representation is more useful than others, play roles in all four areas discussed here. Relative and absolute magnitudes of numbers (2 and 3) and the use of benchmarks (4) are discussed in the section on number magnitude. Linking numeration and operation symbols (5) and understanding the effects of operations on numbers (6) play critical roles in numeration, mental computation, and computational estimation. Using invented strategies to compute mentally (7) is discussed in the section on mental computation, whereas estimation (8) is also addressed in its own section. A disposition toward making sense of numbers (9) is discussed in the section on "Related Issues."

Numeration

An understanding of the many aspects and uses of numbers, particularly those related to cardinal and ordinal meanings and to the notion of place value, is fundamental to the acquisition of number sense. An immature and partial understanding of place value, together with the concomitant violation of place-value conventions, accounts for the majority of errors on whole number computation using standard algorithms (Ashlock, 1982).

Children enter school with informal knowledge of counting and of how cardinal numbers are associated with the counting of sets (Fuson & Hall, 1983; Gelman & Gallistel, 1978; Ginsburg, 1977). The extent of this knowledge varies with the cultural (Case & Griffin, 1990) and socioeconomic (Fuson & Hall, 1983) backgrounds of children. In cultures or families that value quantification, children pay more attention to numbers and acquire counting skills earlier than in families without these values (Resnick, 1989b). Children entering school can also apply number knowledge to solving simple addition and subtraction problems for small numbers presented contextually as "word" problems (Carpenter & Moser, 1984; Riley, Greeno, & Heller, 1983). The research by Carpenter and Moser (1984) and Riley et al. (1983) provides a framework to explain how understanding of addition and subtraction develop, in terms of the sequence of types of problems accessible to children (e.g., join problems are easier than missing addend problems) and in terms of strategies used (e.g., from counting all to counting on). (Research on early number learning is covered in some depth in Fuson, chapter 2, this volume, and so the treatment here is very brief.)

The development of place-value understanding has not been subjected to the same scrutiny as the development of early number concepts. Even so, the theory and research that do exist indicate that more classroom attention needs to be given to place value than is now common in this country. Place value can be viewed as an elaboration of the part–whole schema that allows children to think of numbers as compositions of other numbers (Resnick, 1983). The composition of numbers into ones and tens (and later into hundreds, thousands, etc.) is a special case of grouping numbers, and is subject to regrouping, particularly when performing number operations. Resnick identified three stages in the development of base-ten knowledge. In the first stage, children can uniquely partition numbers into units and tens. Children at this stage should be successful on such tasks as identifying 47 as 4 tens and 7 ones, quickly adding or subtracting ten from quantities, counting up and down by tens, associating numbers (through three digits) with displays such as with Dienes blocks or money, comparing numbers on a left-to-right basis, and eventually adding and subtracting two-digit numbers mentally by counting by tens and then by units (e.g., 24 + 33 is 34, 44, 54; 55, 56, 57).

In the second stage, children can partition numbers into noncanonical representations; that is, 34 can be partitioned into 2 tens and 14 ones rather than 3 tens and 4 ones. They understand that their different partitionings can be equivalent and that there can be more than nine units or tens (or hundreds, etc.). The partitioning in Resnick's (1983) description is dependent on a concrete representation, such as Dienes blocks, in which a ten-for-one trade can be physically undertaken. This partitioning ability becomes semantically linked to written algorithms in the third stage. There is extensive evidence (e.g., Brown & Burton, 1978; Resnick, 1989b; Wearne & Hiebert, 1988a) that many children never make this link and therefore do not reach the third stage.

In order to evaluate understanding of place value and to guide curriculum design, Bednarz and Janvier (1982) undertook an extensive analysis of numeration. They listed several "basic skills" involved: making and unmaking groupings; making groupings of groupings; exchanging one grouping of given order for a unit of higher order and vice versa; coding, that is, moving from a collection reorganized in groupings to the representations of the numbers; decoding; discovering the rules for grouping. These basic skills can be combined into more complex skills. The basic skills, the processes involved in combining them, and the appropriate forms of representation together all characterize numeration. Although many of the basic skills were included in Resnick's (1983) Stage 1 tasks, this list begins at an earlier level because making and unmaking groupings is not place-value dependent. Rather, these skills belong in the class of decomposing and recomposing of numbers without regard to place value (e.g., three fours can be regrouped as six twos).

Bednarz and Janvier (1982) designed several tasks to assess the place-value understanding of children in Grades 1, 3, and 4. In one task, given to third and fourth graders, children were given six cards each with one digit, 0 through 5. They were asked to line up the cards to make the biggest numbers they could; 63% of third graders and 84% of fourth graders were successful. Common errors included placing the digits in random order, using only four digits (because they had not yet studied numbers with more than four digits), eliminating the zero, and placing only the first digits correctly. In another item, the students were given 20 cards, randomly mixed, containing the phrases: 0 ones, 1 one, 2 ones, 3 ones, 4 ones, 5 ones, 10 ones, 11 ones, 12 ones, 3 tens, 4 tens, 5 tens, 40 tens, 41 tens, 42 tens, 43 tens, 45 tens, 51 tens, 3 hundreds, and 5 hundreds. Students were told that the interviewer was thinking of a number between 402 and 513. They were to guess the number and represent it with the cards. The interviewer then told the student if the secret number was more than or less than the represented number, and the game continued. Only 27% of the third graders and 44% of the fourth graders used the cards meaningfully. The problem was very difficult for most children. They would, for example, try to form 445 by taking 4 tens and 5 ones, then search for 4 hundreds and sometimes be unable to proceed without changing their strategies to inappropriate ones such as ignoring the words (ones, tens, hundreds) or ignoring the groupings (e.g., expressing 4,405 as 4 ones, 40 tens, 5 hundreds). Other tasks revealed similar difficulties and misunderstandings. The authors concluded that children "attribute a meaning to hundreds, tens, and ones more in terms of order than in terms of groupings" (p. 53), probably because texts usually represent numbers in this fashion, that is, for example, with the hundreds flats on the left, the tens longs in the middle, the units on the right. They found, as others have, that the concept of borrowing is associated with "crossing out a digit, taking away one, and adjoining one to the next digit"; that is, it is not linked to the idea of exchanging or trading. They also concluded that children have difficulty conceptualizing numbers as entities. Rather, they think of numbers as symbols side by side.

Other studies indicate that children's understandings related to place value continue to be poor as they progress through the grades. This is not too surprising because there is little or no formal instruction on place value in the upper grades beyond naming large numbers, and because children who have already disassociated algorithms and place-value understandings are unlikely to discover this link on their own. In a large-scale British study of 11- to 16-year-olds' understanding of mathematics (Hart, 1981), one component focused on place value and decimals (Brown, 1981). In one task, students were told that a counter at a football turnstyle read 6,399, and were asked what it would read when one more person entered. Only 68% of 12-year-olds could do this problem, with performance increasing to 88% for 15-year-olds. In the same study, success rates progressed from 42% to 57% (ages 12–15 years) on writing four hundred thousand seventy-three in numerals, and from 22% to 43% on telling what the 2 stood for in 521,400.

In some recent data I collected, I gave a meter problem similar to the one used by Brown (1981) to two classes each of fourth, fifth, and sixth graders. Students were required to add one to 47,399. Correct responses ranged from 56% to 80% over the three grade levels. Common incorrect responses were 47,000, 48,400, and 147,399. In a second problem I asked students how many ten-dollar bills could be obtained for $378. Only 26% of fourth graders to 53% of sixth graders could answer this question correctly. Results were even worse, 2%, 6%, and 9% respectively, on a problem requiring students to tell how many boxes of 100 candy bars could be packed from 48,638 candy bars. Incorrect answers were scattered over a wide range of numbers, with no answer gaining more than 11% of the responses.

Yet all of the teachers with whom place value was discussed (four of the seven) said that they thought their students had a fairly good understanding of place value. (The remaining three were not asked.) This belief was probably based on performance on text exercises on place value where students were required to identify the digit in the tens place, in the thousands place, and so on.

In interviews with 20 of these fourth graders, we asked the students how many boxes were needed for 120 bars of soap if 10 bars would fit in one box. Of the 13 who were successful, the most commonly used strategy was to count by tens and keep track of the count. Only two used a number decomposition strategy: "Ten tens in 100, then two more tens." Some had to be prompted by reducing the 120 to 50 and asking students to solve that problem first.

Typically, the present curriculum develops little meaning for place value beyond what is required to read and write numbers, identify the place value of the digits that appear in a number (e.g., there are five tens in 356), and expand numbers (e.g., 356 is 3 hundreds + 5 tens + 5 ones). A small amount of regrouping is thought to be necessary (e.g., trading one ten for ten ones) for learning the algorithms for operations. Place value is considered as a prerequisite to operations rather than as something that develops simultaneously with calculation (Bednarz & Janvier, 1988). But a deeper understanding is needed for the type of flexibility we associate with number sense. Rubenstein (1985) found that the ability to multiply and divide by powers of ten was fundamental to skill in estimation. An understanding of place value that allows an individual to add one to 34,799, to add 400 to 700,300, or to decompose 5,208 into 2,508 + 2,500 + 200 in order to mentally subtract 2,508, does not seem to be too much to ask of a curriculum that intends to develop number sense. These types of problems need to be explored and practiced in school if students are to develop the ability to apply place-value knowledge to obtain solutions to the tasks described in this section.

Number Magnitude

Relative Magnitude. The abilities to compare and order whole numbers and decimal numbers, when these abilities are based on a semantic understanding of the numbers and relations involved, are closely related to the understanding of place value. Few texts, however, devote much space to this topic.

Students appear to be able to develop their own algorithm for comparing whole numbers: First compare the number of digits; if one has more digits it is larger; if the number of digits is the same, begin at the left and compare the numbers digit by digit until a larger digit is found. This algorithm had not been formally taught to students in a study by Sowder and Wheeler (1987), yet most eventually learned it. Second graders had difficulty comparing 400 with 368, or choosing which of 24 and 112 was closer to 87, but this algorithm was successfully applied to comparison of multidigit numbers by fourth graders. Identifying which multidigit number is closer to a third was more difficult for these students. Only 64% of fourth graders, for example, could tell whether 43,724,189 was closer to 43,624,189 or to 43,724,389, although they had been introduced to numbers of this magnitude.

When students do not have a good understanding of place value and its extension to decimal numbers, one error they tend to make is to treat the decimal portion of the number separately from the whole number portion, as when they round 148.26 to 150.3 (Threadgill-Sowder, 1984). Another example of this type of error can be found among students who say that 3.53 is larger than 3.7 because 53 is larger than 7 (Sackur-Grisvard & Leonard, 1985). Similarly, when there are no whole parts associated with the decimal numbers, students treat the decimal parts as though they were whole numbers. Almost half of the sixth and seventh graders interviewed by Hiebert and Wearne (1986) selected .1814 as the largest of .09, .385, .3, and .1814, using a generalization of the "more digits makes bigger" rule. Hiebert and Wearne noted that these students did not distinguish between the conceptual features of whole numbers that can be generalized to decimal numbers, and the syntactic features that cannot. According to Resnick (1987a), these students treat the decimal portions of the numbers as if they were integers. This procedure sometimes yields the correct answer, as when students select 3.683 as larger than 3.53.

On the other hand, students who select 3.683 as larger than 3.7 because "thousandths are larger than tenths" (Sackur-Grisvard & Leonard, 1985) confuse the fractional sizes of the decimal portions. But they too are sometimes correct with this rule, as when they select 3.683 as larger than 3.53. Children who make this error "base their judgments of the relative sizes of numbers entirely on the number and value of the places in the decimal, paying limited or no attention to the digits in these places" (Resnick, 1987a, p. 33). According to Resnick's analysis, children who consistently make this error have a more sophisticated understanding of decimal numbers than children who make the first type of error. In the first case, students are using only whole number knowledge, whereas in the second case, they appear to understand that place value plays a role in the decision making, but they cannot yet coordinate digits and column values.

Some students correct these errors as they gain more experience with decimal numbers. In a study by Sowder and Wheeler (1987), for example, success rates on choosing the larger of .00043 and .0011 increased from 13% to 53% to 95% for students in Grades 6, 8, and 10 respectively.

Instruction that focuses on the place-value interpretation of decimal numbers can be quite successful, if judged by the resulting ability of students to compare and order decimal numbers. Students completing a teaching sequence focusing on semantically based processes for working with decimal fraction symbols (Wearne & Hiebert, 1988b) could choose the larger of two decimal numbers using semantic rather than syntactic processes. In a study I conducted with a colleague (Sowder & Markovits, 1989), students received conceptually based instruction on comparing decimal numbers. Interviews with these students several weeks later showed that they could successfully compare numbers and give semantically reasoned explanations for their comparisons.

Because the ability to find equivalent fractions is necessary for adding and subtracting fractions, this topic receives a substantial amount of instructional attention in elementary school. The ability to compare fractions is considered less useful, and consequently attention to its development is frequently overlooked. When it is attended to, students usually are told to find a common denominator, form equivalent fractions, and compare numerators. Although this algorithm is correct, powerful, and fairly straightforward in its application, it does little to enhance students' fraction number sense. Evidence suggests that the algorithm is often put aside while students attend to the more salient features of the problem, the numerators and/or the denominators of the fractions to be compared. Students often compare numerators if the denominators are equal, and denominators if the numerators are equal (Behr, Wachsmuth, Post, & Lesh, 1984; Sowder & Markovits, 1989; Sowder & Wheeler, 1987). Clearly, their ordering of fractions is dominated by knowledge about ordering whole numbers. Students also frequently misapply the part–whole notion of fractions that dominates instruction on fractional numbers. For example, students will claim that $\frac{2}{3}$ and $\frac{3}{4}$ are equal because "there are the same number of pieces left over" (Peck & Jencks, 1981, p. 344). Students do get better at comparing fractions; success at identifying the larger of $\frac{5}{6}$ and $\frac{5}{9}$ increased from 10% to 19% to 37% to 95% for students in Grades 4, 6, 8, and 10 in the Sowder and Wheeler (1987) study, for example. Although the fact that Grade 10 students are successful may be good news, the low degree of understanding of fractions at the eighth-grade level is unacceptable considering the amount of time eighth graders have devoted to computation on fractional numbers.

Instruction focusing on linking fractions symbols' use to their intended meanings can be quite successful. Behr et al. (1984) had success with children in fourth grade, whereas Kerslake (1986) found that the use of a variety of instances of equivalence increased the ability of 13- and 14-year-olds to solve equivalence tasks. Presumably, a variety of instances also would help students solve nonequivalence tasks.

The Sowder and Markovits (1989) study also included an instructional unit on comparing fractions. After using drawings and manipulatives to formulate rules for comparing fractions with like numerators, then like denominators, students studied patterns and drawings to discover when fractions were close to 0, to $\frac{1}{2}$, and to 1, and whether they were greater or less than $\frac{1}{2}$ or 1. By the end of the instructional unit, students were able to successfully compare fractions with unlike numerators and unlike denominators, often by using benchmarks. The students appeared to have a much better intuitive notion of fractions after instruction than they had before instruction.

Acquiring a quantitative notion for fractions is essential to the development of rational number sense. Behr, Lesh, Post, and Silver (1983) considered this notion to underlie the ability "to order rational numbers, to internalize the concept of equivalent fractions, and to have a meaningful grasp of addition and multiplication of fractions" (p. 122).

Absolute Number Size. Very large numbers are usually introduced by Grade 4, but students have little understanding of what these numbers mean. Some teachers try to make large numbers meaningful. For example, a recent project in a school in Oakland (Johnson, 1989) was begun with the purpose of showing children how much a million is. Relating large numbers to the real world of the student is usually very difficult to do, however. In the Sowder and Wheeler (1987) study, children in Grades 4, 6, 8, and 10 were given several statements and follow-up questions for which they had to select one or more numbers that "made sense" as answers to the questions. On one such task, students were told that a newspaper headline said "Michael Jackson concert a sellout!" They were then asked how many people they thought went to the concert: 65; 300; 40,000; or 5,000,000. At least 35% of the fourth graders thought each response reasonable. Those who said that 40,000 was reasonable ranged from 38% at the fourth grade to 96% at Grade 10. However, many of these same students also thought 5,000,000 was reasonable. We (Sowder & Markovits, 1988) recently asked another group of sixth graders to answer this question during one-on-one interviews. Those who selected only 40,000 said that it made sense because that was about how many people could fit into Jack Murphy Stadium (our local stadium), or because there were not even 5 million people living in the city of San Diego. Other students gave reasons based on Michael Jackson's popularity (or drop in popularity, in one case), but they gave little indication that they understood the magnitude of these numbers.

It is unreasonable to expect children to make sense of large numbers if they are not provided with opportunities for making those numbers meaningful to them. There is evidence that even unschooled Brazilian children can deal with quite large numbers within the Brazilian currency system

(Saxe, 1988). Paulos (1988) has shown us some of the cultural consequences of a poor understanding of the size of numbers. His book *Innumeracy*, though written for adults, provides many examples of how to make
sense of very large and very small numbers.

Mental Computation

There is evidence that instruction on mental computation can lead to both
increased understanding of number and flexibility in working with numbers. In one study (Markovits & Sowder, 1988), fourth- and sixth-grade
students received almost daily instruction on mental computation. The
instruction always allowed for student discussion of varied strategies for
mental computation problems, and students were not presented with rules
other than ones they derived from studying patterns, such as when multiplying by 10. Before instruction, students had a strong inclination to perform the mental analogue of the paper-and-pencil procedure rather than
attempting nonstandard procedures (e.g., using a left-to-right approach to
add multidigit numbers mentally; counting up to solve a subtraction problem such as $65 - 48$: 2 to 50, 10 more to 60, then 5 more, so 17 in all;
recomposing numbers so that 28×4 could be thought of as $[30 - 2] \times 4$).
The use of the standard algorithms dropped from 73% before instruction to
35% following instruction, whereas selection of nonstandard, more efficient mental procedures increased from 8% to 51% over the same period of
time.

But schools are certainly not the only place where people acquire good
mental computation skills. In studies conducted with the Diola people of
the Ivory Coast (Ginsburg, Posner, & Russell, 1981; Petitto & Ginsburg,
1982), unschooled children who worked with their parents in the marketplace developed superior mental computation skills that showed deep
insight into the structure and properties of the whole number system.

Other evidence that skill at mental computation is closely related to an
understanding and flexible use of the structure of the whole number system has been found by studying unskilled and skilled mental calculators
among secondary students (Hope, 1987). Unskilled calculators ignored
even obvious number properties that would help them and depended
wholly on mentally reproducing the standard paper-and-pencil algorithms.
Skilled calculators, on the other hand, used a variety of strategies, worked
usually from left to right, and avoided "carrying" and other procedures with
high memory requirements. They used efficient and accurate procedures
and favored using multiple forms of distributivity and factoring to simplify
their work.

Mental computation can play an important role in developing number sense through explorations that force students to use numbers and number relations in novel ways that are likely to increase awareness of the structure of the number system. This is not, however, the focus of mental computation in most current texts. Rather, mental computation is viewed as doing problems very quickly in one's head, and instruction therefore tends toward drill using chain calculations (e.g., 4 + 15; − 9; × 2; × 3, − 15, ÷ 5 is 9) and on learning "tricks" such as those for multiplying by 9 or by 11. Although such skills are valuable and have a place in the curriculum, they should not be emphasized at the expense of instruction that could lead children to better number sense.

Computational Estimation

In 1976 the mathematics results from the First National Assessment of Educational Progress (NAEP) became available. The analysis of the results showed that students had very weak estimation skills and lacked "quantitative intuition" (Carpenter, Coburn, Reys, & Wilson, 1976). The results of the second NAEP reaffirmed this conclusion (Carpenter, Corbitt, Kepner, Lindquist, & Reys, 1980).

Interposed between these two reports, the landmark position paper of the National Council of Supervisors of Mathematics (1977) on basic skills included estimation and approximation among the 10 basic skill areas in need of development. Both the NAEP reports and the position paper sparked a great deal of interest in learning more about how children (and adults) estimate and how estimation skills develop. In order to acquire a better understanding of children's thinking while answering NAEP problems, I (Threadgill-Sowder, 1984) selected 12 representative NAEP or NAEP-like items and asked 26 sixth through ninth graders to work these problems individually. Because several NAEP items were multiple choice, those same choices (or similar choices) were given to students in the interview setting. Many correct answers were given for the wrong reasons, indicating that NAEP scores were probably somewhat inflated. For example, 62% of my students selected 1,500 as closest to 30.97 × 48.2, given other choices of 120 (4%), 1,200 (19%), and 150 (4%). Of that 62%, however, only 46% of the explanations were judged acceptable. An example of an unacceptable answer was "1,500. That's the biggest, and 30 × 48 has to be pretty big." Three of the 12 problems deserve mention here because the solutions provide a window on the rational number sense possessed by these children. In the first, students were asked to estimate the sum of 148.72 and 51.351. A full 35% of the students gave an estimate with a decimal portion in their answers, usually attached to 199 or 200: "200.071. Well, the sum of 72 and 37 is about 70 plus I added a one to the end, and the 148 and 51 is about 200" or "150.470. Because 148.72 is 100.70 and 51.351 is 50,400. Add these." These children appeared to believe that a decimal number was actually two numbers, to be treated separately. Children's adherence to their interpretations of school-taught rounding rules can be noted both here and in another problem where they were asked to estimate 789×0.52. Only 19% of the students used 0.5 or $\frac{1}{2}$ or 50% as an estimate for 0.52. The majority of students rounded 0.52 to 1 or to 0, 789 to 800, then gave estimates of either 800 or 0. Finally, in the item asking students to estimate $\frac{9}{31} + \frac{4}{9}$, no student saw these numbers as both close to $\frac{1}{3}$, or both less than $\frac{1}{2}$. The 19% who gave acceptable answers used a version of finding least common denominators: "It's $\frac{21}{31}$ because $\frac{4}{9} = \frac{12}{27}$. That's close to the denominator of 31, and 9 and 12 is 21." It was doubtful that these students had any fractional benchmarks that they could use to estimate operations on fractions.

This study, although it provided some insight into performance on NAEP-type items, did not provide information on the range of strategies students use to solve (or attempt to solve) estimation problems. A more comprehensive study of student performance on computational estimation was undertaken by Reys, Rybolt, Bestgen, and Wyatt (1982), who sought to identify and characterize the computational processes used in estimation by in-school students and out-of-school adults. Good estimators were identified as those scoring in the top 10% of each group of students in Grades 7–12 who completed a 55-item computational estimation test. Fifty-nine of these good estimators then were interviewed and asked to describe the strategies they used to estimate on a subset of the problems. Reys and his colleagues were able to identify three key processes. The first, called *reformulation* by the investigators, was a "process of altering numerical data to produce a more mentally manageable form" (p. 187), while leaving the structure of the problem intact. Rounding, truncating (e.g., using $6 + 8 + 4$ to estimate $632 + 879 + 453$), and using compatible numbers (e.g., $7,431 \div 58$ changed to $7,200 \div 60$) are all reformulation techniques. In the second process, called *translation,* the mathematical structure itself is changed to a more manageable form. For example, thinking of $78 + 82 + 77 + 79$ as about 4×80 changes the structure of the problem from one requiring addition to one requiring multiplication. The third process used by good estimators was *compensation.* Adjustments were made both during and after calculation to bring an estimate closer to the exact answer. It was particularly interesting to note that these students often ignored the rules they had been taught for rounding, but rounded instead to numbers more suitable for solving the problem presented. Less-skilled students feel bound to round in the manner in which they were taught (Sowder & Wheeler, 1989). Sometimes teachers, too, resist rounding that does not follow the rules. B. Reys (in Sowder & Schappelle, 1989) recalled an incident where one teacher was quite dismayed when another teacher rounded 26 to 25 in order to estimate the product of 26 and 37.

Poor estimators are limited to using only a rounding strategy and they rarely compensate (Sowder & Wheeler, 1989). Many students prefer to do the exact computation then round to find an estimate, and when they round before calculating, they appear to do so only because they feel they are expected to do so. This preference continues into the college level (Levine, 1982). Levine noted that this strategy did not "require the individual to sense any relationships or to have any 'number sense' to carry it out" (p. 358).

Estimation abilities of younger children have also been investigated. Baroody (1989) analyzed ways in which kindergarten children determine sums before they have these facts established in long-term memory. He based his study on a schema-knowledge view that mental addition tasks are actually estimation exercises for these children. As these children became more developmentally ready for addition, their strategies yielded more plausible answers. In another study with 5- to 9-year-olds, Dowker (1989) found that children frequently used appropriate strategies when problems were at or slightly above their level (levels were set according to performance on straight addition tasks), but not on more difficult problems. The experimenter hypothesized that tasks found to be too difficult demoralized the children and encouraged wild guessing.

There are certain conceptual understandings and skills that appear necessary for the acquisition of skill in computational estimation (Levine, 1982; Reys et al., 1982; Rubenstein, 1985; Sowder & Markovits, 1991). Good estimators have a good grasp of place-value and arithmetic properties; they have quantitative abilities and perform well on mental computation; they are able to compare numbers in terms of relative size and can sometimes use that ability to predict which of two problems will yield the greater answer. In summary, good estimators use a variety of strategies, demonstrating a deep understanding of numbers and of operations. They are flexible in their thinking and are disposed to make sense of numbers. In contrast, poor estimators seem tied to the algorithms they learned to perform with paper and pencil. They have only a vague notion of the nature and purpose of estimation and equate it with guessing (Sowder, in press).

Computational estimation is a complex skill involving two components, converting from exact to approximate numbers, then mentally computing with these numbers. Case and Sowder (1990) theorized that because these components are qualitatively different from one another, solving problems that require completing and coordinating the components is probably not possible for children under 11–12 years of age. In their study testing the application of Case's stage theory (Case, 1985) to the development of computational estimation ability, children from kindergarten through secondary school were asked to perform number size tasks (e.g., is 5 closer to 6 or to 9? [Grade K]); mental computation tasks (e.g., find 23 + 45 in your head [Grade 4]), and estimation tasks (e.g., estimate 1,886 + 2,491 + 2,970

[Grade 9]). Predictions formulated from Case's theory of cognitive growth were remarkably accurate. One extrapolation made by the authors is that educators should not to be in too much of a hurry to teach computational estimation, but rather should first focus on number size concepts, on mental computation skills, and on estimation-type problems that do not require the coordination of complex skills. A fourth grader who can tell whether 352 + 486 is less than or more than 1,000 might not be able to find an estimate of 352 + 486. In another study (Sowder & Wheeler, 1989) of development of computational estimation ability over a wide age range (Grades 3, 5, 7, and 9), a strong developmental trend was found in the willingness of students to accept the fact that there could be multiple processes for finding an estimate, each with a different answer; but there was reluctance (increasing with age) to accept more than one number as "the right answer." (This is not surprising, considering the cumulative effect over years of always looking for the right answer.) Students at all levels (more so at higher levels) preferred the process of finding estimates by computing-then-rounding rather than rounding-then-computing because they felt that the first way gave them a better chance of obtaining a correct answer. The use of rounding became more prevalent as children grew older. This, too, is probably a cumulative effect of school instruction and practice on rounding.

Not only are the results of this study of interest to teachers and curriculum developers, but so are the techniques used to measure understandings and preferences. Students usually were presented with cases showing the strategies and solutions of two (or more) hypothetical students, then asked a series of questions focusing on either the strategies or answers or both. We found that this technique allowed us to explore many strategies, such as truncation and compensation, and a variety of solutions, such as a range of numbers rather than one number, that students very infrequently demonstrated on their own (Sowder & Wheeler, 1987).

There has been little research on the effect of instruction on estimation. Reys, Trafton, Reys, and Zawojewski (1984) designed instructional treatments for Grades 6–9 based on the strategies used by good estimators noted in the earlier Reys et al. (1982) study. The approach used was to provide direct instruction on successful strategies. Postinterviews indicated that students understood that estimation requires computing with approximation numbers, and that students had a better understanding of number concepts.

A more indirect instructional approach was used in a study by Sowder and Markovits (1990). A seventh-grade teacher used discussion of estimation techniques, pattern searching, and cognitive conflict in a unit that focused on making reasonable estimates, particularly with traditionally difficult topics such as estimating products and quotients involving rational numbers. Students become much more flexible when estimating. Four months later they could estimate quite successfully, and even deal with the relative error of estimates (e.g., Which gives a closer estimate of 31×82, 31×80 or 30×82?). An indirect approach to instruction on estimating operations on fractions was also successful for Mack (1988).

Whether estimation strategies should be directly taught to students or whether students should be encouraged to explore and invent strategies through an indirect instructional approach is an important instructional question. The answer depends in part on the rationale for teaching estimation in the first place. There are two reasons commonly given for including instruction on computational estimation in the mathematics curriculum. The first is that estimation can help students develop a better conceptual understanding of number; that is, it can help develop number sense. Indirect instruction seems the more suitable approach to accomplish this goal. The second reason is that estimation is important in its own right and is a skill worth having. Many would argue that direct instruction on strategies is the most efficient and reasonable way to reach this goal. But if the skill we want students to acquire is to be able to use intuitive, sometimes non-routine methods to check the reasonableness of answers, then we might want to consider an indirect approach as a way of assisting students in developing number sense and computational estimation ability.

Another approach is to consider what type of expertise we want students to have, particularly if estimation is a skill worth having in its own right. According to Hatano (1988), there are two kinds of expertise, routine and adaptive. Routine expertise allows an individual to solve routine problems quickly and accurately with the help of automatized procedures. Certainly for textbook and examination problems and even some everyday problems requiring estimation, a routine expertise is quite adequate. Adaptive expertise, on the other hand, requires understanding how and why procedures work and how these procedures can be modified to suit the constraints of a problem. Adaptive expertise allows individuals to solve novel problems that would be unsolvable by someone with only routine expertise. Certainly the good estimators described earlier possessed adaptive expertise. The instructional question is whether adaptive expertise can be acquired through instruction where students are presented with standard procedures for estimation. Will estimation become simply another topic for which students must learn a multitude of rules and procedures? Will the good student routinize these procedures? It seems apparent that adaptive expertise with estimation is more likely to flourish in a classroom where students are encouraged to develop and discuss different approaches to estimation. This is not to say that techniques that are commonly used by experts cannot be suggested to and evaluated by students within the framework of class and group discussions and decision making.

Students need to "own" the mathematics they use if it is ever to be useful to them (Saxe, 1988).

Related Issues

Relating Concepts and Procedures

There is an accumulation of evidence that children are quite capable of learning to solve arithmetic problems, in a very meaningful fashion, without formal instruction (Carraher, Carraher, & Schliemann, 1985, 1987; Carraher, Schliemann, & Carraher, 1988; Ginsburg, 1977; Ginsburg et al., 1981; Saxe, 1988). To the children in these studies, the problems they solved made sense, usually because they were closely related to their livelihoods as street vendors or children of street vendors. They acquired, within the setting of the street and marketplace, a highly developed sense of number, of number properties, and of how to operate on numbers, when those numbers were within the realm of the familiar. Some of these children also received formal mathematical schooling, but they rarely connected the two, and when problems were presented in both the selling context and the school context, they were likely to solve the market problems in idiosyncratic, nonstandard ways, and the school problems in standard algorithmic ways. They were more accurate with their own procedures than with school-learned procedures.

There is other evidence that school-learned procedures are often at odds with self-generated procedures. Cobb (1988) has told of a second grader who easily solved school problems such as $16 + 9$ by counting on. When later given the problem in vertical form, she failed to carry the 1 and obtained 15. She considered both to be correct, 15 for the worksheet problem, 25 when the problem represented 16 cookies plus 9 more. "For her, school arithmetic seemed to be an isolated, self-contained context in which the possibility of doing anything other than attempting to recall prescribed methods did not arise" (p. 98). Resnick and Omanson (1987) had similar results with four children they observed over the period the children were learning to carry in addition. They found that a strong semantic understanding of addition, including the ability to find sums mentally, did not carry over to the written addition requiring the carry procedure.

Silver (1989) has cited evidence from NAEP reports indicating that students are not disposed to make sense out of numbers, that they do not see school mathematics as a sense-making activity. Rather, it is viewed as a collection of facts and rules to be memorized. If mathematics is not required to make sense, then there is no point talking about topics such as "reasonableness of results." Resnick (1986) has hypothesized that the major difference between good mathematics learners and poor mathematics learners is that "good mathematics learners expect to be able to make sense out of rules they are taught, and they apply some energy and time to the task of making sense. By contrast, those less adept in mathematics try to memorize and apply the rules that are taught, but do not attempt to relate these rules to what they know about mathematics at a more intuitive level" (p. 191).

Why do so many students fail to build relationships between their conceptual knowledge and the procedures they are taught in school? Hiebert and Lefevre (1986) hypothesized three reasons. First, there may be deficits in the knowledge base. Students who do not understand the extension of place-value concepts into decimal numbers cannot compare and operate on decimal numbers correctly, for example. Second, students may have difficulties encoding relationships, even those that are obvious to adults. Resnick and Omanson (1987) found, for example, that the mapping from Dienes blocks subtraction to written subtraction was not obvious to students. Third, students tend to compartmentalize knowledge, thus impeding construction of relationships. What is learned out of school is kept separate from what is learned in school. Children tend to separate quantitative and symbolic representations of number; the syntax and semantics of formal mathematics become detached from one another (Resnick, 1987a).

Students must be helped to build connections between their intuitive knowledge and the formal rules taught in school mathematics. Number sense that works only in out-of-school settings will not help a student advance mathematically. Schooling not only should build on intuitive knowledge students bring to the classroom, it should lead students to develop new and more complex intuitions upon which to continue building.

Models

Models of such instruction do exist. In the Cognitively Guided Instruction (CGI) project (Peterson, Fennema, & Carpenter, 1991), first-grade teachers used knowledge from cognitive science, particularly from research on how children solve addition and subtraction problems, to restructure their instruction. The changes were quite radical, in that instruction became entirely student-based rather than text- or program-based. Children did not learn algorithmic procedures, but developed a deep understanding of numbers in their first year of school. The following protocol of a first grader solving 246 + 178 typifies the procedures that children invented, based on their knowledge of numbers:

Well, 2 plus 1 is 3, so I know it's 200 and 100, so now it's somewhere in the three hundreds. And then you have to add the tens on. And the tens are 4 and 7. . . . Well, um. If you started at 70, 80, 90, 100. Right? And that's four hundreds. So now you're already in the three hundreds because of the [100 + 200], but now you're in the four hundreds because of that [40 + 70]. But you've still got one more ten. So if you're doing it 300 plus 40 plus 70, you'd have 410. But you are not doing that. So what you need to do then is add 6 more onto 10, which is 16. And then 8 more: 17, 18, 19, 20, 21, 22, 23, 24. So that's 124. I mean 424. (Carpenter, 1989, p. 90)

In a project with second graders (Cobb, Yackel, & Wood, 1988), instructional materials were developed that reflected as much as possible children's construction of arithmetical knowledge. Teachers received inservice time to help them understand their own teaching and make changes necessary for promoting childrens' construction of their own knowledge. These children, as in the CGI project, were able after instruction to solve symbolic tasks with invented, meaningful algorithms. A basic premise of the program is that for children to learn meaningfully, they must be given more responsibility for their own learning (Cobb & Merkel, 1989). This program, together with the CGI program, have inspired others to undertake like projects, even as far away as South Africa (Olivier, Murray, & Human, 1990).

A third primary program (Resnick, Lesgold, & Bill, 1990) is aimed at developing number sense. It builds on children's invented procedures and their intuitive understanding of number. There is daily conversation in the classroom about numbers, primarily within everyday situations. At the end of its first year in operation, students from all ability levels had made large improvements both in number sense and in computational competence.

A somewhat different approach is taken by Lampert (1988), a teacher–scholar who studies the teaching–learning process in her own fifth-grade mathematics class. Her instructional focus is on making reasoned connections between what students assume about mathematical structure and what she wants them to learn. For example, students in the class used drawings and stories as a symbol system in which they could argue that "it is legitimate to figure out 28×65 by first finding 30×65, and subtracting the product of 2×65 from that" (p. 145).

As part of the Primary Instruction in Mathematics Education (PRIME) project in England (Shuard, 1986), a calculator-aware numbers curriculum is being developed with the following as its main goals: the ability to translate between a situation and the corresponding calculation, a "friendly" feeling for numbers, an understanding of "how numbers work," an understanding of place value, an ability to calculate in the head, the ability to use the calculator sensibly when mental calculation is not appropriate, the early development of algorithmic thinking, and the ability to tackle new problems with confidence and interest. There should soon be reports on the piloting of this project in schools. (It should be noted here that the term *algorithmetic thinking* refers to the ability to develop an appropriate algorithm to solve a particular kind of problem, not to the ability to apply standard, school-taught algorithms.)

Assessment

If we agree that number sense cannot be compartmentalized into discrete parts with lessons or units prepared to teach these parts, if we agree instead that number sense is a way to think, if number sense evokes a way of teaching, then assessment of number sense becomes difficult—perhaps impossible. We can assess some of the components, such as place-value understanding, mental computation, and computational estimation, even though we need to go beyond standardized testing to truly measure these abilities. This is not so bleak a picture as it might first seem. If we know that a child can compose numbers in nonstandard and creative ways, can invent algorithms based on understanding of number structure that will lead to correct answers to computational problems, can judge relative magnitude of numbers, and tries to "make sense" of numbers situations, then we can claim the child capable of each of these things. We can claim the child exhibits number sense, but to say the child has number sense is still questionable, because in another situation the child may fail to demonstrate number sense. Number sense is an enormously large phenomenon encompassing many areas of arithmetic, so that focusing on certain dimensions at any one time is perhaps all that is necessary. If we concentrate on providing ways for students to make links between concepts and procedures, between symbols and meaning, and between different dimensions of number sense, such as number decomposition and mental computation, then number sense has an environment in which to develop, and assessment can focus on measuring the depths of these links.

DEVELOPING NUMBER SENSE AND ESTIMATION SKILLS: ANALYSIS OF SCHOOL PROGRAMS

Four very different school programs are considered here. The first two are current programs developed in the United States, each with a text series for Grades K–8. (Only Grade 1 through Grade 6 are reviewed here.) The two series are quite dissimilar in their sequencing and approach to teaching mathematics. The first text series is probably the better selling of the two, and is more like other elementary mathematics text series currently being marketed. It is referred to here as Current American Program #1 (CAP1), and has a publication date of 1987. The second, called Current American Program #2 (CAP2), has a publication date of 1981.

Only portions of the other two programs are available, but they are included here because they offer interesting contrasts to CAP1 and CAP2, particularly in their coverage of topics relevant to this discussion of number sense. The third program was used in the United States prior to the "new math" era, and is included here toward the end of this section to disprove the widely held belief that instruction on computational estimation and mental computation are fairly new in the curriculum. It is referred to here as Out-of-print American Program (OAP). Only the Grade 3 (1962) and Grade 5 (1956) texts are reviewed. (Other texts were not available to me, but these two are sufficient for comparison purposes.)

The fourth program currently is being used in Soviet schools.[1] The Soviet texts and teacher materials are being translated under the direction of Izaak Wirszup, working with the Resource Development Component of the University of Chicago School Mathematics Project (UCSMP). The mathematics program in the Soviet Union is government mandated, with one set of instructional materials available to all teachers and students. The degree to which teachers adhere to this program is not known, but the same could be said for the United States programs reviewed here. Of the teacher materials, only those from Grade 1 had been translated at the time the materials were reviewed. In the translated student texts, the texts after Grade 1 consist primarily of a large variety of problems, both oral and written, interspersed with some explanation. Although the texts are divided into units, there did not appear to be discrete lessons after Grade 1. The review here is drawn from work by Schappelle (1990), whose master's project included an analysis of the manner in which number sense topics are developed in Soviet and Hungarian mathematics programs. Materials thus far translated and included in her analysis reveal a rich foundation for the acquisition of number sense, and the types of problems given to students are worth studying. This program is referred to here as the Soviet Math Program (SMP).

Overview

The foundations for the development of whole number sense were discussed in the first section. The breakdown here reflects the earlier discus-

---

[1]The Soviet texts have been translated by the Resource Development Component of the University of Chicago School Mathematics Project and are available at the University of

sion. The manner in which texts develop number understanding for small numbers and place-value understanding is first discussed. An important aspect of number sense, noted earlier, is the ability to decompose and recompose numbers. The programs' coverage of this topic, apart from lessons on mental computation, is considered next, followed by an analysis of the approaches taken for comparing whole numbers.

The analysis of the foundations for rational number sense focuses on how fractions and decimal numbers are introduced, that is, how the texts attempt to link meaning to symbols, and then how numbers are compared and ordered. The programs' coverage of mental computation and of computational estimation are covered in the last two sections. These sections include work both with whole numbers and with rational numbers.

Before beginning the analysis of how the different programs treat these topics, it is worthwhile to consider the use of oral exercises within the different programs because of the important role these exercises play in two of the programs reviewed.

The Role of Oral Exercises

Oral exercises are integral parts of the CAP2 and the SMP programs. Much of the instruction that most directly relates to the topics of this chapter, number sense, mental computation, and computational estimation, is approached through whole-classroom oral exercises. In CAP2, these exercises appear in the teachers' pages of each lesson under the heading "Mental Arithmetic" and are intended as a "lively drill" to begin each class. Only a small percentage of these problems require mental computation as defined and discussed earlier in this chapter, particularly if we do not consider review and drill of basic facts as mental computation. Many of the problems require making both gross and fine estimates of sums, differences, products, and quotients. The majority of lessons call for thinking about reasonable answers rather than simply applying a rule or a number fact.

Oral exercises are designed to occupy a large portion of mathematics class time in the Soviet curriculum, particularly in Grades 1–3. Teachers of these grades receive a book of oral mathematics exercises that is intended to be used regularly with children. These exercises include a variety of forms besides mental computation, and cover such topics as properties of operations, dependence between quantities, letter symbolism, composing

Chicago's International Mathematics Education Resource Center. Those referred to here include Goretskii (1979); Kravchenko, Oksman, and Yankovskaya (1979); Markushevich (1980); Moro and Bantova (1980); and Pchelko, Bantova, Moro, and Pyshkalo (1978).

and decomposing numbers, and comparing numbers, all of which play major roles in the development of number sense.

The Soviet teachers' manual on oral exercises (Kravchenko, Oksman, & Yankovskaya, 1979) claims that oral exercises can play a significant role in increasing the effectiveness of a lesson, and that oral exercises are not to be regarded as supplementary, but should be viewed as an organic part of a lesson essential to the students' acquisition of knowledge and skills. The exercises are intended to prepare students to understand new content, to consolidate previously learned content and skills already acquired, and to develop thought processes. They are meant to be used throughout a lesson at whatever times are appropriate. The pace is to be set to meet these objectives. The manual contains many suggestions for doing oral exercises. The richness and variety of the suggested oral exercise are seen in the following sections, where examples of exercises are provided under the appropriate titles.

CAP1 has only occasional oral work. Many lessons contain a "Warm-up" section, and when it is possible to do these exercises orally, it is suggested that they be done so. Almost all of these oral exercises are basic fact reviews.

Foundations for Whole Number Sense

Learning the Numbers 1–10

In CAP1, the first five (of 14) chapters at Grade 1 are devoted to reading, writing, and ordering the cardinal numbers 1–12, sums and differences to 5, counting on and counting back. Addition is presented as the joining of two sets, whereas subtraction is "taking out," "giving away," or "crossing out." After the first chapter, all student practice pages require students to find sums or differences. Teachers are encouraged to use materials, usually counters, to begin each lesson, but the "Lesson Development" sections in the Teacher's Guide use the pictures on the student pages as the focus of each lesson.

CAP2 also devotes about one third of its lessons to these topics. This program uses a great deal of finger manipulation together with a developmental sequence dependent on the use of counters and number strips to develop understanding of cardinality, addition, and subtraction. Fingers are used later for instruction on place value, and after extensive work using fingers students are taught only to visualize the use of fingers while doing computation mentally. The number line is introduced, and students are required to identify what comes after or before a given number. Counting on and counting back also are emphasized with the joining and separating of sets again providing the conceptual foundation for addition and subtraction.

SMP Grade 1 teachers are provided with a long treatise on the preparation for learning numbers. Many examples of counting exercises are provided, and teachers are told that students should be made aware, through their own practical experiences, that counting does not depend on the order in which objects are counted as long as no object is either omitted or counted twice. Emphasis is given to the relations less than, greater than, as many as, and same as. Teachers are told that determining which grouping has fewer, and how many fewer is more difficult than determining which grouping has more and how many more. The problems inherent in equalizing sets is discussed. Each lesson presents many exercises designed to help students arrive at desired generalizations. The text plays a minor role in Grade 1, and most lessons focus on doing practical exercises with concrete objects. Addition and subtraction are introduced through increasing or decreasing amounts by one, then by several, always within a problem situation. Children are expected to change gradually from solving the problems by counting to solving them using numbers facts. Both addition and subtraction problems include comparison (e.g., There are 5 fir trees and 1 more linden than fir. What does that mean? How do you figure out how many linden trees there are? or There are 6 linden trees and 1 fewer fir trees. How many fir trees?). From comparing sets, problems move to comparison of lengths of line segments. Class time is to be spent analyzing the wording of problems then carefully selecting the arithmetic operation needed to solve each, as in:

1. One pack of books weighs 7 kg. A second pack is 3 kg heavier. How much does the second pack weigh?
2. One pack of books weigh 7 kg. A second pack weighs 3 kg. How much heavier is the first pack than the second?
3. One pack of books weighs 7 kg which is 3 kg heavier than a second pack. How much does the second pack weigh?

In the second half of the year, students are given missing subtrahend and missing addend problems, and are required to compare the solution of these problems with the way they solved familiar problems. Examples given are: (a) A girl had some postcards. She gave a friend 4 and then had 6 left. How many did she have to begin with? (b) A girl had some postcards. After a friend gave her 4 postcards, she had 6. How many did she have to begin with?

Summary and Comments. There are two major differences to note between the Soviet approach and the American approach to early work with numbers. Although CAP2 has one early lesson on missing addends and subtrahends (CAP1 problems present missing addend only on an enrichment page that is not used with all children), American teachers are not made aware of the different forms addition and subtraction problems might take. In fact, when comparison subtraction appears in CAP1 in Grade 2, the teacher is not warned that this type of problem is different from all the subtraction problems students have dealt with thus far in the program. The Soviet program, on the other hand, emphasizes the importance of guiding children, through discussion and class analyses of problems, to decide on the correct operation for a problem. The second difference is closely related to this. The American texts, particularly CAP1, contain a good deal of practice aimed at learning the number facts, whereas the learning of facts seems to take a secondary role in SMP at Grade 1.

Within the American texts themselves, CAP1 is more text oriented. It is possible for teachers to teach from CAP1 using few or no manipulatives. But neither text series seems to seriously build upon the intuitive knowledge about number that children bring when they enter school (Carpenter & Moser, 1984).

Place Value

Place-value concepts are introduced in Grade 1 in both American series. CAP1 first shows sets of objects with more than 10 but fewer than 100, with sets of 10 in groups or bundles, and students identify these as, for example, 2 tens and 3 ones, 23. Besides writing the number of elements pictured, students are required to fill in numbers missing from sequences of counting numbers and to tell what comes before and after a number. In Grade 1, trading (one ten for ten ones, and vice versa) is introduced in preparation for adding and subtracting two-digit numbers, and three-digit numbers are introduced via pictures of flats (of 100 squares), longs (of 10 squares), and ones (squares), and also with money. Larger numbers are considered in higher grades.

CAP2 takes a somewhat different approach. Until the last few weeks of Grade 1, two-digit numbers are always verbalized as (x) tens and (y) ones, and when written, the tens digit is printed larger than the ones digit. Fingers are used to represent numbers, so that 43 would require five children, four to demonstrate with 10 fingers and one to show three fingers. Addition and subtraction are demonstrated with fingers, with one addend always 0, 1, or 2. In Grade 2, sets of 10 are to be shown concretely as ice cream sticks bundled in tens or with other materials such as base-ten blocks. Regrouping for addition and subtraction is taught via the concrete materials.

CAP2 also considers larger numbers in higher grades, in addition to other lessons focusing on place-value concepts. For example, in Grade 4 CAP2 begins with an interesting example of place value (10 pins on a strip, 10 strips in a bag, 10 bags in a box, etc.), then continues with two lessons of problems on place value (e.g., using 6, 7, 1, make the biggest number you can). Many games at various grades in this program also call for place-value understanding.

In Grade 1 of SMP numbers larger than ten are divided for instructional purposes into the numbers 11 through 20 and the numbers 21 through 100. Students are expected to acquire the concept of 10 while working with numbers 11 through 20. One bundle of 10 sticks and individual sticks are used to display these numbers. Students are expected to be also measuring line segments and forming relations such as 1 dm 2 cm = 12 cm. Then, using the counting unit 10, students form 30, 40, and so on, and finally all numbers to 100. They are expected to understand the decimal (base-ten) structure of numbers, as a practical tool rather than as a theoretical idea, before they learn algorithms for addition and subtraction.

Many of the Oral Exercises in Grades 2 and 3 continue to require thinking about place value. Some examples from Grades 2 and 3 are the following:

I'm thinking of a number. If the next number is 10,000, what is the number?
Name the numbers that are made up of two hundreds and three tens.
Add 404 and 10,000.
Add to 2,300 as many hundreds as there are thousands in the number.
If one zero is crossed out, tell how that will change 20,300.
List the numbers which can be made up by using the digits 1, 2, 4 and 7 without repeating any: Which is least? Which is greatest?
Name some numbers that have 356 units in the thousands class.
What number is five less than the greatest three-digit number?
Subtract one six times from 1,000,004 and tell what each number is.
Which is greater, a six-digit number written with all 9s, or a seven-digit number written with all 7s?
Find the sum of 20,000,000 and 30,000; the difference of 1,000,000 and 100,000.
Give the numbers of tens in 856 (85 tens), 26,329 (2,632 tens).

Summary and Comments. In the eyes of many elementary teachers, place value appears to be limited to telling how many ones, tens, hundreds, and so on, there are in a particular number. This is not surprising because this is the focus of most place-value lessons in American texts. (CAP2 has some exceptions.) Place-value problems of the type used by Bednarz and

Janvier (1982, discussed earlier) do not appear in our textbooks, nor do problems of the type used in the Soviet program. The restricted attention to place-value understanding in U.S. texts limits children's development of number sense.

Decomposition and Recomposition of Numbers

The ability to decompose and recompose numbers into forms appropriate for the problems at hand is a hallmark of number sense. Howden (1989) has described a class of first graders she visited, in which she asked the children to say the first thing that came to their minds when she said "twenty-four." Students recomposed 24 in several ways: two dimes and four pennies; four nickels and four pennies; take a penny away from a quarter; take six pennies from three dimes; two dozen eggs. Other answers indicated other uses of 24. The teacher of this class spent a great deal of time working with numbers, orally and with concrete materials. In a third-grade class a few days later, Howden asked the same question; only a few responses were given, and none indicated any understanding of the structure of 24. It is easy to agree with her point that the students in the first class have a better understanding of number.

Textbooks traditionally focus on the decomposing and recomposing of numbers only insofar as this work will prepare students for the more "important" tasks of performing operations on numbers using standard algorithms. When learning number facts, children are asked for different ways numbers can add to 5: $0 + 5, 1 + 4, 2 + 3, 3 + 2, 4 + 1$, and $5 + 0$. Later on, numbers are decomposed into component parts according to place value, called *expanded notation* (e.g., $348 = 3 \times 100 + 4 \times 10 + 8 \times 1$, and vice versa). Texts vary in the amount of practice they afford to "regrouping"; that is, 348 is also $2 \times 100 + 14 \times 10 + 8 \times 1$. CAP1 has two lessons on regrouping before introducing the addition algorithm, and three before introducing the subtraction algorithm; CAP2 has four lessons on regrouping before each algorithm is introduced. CAP2 also has some decomposition exercises such as finding 31¢ in stamps, given 2¢, 3¢, 30¢, 5¢, 20¢, and 24¢ stamps, and the program requires some number decomposition in a frequently played number game. It also has some oral exercises in which students are to find "complements"; for example, given one two-digit number, they must produce another such that the sum is 100. Both series use decomposition in strategies used to introduce mental computation, at least to the extent of breaking numbers into hundreds, tens, and ones. Nowhere, however, are students taught to recompose numbers in other ways, such as thinking of 8 as $2 \times 2 \times 2$, so that mentally computing 112×8 could be done by doubling three times, 224, 448, 896, or thinking of 16×25 as $4 \times 4 \times 25$ so that the mental computation is reduced to 4×100.

The SMP program, again through oral exercises, presents substantially more decomposition and recomposition practice in Grades 2, 3, and 4 than the American series do. Some examples of exercises from Grade 1 are:

Which can be expressed as the sum of identical addends: 0, 1, 2, ... 10? What two numbers is 9 the sum of?

Examples from Grade 2 are:

What two numbers can 28 be the sum of? (Note that there are a finite number of answers, using only whole numbers.)

What two numbers can 15 be the difference of? (Note that there are an infinite number of answers.)

Pick out two numbers (given an array) whose sum is 15 from each row; from each column.

Express 40 as the sum of two even numbers; of two odd numbers.

Can 21 be expressed as the sum of two even numbers? of two odd numbers?

Make up some equations using three of these numbers: 24, 2, 8, 8, 2, 4, 6, 2, 3.

And from Grade 3:

Give the numbers that must be added to 700,500 to give 900,500.

Choose two pairs of numbers whose sum is 1,000: 250, 360, 220, 830, 750, 780, 170, 640. (Note that there is more than one correct answer.)

Find pairs of numbers whose product is 60; whose quotient is 10.

What is $395448 \times 9 - 395448 \times 8$?

Summary and Comments. The ability to decompose and recompose numbers is at the heart of flexible mental computation (Greeno, 1989; Resnick, 1989a; Trafton, 1989). American programs allow for little exploration beyond place-value "trading," although CAP2 allows more than CAP1. The Oral Exercises in the Soviet program provide some examples of the kinds of problems that would help students increase their flexibility with number composition. Another way to focus on decomposition and recomposition would be to incorporate this topic more fully into practice with mental computation by suggesting and exploring many ways of doing the same problem. For example, a class might explore and discuss the problem 28×16, which can be mentally computed in many different ways, such as:

$(30 - 2) \times 16 = 480 - 32 = 480 - 30 - 2 = 448.$
$(25 + 3) \times 16 = 25 \times 16 + 48 = (25 \times 4) 4 + 48 = 400 + 48 = 448.$
$28 (10 + 6) = 280 + 25 \times 6 + 3 \times 6 = 280 + 150 + 18 = 430 + 18 = 448.$
28 doubled four times is 56, 112, 224, 448.

Exploration of this problem depends on being able to decompose the numbers 28 and 16 in several different ways.

Comparing the Sizes of Whole Numbers

Comparing two numbers by size begins in Grade 1 in CAP1, where students are given the rule that to compare two two-digit numbers, they need only to compare the tens. The symbols for the relations greater than and less than are introduced in Grade 1, and students compare one- and two-digit numbers. The rule is generalized for larger numbers in Grade 2, and to ordering in Grade 5. There is one lesson at each grade level on comparing whole numbers.

Inequalities (with symbols) are introduced in Grade 1 in CAP2, but at first only with numbers through 18. Students are asked not only to compare two numbers, but also to identify sums greater than or less than a given number. No rule is given for later comparison of two-digit numbers; rather, children having difficulties are asked to consult a number chart. In Grade 2 students are asked to compare numbers such as $10 - 3$ with $10 - 4$, and 30 with $20 + 2$; whereas in Grade 3, they compare $126 - 100$ with $126 - 10$, and $4{,}259 + 675$ with $4{,}259 + 575$. Mental arithmetic becomes a daily part of lessons in Grade 4, and many of the daily drills use an upper or lower bound to compare with sums, differences, products, and quotients. For example, students are to decide whether sums such as $13 + 15$ and $25 + 35$ are greater than 40, and show thumbs up if yes, thumbs down if no. These increase in difficulty by grade; for example, is $750 \div 5$ between 100 and 150? (Grade 5).

Many of the oral exercises in SMP also call for number comparison together with number operations, in many of the same ways as CAP2. However, there are many other problems that call on a deeper understanding of number size and place value. Some examples of these are:

Grade 1: What number with zeros in the ones place can be inserted in the empty squares?
$\square < 90 \qquad 28 + \square > 28 \qquad \square - 1 > 16 - 1$
What signs should replace the asterisks to make these true?
$50 + 20 * 50 + 30 \qquad 18 - 5 * 46 - 5 \qquad 5 + 8 * 8 + 5$

Grade 2: Compare the following:

$(6 + 8) - (2 + 4)$ and $(6 + 4) - (8 + 2)$ $24 - (4 + 10)$ and $24 - 4 + 10$

How much greater is the product 6×7 than 6×6?

Grade 3: Are these true? $25500500 < 25500400$; $865328 > 865000$

Insert a digit in the square so that these numbers are in increasing order:

32,249,677   32,2 □ 9,687   32,299,637

Make these true: $372 > 3 □ 3$, $11111 > 1111 □$

Are these true? $400 - 205 = 450 - 250$; $1320 \times 10 < 1320 \div 10$

Compare: $420 \div 6$ and $420 \div 60$; $1400 - 685$ and $1400 - 554$

Summary and Comments. There is evidence that children can quite easily discover the rules for ordering whole numbers (Sowder & Wheeler, 1987). It would therefore seem pedagogically sound to allow (and guide) this discovery rather than to give rules. Text-given rules are less likely to be as adaptable to the types of exercises found in the SMP as are rules that originate from children. Of the two U.S. programs, CAP2 excels in the variety of ways in which children are introduced to number comparison. The types of problems presented in CAP2 and SMP provide good foundations for strengthening number sense.

Foundations for Rational Number Sense

Rational number sense appears to be somewhat different than whole number sense. Although rational number sense might be characterized in much the same way as whole number sense, individuals can and often do have whole number sense without having rational number sense (Sowder & Schappelle, 1989). Rational number sense is closely associated with the understanding of and the ability to use the rational number symbols, whereas whole number sense can be divorced from written symbols, as it is in the arithmetic of Brazilian street children (Carraher et al., 1985; Saxe, 1988). One facet of rational number sense is, then, the ability to interpret the decimal number and fraction number symbols correctly. This ability often can be assessed through problems requiring ordering and comparing rational numbers. Place-value understanding should extend to decimal numbers. Mental computation with rational numbers rarely is undertaken, except to find fractional parts of whole numbers such as $\frac{2}{3}$ of 60. However, estimation skills with rational numbers are of paramount importance if one is to judge whether or not answers from computations are reasonable. In this section the manner in which the instructional programs under review prepare students to associate meaning with fraction and decimal number symbols and to compare and order rational numbers is explored, followed by a consideration of estimation with fraction and decimal numbers.

Fractions

Fractions $\frac{1}{2}$, $\frac{1}{3}$, and $\frac{1}{4}$ are introduced at the end of Grade 1 in CAP1 as shaded parts of geometric pictures and as parts of discrete sets, and extended to fractions with denominators through 10 at the end of Grade 2. The same topics are included again in four lessons toward the end of Grade 3, with a fifth lesson on equivalent fractions, using different subdivisions of shaded squares. In part of a sixth lesson, equal-size strips are shown subdivided into halves, thirds, fourths, fifths, and tenths. Students then compare fractions (e.g., $\frac{4}{5}$ with $\frac{5}{10}$, $\frac{3}{3}$ with $\frac{2}{5}$) by referring to the strips.

CAP1 devotes major portions of the texts to fractions and decimals in Grades 4, 5, and 6. In each grade, there is a review of concepts introduced in previous grades. In Grade 4, students identify fractions associated with shaded portions of geometric figures and parts of discrete sets (two lessons) and find equivalent fractions (three lessons). To compare fractions, students are shown, through shaded rectangles and on a number line, that fractions with the same denominator can be compared by comparing numerators only.

Students then are told that to compare fractions with unlike denominators, they should write equivalent fractions with the same denominator. Unfortunately, the Grade 3 lesson on comparing fractions by looking at number strips that show $\frac{3}{4} > \frac{3}{5}$, for example, is not repeated in Grade 4 or in higher grades. All skills, whether changing fractions to mixed numbers, finding equivalent fractions, reducing to lowest terms, or performing operations, are presented with a set of rules to be followed. The rules are set in colored boxes with connecting arrows. The Grade 4 lessons are repeated, in abbreviated form, in Grades 5 and 6.

Fractions also are introduced in CAP2 in Grade 1, but students are expected only to find halves of discrete sets and to estimate halves of some measures (length and volume). The fraction symbol is not introduced until Grade 2, and only after experience with the words and pictures representing one half and one fourth. There is a series of eight lessons on fractions in Grade 3. One purpose of the second lesson is "to develop a feel for the relative sizes of halves, thirds, fourths, and fifths of the same object." After lessons on finding fractional parts of sets, students are introduced to equivalent fractions through pictures showing different subdivisions of the same shaded area. The Grade 4 introduction to fractions is similar, but includes probabilities as fractions. Lessons on equivalent fractions contain problems on comparing fractions, implying that they should be compared by the common denominator method.

Addition and subtraction are introduced intuitively at the end of Grade 4, through directions to figure out the answer (sample problem: $\frac{3}{4}$ inch + $\frac{1}{2}$ inch), then draw line segments and measure to check answers. Algorithms for operating on fractions are not introduced until Grade 5, with most operational work coming in Grades 5 and 6.

SMP's approach to fractions is not entirely clear from the materials available at the time of this writing. It appears that fractions are not introduced until Grade 3, because that is when fraction problems first appear in the Oral Exercises. The exercises all require that students find fractional parts of whole numbers. Some examples are: Subtract 17 from half of 80. Which is greater, $\frac{3}{4}$ of 100 or $\frac{1}{2}$ of 60? Text problems include comparing and ordering fractions that are easily converted to equivalent fractions; for example, students are asked to arrange $\frac{7}{8}, \frac{1}{4}, \frac{1}{8}, \frac{1}{2}, \frac{3}{4}, \frac{8}{8}, \frac{3}{8}$, and $\frac{5}{8}$ in increasing order. Grade 4 problems are similar to those in Grade 3. Little operational work appears in the Grade 4 text outline or in the problems. Operations on fractions are postponed until later grades, a situation not unusual in countries where the metric system of measurement requires more and earlier work with decimal numbers and less with fractions.

Summary and Comments. It is worth noting at this point that both of the current American programs depend heavily on the part–whole subconstruct of rational numbers in their introduction to fractions, using both continuous and discrete models. Presenting fractions as quotients seems to have lost favor since OAP, where a lesson at Grade 5 showed fractions resulting from dividing a number by a larger number. In one OAP example given, three cookies were to be divided among four boys, leading to the expression $3 \div 4 = \frac{3}{4}$ as another way of thinking about $3 \times \frac{1}{4} = \frac{3}{4}$. Kerslake (1986) has noted that restricting the interpretation of fractions to parts of whole places limitations on the robustness of children's understanding of rational numbers.

Operations on fractions has proved to be difficult for elementary school children, primarily because they develop computational procedures without first acquiring a conceptual base for operation work (Kouba, Carpenter, & Swafford, 1989). In many other countries fraction work is postponed until later grades, and operations on decimal numbers is first emphasized. However, as long as the United States continues to favor English over metric units of measure, it is doubtful that computation with fractions will be postponed.

Decimal Numbers

Decimals (in tenths) are introduced in CAP1, Grade 3, as a new way to write fractions with denominators of 10. Adding decimal numbers is introduced next, with the rule given to line up decimal points. One demonstration that $0.8 + 0.6$ is 1.4 is given, and the text justifies the algorithm by showing via a picture that the decimal parts in $2.6 + 1.7$ give 1 whole and 3 tenths. No attempt appears to be made in this grade to relate decimals to previously acquired place-value concepts.

Decimals in Grade 4 again are introduced as different ways of writing fractions with denominators of 10 or 100, and related to metric measures (e.g., a straw 4 and 8 tenths centimeters long is 4.8 cm long). Money is also used to develop the concepts of decimal parts. A lesson then is given on comparing decimal numbers. The rules given for comparing decimal numbers tell students to line up the decimal points and, starting from the left, to compare digits. No pictorial assistance is given in the lesson on comparing, nor are there any suggestions given to the teacher about ways of comparing decimal numbers other than by following the rules.

Decimals first appear in Grade 3 in CAP2, in a series of 14 lessons. Tenths are introduced in terms of money and metric length units (e.g., 2.3 m = 23 dm). Hundredths are introduced as tenths of tenths. In the eighth lesson, students compare decimal numbers. It is suggested that teachers explain that it is easier to compare 0.40 and 0.32 than 0.4 and 0.32 and that students should convert one number so that the numbers have the same number of decimal places. Addition and subtraction of decimals are presented through demonstrations with money and metric measures that the results of adding numbers with decimal points is the same as adding as though the decimal points were not there—as long as the decimal points are lined up.

Decimal number instruction in Grade 4 is more traditional, with wholes (squares) being divided into ten or one hundred parts, and ten squares divided into a thousand parts. Students again compare decimal numbers by annexing zeros before operations and algorithms are introduced. By Grade 5, work with decimal numbers (except for long division) is mostly treated as review.

SMP Grade 4 includes quite a thorough treatment of decimal numbers, introduced through comparison of metric units, and fractions with denominators of 10, 100, and 1000. Decimal numbers are compared by annexing zeros until both numbers have the same number of places to the right of the decimal point. Addition and subtraction are introduced by first writing the numbers in expanded notation, then using the rule of lining up decimal points. Multiplication is introduced by converting decimal numbers in metric units to nondecimal numbers (e.g., 0.5 dm and 0.3 dm to 5 cm and 3 cm), multiplying to find area, then converting back again (15 cm^2 = 0.15 dm^2).

Summary and Comments. Comparing and operating on decimal numbers is very rule oriented in both the American and Soviet programs. Of particular interest here is the rule given in all three programs for comparing decimal numbers for which the whole number portions are equal, that is, to annex zeros until all numbers have the same number of places to the right of the decimal point. Data reported in the first section indicate that comparing decimals is not so simple as text authors make it appear. Again, this notion of decimal size needs to be very carefully developed before algorithmic work begins. The NAEP results on decimal understanding (Kouba et al., 1989) are similar to those discussed for fraction understanding, namely, that students are beginning computational work before they learn basic decimal concepts. Wearne and Hiebert (1988b) have shown that once students have learned algorithms for performing operations on decimal numbers, often incorrectly, it is extremely difficult for then to relearn these algorithms semantically.

Mental Computation

CAP1 begins instruction in mental computation (other than the learning of basic facts) in Grade 3. One lesson contains mental mathematics problems such as 30 + 50 and 400 + 900. Another suggests adding 46 + 22 in a left-to-right manner as 40 + 60, then 6 + 2, so 68. (No problems in this lesson require regrouping.) A third lesson requires sums of two-digit and one-digit numbers; a fourth uses a count-down method to do problems such as 402 − 398. In a fifth lesson, children are told to find products such as 6 × 30 by thinking 6 × 3 tens is 18 tens, so one hundred, eight tens. A few more such lessons are distributed throughout the text, for the most part without suggestions for strategies and without suggestions to the teachers to discuss strategies children use. At Grade 4, mental addition from left to right is encouraged, as is (where appropriate) using multiples of 10 (e.g., to compute 15 + 7: 15 + 5 is 20, + 2 is 22; 16 + 16: 16 + 4 is 20, + 12 is 32.) The distributive property is used to teach mental multiplication. None of the sums of two-digit addends requires regrouping. Some mental multiplications and divisions of the type "9 × 8 = 72 so 9 × 80 = 720; 18 ÷ 3 = 6 so 180 ÷ 3 is 60" occur in Grade 5. These skills are practiced and extended in Grade 6. There is some encouragement given to use mental computation on problems other than those that appear as "Mental Computation."

Contrary to first appearances, there is actually little mental computation required of students in the early grades of the CAP2 program beyond basic fact learning. The Grade 4 text contains a lesson on mental computation requiring answers to problems such as 20 + 35 and 1735 − 705. The emphasis in this lesson is on place value. A later lesson requires multiplication and division by multiples of 10 (e.g., 2 × 40 = 80). In that lesson, children next are given the problem 2 × 39 as a follow-up to 2 × 40. This extension is not the norm, however, until Grade 6, where several such pairs or sets of problems appear. The Grade 5 text has a few lessons containing multidigit addition and subtraction, and this is considerably extended in Grade 6. Only two illustrations, one for addition and one for subtraction, are given as procedures for carrying out mental calculation, so students do not see a variety of strategies that work, possibly leading them to believe that there is only one correct way to do these problems. There are lessons on multiplying and dividing whole numbers and decimal numbers by powers of ten in both text series.

Because of the Soviet's curricular emphasis on oral exercises, there is a good deal more mental math, presented in a variety of ways, in SMP. The contrast with American texts is striking, and so several examples of exercises from SMP are given here. The following is an example of an oral exercise given in Grade 1:

	1	2	3	4	5	6	7
1	10	18	40	15	36	20	60
2	14	38	50	45	39	23	77
3	11	48	60	95	39	25	93
4	16	58	70	65	34	29	64
5	12	98	80	25	33	24	98

Subtract 10 from each number in row 3; from each number in the fourth column.
Add 10 to each number in row 3, to each number in the fourth column.
Add 2 to each number in row 1.
Reduce the numbers in the seventh column by 20, by 60, by 7.
Add the corresponding numbers in the first and third columns together.

Several other questions were also suggested for this table. The variety of problems dealing with this one table requires as much mental computation as appears in a full year of mental computation in some American texts. Problems of the type just shown appear, in more advanced forms, at succeeding grade levels.

Mental computation also appears in several problem contexts in SMP where there is more than one correct answer:

Grade 1: Think up two numbers, one 16 greater than the other.
Grade 2: Find a pair of numbers whose product is 60.

Sometimes students are asked whether or not a computation is correct:

Grade 1: $24 + 35 = 59$.
Grade 3: When not, older children are asked to put in parentheses to make it true:
$$32 - 2 \times 6 + 3 = 183.$$

Problems frequently are presented algebraically:

Grade 1: Solve $x + 160 = 360$.
Grade 2: Is 25 a solution to any of these? $x - 25 = 25, x + 0 = 25, x + 14 = 28$.
Grade 3: $a \times 50 - 50 = 0; b - 999 = 1$.
Grade 4: $21 \times 8 \times a = 168$.

Students also may be required to identify the operation, such as in:

Grade 3: Name the operation performed to get the next numbers:
$3,000 \rightarrow 3,900 \rightarrow 2,900 \rightarrow 2,000$.

Many SMP problems require students to know certain terminology:

Grade 1: One addend is 34, the other is 9; find the sum.
Grade 3: Find the sum of all the odd numbers between 18 and 26.

Reflecting on problems before beginning to compute is encouraged through problems such as:

Grade 1: Solve in any appropriate way: $(7 + 8) + 3; 14 + (20 + 6)$.
Grade 3: Calculate the easiest way: $145 + 61 + 55 + 39; 395,448 \times 9 - 395,448 \times 8$.
    Using the equation $421 - 285 = 136$, evaluate this second expression:
    $421 - (285 + 4) = ?$
Grade 4: Use a convenient order to add $221 + 427 + 373$.

There are also, of course, many examples of straightforward mental computation:

Grade 3: Find 27×7, 34×9, 120×11

It is not clear, from the translated materials available at this time, whether students are encouraged to try different strategies when presented with problems of this sort. On one problem in the oral exercises, however, students were asked to use a "rounding-off" procedure to evaluate problems such as $35 + 17$ and $62 - 19$. This meant, for example, that $35 + 17$ could become $35 + 20 - 3$, and $62 - 19$ could become $62 - 20 + 1$.

Summary and Comments. As discussed earlier, mental computation has several meanings, not only for teachers but for curriculum writers. In its initial stages, learning basic facts certainly requires some mental computing, but one could argue that drill intended to facilitate recall of facts from memory no longer can be said to require mental computation. Many of the chain calculation drills that are viewed as mental computation, such as $13 - 5$, $\div 2$, $+ 7$, $+ 4$, $\div 3$, $\times 5$, also simply require recall of basic facts (Sowder & Schappelle, 1989). Both American texts include chain calculations and basic fact review as mental calculation. Both texts, however, devote several lessons to mental computation in the higher grades. Students in both programs have several opportunities to mentally practice multidigit addition and subtraction with nonstandard algorithms, and to practice multiplying and dividing by powers of ten, multiplying by multiples of ten and one hundred, working with simple percents, finding fractions of whole numbers, transferring between decimal and fraction notation, and converting metric measures.

Neither of the American programs reviewed approaches mental computation in the manner advocated by Markovits and Sowder (1988) for increasing number sense, that is, treating mental computation as a higher order thinking skill, with instruction focusing on number and operation concepts in order to develop flexibility in selecting and inventing appropriate strategies for the computational task at hand. The oldest curriculum, OAP, perhaps came closest to this view on mental computation in instruction in Grade 3, such as:

Here are two ways to find $83 + 45$ without a pencil. Explain each way.

- Think: $80 + 40 = 120$; $120 + 8 = 128$.
- Think: $83 + 40 = 123$; $123 + 5 = 128$.

Which way do you like better? Tell how you could think to find these sums.

The OAP method of mental subtraction is essentially the same as one appearing in SMP:

To find $40 - 13$, think $40 - 10 = 30, 30 - 3 = 27$ (Grade 3);

and in CAP1:

$235 - 97$ is $235 - 100 + 3$ (Grade 4).

In my own research, I have found the technique of rounding then compensating to be very confusing to some children, who have difficulty figuring out which way to compensate. For example, $41 - 23$ frequently is computed as $41 - 20$ is $21, + 3$ is 24, rather than $- 3$ is 18, unless children are assisted in thinking "I need to take away 23, so if I take away 20, then 3 more, that is 23 in all." It is surprising that other, less error-prone strategies are so infrequently discussed in texts. CAP2 does give examples of the strategy of adding or subtracting the same amount from each number:

$317 - 198$ is $319 - 200$, is $119; 321 - 102$ is $319 - 100$ is 219.

I have found that the method of counting up also works well for some children; that is, to find $317 - 198$, count up 2 to 200, then 100 to get 300, then 17 more, or 119 in all. If presented in texts at all, this strategy appears as a way in which to count change in money problems and is not generalized to other subtraction situations. Both the counting-up method and the equal-additions (or subtractions) method are less error prone than rounding then compensating.

Computational Estimation

American texts published in the last few years have included sections on estimation, and many teachers believe that this topic is new in the elementary curriculum. But the OAP series from the 1950s contained several lessons and exercises requiring estimation. In a third-grade example, a boy named Joe was shown buying a 49¢ hat and a 29¢ ball, for 78¢. Joe asked himself whether this was a reasonable answer. So he rounded the addends to 50 and 30, and obtained an estimate of 80. The accompanying rhyme, "A wise boy is Joe Bates, When he adds he estimates," was intended to help students see value in estimation. Throughout the text, lesson headings include "Using Common Sense"; "Sensible Answers in Subtraction"; and "What Price is Sensible?". Incorrect answers (worked out) are shown for problems, and students are required to find the errors and tell how estimating helped them do this. Similar problems, but with more complex computations, can be found in the OAP Grade 5 text. Multiple ways are suggested for estimating, as in the following:

Estimate the quotient $1,215 \div 52$.
Method 1: 52 is about 50, two 50s is 100, and 1,200 has 24 50s, so 24.
Method 2: $10 \times 52 < 1,215$ and $100 \times 52 > 1,215$. First digit is 2, so 20 something.
Method 3: $10 \times 52 - 520$, $20 \times 52 = 1,040$, $30 \times 52 = 1,560$. So 20 something, closer to 20 than 30, so less than 25.

Students are asked which method they like; they are told to try them all and decide which is easiest for themselves.

The approach to computational estimation in CAP1 is quite different. Strategies for estimating are explicitly taught, and students are told, for the most part, which strategy to use when. Students first encounter estimation in Grade 3, where they are required to estimate sums, differences, and products using rounding. They are told, for example, to estimate $789 - 207$ by rounding both numbers to the nearest hundred before subtracting. In at least one instance, students are told to estimate to see whether their answers to word problems make sense, but such directions are not consistently given. These estimation lessons are more fully developed in Grade 4, where students are also asked to estimate quotients after rounding to the nearest ten or nearest dollar. In Grade 5, students use rounding to estimate decimal sums. They also are taught to look for compatible numbers; for example, to estimate $53.2 + 79.1 + 51$, they are to note that $53.2 + 51$ is about $50 + 50$, so that the answer is about 180. Front-end estimation, with compensation, is introduced for sums and differences, as is estimating sums using clustering. Fractions (mixed) and decimal numbers are rounded to the closest whole number to estimate sums and differences. It should be noted that teaching students to round fractions to the closest whole number can cause difficulties such as the one noted by Threadgill-Sowder (1984), where several students estimated 0.52×789 as 1×800. Rounding to $\frac{1}{2}$ does appear in the Grade 5 text, but only on an enrichment page. These strategies are individually reviewed and practiced in Grade 6. Students are also introduced to deciding on estimates of more than x, less than x, or between x and y, rather than finding one estimate obtained by applying a particular procedure.

In CAP1, estimation is a major strand, and lessons at each grade level focus on particular estimation strategies. CAP2 takes yet another approach to computational estimation. There are only a few lessons on estimation but students frequently are exposed to problems requiring estimation. Estimating sums and differences begins in CAP2 at Grade 3. Early in the year, children are required to place relation symbols between expressions such as $126 - 100$ and $126 - 10$, and later in the year between expressions such as 25×25 and 6×10. In another lesson, they are required to estimate and then choose the correct answers to problems such as $51 + 51$ and $200 - 22$ from a set of answers that includes 102, 150, 178, 304, and 500. The Mental Arithmetic sections of the Grades 4–6 texts provide an abundance of estimation practice, although students are not required to learn particular techniques or to give estimates for particular problems. In some problems, students are told they have money, such as $10, then asked if they have enough to buy items costing $7.97 and $0.97 (Grade 4). Sometimes students are required to tell whether answers are obviously wrong or possibly correct, such as with $310 + 306 = 596$ and $1,000 - 17 = 983$ (Grade 4), or $700 + 120 = 620$ and $15.9 - 6 = 15.3$ (Grade 6). Other times students must find the answer by eliminating two choices through estimation, such as with answers of 20,002; 2,372; and 23,712 for 593×42, and yet other times by telling whether the result of an operation is "within bounds"; for example: Is 53×4 between 500 and 600? Is $\frac{1}{2} + \frac{3}{4}$ less than 1? (Grade 5). Another type of estimation problem sometimes given on student pages is the "ink-blot" problem, where some digits are blackened, and students must select an answer to a problem without knowing what all the digits are; for example, which of 482, 607, and 758 could be the answer to $8XX - 3X5$, where the Xs here represent the inked-out digits (Grade 4). Teachers are advised to keep in mind that students want the security of exact answers and that not every student will master these types of problems.

SMP does not seem to emphasize estimation. Many of the oral exercises can be more easily solved by using estimation than by calculating, but it is not clear whether students are encouraged to solve these exercises by estimating. Some examples of such problems are as follows:

Grade 1: $178 + x = 360$. Guess what could be the solution: 5, 182, 237, 375, 25.

Which numbers in the second column match the expression in the first column?

$7,155 \div 795$	106
$84,270 \div 795$	64
$50,880 \div 795$	12
$9,540 \div 795$	9

Text problems also require some estimating, although estimation is not always indicated. Two examples are:

Grade 3: Without computing, how can you estimate whether the following are correct:

$$51,054 \div 127 = 4.2 \qquad 40,945 \div 135 = 307$$

Grade 4: Find two values for the variable that make each statement true and two values that make each statement false:

$$a < 206 \times 504 - 208 \times 401$$
$$y < 12,322 \div 61 - 3,328 \div 32$$

Summary and Comments. Rounding numbers and then computing with the approximated numbers is presented in CAP1 as the primary way in which to carry out computational estimation. This is certainly an acceptable way in which to estimate computations. Several other ways are suggested also, such as front-end and clustering. However, students usually are told which method to use, and so they have little or no opportunity to develop the skill of choosing an appropriate method. Even though the CAP1 approach is easier to teach, because for each problem there is usually only one right process and one right answer, this approach seems contrary to the spirit of estimation, and may not develop the adaptive expertise (Hatano, 1988) needed to solve novel problems.

The CAP2 authors seem to recognize that computational estimation is a difficult skill to develop, particularly at the elementary school level. There use of problems requiring students to find whether the result of an operations is within given bounds is an excellent way to begin work on estimation. This approach is more in keeping with the developmental levels of learning estimation noted by Case and Sowder (1990).

There does not appear to be a conscious focus on estimation in SMP, although some of the exercises presented could be more easily solved by estimation than by exact computation.

A Caveat

The preceding analysis focused on number sense and related topics. It is to be expected that not all text series would treat these topics in the same manner, and that an individual familiar with this area would have particular biases leading him or her to favor one approach to instruction on these topics over another approach. I am sure my biases are evident to the reader. However, the reader should keep in mind that this analysis was limited to particular topics, and that an analysis of other topics might lead to quite different conclusions regarding which text series' approach is favored. The two U.S. programs were selected before any analysis was undertaken; thus there was no intention of showing one to be "better" than the other. Exemplary problems from the U.S. texts were not shown as abundantly as those from SMP because U.S. texts are quite easily accessible, and SMP materials are not.

CONCLUSION

One theme of this chapter has been that number sense has many dimensions, all interrelated, and cannot be taught as a series of discrete components. Number sense is a way of thinking about numbers. Another characterization of number sense, different from and yet complementary to the dimensional analysis in this chapter, was made by substituting number sense for the original term "higher order thinking" in Resnick's (1987b) characterization of thinking skill in *Education and Learning to Think:*

> Number sense resists the precise forms of definition we have come to associate with the setting of specified objectives for schooling. Nevertheless, it is relatively easy to list some key features of number sense. When we do this, we become aware that, although we cannot define it exactly, we can recognize number sense when it occurs. Consider the following:
>
> Number sense is nonalgorithmic.
> Number sense tends to be complex.
> Number sense often yields multiple solutions, each with costs and benefits, rather than unique solutions.
> Number sense involves nuanced judgment and interpretation.
> Numbers sense involves the application of multiple criteria.
> Number sense often involves uncertainty.
> Number sense involves self-regulation of the thinking process.
> Number sense involves imposing meaning.
> Number sense is effortful. (Resnick, 1989a, p. 37)

Thinking about number sense in the same way we think of higher order thinking reinforces the notion that children will not develop number sense if it is considered another "add-on" to the curriculum rather than an environment within which number work takes place. "Isolated instruction on individual components of number sense, regardless of how well the instruction is designed, is unlikely to lead to the development of the kind of sense-making with respect to quantitative processes and products that we seek. . . . Our curriculum and instructional methods must be restructured to emphasize sense-making in all areas of mathematics instruction" (Silver, 1989, p. 96).

Use of the metaphor of an environment suggests a more global treatment of number sense, where "flexible mental computation, computational estimation, and quantitative judgment and inference [would be treated] as symptoms of a more basic and general condition of knowing in the conceptual domain of numbers and quantities" (Greeno, 1989, p. 44). In this environment, people would know where they are, "which things are nearby, which things are easy to reach from where they are, and how routes can be combined flexibly to reach other places efficiently" (p. 46). Greeno noted that thinking of number sense as an environment highlights its multileveled and multiconnected nature. He also noted that this view of number sense has implications for instruction. Although it may be a good idea to design activities to develop abilities in quantitative judgment, mental computation, and computational estimation, we also need to think about how all the activities in the mathematics program can be designed and organized to promote the growth of number sense. Problem solving and active exploration are some of the ways one learns to move about in this environment. The social group plays a paramount role in learning within this environment.

Textbooks cannot create this sort of environment. We need to be more concerned that texts do not negatively affect the development of number sense than that texts will do it all for us. The analysis presented here gives examples both of how texts can hinder and of how texts can assist teachers in creating the environment children need in order to make sense of numbers.

ACKNOWLEDGMENT

The preparation of this manuscript was partly supported by the National Science Foundation (Grant No. MDR 8751373). The opinions expressed here do not necessarily reflect the position, policy, or endorsement of the National Science Foundation.

REFERENCES

Ashlock, R. B. (1982). *Error patterns in computation: A semi-programmed approach.* Columbus, OH: Merrill.

Baroody, A. J. (1989). Kindergartners' mental addition with single-digit combinations. *Journal for Research in Mathematics Education, 20*(2), 159–172.

Bednarz, N., & Janvier, B. (1982). The understanding of numeration in primary school. *Educational Studies in Mathematics, 13,* 33–57.

Bednarz, N., & Janvier, B. (1988). A constructivist approach to numeration in primary school: Results of a three year intervention with the same group of children. *Educational Studies in Mathematics, 19,* 299–331.

Behr, M. J. (1989). Reflections on the conference. In J. T. Sowder & B. P. Schappelle (Eds.), *Establishing foundations for research on number sense and related topics: Report of a conference* (pp. 85–88). San Diego: San Diego State University Center for Research in Mathematics and Science Education.

Behr, M. J., Lesh, R., Post, T. R., & Silver, E. A. (1983). Rational-number concepts. In R. Lesh & M. Landau (Eds.), *Acquisition of mathematics concepts and processes* (pp. 91–126). New York: Academic.

Behr, M. J., Wachsmuth, I., Post, T. R., & Lesh, R. (1984). Order and equivalence of rational numbers: A clinical teaching experiment. *Journal for Research in Mathematics Education, 15,* 323–341.

Brown, J. S., & Burton, R. R. (1978). Diagnostic models for procedural bugs in basic mathematical skills. *Cognitive Science, 2,* 155–192.

Brown, M. (1981). Place value and decimals. In K. M. Hart (Ed.), *Children's understanding of mathematics: 11–16* (pp. 48–65). London: John Murray.

Carpenter, T. P. (1989). Number sense and other nonsense. In J. T. Sowder & B. P. Schappelle (Eds.), *Establishing foundations for research on number sense and related topics: Report of a conference* (pp. 89–91). San Diego: San Diego State University Center for Research in Mathematics and Science Education.

Carpenter, T. P., Coburn, T. G., Reys, R. E., & Wilson, J. W. (1976). Notes from National Assessment: Estimation. *Arithmetic Teacher, 23,* 296–302.

Carpenter, T. P., Corbitt, M. K., Kepner, H. S., Jr., Lindquist, M. M., & Reys, R. E. (1980). National assessment: A perspective of students' mastery of basic mathematics skills. In M. M. Lindquist (Ed.), *Selected issues in mathematics education* (pp. 215–257). Chicago: National Society for the Study of Education, & Reston, VA: NCTM.

Carpenter, T. P., & Moser, J. M. (1984). The acquisition of addition and subtraction concepts in grades one through three. *Journal for Research in Mathematics Education, 15*(3), 179–202.

Carraher, T. N., Carraher, D. W., & Schliemann, A. D. (1985). Mathematics in the streets and in schools. *British Journal of Developmental Psychology, 3,* 21–29.

Carraher, T. N., Carraher, D. W., & Schliemann, A. D. (1987). Written and oral mathematics. *Journal for Research in Mathematics Education, 18*(2), 83–97.

Carraher, T. N., Schliemann, A. D., & Carraher, D. W. (1988). Mathematical concepts in everyday life. In G. B. Saxe & M. Gearhart (Eds.), *New directions for child development, #41: Children's mathematics* (pp. 71–87). San Francisco: Jossey-Bass.

Case, R. (1985). *Intellectual development.* Orlando, FL: Academic.

Case, R., & Griffin, S. (1990). Child cognitive development: The role of central conceptual structures in the development of scientific and social thought. In C. A. Hauert (Ed.), *Advances in psychology—Developmental psychology: Cognitive, perceptuo-motor and neurological perspectives* (pp. 193–230). Amsterdam: North Holland.

Case, R., & Sowder, J. T. (1990). The development of computational estimation: A neo-Piagetian analysis. *Cognition and Instruction, 7*(2), 79–104.

Cobb, P. (1988). The tension between theories of learning and instruction in mathematics education. *Educational Psychologist, 23*(2), 87–103.

Cobb, P., & Merkel, G. (1989). Thinking strategies: Teaching arithmetic through problem solving. In P. R. Trafton & A. P. Shulte (Eds.), *New directions for elementary school mathematics* (pp. 70–81). Reston, VA: NCTM.

Cobb, P., Yackel, E., & Wood, T. (1988). Curriculum and teacher development: Psychological and anthropological perspectives. In E. Fennema, T. P. Carpenter, & S. J. Lamon (Eds.), *Integrating research on teaching and learning mathematics* (pp. 92–130). Madison, WI: National Center for Research in Mathematical Sciences Education.

Dowker, A. D. (1989, May). *Computational estimation by young children.* Paper presented at the Conference of the British Society for Research into Learning Mathematics, Brighton Polytechnic, Brighton, England.

Fuson, K. C., & Hall, J. W. (1983). The acquisition of early number word meanings: A conceptual analysis and review. In H. P. Ginsburg (Ed.), *The development of mathematical thinking* (pp. 49–107). New York: Academic.

Gelman, R., & Gallistel, C. R. (1978). *The child's understanding of number.* Cambridge, MA: Harvard University Press.

Ginsburg, H. (1977). *Children's arithmetic: The learning process.* New York: Van Nostrand.

Ginsburg, H. P., Posner, J. K., & Russell, R. L. (1981). The development of mental addition as a function of schooling and culture. *Journal of Cross-Cultural Psychology, 12*(2), 163–178.

Goretskii, V. G. (Ed.). (1979). *Teaching mathematics in grade one: Handbook for teachers.* Moscow: Prosveshchenie.

Greeno, J. G. (1989). Some conjectures about number sense. In J. T. Sowder & B. P. Schappelle (Eds.), *Establishing foundations for research on number sense and related topics: Report of a conference* (pp. 43–56). San Diego: San Diego State University Center for Research in Mathematics and Science Education.

Hart, K. (1981). *Children's understanding of mathematics: 11–16.* London: John Murray.

Hatano, G. (1988). Social and motivational bases for mathematical understanding. In G. B. Saxe & M. Gearhart (Eds.), *New directions for child development, #41: Children's mathematics* (pp. 55–70). San Francisco: Jossey-Bass.

Hiebert, J. (1989). Reflections after the conference on number sense. In J. T. Sowder & B. P. Schappelle (Eds.), *Establishing foundations for research on number sense and related topics: Report of a conference* (pp. 82–84). San Diego: San Diego State University Center for Research in Mathematics and Science Education.

Hiebert, J., & Lefevre, P. (1986). Conceptual and procedural knowledge in mathematics: An introductory analysis. In J. Hiebert (Ed.), *Conceptual and procedural knowledge: The case of mathematics* (pp. 1–27). Hillsdale, NJ: Lawrence Erlbaum Associates.

Hiebert, J., & Wearne, D. (1986). Procedures over concepts: The acquisition of decimal number knowledge. In J. Hiebert (Ed.), *Conceptual and procedural knowledge: The case of mathematics* (pp. 199–223). Hillsdale, NJ: Lawrence Erlbaum Associates.

Hope, J. A. (1987). A case study of a highly skilled mental calculator. *Journal for Research in Mathematics Education, 18*(5), 331–342.

Howden, H. (1989). Teaching number sense. *Arithmetic Teacher, 36*(6), 6–11.

Johnson, S. (1989). Milking a million. *The Elementary Mathematician, 3*(3), 3–5.

Kerslake, D. (1986). *Fractions: Children's strategies and errors.* Windsor, England: NFER-NELSON.

Kouba, V. L., Carpenter, T. P., & Swafford, J. O. (1989). Number and operations. In M. M. Lindquist (Ed.), *Results from the Fourth Mathematics Assessment of the National Assessment of Educational Progress* (pp. 64–93). Reston, VA: NCTM.

Kravchenko, V. S., Oksman, L. S., & Yankovskaya, N. A. (1979). *Oral exercises in mathematics, Grades 1–3.* Moscow: Proveshchenie.

Lampert, M. (1988). Connecting mathematical teaching and learning. In E. Fennema, T. P. Carpenter, & S. J. Lamon (Eds.), *Integrating research on teaching and learning mathematics* (pp. 132–165). Madison, WI: National Center for Research in Mathematical Sciences Education.

Levine, D. R. (1982). Strategy use and estimation ability of college students. *Journal for Research in Mathematics Education, 13*(5), 350–359.

Mack, N. K. (1988, April). *Using estimation to learn fractions with understanding.* Paper presented at the annual meeting of the American Educational Research Association, New Orleans.

Markovits, Z. (1989). Reactions to the number sense conference. In J. T. Sowder & B. P. Schappelle (Eds.), *Establishing foundations for research on number sense and related topics: Report of a conference* (pp. 78–81). San Diego: San Diego State University Center for Research in Mathematics and Science Education.

Markovits, Z., & Sowder, J. (1988). Mental computation and number sense. In M. J. Behr, C. B. Lacampagne, & M. M. Wheeler (Eds.), *PME-NA: Proceedings of the Tenth Annual Meeting* (pp. 58–64). DeKalb: Northern Illinois University.

Markushevich, A. E. (Ed.). (1980). *Mathematics: Textbook for grade 4.* Moscow: Prosveshchenie.

Moro, M. I., & Bantova, M. A. (1980). *Mathematics: Textbook for grade 2.* Moscow: Prosveshchenie.

National Council of Supervisors of Mathematics. (1977). Position paper on basic skills. *Arithmetic Teacher, 25*(1), 19–22.

National Council of Teachers of Mathematics. (1989). *Curriculum and evaluation standards for school mathematics.* Reston, VA: Author.

Olivier, A. I., Murray, H., & Human, P. (1990). Building on young children's informal arithmetical knowledge. In G. Booker, P. Cobb, & T. de Mendicuti (Eds.), *Proceedings of the fourteenth annual meeting: International Group for the Psychology of Mathematics Education* (Vol. 3, pp. 297–304). Gobierno del Estado de Morelos, Mexico: CONACYT.

Paulos, J. A. (1988). *Innumeracy: Mathematical illiteracy and its consequences.* New York: Hill & Wang.

Pchelko, A. S., Bantova, M. A., Moro, M. I., & Pyshkalo, A. M. (1978). *Mathematics: Textbook for grade 3.* Moscow: Prosveshchenie.

Peck, D. M., & Jencks, S. M. (1981). Conceptual issues in the teaching and learning of fractions. *Journal for Research in Mathematics Education, 12*(5), 339–348.

Peterson, P. L., Fennema, E., & Carpenter, T. P. (1991). Teacher's knowledge of students' mathematics problem solving knowledge. In J. E. Brophy (Ed.), *Advances in research on teaching: Vol. 2. Teachers' subject matter knowledge,* (pp. 49–86). Greenwich, CT: JAI Press.

Petitto, A. L., & Ginsburg, H. P. (1982). Mental arithmetic in Africa and America: Strategies, principles, and explanations. *International Journal of Psychology, 17,* 81–102.

Resnick, L. B. (1983). A developmental theory of number understanding. In H. P. Ginsburg (Ed.), *The development of mathematical thinking* (pp. 109–151). Orlando, FL: Academic.

Resnick, L. B. (1986). The development of mathematical intuition. In M. Perlmutter (Ed.), *Perspectives on intellectual development: The Minnesota Symposia on Child Psychology* (pp. 159–194). Hillsdale, NJ: Lawrence Erlbaum Associates.

Resnick, L. B. (1987a). Constructing knowledge in school. In L. S. Liben (Ed.), *Development and learning: Conflict or congruence?* (pp. 19–50). Hillsdale, NJ: Lawrence Erlbaum Associates.

Resnick, L. B. (1987b). *Education and learning to think.* Washington, DC: National Academy Press.

Resnick, L. B. (1989a). Defining, assessing, and teaching number sense. In J. T. Sowder & B. P. Schappelle (Eds.), *Establishing foundations for research on number sense and related topics: Report of a conference* (pp. 35–39). San Diego: San Diego State University Center for Research in Mathematics and Science Education.

Resnick, L. B. (1989b). Developing mathematical knowledge. *American Psychologist, 44*(2), 162–169.

Resnick, L. B., Lesgold, S., & Bill, V. (1990). From protoquantities to number sense. In G. Booker, P. Cobb, & T. de Mendicuti (Eds.) *Proceedings of the fourteenth annual meeting: International Group for the Psychology of Mathematics Education* (Vol. 3, pp. 305–311). Gobierno del Estado de Morelos, Mexico: CONACYT.

Resnick, L. B., & Omanson, S. F. (1987). Learning to understand arithmetic. In R. Glaser (Ed.),

Advances in instructional psychology (pp. 41–95). Hillsdale, NJ: Lawrence Erlbaum Associates.

Reys, B. B. (1989). Conference on number sense: Reflections. In J. T. Sowder & B. P. Schappelle (Eds.), *Establishing foundations for research on number sense and related topics: Report of a conference* (pp. 70–73). San Diego: San Diego State University Center for Research in Mathematics and Science Education.

Reys, R. E. (1989). Some personal reflections on the conference on number sense, mental computation, and estimation. In J. T. Sowder & B. P. Schappelle (Eds.), *Establishing foundations for research on number sense and related topics: Report of a conference* (pp. 65–66). San Diego: San Diego State University Center for Research in Mathematics and Science Education.

Reys, R. E., Rybolt, J. F., Bestgen, B. J., & Wyatt, J. W. (1982). Processes used by good computational estimators. *Journal for Research in Mathematics Education, 13*(3), 183–201.

Reys, R. E., Trafton, P. R., Reys, B. B., & Zawojewski, J. (1984). *Developing computational estimation materials for the middle grades.* Final Report of NSF Grant No. NSF 81-13601.

Riley, M. S., Greeno, J. G., & Heller, J. I. (1983). Development of children's problem-solving ability in arithmetic. In H. P. Ginsburg (Ed.), *The development of mathematical thinking* (pp. 153–196). New York: Academic.

Rosch, E. (1973). On the internal structure of perceptual and semantic categories. In T. E. Moore (Ed.), *Cognitive development and acquisition of language.* New York: Academic.

Rubenstein, R. N. (1985). Computational estimation and related mathematical skills. *Journal for Research in Mathematics Education, 16*(2), 106–119.

Sackur-Grisvard, C., & Leonard, F. (1985). Intermediate cognitive organizations in the process of learning a mathematical concept: The order of positive decimal numbers. *Cognition and Instruction, 2*(2), 157–174.

Saxe, G. B. (1988). Candy selling and math learning. *Educational Researcher, 6*(6), 14–21.

Schappelle, B. P. (1990). A search for a curriculum to promote number sense: Contributions from the Soviet Union and Hungary. San Diego: San Diego State University Center for Research in Mathematics and Science Education.

Shuard, H. (1986). *Primary mathematics in the calculator/computer age.* Unpublished manuscript.

Silver, E. A. (1989). On making sense of number sense. In J. T. Sowder & B. P. Schappelle (Eds.), *Establishing foundations for research on number sense and related topics: Report of a conference* (pp. 92–96). San Diego: San Diego State University Center for Research in Mathematics and Science Education.

Sowder, J. T. (in press). Estimation and related topics. In D. A. Grouws (Ed.), *Handbook of research on teaching and learning mathematics.* New York: Macmillan.

Sowder, J. T., & Markovits, Z. (1988). [Number size: Interview data]. Unpublished raw data.

Sowder, J. T., & Markovits, Z. (1989). Effects of instruction on number magnitude. In C. A. Maher, G. A. Goldin, & R. B. Davis (Eds.), *Proceedings of the eleventh annual meeting: North American Chapter of the International Group for the Psychology of Mathematics Education* (pp. 105–110). New Brunswick, NJ: Center for Mathematics, Science, and Computer Education, Rutgers—The State University of New Jersey.

Sowder, J. T., & Markovits, Z. (1990). Relative and absolute error in computational estimation. In G. Booker, P. Cobb, & T. de Mendicuti (Eds.), *Proceedings of the fourteenth annual meeting: International Group for the Psychology of Mathematics Education* (Vol. 3, pp. 321–328). Gobierno del Estado de Morelos, Mexico: CONACYT.

Sowder, J. T., & Markovits, Z. (1991). *Learning computational estimation.* Unpublished manuscript.

Sowder, J. T., & Schappelle, B. P. (Eds.). (1989). *Establishing foundations for research on number sense and related topics: Report of a conference.* San Diego, CA: San Diego State University Center for Research in Mathematics and Science Education.

Sowder, J. T., & Wheeler, M. M. (1987). *The development of computational estimation and number sense: Two exploratory studies* (Research Report). San Diego: San Diego State University Center for Research in Mathematics and Science Education.

Sowder, J. T., & Wheeler, M. M. (1989). The development of concepts and strategies used in computational estimation. *Journal for Research in Mathematics Education, 20*(2), 130–146.

Threadgill-Sowder, J. (1984). Computational estimation procedures of school children. *Journal of Educational Research, 77*(6), 332–336.

Trafton, P. R. (1989). Reflections on the number sense conference. In J. T. Sowder & B. P. Schappelle (Eds.), *Establishing foundations for research on number sense and related topics: Report of a conference* (pp. 74–77). San Diego: San Diego State University Center for Research in Mathematics and Science Education.

Wearne, D., & Hiebert, J. (1988a). Constructing and using meaning for mathematical symbols: The case of decimal fractions. In J. Hiebert & M. Behr (Eds.), *Number concepts and operations in the middle grades* (pp. 220–235). Hillsdale, NJ: Lawrence Erlbaum Associates and Reston, VA: NCTM.

Wearne, D., & Hiebert, J. (1988b). A cognitive approach to meaningful mathematics instruction: Testing a local theory using decimal numbers. *Journal for Research in Mathematics Education, 19*(5), 371–384.

2

RESEARCH ON LEARNING AND TEACHING ADDITION AND SUBTRACTION OF WHOLE NUMBERS

Karen C. Fuson
Northwestern University

Contents

This chapter summarizes current research that is relevant to the learning and teaching of addition and subtraction of whole numbers ranging from simple small number situations through the multidigit algorithms. There is a considerable amount of research on how children think about addition and subtraction situations. We now are able to describe developmental progressions in this thinking from the preschool years through the third grade. However, we do not yet have very clear understandings of how or why children move from one level of thinking to a more advanced level. There is considerably less research directly concerning the teaching of addition and subtraction. Some of this research uses the research on children's thinking to devise and test teaching approaches, some examines textbook treatments of addition and subtraction as a way to understand children's current learning environments, some focuses on analyses of the mathematical conceptual attributes of what is to be learned, and some focuses on aspects of the teaching process itself. This chapter summarizes results from these areas of research but, because of the relative amounts of research available, concentrates most heavily on children's thinking.

The chapter is divided into three major sections. The first section focuses on simple addition and subtraction of sums through 10. It includes discussion of learning the number-word sequence, counting objects, reading and writing symbols to 20, and solving simple addition and subtraction word problems. The second section concerns single-digit sums and differences between 10 and 18, more complex addition and subtraction situations (and word problems), and the several more complex solution procedures children use to solve such situations. The final section covers multidigit whole numbers (i.e., the base-ten system of numeration) and multidigit addition and subtraction. The grade levels for these sections are overlapping: The first section is directed toward teaching from the preschool through the first grade, the second toward first and second grades, and the third toward second through sixth grades. Thus, this chapter moves from very simple addition and subtraction as comprehended by preschool children through the most difficult addition and subtraction problems treated in the elementary school mathematics curriculum.

Each main section is divided into three parts: research on children's thinking, research on instruction, and a vision of the future called "What Can Be: Supporting Children's Thinking in the Classroom." This organization stems from contradictions that emerge between the research on children's thinking and the research on instruction. The research on children's thinking unequivocally reveals children to be constructors of their own knowledge who see a given situation according to their own conceptual structures for that situation. These conceptual structures change and become more sophisticated and efficient, enabling children to see and do different things at different times even for the same given situation. In sharp contrast, much of the past practice of mathematics instruction, as reflected in textbooks (the primary vehicle for mathematics teaching), in teachers' knowledge about mathematics and how to teach mathematics (resulting from their own mathematics classroom learning experiences), and in children's mathematics performance, is directed toward producing calculators—people who can add, subtract, multiply, and divide whole numbers, fractions, decimals, and integers (and later, who can solve equations, use formulas, solve triangles, integrate, differentiate). For hundreds of years human societies needed such calculators. Societies devised institutions for producing such calculators (apprentices, universities, schools), and the calculators-to-be spent a great deal of time learning the written symbols of mathematics, learning the rules to combine these symbols, and automatizing these rules. Our present mathematics education is the legacy of this tradition: The words "instruction" and even "teaching" imply that one need only tell or demonstrate the rules and the calculator-to-be will learn to follow them.

The problem, of course, is not only the strong conflict between our present view of children as active thinkers who have different conceptual structures for a given mathematical situation and the passive view of the learner taken by schools, textbooks, and many teachers (because of their own educational backgrounds). The very goals of mathematics education now have to change with the widespread availability all over the world of inexpensive calculators that can carry out the rules of calculation more quickly and more accurately than can most (and for larger problems, all) people. The increasing availability of powerful computers also will continue to change the goals of mathematics education for years to come. These calculating machines are powerful calculators, but they are extraordinarily weak at interpreting, at making meanings, at deciding what rules or what operations to use in a given situation. These are the special capabilities of humans. Children now need to be problem solvers and problem posers, not just calculators. Therefore, it is now crucial that mathematics education emphasize and develop children's abilities to understand and connect meanings to mathematical symbols. Mathematics education must shift from concentrating on teaching children what to do when they see mathematical symbols to concentrating on helping children think when they see mathematical symbols or a mathematical situation. This view does not imply that children learn no aspects of computation, but it does emphasize that these aspects must be linked to meanings so that the computational results can be interpreted sensibly. There is sufficient research at present to indicate ways in which teachers can teach for meaning. This changed emphasis can make teaching mathematics to young children much more enjoyable and more human than the past emphasis on children as calculating machines.

Teaching mathematics meaningfully requires helping children construct concepts for spoken mathematical words and written mathematical symbols. The latter is called *mathematical marks* to avoid the ambiguities of the various uses of the word "symbol" and to emphasize that these squiggles written on paper (or on the chalkboard) must be interpreted, must be given some meaning, by each viewer. This term, then, is a constant reminder that it is the task of the mathematics classroom to help children toward fruitful interpretations of these marks and that some of these interpretations may not be obvious. The mathematical marks required for addition and subtraction of whole numbers are really quite few: 0, 1, 2, 3, 4, 5, 6, 7, 8, 9, $+$, $-$, $=$, $<$, $>$. With these 15 marks and some rules for combining the marks (e.g., for whole numbers one can write 5038 and $8 - 2$ but not $5 + 3$ $-$ or $2 - 8$), one can assess the cardinal aspects of a truly amazing number of addition and subtraction situations. One pays for this efficiency, sometimes called the unreasonable power of mathematics, by complexities in the use of the marks and by multiple meanings attached to several of them. It is the task of the teacher to help children understand these complexities and multiple meanings so that they can take advantage of the power of the marks. The goal of this chapter is to help teachers and those who work with teachers understand these complexities and multiple meanings, and how children think about them, so that they can better meet the challenge of their roles. Thus, a number is an idea, a concept, and children think about numbers in various ways. Concepts of numbers are very concrete for young children, and they become increasingly abstract. When young children hear a number word (e.g., eight) or see a written number mark (e.g., 8) they may have a different concept of number for that word or mark than adults do. This chapter describes these different conceptual structures for number that children have.

By the time children enter school, they already possess considerable mathematical understanding. This understanding sometimes has been characterized as informal understanding or informal mathematics, in contrast to the formal mathematical knowledge that is the focus of school instruction. Many researchers suggest that the teaching of the formal school mathematics be linked to children's informal mathematics (e.g., Baroody, 1987a; Carpenter & Moser, 1982; Ginsburg, 1977; Hiebert, 1984). This chapter presents a similar position but casts the issue in terms of children's conceptual structures for the mathematics to be learned rather than in terms of informal/formal knowledge. The latter terms may convey some sense of informal mathematics as being less organized, less correct, less efficient than formal mathematics, and this may not be true. The more central issue here is that all children will use conceptual structures for the formal mathematical words and marks used in the school mathematics classroom; they must do so in order to process and react to those words and marks. Therefore, children either will use conceptual structures they already bring into the classroom or they will construct new conceptual structures from experiences in the classroom. Some of these conceptual structures are accurate and some are not; some are efficient and some are not; some are advanced and some are simple. To help children function effectively in mathematics, teachers need to reflect on how the classroom experiences they are providing their children are supporting children's construction of accurate, efficient, and advanced conceptual structures for the mathematical marks, procedures, and concepts addressed in the classroom. Knowing the range of conceptual structures used by their children obviously can aid in this reflective process.

It is important to keep in mind that most of the research discussed in this chapter concerns children who have received traditional school mathematics instruction focused on teaching children to be doers rather than thinkers. This approach considerably underestimates what children can learn. Thus, these results should not be viewed as inevitable or as norms of what children of certain ages can learn but rather as the consequences of the cultural practices in U.S. mathematics classrooms.

SIMPLE ADDITION AND SUBTRACTION
WITH SUMS AND DIFFERENCES TO TEN:
PATTERN NUMBER AND COUNTED NUMBER

Research on Children's Early
Numerical Thinking

Pattern Number

Cardinal number situations involve some set of discrete entities; the cardinal number refers to the whole set of entities (not to any of the individual entities) and describes the manyness of the set. Some children begin to label cardinal situations with a number word even before 2 years of age (Durkin, Shire, Riem, Crowther, & Rutter, 1986; Fuson, 1988a; Wagner & Walters, 1982; Walters & Wagner, 1981). Up until age 3 years or so, and perhaps even beyond, such labelings are mostly the word "two," with less use of "three" and "four" and very little use of any larger number words. Preschool children as young as 3 and 4 years show some understanding of very simple cardinal addition and subtraction situations in which addition is viewed as "getting some more" and subtraction is viewed as "losing some" (Brush, 1978; Cooper, 1984; Fuson, 1988a; Gelman & Gallistel, 1978; Ginsburg, 1977; Ginsburg & Russell, 1981; Saxe, Guberman, & Gearhart, 1987; Starkey, 1987; Starkey & Gelman, 1982). All of these cardinal situations involve very small numbers, usually addends of 1, 2, and 3. Apparently young children can process very small numbers such as 1, 2, and 3 much more easily than larger numbers; this ability to see and label very small numbers has been called subitizing (Kaufman, Lord, Reese, & Volkmann, 1949). How children think about such very small numbers is not known, but most theories hypothesize that they use visual or auditory patterns for these very small numbers (e.g., Chi & Klahr, 1975; Cooper, 1984; Klahr & Wallace, 1973, 1976; Mandler & Shebo, 1982; von Glasersfeld, 1982). Because these numbers involve special perceptual processes that do not generalize to larger numbers, facility with such small "perceptual" numbers does not necessarily indicate facility with larger numbers. Sometime between ages 4 and 6 years many children extend their range of perceptual numbers to somewhat larger numbers by making combinations of the smaller subitized numbers and "seeing" these smaller numbers within a larger number (von Glasersfeld, 1982, called this figural joining). A child may say, for example, "There are six because there are three and three." These patterns can be useful supports for learning sums below ten, especially those of eight or less.

Learning the Number-Word Sequence

Learning the English sequence of number words to one hundred is a protracted task that begins for most children in their third year and may last until first or second grade. Most middle-class children below age $3\frac{1}{2}$ years are working on learning the sequence to ten (Fuson, Richards, & Briars, 1982; Saxe et al., 1987), and most children between ages $3\frac{1}{2}$ and $4\frac{1}{2}$ years are working on learning the sequence between ten and twenty (Fuson et al., 1982; Saxe et al., 1987). A substantial proportion of children between $4\frac{1}{2}$ and 6 years of age still make errors in the sequence between fourteen and twenty but many are working on the decades from twenty through seventy (Fuson et al., 1982; Siegler & Robinson, 1982). Most kindergarten children are learning the decades between twenty and seventy, but a substantial number of them are working on the sequence between one hundred and two hundred (Bell & Bell, 1988; Fuson et al., 1982). Roughly half the first graders and almost all the second and third graders in the Bell and Bell (1988) sample knew the sequence to one hundred and were working on the sequence above one hundred. Of course, children's ability to say the correct sequence of number words is strongly affected by the opportunity to learn and to practice this sequence.[1] Children within a given age group show considerable variability in the length of their correct sequence. Frequent exposure to "Sesame Street" or to parents, older siblings, or teachers

---

[1]The Bell and Bell study (1988) is based on 500 working-, middle-, and upper-middle-class children from urban, suburban, public, and private schools. The Fuson et al. (1982) sample consisted of 60 $3\frac{1}{2}$-though 6-year-old children from a Chicago public magnet school with a population computer selected to match that of the city and 26 children of the same age from

who provide frequent counting practice undoubtedly enables a child to say longer accurate sequences at a younger age.

The incorrect sequences produced by children before they have learned the standard sequence have a characteristic structure (Fuson et al., 1982). For sequences up to thirty, the characteristic form of most sequences produced by children is a first portion consisting of an accurate number-word portion, followed by a 2- to 5- or 6-word stable incorrect portion that is produced with some consistency over repeated trials, followed by a final nonstable incorrect portion that varies over trials and may consist of many words. For example, in the sequence "1, 2, 3, 4, 5, 8, 9, 10, 12, 16, 18, 5, 9, 3, 16, 3, 10, 14, 16, 3, 16," the accurate number-word portion is "1, 2, 3, 4, 5" and the stable incorrect portion might be "8, 9, 10, 12" if these number words always or usually followed "1, 2, 3, 4, 5." The final nonstable incorrect portion is the rest of the number words after the stable portion. One cannot differentiate the stable and nonstable portions until one has heard a given child say the sequence several times. Almost all stable incorrect portions have words in the conventional order but some words are omitted (e.g., "fourteen, sixteen" or "twelve, fourteen, eighteen, nineteen"). The nonstable incorrect portion may contain words from the accurate and stable incorrect portions and some number words may be said several times.

The patterns of omissions and other data indicate that most children learn the words to twenty as a rote sequence of new words (except possibly for "eighteen, nineteen") rather than observing and using the somewhat irregular pattern of the teen words.[2] Children do see the decade pattern of repeated cycles of words from x-ty to x-ty-nine (Fuson et al., 1982; Siegler & Robinson, 1982), and their incorrect sequences will show these decade cycles. However, the decade problem of learning the English decade names and their conventional order takes a long time to solve (as much as a year and a half). During this time children may say the twenties, then the forties, then the sixties, then the forties again, then the thirties, and so on. Evidently it is difficult for children to see the pattern of the decade words because the words twenty, thirty, and fifty (rather than twoty, threety, and fivety) obscure the pattern in forty and sixty through ninety.

This characteristic form of incorrect sequences seems to result from the English irregularities between ten and twenty and the irregularities in the decade words. Number-word sequences with different structures do not

---

an upper-middle-class educational demonstration school. The Siegler and Robinson (1982) sample attended a university laboratory school and was considerably above average in ability. Obviously, sequence performance might differ for different populations of children, especially those for whom English is not the first language.

[2]See Fuson (1988a, pp. 39–41) for a discussion of the evidence concerning this issue.

show these same errors. For example, deaf children learning American Sign Language (ASL; Secada, 1985) show different errors that are related to hand positions that are difficult to make, and 4-, 5-, and 6-year-old Chinese children show few errors up to twenty with the regular Chinese number words (. . . , nine, ten, ten one, ten two, ten three, . . . , ten nine, two ten) (Miller & Stigler, 1987). The irregularities in English also suggest that one of the first experiences of English-speaking children with a mathematical structure (the English sequence of number words) is that it is complex, irregular, and must be memorized laboriously rather than that it has a clear and obvious pattern that is easy to learn. The negative consequences of these irregularities in English number words is a recurring issue in this chapter. In a very real way, English-speaking primary school children are culturally disadvantaged with respect to addition and subtraction of whole numbers compared to Asian children who have number words based on the regular Chinese sequence of number words in which the tens within each number are explicitly named. The task of the teacher of English-speaking children is therefore more complex, for the teacher must provide extra support to help children relate these irregular English words to the regular written number marks. The contrast in this chapter between children speaking English and children speaking an Asian language with number words that follow the regular named-ten Chinese pattern is between English-speaking children learning addition and subtraction in English and Asian-speaking children learning addition and subtraction in their regular Chinese pattern language. It is not clear at present the extent to which Asian-speaking children learning addition and subtraction in English (e.g., in classrooms in the United States) benefit from the regular named tens in their native language.

Learning with respect to the number-word sequence does not stop when a child can say the number words correctly. This sequence itself becomes the way in which children think about and add and subtract numbers (see section on "Research on Children's Later Numerical Thinking"). The sequence goes through developmental levels in which it becomes an increasingly efficient representational tool for solving addition and subtraction situations (Fuson et al., 1982). Children become able to think about the sequence, not just say it. They can start counting from a given number in the sequence and can give the word just before or just after a given word. Therefore, children need to continue to receive much practice in saying the number-word sequence and in counting objects with this sequence even after they can say the number-word sequence correctly.

Counting Objects

Counting objects in space is a complex activity. Such counting by young children has the following features (see Fuson, 1988a, for more details):

the production of *a sequence of counting words* (e.g., saying "one, two, three, four, five"),

isolation of perceptual unit items to be counted (e.g., the counter must take each of the five objects as a thing-to-be-counted; see Steffe, von Glasersfeld, Richards, & Cobb, 1983),

the use of a strategy for *sequencing the objects* so that every object is indicated and no object is indicated more than once,

the production of *a sequence of indicating acts* (such as pointing) that relates the sequence of words said in time ("one, two, three, four, five") to the objects distributed in space (the five scattered objects) by creating time-space units that coordinate two sequences of one-to-one correspondences: a *word–indicating act correspondence* occurring in time between the sequence of words and the sequence of indicating acts ("one" said while pointing to one object, "two" said while pointing to one object, etc.) and an *indicating act–object correspondence* occurring in space between the sequence of spatial locations indicated by the indicating acts and the spatial locations of the objects to be counted (the location of the first point is the same as the location of one object, the location of the second point is the same as the location of one object, etc.).

The indicating act of pointing (or moving objects or gaze fixation) connects the number words spoken over time to the objects scattered in space because each point is done in time with saying a word and that same point indicates (points at) an object.

The counting of young children very early displays all of these distinctive features (Fuson, 1988a; Gelman & Gallistel, 1978). It also fairly frequently violates one of the various correspondences (Fuson, 1988a). Even 3-year-olds use a linear sequence if objects are given in a row, but 5-year-olds still show difficulties in sequencing large disorganized arrays so some objects are never counted and others are counted twice. Three- and 4-year-olds violate the word-indicating act correspondence in two different ways: by pointing to an object without saying a word and by pointing to an object and saying two or more words. They violate the indicating act–object correspondence by skipping over objects (given them no point and no word) and by double counting objects (giving them a point and a word and then immediately another point and another word). Other more complex errors made less frequently are discussed in Fuson (1988a). Many individual entities are counted correctly, but these various errors scattered among correct correspondences frequently result in an inaccurate final count name. Five-year-olds make comparatively few errors, and many can count even fairly large rows accurately (up to 20 or even 30 objects). However, the counting of 5-year-olds does suffer from two factors that decreases the accuracy of their counting: lack of effort and internalization of counting. The accuracy of children's counting varies considerably with effort (Fuson,

1988a) and asking children to "try real hard" substantially reduces errors. Five-year-olds have begun to internalize both aspects of counting: They may say the words silently or with lip movements only and they may use eye fixation rather than pointing as the indicating act. The latter can greatly increase errors. Therefore, it is important for teachers of young children to accept counting in their classes (so that it will not go underground and become more errorful) and even to suggest that children who make errors should point and count out loud rather than look and count silently. Similarly, it would be useful to stress that one needs to count carefully because counting accurately is hard work rather than viewing counting as easy and/or babylike. As becomes clear in the section on addition and subtraction, counting for children at this developmental level is not a crutch to be abandoned as soon as possible. Rather, counting objects is their primary way of making numbers meaningful (i.e., of presenting and thinking about numbers) and this counting is crucial for the construction of later more efficient addition and subtraction procedures.

Counting and Cardinality

Counting for cardinal purposes is not part of children's early counting (Fuson, 1988a; Gelman & Gallistel, 1978; Ginsburg & Russell, 1981; Schaeffer, Eggleston, & Scott, 1974). Early counting has no result other than the activity of counting. Many 2- and 3-year-old children who are asked "how many" after counting typically count again (and continue to do so after each such request); they also may answer by saying a number word that is not the last word said in counting or by saying a sequence of number words (frequently not the sequence just said in counting). Most children during this period remember the last word they said in counting, so these responses are not due to limited memory resources (Fuson, 1988a). Children eventually come to make a *count-to-cardinal transition* in which they shift from the counting meaning of the last word said in counting as referring to the last counted object to a cardinal meaning of this word as referring to the manyness of the whole counted set of objects (Fuson, 1988a; Fuson & Hall, 1983). So, for example, when asked to show "the five cars" after having counted them, a child will indicate all five cars and not the last car where the child actually said "five" (during counting, "five" has a counting meaning paired with that object and does not have the cardinal meaning "all five cars"). A similar *count-to-ordinal transition* is required for counting in ordinal situations; this shift is more obvious because it requires a change in the number words; for example, "one, two, three, four, *five* (where five is the count name of the last counted object). This is the *fifth* candy." Some children show a transitional last-word response in which they will respond to a how-many question with the last word in counting, but the last word does not refer to the whole counted set—it does not yet have cardinal meaning. For example, such children will point to the last object where they said "five" and say, "This is the five cars." Almost all 5-year-olds do give last-word responses, and most of these are count-to-cardinal transitions in which the last counted word does shift in the child's thinking to refer to the manyness of the whole counted set.

Even with count-to-cardinal transitions, the cardinal word still does not have its full adult meaning. At this developmental level the cardinal word is only pattern number or counted number for children. The cardinal conceptual structures still have to go through the developments described in the second section, including Piaget's conservation of discrete quantity (Piaget, 1941/1965). Conservation is discussed here because many followers of Piaget have suggested that it is fruitless for children to work on addition or subtraction situations until they have conservation of number. Understanding conservation of number is assessed by making a row of objects and asking a child to make a row equivalent to the given row of objects. Even most 4-year-olds can make such a row and can judge the two rows in visual one-to-one correspondence (objects directly across from each other) to be equivalent (i.e., to have the same number of objects). However, if one row is made longer by moving the objects apart (or made shorter by moving the objects closer together), young children are drawn by the length of the rows and judge the longer row to have more (or, occasionally, use density and judge the shorter row to have more). Children who conserve (some 5-year-olds, many 6-year-olds, and most 7-years-olds) know that the transformation of the objects does not affect their quantity and respond even without counting the two rows that the two rows still have the same number. Piaget discounted the role of counting in the child's construction of the concept of number, and it is true that children at a certain point will count each row and obtain the same counted number but still say that the longer row has more (even saying something like "this seven is more than that seven"). However, there is now considerable evidence that if 5-year-old children are asked to count in the conservation situation, they can use the count information to judge the rows to be equivalent, and older 5-year-olds will count spontaneously to obtain such information in the conservation situation (Fuson, 1988a; Michie, 1984a, 1984b; Secada, Fuson, & Hall, 1983; Siegler, 1981). Thus, for most 5-year-olds counted number is sufficient to ascertain the equivalence or non-equivalence of two sets. Therefore, a lack of conservation of numerical equivalence does not prevent children from meaningful engagement with counted or patterned number situations, including simple addition and subtraction situations.

TABLE 2.1
Simple Addition and Subtraction Situations

Action Unary	*Static Binary*
Simple Addition Situations	
Change-Add-To: Missing End	*Put-Together: Missing All*
Joe had 5 marbles. Then Tom gave him 3 more marbles. How many marbles does Joe have now? COUNT ALL	Joe has 3 marbles. Tom has 5 marbles. How many marbles do they have altogether? COUNT ALL
Simple Subtraction Situations	
Change-Take-From: Missing End	*Equalize Compare: Missing Difference*
Connie had 8 marbles. Then she gave 3 marbles to Jim. How many marbles does she have left? SEPARATE FROM	Susan has 8 marbles. Fred has 5 marbles. How many more marbles does Fred have to get to have as many marbles as Susan has? (or: How many marbles does Susan have to lose to have as many marbles as Fred?) MATCH or COUNT SMALLER AND COUNT THE REST
	Won't Get Compare: Missing Difference
	There are 6 birds and 4 worms. Suppose the birds all race over and each one tries to get a worm? How many birds won't get a worm? MATCH or COUNT SMALLER AND COUNT THE REST

(Continued)

Simple Addition and Subtraction Situations

The mathematical marks + and − need to be given some meaning. Typically only one meaning has been given for + (it means to get more) and one meaning has been given for − (it means to take away some). However, research indicates that there are several different simple addition and subtraction situations that kindergarteners and early first graders can readily understand and solve. Some of these can be solved without any previous experience, whereas some require a bit of discussion and practice. Children solve these problems by directly modeling the action or situation with objects, for example, with blocks, fingers, or drawings on paper (Bergeron & Herscovics, 1990; Carpenter & Moser, 1983; Riley, Greeno, & Heller, 1983). These objects are not just answer-getting devices for the children. They present the problem situation and the problem numbers to the child and suggest the solution procedure, which is then carried out on the available numerical presentation (i.e., with the objects).

TABLE 2.1
(continued)

Action Unary	Static Binary
	Fairly Simple Subtraction Situations
Change-Take-From: Missing Change	Compare: Missing Difference
Joe had 8 marbles. Then he gave some marbles to Tom. Now Joe has 3 marbles. How many marbles did he give to Tom? SEPARATE TO	Joe has 8 marbles. Tom has 5 marbles. How many more marbles does Joe have than Tom? (or: How many fewer marbles does Tom have than Joe?) MATCH
Change-Add-To: Missing Change	Put-Together: Missing Part
Kathy has 9 pencils. How many more pencils does she have to put with them so she has 15 pencils altogether? ADD ON UP TO SUM[a]	There are 6 children on the playground. 4 are boys [and the rest are girls.] How many girls are on the playground?
	Together, Tom and Joe have 8 apples. 3 [of these apples] belong to Tom. How many [of them] belong to Joe?
	Tom and Ann have 9 nuts altogether. Three of these nuts belong to Tom. [The rest belong to Ann.] How many nuts does Ann have? SEPARATE FROM (if make All first) ADD ON (if make Part first)[a]

Note: The direct modeling object solution procedure is given in capital letters under each word problem. Words in [ ] make the problem easier because they make the problem structure clearer to the children.

[a]These procedures require keeping the added-on objects separate from the initial objects, so some sense of double role objects is required.

The addition and subtraction situations that are clearly appropriate in kindergarten and at the beginning of the first grade are given in Table 2.1.[3] The simple addition and simple subtraction situations in Table 2.1 are those solvable by direct modeling with objects by many children even at the beginning of kindergarten, whereas the situations called "fairly simple subtraction situations" may require some facilitation, discussion, and ex-

---

[3]These terms for the situations are simplifications of the terms used in Fuson (1988a) and in an instructional project with first and second graders (Fuson, 1988b, 1991; Fuson & Willis, 1989) because they are easier for children than are the standard terms. Change-Join, Change-Separate, and Combine (for Put Together) are the more usual terms. We changed here the terms Change-Get-More and Change-Get-Less to Change-Add-To and Change-Take-From to emphasize the action rather than the result and to use terms appropriate for integers as well as for whole numbers (e.g., when you add a negative number, you do not get more).

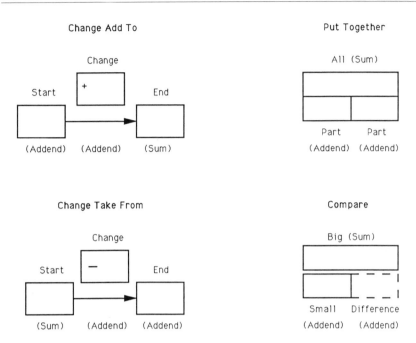

FIG. 2.1.   Schematic drawings to show word problems.

perience in order for most kindergarteners or early first graders to solve successfully using objects. Schematic drawings that show the four basic types of situations are shown in Fig. 2.1. The action unary Change-Add-To and Change-Take-From situations involve an initial quantity (Start), a Change quantity, and a final End quantity. The Put Together situation is composed of two Parts that when put together make All. The Compare situation involves a comparison of two quantities, a Big and a Small, that yields a Difference (the amount the Big is bigger than the Small and the amount the Small is smaller than the Big). The difficulty of a given problem depends heavily on which quantity is unknown; these relative difficulty levels are given in Fig. 2.2.

The direct modeling solution procedures children use to solve each kind of problem are typed in capital letters in Table 2.1. For both kinds of Change problems and for the Put Together problem, the sum is made out of the same objects that make both addends.[4] Objects are used to make one addend, and then other objects are used to make the other addend. These

<hr />

[4]We use the terms *sum, addend, addend* for subtraction situations because they emphasize the inverse relation of addition and subtraction and are easier to comprehend than the usual *minuend, subtrahend, difference* terms.

addends are combined to make the sum objects, or the sum is made with objects first and then separated somehow into the two addends. Thus, these solution procedures all occur over time, and each object plays two roles (as composing an addend and as composing the sum). However, it only plays one of these roles at a time: At a given moment it is either a sum object or an addend object.

The two simple addition situations suggest somewhat different actions with objects. The Change situation suggests making objects for the initial starting set, adding to that set the number of objects in the change set, and then counting all of the objects to ascertain the result. The Put Together situation suggests making objects for one addend, making objects for the other addend, and then putting these objects together to find out how many they make together or just counting the two sets altogether without moving them. Many first graders do differentiate between these problem types by solving them in these different ways (De Corte & Verschaffel, 1987a). Moser (in Bergeron & Herscovics, 1990) made further differentiations within Change procedures depending on whether objects for the second addend were added to the first addend objects one at a time or gathered separately and added all at once. He also differentiated Put Together solutions in which the objects for both addends were moved to-

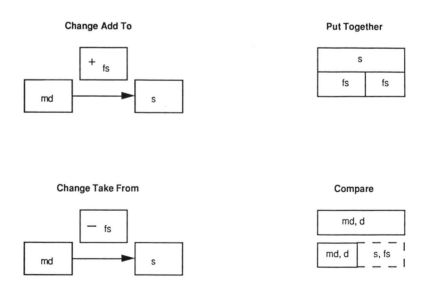

FIG. 2.2.   Difficulty level of word problems with different unknown quantities. *Note:* The small letters within the drawings indicate the difficulty level of a problem in which that quantity is unknown: s is simple, fs is fairly simple, and md is more difficult. The difficulty of the Compare problems depends heavily on whether the question cues the solution procedures, so these problems have multiple difficulty classifications that depend on the nature of the question.

gether and those in which all of the objects were counted as the sum without moving any objects. However, these differences seldom have been noted or described by researchers. Because in all of these procedures all of the objects are counted to determine the sum, all of these procedures have usually just been called Counting All.

Change-Take-From: missing End is usually solved by a take-away procedure called Separate From because the sum set (the starting set in the Change-Take-From problem) objects are made and then the change objects are removed from (separated from) these sum objects. The remaining objects are the result. In Change-Take-From: missing Change, children usually Separate To: They make objects for the starting sum and then remove objects until only the specified number of End objects remain. The removed objects then tell the missing Change amount (unless the removed objects have been put with other objects not used in the problem, in which case the problem is not solved). Change-Add-To: missing Change problems have been found to be more difficult than the Change-Take-From: missing Change problems if there is no action cue as in Table 2.1. For problems as in Table 2.1, children use Add On Up To the Sum: They make objects for the Start set, add on objects of a different color (or objects otherwise differentiated from the start objects) until they have the known End number of sum objects, and then count the number of objects they have added on. This procedure requires at least a minimal double role for objects as being in the sum and in an addend, for the child must use different colored objects for the second unknown addend or keep the added on objects separate from the first addend objects to carry out this procedure successfully. In contrast, a child can just follow the action sequence in the Change-Take-From: missing Change problem and the answer is left as a separate pile of objects.

Young children's performance on Put-Together: missing Part problems varies considerably with differences in phrasing. Language clarifying the relationship between the parts and the all in such problems facilitates performance in kindergarteners and first graders. Three such examples are given in Table 2.1; they are taken from Carpenter, Hiebert, and Moser (1981), De Corte, Verschaffel, and De Win (1985), and Lindvall and Ibarra (1980). Obviously, set–subset problems such as the boys/girls/children problem also can vary in how easy it is for children to relate the subsets to the sum set. Such problems can be a good place for language practice of various kinds, and children might get quite involved in making up and keeping a record of many such sets/subsets. These problems also can vary in whether the sum or the known addend is mentioned first. This feature can affect how the problem is modeled with objects. If the known sum is mentioned first, this sum can be made with objects and then the known part separated from the sum to leave the unknown part (e.g., Carpenter &

Moser, 1984). If the known part is mentioned first, objects can be added on to make the sum objects (De Corte & Verschaffel, 1987a). In this case, the unknown part objects added on must be kept separate from the known objects (by using a different color or location); as discussed previously, this requires at least some anticipation of a double use for these objects as objects for the known part and also for the sum.

For all of the comparison situations (Equalize, Won't Get, and ordinary Compare), objects are used to make each of the compared sets (the Big set and the Small set). The objects for these two sets are matched, and the missing difference is equivalent to the extra objects in the Big set (i.e., to that part of the Big set that is more than the Small set). This matching procedure is fairly simple for children to carry out. Children also solve these problems by counting the Small set, counting that many in the Big set of objects, and then counting the rest of the Big set. Children's main difficulties with the Compare problems are in thinking to use matching initially and in understanding the meaning of the usual Compare question, that is, the meaning of the words "more," "less," and "fewer."[5] Helping children interpret this question in the Equalize question form can facilitate understanding of Compare problems because the Equalize questions suggest solution actions and are often easier for children than are Compare problems (e.g, Fuson & Willis, 1986).

We have at present no data concerning how first graders do in solving addition and subtraction situations if they have a supportive challenging numerical environment in kindergarten. Data based on present instructional methods indicate that with no previous instruction and using objects, more than 90% of kindergarten children were able to solve both simple Change: missing End situations, the Put-Together: missing All situation, the Change-Take-From: missing Change situation (Riley, 1981; see Riley et al., 1983), and the Won't Get Compare: missing Difference situation (Hudson, 1983). With no previous instruction and using objects, more than 90% of first graders were able to solve the Equalize Compare: missing Difference problem situations with both forms of the questions (Carpenter et al., 1981) and the Change-Add-To: missing Change with phrasing like that in Table 2.1 (Carpenter & Moser, 1984). Performance on the Compare: missing Difference ordinary static language form is quite variable, depending on children's opportunity to learn the meaning of "How many more than?" or "How many less than?" and to use the matching strategy that is natural in answering this question. First graders who had such an opportunity got 80% of such problems correct even for problems with sums between 11

---

[5]Technically, fewer refers to discrete (countable) quantities and less refers to continuous quantity, but less often is used in Compare word problems about discrete objects because it seems simpler or more familiar than fewer.

and 16 (Carpenter et al., 1981). First graders who had an opportunity to solve Put-Together: missing Part problems using objects and a part–whole drawing solved 77% of such problems correctly when the problems were the full information form such as in brackets in Table 2.1 (Carpenter et al., 1981).

Addition and Subtraction Mathematical Marks Problems

When children first begin to solve addition and subtraction problems written with mathematical marks (e.g., 4 + 2 or 5 − 3), they use objects to model each problem. How they use objects depends on the meanings they have learned for the + and − marks. Given the typical interpretations of + as Change-Add-To and of − as Change-Take-From (i.e., take away), children initially solve + problems by counting all and solve − problems by separating from. They may use objects or, particularly when both addends are 5 or less, use fingers. Addition and subtraction combinations sometimes are presented orally in research studies and in the classroom. The + sign is usually said as "plus" but sometimes as "and" ("four plus two" or "four and two"). The − sign is frequently said as "take away" ("four take away two"), but "minus" is a neutral word that can indicate either take-away or comparison subtraction. The solution procedures discussed here have been used to solve oral and written marks problems.

In the most primitive solution procedure for addition problems, each finger is counted as it is extended to make the first addend, the second addend is made on the other hand by counting each finger as it is extended, and then all of the fingers for both addends are counted (Baroody, 1987b). Eventually, patterns of fingers may become known, and the requisite addend fingers each may be extended as a pattern on separate hands and then counted altogether or extended and the sum recognized as a pattern (Baroody, 1987b; Siegler & Robinson, 1982; Siegler & Shrager, 1984). Later, the initial production of the addend finger patterns may be omitted, and all of the fingers just counted as fingers for each addend are sequentially extended (Baroody, 1987b); this requires attending to the second addend fingers during this sum count of the second addend and stopping the count when fingers for the second addend have been extended. Eventually counting all may be done without any observable objects: The final sum counting all is just said out loud (Baroody, 1984; Baroody & Gannon, 1984; Baroody & Ginsburg, 1986; Siegler & Robinson, 1982; Siegler & Shrager, 1984). This counting all may be done in the order in which the addends are given or a child may start by counting the larger number first, thus minimizing the difficulty of the demanding keeping-track process for the second addend. Children may count all from the larger number without necessarily understanding commutativity, that is, without understanding that counting from the larger number will produce the same answer as counting from the first number given (see Baroody & Ginsburg, 1986, for a discussion).

Subtraction procedures for sums of ten and less have been studied much less than have addition procedures, but Siegler and Shipley (1987) reported that kindergarteners and first graders model separating procedures for a subtraction combination in four ways similar to those used for addition by preschoolers: counting fingers (counting out the sum by successively extending fingers, counting the known addend by successively putting down each finger while counting, and then counting the remaining fingers to find the unknown addend), producing fingers (putting out a finger pattern for the sum, putting down a finger pattern for the known addend, and then recognizing and labeling the finger pattern for the remaining unknown addend), counting (without any observable objects), and remembering the answer.

Eventually children simply remember the sum or the difference of two given numbers. They remember sums before remembering differences, and remembering differences seems to depend on and is frequently derived from the sum (Briars & Larkin, 1984; Steinberg, 1984). Siegler has proposed a distributions of associations model of such fact learning in which a child first tries to generate an answer to a given problem (Siegler & Shipley, 1987; Siegler & Shrager, 1984). If no answer is stored with a sufficiently high probability, the child will use one of the nonmemory solution procedures described previously. Gradually over time and with practice, distributions of particular answers begin to build up for particular problems. If the initial solution procedures for a given problem are carried out accurately, the associations for that problem will become peaked at the right answer fairly early. If a child instead guesses or uses inadequate solution procedures, several different answers will become associated to that problem, greatly delaying the time at which the child will be able to recall the correct answer. This model thus underscores the importance of teachers supporting children's construction and use of accurate solution procedures, even if the procedures seem primitive to the teacher. It is also important to create a classroom environment where accuracy and meaningful solutions are more important than rapidly produced answers, because stress on the latter leads to increased associations with incorrect answers for good and not-so-good students, who tend to set low thresholds for generating an answer without solving the problem (Siegler, 1988). A more recent strategy-choice model currently is being developed. In this model the choice among all available strategies reflects specific associations between a given strategy and the particular given number pair and more general associations with related number pairs and with pairs on which that strategy has been used (Siegler & Jenkins, 1989). We know relatively little at the moment about how children make choices among various strategies they possess. Baroody and Ginsburg (1986) stressed that children also learn many facts by noticing patterns across facts, for example, the 0 facts (in which the sum is the greater addend) and the doubles (1 + 1, 2 + 2, 3 + 3, etc. in which the sums go up by alternating numbers). Children also learn many of the smaller sums by subitizing and adding objects for the sum, leading to a pattern-based knowledge of the sum (e.g., seeing 6 objects as 3 objects and 3 objects or as 4 objects and 2 objects).

Learning the Mathematical Marks from 1 to 20

At present, we do not have very much information about how or at what ages children learn the mathematical marks for numbers. However, it is clear that many children bring to school considerable knowledge regarding both reading and writing such marks. Bell and Bell (1988; see also Hedges, Stodolsky, & Mathieson, 1987) found quite good facility concerning marks from 1 to 20 in kindergarten children from a range of schools (public and private, urban and suburban, working-class through upper-middle-class, 20% through 100% African-American populations) and found considerable competence concerning marks between 20 and 100. In October, 95% of the kindergarten children could read 3 and 80% of them could write 3. The percentages for 9, 17, 57, and 100 were 74%, 54%, 26%, and 41% for reading and 53%, 21%, 30%, and 31% for writing. By May reading and writing of both 3 and 9 were above 93%, and reading and writing of 17, 57, and 100 ranged between 55% and 80%. The reversal in the English teens words created special problems. We say the four first in fourteen but write the four second; we also say the four second in all the decade words such as twenty-four, thirty-four, and so on. Children followed the order of the English words, creating correct 2-digit marks for words above twenty but incorrect marks for teens: Many children wrote 71 instead of 17 for seventeen, whereas considerably fewer made such a reversal for 57. Reversals of individual digits (i.e., writing a 3 opening to the right) were frequent and were counted as correct in the scoring, because digit and letter reversals occur frequently with younger children and will be outgrown. Thus, many children seem to enter kindergarten already reading and writing many of the mathematical marks for cardinal numbers. Bergeron, Herscovics, and Bergeron (1987) even reported a case-study of a French-speaking Quebec kindergarten child who could say French number words only through fourteen but wrote mathematical marks from 1 through 19. Evidently he knew the marks 1 through 9 and saw the regular pattern from 11 through 19 but had not yet learned the irregular French teen words.

English- and French-speaking children learn the marks between ten and twenty as a concatenation of two single digits with no sense of the 12 as one ten and two ones (Bergeron, Herscovics, & Bergeron, 1986; Ginsburg, 1977; C. K. Kamii, 1985; Kamii & Joseph, 1988; M. Kamii, 1982; Miura, 1987; Ross, 1986). Instead, these marks (10, 11, 12, 13 . . . , 18, 19, 20) refer either to sequence meanings (the spoken sequence of number words, e.g., twelve as coming just after eleven and just before thirteen) or to cardinal meanings (twelve as a pile of twelve single objects). It may take several years for English-speaking children to build concepts of tens and ones and associate these with the 2-digit mathematical marks (Kamii, 1989; Ross, 1986; Steffe & von Glaserfeld, 1983). In contrast, first-grade children whose Asian languages (Chinese, Japanese, Korean) have regular named values for all 2-digit numbers (11 is said as ten one, 18 as ten eight, 23 as two ten three, 57 as five ten seven) show understanding of the marks between ten and twenty as being composed of one ten and some ones (Miura, 1987; Miura, Kim, Chang, & Okamoto, 1988; Miura & Okamoto, 1989). For these languages, the number words and the number marks have the same regular pattern for all words from one to one hundred. English-speaking children evidently are culturally (linguistically) disadvantaged by the English irregularities and need some kind of special support in learning correct 2-digit mathematical marks, especially for the reversed teens, and later in learning ten-structured meanings for these marks. These issues are discussed further in the second and third sections.

Summary

Children initially think about a cardinal number by thinking about objects. They either immediately label the objects with a number using a pattern-based response (e.g., "There are 2 cats."), or they count the objects and label the whole group of objects with the last counted word. These conceptual constructions have been called here pattern number (directly "seeing" the number in an object situation) and counted number. With these two conceptual structures for numbers children can solve a variety of addition and subtraction situations by directly modeling the situation with objects. These different situations can provide different meanings for the mathematical marks + and − and thus enable children to solve mathematical marks problems (e.g., 6 − 4) in different ways. Kindergarten children already understand a great deal about addition and subtraction and can learn considerably more in developmentally appropriate and empowering ways. The object solutions based on pattern number and on counted number are also developmentally important because the more advanced solutions described in the second section are all abbreviations of these object solutions. These solutions therefore are not crutches to be abandoned as soon as possible but instead are the basic numerical "walking" procedures out of which later numerical "running" and "jumping" will develop.

Research on Early Numerical
Instruction

What Do Textbooks Present?

Children have to attach meanings to mathematical marks such as $4 + 2$ or $3 - 1$ in order to find the result of these addition and subtraction operations. In most textbooks,[6] only one meaning is given to each of these, the Change meaning: $a + b$ is interpreted as Change-Add-To: "having a and then getting b more" and $a - b$ is interpreted as Change-Take-From: "having a and then taking away b." Pictures are drawn in first-grade workbooks to convey these meanings (e.g., birds fly in to join some that are there, birds fly away), and children solve mathematical marks problems using these pictures. After some number of pages, pictures no longer are given, and children do pages and pages of mathematical marks problems. Eventually, when children are good enough at these marks problems, they are given word problems to which they are to apply their knowledge of mathematical marks. They are supposed to write a mathematical marks sentence (e.g., $4 + 3 =$ or $5 - 2 =$) for each word problem and then solve the marks problem. The addition and subtraction word problems that are presented in textbooks in the United States, even in the later grades, are very simple ones; they consist almost entirely of only those simple types that many children can already solve when they enter school (Stigler, Fuson, Ham, & Kim, 1986). This is in contrast to texts in the Soviet Union in which a great variety of addition and subtraction problems, even many two-step problems, are presented in first grade (Stigler et al., 1986). Textbooks also contain more easy single-digit written marks combinations than difficult single-digit combinations (Hamann & Ashcraft, 1986), thereby giving children insufficient opportunity to solve problems with larger sums (sums between 10 and 18).

The research on children's thinking reviewed earlier indicates that there are major problems with this typical textbook approach to addition and subtraction. It is extremely and unnecessarily restrictive in the meanings given to addition and subtraction, it ignores the evidence concerning the many direct modeling ways in which children solve addition and subtraction situations, its mathematical marks/then word problems order is backward (word problems need to be used to give meaning to the mathematical marks), and writing solution sentences to solve simple word problems

---

[6]These generalizations are based on the five widely used textbooks analyzed for Stigler et al. (1986), but also were true for textbooks in the early 1970s when Bell et al. (1976) discussed for teachers the varying meanings of addition and subtraction not usually given in textbooks.

does not mirror how children think about and solve simple word problems. Even kindergarten children in the United States understand several different kinds of addition and subtraction word problems and can solve them with concrete objects. Thus, teaching children only one meaning for + and only one meaning for − severely limits their ability to understand and apply these mathematical marks to other situations. Furthermore, because most children can understand and solve a range of addition and subtraction situations when they enter school, these different situations can be used to define meanings for the + and − marks. Trying in some other way to give some meaning to the marks and then presenting addition and subtraction word situations only as applications of + and − ignores what young children know and understand (e.g., Hiebert, 1984).

Furthermore, children initially solve word problems by directly modeling the problem situation with objects (e.g., chips, buttons, fingers, tallies on paper). Most simple addition and subtraction situations direct the solution by suggesting actions to be carried out on these objects. Thus, the objects present the problem situation and also present the solution procedure required to solve the problem, as the objects are moved in carrying out the solution procedure. Therefore no separate presentation of the solution as a solution number sentence is needed before children solve the problem. This lack of necessity is reflected by the fact that, if forced by instruction to write such sentences, children frequently write such sentences after writing the answer to a problem (Carpenter, Hiebert, & Moser, 1983) or are unable to write a number sentence even if they have solved the problem correctly (De Corte & Verschaffel, 1985a; Thompson & Hendrickson, 1983). It may be useful for children to write number sentences to present the problem for certain kinds of more difficult problems (see discussion entitled "Level IV: Triad Number and Recomposible Triads"), but writing the solution sentence before solving the problem at this developmental level is either unnecessary (because the child already has presented and solved the problem concretely) or impossible (because the child cannot present or solve the problem). It is fine for children to write equations to show in written marks what they have done for a particular problem, but teachers should recognize that children do not need to do this before they can solve simple addition and subtraction situations. Finally, using pictures for problems for all children and then abruptly abandoning them at one time for all children ignores the developmental sequence of different solutions children devise for addition and subtraction situations; a typical kindergarten or first-grade class is distributed across this whole sequence. Carpenter (1985) pointed out how crucial this first experience with problem solving is for children in that this typical textbook approach actually teaches children to ignore the meaning, the semantic structure of the situation. This "lesson" is underscored by data on children's eye movements in solving word problems: Some children only look at the numbers in a problem and do not even look at the words (De Corte & Verschaffel, 1986).

Textbooks typically do not use well either of children's major conceptual structures for early number—pattern number and counted number—and they do not extend and support the conceptual structure that will become very important in the next developmental phase, sequence number. It would be easy to strengthen children's concepts of pattern number by providing experience with various patterns for the small numbers, but textbooks do not do this. Even the pictures that are given for the small addition and subtraction problems may be so busy and confusing that it is difficult to see the "twoness" or "threeness" or "fourness" in the picture. There are few pattern recognition or pattern generation activities provided or even suggested. Counted number suffers from the opposite problem. Children's ability to count objects in kindergarten and first grade typically far outstrips the small sets pictured in texts to be counted, so this ability to count objects is not used much or extended. Finally, virtually no experiences are given in choral or individual saying of the number-word sequence past ten (or perhaps some teen numbers), so children have no opportunity to extend or even to practice their number-word sequence. As is seen in the second section, the sequence needs to be highly overlearned, and children need to be able to begin counting at a given word and to count forward a given number of words. This requires repeated practice. If such practice is not given in the classroom, children with less home experience in saying the number-word sequence cannot catch up with children who have had such experiences at home. All three of these abilities (pattern number, counted number, and a highly automatized number-word sequence) are needed for the conceptual structures at the next level. Counting and saying the number-word sequence need to be overlearned—very automatized and familiar—in order for the conceptual structures of the second level to develop (see "Research on Children's Later Numerical Thinking"). Textbooks support none of the practice in these three areas that is needed for children to construct more advanced solution procedures.

How Are U.S. Children Doing?

The research evidence indicates that many U.S. children enter kindergarten with numerical abilities that are not even used by the first-grade textbook. Many kindergarteners can say the number-word sequence farther and count accurately larger sets of objects than are used in first-grade texts, and many kindergarteners understand and can solve kinds of addition and subtraction situations that are not even posed in first-grade texts. Thus, for many children, for a long time their experiences in math class are trivial ones, way beneath their capabilities. United States texts present addition and subtraction considerably more slowly than do texts in Japan, Mainland China, Taiwan, and the Soviet Union (Fuson, Stigler, & Bartsch, 1988). Many U.S. texts did not even get to all the sums and differences to 18 in first grade (one text series did not even get to all of these difficult subtraction facts until the second half of second grade), whereas all of the texts of these other countries did so, with Mainland China even reaching these in the first half of the first grade. Many U.S. children's capabilities considerably outstrip the very slow pace of U.S. first-grade texts.

Other Research on Teaching

The University of Chicago School Mathematics Project (UCSMP) kinder-garten materials (UCSMP, 1987) remedy certain of the shortcomings in textbooks. These materials emphasize counting aloud and counting larger numbers of objects, include a wider range of addition and subtraction situations, and focus on "seeing" number situations in classroom and life situations. An evaluation indicates that the materials result in a consider-able amount of learning of various kinds (Hedges et al. 1987), and informal reports indicate that even inner-city children can become very involved in addition and subtraction activities—becoming enthusiastic solvers and posers of word problems and even making up two-step problems for each other (D. Briars, personal communication, April, 1988).

In the Cognitively Guided Instruction (CGI) research study (Carpenter, Fennema, Peterson, Chiang, & Loef, 1989), experimental first-grade teach-ers spent 3 weeks in the summer learning about children's thinking about addition and subtraction and then planning their teaching for the coming year with this knowledge in mind. These teachers spent more whole-group class time on word problems and less on basic facts (i.e., on marks prob-lems) than did control teachers, but the experimental children learned more addition and subtraction facts at the recall level and solved moder-ately difficult word problems better than did the control children given usual instruction. Most children in both groups solved simple addition and subtraction word problems entirely correctly, so the groups could show no difference on these. However, for the classes with very low performance at the beginning of the year, children in the experimental classes solved simple word problems better at the end of the year than did control chil-dren in these lower achieving classes.

Kamii (1985) describes a first-grade classroom based on several aspects of Piaget's theory. Children's conceptual autonomy is emphasized, and children's concepts of addition and subtraction grow out of their experiences in daily living and with arithmetic games that involve social interaction. Children discuss their alternative solution strategies under the leadership of the teacher. A measure of quickly stating the answer to given addition combinations revealed performance roughly equivalent to control children who had instruction emphasizing memorizing facts, but the experimental children were more mentally active and autonomous than were the control children.

Evaluation of all three of the above projects suffered from the fact that no tasks presently exist to measure the attitudes and conceptual competencies emphasized in these approaches or in any approach supporting children's thinking. The results all indicate that children having more extensive and active experiences with addition and subtraction situations will perform at least as well as children receiving standard textbook instruction on the usual measures of known addition facts and will also show a range of other conceptual, attitudinal, and motivational strengths (albeit not measured very well) that will enable them to take advantage of later experiences in mathematical thinking. Thus, shifting to a more problem-focused approach seems to be a low-risk endeavor that is quite likely to exceed current levels of performance.

What Can Be: Supporting Children's Early Numerical Thinking in the Kindergarten and First-Grade Classrooms

It is fairly clear how to support children's early numerical thinking in developmentally appropriate and empowering ways. Children need the opportunity to develop their pattern number and counting number conceptual structures by participating in activities that help them link number words and number marks to patterns of small numbers and help them link number words and number marks to sets of counted objects, small or large depending on a child's counting ability. They need practice in saying and extending their accurate number-word sequence and then practice in the number-word sequence skills necessary for Level 2: saying the sequence starting from an arbitrary word and being able to say the word that comes just after or just before a given word. They need practice in making the mathematical marks for numbers 1 to 20 (suggestions concerning overcoming problems with the teens marks are discussed in the section "What Can Be: Supporting Children's Multidigit Thinking in the Classroom"). For addition and subtraction they need to be introduced to the various simple meanings for these words and for the + and − marks given in Table 2.1.

Thus, addition and subtraction situations should be the initial introduction to addition and subtraction, and written marks problems (3 + 1 or 4 − 2) should stem from these situations. Written word problems can be used as soon as children can read and write, and children can write problems they see at home and at school for other children to solve.

Children need a rich problem-solving and problem-posing environment that emphasizes (a) seeing addition and subtraction situations in the classroom, home, and neighborhood so that the whole range of meanings for the mathematical marks + and − can be learned, (b) posing and solving a wide range of problems, (c) using this range of meanings to solve and to interpret marks problems, and (d) allowing children to use solution procedures comprehensible to them and explainable by them. Such an environment avoids stereotyped problems in which key words give away the problem type and includes problems in which children can create two problems with different solution procedures by varying the question posed (e.g., Nesher, 1986; Nesher & Katriel, 1977). Many children in kindergarten and first grade will use the direct modeling solution procedures discussed in the section called "Simple Addition and Subtraction Situations", but many other children will use the more sophisticated procedures discussed in the "Levels of Solution Procedures" section.

This whole approach is an informal problem-solving one focused on children's thinking and talking about problems rather than their just working on pages of mathematical marks by themselves individually. In this problem-solving approach the focus of the teacher is on how a problem is solved by a given child, not on getting an answer as rapidly as possible. The approach involves considerable discussion among children about how different children solved a given word or mathematical marks problem. All of these discussions—oral and written communication about addition and subtraction—and the validation of children's individual approaches to problems (e.g., Cobb, Yackel, Wood, Wheatley, & Merkel, 1988) emphasize thinking. This approach presents mathematics as a thinking and involving activity about which one can communicate rather than presenting mathematics as completing as many workbook pages as quickly and trivially as one can (e.g., Mumme & Shepherd, 1990). It allows for the enormous range of individual differences in early numerical knowledge that is present in most classrooms and uses this range to support the learning of individuals with and from each other. There is not yet research about the best ways to organize classrooms to achieve these informal problem-solving goals. There are probably several different effective ways to design such classrooms. But the emphasis on mathematics as meaning requires discussion of different student's interpretations of various mathematical situations.

This description raises the question of whether workbooks are necessary or even helpful for this early numerical learning. In addition to the considerable limitations of the content of most present textbook series, there are inherent limitations to the textbook or workbook format. Many kindergarteners or first graders cannot read, so word-problem situations have to be posed orally. Ironically, all the interpretations of addition and subtraction that are used in texts are difficult to "book"—to portray by a static picture—whereas the only simple addition and subtraction that is really easy to book—the compare situation—is ignored in most texts. The Change pictures used so typically for $+$ and for $-$ use a single picture to portray three different points in time—the initial state, the change, and then the final state. This is confusing to many children, who need to see the action directly modeled, not embedded in a single static picture. For Put Together problems there is also an action sequence in which the parts are first given and then physically or mentally put together to make the All. Again either one picture is given showing the Parts and the All must then be made mentally, or a before and after picture is given that is confusing because twice as many objects are shown as are really involved in the situation. Compare situations in which two sets are compared to see how many more one set has are easy to book clearly in ways that facilitate the matching procedure by children, but these rarely are given in books.

Many of the necessary supporting learning activities then occur over time with things and between people using words and mathematical marks. An individual and small-group activity-centered approach such as discussed in *Workjobs* (Lorton, 1972) or used in Montessori classrooms, supplemented with some whole-class activities from *Mathematics Their Way* (Lorton, 1976) and problem situations from Real Math or developed from Table 2.1, seems much more likely to support children's early numerical thinking. Although there are pieces of programs here and there that are clearly helpful, almost all programs have been conservative in the kinds of addition and subtraction situations that have been used with children. We do not really even know what kindergarten and first-grade children can learn with a supportive teacher and enabling environment because to date kindergarten children in this country have been given only very simple situations. Kindergarten children can learn a considerable amount about addition and subtraction and learn it in ways that contribute to their self-confidence and that are developmentally appropriate. When this learning potential is used, first graders with such a kindergarten experience will be able to learn much more than in the past. Most of the research reported in the following section is therefore conservative: The word-problem performance is based on no instruction or experience with the problems or stems from instruction that is inconsistent with how children think, and the performance with mathematical marks is based in most cases on no instruction or support for children's thinking but merely on the opportunity to practice marks problems.

ADDITION AND SUBTRACTION WITH SUMS
AND DIFFERENCES TO 18: EMBEDDED
NUMBER, TRIAD NUMBER,
AND RECOMPOSIBLE TRIADS

Research on Children's Later
Numerical Thinking

The first and second parts of this chapter differentiate children's conceptual structures by developmental level (pattern number and counted number versus embedded number, triad number, and recomposible triads) and
by the size of the numbers added and subtracted (sums to 10 and sums
between 10 and 18). The level of conceptual structure is the important
focus of the two sections, and the size of the sum is only a rough guide to
children's thinking. Children can use the Level I conceptual structures to
add and subtract numbers with sums through 18 and even sums to 40 or 50,
though these methods become cumbersome and often inaccurate. There
are some factors that add particular complexities to sums over ten: Children run out of fingers to show sums over ten in a simple way, and they
must learn the intricacies of the English teen words and relate these to our
two-digit marks for writing numbers between ten and eighteen. Simple
pattern number is also seldom useful for these larger sums, though patterns of patterns (e.g., six is two threes) may be used. It is also useful to
repeat the caveat given at the beginning of this chapter concerning the
conservatism of most of the present research concerning U.S. children's
conceptual structures: This research for the most part was done with
children receiving standard U.S. instruction. Because this instruction greatly underestimates what children can learn and fails to support children's
ways of thinking, children can learn more rapidly and more deeply than
described by the present literature.

Levels of Solution Procedures

Children's conceptual structures for numbers, and therefore their solution
procedures for single-digit addition and subtraction situations, go through
at least three more levels beyond the concrete modeling of an addend or a
sum described in the section "Simple Addition and Subtraction Situations."
Various aspects of these conceptual structures for the different levels are
given in Table 2.2.[7] The solution procedures fall into four different struc-

---

[7]The evidence concerning these levels of solution procedures comes from many sources
(e.g., Baroody & Ginsburg, 1986; Briars & Larkin, 1984; Carpenter & Moser, 1984; Fuson &

tural forms: two additive (forward) solutions, one in which two addends are known and one in which one addend and the sum are known, and two subtractive (backward) solutions, for both of which the sum and one addend are known. In Levels II and III, the four Level I concrete counting procedures described in "Simple Addition and Subtraction Situations" (count all, add on, separate from, separate to) become abbreviated to the more abstract and efficient counting procedures listed in the corresponding positions in Table 2.2 and shown in Table 2.3. In both of these levels the addends become embedded within the sum; that is, entities simultaneously can present an addend and the sum to a child rather than only presenting one of these at a time as in Level I. Level II involves two different transitional levels, each of which marks conceptual progress with respect to one of the addends. In Level III these two separate advances are combined into abbreviated general sequence procedures. In Level IV, the two addends and the sum become three separate numbers that are related to each other in a triad addend-addend-sum structure; later in this level each of these three separate numbers can be decomposed and recomposed while remaining within this triad structure, permitting complex thinking strategies to be carried out. The solution procedures in Tables 2.2 and 2.3 are used to solve word problems, mathematical marks problems, and oral number-word problems (e.g., "eight plus six is what?"). The solution procedures for mathematical marks problems vary with the interpretation given to the + and − marks by the solver of the marks problem. The use of fingers in the solution procedures shown in Table 2.3 are typical for many children in the United States. Children in other countries may show numbers on fingers in different ways; for example, many Europeans begin counting on the thumb. Other ways of using fingers to show sums and differences are discussed in later sections. The sketches in Table 2.3 are meant to be illustrative of some ways U.S. children use fingers to show various solution procedures at each level. Children also carry out all of the solution procedures at the first three levels using objects other than fingers.

Level II: Object Embedded Number and Sequence
Nonabbreviated Number

Level II consists of two transitional paths from Level I to Level III, each involving a conceptual advance with respect to one addend.[8] One path (Level II First Addend Abbreviated) involves conceptual advances with

---

Secada, 1986; Riley et al. 1983; Steffe et al., 1983; Steffe & Cobb, 1988). Table 2.2 is a modification of Table 8-3 in Fuson (1988a); the evidence concerning these developmental levels is summarized in Fuson (1988a, chapter 8). The terminology used here is from that source; see Steffe et al., 1983, and Steffe and Cobb, 1988, for somewhat different terminology.

[8]First and second addend always mean the addends chosen as the first and second addends by the child. These may not be the way the addends are given in the situation. For

respect to the first addend: That addend becomes embedded within the sum and abbreviated so that entities for the first addend do not have to be counted in the sum count. The counting of these first addend entities within the sum count is seen to be unnecessary. The other path (Level II Second Addend Keeping Track) involves conceptual advances with respect to the second addend: The entities for the second addend can be paired with some method of keeping track of how many second addend entities are produced. Thus, entities do not have to be produced for the second addend before the final sum count; they can be produced sequentially during the final sum count. This enables children to carry out sequence counting procedures in which both addends are presented by sequence words rather than by physically present visuo-spatial objects. Changes occur for both addends in each of these transitional levels, but the transition occurs because of a major change in the conception of the first addend (Level II First Addend Abbreviated) or second addend (Level II Second Addend Keeping Track).

In the research to date, particular studies have focused on one or the other of these transitions, so little evidence is available to determine how many children make the first addend advance before the second addend advance and vice versa. Ascertaining the developmental relationship between these advances will be complicated by the roles played by pattern number in these transitions: Children can use pattern number methods of keeping track of the second addend for small addends long before they develop general keeping-track methods that work for second addends of five and more. Present research concerning Level II Second Addend Keeping Track procedures is largely confined to sums of tens or less, where the second addend is usually small. The Level II First Addend Abbreviated procedures use perceptual unit items and thus usually involve counted number, so pattern number does not facilitate the use of these procedures. The use of counting on (the first Level II First Addend Abbreviated procedure) may even be facilitated by large first addends because such addends make it more worthwhile to rethink whether counting the first addend is necessary (Secada, 1982; Siegler & Jenkins, 1989); it is very easy just to run through the counting of small first addends. Therefore data on the developmental relationship between these two advances will be quite affected by the size of problems children have had an opportunity to solve.

Level II First Addend Abbreviated: Object Embedded Number. In Level II First Addend Abbreviated, children still require objects from which to make perceptual unit items for presenting and solving addition and subtraction problems. However, their conceptual structures are now sufficient for a given perceptual unit item simultaneously to present an object in an

---

example, a child may count on from the larger number even though it is the second given addend.

TABLE 2.2

Developmental Levels of Conceptual Structures and Solution Procedures

Level	Conceptual Unit Items and Cardinal Operations		Cardinal Conceptual Structures	Additive (Forward) Solutions	Subtractive (Backward) Solutions
	First Addend	Second Addend			
				addend + addend = [sum]	sum − addend = [addend]
				addend + [addend] = sum	sum − [addend] = addend
I	Perceptual unit items Single presentation of the addend or the sum Simple cardinal integration	Perceptual unit items Single presentation of the addend or the sum Simple cardinal integration	(diagrams)	Count all	Separate from (take away)
				Add on up to sum	Separate to a known quantity
II Fst Add Abb	Unproduced unit items Simultaneous nonpresentation of the addend within the sum Embedded and abbreviated by a cardinal-to-count transition	Perceptual unit items Simultaneous presentation of the addend within the sum Embedded cardinal integration of the second addend entities	(diagrams)	Count on known addend with objects	Count down known addend with objects
				Count up from known addend to sum with objects	Count down to known addend with objects

	First addend representation	Second addend representation			Count up strategies	Count down strategies
II **Sec** **Add** **KT**	Sequence unit items Simultaneous presentation of the addend within the sum Embedded cardinal integration of the first addend entities	Sequence unit items (and keeping-track unit items) Simultaneous presentation of the addend within the sum (Paired integrations of the keeping-track unit items and the sequence second addend items)	[box: •••• / •••••]	[box: •••• / •••••]	Sequence count all Sequence count up from one to known addend and then up to known sum	Sequence count down known addend and then count down to one Sequence count down to known addend and then count down to one
III	Unproduced unit items Simultaneous nonpresentation of the addend within the sum Embedded and abbreviated by a cardinal-to-sequence transition	Sequence unit items and keeping-track unit items Simultaneous presentation of the addend within the sum Paired integrations of the keeping-track unit items and the sequence second addend items	[box: PI]	[box: PI]	Sequence count on known addend Sequence count up to sum	Sequence count down known addend Sequence count down to known addend

TABLE 2.2
(continued)

Level	Conceptual Unit Items and Cardinal Operations		Cardinal Conceptual Structures	Additive (Forward) Solutions	Subtractive (Backward) Solutions
	First Addend	Second Addend			
IV	Chunked numerical unit items Simultaneous nonembedded mental presentation of both addends and the sum Numerical addition and numerical equivalence	Chunked numerical unit items Simultaneous nonembedded mental presentation of both addends and the sum Numerical addition and numerical equivalence		Forward thinking strategy to find sum

Forward missing addend thinking strategy | Backward thinking strategy to take away known addend

Backward missing addend thinking strategy |

Note: Dotted lines enclose unknown quantities, and solid lines enclose known quantities. Abb is abbreviated, KT is keeping track, PI is paired integration of the keeping-track entities and the second addend entities. Brackets enclose unknown quantities. II Fst Add Abb and II Sec Add KT are transitional levels in which a conceptual advance is made in the conceptual structure of the first addend (II Fst Add Abb: The first addend is abbreviated) or the second addend (II Sec Add KT: A keeping-track procedure is used for the second addend items). Level III reflects both of these advances.

addend and in the sum. This distinction was termed using "double-role counters" in the word-problem model proposed by Briars and Larkin (1984). The cardinal conceptual operation that organizes these individual perceptual unit items into addends and the sum is embedded integration: A given set of objects is mentally integrated to form an addend embedded within a sum (see the sketch in Table 2.2). Now the child can think of the sum objects and simultaneously can think of the objects for one addend as being some of those sum objects. This simultaneous presentation permits children to carry out count-to-cardinal and cardinal-to-count transitions for the addend within the counting of the sum. Such transitions enable children to use the more efficient object counting procedures listed in Table 2.2 and shown in Table 2.3: count on a, count up to s, count down a, and count down to a. In all of these procedures, only one addend is counted, but it is counted as the second addend embedded within the sum; at Level I, counting of the addends and of the sum were different counting operations.

To count on a with objects, the number for the first addend is stated, and the counting of the sum continues on across the objects for the second addend. For example, for $8 + 5$, the child says, "8 (pointing at the first addend), 9, 10, 11, 12, 13 (pointing at each object in the second addend)" rather than counting from 1 to 13 while pointing to the first addend objects and then the second addend objects. To count down a with objects, a child reverses the counting-on procedure. For example, for $13 - 5$, the child says, "13, 12, 11, 10, 9 (while pointing at each second addend object starting with the last and moving toward the first addend), 8 (pointing at the first addend). $13 - 5$ is 8." Counting up to s and counting down to a are similar to the procedures counting on a and counting down a, respectively, except that they each require an auditory feedback loop during the counting of the second addend; this auditory loop determines when the counting stops. This feedback loop for count up to s is controlled by the sum: To count up from 8 to 13, the child says, "8 (pointing to the first addend), 9, 10, 11, 12, 13 (while pointing to objects for the second addend and stopping when the child hears 13)." The objects that have been counted up beyond the first addend 8 are then counted to find the missing addend. The feedback loop for count down to a is controlled by the known addend: To count down from 13 to 8, the count of the unknown second addend begins at 13 and ends with the first addend word, 8. The objects that have been counted down in the second addend (those for which 13, 12, 11, 10, and 9 were said) are then counted to find the missing addend.

These more efficient counting procedures are not just trivial abbreviations of the Level I object-counting procedures. These Level II procedures require the new conceptual unit items and cardinal operations identified in Table 2.2. For example, Secada et al. (1983) found that children who

TABLE 2.3
Developmental Levels of Addition and Subtraction Solution Procedures

Level	Addend + Addend = [Sum]	Addend + [Addend] = Sum	Sum − Addend = [Addend]	Sum − [Addend] = Addend

LI

count all

$4 + 3 \rightarrow 7$

add on up to sum

$4 + ? = 7 \quad ? = 3$

take away known addend

$7 - 3 = 4$

take away to known addend

$7 - ? = 4 \rightarrow ? = 3$

LII Fst Add Abb

object count on

$4 + 3 \rightarrow 7$

object count up to sum

$4 + ? = 7 \quad ? = 3$

object count down known addend

$7 - 3 = 4$

object count down to known addend

$7 - ? = 4 \rightarrow ? = 3$

LII Sec Add KT

sequence count all

hear 3 words (3)

$4 + 3 \rightarrow 7$

sequence count all up to sum

hear 3 words (3)

$4 + ? = 7 \rightarrow ? = 3$

sequence count down known addend and then down to one

hear 3 words (3)

$7 - 3 = 4$

sequence count down to known addend and then down to one

hear 3 words before hear (4)

$7 - ? = 4 \rightarrow ? = 3$

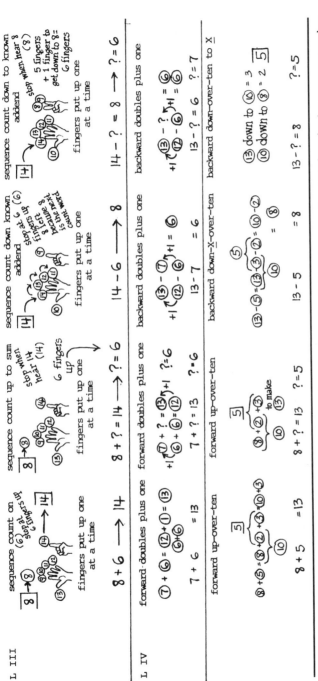

Note: A number in a right-hand bracket, 4], means a cardinal number (a number that tells how many); a circled number is a sequence number (a number within the counting sequence); and a number in parentheses, (4), means that this number is monitored in a keeping-track process so that some count can end at that number or after that many numbers have been said.

89

counted on with objects possessed three abilities and children who counted all lacked one or more of these abilities.[9] The first ability is the number-word sequence skill of being able to start counting up from an arbitrary word in the number-word sequence (see also Fuson et al., 1982). The second and third abilities are relationships between counting and cardinality meanings; the tasks used to assess these abilities are shown in Fig. 2.3. The first task requires a cardinal-count transition, a shift from the given cardinal meaning of the first addend number word as how many there are in the first addend to its count reference to the last counted object of the first addend. Though this task looks trivial to adults, a good number of first graders did not know that they would say the first addend number (eight, in the example in Fig. 2.3) for the last object if they counted the first addend objects. The second task requires an object-embedded count extension to the second addend within the sum count, the ability to continue the count initiated by the cardinal-to-count transition (here, saying eight) by counting the first entity in the second addend as the next count word (here, nine) (see also Steffe et al., 1983; Steffe & Cobb, 1988). Counting-all children who failed to continue the count on to the second addend often gave the answer "one" or gave the cardinality of the second addend in response to the second task. Thus, these children seemed to be unable to consider that first object of the second addend as both an object in the addend and as an object within the total sum set. Fuson (1988a) identified a third conceptual ability required for counting on: a count-to-cardinal transition for the sum made at the end of counting; this is pictured as the last sketch in Fig. 2.3.

Counting down *a* requires a child to count backward (count down) rather than forward and requires the reverse of the counting/cardinal conceptual transitions used in the forward counting on (see Fuson, 1988a, chapter 8 for a discussion). Because making the backward transitions would seem to require considerable experience with the forward transitions and because just counting backward is much more difficult for children than is counting forward (Bell & Bell, 1988; Fuson et al., 1982), it would seem that children would learn the backward counting transitions later than the forward transitions. Secada (1982) found that counting on preceded all forms of Level II counting for subtraction, and Baroody (1984) and Fuson (1984) discussed the difficulties children have in counting down. Carpenter and Moser (1984) found complex relationships among these procedures for word problems. The tendency of children not always to use their most sophisticated procedure complicates this issue. There is at the

---

[9]Somewhat different terms were used in Secada et al. (1983); this terminology is taken from Fuson (1988a). Steffe et al. (1983) used the word *extension* to describe the third ability; that word was used here for both Levels II and III.

Object-embedded cardinal-to-count transition of first addend within the sum count
(Embedded integration of first addend)

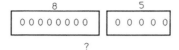

If I counted all these dots, what
would I say for this (?) dot?

Object-embedded count extension to second
addend within the sum count
(Embedded integration of second addend)

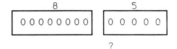

If I counted all these dots, what
would I say for this (?) dot?

Object-embedded count-to-cardinal
transition of the sum
(Embedded integration of the sum entities)

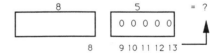

How many dots are there?

FIG. 2.3. Understandings required by counting on.

moment no definitive evidence concerning the developmental relationships among Level II First Addend Abbreviated counting on *a,* counting up
to *s,* counting down to *a,* and counting down *a.*

*Level II Second Addend Keeping Track: Sequence Nonabbreviated Num-
ber.* The solution procedures at the transitional Level II Second Addend
Abbreviated are sequence solution procedures in which both addends are
presented by sequence unit items, that is, by number words each taken as a
single equivalent unit that will be integrated with other sequence units to
form the first and second addends embedded within the sum. With these
sequence procedures, numbers are not presented by a certain quantity of
objects as at Level 1; instead, numbers are presented by saying a certain
quantity of sequence number words. At this level, the child cannot yet

abbreviate the counting for either addend but must produce all of the words from one (or to one, in the backward procedures). The number words said for the first addend (the words that eventually will be seen as redundant and unnecessary and will not be produced in the Level III solution procedures) may in some cases be produced in a very rapid somewhat pro forma fashion, as if the child knows that their status is different from the second addend words but nevertheless is compelled to say all of them in order to present the first addend in the solution procedure. Some children in Fuson (1982) did this, and Siegler and Steffe have both reported such behaviors in their subjects in personal communications to this author (March, 1989, and August, 1980).

Most of the present data concerning Level II Second Addend Keeping Track procedures involve small second addends in which pattern number can be used as the keeping-track procedure: Children can hear themselves say one or two or three more words past the first addend words. When pattern number is the keeping-track procedure for the second addend, the conceptual advances in parentheses in Table 2.2 (keeping-track unit items for the second addend, paired integrations of the keeping-track unit items and the sequence second addend items) are not really required. Keeping track by pattern number does not require the decided-upon-in-advance production of keeping-track units that are produced in synchrony with the second addend units; it only requires the ex post facto recognition that one has said a pattern of one, or two, or three more words after the first addend. Pattern number keeping track therefore is much less advanced conceptually than are general methods that will work for larger numbers. Because at present most data about the Level II Second Addend Keeping Track nonabbreviated sequence procedures seem to involve the use of pattern number methods of keeping track of the second addend, it is not really clear whether the conceptions in parentheses are used at this level, and indeed whether children use general nonpattern methods of keeping track of the second addend before they abbreviate the counting of the first addend. Future research may indicate that the conceptual advances in parentheses in Level II Second Addend Keeping Track do not really occur at this level but only in the Level III abbreviated sequence procedures. Level II Second Addend Keeping Track procedures then will be seen as confined to pattern number methods of keeping track of the second addend, as shown in Table 2.3.

The forward Level II Second Addend Keeping Track sequence solution procedures sound just like their Level I object-counting counterparts, but the words said in Level I counting all and adding on up to sum refer to physically present entities whereas those said in Level II sequence counting all and sequence counting up from one to the known addend and then up to the known sum do not refer to physically present objects. The Level II subtractive backward sequence solution procedures do not sound like their Level I counterparts because all Level I solutions involve only forward counts. The Level II First Addend Abbreviated and Level II Second Addend Keeping Track subtractive backward solutions all involve counting backward. For most children it is much more difficult to produce the number-word sequence backward from some number than it is to say it forward (Fuson et al., 1982), and children show special difficulties in these backward solution procedures (Baroody, 1984; Fuson, 1984; Steffe et al. 1983). Very little has been reported about the backward Level II Second Addend Keeping Track sequence solution procedures. They may not be used by many children because they may be so difficult that a child is capable of Level III abbreviated sequence solutions by the time a keeping-track procedure can be used with backward counting. These Level II subtractive backward solutions arise from a take-away (Change Take From) meaning of −, so they are much more likely to be used when that is the only interpretation available to children for − or for subtraction.

Level III: Sequence Embedded Number

Eventually, counting becomes abstracted from the objects being counted and the words in the number-word sequence are taken as the entities, or the units, presenting the addends and the sum (Fuson et al. 1982; Steffe et al., 1983). Each number word is taken as an equivalent single unit regardless of the cardinal value of that word; that is, a sequence unit item is mentally made for each word in the sequence. The conceptual operation of embedded integration forms these sequence unit items into cardinal situations and permits these sequence unit items to present cardinal addition and subtraction. As with counting objects, the ordered list of sequence words ensures that the last named sequence word will tell how many sequence words have been said: Saying the words from one through seven will generate seven sequence unit items, seven words. These conceptual sequence unit items and cardinal embedded integrations enable children to carry out Level III sequence solution procedures (see Tables 2.2 and 2.3). For the first addend, these sequence solution procedures require an embedded integration, a cardinal-to-count transition, and a count-to-cardinal transition like those required by the Level II abbreviated object procedures, but at Level III these are carried out on sequence unit items (on the sequence words) rather than on objects.

For the second addend, the sequence solution procedures require general methods of keeping track of the number of second addend words said. For small second addends, simple pattern number may be sufficient for a child to hear one, or two, or three words counted on. But when the second addend (or the addend taken as the second addend by the child) is very large, all the sequence procedures in Level III require some method of keeping track of the number of words said for the second addend. In the Level II abbreviated procedures, objects presented the second addend and were counted in the final sum count. For the Level III sequence procedures, some other means must be used to ensure that the number of second addend words said fits the known second addend quantity (for sequence counting on a and counting down a) or to record the number of second addend words said so this unknown addend can be found (for sequence counting up to s and counting down to a). Three general ways in which children keep track of the second addend (Fuson, 1982; Steffe et al., 1983) are (a) by saying the second addend words in a complex auditory pattern of patterns (for example for $8 + 6$, and auditory pattern of two threes can be used for the 6 in sequence counting on: "8   9 10 11   12 13 14"); (b) by using known finger patterns (for example, one hand plus one finger is 6) and matching each second addend word to a finger extended as the word is said; and (c) by double counting (that is, counting each second addend word as it is said "8, 9 is 1, 10 is 2, 11 is 3, 12 is 4, 13 is 5, 14 is 6"). All of these general keeping-track methods require the choice of a keeping-track method before the procedure begins: The child must intend to say a pattern of six more words or make a pattern of six fingers or double count to six. These methods thus require the child to conceptualize in advance keeping-track unit items for the second addend (an auditory pattern of patterns for six, a finger pattern of six, or a count to six) and then to make paired integrations of these keeping-track unit items and the sequence unit items for the second addend. This pairing permits the keeping-track methods to function accurately for large second addends. Children do demonstrate these sequence counting procedures with very small second addends (Fuson et al., 1982; Steffe et al., 1983) much earlier than they invent and use an adequate method of keeping track of larger addends; the distinction here is that made earlier with respect to Level II Second Addend Keeping Track: Simple pattern number can be used to recognize the number of words said, so such problems do not require the conceptual advances described here for using general methods of keeping track that are chosen by a child in advance of carrying out the solution. The Level III sequence procedures given in Tables 2.2 and 2.3 assume that a general keeping-track procedure can be used, and these procedures involve the conceptual advances indicated in Table 2.2 for the second addend.

Children actually use two different sequence counting-down a procedures (Carraher & Schliemann, 1985; Fuson, 1984; Steinberg, 1984). One procedure is the reverse of counting on a: A words (the words presenting the second addend in the backward sum count) are generated in reverse order (from the sum down to the first addend) and the next word down is the cardinality of the first addend (the remainder in a take-away situation).

For 14 − 6, this procedure is "fourteen, thirteen, twelve, eleven, ten, nine (that is six words said), so eight is the answer (the next word down is the cardinal value of the first addend words—the rest of the counted-down words that I do not need to say)." The other counting-down procedure may not be linked so well to cardinal understandings. It is the procedural (rather than conceptual) backward analogue[10] to the counting-on procedure. For 14 − 6, this would be: Say a word (fourteen), say six more words (thirteen, twelve, eleven, ten, nine, eight), and the last word said is the answer (8). A possible meaningful interpretation of this procedure is the one given in Baroody (1984): fourteen (words in all), thirteen (that's one taken away), twelve (that's two taken away), eleven (three taken), ten (four taken), nine (five words taken), eight (six words taken). Most reports of counting down have not differentiated these two procedures, so their relative prevalence is not clear. However, children sometimes confuse these two procedures, and both kinds of possible mistaken combinations of them are made (Steinberg, 1984). This indicates that some children may invent and use counting down in a procedural way without close ties to cardinality.

Level IV: Triad Number and Recomposible Triads

At Level IV numbers for the first time can be related in a triad structure of three separate quantities in which the addends are outside and equivalent to the sum (see Table 2.2) rather than the addends becoming the sum in Level I or being embedded within the sum as in Levels II and III. This triad conceptual structure was called numerical equivalence by Fuson (1988a) and a part–whole structure by Resnick (1983) and Steffe and Cobb (1988). The availability of triad numbers as conceptual units enables children to use new methods of addition and subtraction and to be quite flexible in their problem solving. Children no longer are bound by the action sequence within a problem situation (or within their interpretation of a mathematical marks problem) but can reflect about that situation using the triad structure and then can choose a preferred solution procedure that may not directly model the problem situation. This procedure may be chosen for its relative ease or efficiency (e.g., Baroody & Ginsburg, 1986; Carpenter & Moser, 1984; Woods, Resnick, & Groen, 1975).

Children later in this level[11] also become able to chunk numerical unit items within each addend and within the sum and thus to recompose the

---

[10]As acknowledged in Fuson, 1984, this possibility was pointed out to be by both Jim Moser and Ruth Steinberg.

[11]There has been relatively little work done on Level IV solutions. This level eventually may be differentiated into more than one level.

triad numbers into a different related triad. These recomposible triad conceptual structures enable children to carry out solution procedures based on a known fact related to a triad with an unknown quantity: Such solutions have been called derived facts, thinking strategies, heuristic strategies, and indirect solutions (e.g., Baroody & Ginsburg, 1986; Carpenter & Moser, 1984; Houlihan & Ginsburg, 1981; Rathmell, 1978; Steffe & Cobb, 1988; Steinberg, 1984, 1985; Thornton, 1978). These methods all involve operating on numbers as numbers and relating a triad with all three quantities known to a triad with an unknown quantity (see Table 2.3 for some examples). Two major kinds of derived-fact strategies are (a) those that involve increasing (or decreasing) one addend and the sum by the same amount and (b) those that involve compensation (moving entities from one addend to the other while keeping the same sum). An example of the former is to find $6 + 7$ by relating it to the known triad $6 + 6 = 12$: The 7 is 1 more than 6, so the unknown sum would be one more than the sum of the known triad ($6 + 6 = 12 + 1 = 13$). An example of compensation is to find $8 + 6$ by relating it to the known triad $7 + 7 = 14$: One unit item moved from 8 to 6 makes 7 and 7; because the sum of 7 and 7 is 14, the sum of 8 and 6 is the same, 14. Another example of compensation is the up-over-ten method in which one addend (usually the larger) is compensated to ten (added to from the other addend to make ten); the sum is then just ten plus the rest of that other addend: $8 + 6$ is eight plus two (to make ten) plus four (left from the 6) which makes ten plus four which is fourteen. Doubles ($a + a$) often are used as the basis for derived facts because they are learned so early and seem to be easy to think about. Some derived-fact strategies that require only adding or subtracting one may be learned before more complex derived-fact strategies involving adding or compensating more than one. As with other precocious conceptual advances that require only pattern number, it is not clear whether such simple derived-fact strategies should really be considered as Level IV recomposible triad strategies or whether Level IV recomposible triad strategies should require the ability to use more general derived-fact strategies. At the moment, little is known about the conceptual structures required by various derived-fact strategies (see Putnam, deBettencourt, & Leinhardt, 1990, for one analysis) or about the relationships between the availability of these strategies and the sequence counting strategies. Children's inconsistency in solving the same kinds of problems even within the same session (e.g., Carpenter & Moser, 1984; Steinberg, 1984) and the dependency of children's sequence counting strategies on their meanings for subtraction promise to make these issues difficult to resolve.

Level IV solution procedures include the direct recall of single-digit sums and differences. Because children can recall sums of some small numbers (e.g., two plus two is four) before they can carry out even Level II procedures for large single-digit numbers (e.g., 8 + 7), many children clearly function at multiple levels that vary by the size of the numbers in the addition or subtraction situation. Although much research has been directed at the issue of how recalled addition and subtraction "facts" are presented and organized mentally and how they are recalled by children and by adults, there is still considerable debate about the nature of this mental organization and presentation and even about whether all facts are actually recalled as opposed to reconstructed or generated from a rule (e.g., Ashcraft & Fierman, 1982; Ashcraft & Stazyk, 1981; Baroody, 1983; Bisanz & LeFevre, 1990; Cobb, 1986b; Groen & Parkman, 1972; Hamann & Ashcraft, 1986; Kaye, Post, Hall, & Dineen, 1986; McCloskey, Sokol, & Goodman, 1986; Resnick, 1983; Siegler, 1987a, 1987b, 1989; Siegler & Campbell, 1990; Woods et al., 1975). This work all has concentrated on what children do in school or on what children or adults do in laboratory experiments. It is even less clear how adults find single-digit sums or differences in ordinary life. Conversations with many teachers suggest to me that many adults may continue to use counting or sequence solution procedures or derived facts when "it really matters." For example, a researcher whose results figure prominently in this chapter reported at a small conference that s/he counted on when balancing the checkbook. Thus, it may be that a sensible goal for addition and subtraction of single-digit numbers is that a child learn several procedures, at least one of which will be efficient enough to be used in multidigit calculations and in other more complex procedures requiring knowledge of addition and subtraction. In any case, it is a damaging and erroneous oversimplification for textbooks, teachers, or researchers to assume that children move directly from Level I direct modeling object solutions to memorized facts for all, or even most, single-digit sums and differences.

Developmental Changes in Conceptual Structures for the Number-Word Sequence

The changes in conceptual knowledge and the resulting changes in addition and subtraction solution procedures over Levels II, III, and IV require prerequisite changes in abilities children can display with the number-word sequence. Thus, there are developmental levels of changes within a child's mental number-word sequence that precede the developmental levels of conceptual structures described in Table 2.2 and that are reflected in new abilities that are not yet connected to cardinal and counting knowledge (see Fuson et al., 1982, concerning these). The advance in sequence ability at each level is followed by the Table 2.2 changes in conceptual structures so that over these developmental levels sequence, counting, and cardinal meanings become increasingly closely related and integrated within the sequence itself (Fuson et al., 1982; Fuson, 1988a). Table 2.4 displays major aspects of this increasing integration. Levels II, III, and IV from Tables 2.2 and 2.3 correspond to the Breakable chain, Numerable chain, and Bidirectional Chain/Truly Numerical Counting levels in Table 2.4.

At the first "string" conceptual level (see Table 2.4), the sequence is not

TABLE 2.4
Developmental Levels Within the Number-Word Sequence

Sequence Level	Meanings Related	Conceptual Structure Within the Sequence and Relationships Among Different Number-Word Meanings	
String	Sequence	onetwothreefourfivesixseven	Words may not be differentiated.
Unbreakable List	Sequence	one-two-three-four-five-six-seven-	Words are differentiated.
	Sequence-Count	one-two-three-four-five-six-seven	Words are paired with objects.
	Sequence-Count-Cardinal	one-two-three-four-five-six-seven→[seven]	Counting objects has a cardinal result.
Breakable Chain	Sequence-Count-Cardinal	[four]→ four-five-six-seven →[seven]	The addends are embedded within the sum count; the embedded first addend count is abbreviated via a cardinal-to-count transition in word meaning.
Numerable Chain	Sequence-Count-Cardinal		The sequence words become cardinal entities; a correspondence is made between the embedded second addend and some other presentation of the second addend.
Bidirectional Chain/Truly Numerical Counting	Sequence-Count-Cardinal ↕ Sequence-Count-Cardinal		The sequence becomes a unitized seriated embedded numerical sequence; both addends exist outside of and equivalent to the sum; relationships between two different addend/addend/sum structures can be established; addends can be partioned.

Note: A rectangle drawn around related meanings indicates meanings that have become integrated. A number word alone has a sequence or count meaning; a number word enclosed by a bracket has a cardinal meaning.

related to any other situation; children just say it for the purpose of saying it, like saying the alphabet. Words may not be completely differentiated. At the Unbreakable List level, children can use the sequence in counting, that is, can establish one-to-one correspondences between sequence words and perceptual unit items "seen" by the counter in the counting situation (i.e., objects taken as individual "countables"). Later in the Unbreakable List level, the conceptual operation of cardinal integration enables a counter to make a count-to-cardinal transition and thus to use counting for cardinal purposes. These conceptual tools are sufficient to carry out all of the object addition and subtraction Level 1 solution procedures discussed in the section "Simple Addition and Subtraction Situations." This Unbreakable List level corresponds roughly to Resnick's (1983) mental number line described as preschooler's representation of number. The description there is accurate, but the term *number line* is misleading because a number line is a measure model in which numbers are presented by lengths on the line (e.g., 5 is the length from 0 to 5). In contrast, children's early presentations of number clearly are based on counting and on the number-word sequence; that is, they are based on discrete entities, not lengths. Therefore the term *mental number list* is a more accurate one than is *mental number line.*[12] At the Breakable Chain level a cardinal-to-count transition for the first addend enables a child to count on by moving from the cardinal meaning of the first addend (*eight* in Table 2.4) to the count meaning as paired with the last entity in the first addend; an embedded extension then enables the count to continue on to the entities presenting the second addend. At the Numerable Chain level no entities need to be present. The same embedded cardinal-to-count and count-to-cardinal transitions occur, but now the cardinal situations are presented by sets of number words, by sequence unit items. A paired integration is used to match the sequence unit items for the second addend with the unit items for the keeping-track process.

The evidence clearly supports the developmental progression outlined in Table 2.4 up to this level (see Fuson, 1988a; Steffe et al., 1983; Steffe & Cobb, 1988). The last level in the table includes several aspects of relationships among sequence, counting, and cardinal situations and of relationships between cardinal and ordinal situations that occur after these earlier ones. Research concerning these different aspects, and how they might relate to various derived-fact strategies children use for addition and subtraction, clearly is needed.

The term Bidirectional Counting refers to the ability of a child to relate forward and backward sequence solution procedures (see Steffe et al.,

---

[12]Children's and teacher's confusions of discrete and length (such as number line) models of number are a considerable problem in primary school mathematics instruction. This point is discussed in "What Do Textbooks Present?"

1983; Steffe & Cobb, 1988). This ability combined with the triad conceptual structure enables children to free themselves from a particular subtraction situation and see that situation as a triad of three quantities in which the unknown quantity may be able to be found by either a forward or a backward procedure. Thus, a backward take-away situation might be solved by a forward counting up to s solution procedure.

The truly numerical counting label and several other understandings identified at this level come partially from Piaget (1941/1965), who proposed a fourth postconservation stage of truly numerical counting (see Fuson, 1988a, chapter 9 for a discussion). One aspect of this truly numerical counting level is that the sequence is now both seriated and embedded. Each word of the sequence is now an ideal identical iterable *one,* and each word is now both a sequence word and a cardinal word that can refer to all of the words up to and including itself. Therefore, each next word presents a cardinal number that is one larger than (using the cardinal as well as the sequence meaning) the earlier word. This cardinalized sequence thus displays both class inclusion (the embeddedness of each cardinal number within the next) and seriation. These were the requirements of a truly operational cardinal number for Piaget (1941/1965; also see C. Kamii, 1986). The child at this level then is capable of the progressive summation of sequence/counting/cardinal words. The term *progressive summation* is taken from Saxe (1982), who defined counting as the "progressive summation of correspondences." Any given cardinal number also can be seen as composed of all possible combinations of smaller numbers, so the child can now decompose any number methodically into all such possible combinations (an example for the number 5 is given in Table 2.4). The triad addend-addend-sum structure enables addition and subtraction to be related to each other so that either operation can be used to find the other. For example, one could use the information that $72 - 26 = 46$ to solve $72 - 46$ or $26 + 46$ without calculating. Finally, cardinal and ordinal situations are related via the embedded seriated numerical sequence so that a child knows that there are $n - 1$ entities in the cardinal set preceding the nth ordinal entity. This can be accomplished by an ordinal-to-count transition from the nth ordinal entity to the sequence n, which is now a cardinal as well as a sequence number for the child and thus is known to have $n - 1$ entities before the n. For example, in Piaget's staircase problem, a child at this conceptual level who looks at a doll standing on the eighth stair could make a cardinal integration of the stairs preceding this eighth stair and use the backward chain to know that the cardinality of those stairs would be the sequence word before eight, that is, would be seven. These decomposible and relational abilities then lead to recomposible triads and derived-fact solution procedures as discussed earlier.

Solution Procedures and Conceptual Structures
for Word Problems: Solving Word Problems

The more advanced conceptual unit items and cardinal conceptual operations that allow children to carry out Level II, III, and IV solution procedures also allow them to present and solve more difficult addition and subtraction situations. The four major types of addition and subtraction problems (Change-Add-To, Change-Take-From, Put-Together, and Compare) were discussed in the section "Simple Addition and Subtraction Situations" (Equalize problems were viewed as an action-cueing Change form of Compare), and seven simple and fairly simple problem subtypes capable of solution by kindergarteners and early first graders were presented in Table 2.1.

The remaining four addition and subtraction subtypes are the most difficult to solve. These are the two Change problems with the Start quantity unknown (Change-Add-To: missing Start and Change-Take-From: missing Start) and the Compare problems with the Big or Small quantities unknown (Compare: missing Big and Compare: missing Small). The Change problems with unknown Start quantities are difficult to solve because one must transform the situation in some way in order to change these $? + b = c$ and $? - b = c$ situations to one of the four addition and subtraction solution procedures in Table 2.2 if one is going to use anything other than a trial and error solution. The difficulty of the Compare problems depends on how the comparing statement is phrased. This statement can use the Compare form or an Equalize form that embeds a Change situation within the Compare situation (see Figure 2.4 and Table 2.5); the Equalize form is action-based and can be simpler because it can cue the correct solution procedure. For a given Compare situation, the comparing statement can be said in one of two different ways by using two different words: the words "more" or "less" (in the Compare form) and the words "add to" or "take from" (in the Equalize form). For any given Compare or Equalize situation, one of these phrasings will be consistent with the solution procedure required to solve the situation and the other will be inconsistent. In the consistent forms, (a) the situation requires addition and the comparing statement uses "more" or "add to" or (b) one must subtract to solve the situation and the problem says "less" or "take from." If the opposite phrasings are used for those situations, the words will conflict with the required solution procedure. For this reason, Briars and Larkin (1984) differentiated these problems into those with consistent language and those with conflict language (see Table 2.5 for problem examples). Fuson and Willis (1986) did find that the consistent problems were easier than the conflict problems, probably because the consistent comparison terms help to cue the correct

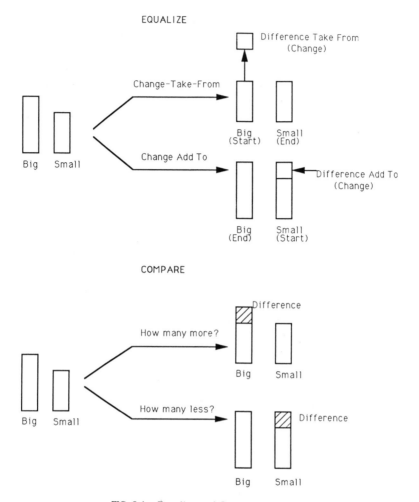

FIG. 2.4. Equalize and Compare situations.

solution procedure. The problems requiring subtraction but using addition words seemed to be the most difficult of all to solve. All of these more difficult problem subtypes are discussed further in the two sections "Level III Word Problems" and "Level IV Word Problems."

The conceptual structures that underlie the four different classes of solution procedures discussed in Table 2.2 (the two forward and two backward procedures) also are used by children in understanding different addition and subtraction situations. How the problem is understood and presented by a child dictates the solution procedure the child will use to solve the problem: The presentation of the problem and of the solution procedure are identical or very closely related at the lower levels. Initially, each problem subtype is understood as (assimilated to) the conceptual structure that directly models the situation. By Level IV there may be considerable separation between the child's conceptual structure for the problem situation and the conceptual structure used for the solution procedure, and children's problem solving becomes more flexible and more individual. Word-problem subtypes children can solve at each conceptual level are outlined in Table 2.6. The conceptual structures used to present

TABLE 2.5
More Difficult Addition and Subtraction Situations

Action Unary

Change-Add-To: Missing Start	*Change-Take-From: Missing Start*
Joe had some marbles. Then Tom gave him 5 more marbles. Now Joe has 8 marbles. How many marbles did Joe have in the beginning?	Joe had some marbles. Then he gave 5 marbles to Tom. Now Joe has 3 marbles. How many marbles did Joe have in the beginning?

Action Unary Within Static Binary: Equalize	*Static Binary: Compare*

Consistent Language

Equalize-Add-To: Missing Big	*Compare-More: Missing Big*
Joe has 3 marbles. If Joe gets 5 more marbles, he will have as many as Tom. How many marbles does Tom have?	Joe has 3 marbles. Tom has 5 more marbles than Joe. How many marbles does Tom have?

Equalize-Take-From: Missing Small	*Compare-Fewer: Missing Small*
Joe has 8 marbles. If Joe gives away 5 of his marbles, he will have as many marbles as Tom has. How many marbles does Tom have?	Joe has 8 marbles. Tom has 5 fewer marbles than Joe has. How many marbles does Tom have?

Conflict Language

Equalize-Take-From: Missing Big	*Compare-Fewer: Missing Big*
Joe has 3 marbles. If Tom gives away 5 marbles, he will have as many marbles as Joe. How many marbles does Tom have?	Joe has 3 marbles. He has 5 fewer marbles than Tom has. How many marbles does Tom have?

Equalize-Add-To: Missing Small	*Compare-More: Missing Small*
Joe had 8 marbles. If Tom gets 5 more marbles, he will have as many marbles as Joe. How many marbles does Tom have?	Joe has 8 marbles. He has 5 more marbles than Tom has. How many marbles does Tom have?

TABLE 2.6
Developmental Levels of Word Problem Solutions

Additive (Forward) Solution Procedures	Subtractive (Backward) Solution Procedures
addend + addend = [sum]	sum − addend = [addend]
addend + [addend] = sum	sum − [addend] = addend

Level I: Object Solution Procedures

Count All (A or PT)	Take Away a (TA)
ChAdd: Start **A** Change → [End]	ChTA: Start **TA** Change → [End]
PT: Part **PT** Part → [All]	PT: All **TA** Part → [Part]
EqAdd: Small/Start **A** Diff/Ch → [Big/End]	EqTA: Big/Start **TA** Diff/Ch → [Small/End]
Cm: Small **A** Diff → Big	Cm: Big **TA** Small → [Diff]

Add on up to s (AOUT or PTUT)	Separate to a (ST)
ChAdd: Start **AOUT** [Change] → End	ChTA: Start **ST** [Change] → End
PT: Part **PTUT** [Part] → All	EqTA: Big/Start **ST** [Diff/Ch] = Small/End
EqAdd: Small/Start **AOUT** [Diff/Ch] = Big/End	
Cm: Small **AOUT** [Diff] → Big	

Match (M)

Cm: Big **M** small → [Diff]
Eq: Big **M** Small → [Diff]

Level III: Sequence Solution Procedures

	Sequence Count On a (CO)		Sequence Count Down a (CD)
	ChAdd: Start# **CO** Change → [End]		ChTa: Start# **CD** Change → [End]
	PT: Part# **CO** Part → [All]		PT: All# **CD** Part → [Part]
	EqAdd: Small/St# **CO** Diff/Ch → [Big/End]		EqTA: Big/Start# **CD** Diff/Ch → [Small/End]
*Opp	Cm^m: Small# **CO** Diff → [Big]		Cm: Big# **CD** Small → [Diff]
*Rev	Cm^l: Small# **CO** Diff → [Big]		Cm^l: Big# **CD** Diff → [Small]
	EqTA: Small/End# **CO** Diff/Ch →	*	Cm^m: Big# **CD** Diff → [Small]
*Rev	[Big/St]	*Opp	ChA: End# **CD** Change → [Start]
	ChTA: End# **CO** Change → [Start]	*Rev	ChTA: Start# **CD** End → [Change]
		*SE	

(Continued)

TABLE 2.6
(*continued*)

Additive (Forward) Solution Procedures	*Subtractive (Backward) Solution Procedures*
Sequence Count Up to s (CU)	*Sequence Count Down to a (CDT)*

	ChAdd: Start# **CU** [*Change*] → End	ChTA: S# **CDT** [*Change*] → End
	PT: Part# **CU** [*Part*] → All	EqTA: Big/Start# **CDT** [*Diff/Ch*]
	EqAdd: Small/St# **CU** [*Diff/Ch*]	= Small/End
	= Big/End	
	Cm: Small# **CU** [*Diff*] → Big	
•	Cm[l]: Diff# **CU** [*Small*] → Big	
*Opp	Cm[m]: Diff# **CU** [*Small*] → Big	
*Opp	EqAdd: Diff/Ch# **CU** [*Small/St*] →	
	Big/End	
*Rev	ChTA: End# **CU** [*Change*] → Start	
*SE	ChAdd: Change # **CU** [*Start*] → End	
*R,SE	ChTA: Change# **CU** [*End*] → Start	

Level IV: Numerical Thinking Strategy Solution Procedures

Direct Additive Derived and Known Facts	*Direct Subtractive Derived and Known Facts*
PT [End]: to find 7 + 5 use up over ten: 7 + 3 + 2 = 10 + 2 = 12	ChTA [End]: to find 13 − 7 use down over ten: 13 − 3 − 4 = 10 − 4 = 6

Indirect Additive Derived and Known Facts

ChAdd [Change]: to find 5 knowing
7 and 12 use
up over ten: 7 + 3 [is ten] + 2
more is 12 so 3 and 2 is 5

Note: Brackets enclose the unknown, quantities in italics require paired integration with entities in a keeping-track procedure, and quantity labels followed by # denote an abbreviated first addend (a single sequence number word produced for that quantity). Diff is Difference, Ch is Change, PT is Put Together, Cm is Compare, and Eq is Equalize. Problem subtypes newly solvable at a given level are marked with *. Opp denotes a solution procedure opposite to the difference sentence. Rev or R denotes reversibility and SE denotes subset equivalence used on the original problem situation. Problem types given in Level IV are exemplary only. Solution procedures are in boldface: **A** is add to, **PT** is put together, **TA** is take away, **AOUT** is add on up to, **PTUT** is put together up to, **ST** is separate to, **M** is match, **CO** is count on, **CD** is count down, **CU** is count up to, **CDT** is count down to. The superscripts [m] and [l] refer to the word "more" or "less" used in a compare problem. The transitional levels II Fst and II Sec are not given in the table because so few data exist concerning their use in solving word problems. Table adapted from Fuson, 1988a.

the problem and the solution at each level fall within the four types of addend/addend/sum structures given at the top of the table; these vary by the direction of the solution/situation and by the nature and position of the unknown quantity. The evidence supporting the placement of given subtypes in each level is not discussed in detail here (see Fuson, 1988a, chapter 8, for that discussion). However, each level is discussed briefly in order to give some flavor of the thinking at that level. The conceptual structures and solution procedures used at each level are those appearing in the same levels in Tables 2.2 and 2.3; the solution procedures are named in Table 2.6. At each higher level, word problems solvable at an earlier level are still solvable but they may now be solved by the more advanced solution procedures of that higher level. New kinds of word problems become solvable at each level; these are marked in the table by a *.

The relationship between the conceptual structures children possess and the word problems they solve (and the solutions they use to solve the problem) is complicated by two factors. First, children do not always solve word problems (or mathematical marks problems) by the most advanced procedure they possess (e.g., Carpenter & Moser, 1984; Steinberg, 1984). The levels in Table 2.6 indicate the highest performance of which children at a certain level are capable and will show at least sometimes. Second, addition and subtraction subtypes are differentially capable of being solved by trial and error procedures that do not require the full conceptual structures necessary for a planned prechosen solution procedure. Thus, children may also sometimes solve by trial and error or by partial cues a given problem subtype that is above the level of their conceptual structures. For example, a child given the Change-Take-From: missing Change problem "Tanika has 15 ribbons and gives some to her sister. She has 7 left. How many did she give to her sister?" may make a set of 15 objects and take away 7 of them because the situation is a Change-Take-From situation. These actions result in a set of 8 objects that may be then recognized as the objects given to the sister. This is a partially cued solution that serindipitously gives the correct answer. It requires much less knowledge than an embedded structure in which the known End 7 objects are counted from the 15 objects in order to leave the missing Change objects.

Level II Word Problems: Embedded Object
and Nonabbreviated Sequence Solutions

Level II is not included in Table 2.5 because there is little unambiguous evidence concerning the use of the transitional Level II solution procedures in presenting or solving word problems. Word problems at Level II can be presented by the conceptual structures for Level II First Addend Abbreviated, that is, by perceptual unit items that simultaneously present the addend within the sum and by conceptual understandings that allow the first addend count to be abbreviated. Thus, for example, the Put Together: missing Part problem now does not have to be solved by counting out the sum objects first. It now can be presented by "addend + a = sum" and solved by counting up to s with objects (Briars & Larkin, 1984; Riley et al., 1983), as can the Change-Add-To: missing Change problem.[13] Children now have two choices for solving the missing Difference form of the Compare problem: by counting up to s with objects and by counting down a.[14] Fuson and Willis (1988) reported that first graders who had been taught to count on with objects to solve mathematical marks addition problems solved these Compare problems much more frequently (10 solutions versus 1 solution) by counting up to s with objects than by counting down a; the predominance of counting up was even stronger for the Equalize form of this problem, where the wording of the problem gave an addition cue (17 count up solutions versus 2 count down solutions). Carpenter and Moser (1984) found in their longitudinal study that most children who did not use matching could not solve the regular Compare form until they could use count up to s. However, these authors did not make a distinction between counting up with objects and counting up as a sequence procedure (Level III), so the extent to which their children used Level II count up to s with objects is not clear. The two remaining subtypes of Compare and Equalize problems are able to be presented and solved at Level II if they have the comparison sentence consistent with the required solution procedure, that is, missing Small using "less than" or "take from" and missing Big using "more than" or "add to" because these phrasings suggest the required solution activity.

Level III Word Problems: Embedded Sequence Solutions

There is considerable consensus that initially at Level III problems are presented and solved by the Level III conceptual structures in Table 2.2: by sequence unit items that simultaneously present an addend and the sum so that the addends are embedded within the sum and one addend is abbrevi-

---

[13]The Put-Together: missing Part problem was not placed in Level I in the original Table 4 in Fuson (1988a) because I was not aware of any evidence that indicated that children spontaneously solved such problems by adding on. It was put into Table 2.1 as a fairly simple subtraction problem because it seemed probable that with instructional and peer support, children could solve these problems by adding on. The Carpenter and Moser (1984) evidence that children added on to solve the Change-Add-To: missing Change problem is actually ambiguous about whether children began the adding on of the second addend objects by beginning the count with "one" and counting the first addend objects, in which case it is a Level I solution, or whether the count began with the first addend word and counted only the second addend objects, in which case it is Level II counting up to s.

[14]One can solve such a missing Difference problem by counting down to a, but the problem was not entered in the Fuson 1988a Table 4 in this location because there was no evidence of such child solutions known to me.

ated. Solution of the old Level I and Level II problems by sequence solution procedures was reported by Carpenter and Moser (1984); the new Compare problem entries in Level III are based on Fuson and Willis (1986, 1987). Children use these embedded sequence solutions to solve all of the word-problem subtypes. There is, however, considerable disagreement concerning how children present problem situations at this level and how they move from the problem presentation to the problem solution. The two major computer models of word-problem solutions both postulate considerable separation between the child's presentation of the problem situation and the presentation of the solution procedure; both propose that the child uses a general problem schemata to present the word-problem situation and then transforms this presentation of the situation to enable a solution procedure to be carried out. Others suggest that the separation between problem presentation and problem solution may not be so major or so clear and that children may not use general problem schemata removed from the quantities in the problem situation. There has been much less research about these more difficult problems, so these issues are not presently resolved.

Briars and Larkin (1984) in their computer model proposed that children use the mental operations reversibility (R) and/or subset equivalence (SE) to solve the more difficult Change problems. Children first present the Change situation to themselves and then use reversibility and/or subset equivalence to transform the situation so that one of the solution procedures in Table 2.2 can be used to solve the problem. For example, to solve a Change-Add-To: missing Start problem the child first presents this as a Change-Add-To situation: [Start] + Change = End. The child then operates conceptually on this problem presentation by using reversibility: A child would think of starting with the End sum (the marbles Joe has at the end), giving back the Change marbles that were given to Joe (taking away the Change marbles), and ending up with the Start marbles Joe had at the beginning (End take away Change = [Start]). To solve this problem by subset equivalence, the child considers the Start and Change amounts to be interchangeable and thus changes the [Start] + Change = End presentation to Change + [Start] = End, which can be solved by sequence counting up. Cobb (1986a) reported that reversibility seemed to precede the use of subset equivalence in Change problems, so these conceptual operations may not be learned at the same time.

Riley et al. (1983), Kintsch and Greeno (1985), and Riley and Greeno (1988) also proposed computer models that operate on the problem presentation at the highest level. However, these models do not just change around the parts of a specific problem as does the Briars and Larkin (1984) model. Instead, one problem main type is changed into another main type and then solved as this type. For example, these models solve the Change:

missing Start problems by presenting such a problem as a Change problem and then re-presenting it as a Put-Together: missing Part problem which is then solved as in Table 2.6. However, De Corte and Verschaffel (1986) found a sizable number of children who could solve Change-Take-From: missing Start problems but not the hypothetically required Put-Together: missing Part problems. Thus, initially at least, children seem to have some presentation of Change-Take-From: missing Start problems that enables them to solve this problem without re-presenting it as a Put Together problem. Willis and Fuson (1988) and Fuson and Willis (1989) also reported data from instructional studies with second graders suggesting that most successful solvers did not present these Change problems as Put Together problems.

The experiences that lead to children's use of subset equivalence and reversibility are not clear at present. The transitional procedures at Level II serve to differentiate the addends because different conceptual operations are used with each addend. Thus, it may take some time of using the Level III sequence procedures in order to make both addends quite salient within the sum. Both reversibility and subset equivalence require a conceptual overview of the similar functioning of the addends within the sum, and use of the embedded sequence procedures may help to provide this.

Fuson (1988a) questioned whether children at this level actually first present problem situations and then re-present them by reversibility or subset equivalence. Observations of second graders asked to use dolls and objects to "show what is happening in the problem" for the conflict language Compare problems (missing Small using "has more" and missing Big using "has less") suggested that children seemed to assimilate the problem directly into a presentation that led to a solution: As they read the problem, they constructed a coherent presentation that then led to a solution procedure. Data on retelling the story supported this view, for some children retold a story consistent with their solution procedure rather than with the original story: The solution procedure and the explanation were correct and consistent with each other but the original problem was lost (or never was presented by the child). Even when reversibility and subset equivalence are used, the child's consideration of the problem situation may be closely tied to the specific quantities used in that problem situation rather than based on a general problem schema. The initial conceptual presentation of the problem may involve sequence unit items that present the specific numbers given in the problem, and these specific sequence quantities may then be reversed by reversibility or subset equivalence.

Carpenter, Fennema, Peterson, and Carey (1988) reported that teachers overestimated their children's use of Level I direct modeling and Level IV number recall to solve word problems and underestimated use of Level II and Level III embedded and abbreviated counting strategies. The importance of children's use of the Level II and Level III counting strategies to present problem situations as well as to present solution procedures suggests that teachers need to know about these developmental stages in children's conceptions of addition and subtraction and be encouraged to listen to, discuss, and support such solutions in their classrooms.

Level IV Word Problems: Triad Number Solutions

With the triad conceptual structures available at this level, the child can be conscious of wanting to add or to subtract and may carry out these operations in ways that do not directly model the problem situation. Thus, at this level there may be a definite separation of and difference between the child's presentation of the problem and of the solution procedure by which the problem will be solved. For example, children may choose a particular solution procedure and use it consistently to solve a range of word problems requiring subtraction. Carpenter and Moser (1984) found that sometime in second or third grade many children shifted to a consistent use of counting up to s to solve four problems with different situational subtraction structures: Change-Add-To: missing Change, Change-Take-From: missing End, Put Together: missing Part, and Compare: missing Difference. Earlier these children had solved each problem with a sequence solution that modeled the problem structure (e.g., solving Change-Take-From: missing End by counting down a). Thus, the child may be using Level IV Triad or Recomposible Triad conceptual structures to present the situation but only using Level III embedded sequence solution procedures to solve the modified situation.

Recent evidence indicates that children may also do the opposite: They may use Level IV Triad or Recomposible Triad conceptual structures for the solution procedure but use lower level direct modeling structures to present the problem situation. Thus, Level IV known facts or derived facts may be used to model a word problem directly. De Corte and Verschaffel (1987b, 1987c) distinguished among known and derived facts that paralleled counting on, counting up to, and counting down from; they called these direct additive, indirect additive, and direct subtractive procedures. These procedures are shown in the first, second, and third columns of Level IV in Table 2.3. De Corte and Verschaffel found that first and second graders' use of known facts and derived facts modeled the semantic structure of the word problem just as did these sequence solution procedures. For example, a child would use the fact $7 + 6 = 13$ or the derived-fact strategy "up-over-ten" ($7 + 3 + 3 = 13$) for a Put Together: missing All problem whose Parts were 7 and 6 or for a Change-Add-To: missing Change problem with a Start of 7 and an End of 13. However, they would use the fact $13 - 7 = 6$ or the derived-fact strategy "down-over-ten" ($13 - 3 - 4 = 6$)

for a Change-Take-From problem with a Start of 13 and an End of 7. De Corte and Verschaffel also reported that the order in which the sum and the addend are stated affects the solution procedure, and this order interacts with specific word-problem types. Giving the sum number before the known addend number induced more direct subtractive solutions and giving the addend number first led to more indirect additive solutions; this effect was stronger for Put Together: missing Part problems than for Change-Add-To: missing Change problems. Thus, the numbers may serve to provide a separate problem presentation that may compete with or replace the problem presentation based on the semantic structure of the problem. Further research is needed concerning known facts and derived facts and how these relate to problem presentations and solutions; in earlier research no distinction was made among the kinds of known or derived facts used in a problem.

There is at present very little evidence about children's later presentations of word problems. Fuson (1988a) suggested that the next step in problem presentations may be the building of explicit connections between different problem types. The most obvious links are between the two unary Change situations and between the two binary situations Put Together and Compare. Reversibility would seem to provide an important link between the unary Change-Add-To and Change-Take-From problems. After some experience in using reversibility to solve particular problem situations, these two problem types might become integrated into a single Reversible Unary Change problem presentation that could facilitate the choice of addition or subtraction as a solution procedure. The similarities between the two binary situations, the Put Together and the Compare situations, also might become obvious to children, leading to the integration of these two problem types within a static Small-Small-Big presentation. A common "error" of children who had been taught to make schematic drawings of Put-Together and Compare problems was in fact to put the numbers for a Put-Together: missing Part problem into a Compare drawing (Fuson & Willis, 1989; Willis & Fuson, 1988); children argued that the Put-Together: missing Part problem was asking them to compare the smaller part to the larger whole. A common static Small-Small-Big situation conception might be facilitated by experience with the more difficult Compare problems, because the role of the Small and the Difference as together being equivalent to the Big becomes clearer in these more difficult forms. The formation of such a static presentation also would seem to draw fairly heavily upon children's many addition and subtraction experiences with triads of numbers related in the same Small-Small-Big way: 5, 3, 8; 9, 6, 15; and so forth. Finally, the different problem schemata, the four separate solution procedure structures (addend + addend = s, addend + a = sum, sum − addend = a, and sum − a = addend), and many experiences with specific cardinal number triads all may become integrated into a single ADDEND-ADDEND-SUM schema. Addition then could be seen generally as any situation in which two addends are known, and subtraction would be viewed as any situation in which the sum and one addend are known. This schema would provide enormous flexibility and creativity for solving addition and subtraction problems of all types, especially when larger multidigit numbers are involved and one needs to choose to carry out an addition or subtraction operation.

Resnick (1983) proposed that during early school arithmetic, a part–whole schema knowledge structure is used by children to relate triads of numbers and to interpret various kinds of word problems so that the problems can be solved by informal arithmetic methods or by more formal methods taught in schools. Rathmell (1986) reported considerable success in a 2-year program helping children interpret all word problems within a part–part–whole structure; second graders reached ceiling on most problem types with sums and differences to ten. However, considerable other evidence indicates that children first have many different experiences with different situations and they present these situations concretely and thus differently, even though many of the situations share a deep underlying common part–part–whole structure. For example, De Corte and Verschaffel (1985b) reported that an instructional attempt to use a single schematic part–part–whole drawing (similar to the top right-hand drawing in Fig. 2.1) was not as successful as one in which children filled numbers into three different kinds of drawings for Change, Put Together, and Compare problems. Willis and Fuson (1988) reported that children who used a Put Together drawing for Change problems were less successful at solving them than were children who used a Change drawing, and Fuson (1988b) and Fuson and Willis (1989) reported little tendency for second graders to present all problems as Put Together problems. An intervention with three different kinds of drawings helped second graders reach ceiling on problems with sums and differences to 18 and do well on many problems with 3-digit numbers involving trading. Thus, a general pervasive part–whole schema may be something that is salient to adult researchers in all aspects of addition and subtraction but is not salient to children until they have had many different experiences with addition and subtraction problem situations and with many specific addition and subtraction number triads.

Caveats

The developmental course of the relationship between children's presentations of problem situations and their presentations of solution procedures is not yet fully established. It is fairly clear that a single presentation is used initially for both and that several years later children generate and use separate presentations. Exactly what happens in between and how problem type variations or instruction influence the developmental course is not so clear. As a wider range of problems than those simple addition and subtraction problems appearing in present textbooks come to be commonly experienced by children, children's potential in these areas will be more easily discovered. Other research issues concerning our present research knowledge base are discussed in Fuson (in press).

The contrast in much of the preceding discussion (and in the literature) is between a child thinking of a problem situation with a general schema ("This problem is about having some and getting some more." or "This problem is about comparing two numbers to find how much bigger one number is.") or as a solution procedure that will operate on the known quantities to give the unknown quantity ("I have to add six to eight" or "I have to make six and make eight and match them to find out how much bigger eight is."). In this contrast word-problem schemata do not involve numbers and solution procedures do. But in fact the quantities themselves may for a long time be quite salient to children, and children may generate a single version of the problem situation that focuses on the quantities but places these within the situational context (e.g., "This problem is about having eight and getting six more." or "This problem is about comparing 57 to 28 to find out how much bigger 57 is.").

Research on Later Numerical Instruction

What Do Textbooks Present?

Textbooks in the United States have three features that limit their effectiveness as the primary source of instruction for mathematical marks sums and differences between 10 and 18: (a) Such problems are delayed compared to their placement in other countries, (b) no method of solving such problems is supported in the text, and (c) there are fewer such problems given than are given for the easier problems. First, in the United States learning these more difficult sums and differences between 10 and 18 is primarily a second-grade task, whereas in several countries noted for the mathematics learning of their children (Japan, Korea, Mainland China, the Soviet Union, Taiwan) such learning is primarily a first-grade task (Fuson & Kwon, in press-a; Fuson et al., 1988). Three of the five prominent U.S. text series analyzed in the latter study did not even include nonoptional work on such sums and differences in first grade, one series did not introduce all such subtraction problems until the second half of second grade, and an average of 23% of the pages of U.S. second-grade texts (the five series ranged between 19% and 31%) was devoted to sums and differences to 18 compared to percentages ranging between 0% and 3% of the pages of the other countries. Five commonly used series published in the late 1980s were examined for this chapter. The situation had improved somewhat with respect to the availability of all sums and differences to 18 in the first-grade texts; all five series now had such a chapter in their first-grade text. However, the chapter with sums and differences between 12 and 18 was the last chapter in the book in three of the five series (i.e., it is unlikely that all first graders reach that chapter). Learning these single-digit sums and differences was still a major focus of the second-grade texts, with a mean of 24% of the pages focusing on such problems.

Second, no method of addition or subtraction was supported in the U.S. texts. Initially, pictures were given with small problems to show a Change-Add-To procedure for addition and a Change-Take-From (separate/take away) procedure for subtraction; then suddenly no pictures were given with the mathematical marks.[15] In contrast, for sums between 10 and 18 methods that recompose numbers around ten were taught in the other countries.[16] These methods can be carried out mentally and rapidly and are easily used in multidigit addition and subtraction. They are discussed further in "Research on Ten-Structured Methods of Addition and Subtraction." These characteristics were shared by the newer texts reviewed for this chapter, with the exception of the Addison-Wesley series whose support of various solution procedures is discussed later. Two aspects of the pictures given initially in many of the older and the new texts interfere with children's use of those pictures for Level I solution procedures. First, the initial state, change, and final state of these Change situations are all given in a single picture. This is potentially confusing for many children who have to see the birds that were there initially by mentally combining the birds still there and the birds flying away. Two of the newer texts did for two to four pages show three different pictures for a given addition or subtraction situation: the initial state, the change state, and the final state. But then all the other pictures in the text were of the single picture type. Second, the pictures are sometimes (in some series, more often than sometimes) very complex and confusing. They frequently show no pattern that can be subitized even with a pattern of patterns because each picture is so complex and they are sometimes crowded together. No standard pattern arrange-

---

[15]The Harper and Row books did for some problems support counting on, doubles plus one, and the nines over ten, and the new Addison-Wesley series does contain some exercises for counting on 1, 2, or 3. However, no general method and no combination of procedures that would work with all problems is given in any U.S. text, and most had no procedure other than Level I counting procedures.

[16]The over-ten method is not demonstrated very much in the Soviet textbooks, but the teacher's handbook directs teachers to teach this method.

ment is used, though that would support pattern number solutions of smaller sums. Some pictures are even difficult to count.

Third, even though the problems with sums above ten are the most difficult, they do not appear in U.S. texts as often as do easier problems (Hamann & Ashcraft, 1986). This predominance of smaller easier problems over the larger more difficult problems also was reported in a similar analysis in 1924 (Clapp, 1924; discussed in Hamann & Ashcraft, 1986), suggesting that this pattern may be a very long-term one in the United States. Adults' ratings of problem difficulty verified that these larger problems given less frequently are indeed the more difficult problems. This counterproductive distribution of mathematical marks problems is clearly exacerbated, and probably created by, the delay of the more difficult facts until second grade. Many more text pages are spent on single-digit sums in the first grade (a mean of 36% for five series), where the focus is on sums to ten, than in the second grade, where both sums below and above ten are covered (a mean of 23% of second-grade text pages are spent on all single-digit sums) (Fuson et al., 1988). In the newer textbooks analyzed for this chapter, the dominance of sums and differences to 10 over the more difficult sums and differences between 10 and 18 was reduced if one assumes that teachers will actually get to the last chapter in the first-grade book (that containing the sums between 12 and 18 in 3 of the 5 text series): 25% of the first-grade text pages were on sums to 10, and 17% were on sums between 10 and 18. In the three series that had separate chapters for sums below and above ten in the second-grade texts (the other two series had chapters for sums to 12 and for sums between 12 and 18), two series had twice as many pages on sums between 10 and 18 as on sums to 10, and the other series had about equal numbers of pages on these two topics.

Most textbooks in the United States also have several characteristics that interfere with their ability to support understanding of various meanings of addition and subtraction and the ability to solve addition and subtraction word problems: The + and − marks are given only a single meaning (or the take-away meaning for − is introduced very much earlier than are the comparison or missing part meanings), the kinds of word problems are restricted to the easy addition and subtraction problems discussed in the "Simple Addition and Subtraction Situations" section, most pages of word problems are all addition problems so that the problem does not even have to be read, the language and types of problems even within a given subtype are very restricted and stereotyped so that a key word approach can be used, word problems are concentrated on a few word-problem pages rather than being maximally distributed throughout the text (as are problems in Soviet textbooks), practically no problems are two-step problems involving two different problem subtypes (in contrast to the Soviet first- and second-grade texts, where 37% and 53% of the addition and subtraction word problems are two-step problems) (Stigler et al., 1986), and children are expected to write solution equations for a word problem instead of equations that present the problem situation. Several of these features were discussed in "What Do Textbooks Present?" in the first section of this chapter, but the restrictiveness is even more striking given the more extensive range of possible addition and subtraction situations evident in Tables 2.1 and 2.5 combined and in Figs. 2.1 and 2.2. Only 42 of the 1,527 addition and subtraction problems given in widely used U.S. texts (3%) were of the more difficult addition and subtraction problems shown in Table 2.5. Strikingly, in the first-grade textbooks of the Soviet Union the number of problems is almost equal across the 12 possible problem sub-types, almost as if the Soviet authors had used a problem-type classification like that in Fig. 2.1. The existence of the whole range of problem subtypes and the large numbers of two-step problems in the Soviet text-books indicate that the poverty and oversimplicity of word problems in U.S. texts is not a developmental necessity.

Finally, many textbooks at some grade level use a number line to demonstrate addition and subtraction. Numbers usually are demonstrated as being composed of hops (6 is 6 hops) on the number line. Hops do show the number line meaning of a number as a measure of length: A 6 on the number line means the length from the 0 to the 6. But because the number line involves intervals and interval marks, and there is always one more interval mark than interval, children frequently confuse these two.[17] This may be exacerbated by the fact that a child doing hops on a number line does not write the little hop marks on the number line because the same number line must be reused for many problems. So the child loses the sense of a number as a length, as a trip of several hops, and sees the number only as the name for the interval mark below which it is written. If the child then begins using this meaning of number on the number line and starts counting interval marks (essentially turning the length measure number line into a count model of discrete entities), answers may begin to be off by one because the 6 is written below the seventh interval mark to show the length six intervals from 0. A centimeter number line, used in conjunction with numbered strips or Cuisenaire rods, may help children retain the length meaning of number on a number line. An alternative that may be more consistent with children's conceptual structures of number is a number list consisting of a row or a column of numerals. This number list is a count model that works just like counting objects works: There are six numbers up to and including the 6. Because many primary children con-

---

[17]These observations about the number line are based on 20 years work with in-service and preservice teachers; they reflect teachers' own confusions about the number line and their reports of children's confusions.

fuse left and right, a vertical number list that increases as it rises (consistent with people getting older as they get taller) might prove to be an especially strong conceptual support for many children.

How Are U.S. Children Doing?

There are few hard data on how well children in the United States do on the more difficult addition and subtraction facts between 10 and 18. Thornton and Smith (1988) reported that even a relatively high testing class of first-grade children (92% percentile on the Iowa Test of Basic Skills) who used the regular textbook only solved correctly 36% of the hard addition facts (nondouble facts above 11) and only solved 23% of such subtraction facts correctly. Correct percentages for two later classes of children about at the mean for the State of Illinois were 20% and 18% of such subtraction facts (Thornton, 1990). Softer data (newspapers, teacher complaints at inservice sessions, talks at professional meetings) indicate that children cannot solve these problems nearly as accurately or quickly as teachers and others wish. Song and Ginsburg (1987) reported that U.S. first, second, and third graders performed much more poorly than their Korean counterparts on these problems,[18] and Fuson and Kwon (in press-a) reported that the majority of Korean children interviewed at the end of the first semester of first grade already could do the methods structured around ten for addition and subtraction (see "Level IV Word Problems: Triad Number Solutions") and were quite accurate on these even though these children do not learn such methods in school until the second semester of first grade. This is in contrast to the United States, where many texts do not even introduce all of the facts between 10 and 18 until second grade (or the very end of first grade).

Other Research on Teaching

What Happens in U.S. First-Grade Mathematics Classrooms?

Two studies indicate that U.S. first graders spend a considerable amount of time working individually on paper-and-pencil tasks. Bell and Burns (1981) reported that over 80% of the classtime of first- through third-grade children is spent working by themselves on textbook or teacher worksheets. School work rarely indicated any uses of numbers or of arithmetic

---

[18]The criterion was giving the answer within 2 seconds. It is possible that the U.S. children would have been fairly accurate but many could not answer in this time; Korean children might have been doing the strategies structured around ten in this time period.

procedures; these were practiced in isolation of any addition or subtraction situations. Stigler, Lee, and Stevenson (1987) found that U.S. children in 20 representative classrooms spent averages of 52% of their mathematics instructional time working alone, 41% as a whole class, and 8% working in small groups. This study provided comparative data on classrooms in Japan and Taiwan. U.S. and Japanese teachers spent similar amount of their time imparting information (25% and 33%), however the Japanese but not the American teachers often conveyed information indirectly by seeking answers, responses, and explanations from their students. Another study (Stigler, 1988) followed up this difference and found that Japanese first-grade teachers gave, and asked students to give, lengthy verbal explanations of mathematical concepts and algorithms. The Japanese explanations were more complicated and abstract than were the U.S. explanations. Nearly half of all Japanese first-grade classroom segments contained verbal explanations, compared to only 20% of the U.S. first-grade segments. Japanese teachers moved at a slower pace than did U.S. teachers, covering fewer problems in depth. Thus, these complex verbal explanations always were linked to particular problem situations. Incorrect solutions were commonly put on the board and discussed and corrected in Japanese classrooms, whereas public evaluations in U.S. classrooms usually were limited to reporting how many problems had been answered correctly or praising correct answers, thereby losing the opportunity for children to correct their misunderstandings.

A number of factors combined to result in U.S. first graders having considerably less opportunity to learn mathematics than did Japanese or Taiwanese children. Lower percentages of time in U.S. classes were devoted to academic classes overall and to mathematics within that total academic class time, resulting in a mean of 2.9 hours a week spent on mathematics compared to 6.0 in Japan and 3.9 in Taiwan. In nearly a third of the U.S. classrooms teachers spent less than 10% of the classroom time on mathematics. In spite of average first-grade class sizes of 22 in the United States compared to 45 in Japan and 39 in Taiwan, in U.S. classrooms almost 20% of individual first graders' time in mathematics class was spent in inappropriate off-task activity, compared to only 10% for the other two countries. A substantial portion, 30%, of the academic class time of U.S. first-grade classes was spent in nonacademic transition activities compared to 8% in Japan and 20% in Taiwan.

Research on Instruction Based on Children's Thinking

Some research indicates that children in the United States can learn much more than is presented to them now if instruction is consistent with their thinking. One major area of research has been the work of Thornton,

Rathmell, Steinberg, and others on teaching thinking strategies. Thornton (1978) taught to second graders derived-fact strategies (known fact plus or minus a number) for particular facts. These children improved significantly more in 8 weeks of instruction than did a control group using the teaching suggestions of the text and teacher-made drills: means of 62 and 42 on the 3-minute 98-fact test in addition and subtraction, respectively, compared to means of 40 and 21 in the control group. Steinberg (1984, 1985) reported the results of teaching a second-grade class an 8-week unit on addition and subtraction derived-fact strategies (double and nondouble known facts plus or minus a number, up-over-ten for addition, compensation to a double). Children who used some derived-fact strategies on the pretest increased substantially their use of derived-fact strategies; they also recalled many facts on the posttest. Some of the children who on the pretest were very fast at sequence counting on continued to use this method rather than changing to derived-fact strategies. The remaining children mainly used derived-fact strategies in the later interviews, using them more in addition than subtraction. Children improved on a timed test (2 seconds for each problem) in both addition and subtraction, solving almost all of the sums less than 10, two thirds of the addition and half of the subtraction sums above 10 in this time. Children used sequence counting, derived-fact strategies, and recall to solve these problems within 2 seconds. On the posttest 65% of the derived-fact strategies used on subtraction problems involved a related addition problem, but two fifths of the children never used additive strategies to solve subtraction problems. The use of direct subtractive derived-fact strategies was found to be difficult for many children (Steinberg, 1984, 1985).

Thornton and Smith (1988) reported one year-long study and Thornton (1990) reported two year-long studies teaching addition and subtraction strategies to first graders. Most of these strategies were simpler than the complex thinking strategies discussed earlier. The addition and subtraction combinations were organized by the solution procedure that was easy to use rather than by the sum, as is ordinarily done in textbooks. Seventy-four easy addition and subtraction facts were taught by counting on, counting back, and counting up 1, 2, or 3 (auditory patterns were used to keep track of the words counted on, back, or up) and by memorizing with pattern-based experiences sums that made 10, facts with 0, and doubles. Doubles +1 and −1 were taught, and up-over-ten was used for nines and five other facts plus their commutatives. Subtraction instruction was delayed until children knew 74 easy addition facts. Solving a subtraction combination by using the related addition fact also was emphasized. There was considerable class discussion about how individual children solved particular problems. The control class used the school-adopted text and worked through the text material in order; they thus worked on problems by sum (problems with sums to 8, sums to 10, etc.) and later work emphasized fact families—the four related addition and subtraction sentences coming from a single triad of numbers. The control group children were drawn from a second school by matching their performance on the Steffe counting model (Steffe et al., 1983) to that of the control children. In Thornton and Smith (1988) children in both groups were high performers in mathematics (each group had a mean of the 93rd percentile on the Iowa Test of Basic Skills), and in the Thornton (1990) study both groups were ethnically mixed and were near the Illinois state average on standardized tests. In all studies on the posttest, the Strategy children gave correct rapid answers at a considerably higher rate than did the Control children on doubles, count on/count up, count back, sums of ten, and hard facts (those other than the 74 easy facts) problems. On written tests, Strategy children solved more than 85% of the first four kinds of subtraction problems correctly, whereas Control children only solved 20% to 50% of such problems correctly. Over the three studies, Strategy children solved 47%, 48%, and 75% of the hard fact subtraction problems correctly, and Control children solved only 23%, 20%, and 18% correctly. Many Control children did not attempt to solve a problem they had not yet studied, whereas virtually all Strategy children could count on to solve difficult addition facts and count up to solve difficult subtraction facts. Thus, this approach was considerably more effective than the usual textbook approach.

The Addison-Wesley series implements the Thornton thinking strategy approach to sums and differences to 18. It is of course a major improvement to have a textbook support children's solution procedures beyond the Level I direct modeling procedures. However, the particular implementation has some problems that need to be avoided in future textbook implementations of research on children's thinking. The counting on is approached in a rote fashion, with no acknowledgment of or support given to the conceptual connections that need to be made for counting on. In the Thornton studies count ons, count ups, and count backs were supported by children's use of physical materials in which they added on or took off one, two, or three objects as they counted on, up, or back. In the text no such pictures are used; instead little cartoons show someone doing the counting with numerals in little thought balloons. Because these are not connected to objects, they are potentially confusing because two numerals are shown when one is counting on one, three numerals are shown when one is counting on two, and so on. Pictures or pattern supports are used for some other strategies, but usually only for a page or two. These pictures are sometimes confusing rather than helpful because they are so busy and complicated that it is difficult to see the pattern. Different pattern layouts are used on different pages instead of one clear pattern being used consistently. The approach emphasizes that there is one way to solve each particular marks problem, and a collection of several different methods are taught. Thus, the first step for solving any marks problem is deciding what kind of a problem it is. This conveys the old idea that math is a collection of different procedures, and one must learn the correct procedure for each problem. An acknowledgment that all addition problems can be solved in several different ways, as can all subtraction problems, and that one can choose less and more efficient ways to do these problems is a more accurate and empowering approach. This seems to have been done in the Thornton studies by class discussions of how various children solved a particular problem ("And how did you solve it?") within a context of acceptance of various solution procedures (Thornton, 1990). The textbook series does not convey this carefully enough. Finally, the teacher text states that counting on and counting up with numbers more than 3 are not as accurate for most children as are other strategies introduced in the text, and it tells teachers to discourage such counting on and counting up. Research indicates that this position is in error. Counting on and counting up are almost universally invented by U.S. children, and they are powerful and accurate procedures that can be learned by almost all first graders (see following discussion). In contrast, the evidence on derived-fact strategies, especially on subtraction derived-fact strategies, suggests that many of the more difficult strategies are not easily accessible to first graders (and not even to second graders). Even the strategy children in Thornton's own studies used counting on as a general solution method for solving difficult addition problems and counting up as a general solution method for solving difficult subtraction problems. It may be acceptable to suggest that teachers encourage children to move on from these general methods when children can do so (though recognizing how long some children may remain at Level II or Level III), but telling teachers to discourage children from using these methods robs children who are at Level II and Level III of their most natural and powerful methods and sends wrong messages about who "owns" mathematical thinking in the classroom.

My own work on counting on for addition and counting up for subtraction indicated that one can help first graders of all achievement levels move through the usual developmental levels of solution procedures (from counting all with objects to counting on with objects to sequence counting on) to the efficient and general Level III sequence solution procedures by the end of first grade (Fuson, 1986b; Fuson & Fuson, in press; Fuson & Secada, 1986; Fuson & Willis, 1988). The instruction used the results of Secada, Fuson, and Hall (1983) concerning the understandings possessed by children who count on to help children move from counting all to counting on with objects. Because most kindergarten children possess the first skill, counting up from an arbitrary number (Fuson et al., 1982), this was not taught. Instruction focused on the three tasks discussed earlier and pictured in Fig. 2.3. Teachers of eleven classes of first-grade children of all achievement levels successfully helped children build the understandings in Fig. 2.3 in from one to four class periods (see Fuson, 1987, and Fuson & Secada, 1986, for details of the instruction). The rapidity of this learning suggests that most first graders already have the conceptual understanding required for counting on with objects and that the instruction merely permits them to reflect on and organize their knowledge to bring about this conceptual advance of counting on. However, without instructional support it evidently takes some children until third grade to begin to count on spontaneously (Carpenter & Moser, 1983). Children in these instructional studies then learned sequence counting on that was related to their object counting on. We had found in earlier work that children's usual methods of keeping track were difficult to do while writing mathematical marks with a pencil, because many children would put down their pencil to keep track with both hands, pick up their pencil to write the answer, put down the pencil to use both hands for the next problem, and so forth. Thus, much of the child's time was spent putting down and picking up the pencil. Therefore, a method of keeping track that only required one hand was taught so that the child could always keep the pencil in the writing hand (see Fig. 2.5). Learning these one-handed finger patterns and sequence counting on using these finger patterns to keep track took from 10 to 14 class periods and was quite successful (see Fuson, 1987, Fuson & Fuson, in press, and Fuson & Secada, 1986, for details of the instruction and results). First and second graders added any two single-digit numbers with sums over ten quite accurately; the high-achieving first graders and all achievement levels of second graders added quite rapidly, whereas the average- and low-achieving first graders added accurately but more slowly. Counting on with one-handed finger patterns was efficient enough to be used in solving 3- to 10-digit problems requiring trading (Fuson, 1986a; Fuson & Briars, 1990). Thus, children in the United States can solve sums to 18 as early as children in China, Japan, the Soviet Union, and Taiwan if they receive instruction that helps them to move through the developmental levels of solution procedures to Level III sequence counting on using an efficient method of keeping track. Lower achieving first and second graders in this study were very proud of their ability to solve such "large problems."

There is considerable evidence that the backward counting-down procedures are much more difficult for children than are the forward counting-on and counting-up procedures (e.g., Baroody, 1984; Fuson, 1984; Secada, 1982; Steffe et al., 1983), and children shift to using counting up to solve a range of subtraction situations when they have advanced flexible conceptual structures (Carpenter & Moser, 1984). These results led me to try to support children's learning to subtract mathematical marks problems by sequence counting up to s. After the eleven classes of first- and

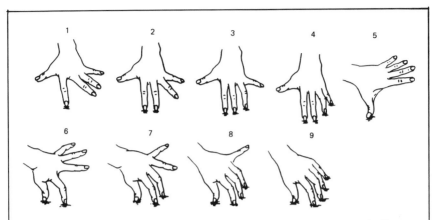

The finger patterns for 1 through 9 are made by touching certain fingers and/or the thumb to some surface such as a table. Thus, there is a kinesthetic as well as visual feedback for the finger patterns. The finger patterns use a subbase of 5. The thumb is 5, and 6 is the thumb plus the 1 finger (6 = 5+ 1), 7 is the thumb plus the two fingers (7 = 5 + 2), etc. The motion from 4 to 5 is a very strong and definite motion—the fingers all go up and the thumb goes down, all in one sharp motion with the wrist twisting.

Words said: "8"   "9"   "10"   "11"   "12"   "13"

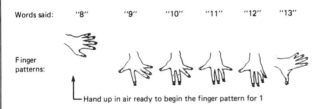

Finger patterns:

└ Hand up in air ready to begin the finger pattern for 1

Children should do the finger patterns with their non-writing hand. To help children remember at which word they should stop, we had them place their pencils to the number word they were counting on.

Addition	*Subtraction*
8 + 5 = ?	13 − 8 = ?

The counting-on procedure:
1. Count on 5 more words from 8.
2. Stop when finger pattern for 5 is made.
3. Answer is *last* word said (13).

The counting-up procedure:
1 Count up from 8 to 13.
2. Stop when say 13.
3. Answer is what the *hand* says—the finger pattern for 5.

FIG. 2.5.   Counting on and counting up with one-handed finger patterns.

second-grade children had learned to sequence count on with one-handed finger patterns to add, their teachers introduced the − sign as having three different meanings: a take-away, a compare, and an equalize meaning (Fuson, 1986b). These meanings then supported counting up for subtraction (even take away can be thought of as "the part taken away plus how much more to get the original?"). It was very easy for children to learn to count up from 8 to 14 to solve 14 − 8 using one-handed finger patterns to keep track (see Fig. 2.5 and Fuson, 1988c). Even below-average first graders were able to solve the most difficult subtraction marks problems with single-digit addends and sums through 18 (Fuson, 1986b; Fuson & Willis, 1988). Because counting up does not require the finger patterns to be overlearned (one merely listens for the sum and then looks at the finger pattern for the unknown addend), counting up for subtraction is actually easier than is counting on for addition. Teachers reported that they were astounded by how rapidly children learned counting up and how much easier subtraction was for these children than it had ever been.

These children were as accurate and as fast at subtracting as at adding sums to 18 (Fuson & Fuson, in press; Hall, Fuson, & Willis, 1985). As with addition, counting up with the one-handed finger patterns was efficient enough to be used in solving large multidigit subtraction problems with trading (Fuson, 1986b; Fuson & Briars, 1990). Some children did show interference between counting on and counting up and required further experiences focused on differentiating and remembering meanings for the marks + and − and differentiating and remembering the counting-on and counting-up procedures; this experience was successful in reducing this interference. Learning subtraction as counting up did not interfere with children's understanding of take-away problems (Fuson & Willis, 1988), and children were able to solve compare and equalize problems as well as take-away problems (Fuson, 1986b; Fuson & Willis, 1988). Children, especially the lower achieving children, were very proud of their ability to subtract these large problems. Thus, expanding the meanings for − to include equalize and compare situations enabled first-grade children to learn an efficient sequence counting procedure for subtraction (counting up to) that made subtraction mathematical marks problems as easy as addition problems. Neither counting on for addition nor counting up for subtraction was learned merely as a rote procedure: Most of the children spontaneously generalized the use of these procedures to addition and subtraction word problems of several kinds.

Counting up for subtraction seems to be a powerful and natural approach for children. Children given the opportunity to think of subtraction as a forward procedure will choose to solve difficult subtraction marks problems in that way (Thornton, 1990). The Strategy children were not taught general counting on for addition and counting up for subtraction because the Thornton strategy approach emphasizes that there is an easy way to solve each problem and counting on and counting up are limited to second addends of 1, 2, or 3. But virtually all of the Strategy children solved the difficult addition problems they did not know by counting on and the difficult subtraction facts they did not know by counting up. The Strategy approach did offer both forward and backward counting views of subtraction to these children: Subtraction combinations in which the subtrahend is close to (within three of) the sum (e.g., $9 - 8, 6 - 4$) were to be solved by counting up from the smaller to the larger number and subtraction combinations in which the subtrahend is 1, 2, or 3 (e.g., $9 - 2, 5 - 3$) were to be solved by counting back. The one, two, or three words counted on or counted back were subitized using auditory patterns that children practiced separately. However, evidently all children generalized counting up to all subtraction combinations and invented some method of keeping track of more than three words counted up. This view of subtraction as a forward procedure also may have been facilitated by the emphasis on using an addition fact to solve a subtraction problem. The fact that these Strategy children were not as correct on the difficult subtraction problems as were the children in the Fuson studies discussed earlier who learned general counting up in a conceptual fashion and who learned a general efficient method of keeping track of the second addend (correct solutions of 48% and 75% compared to 89%) seems to indicate that some children need support for these aspects of general counting up.

There is some evidence that many first graders and most second graders can learn to solve many of the more difficult word problems if they are given an opportunity to do so and are provided with some kind of instructional support for thinking about these problems. What kind of instructional support is maximal and whether this support should be differentiated for different problem types is still not clear. Rathmell (1986) reported high levels of success with small numbers (sums and differences to 10) in a 2-year teaching study in which he helped children to analyze all problem types within a part–part–whole joining/separating context. The quantities in a word problem were labeled as parts or wholes and then solved by Change-Add-To or Change-Take-From (joining or separating) procedures. Second graders at the end of the year were at ceiling on all problem types except the most difficult Compare problems. However, De Corte and Verschaffel (1985b) reported that a first-grade class using a different schematic drawing for Change, Put Together, and Compare problems performed better at the end of the year than a class using the traditional approach of a single drawing, and Wolters (1983) found that use of a part–part–whole schema had positive effects on Put Together problems but negative effects on Change and Compare problems. Lindvall and Tamburino (Greeno, 1987; Tamburino, 1982) found that eight different kinds of drawings used for eight different kinds of word problems improved performance on these problems and on a test of transfer. Colleagues and I (Fuson, 1988b; Fuson & Willis, 1989; Willis & Fuson, 1985, 1988) found that teacher's use with first and second graders of three different schematic drawings for Change, Put Together, and Compare problems led to much higher levels of performance on the whole range of problem types than has been reported elsewhere in this country: High-achieving first graders reached ceiling on almost all problem subtypes with sums and differences to 18, high-achieving second graders reached very high levels of performance on almost all subtypes with 3-digit numbers requiring trading, and average-achieving first graders and low-achieving second graders showed progress over the year for many subtypes with sums and differences to 18. At the very least, the drawings support a vocabulary and organization of the problem elements that facilitate discussion among problem solvers. Some children seemed to use the drawings to present the problem situation, whereas other children seemed to focus more on the quantities in the word problem and use the drawings to present the solution procedure. It is clear that more research is need in this area of facilitating children's solution of the whole range of addition and subtraction situations and in understanding relationships between children's conceptions of problem situations and of addition and subtraction solution procedures. The success of various approaches does indicate that first graders can profitably work on the whole range of such problems using sums and differences to 18 and that second graders can work on the whole range of problems using three-digit numbers.

Research on Ten-Structured Methods of Addition and Subtraction

In Japan, Korea, Mainland China, and Taiwan children are taught specific methods of adding and subtracting single-digit numbers with sums between 10 and 18. These methods are structured around ten: The sums between 10 and 18 are decomposed into a ten and the rest of the number. These methods are facilitated by the structure of number words in these countries: The numbers between 10 and 18 all name ten (11 is ten one, 12 is ten two, . . . , 15 is ten five, . . .). The ten-structured method taught for addition is up-over-ten. Up-over-ten is a thinking strategy short-cut of counting on in which one number (usually the smaller number) is split into (a) the quantity that will make ten with the other number and (b) the left-over quantity. For example, $7 + 5 =$ "seven plus three (to make ten) plus two (because five is three plus two) = ten plus two = ten two." In Chinese, Japanese, and Korean (and any language with the regular named ten) the regular named ten in the words between 10 and 18 makes the last step trivial, and in practice the "ten plus two" step can be omitted. To do the up-over-ten method in these languages, one really just has to separate the smaller number (here, the 5) into the part to make ten and the part over ten, and the answer is then just "ten the-part-over-ten," that is, here, ten two. In the United States this last step is not trivial. Steinberg (1985) reported that more than a third of her middle-class second graders did not know this "ten plus x" prerequisite for the up-over-ten method; they had to count to find the English word for "ten plus two" or "ten plus four" and so forth. Furthermore, many children did not possess another prerequisite for this strategy: Half of these second graders did not recall combinations that sum to ten (i.e., given seven, they had to count to find out that three more made ten). Of course, these results reflect first-grade experiences that neglect both of these prerequisites.

In Japan, Korea, Mainland China, and Taiwan, subtraction is taught by two methods structured around ten. One is the reverse of up-over-ten. In this down-over-ten procedure, one splits the known addend into the part over ten and then subtracts the rest from ten: $12 - 5 =$ "ten two minus five $=$ ten two minus two (to make ten) minus three (the rest of the five) $=$ ten minus three is seven." In the subtract-from-ten method, the known addend is subtracted from ten and the remainder is added to the part over ten: $12 - 5 =$ "ten two minus five $=$ ten minus five is five plus the two from the ten two is seven." Both of these subtraction methods are easier to carry out in the languages that name ten because the two-digit sum is decomposed by the number words into a ten and the ones, and thus the ten is present as a separate entity to be subtracted from or to be subtracted down over. Children in these countries prepare in the first half of first grade for these addition and subtraction methods structured around ten by doing activities focusing on the two prerequisites for these methods: decomposing a single-digit number into all of the various pairs of numbers whose sum is that number and working on finding complements to ten (the number that makes ten with a given number) (Fuson et al., 1988).

In Korea and Japan further supports are available to help children learn these ten-structured methods. Korean children may learn traditional Korean methods of folding or unfolding fingers to show addition and subtraction (Fuson & Kwon, in press-a). For sums over ten (e.g., $8 + 6$), children using the unfolding method would begin with all ten fingers folded down, then would unfold (extend) eight fingers either sequentially while counting from one to eight or by using a known pattern of eight fingers. To add 6, they then would start counting from one while unfolding the rest of the ten fingers ("one, two") and then fold fingers down to show the rest of the six added on (say "three, four, five, six") while folding down four fingers (see Table 2.7). The fingers then would show the sum "ten four" because ten fingers had been unfolded and four had been folded again. The fingers support the mental up-over-ten method because one can see the eight

TABLE 2.7
Korean and Japanese supports for ten-structured methods of addition

Support	The ten-structured method of addition

Adding Up Over Ten

Korean finger unfolding and folding

8   2 more   + 4 more = 6

8   + 2 = 10

ten unfolded + four folded = ten four = 14

Japanese TILEs

8   +   6   ten four = 14

Combine Fives to Make Ten

Korean one-handed unfolding and folding

left hand   right hand   7 + 8   I had

five unfolded in 7
five unfolded in 8
ten unfolded

5   2   5   3   2   3   5
unfolded folded   unfolded folded   folded folded folded   ten five

5 + 2 = 7   5 + 3 = 8   15

Japanese TILEs

2 fives = ten

ten four
14

8 + 6   3 + 1 = 4

Note: The Korean methods may begin with the little finger and move toward the thumb, and they may begin with the hands open, fold fingers down, and then unfold them over ten (or over five). The TILEs are cut from cardboard.

(fingers), the two more (fingers) to make ten, and the four more from the six that make ten four. The folding method works similarly, with the fingers all unfolded (extended) to start, folded down to show the first addend and then the part of the second addend that makes ten, and then unfolded to show the part of the second addend over ten. The five fingers on each hand provide a subbase of five so that the larger single-digit numbers can be thought of as five plus one, five plus two, five plus three, five plus four. In Japan tiles that show the numbers 1 through 10 within a two-by-five rectangle of squares also structure numbers by a subbase of five and support the ten-structured methods (see Table 2.7 and Hatano, 1982). An 8 tile is a row of five squares beside a row of three squares; the missing two squares show the complement to ten: Two squares are needed to make ten with eight. These tiles were developed for use with retarded children, but now are used fairly widely with all children to support understanding of the ten-structured methods. Wirtz (1980) used a similar pattern to show complements to ten, and Thornton (1990) used the Wirtz approach in teaching ten-facts (complements to ten).

There are also ten-structured methods that involve combining fives from numbers five through nine. Some Korean children used the Korean folding/unfolding method to put each addend on a single hand (see Table 2.7). For 8 + 6, one hand was unfolded and then three fingers were folded down (to make 8), and the other hand was unfolded and one finger was folded down (to make 6). The child then said that the two fives made ten, the three plus one made four, so the sum was ten four. The one-handed finger patterns (see Fig. 2.5) used to keep track of the second addend in the counting-on studies discussed earlier (Fuson & Secada, 1986) also are structured with a subbase of five: The thumb shows five, and 6 through 9 are thumb plus one, thumb plus two, thumb plus three, and thumb plus four. Some children in those studies used these one-handed finger patterns to add in this combining five method: They made each number on a separate hand (e.g., 8 is a thumb and three fingers down and six is a thumb and one finger down) and said that the two thumbs made ten, the fingers made four, so the sum was fourteen. The last step of course is more difficult in English than in the named-ten Asian languages because children have to know how to say ten plus four; it is not given in the language as "ten four."

Research on Mathematics as Thinking

Structuring the mathematics classroom with a focus on mathematics learning as thinking can have affective and attitudinal benefits at no cost to mathematics achievement.[19] A second-grade classroom was organized with the following features: Children worked in pairs or trios on mathematical tasks and had to reach a consensus on the solution of a given task, working hard rather than completing many problems was emphasized, and children verbalized and discussed their solution attempts in an atmo-

---

[19]Formal data on mathematics achievement have not yet been published by this project, but the children in the experimental classroom did at least as well on standardized tests as had previous classes taught by the same teacher, and the same was true in the following year in an expanded set of classrooms (personal communication, P. Cobb, April, 1989).

sphere in which everyone's thinking was accepted and errors were perceived as natural and informing rather than as sources of embarrassment. Reaching consensus in the pairs or groups and discussing problems as a total class provided many opportunities for reflection and cognitive reorganization. Observers reported positive emotional tone: Children were enthusiastic and persistent and experienced joy when they solved a problem that was personally challenging (Cobb, Wood, & Yackel, 1991). Children displayed considerable intellectual autonomy and sought to solve problems on their own and in their own way, protesting when peers told them answers (Cobb, Yackel, & Wood, 1989). Children in this constructivist classroom had higher task orientation, stronger beliefs that success depends on effort, more attempts to understand, more cooperation with peers, less desire for superiority over their friends, less desire to avoid work, and less belief that success depends on superior ability than did children in traditional second-grade classrooms (Nicholls, Cobb, Wood, Yackel, & Patashnick, 1990). The teacher created the new social norms required for this cooperative learning by intervening to support the discussion of problem solutions and then sharing such interventions with the whole class (Cobb et al., 1988; Yackel, Cobb, & Wood, 1991).

What Can Be: Supporting Children's
Later Numerical Thinking
in the Classroom

Kindergarten and early first-grade children who have had learning opportunities like those discussed in the first "What Can Be" section would be well equipped to tackle the more difficult word problems discussed in this section. They would not be hampered by a single take-away meaning of $-$, subtract, or minus, and they would approach problem situations with confidence and a focus on the meaning of the situation, not on surface features such as the numbers or key words. Such children in late first grade and in second grade could be provided with many opportunities to solve the more difficult word-problem subtypes discussed in the second section, and children's interpretations and solution procedures for problems would be a focus of frequent discussions. Children also would attack many different kinds of two-step problems composed from different one-step problem types (see Table 2.8 for some examples of two-step problems taken from the Soviet first-grade text). Work on word problems should allow for individual interpretations because a given problem can be thought of as more than one type. For example, many children thought of Put Together: missing Part problems as Compare problems in which the known part and

TABLE 2.8
Examples of Two-Step Addition and Subtraction Word Problems
in the Soviet First-Grade Textbook

Type of Problem	Problem
Put Together Change-Take-From	Some October Scouts prepared 6 kg of mountain ash seeds and 4 kg of linden seeds for the birds. Over the winter they fed the birds 9 kg of seed. How many kilograms of seed were left?
Compare Put Together	There are 10 green lights lit on a New Year's tree, and 5 fewer red lights than green lights. How many lights in all are lit on the New Year's tree? Change the question so that it can be answered in a single operation.
Change-Take-From Change-Add-To	Kolya had 15 kopecks. He spent 10 kopecks on breakfast, and then his mother gave him 20 kopecks more. How much money does he now have?
Change-Take-From Change-Take-From	12 children were playing hide-and-seek. First 3 girls went home, and then 2 boys. How many children were left playing hide-and-seek?
Compare Put Together	Two boys measured the length of a bridge from either end, walking toward each other. One measured off 45 m before meeting the other, who measured off 6 m less. How long is the bridge?
Put Together Compare	There were 12 pencils in the first box, 9 in the second box, and 3 fewer pencils in the third box than in the first and second boxes together. How many pencils were in the third box?
Change-Add-To Change-Add-To	It is 50 m from my house to school. I left for school, but after I walked 20 m, I remembered that I had forgotten my book. I returned home, got the book, and went to school. What distance did I walk?

known whole were compared to each other (Fuson, 1988b). Accepting such different views (if they are articulated and defended by a child) both supports individual thinking of children and provides opportunities for relating the problem types to each other; the latter can lead to the eventual formation of a single rich addend-addend-sum schema relating all problem types. First graders without the richer learning opportunities outlined in "What Can Be" would need to be provided with some of those learning opportunities first and then have their word problems extended to the more difficult kinds discussed in the section entitled "Solution Procedures and Conceptual Structures for Word Problems."

Both the results of the research studies discussed in "Other Research on Teaching" and the work on conceptual analyses of sequence counting and of thinking strategies suggest that children can successfully learn general sequence counting on and counting up with one-handed finger patterns to keep track before many of them can learn thinking strategies for all of the facts. The first-grade children in the sequence instructional studies were considerably more accurate on marks problems with sums above ten than the children in the thinking-strategy studies, especially in subtraction, and the sequence children clearly could also use the sequence strategies to solve word problems of various kinds. These instructional results suggest that it would be helpful for most children to learn conceptually based[20] counting on and counting up as general fall-back methods sometime during first grade. This enables them to solve all single-digit addition and subtraction situations in an efficient and comprehensible way. The Siegler and Shrager (1984) model underscores the importance of children having an accurate fall-back method. Given the irregularities in the English language that make the ten-structured methods so much more difficult for U.S. than for Asian children and the fact that most U.S. children eventually invent counting on and counting up (though with less efficient keeping-track methods than the one-handed finger patterns), counting on and counting up with one-handed finger patterns seem to be culturally appropriate candidates for such general fall-back methods. Such learning should be preceded by pattern and counting work for small sums and differences (see the first "What Can Be" section) resulting in understanding of mean-meanings of addition and subtraction and recall of small sums and differences and then by conceptually based counting on with objects. The one-handed finger patterns can be taught separately as pattern number activities any time before this. Conceptually based counting on requires some kind of object or picture situations such as those in Fig. 2.3 that permit children to make the count/cardinal connections that are necessary for counting on and counting up to be meaningfully related to their old count-all and take-away schemes and to be seen as abbreviations of these procedures. Compare and equalize situations are particularly supportive of counting up and should be used to introduce it.

Although the one-handed finger patterns can be learned easily by first graders, any general method of keeping track of large second addends (at least up to nine) can be used by children. Some children use auditory patterns of patterns as they say the second addend words (e.g., say seven more words by saying three words then three words then one word). In the pilot work for the instructional studies we initially tried using such auditory patterns, but many children had trouble learning them. We then moved to the one-handed finger patterns, with which few children had difficulty and which they could do without constantly putting down and picking up

---

[20]Conceptually based instruction means that children must be supported in their construction of the conceptual prerequisites for object counting on and counting up, and children must link these solution procedures to object situations so that the requisite links among the counting, cardinal, and sequence number-word meanings can be made.

their pencil. The Korean one-handed methods of folding/unfolding with a subbase five (see Table 2.7) might be tried instead of the one-handed finger patterns. The Korean one-handed method might be simpler than the finger method in Fig. 2.5 because the five is five fingers rather than a thumb (see Fig. 2.5), or it might be more difficult because children confuse the Korean numbers under five and over five (e.g., seven and three both show three fingers unfolded in the unfolding method). The Touch Math patterns of using particular spots on numerals to keep track of the second addend can also be used to count on (e.g., Flexer & Rosenberger, 1987), but they cannot be used to count up for subtraction because the second addend is unknown in subtraction so the numeral is not there to provide the keeping-track pattern. The real issue concerning the acceptibility of a keeping-track method is whether it is efficient enough to be used in more advanced uses of single-digit addition and subtraction—in multidigit addition and subtraction, column addition, and addition within multiplication. One-handed finger patterns are efficient enough for all of these purposes, so children who are still using these fall-back methods when they are learning these more complicated topics are not at a disadvantage. Second graders in the instructional studies even spontaneously used them in their first multiplication experiences to keep track of how many fours (or fives or sixes) they had counted. The efficiency and sufficiency of a general fall-back method, rather than emotional judgments about "crutches," should be the real criteria for choosing which general methods to support in a classroom.

Because children in a heterogeneous classroom will span two or three different developmental levels of Tables 2.2 and 2.3, discussion of various thinking strategies will arise as the more advanced children construct and use them. Various object and pattern supports can be provided for those children who are ready to learn these strategies. We do not at this time have any data on how difficult it would be for English-speaking children in the United States to learn the methods structured around ten if they had experiences in kindergarten and early first grade that supported learning of the three prerequisites of these methods: learning complements to ten (what makes ten with any number), being able to find an unknown addend for any known addend and sum below ten (e.g., two and what makes six?), and knowing all the sums of single-digit numbers with ten (e.g., ten and three are thirteen). It may be that using "tens words" for numbers between ten and twenty (11 is "ten one" or "ten and one," 12 is "ten two" or "ten and two," 13 is "ten three" or "ten and three") instead of English names (or Spanish names or other language names) would be an extraordinarily powerful conceptual support for children's learning in several areas discussed in the first part of the chapter as well as support the ten-structured methods. Use of the "tens words" would make it much easier to learn the written numerals, to count above ten, and to use the ten-structured methods because the aforementioned third step would be unnecessary and the ten would be present as a separate entity in every sum over ten. The verbal presence of this ten then could support the up-over-ten, down-over-ten, and subtract-from-ten methods. With the support of the "tens words" and visual supports such as the Korean folding-unfolding fingers that show the ten-structured methods, it might be very much easier for children in this country to learn these ten-structured methods than it is now. Now they are clearly advanced Level IV methods. With the proper learning opportunities from early kindergarten, it might even be that the unitary Level III fall-back sequence counting-on and counting-up methods would be unnecessary for most children (or would be a brief developmental waystation); they might then just be supported for a few children who need them for an extended period before they can completely put together the components of the ten-structured methods. Children could learn the traditional English names and use them to say numerals (many kindergarten children already know these connections) but use the "tens words" when they are thinking about mathematical situations. This is actually what happens in Korea and Japan right now: Children use the formal "tens words" in all school mathematics but also learn the traditional informal counting system(s) and various word endings and use them for counting objects. Korean and Japanese children's strong performance in addition and subtraction indicates that children can deal with more than one counting system. The "tens words" also would be supportive of general conceptual methods of adding and subtracting two-digit and larger multidigit numbers (this language issue with respect to multidigit numbers is discussed further in the next section).

We know little at this time about how adults and children use fingers to show addition and subtraction in various subcultures within this country, though it is clear that children in Sweden, Korea, and the United States exhibit differences in such uses (Fuson & Kwon, 1991). It would seem to be helpful for teachers to find out methods already used by their children. There may yet be methods that are particularly clear with respect to structuring around ten that would be good to share with all children. The teacher can act as the repository of such useful methods (gleaned from reading as well as from children in past classes) and can share them as methods that "some other children have shown me" so that they are not perceived by children as "the correct teacher methods."

The research on teaching suggests several other fundamental classroom changes that can facilitate children's learning, emotional state, and attitudes toward mathematics: shifting the classroom from individual work on many paper-and-pencil tasks with an emphasis on carrying out the correct rotely learned procedure quickly on many problems with little discussion or explanation of solution procedures to a classroom in which individual solution procedures are accepted, explained, defended, and discussed, a wide range of addition and subtraction situations are considered, and the norms validate sustained and cooperative effort rather than beating other children with "the" answer. The Japanese model of working thoughtfully and deeply and discussing alternative solution procedures for a few problems rather than quickly "covering" many problems seems to facilitate mathematical thinking and to be more natural to children's slower pace of thinking. Public acceptance of and discussion of mistakes in a context in which mistakes are viewed as a way for everyone to learn is also helpful. Because young children are novices at verbal explanations, the teacher may need—at least initially—to model full explanations, expand on (or have other children expand on) incomplete explanations, and relate various solution procedures. Japanese classrooms indicate that even first graders can become quite expert explainers if given opportunities to do so.

Finally, with respect to both the last section and this section, the question must be raised: Can mathematics for young children be booked? Do mathematics textbooks or workbooks make any sense at all for kindergarten, first, and second graders? Given that children at these ages must, at least initially, be interacting with physical objects in order to present addition and subtraction situations to themselves, what are sensible roles of worksheets? Pictures do not allow the range of actions enabled by physical objects. Radical changes need to be made in the nature of the supports provided in all mathematics classrooms for children, and workbooks may interfere with rather than provide such supports. At the very least children need their own mathematics box of objects that provide conceptual supports for their mathematical activities, and the classroom needs to have further object supports available for particular topics.

MULTIDIGIT ADDITION AND SUBTRACTION: NAMED-MULTIUNIT AND POSITIONAL NUMBERS

Research on Children's Named-Multiunit and Positional Thinking

The Mathematical Structure of English Number Words and Written Marks

All systems of written marks and spoken number words for large numbers use multiunits of particular quantities to build up the large numbers. A wide variety of different multiunit quantities have been used in different systems (e.g., Menninger, 1969). The system of written multidigit marks that is now used worldwide and the English system of number words use the same multiunit quantities to compose large numbers. These multiunit quantities are made in a particular regular way: Each larger multiunit is ten times larger than its next smaller multiunit. Both the written marks and the English words reuse their symbols for the first nine numbers to tell how many of a given multiunit is in a larger number. So large numbers are built up in a similar fashion by both systems: They are composed of multiunit quantities that are powers of ten, and a symbol for the small numbers one through nine is used to tell the number of each kind of multiunit in a given large number.

The system of multidigit written number marks and the spoken system of English number words also have several features that differ from each other. Most adults have long since constructed such strong links between the English number words and written number marks that it now may be difficult for them to see the differences between these systems and to appreciate how much children have to learn about each system. The system of English number words is an irregular named-multiunit system, and the system of written marks is a regular relative positional system. Features of each of these attributes are listed in Table 2.9; they are discussed in more detail in Fuson (1990a) and Bell, Fuson, and Lesh (1976, chapters B1, B2, B7). English words are regular for the hundreds and thousands, but they are irregular in several ways for two-digit numbers. These irregularities, and their negative consequences, are discussed in the section "The Special Difficulties Caused by the Irregularities in English Number Words." Written number marks are completely regular. The English number words are a named-multiunit system in which each kind of multiunit has a different name. A large number is made by saying the number of each kind of multiunit followed by the multiunit name: "four thousand nine hundred twenty eight." This named-multiunit system is similar to a measurement system in which we say "four miles nine yards two feet eight inches" in that both systems are composed of number/measure quantity pairs that tell how many of each kind of measure make up the large number or length. The named multiunits in the English words are particularly nice ones— regular ten-for-one trades connect each larger named multiunit—in contrast to English systems of measure like this length example in which the trade rules are irregular as the measure units get larger (twelve-for one, three-for-one, seventeen hundred sixty-for-one). Just as one can derive trade rules for any two measure units (e.g., how many inches in a mile), one can derive trade rules for any two named-multiunit quantities (e.g., how many tens in a thousand). However, the primary meanings of the English named multiunit quantities are the number of ones they contain; for example, a thousand says how many ones are in that multiunit quantity. With English number words, one is allowed to use values over nine (fifteen hundred is an acceptable phrase), one can disorder some number/named-

TABLE 2.9

Structural Differences Between English Named-Multiunit Words
and Unnamed Positional Number Marks

Attribute	English Number Words Named-Multiunit System	Written Number Marks Relative Position System
Regularity of the system	Irregular in the teen (one ten) words, in the decade prefixes, and in the decade names	Totally regular
Quantity of each named multiunit/ position	Each named multiunit (tens, hundreds, thousands) is relative to the ones (e.g., a thousand is one thousand ones); multiunits are collections of single units	The multiunit quantity of any position is derived from the number of one/ten trades to get to it from the ones position; multiunits are products of ten (e.g., the thousands place is ten × ten × ten)
Explicitness of the values	Multiunits are named explicitly after each digit	Multiunits are implicit in the relative position of a digit
Trades between values	Quantities of each multiunit can direct fair (one/ten) trades; trades can be derived from multiunits	One/ten trades are dictated by the limit of only nine digits; i.e., one/ten trades are a feature of the positional system
Number of multi-units/positions	Number of multiunits limited to known names	Number of places can go on and on
Need for order	The quantity of an English number word is conserved if the named multiunit/digit pairs are out of order	The quantity is not conserved if digits are out of order
Need for zero	Need no zero; just do not name that multiunit	Need zero to keep the other digits in their places

Implications for Multidigit Addition and Subtraction

What is added and subtracted?	Quantities of each multiunit direct addition and subtraction of like multiunits	Addition and subtraction directed only by meaning of positions built up by trades
How does trading arise?	Trading for too many (+) and for not enough (−) are directed by the multiunit quantities or by the counting pattern	Trading for too many (+) and for not enough (−) are directed by the regular one/ten trades
Limits to the quantity of a named multiunit/ position	Some multiunits can have ten or more of that value, e.g., fifteen hundred is acceptable and fifteen tens is not standard but it is not ambiguous	No place can have ten or more because those two digits push digits that are on the left one place to the left; this is disobeyed temporarily in subtracting but not for the final answer

multiunit pairs and maintain the meaning of the multidigit number (five-thousand ninety three-hundred six is meaningful even if it is not usual), and a zero is not needed (one just does not say empty multiunits: five thousand six and not five thousand no hundred noty six).

The system of written number marks is an unnamed relative positional system in which multiunits are not named but are implicit in the relative position of a given mark, that is, in its position relative to the rightmost mark. Each position to the left is a multiunit that is ten times as large as the multiunit to its right. Thus, the multiunits in the written multidigit marks system are successively built up by ten-for-one trades from the units position. A mark for some number between one and nine is put into each relative position to tell how many of that multiunit there are. So when one looks at written multidigit marks, one sees only single-digit small numbers. One has to know the one/ten trade rules or the multiunit quantities for each relative position in order to understand the quantity in the large multidigit number shown by the single-digit marks. Because these positions are relative, a special new mark is needed when there is not any of a given kind of multiunit. Without this special mark all of the positions to the left of that multiunit would move over to the right and thereby be in the wrong position. The mark used to show there is none of a given multiunit is 0. Because new multiunit quantities are made by a ten-for-one trade from the next largest multiunit, and this is just written in the next position to the left, one can go on and on making and writing larger and larger multiunits. With number words, one has to invent a new name for each larger multiunit, so these multiunits cannot really go on and on.

Each of these systems contributes different aspects to multidigit addition and subtraction. The named-multiunit words can direct the basic insight underlying multidigit addition and subtraction: that like multiunit quantities are added to or subtracted from each other. They also can direct and constrain correct trade rules when one has too many or not enough of a given multiunit quantity. But it is the written marks that require trading (borrowing, carrying, regrouping) in multidigit addition and subtraction because only they limit the number of each multiunit quantity to nine or less. This limitation arises because the relative positional nature of the written marks means that using more than one mark for a given multiunit (i.e., writing any number larger than nine) pushes all of the larger multiunits one place too far to the left. Thus, addition and subtraction of multidigit numbers of several places can help clarify several positional features: the regular ten-for-one trade rules that make each larger value in each position to the left, the need for zero to keep each mark in its correct relative position, the lack of conservation of multiunit quantities if the positions of marks are changed, and the continued generation of larger numbers by trading to the left again and again. Learning experiences that can help children understand the features of the system of English number words and the system of written number marks and understand how multidigit addition and subtraction are related to each of these systems are discussed in the section "What Can Be: Supporting Children's Multidigit Thinking in the Classroom."

Children's Conceptual Structures for Multidigit Numbers

Compared to addition and subtraction of single-digit numbers, there has been relatively little theoretical or empirical work on children's conceptual structures for multidigit numbers. Resnick (1983) described three stages of decimal (i.e., multidigit) knowledge: (a) unique partitioning of multidigit numbers (two-digit numbers as a part–whole schema with the special restriction that one part is a multiple of ten), (b) multiple partitionings of multidigit numbers (using one/ten trades to make an equivalent multiunit number), and (c) application of part–whole to written arithmetic (carrying out the trades in written marks problems). Knowledge is organized into nodes related to each mark's position. Fuson (1990a) specified ten conceptual structures for multiunit numbers, six of which are sufficient for addition and subtraction of multiunit numbers. The latter analysis is summarized here because it is more extensive.

Conceptual structures for multiunit numbers are described in Table 2.10 (taken from Fuson, 1990a). The first and third structures contain knowledge about the surface features of the written marks (single digits appear in horizontal layout) and of the spoken words (special new words are used). The second and fourth structures contain the knowledge that the components of the marks and the words are ordered and have a specified direction of increasing quantity. These four structures contain no knowledge about the multiunits that are put together to compose large marks and words. Such lack of knowledge is in fact demonstrated by many children, who behave as if the written marks are concatenated single digits (see later discussion in "How Are U.S. Children Doing?") or who do not have any notion of "ten" (or larger multiunits) as a multiunit quantity—the ten is just a name. The list of Chinese words for the first five multiunit quantities is given in Table 2.10 for the multiunit names conceptual structure to indicate that children may learn their own multiunit name list, and how to use it to compose large numbers, without having any notion of what the words mean (just as most English-speaking readers of this chapter do not have a meaning for the Chinese multiunit-quantity words). Two multiunit conceptual structures must be constructed and related to the marks and words conceptual structures for the marks or words to be understood as referring to large numbers that are composed of certain numbers of partic-

TABLE 2.10
Conceptual Structures for Multiunit Numbers

Name of the Conceptual Structure	Nature of the Conceptual Structure				
	Fifth	Fourth	Third	Second	First
Features of the marks					
Visual layout					
Positions ordered in increasing value from the right	—	—	—	—	—
Features of the words					
Multiunit names	*Wan*	*Qian*	*Bai*	*Shi*	*Yi*
Words ordered in decreasing value as they are said	Ten-thousand	Thousand	Hundred	Ten	Ones
Multiunit structures					
Multiunit quantities					

Regular ten-for-one and one-for-one trades	Ten thousands	one ↔	Ten hundreds	one ↔	Ten tens	one ↔	Ten ones	one ↔	ten
		ten		ten		ten		ten	
Positions/values as cumulative trades	Four trades		Three trades		Two trades		One trade		No trades
Positions/values as cumulative multiples of ten	Four multiples of ten t×t×t×t		Three multiples of ten t×t×t		Two multiples of ten t×t		One multiple of ten t		No multiples of ten
Positions/values as exponential words for multiples of ten	ten to the fourth power		ten to the third power		ten to the second power		ten to the first power		ten to the zero power
Positions/values as exponential marks for multiples of ten	10^4		10^3		10^2		10^1		10^0

Note: The multiunit names are the Chinese words to recreate for readers not speaking Chinese the initial experience of a child who must learn meanings for these words.

141

ular multiunit quantities. The multiunit quantities structure contains knowledge about "how large" each multiunit is in terms of single units; each multiunit quantity is seen as a collection of single units. The regular ten-for-one and one-for-ten conceptual structures focus on the regular one/ten relationship between contiguous multiunits. Strong relationships among all six of these conceptual structures enable a child to understand multidigit numeration, addition, and subtraction. The last four rows of Table 2.10 describe more advanced multiunit conceptual structures that are required for understanding multidigit multiplication and division, exponents, and scientific notation. They each arise from reflecting about the conceptual structure in the level above.

There are several kinds of problems children have in relating the features of the marks to the features of the words. Translating from spoken words to written marks is easy: One simply writes the mark for each word between one and nine that tells how many of a given kind of multiunit and ignores the multiunit word. However, the latter is difficult for many children to do. They want to write marks that show the small number/multiunit pairs, leading to errors such as 300406 (three hundred then forty then six). Such constructions are wrong because they look like positional marks but are really named-multiunit marks. Unambiguous named-multiunit marks can be made if new marks are used for the English multiunit names: 3 H 4 T 6. Translating from written marks to spoken words requires one to start from the ones mark and move left to find the position of the mark with the greatest value. This requires backward counting or subitizing from the right, that is, processing in an order opposite to the order of writing. In the United States commas are used to separate groups of three marks in order to make the largest position accessible by pattern and to signal the overlying base-thousand structure of our words. Using these patterns and how they relate to the base-thousand structure of the English words must be learned.

The conceptual structures for number discussed in the first two major parts of this chapter were all unitary structures: The unit items composing a number each had a single unit value. These unitary structures are adequate for addition and subtraction of fairly small two-digit numbers, but they rapidly become time consuming and error-prone for larger two-digit numbers (e.g., 87 + 75). Children in the United States who receive traditional instruction seem to construct two different kinds of multiunit quantities conceptual structures for use in multidigit addition and subtraction: collected multiunits and sequence multiunits. The collected multiunits are collections of single units: A ten-unit item is a collection of ten single unit items, a hundred-unit item is a collection of one hundred single unit items, a thousand-unit item is a collection of one thousand single unit items, and so forth. Addition of collected multiunits consists of putting together all the like collected multiunit items (tens with tens, hundreds with hundreds, etc.), and ten of one kind of multiunit can be traded for one of the next larger multiunit if this seems desirable. Subtraction consists of subtracting like multiunit items from each other, with a larger multiunit item being traded for ten smaller multiunits if more of those smaller multiunits are needed.

The sequence multiunits are extensions of the unitary sequence solution procedures in which the multiunits are chunked units of counting words within the number-word sequence: sequence ten-units, hundred-units, and thousand-units. A sequence multiunit number is an entity within the number-word sequence: "Five thousand six hundred eighty nine" is the word after five thousand six hundred eighty eight and the word before five thousand six hundred ninety. Addition is carried out by counting on from one number using the sequence multiunits or by counting within sequence values by these sequence multiunits. So 546 + 689 can be found by counting on from 689 by hundreds and then by tens and then by ones: six hundred eighty nine, seven hundred eighty nine, eight hundred eighty nine, nine hundred eighty nine, ten hundred eighty nine (or one thousand eighty nine), eleven hundred eighty nine (that is five hundreds counted on, so shift to counting on by tens), eleven hundred ninety nine, eleven hundred one hundred nine is twelve hundred nine, twelve hundred nineteen, twelve hundred twenty nine (that is forty counted on, so shift to counting on by ones), twelve hundred thirty, twelve hundred thirty one, twelve hundred thirty two, twelve hundred thirty three, twelve hundred thirty four, twelve hundred thirty five. Counting within values would be: six hundred, seven hundred, eight hundred, nine hundred, ten hundred, eleven hundred; then eighty, ninety, one hundred, one hundred ten, one hundred twenty plus the eleven hundred is twelve hundred twenty; nine plus six is fifteen plus the twelve hundred twenty is twelve hundred thirty five. One must remember the partial sums so that they can be added as one goes along. Both of these methods require a lot of memory space and well-automated sequence counting skills. The former method requires difficult counts over multiunit value changes, and the latter requires combining different value sums. Subtraction can be carried out by counting down from, down to, or up to by hundreds, tens, and ones from one whole number or within sequence values.

Just as children's first conceptions of small numbers required perceptual unit items (objects whose numerosity is obtainable by pattern or by counting), so children need perceptual support for their construction of multiunits. With collected multiunits children re-present to themselves and reflect on collections of objects (groups of ten, hundred, or a thousand collected single-unit items), and with sequence multiunits children re-present to themselves and reflect on their own counting activity as they count by tens, hundreds, or thousands. Labinowicz (1989) described this difference as counting of tens versus counting by tens. Materials that present collections of tens, hundreds, and thousands help children construct both kinds of multiunits (Fuson, 1986a; Fuson & Briars, 1990; Labinowicz, 1985; Resnick, 1983; Resnick & Omanson, 1987; Steffe & Cobb, 1988; Thompson, 1982). Fuson (1990a) called such object collections perceptual "collectible" multiunits to emphasize that they are only potential supports for conceptual multiunits and called the conceptual multiunits constructed from these objects "collected" multiunits to indicate that each child must do the conceptual collecting to make a collected multiunit (see also Cobb, 1987, concerning this point). For children receiving traditional school experiences, the initial construction of these two kinds of multiunits for two-digit numbers may be independent: Cobb and Wheatley (1988) found that many second graders constructed sequence ten-unit items or collected ten-unit items but not both. However, Thompson (1982) found that children could do tasks involving collected multiunits before they could do similar tasks requiring sequence multiunits. Much evidence also exists concerning how difficult it seems to be for many first and second graders to count on by tens (Cobb & Wheatley, 1988; Steffe & Cobb, 1988) and for second and third graders to count on by hundreds, tens, and ones, even when collections of objects are present to support such counting (Labinowicz, 1985; Resnick, 1983; Thompson, 1982). Counting over decade or hundred changes presents particular difficulties. For example, Bell and Burns (1981) found that 9 of 30 third graders could not count by tens from 180 to 210, and Labinowicz (1985) found that 20 of 29 third graders made errors in counting by tens between 94 and 124.

In contrast, second graders of all achievement levels and high-achieving first graders, when provided with a learning/teaching setting that supported the construction of relationships among collectible multiunits (base-ten blocks that showed thousands, hundreds, tens, and units), written marks, and English words, were able to construct collected multiunits for four-digit numbers and use these conceptual collected multiunits to add and subtract such numbers accurately and meaningfully (Fuson, 1986a; Fuson & Briars, 1990). Most second graders who made multidigit addition and subtraction errors at the end of this learning self-corrected their own errors when told to "think about the blocks" and explained these corrections by using the sizes of the nonpresent blocks, that is, by using conceptual collected multiunits (Fuson, 1986a). No similar effort has been made to date to try to help second graders construct sequence ten-unit, hundred-unit, or thousand-unit items (to count on by tens, hundreds, and thousands), so the comparative difficulty of this task is not clear. However, the evidence at this time indicates that the developmental sequence for constructing multiunits for hundreds and thousands, and perhaps for tens, follows the order for the earlier single-digit numbers: Numbers are presented by collections of objects before they are presented by one's counting activity separated from objects.

The Special Difficulties Caused
by the Irregularities in English

English number words do not directly name the ten and the one quantities in the numbers between nine and one hundred, and these number words are also irregular in several ways. The ten and one structure of two-digit number marks is masked in English by (a) the existence of the arbitrary number words "eleven" and "twelve" that do not indicate their composition as "ten and one" and "ten and two"; (b) the irregular pronunciation of "three" in "thirteen" and "five" in "fifteen" that obfuscate the "ones-number teen" pattern between thirteen and nineteen; (c) the tens/ones reversal in the teen words (one says the ones word before the tens word: "fourteen" instead of "teenfour" or "ten four") that contrasts with the tens-then-ones order for all words between twenty and one hundred (twenty four and not four twenty) and that contrasts with the order of writing the marks for the teens (one writes the ones numeral after the tens numeral (14 and not 41) but says the ones word before the tens word: fourteen); (d) the use of two different modifications of "ten" (i.e., "teen" and "ty") instead of the word "ten"; and (e) the irregular pronunciation of the decade words "twenty," "thirty," and "fifty" that mask for many children the relationship of the decade names to the first nine number words (Fuson et al., 1982; Siegler & Robinson, 1982).

This obfuscation of the underlying tens structure prolongs the use by English-speaking children of their first unitary counting/sequence and cardinal conceptual structures for number, and these unitary conceptions interfere with the construction and use of more advanced multiunit conceptual structures for multidigit numbers. This is in contrast to children who speak Asian languages based on Chinese, a totally regular named-multiunit system (for example, 12 is said "ten two," 25 is "two ten five," and 53 is "five ten three"). These regular named multiunits for two-digit numbers evidently help children construct and use conceptual multiunits. Miura (1987) found that Japanese-speaking first graders living in the San Francisco area used the tens blocks in base-ten blocks (tens blocks are longs of ten connected units, ones blocks are single unit blocks) to present five numbers between 11 and 42 considerably more than did English-speaking first graders; the Japanese children showed numbers using the tens blocks and single blocks, whereas the English-speaking children counted out piles of unit blocks (28 little cubes instead of two longs and eight units). Similar results were reported for Chinese, Japanese, and Korean children compared to U.S. children (Miura et al., 1988) and even for Japanese first graders before any work on tens compared to U.S. first graders after instruction on tens (Miura & Okamoto, 1989). The failure of English-speaking children to use perceptual collectible ten-unit items to present two-digit numbers also is reported by M. Kamii (1982), Richards and Carter (1982), and C. Kamii (1985, 1986). The persistence of this unitary view of number even in U.S. adults is indicated by the difficulty adults had accessing a multiunit tens and ones rather than a unitary sequence/counting meaning for a two-digit number even when it would help them in a task (Heinrichs, Yurko, & Hu, 1981). Thus, it is no wonder that so much two-digit place-value and addition and subtraction instruction goes awry in the United States: Teachers talk about tens and ones but children see and think about unitary sequence/counting numbers in which the two digits are not separable or they see two single digits beside each other.

The irregularities in English pose difficulties in learning multidigit addition and subtraction meaningfully and in carrying out multidigit addition and subtraction accurately, at least compared to the regular Chinese-based languages (see Fuson, 1990a; Fuson & Kwon, in press-b, for a fuller discussion). When U.S. children add single-digit numbers within a multidigit addition problem, they do so using a unitary presentation even for sums between ten and eighteen. Even if they recall an addition fact, this sum initially is presented with a unitary representation as "fourteen" (fourteen ones not one ten and four ones). U.S. children must shift from this unitary presentation to a multiunit conception in order to trade ten ones for the next larger multiunit. This shift is difficult initially because many U.S. children do not know how many tens and ones are in a given number word between ten and eighteen. This lack of knowledge and the necessity to shift conceptions was underscored by the extra step for multidigit addition that was invented by first graders in Fuson (1986a) and used by many second graders in Fuson and Briars (1990). At the beginning of the addition learning, some children would find the sum of a given column (for example, that seven plus five is twelve). However, they would not know how many tens and ones were in twelve because twelve had only a unitary sequence/counting meaning for them as twelve single units. They would therefore use an available word-numeral pattern association to write the marks for twelve to the right of the problem. They could then look at the 12 and think of it as "one two" or as "one ten two ones" in order to find that twelve has one ten and two ones. They would then trade the 1 ten over to the top of the tens column and record the 2 in the ones column. Asian children have no need for such a translation across conceptions, for their language gives all sums over ten in a usable tens and ones form: They just say "seven plus five is ten two." Even if the Asian child does unitary counting on from seven, the answer will be in a tens and ones form: "seven, eight, nine, ten, ten one, ten two." Not only do Asian children not have to translate from unitary to multiunit conceptions, but their number words actually suggest the multidigit procedure: Put the ten with the tens.

The named ten in Asian number words facilitates several aspects of Asian children's numerical experiences structured around tens. Sums between ten and eighteen (ten eight in Chinese) are given as tens and ones, and as discussed in "Research on Ten-Structured Methods of Addition and Subtraction," particular methods of single-digit addition and subtraction structured around ten are taught. It is clearer in Chinese than in English that one hundred is ten tens because ninety is said "nine ten" and ninety nine is said "nine ten nine." In English one more added to ninety-nine just makes the collection one hundred, and the tens are not obvious within this new hundred unit. In Chinese one more added to nine ten nine (99) makes nine ten and one more ten, which is ten tens, so one hundred is ten tens. The lack of regularity in English makes it more difficult for U.S. children to learn to count above one hundred: 8 of the 13 U.S. 6-year-olds who could count above one hundred (these were the brightest U.S. children) shifted to counting by hundreds after 109 (said "one hundred nine, two hundred, three hundred") whereas no Chinese 6-year-old made such a shift (Miller & Stigler, 1987). English-speaking children in the United States also do not experience clear ten-structures in their systems of measure or of money. The metric system with its regular ten-for-one trades is used in almost every other country in the world and can provide meanings for and make salient ten/one trades. The English system of measure has many different trade rules, none of which are ten/one trades. Our money also does not clearly use tens: The large nickels and quarters obfuscate the one/ten trade structure of pennies, dimes, and dollars. Dimes and pennies are also really meanings for decimals less than one (a dime is a tenth of a dollar and a penny is a hundredth), though most textbooks pretend that they are whole numbers (and thus lose an excellent way to make decimal fractions meaningful to U.S. children). Thus, U.S. children have little opportunity to develop ten-structured multiunit conceptual structures outside of school, making it vital that such experiences are provided within the classroom. The characteristics of such experiences are discussed in "Other Research in Teaching" and in "What Can Be: Supporting Children's Multidigit Thinking in the Classroom" after textbook treatments and children's performance on multidigit addition and subtraction are briefly summarized.

Research on Multidigit Instruction

What Do Textbooks Present?

Present addition and subtraction multidigit instruction in the United States takes much more time and is considerably more prolonged than such instruction in some other countries. In the United States, instruction in the addition and subtraction of whole numbers typically has been distributed across the first five or six grades, with the single-digit sums and differences to 18 consuming much of the first two grades. The multidigit algorithms with trading (carrying and borrowing) are distributed over 4 or 5 years beginning with two-digit problems in second grade, and one or two more places are added each year (Fuson et al., 1988). In contrast, countries that have been characterized as fostering high mathematics achievement—China, Japan, Taiwan, and the Soviet Union—stress mastery of sums and differences to 18 in the first grade, and they complete multidigit instruction by the third grade (Fuson et al., 1988).

This pattern continued to be true for eight texts copyrighted in 1987 or 1988 and examined for this chapter. These and other features of the textbook placement of initial place-value and multidigit instruction are given in Table 2.11. For a country that supposedly does not have a national curricula, the grade-level placements of these topics are astonishingly similar. Most of these texts had different numbers of pages, so the uniformity in Table 2.11 reflects proportional assignment of topics to pages and similar orderings within the texts. Topical material in all texts was tightly organized into chapters, and topics were not repeated within a given year (except in some cases on a review page at the end of a chapter). Thus, the figures in the table index the placement of the topic within the school year. Textbook presentation of place value and multidigit addition and subtraction has the following features in all or most texts:

Instruction on two-digit place value precedes instruction on two-digit addition and subtraction by 2 to $4\frac{1}{2}$ months.

Initial instruction on two-digit addition precedes that on all sums between 10 and 18, which in half the texts is the last chapter in the first-grade text and therefore may never be reached in many classrooms.

Two-digit addition with no trading precedes two-digit addition with trading by 9 to 10 months.

Two-digit addition with trading precedes three-digit addition by $2\frac{1}{2}$ to 12 months.

Three-digit addition with trading precedes four-digit addition by 5 to $7\frac{1}{2}$ months.

TABLE 2.11

Textbook Grade Placement of Initial Place-Value and Multidigit Addition Instruction

Topic	Addison-Wesley	Heath	Holt, Rinehart, & Winston	Houghton Mifflin	McGraw-Hill	Merrill	Silver Burdett	Scott, Foresman
Place value: 2-digit	1.34	1.46	1.33	1.38	1.37	1.38	1.35	1.58
Place value: 3-digit	2.72	2.84	2.76	2.73	2.68	2.85	2.42	2.90
Sums and differences from 10 to 18	1.87	1.93	1.69	1.94	1.92	1.91	1.95	1.82
Add: 2-digit no trade	1.77	1.81	1.53	1.78	1.76	1.84	1.86	1.95
Add: 2-digit with trade	2.46	2.46	1.94	2.59	2.41	2.61	2.55	1.95[a]
Add: 3-digit with trade	2.78	2.94[b]	2.84	2.77[b]	2.76	2.88[b]	2.86[b]	2.92
Add: 4-digit with trade	3.21	3.26	3.28	3.21	3.24	3.32	3.21	3.17
Add: 5-digit with trade	4.13	5.10	4.12	4.11	4.17	4.18	4.13	5.05
Trades from								
ones to tens	2.46	2.46	1.94	2.59	2.41	2.61	2.55	1.95[a]
tens to hundreds	2.79	3.24	2.85	3.17	2.78	3.18	2.60	2.92
ones to tens and tens to hundreds	3.18	3.24	2.86[c]	3.17	3.23	3.18	3.18	3.17
hundreds to thousands	3.21	3.25	3.29	3.21	3.24	3.32	3.21	3.17

Notes: Values were calculated by dividing the page number of the first occurrence of a topic by the number of pages in the textbook; these page numbers were always the first page of a whole chapter on the topic. All decimals values between .90 and .99 are in the final chapter. Subtraction occurred within .12 of addition unless noted.
[a]These were all with pictures; 2-digit ones-to-tens trades without pictures began at 2.61. [b]Only trades from ones to tens. [c]Subtraction with two trades first occurred at 3.35.

Four-digit addition with trading precedes five-digit addition by $11\frac{1}{2}$ to 23 months.

Trading tens precedes trading hundreds by 3 to 12 months.

Trading hundreds precedes trading both tens and hundreds in the same problem by 5 to 9 months (in half the texts).

The approach to these problems in most texts is rule based: Add the ones and then add the tens and then add the hundreds. The procedure frequently is stated as a rule for the very first example given in the text. Although pictures of different size objects for each place (i.e., collectible multiunits) may be used to explain or justify the procedures, these are soon abandoned in most texts. The layout of these pictures and the written marks is also so confusing in some texts that it is difficult even for an experienced adult to see how the pictures relate to the marks. Because adding the ones and adding the tens is stressed from the start and problems are given vertically with these places aligned, children are not able to use addition methods suggested by their available unitary counting/sequence representations (e.g., counting on by ones). Because the few pictures provided are not sufficient to learn or to apply multiunit quantities or ten/one trade conceptual structures for these problems, this approach sets children up to focus on the vertical column of digits and ignore any meanings for the horizontal row of digits that is the multiunit written number. The focus on individual digits rather than on the whole multidigit number is initiated and reinforced by the use in first grade of many two-digit problems without trading: Children just do single-digit addition (or subtraction) focusing on each column. Other kinds of multidigit addition and subtraction problems are approached piecemeal and slowly, with problems with a trade from ones to tens done long before those with a trade from tens to hundreds, and problems with a single trade are done before problems with more than one trade. This approach then supports children's construction of the incorrect concatenated single-digit representation of multidigit numbers (discussed in "How Are U.S. Children Doing?") and indicates that there are many different addition and subtraction procedures and that one must learn the rules for all of these procedures in order to be able to do them correctly.

Another issue raised by textbooks is the confusing nature of the expanded notation commonly appearing in texts. A number such as 5,783 is written in expanded notation as $5,000 + 700 + 80 + 3$. What is ignored in such use is that both the 5,783 and its expanded notation are positional and not named-multiunit marks. If one does not understand the 5,783 as positional marks, the expanded notation does not seem likely to elucidate the positional structure. Expanded notation seems to be a misguided attempt to link the positional marks to the more explicit named-multiunit words by saying that 5,783 is just 5 thousand (5,000) + 7 hundred (700) + eighty (80) + 3. Such linking is a sensible strategy, but expanded notation carries the risk that children will concatenate (place adjacent in time or space) the small number/named-multiunit pairs just as they do in the English words and thus will make the common errors of writing 5000700803 or somewhat shorter versions of such named-value forms. For example, Bell and Bell (1988) reported frequent such errors by primary school children, and medieval Europeans frequently made such errors when first changing from the concatenated Roman numerals to the new Arabic positional notation (Menninger, 1969). Thus, this pedagogic invention of expanded notation itself might be responsible for increasing children's errors in writing multidigit marks. The forms of expanded notation in which cards for smaller multiunits are placed on top of the larger ones (a 700 card covers the 000 in the 5,000 card, a 80 card then covers the 00 in 700, and a 3 card then covers the 0 in 80 so that 5,783 shows), like those used in Montessori schools, are not as misleading as the school textbook forms. But such cards require activity in time—the placing of the cards on top of each other, and this is quite difficult to show in a written text. Therefore, substituting an obvious named-multiunit notation like 5 Th 7 H 8 T 3 seems the better course, especially because such a notation can be regular in the tens place, possibly reducing the debilitating effect of the irregularities in English number words for two-digit numbers.

How Are U.S. Children Doing?

Even though multidigit instruction is delayed and prolonged in the United States relative to that in some other countries, this instruction yields neither adequate understanding of multidigit addition and subtraction or of positional numeration nor adequate procedural mathematical marks performance: Many children still make many kinds of addition and subtraction errors. Usual school experiences fail to help many children build adequate conceptual structures for multidigit numbers and use these conceptual structures in adding and subtracting multidigit numbers. The National Assessment of Educational Progress found that fewer than half the third graders could do items identifying the hundreds digit and only 65% did items identifying the tens digit correctly (Kouba et al., 1988). Labinowicz (1985) reported that less than half his sample of third graders identified tens and hundreds in 3-digit numerals. Ross (1986) reported that 43% of a heterogeneous sample of second through fifth graders showed no understanding of tens and ones when asked to relate the digits in a two-digit numeral to grouped objects (this was true of 33% of the fifth graders), and another 13% showed only partial or confused understandings. Kamii and Joseph (1988) reported that at the end of the year only one third of the third graders and half of the fourth graders interviewed showed for a set of sixteen objects that the 1 in 16 referred to ten of the objects and the 6 referred to the remaining six objects; the other children said that the 1 referred to one object. Ross (1986, 1989) also reported that many children who knew the names for tens and ones had "face value" rather than actual "named-value" meanings for marks because they associated tens and ones digits with groupings that contained values other than tens and ones; for example, when shown a written 26 and twenty-six objects grouped into six groups of four and two single objects, they said that the 6 referred to the six groups of four and the 2 referred to the two ones.

Children receiving traditional instruction also have difficulty with many aspects of multidigit addition and subtraction. Children frequently do not understand that like multiunit quantities are added to and subtracted from each other: When writing marks problems vertically for adding or subtracting, they do not align the ones under the ones, the tens under the tens, and so on. Tougher (1981) found that less than half of a class of third graders aligned numbers correctly, Ginsburg (1977) reported that many interviewed children wrote down marks aligned on the left, and Labinowicz (1985) found that only 5 of 21 third graders identified marks aligned on the left as misaligned. Written number marks have for many children only their single-digit meanings regardless of where they appear. For example, the 1 traded[21] into the tens or hundreds column and written above that column is often identified only as a one rather than as a ten or a hundred: Every third grader interviewed by Resnick (1983, see also Resnick & Omanson, 1987) said that the traded one ten written above the tens column as a 1 was a one, and half the third graders who added correctly said this in spite of probes such as "What is the 1 worth?" used by Labinowicz (1985). Children make many errors in multidigit addition and subtraction that reveal their conceptual structure for multidigit addition and subtraction as a vertical arrangement of single-digit numbers (see Table 2.12). The digits may not even stay together to form the original two multidigit numbers, and positional multiunit values of the digits do not exist so they do not constrain where digits are written and cannot direct trades for too many or too few.

This inadequate valueless conceptual structure for multidigit numbers has been termed a "concatenated single-digit" structure (Fuson, 1990a). This concatenated single-digit view of multidigit addition and subtraction

---

[21]The word *trading* is used in this chapter instead of *regrouping*, because trading implies the fair exchange of some of a given value for some of a different value whereas regrouping implies nothing about exchanges of different values, can refer to clustering of individual unit items within a collection (e.g., 4 + 2 can be regrouped as 3 + 3), and can refer to regrouping of items within another base structure (e.g., making groups of four instead of groups of ten). Neither of the latter two meanings is related to multidigit addition or subtraction of base-ten numbers.

TABLE 2.12
Multidigit Addition and Subtraction Errors that Reflect
a Concatenated Single-Digit Conceptual Structure

Addition Errors	*Subtraction Errors*
Write sum for each column (FB, F 47-8)	Smaller from larger (DMPE/D 115; FB, F 48-9; L 341; VL 174)

Addition:
```
  5  6  8
  7  7  8
  2 13 16
```

Subtraction:
```
2 5 2
1 1 8
1 4 6
```

Vanish the one (FB, F 47-8)

Top smaller write zero (FB; VL 176)

```
5 6 8
7 7 8
2 3 6
```

```
2 5 2
1 1 8
1 4 0
```

Carry to the leftmost (B 229)

Borrow unit difference (VL 150)

```
 ¹¹1 6 8
   1 5 6
   4 1 4
```

```
  4 9
  ᴼ ᴼ
  1 9
  3 0
```

Wrong align long algorithm (G 116)

```
  8 7
  3 9
  1 6
  1 1
  2 7
```

Always borrow left (VL 149)

```
   2
  ᴼ 6 ¹5
  1 0 9
  1 6 6
```

Add extra digit into column (F/D 114)

Stops borrow at zero (VL 175)

```
  6 3
    2
  1 1
```

```
   6
  ᴼ¹0¹0¹2
    3 2 5
  6 7 8 7
```

Reuse digit if uneven (F/D 113)

Borrow across zero (D 325, VL 167)

```
  6 3
    2
  8 5
```

```
  5 ᴼ
  ᴼ 0¹0¹2
      2 5
  5 0 8 7
```

Ignore extra digits (F/D 114)

Reuse digit in uneven (F/D 115)

```
  6 3
    2
    5
```

```
  7 8
    6
  1 2
```

Note: Initials in parentheses are the source references and page numbers as follows: B is Baroody, 1987a; DMPE/D is Davis, McKnight, Parker, & Elrick, 1979, in Davis, 1984; F/D is Friend, 1979; F is Fuson, 1986a; FB is Fuson & Briars, 1990; G is Ginsburg, 1977; L is Labinowicz, 1985; VL is VanLehn, 1986.

frequently results from usual school instruction. Solving multidigit addition and subtraction problems seems to occur for many children within a separate written marks world in which no meanings are attached to the marks other than the single-digit meanings for each numeral. In this marks world one simply carries out rule-dictated procedures on the marks, especially if the problems are presented in the usual vertical form. Children do not use unitary counting/sequence or cardinal conceptual structures they have for two-digit numbers in solving vertical two-digit marks problems (Cobb & Wheatley, 1988), and they even find it perfectly acceptable to get different answers when they use their unitary counting/sequence structures and when they use their rule-based marks procedures. For example, children may find 37 + 8 to be 45 by counting on 8 from 37 but find the marks answer to be 315 or 117 when 37 and 8 are written vertically as a marks problem (Cobb & Wheatley, 1988). Many children also find it acceptable to get different answers to a single written marks problem (Cobb & Wheatley, 1988; Davis, 1984; Davis & McKnight, 1980). Even when children do possess some multiunit quantity understanding, they usually do not link this understanding to the addition and subtraction marks procedures (Resnick, 1982, 1983; Resnick & Omanson, 1987). Thus, marks procedures are not constrained by multiunit meanings for the marks but only by memorized rules that are easy to mislearn initially or to confuse over time (see discussions by Fuson, 1990a, and VanLehn, 1986).

With respect to procedural performance, the National Assessment of Educational Progress indicated that a third of the third graders were incorrect on a two-digit subtraction problem with trading, and half were incorrect on three-digit problems (Kouba et al., 1988). Bell and Burns (1981) found that only 4 of 24 third graders could solve 65 − 37 correctly. Davis and McKnight (1980) found in interviewing third and fourth graders from several schools with above-average students and instruction that not a single child solved 7,000 − 2 correctly. Ashlock (1982), Baroody (1987a), Brown and VanLehn (1982), Ginsburg (1977), Labinowicz (1985), VanLehn (1986), and others have documented many errors made by children in multidigit addition and subtraction. U.S. second and third graders perform much more poorly on multidigit addition and subtraction tasks than do Korean second and third graders (Fuson & Kwon, in press-b; Song & Ginsburg, 1987), and U.S. first and fifth graders do much worse on such problems and on place-value tasks than do Japanese and Taiwanese first and fifth graders (Stigler, Lee, & Stevenson, 1990).

In the area of place-value concepts and multidigit addition and subtraction, it seems clear that many normal U.S. children are, to use the terms of Hendrickson (1983), curriculum disabled and textbook disabled. This, in combination with the linguistic and cultural disadvantage of irregular English number words, no metric system, and no clear ten-based structure in money, means that all teachers have a considerable compensatory task to undertake in the elementary mathematics classroom.

Other Research on Teaching

Direct Multidigit Instruction

Leinhardt (1987) analyzed the attributes of the explanations within a series of lessons on two-digit subtraction problems with trading given by an expert second-grade inner-city teacher whose children performed unusually well on such problems. Children were interviewed throughout the instructional period to ascertain the effects of lessons on their knowledge. This successful series of lessons had the following attributes:

1. Necessary knowledge was reviewed.
2. The teacher created suspense about how to solve these problems requiring trading.
3. The renaming (traded) marks procedure was connected to trading of felt strips.
4. Children were continuously asked why they had to trade for certain problems.
5. There was considerable repetition and consistency within the lessons.
6. The top children were overrehearsed for the benefit of the slower children.
7. The new procedure was related to more familiar ones in several ways.

Attributes 5 and 6 particularly aided the weaker children, but the overrehearsal also benefited the top children, who showed subtle changes in understanding over these lessons.

How teachers diagnose and remediate student errors in multidigit addition was explored by Putnam (1987). Six experienced teachers interacted with one real student and with a computer program that made particular errors. These teachers engaged in practically no diagnosis; that is, they did not try to understand the kind of error the student was making or the nature of the misunderstanding by the student that led to the error. Instead, the primary goal of the teachers was to help the student get the immediate problem right. There were few attempts to teach more general facts, procedures, or concepts. The teachers' overarching curriculum plan was not based on helping students understand the multidigit procedure.

Rather they followed a curriculum script based on assumed problem difficulty: They moved from small problems with no trading to larger problems with trading from the ones to problems with trading from the tens to problems with trading from the hundreds, and so forth. This script mimics the presentation of problems in many textbook series. Putnam concluded that teachers need to be provided with better curriculum scripts, ones that are based on pedagogical subject-matter knowledge that can permit teachers to teach with more adequate understanding.

An analysis of mathematics learning and teaching by Skemp (1979) underscored the complexities of teaching when the goal is understanding by the students. Such teaching is an intervention in the learning of another person. Skemp identified the following several tasks the teacher must do in order to carry out intelligent teaching directed toward intelligent learning by the child:

1. Build a model of primitive and of intelligent processes of human learning.
2. Build a model of the processes by which the teacher can interact with the planning goal-directed systems of the learner.
3. Consciously apply the models in 1 and 2 to the subject matter being learned.
4. Develop a repertoire of routine plans by which the teacher's conscious attention can be largely freed to deal with the succession of nonroutine situations that are almost inevitable during a teaching and learning situation.
5. Regularly reflect on one's own activities as a teacher in order to learn intelligently from one's own teaching experiences.

However, general knowledge of learning and teaching is not sufficient. These more general attributes of professional teaching must then be carried out within the context of an analysis of the particular subject matter being taught. The teacher must be aware of the conceptual structure of the topics being taught so that this teaching can enable the learner to resynthesize this structure in her own mind as a schema. Thus, with respect to place value and multidigit addition and subtraction, the teacher must understand the named-multiunit nature of the system of English number words and the positional nature of the system of written marks, the unitary nature of children's initial conceptual structures for two-digit numbers, and how much perceptual and linguistic support children may need in order to construct multiunit conceptual structures for multidigit numbers that are sufficient to make place value and multidigit addition and subtraction comprehensible to them.

Using Embodiments to Help Children Construct
Multiunit Meanings

Resnick (1987) discussed the need for a new psychological theory of instruction, one that places the learner's active mental construction at the heart of the instructional exchange. Such a theory could then guide the design of interventions that aim to place learners in situations where their constructions will be powerful and correct. This theory is necessary, Resnick argued, because a hands-off attitude toward children's constructive capacities, as suggested by some, does not adequately guide and constrain children's knowledge construction. Some decision is made by someone about what will occur in a given mathematics classroom. Whatever does occur will provide the material upon which children's constructive mental processes will work. At present the material provided is primarily textbook pages giving vertically arranged multidigit addition and subtraction, and this material results for many children in a concatenated single-digit conception of multidigit numbers.

Skemp's (1979) theory of mathematics learning and teaching is a good start toward such a psychology of instruction. Some aspects of his analysis of teaching were discussed earlier. Central to this theory is symbolic understanding, defined as mutual assimilation between a symbol system (what we have been calling here a system of written marks) and an appropriate conceptual structure, with this mutual assimilation dominated by the conceptual structure (Skemp, 1981). Nesher (1986) suggested that mutual assimilation between multidigit addition/subtraction procedures and place-value concepts is crucial and that knowing the algorithms and procedures contributes to the student's understanding of these concepts. Resnick (1982, 1983) documented how the symbol system procedure and the conceptual structures[22] for multidigit subtraction with trading have little or no mutual assimilation under usual school instruction (see "How Are U.S. Children Doing?"). How to facilitate children's opportunities for such mutual assimilation is then the central task of instruction on multidigit addition/subtraction and place value.

Dienes (1960, 1963) invented base-ten blocks exactly to provide conceptual support for multiunit quantities.[23] These blocks are a size embodiment

---

[22]Resnick called the symbolic (marks) procedure the *syntax* and the conceptual structure underlying this procedure the *semantics.* This distinction is important, but these terms are misleading because the syntax of most natural languages is arbitrary (e.g., the subject customarily can occur first in one language and last in another language without altering the meaning) whereas the syntax of multidigit subtraction with trading is not arbitrary—it is almost entirely derivable from the semantics of that procedure.

[23]Dienes used block sets for various bases (e.g., base-two blocks, base-three blocks, etc.) in order to support understanding of base systems in general. Under his theory understanding

of the English named-multiunit words in which different size pieces of wood present the units, tens, hundreds, and thousands. A ten-unit is a single long stick equal to ten small unit cubes stuck together, a hundred-unit is a flat piece of wood equal to one hundred small cubes (it is a long on each side and one unit thick; i.e., it is a ten-unit by a ten-unit by a one unit), and the thousand-unit is a large cube equal to a thousand small cubes (it is a long by a long by a long). The usual block names for these multiunits are long, flat, and big cube. Thus, five thousand six hundred thirty four would be shown by five big cubes six flats three longs and four units. Use of these blocks to support correct written marks performance and understanding has been discussed in a general way by many authors and this use has had many different labels: an analogy (VanLehn, 1986), an assimilation paradigm (Davis, 1984, 1986), embodiment of the mathematical concepts (Bell et al., 1976; Dienes, 1960, 1963), linking form and understanding (Hiebert, 1984), metaphorical representation (Resnick & Ford, 1981), a morphism between a reference domain (which can be thought of as a reference world and as a symbol system) and a symbol system (positional arithmetic) (Schoenfeld, 1986), semantic understanding that is linked to the syntax of the symbolic procedure (Resnick, 1982, 1983), and use of manipulatives (Fuson, 1975). Use of the blocks is said to result in an abstraction (Schoenfeld, 1986), in a generalization (Greeno, 1983) across the object and symbolic procedures, or in a relationship between conceptual structures (Fuson, 1990a). However, few authors have noted that positional blocks embody the English words and not the written marks: The blocks present different collectible multiunits that are named by the English multiunit words. These collectible multiunit quantities can be related to the marks positions and thus give quantitative meaning to the different marks positions, and the differing sizes of the blocks can also support construction of the one/ten trade conceptual structures. But the blocks themselves are an explicit multiunit system and not an implicit multiunit positional system.

A central issue in the use of such embodiments is that the embodiments only present the mathematical concepts they embody. Only people can construct the concepts presented by embodiments and later re-present these concepts to themselves. Concepts presented by particular materials may or may not be noticed by an observer, and unintended features may instead be noticed. Cobb (1987) focused his discussion of several of the aforementioned analyses of embodiments on how children "see" the blocks and cautioned against assuming that children see what adults see in the blocks. Labinowicz (1985) gave some examples of ways in which children see these blocks differently. Use of the blocks with children does not auto-

---

of the base-ten system was to be set within this more general understanding. The discussion here focuses only on the base-ten system.

matically result in understanding or in accurate computation (Resnick & Omanson, 1987). This distinction is captured in the labels "collectible" embodiments and "collected" conceptual multiunits (Fuson, 1990a).

However, use of base-ten blocks with second graders can result in considerable place-value understanding, accurate multidigit addition and subtraction of large marks problems (up to ten digits), and verbalizable understanding of the trading involved in multidigit addition and subtraction (Fuson, 1986a; Fuson & Briars, 1990). A large number of second graders from a wide range of achievement and SES levels (43 classrooms over three studies) showed considerably higher levels of performance than that reported in the section "How Are U.S. Children Doing?" for third graders under usual instruction. Almost every child[24] identified the tens and hundreds places, correctly aligned like places when they rewrote marks problems vertically, correctly identified the 1 mark as a traded ten, added multidigit problems with correct trading in at least four places, and correctly identified already solved multidigit addition and subtraction problems as solved correctly or incorrectly. Most attended to English words as well as digits and correctly unscrambled disordered digit/English name pairs into positional marks, described and justified quantitatively the addition ten-for-one trading procedure and its marks recording, described and justified quantitatively the subtraction one-for-ten trading and its marks recording, and subtracted multidigit problems with correct trading.

The base-ten blocks were used as part of a learning/teaching setting that supported the construction of relationships among the six conceptual structures required for multidigit addition and subtraction and multidigit numeration. Features of this setting and ways in which the setting supported children's construction of the necessary relationships are identified and discussed in the next section. Some of these have been reported and discussed in Fuson and Briars (1990) and Fuson (1990a, 1990b), and several are discussed in more detail in Fuson (1990a). This discussion indicates some of the complexities of building relationships among the various conceptual structures and identifies features that are important for classroom support of children's learning of multidigit numeration, addition, and subtraction. The learning/teaching setting evolved during 20 years of teaching these topics to preservice and in-service teachers and was revised in response to this teaching and to teacher's use with children of the setting. A base-four version of the setting was used in Bell et al. (1976). The features identified are those that were used both in studies in which teachers supported a particular multidigit addition procedure and a particular subtraction procedure by modeling or by directed questioning of children adding

---

[24]Some of these measures were done with only part of the sample; the "almost all" or "most" then refers to the proportion of tested children responding as described.

or subtracting with the blocks (Fuson, 1986a; Fuson & Briars, 1990) and in a study in which small groups of second graders invented their own procedures for adding and subtracting four-digit numbers (Burghardt & Fuson, 1992; Fuson, Fraivillig, & Burghardt, in press).

Supporting Children's Construction
of Relationships Among Conceptual Structures
for Multidigit Marks, Words, and Multiunit
Quantities

In order to use and understand English named-multiunit words and positional written marks, and in order to add and subtract multidigit numbers with understanding, children need to link the words and the marks to each other and need to give quantitative multiunit meanings to both the words and the marks. An example of a learning/teaching setting that supports the construction of these conceptual relationships is given in Fig. 2.6. Because of the different features of the words and the marks, one physical embodiment (base-ten blocks) was used for the words, and a different embodiment (digit index cards) was used for the marks. Each embodiment helped to direct children's attention to crucial meanings and attributes of the embodied system and could constrain children's actions with each embodiment to those consistent with the mathematical features of the embodied system. The digit cards were 3×5 index cards, each with one large digit between 0 and 9 written on it; the cards were kept in order in a small file box, with file separators listing each digit. The other components of the learning/teaching setting were three sets of words: English words, block embodiment words, and positional words (see Fig. 2.6). The same set of positional words was used for the mathematical marks and the digit cards because they were so similar. These three sets of words helped direct children's attention to critical features of the mathematical systems and embodiments, facilitated communication among the participants in the learning/teaching setting, and supported the construction of links among the different systems and embodiments. The desired conceptual relationships among words, marks, and the collectible multiunit quantities in the blocks are indicated by arrows. Single arrows show isomorphic relationships between similarly structured systems, and double arrows show the more difficult relationships between nonisomorphic systems.

The tasks of building named-multiunit meanings for the English words and positional meanings for the written marks, relating words to marks and vice versa, and relating multiunit quantities to the words and to the marks are complex. After an initial period of exploration of the base-ten blocks[25]

---

[25]Ones and tens are quite inexpensive, but the flats and big cubes are fairly expensive. Some purchased examples of the latter were mixed with inexpensive substitutes. Plain wood-

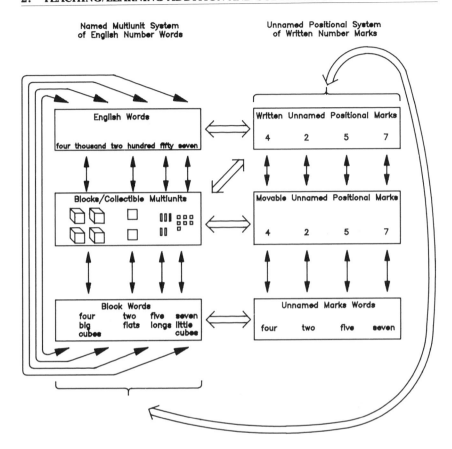

FIG. 2.6.   Relationships among words, marks, and multiunit conceptual structures.

and establishment of the relationships among different sized blocks, including the consistent ten-for-one trades between contiguous multiunits,
this goal of supporting the construction of the multiple relationships portrayed in Fig. 2.6 was addressed by continually emphasizing the links
among the various parts of the setting. Large calculating cardboards were
used to keep the blocks organized in a way that would easily relate to the
standard written marks procedure. Figs. 2.7 and 2.8 show how the blocks
and digit cards were tightly linked together in demonstrating particular
multidigit addition and subtraction procedures. This tight linking has at
least three important aspects.

en flats were cut at a local lumberyard (which did the cutting free because the materials were
for a school), and large cubes were made of cardboard folded up to make a hollow cube. Some
cardboard flats also were made by folding up and taping a two-dimensional pattern. Only the
expensive perfect blocks were used in the initial exploration of relationships. Children easily
used the cheaper blocks in addition and subtraction activities.

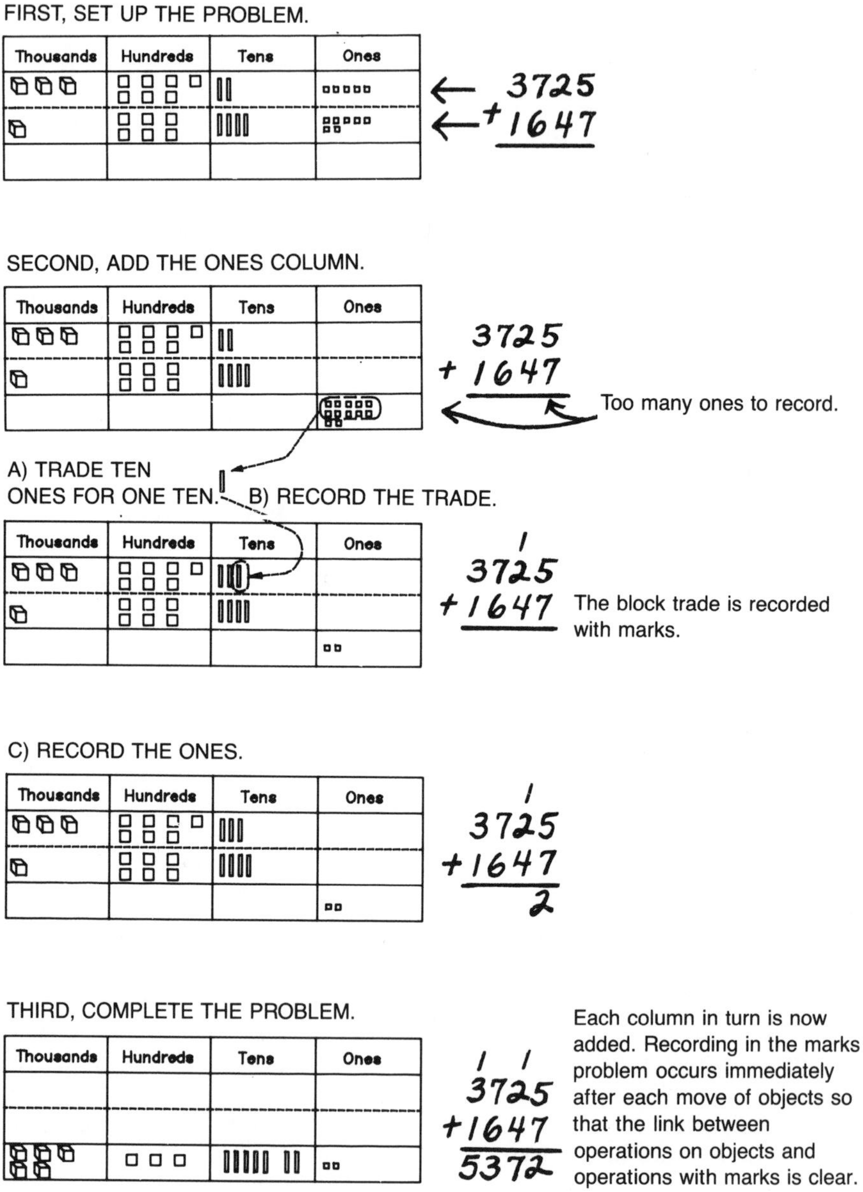

FIRST, SET UP THE PROBLEM.

Thousands	Hundreds	Tens	Ones
🔟🔟🔟	⬜⬜⬜⬜	‖	▫▫▫▫▫
🔟	⬜⬜⬜	‖‖‖	▪▪▫▫▫

← 3725
←⁺1647

SECOND, ADD THE ONES COLUMN.

Thousands	Hundreds	Tens	Ones
🔟🔟🔟	⬜⬜⬜⬜	‖	
🔟	⬜⬜⬜	‖‖‖	
			⬛⬛⬛

3725
+ 1647   ⟵ Too many ones to record.

A) TRADE TEN
ONES FOR ONE TEN.   B) RECORD THE TRADE.

Thousands	Hundreds	Tens	Ones
🔟🔟🔟	⬜⬜⬜⬜	‖◖	
🔟	⬜⬜⬜	‖‖‖	
			▫▫

   ¹
3725
+1647   The block trade is recorded
               with marks.

C) RECORD THE ONES.

Thousands	Hundreds	Tens	Ones
🔟🔟🔟	⬜⬜⬜⬜	‖‖	
🔟	⬜⬜⬜	‖‖‖	
			▫▫

   ¹
3725
+1647
    2

THIRD, COMPLETE THE PROBLEM.

Thousands	Hundreds	Tens	Ones
🔟🔟🔟🔟🔟	⬜⬜⬜	‖‖‖‖‖‖‖	▫▫

  ¹ ¹
3725
+1647
5372

Each column in turn is now added. Recording in the marks problem occurs immediately after each move of objects so that the link between operations on objects and operations with marks is clear.

FIG. 2.7. Multidigit adding and recording with the multiunit embodiment. Note that there was not enough space to draw the hundreds and thousands blocks to scale.

FIRST, SET UP THE PROBLEM.

Thousands	Hundreds	Tens	Ones
	□ □ □	‖‖‖‖‖	▫ ▫
		‖‖‖	

← 5372
← ⁻1647

SECOND, DO ALL
TRADING.

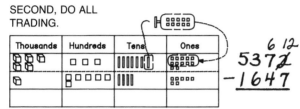

Thousands	Hundreds	Tens	Ones
	□ □ □	‖‖‖‖	
		‖‖‖	

Need more ones in order to
subtract. Trade one ten for ten
ones.

$$\begin{array}{r} 6\ \ 12 \\ 537\!\!\!/2 \\ -1647 \end{array}$$

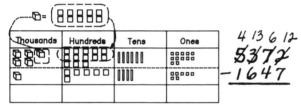

Thousands	Hundreds	Tens	Ones
		‖‖‖‖‖	
		‖‖‖	

$$\begin{array}{r} 4\ \ 13\ \ 6\ \ 12 \\ 537\!\!\!/2 \\ -1647 \end{array}$$

Now make each necessary
trade, recording each trade on
the marks problem immediately
after block trade is made.

THIRD, DO ALL SUBTRACTING.

Thousands	Hundreds	Tens	Ones
		‖‖‖‖‖	
		‖‖‖	
			▫ ▫ ▫

$$\begin{array}{r} 4\ \ 13\ \ 6\ \ 12 \\ 537\!\!\!/2 \\ -1647 \\ \hline 5 \end{array}$$

To subtract 12 − 7, a child can
count up from 7 to 12, know
the fact, go over 10 (7 + 3 +
2), or use any other method.
We matched the blocks and
put the extra from the top into
the bottom, but other methods
can be used.

FOURTH, COMPLETE THE PROBLEM.

Thousands	Hundreds	Tens	Ones
		‖‖‖‖‖	
		‖‖‖	▫ ▫ ▫
	□ □ □	‖	▫ ▫ ▫
	□ □ □		

$$\begin{array}{r} 4\ \ 13\ \ 6\ \ 12 \\ 537\!\!\!/2 \\ -1647 \\ \hline 3725 \end{array}$$

Each column in turn is now
subtracted. Recording in the
marks problem occurs
immediately after each move
of objects. Each column is
recorded before the next
column is subtracted with the
objects.

FIG. 2.8. Multidigit subtracting and recording with the multiunit embodiment. Note that
there was not enough space to draw the hundreds and thousands blocks to scale.

First, in the teacher-led studies links among the English words, multiunit blocks, positional marks, and digit cards were strengthened by verbal descriptions of block displays and of digit card and written marks recordings of block displays. All three sets of words—the English words, block multiunit embodiment words, and positional words—might be used in these descriptions, with many readings using two different sets of words. Operations on the blocks were described as they were being carried out, frequently with at least two sets of words. For example, while trading ten small cubes for one long, the trader would say, "I'm trading ten of these baby cubes for a long, ten ones for one ten, and I'm putting the traded long here at the top of the longs column, the tens column." These running commentaries served to help hold children's attention and direct their attention to the particular important features of a given situation, for example, that the trade was ten ones for one ten and not just many (unspecified) for one. This emphasis on verbalization is consistent with results reported by Resnick and Omanson (1987) concerning a positive relationship between the amount of verbalizing and the amount of learning with the blocks. The positional words were particularly useful early in instruction in facilitating the participation of children having difficulty with the English words and late in instruction when the positional words facilitated discussion of the importance of the position of the word or digit.

Second, when adding and subtracting with the blocks, the blocks-to-written-marks links were made strongly and tightly: Each step with the blocks was immediately recorded with the mathematical marks. In earlier work with multibase blocks with children and with teachers (work that preceded the tight-link approach used in Fuson, 1975, and in Bell et al., 1976), children or teachers allowed to do whole problems with the blocks did not learn what to do with the written marks and these marks did not "take on" the meanings of the blocks. The blocks instead were just calculating devices for finding the answer. When instead children (or teachers) were forced to record with written marks what they did with the blocks for each column (i.e., for each multiunit), the marks and the marks procedures did take on the block multiunit meanings. It is beyond the ability of most children to reflect on the whole blocks procedure and relate it to the whole written marks procedure, but they can do this reflection and relating for each multiunit. Thus, the teacher must set up children's experiences with the blocks to maximize children's opportunities to make these links. This takes some effort, because the use of the blocks is so involving and interesting that children (and teachers) do not want to stop after a column and record their results; they want to finish the problem with the blocks. For all of these reasons, when teachers were supporting the learning of the standard procedures, not only was recording done with the digit cards after each step with the blocks, but each child had a worksheet and did the recording on his or her own paper.

In the child-inventing groups, it was sometimes quite difficult to enforce the links between the blocks and the written marks. Children easily understood and invented accurate multiunit addition procedures with the blocks even though all multidigit problems were given in horizontal rather than vertical form. After a group had sorted through the difficulties of the directionality of subtraction and the trading requirements, groups also invented accurate subtraction procedures with the blocks. But some groups resisted linking each step with blocks to recording with written marks, so different blocks and marks procedures were used. Some groups had difficulties organizing the blocks and the digit cards so that it was easy to make the links between blocks and written marks, and making the digit card marks recordings was very time consuming for some groups. For these reasons, the digit cards were abandoned after the first three groups, and a "Magic Pad" that needed to have children make marks recordings any time something was done with blocks was used instead. This worked better, but errors still were made frequently by some children when they did not connect the blocks to the marks. Incorrect procedures were invented when children added in a marks world unconnected to the blocks world. When experimenters forced children to connect these marks procedures to the blocks, the multiunit quantities in the blocks always could help the children self-correct the incorrect marks procedure. But some children did not make these connections spontaneously. Many teachers also evidently underestimate the need to make very tight connections between the blocks and the mathematical marks. Hart (1987) reported that in England this need is not necessarily seen by teachers using the blocks, who frequently make minimal or even no links between these two, abandoning the blocks very soon after introducing the written marks (much as is done in most U.S. textbooks that use pictures of the blocks).

A computer program can build in the links between the blocks and the written marks. Thompson (1991) wrote such a program in which modifying a block display automatically changed the marks display and vice versa. This program was more effective with fifth graders inventing computational procedures for decimal fractions than a comparison treatment using real blocks.

Recording with written marks the actions of the blocks can direct children's attention to the critical aspects of multidigit addition because one has to write down a certain number in a certain location. Because the written marks are similar across different multiunit positions (in contrast to the blocks and words that look or sound different across different multiunits), recorded marks problems provide a simpler context from which children can generalize the similarities in their procedure across positions: The traded 1 marks look alike whereas the traded long, or flat, or big cube do not. In all of the Fuson studies, recording with written marks began at the very beginning of addition with the blocks. Thus, this simpler context was available from the very beginning but was always accompanied by the blocks so that the different multiunits as well as the similar marks could be apparent.

Third, when children finally carry out multidigit addition and subtraction only with the written marks, the written-marks-to-blocks link needs to be reinforced frequently. Many discussions of the use of physical embodiments to support the construction of meaning for mathematical marks emphasize the importance of helping children construct initial embodiment-to-marks links. The necessity of emphasizing the reverse marks-to-block links has been discussed much less frequently. It was recognized by Dienes (1963) when discussing how easy it is for symbolism to become autonomous (i.e., removed from meanings) without occasional feedback to the experiences from which the symbolism has been derived. Without such marks-to-blocks feedback, errors may creep in. Resnick and Omanson (1987) found that children who had overcome errors when using the blocks made the errors again several months later, and Fuson (1986a) reported that monthly multidigit calculation tests indicated that some children who had earlier calculated correctly began to make mistakes. However, in the latter case, for most interviewed second graders making such marks errors, asking them to "think about the blocks" was sufficient for them to self-correct their own errors, even for subtraction problems with zeros in the top number. Thus, their mental presentations of the blocks were strong enough to direct the correct marks procedure, but they did not access the blocks even occasionally to check their written marks procedure. Frequent practice of a few multidigit addition and subtraction problems during which children are asked to think about the blocks and check the accuracy of their procedures or are asked to explain and justify the procedure may serve to prevent errors from creeping into written procedures and increase the frequency with which children will spontaneously make the marks-to-block link in order to check on their own procedures.

Building the conceptual structures and making all of the relationships in Fig. 2.6 requires protracted experience with the learning/teaching setting. The second graders in the Fuson block studies varied considerably in the time they needed to construct multiunit items and make all of the links among the components of the learning/teaching setting. Children were to continue to use the blocks and record the results until they felt ready to try problems without the blocks. Some children were ready to work without the blocks within several days whereas others only felt ready after many days (a few children took several weeks) of work with the blocks. One criterion for deciding when a child is ready to work with marks alone is if the child can describe and justify a marks problem using the block words and English words. Being able to explain when and why and what one trades for specific problems is a good indication that the child has built meaningful multiunit conceptual structures for the written marks and can use these structures in operating with the marks.

Addition began with four-digit problems except with the low-achieving second graders who began with two-digit problems and moved immediately to four-digit problems. These four-digit problems allowed children to see addition and subtraction functioning with several different multiunits and with all possibilities of trades (some problems had no trades and some had trades for every multiunit). This facilitated the reflective abstraction of the common features of the procedures across positions. This initial work over the whole range of possible multidigit problems prevented children from inventing errors when confronted with unfamiliar problem types, a frequent source of children's errors on multidigit algorithms (see the discussion by VanLehn, 1986). The work on four-digit addition and subtraction highlighted and reinforced several crucial place-value concepts, thus allowing children to learn multidigit numeration within the context of addition and subtraction. Children got a great deal of practice seeing and saying the words for all four places, they saw similar one-for-ten trades connecting contiguous places and had to use this trade knowledge in adding, they saw and used the reverse one-for-ten trades for subtraction, and the need for a 0 was more obvious than with the already learned two-digit marks, where the 0 just marks the decade words (which do not at first mean tens and ones). Thus, unlike textbooks in which a long chapter on multidigit numeration precedes multidigit addition and subtraction, this approach allowed children to learn multidigit numeration while learning multidigit addition and subtraction. The use of three- and four-digit numbers allowed the use of English words that are regular for the first places said (the thousand and hundreds places). This regularity supported the named-multiunit blocks structure and avoided eliciting the unitary conceptions that are common for two-digit numbers. The second graders in the studies felt empowered and very proud of their knowledge about these big problems.

Addition and subtraction can be done in various ways with the blocks, can be phrased in different ways in words, and can be recorded in different ways with the marks. For example, to find $12 - 7$, one can think "7 plus how many to make 12?" or "12 minus 7 is how many?" or "12 take away 7 is how many?" If one makes both multidigit numbers with the blocks in a vertical arrangement, one can (a) add blocks into the third row of the calculating sheet so that the new blocks plus the 7 blocks equal the 12 blocks on the top, or (b) can match the 7 blocks to the 12 blocks and put the extra down in the third row as the difference, (c) can match the 7 blocks to the 12 blocks and leave the difference as part of the minuend blocks, or (d) can match 7 of the 12 blocks to the 7 blocks and take both amounts of 7 blocks away. One can also just make the minuend with blocks and take away the multiunits for the subtrahend. The choice depends on the meanings of subtraction available to the children and on individual preferences. The children from the Chicago area had compare and take-away meanings of subtraction, and their teachers found (b) and (c) to be quite clear because these methods showed all three multidigit numbers with the blocks. Children and teachers from Pittsburgh had only take-away meanings, so they usually made only the minuend with blocks. Second graders who were inventing procedures in small groups usually made both numbers when adding and usually aligned the blocks vertically, and almost all groups began subtracting by making both numbers and taking away blocks because they had only a take-away meaning for subtraction. The directionality of subtraction proved to be so problematic for several groups (there were long arguments concerning whether $2 - 8$ is "two take away eight" or "eight take away two" or "two from eight" or "eight from two" or "take two from eight" or "take eight from two" or "two minus eight" or "eight minus two") that the experimenters finally suggested that they just make the minuend with blocks.

The trading can be carried out and recorded in different ways also. Two groups of second graders invented an addition procedure in which all the adding was done first and then all of the trading was done (Fuson et al., in press). Like multiunits were added and recorded, even if the sums were two-digit sums, and then all of the two-digit sums were "fixed" by trading so that the sum could be written in standard marks form (see the top left method in Table 2.13). The reverse of this procedure was used for subtraction by the teachers in the teacher-supported studies (see Fig. 2.8 and Table 2.13). Children first checked each top digit to be sure that it was big enough (equal to or larger than the bottom digit in that column). If it was not, a one-for-ten trade (borrow, regrouping) was made from the column on the left. After all the necessary trading had been done to the top number (i.e., after the top number was "fixed" so that each multiunit in the minuend was as large as or larger than each subtrahend multiunit), the single-digit subtraction was done with each multiunit (column by column). In both these procedures, the trading and the adding/subtracting can be done from either direction or even on the multiunits in any order. These procedures eliminate the necessity of switching between unitary and multiunit conceptual structures as is required when one alternates between adding/subtracting and trading for each multiunit (column). They focus successively on two major components of multiunit addition and subtraction: (a) adding/subtracting like multiunits and (b) trading multiunits so that the addition can be recorded or the subtraction actually carried out. This procedure is similar to the low-stress procedure described by Hutchings (1975).

TABLE 2.13
Alternative Multidigit Addition and Subtraction Procedures

Type of Procedure	Procedure	
Do all adding/subtracting	3 7 6 5	16
Do all fixing of multiunit	+1 9 6 3	4 $\cancel{6}$ 12
quantities	4 16 12 8	$\cancel{5}$ $\cancel{7}$ $\cancel{2}$ 8
	5 6	−1 9 6 3
	5 7 2 8	3 7 6 5
Procedures that simplify	4	
the addition of the	4 $\cancel{7}$ 8	4 3 8
traded number	+3 5 6	+3 5$^{|}$6
	7 9 4	7 9 4
Two U.S. versions of a	4	16
traded ten	8 $\cancel{5}$ $^{|}$6	8 $\cancel{6}$ $\cancel{6}$
	−3 2 9	−3 2 9
	5 2 7	5 2 7
The Korean method of	4 10	
writing a traded ten	8 $\cancel{6}$ 6	
	−3 2 9	
	5 2 7	

Table 2.13 shows two other methods of recording trading in addition and three other methods for subtraction. For addition the most common method in the United States and in Korea is to write the new multiunit above the other multiunits that are like it. The two addition methods shown in the second row of Table 2.13 are variants of this method that make it easier to carry out the addition of three numbers in a traded multiunit. The first method of crossing out the top multiunit and writing the sum of that multiunit and the new traded multiunit was used in Fuson (1986a) and was also invented in the children's invention study (Fuson & Burghardt, 1991). Some children find it difficult to hold in their mind the number one larger than the top multiunit while adding that number to the bottom multiunit number. But some children already had learned the standard method of writing the little 1 above, and this crossing-out method caused confusion in some of them. So in Fuson and Briars (1990) this method was only suggested to children who were having difficulty adding. The second method is used in the People's Republic of China: The traded 1 is added into the larger number (which may be in the top or the bottom number) to make the addition easier. The first subtraction method shown in the third row is the method commonly used in U.S. textbooks. It may increase children's tendency to view the 1 as a one rather than as a ten. The second method was used in the blocks studies to reduce this possibility. The third method is

used in Korea. It shows explicitly that a ten was traded over, and the separation of the top multiunit into its ten and ones components supported the Korean subtraction methods structured around ten (see "Research on Ten-Structured Methods of Addition and Subtraction"). There are also other ways to carry out multiunit addition and subtraction. Many Europeans use the equal additions subtraction procedure in which a trade from the top number is compensated for by adding one to that multiunit on the bottom (instead of reducing that top multiunit by one). Children can explore and compare any of these procedures as well as other procedures they may invent with the blocks or other embodiments of multiunit quantities.

In the teacher-led work with the blocks, the calculating sheets shown in Figs. 2.7 and 2.8 provided an organizing frame for the block multiunit numbers and for the vertical arrangement of these numbers so that like multiunits could easily be added, subtracted, and traded. Because the vertical arrangement of either marks or blocks seems to elicit a vertical "column" orientation by children in which the horizontal multiunit numbers may disappear, teachers provided by verbalization and gesture the simultaneous horizontal frame to maintain the multiunit numbers within children's attention. In the child-invention study, neither source of framing was present, and some groups of children, especially lower-achieving groups, experienced considerable difficulty in organizing the blocks so that links could easily be made with marks or so that they could attend to like multiunits in both multiunit numbers without losing the identity of each whole large multiunit number. There were two other kinds of organizational problems with the blocks. Blocks in multiunit numbers sometimes edged into the extra pile of blocks so that it was not clear which blocks belonged to the multiunit number, and children sometimes took blocks out of the multiunit number in order to play with them. Both of these nonobvious sources of change in the block multiunit number sometimes led to prolonged frustrating periods in which differences existed between the blocks and marks multiunit numbers, and children had difficulty ascertaining the source of the difference. Thus, it may be helpful to provide a cardboard or wooden frame with four horizontal sections into which blocks can be placed for each four-digit multiunit blocks number; the frame should be large enough to permit trading within the frame. Such horizontal frames might eliminate the confusions, maintain children's awareness of the whole multiunit number, allow children to see conservation of the quantity of the multiunit number after trading, and allow children to move whole multiunit numbers around to explore different ways of writing or carrying out multiunit addition or subtraction.

At present there is little research concerning how and when children can learn general methods of multidigit addition and subtraction as a problem-solving activity similar to that discussed in the section "What Can Be: Supporting Children's Later Numerical Thinking in the Classroom" other than the preliminary results of the child-invention study summarized earlier and the results of Madell (1985). Labinowicz (1985, chapter 14) reviewed several efforts at supporting children's individual inventions of multiunit addition and subtraction, and Kamii (1989) reported the efforts in Piagetian second- and third-grade classrooms. Almost all of the reported invented procedures use sequence multiunits and are limited to two-digit computation. It is not clear that these procedures are generalizable to computation with numbers of several places. Research directed at the issues of the generalizability of various child-invented procedures and the kind of conceptual structures used by each procedure would be helpful in determining how successful various problem-solving approaches might be. The methods reported to date take a long time for children to construct, with third graders still struggling with written methods for two-digit subtraction. However, this may be because no efforts have provided embodiments of multiunit quantities through thousands and allowed children to work on general addition and subtraction with the support of the regular English named-multiunit hundred and thousand words and the support of collectible multiunit quantities. Some anecdotal evidence from Cognitively Guided Instruction classrooms (Carpenter et al., 1989) does indicate that allowing first and second graders to work with problem situations involving large numbers (sometimes even larger than four digits) is quite motivating and does engender invented child procedures for adding these large numbers (Carey, personal communication, November, 1988).

What Can Be: Supporting Children's Multiunit Thinking in the Classroom

Labinowicz (1985, chapter 15) identified and discussed three approaches to multidigit computation: as isolated skills, in the context of meanings, and as an area of problem solving. The first approach is the approach now taken in most textbooks and most classrooms, though there are some steps toward the second. Recent evidence concerning the use of embodiments that present collectible multiunits indicates that children can learn multidigit addition and subtraction in the context of meanings and that this can be a powerful approach. Computation as an area of problem solving clearly must be built upon computation in the context of meanings: Children only can invent accurate multidigit computational procedures if they are helped to construct accurate and powerful multiunit conceptual structures related to the English number words and positional written marks. Thus, creating a classroom in which children approach multidigit computation as a problem-solving activity, that is, in which children invent methods of multi-unit addition and subtraction, requires providing a setting within which children can suggest and then test various computational procedures by checking whether they are consistent with their multiunit conceptual structures. Such an approach would be facilitated by earlier experiences in a meaningful problem-solving classroom at the kindergarten and first-grade levels such as discussed in the sections "What Can Be: Supporting Children's Early Numerical Thinking in the Kindergarten and First-Grade Classroom" and "What Can Be: Supporting Children's Later Numerical Thinking in the Classroom," and perhaps especially facilitated by experiences that help children hear, see, and say the tens and ones in the irregular English words. Thus, ascertaining the full potential of a problem-solving approach to multidigit computation may need to await successful implementation of problem-solving approaches to addition and subtraction of single-digit numbers.

Several aspects of the present order and placement of multidigit topics within the elementary school curriculum need to be questioned. First, the present textbook organization and presentation of these topics rests on a skills analysis of performance rather than on recent evidence concerning children's thinking about multiunit numbers. One aspect that needs to be rethought is the introduction of two-digit place value and two-digit addition and subtraction with no trading before adding and subtracting all single-digit sums and differences to 18. The present order results from the assumptions that children need to have multiunit conceptual structures in order to understand how to read and write two-digit marks and that it is easier for children to add and subtract quantities of different multiunits (tens and ones whose sum is nine or less: $43 + 54$) than to add unitary numbers whose sum happens to exceed ten ($8 + 7$).

Neither assumption is warranted by the evidence. First, kindergarten and first-grade children learn to read and write two-digit marks even though they do not understand these marks as tens and ones but only as counting/sequence unitary numbers: They link the patterns in these marks to the decade pattern in the number-word sequence. Making such links is fairly straightforward for numbers between twenty and one hundred because the decade word is said first and the decade mark is written first. The opposite order of the teen words and the teen marks (saying sixteen but writing 16 rather than 61) needs to be discussed explicitly because this reversal in saying English teen words creates difficulty for English-speaking children—they show more difficulty in writing teen words than nonteen words. Children might be invited to invent "better" ways of reading our two-digit marks, especially the teen marks, as an English child did when she adamantly proclaimed that whoever made the teen words was stupid and that 12 (for example) ought to be called onety-two (Wheeler, 1977). Using "tens words" between ten and two ten (and later to nine ten nine) in an English version of Chinese (using English instead of Chinese words for one through ten) might be explored as a way to support learning the marks for the teens and as a potential future support for the construction of multiunit conceptual structures. Second, children clearly construct unitary conceptual structures for numbers and use these conceptual structures for a long time before they are able to construct multiunit conceptual structures for two-digit numbers. These unitary conceptions are sufficient for them to add and subtract all single-digit numbers (sums and differences to 18) and even small two-digit numbers. The ability to think about two different kinds of units at the same time—single units and collected ten-unit items—follows the construction and use of the increasingly more abstract and efficient unitary conceptual structures for number discussed in "What Can Be: Supporting Children's Later Numerical Thinking in the Classroom." So children need to have in first grade a considerable amount of experience with all sums and differences to 18 in order to build more advanced unitary conceptions before beginning experiences to support the construction of multiunit conceptions.

Second, the skill-based step-by-step piecemeal approach now used for multidigit addition and subtraction clearly is not necessary if the classroom provides children with learning/teaching settings in which they can construct multiunit conceptual structures for multidigit numbers. Most second graders can construct such conceptions for four-digit numbers, and working with such large numbers initially may facilitate understanding of the general repetitive ten/one features of the English number words and written number marks. It also seems to be easy for most second graders to generalize procedures for four-digit numbers to problems with many digits (Fuson, 1986a; Fuson & Briars, 1990). So an initial in-depth effort can result in general learning of multidigit addition and subtraction, eliminating the present need for extensions year after year to larger numbers.

Third, the relationship between place-value concepts and multidigit addition and subtraction is not just the simple one usually found in textbooks: place value preceding and providing the foundation for addition and subtraction. Multidigit addition and subtraction are problem situations that permit crucial attributes of the named-multiunit words and the positional written marks to become evident and thus are excellent contexts within which children can construct place-value understandings. For example, the initial introduction to multidigit addition can provide a setting for discussing the fourth, sixth, eight, ninth, and tenth features of the English named-multiunit words and the positional marks listed in Table 2.8. In such an introduction the initial problem situation might be to show and to find 735 + 647 with blocks and with the digit cards. This addition problem can be made with the blocks by generalizing from single-digit addition: Make a pile of blocks for 735 (i.e., make 7F 3L 5SC) and a pile of blocks for 647 (make 6F 4L 7SC) and then push the piles together to add them. One can then say and record the resulting sum jumble of blocks in many ways (e.g., "nine flats two longs one long four flats six small cubes three longs six small cubes one long"). However, a simple, adequate, and accurate description is "thirteen flats seven longs twelve small cubes." Likewise the English version of this sum ("thirteen hundred seventy twelve") is quite well defined and clear (even if nonstandard, though "thirteen hundred" is a frequent acceptable alternative for 1,300). The block embodiment and the English and block words can support understanding of one of the primary features of multidigit addition: Only multiunit items that are alike can be added to each other. Two longs and three flats are not 5 longs or 5 flats—they cannot be added as if they were both single-digit numbers.

Applying a single-digit meaning of addition to the index cards creates problems and can facilitate focusing on the third, sixth, and tenth crucial aspects of positional multidigit addition: Put out index cards 735 in that order, put out index cards 647 in that order, and then push all the index cards together to add as one added with the blocks. The resulting sum is not well defined: Depending on how one pushed the cards together, one gets many different 6-digit answers (e.g., 734675). Furthermore, if the digit card sum records the blocks sum, this digit card sum must be wrong, because even if one trades in ten flats for one big cube, the block sum has only one thousand/big cube. Thus, unless one wants to allow addition of multidigit marks to be done in many different ways, one needs to agree to let the block multiunit meanings of the written marks direct addition of marks (of the cards): The 7 flats and the 6 flats make 13 flats, the 3 longs and the 4 longs make 7 longs, and the 5 small cubes and 7 small cubes make 12 small cubes. However, there is still a problem with making this sum in index cards: 13712 is still too many places. The problem with the cards is that the biggest card is 9, and as soon as you try to make a bigger number, you have to use two cards. This pushes the other cards over a place and makes the wrong multiunit number. The question then is, "How can one say/write 'thirteen flats seven longs twelve small cubes' using only the words from one through nine?"[26] Such a discussion can lead to the idea of trading some of the blocks where there are too many, and the size of the blocks can help suggest fair ten-for-one trades.

The more general point from this approach, and one that can be articulated and repeated, is that one cannot just jumble written marks around

---

[26]The answer may have been discovered already by some in the search for different ways to write the sum of the blocks. We are presenting here only a summary version of what may be a prolonged activity carried out in different ways.

arbitrarily, as one jumbled around the index cards. What one does with written marks needs to fit the meaning of those marks. If you know the meaning, you can figure out what to do with the marks—you do not even have to be told what to do. Some marks written in mathematics have more than one meaning (e.g., − means take away and compare). Then you need to choose a meaning that makes sense for the situation in which you are using the marks. If you do not know what to do with some written marks, you do not have to ask someone else what to do with them. You ask what the marks mean. Then you can figure out what to do with the marks.

Furthermore, the simplistic view of place-value understanding preceding multiunit addition and subtraction is inaccurate because place value has some characteristics (the third through sixth multiunit conceptual structures listed in Table 2.9) that are not required for understanding of multiunit addition and subtraction. Understanding and using these more abstract features of the named-multiunit English words and positional written marks—truly understanding place value—may take a long period of time, much longer than just learning to add and subtract multidigit numbers.

Fourth, constructing multiunit conceptual structures and relating them to English words and positional marks may take a long time, considerably longer than is allotted in a single textbook chapter. Textbooks spend much more time on single-digit sums and differences, for which children already possess initial unitary conceptual structures when they enter school, than they do on multidigit addition and subtraction, for which children must construct new multiunit conceptions. Constructing these multiunit conceptual structures for three- and four-digit numbers may be the major accomplishment of second grade, requiring sustained experiences with multiunit learning/teaching settings initially and then repeated discussions and uses of these multiunit structures throughout the year as other mathematics topics are treated. Much less time would then be required for multidigit addition and subtraction in subsequent years, where it presently consumes much or part of every fall, because children would have adequate conceptual structures to support any written procedures they do carry out and because they would have devised general multidigit procedures that would work for large multidigit problems already. Such sustained experiences would be an excellent foundation for considering and building the later multiunit conceptual structures for English words and positional marks.

The learning and teaching of multidigit numbers are different in two ways from the learning and teaching of small whole numbers. These differences are typical of much of later school mathematics, so the learning and teaching of multidigit numbers can set powerful expectations that will influence later mathematics learning. First, as discussed earlier, U.S. children have relatively few supports within the culture for constructing ten-based multiunits. The irregular English language, the irregular nonten English measure units, and the existence within our money of distracting nonten units all contribute to a lack of salience of ten as an underlying trading unit in our culture. Therefore, the mathematics classroom needs to provide experiences of multiunits of ten, hundred, and thousand so that children can build the conceptual structures for multidigit numbers and support the mutual assimilation of these conceptual structures to marks and marks procedures. Any size embodiment that clearly presents collectible multiunits might suffice to support the construction of multiunit items, but metric positional blocks are a particularly useful size embodiment because they also can support the construction of metric intuitions. A small cube has a length of one centimeter, a liter is a big cube filled with water, a gram is the weight of a small cube filled with water, and a flat is a square decimeter (on its flat surface). Work with the metric system can further support children's use of multiunits based on ten, providing different concrete situations in which thinking in such multiunits is helpful. For example, "How many square decimeters in a square meter?" or "How many little cubes are in a cubic meter?" (where a cubic meter is made by outlining a cube by meter sticks)[27] permit exploration of relationships between different metric measures. The latter question could motivate the learning of large English number words and written numbers as children discuss building in various ways up to one million and even larger numbers (see Joslyn, 1990, for an excellent discussion). Construction and use of ten-based multiunits also would be facilitated by classroom activities in which children had many experiences with large amounts of money—single dollars, tens, hundreds, and thousands. Realistic play money versions of such bills might be laminated for use in these activities. Children might have bank accounts (envelopes filled with their money) that they can increment through various means (many activities might lead to earning pretend money) and then spend on various pretend purchases. These activities would only be meaningful, of course, if the meanings of a hundred dollars or a thousand dollars were built up through trading and through association with real costs, real incremented earnings, and with size embodiment collectible multiunit meanings from other multidigit activities.

Materials that embody neither collectible multiunits nor an implicit

---

[27]Meter sticks can be made inexpensively by cutting 6-foot or 8-foot-$\frac{3}{8}$-inch wood stock into meter lengths. The $\frac{3}{8}$-inch wood stock is about one centimeter square, so these meter sticks look just like long Cuisenaire rods—ten orange rods placed end to end are the same length and shape as this meter stick. Having many of these sticks available in the classroom facilitates measuring by using several meter sticks placed end-to-end, and their lack of smaller marks makes them less confusing initially.

multiunit positional system are not as helpful as materials that present one of these systems, and materials that present neither set of attributes may even be confusing. For example, colored chips and chip trading for different values do not present collectible multiunits, and they are not a positional embodiment because position is not required to present a number (you can mix up colored chips and still tell the value of the number). Showing 3-digit numbers in colored chips induced some third graders to focus only on the size of the digits rather than on their position and say that 198 was larger than 231 (Labinowicz, 1985). Such mixed embodiments seem rather to support the inadequate face-value meanings reported by Ross (1988) in which children focus on the number of groups but not on the value of the groups.

A second way in which multidigit numbers are like later mathematical topics is that the multidigit written marks look like those used earlier for simpler concepts but they now take on different meanings in the new multidigit domain: They look like concatenated single digits but really number different multiunits. These old single-digit meanings can interfere with the new multiunit meanings. Therefore the classroom needs to provide some inhibitory mechanism that will prevent the child's accessing the more familiar misleading meaning for the written marks until the new accurate conceptual structures for the domain can be constructed and the elicitation of these new structures facilitated. Such misinterpretations of reused old written marks continue to occur throughout mathematics, and inhibiting these wrong generalizations of earlier meanings is important. For example, children have considerable difficulty with multiplication by decimals less than one, where multiplication makes smaller, because multiplication with whole numbers means making bigger, and the top and bottom marks in fractions look like they are whole numbers, leading to adding and subtracting these whole numbers instead of finding common names (denominators) for the fractions.

CONCLUSION

The considerable amount of knowledge we now have about how children think about numbers and about addition and subtraction of numbers enables us to restructure children's experiences in mathematics classrooms. Classrooms now can become places where the human potential of children can blossom as children use their human capacities for meaning making and complex thinking. The economic and cultural need to turn humans into calculators has been superseded by the technological development of inexpensive reliable machines that calculate. Humans now need to develop their capacities to use these machine calculators to solve human problems and to understand mathematical concepts and written marks and words for these mathematical concepts. This is a liberating change for teachers, for they are now freed from overseeing the mechanical development of human calculators and instead can participate in and facilitate each child's marvelous re-creation of single-digit and multiunit addition and subtraction concepts.

REFERENCES

Ashcraft, M. H., & Fierman, B. A. (1982). Mental addition in third, fourth, and sixth graders. *Journal of Experimental Child Psychology, 33,* 216–234.

Ashcraft, M. H., & Stazyk, E. H. (1981). Mental addition: A test of three verification models. *Memory & Cognition, 9,* 185–196.

Ashlock, R. B. (1982). *Error patterns in computation.* Columbus, OH: Merrill.

Baroody, A. J. (1983). The development of procedural knowledge: An alternative explanation for chronometric trends of mental arithmetic. *Developmental Review, 3,* 225–230.

Baroody, A. J. (1984). Children's difficulties in subtraction: Some causes and questions. *Journal for Research in Mathematics Education, 15,* 203–213.

Baroody, A. J. (1987a). *Children's mathematical thinking: A developmental framework for preschool, primary, and special education teachers.* New York: Teachers College Press.

Baroody, A. J. (1987b). The development of counting strategies for single-digit addition. *Journal for Research in Mathematics Education, 18,* 141–157.

Baroody, A. J., & Gannon, K. E. (1984). The development of the commutativity principle and economical addition strategies. *Cognition and Instruction, 1,* 321–339.

Baroody, A. J., & Ginsburg, H. P. (1986). The relationship between initial meaningful and mechanical knowledge of arithmetic. In J. Hiebert (Ed.), *Conceptual and procedural knowledge: The case of mathematics* (pp. 75–112). Hillsdale, NJ: Lawrence Erlbaum Associates.

Bell, M. S., & Bell, J. B. (1988). *Assessing and enhancing the counting and numeration capabilities and basic operation concepts of primary school children.* Unpublished manuscript, University of Chicago.

Bell, M., & Burns, J. (1981). Counting and numeration capabilities of primary school children: A preliminary report. In T. R. Post & M. P. Roberts (Eds.), *Proceedings of the third annual meeting of the North American chapter of the International Group for the Psychology of Mathematics Education* (pp. 17–23). Minneapolis: University of Minnesota.

Bell, M. S., Fuson, K. C., & Lesh, R. A. (1976). *Algebraic and arithmetic structures: A concrete approach for elementary school teachers.* New York: Free Press.

Bergeron, J. C., & Herscovics, N. (1990). Psychological aspects of learning early arithmetic. In P. Nesher & J. Kilpatrick (Eds.), *Mathematics and cognition: A research synthesis by the International Group for the Psychology of Mathematics Education* (pp. 31–52). Cambridge, England: Cambridge University Press.

Bergeron, A., Herscovics, N., & Bergeron, J. C. (1986). Counting tasks involving some hidden elements. In G. Lappan & R. Even (Eds.), *Proceedings of the eighth annual meeting of the North American chapter of the International Group for the Psychology of Mathematics Education* (pp. 21–27). East Lansing, Michigan.

Bergeron, A., Herscovics, N., & Bergeron, J. C. (1987). Kindergarteners' knowledge of numbers: A longitudinal case study. Part II: Abstraction and formalization. In J. C. Bergeron, N.

Herscovics, & C. Kieran (Eds.), *Proceedings from the Eleventh International Conference for the Psychology of Mathematics Education* (Vol. II, pp. 352–360). Montreal.

Bisanz, J., & LeFevre, J. (1990). Strategic and nonstrategic processing in the development of mathematical cognition. In D. Bjorklund (Ed.), *Children's strategies: Contemporary views of cognitive development* (pp. 213–244). Hillsdale, NJ: Lawrence Erlbaum Associates.

Briars, D. J., & Larkin, J. H. (1984). An integrated model of skills in solving elementary word problems. *Cognition and Instruction, 1,* 245–296.

Brown, J. S., & VanLehn, K. (1982). Toward a generative theory of bugs in procedural skills. In T. P. Carpenter, J. M. Moser, & T. A. Romberg (Eds.), *Addition and subtraction: A cognitive perspective* (pp. 117–135). Hillsdale, NJ: Lawrence Erlbaum Associates.

Brush, L. R. (1978). Preschool children's knowledge of addition and subtraction. *Journal for Research in Mathematics Education, 9,* 44–54.

Burghardt, B. H., & Fuson, K. C. (1992). *Children's multiunit learning moments in small groups.* Manuscript in preparation.

Carpenter, T. P. (1985). Learning to add and subtract: An exercise in problem solving. In E. A. Silver (Ed.), *Teaching and learning mathematical problem solving* (pp. 17–40). Hillsdale, NJ: Lawrence Erlbaum Associates.

Carpenter, T. P., Fennema, E., Peterson, P. L., & Carey, D. A. (1988). Teachers' pedagogical content knowledge in mathematics. *Journal for Research in Mathematics Education, 19,* 385–401.

Carpenter, T. P., Fennema, E., Peterson, P. L., Chiang, C., & Loef, M. (1989). Using knowledge of children's mathematics thinking in classroom teaching: An experimental study. *American Educational Research Journal, 26,* 499–531.

Carpenter, T., Hiebert, J., & Moser, F. (1981). The effect of problem structure on first graders' initial solution procedures for simple addition and subtraction problems. *Journal for Research in Mathematics Education, 12,* 27–29.

Carpenter, T. P., Hiebert, J., & Moser, J. M. (1983). The effect of instruction on children's solutions of addition and subtraction word problems. *Educational Studies in Mathematics, 14,* 55–72.

Carpenter, T. P., & Moser, J. M. (1982). The development of addition and subtraction problem-solving skills. In T. P. Carpenter, J. M. Moser, & T. Romberg (Eds.), *Addition and subtraction: A cognitive perspective* (pp. 9–24). Hillsdale, N.J.: Lawrence Erlbaum Associates.

Carpenter, T. P., & Moser, J. M. (1983). The acquisition of addition and subtraction concepts. In R. Lesh & M. Landau (Eds.), *Acquisition of mathematics: Concepts and processes* (pp. 7–44). New York: Academic.

Carpenter, T. P., & Moser, J. M. (1984). The acquisition of addition and subtraction concepts in grades one through three. *Journal for Research in Mathematics Education, 15,* 179–202.

Carraher, T. N., & Schliemann, A. D. (1985). Computation routines prescribed by schools: Help or hindrance? *Journal for Research in Mathematics Education, 16,* 37–44.

Chi, M. T., & Klahr, D. (1975). Span and rate of apprehension in children and adults. *Journal of Experimental Child Psychology, 19,* 434–439.

Clapp, F. L. (1924). The number combinations: Their relative difficulty and the frequency of their appearance in textbooks. *University of Wisconsin Bureau of Educational Research Bulletin No. 2.*

Cobb, P. (1986a, April). *Counting types and word problems.* Paper presented at the annual meeting of the American Educational Research Association, San Francisco.

Cobb, P. (1986b). An investigation into the sensory-motor and conceptual origins of the basic addition facts. *Proceedings of the tenth international conference of the International Group for the Psychology of Mathematics Education* (pp. 141–146). London: University of London Institute of Education.

Cobb, P. (1987). Information-processing psychology and mathematics education—A constructivist perspective. *The Journal of Mathematical Behavior, 6,* 3–40.

Cobb, P., & Wheatley, G. (1988). Children's initial understandings of ten. *Focus on Learning Problems in Mathematics, 10,* 1–28.

Cobb, P., Wood, T., & Yackel, E. (1991). A constructivist approach to second-grade mathematics. In E. von Glasersfeld (Ed.), *Constructivism in mathematics education* (pp. 157–176). Dordrecht, Netherlands: Kluwer.

Cobb, P., Yackel, E., & Wood, T. (1989). Young children's emotional acts while doing mathematical problem solving. In D. B. McLeod & V. M. Adams (Eds.), *Affect and mathematical problem solving: A new perspective* (pp. 117–148). New York: Springer-Verlag.

Cobb, P., Yackel, E., Wood, T., Wheatley, G., & Merkel, G. (1988). Creating a problem-solving atmosphere. *Arithmetic Teacher, 36*(1), 46–47.

Cooper, R. G. (1984). Early number development: Discovering number space with addition and subtraction. In C. Sophian (Ed.), *Origins of cognitive skills* (pp. 157–192). Hillsdale, NJ: Lawrence Erlbaum Associates.

Davis, R. B. (1984). *Learning mathematics: The cognitive science approach to mathematics education,* Norwood, NJ: Ablex.

Davis, R. B. (1986). Conceptual and procedural knowledge in mathematics: A summary analysis. In J. Hiebert (Ed.), *Conceptual and procedural knowledge: The case of mathematics* (pp. 265–300). Hillsdale, NJ: Lawrence Erlbaum Associates.

Davis, R. B., & McKnight, C. C. (1980). The influence of semantic content on algorithmic behavior. *Journal of Children's Mathematical Behavior, 3,* 39–87.

De Corte, E., & Verschaffel, L. (1985a). Beginning first graders' initial representation of arithmetic word problems. *Journal of Mathematical Behavior, 1,* 3–21.

De Corte, E., & Verschaffel, L. (1985b). Working with simple word problems in early mathematics instruction. In L. Streefland (Ed.), *Proceedings of the Ninth International Conference for the Psychology of Mathematics Education* (pp. 304–309). Utrecht, Netherlands: Research Group on Mathematics Education and Educational Computer Center.

De Corte, E., & Verschaffel, L. (1986, April). *Eye-movement data as access to solution processes of elementary addition and subtraction problems.* Paper presented at the meeting of the American Educational Research Association, San Francisco.

De Corte, E., & Verschaffel, L. (1987a). The effects of semantic structure on first-graders' strategies for solving addition and subtraction word problems. *Journal for Research in Mathematics Education, 18,* 363–381.

De Corte, E., & Verschaffel, L. (1987b, April). *The influence of some non-semantic factors on solving addition and subtraction word problems.* Paper presented at the meeting of the American Educational Research Association, Washington, DC.

De Corte, E., & Verschaffel, L. (1987c, April). *Word problems in the primary grades: Implications of recent research.* Paper presented at the 65th annual meeting of the National Council of Teachers of Mathematics, Anaheim, CA.

De Corte, E., Verschaffel, L., & De Win, L. (1985). The influence of rewording verbal problems on childrens' problem representations and solutions. *Journal of Educational Psychology, 77,* 460–470.

Dienes, Z. P. (1960). *Building up mathematics* (4th ed.). London: Hutchinson Educational, Ltd.

Dienes, Z. P. (1963). *An experimental study of mathematics learning.* London: Hutchinson Educational, Ltd.

Durkin, K., Shire, B., Riem, R., Crowther, R. D., & Rutter, D. R. (1986). The social and linguistic context of early number word use. *British Journal of Developmental Psychology, 4,* 269–288.

Flexer, R. J., & Rosenberger, N. (1987). Beware of tapping pencils. *Arithmetic Teacher, 34*(5), 6–10.

Friend, J. E. (1979). Column addition skills. *Journal of Mathematical Behavior, 2*(2), 29–57.

Fuson, K. (1975). The effects on preservice elementary teachers of learning mathematics and means of teaching mathematics through the active manipulation of materials. *Journal for Research in Mathematics Education, 6,* 51–63.

Fuson, K. C. (1982). An analysis of the counting-on solution procedure in addition. In T. P. Carpenter, J. M. Moser, & T. A. Romberg (Eds.), *Addition and subtraction: A cognitive perspective* (pp. 67–81). Hillsdale, NJ: Lawrence Erlbaum Associates.

Fuson, K. C. (1984). More complexities in subtraction. *Journal for Research in Mathematics Education, 15,* 214–225.

Fuson, K. C. (1986a). Roles of representation and verbalization in the teaching of multi-digit addition and subtraction. *European Journal of Psychology of Education, 1,* 35–56.

Fuson, K. C. (1986b). Teaching children to subtract by counting up. *Journal for Research in Mathematics Education, 17,* 172–189.

Fuson, K. C. (1987). Research into practice: Adding by counting on with one-handed finger patterns. *Arithmetic Teacher, 35*(1), 38–41.

Fuson, K. C. (1988a). *Children's counting and concepts of number.* New York: Springer-Verlag.

Fuson, K. C. (1988b). First and second graders' ability to use schematic drawings in solving twelve kinds of addition and subtraction word problems. In M. J. Behr, C. B. Lacampagne, & M. M. Wheeler (Eds.), *Proceedings of the tenth annual meeting of the North American chapter of the International Group for the Psychology of Mathematics Education* (pp. 364–370). DeKalb: Northern Illinois University.

Fuson, K. C. (1988c). Research into practice: Subtracting by counting up with one-handed finger patterns. *Arithmetic Teacher, 35*(5), 29–31.

Fuson, K. C. (1990a). Conceptual structures for multiunit numbers: Implications for learning and teaching multidigit addition, subtraction, and place value. *Cognition and Instruction, 7,* 343–404.

Fuson, K. C. (1990b). Issues in place-value and multidigit addition and subtraction learning. *Journal for Research in Mathematics Education, 21,* 273–280.

Fuson, K. C. (1991). *Addition and subtraction word problems: An instructional intervention using schematic drawings.* Manuscript in preparation.

Fuson, K. C. (in press). Research on whole number addition and subtraction. In D. Grouws (Ed.), *Handbook of research on mathematics teaching and learning.* New York Macmillan.

Fuson, K. C., & Briars, D. J. (1990). Using a base-ten blocks learning/teaching approach for first- and second-grade place-value and multidigit addition and subtraction. *Journal for Research in Mathematics Education, 21,* 180–206.

Fuson, K. C., & Burghardt, B. H. (1991). *Children's invented procedures for multidigit addition and subtraction.* Manuscript in preparation.

Fuson, K. C., Fraivillig, J. L., & Burghardt, B. H. (in press). Relationships children construct among English number words, multiunit base-ten blocks, and written multidigit addition. In J. Campbell (Ed.), *The nature and origins of mathematical skills.* North Holland: Elsevier Science.

Fuson, K. C., & Fuson, A. (in press). Instruction supporting children's counting on for addition and counting up for subtraction. *Journal for Research in Mathematics Education.*

Fuson, K. C., & Hall, J. W. (1983). The acquisition of early number word meanings. In H. Ginsburg (Ed.), *The development of children's mathematical thinking* (pp. 49–107). New York: Academic.

Fuson, K. C., & Kwon, Y. (1991). Learning addition and subtraction: Effects of number words and other cultural tools [Systemes de mots nombres et autres outils culturels: effets sur les premiers calculs de l'enfant]. In J. Bideaud, C. Meljac, & J. P. Fischer (Eds.), *Les chemins du nombre (Pathways to number)* (pp. 351–374). Villeneuve d'Ascq, France: Presses Universitaire de Lille and Hillsdale, NJ: Lawrence Erlbaum Associates.

Fuson, K. C., & Kwon, Y. (in press-a). Korean children's single-digit addition and subtraction: Numbers structured by ten. *Journal for Research in Mathematics Education.*

Fuson, K. C., & Kwon, Y. (in press-b). Korean children's understanding of multidigit addition and subtraction. *Child Development.*

Fuson, K. C., Richards, J., & Briars, D. J. (1982). The acquisition and elaboration of the number word sequence. In C. Brainerd (Ed.), *Progress in cognitive development research: Vol. 1. Children's logical and mathematical cognition* (pp. 33–92). New York: Springer-Verlag.

Fuson, K. C., & Secada, W. G. (1986). Teaching children to add by counting on with finger patterns. *Cognition and Instruction, 3,* 229–260.

Fuson, K. C., Stigler, J. W., & Bartsch, K. (1988). Grade placement of addition and subtraction topics in China, Japan, the Soviet Union, Taiwan, and the United States. *Journal for Research in Mathematics Education, 19,* 449–458.

Fuson, K. C., & Willis, G. B. (1986). First and second graders' performance on compare and equalize word problems. In *Proceedings of the Tenth International Conference on the Psychology of Mathematics Education* (pp. 19–24). London: University of London Institute of Education.

Fuson, K. C., & Willis, G. B. (1987). [Children's conceptual structures and solution procedures for Compare word problems]. Unpublished raw data.

Fuson, K. C., & Willis, G. B. (1988). Subtracting by counting up: More evidence. *Journal for Research in Mathematics Education, 19,* 402–420.

Fuson, K. C., & Willis, G. B. (1989). Second graders' use of schematic drawings in solving addition & subtraction word problems. *Journal of Educational Psychology, 81,* 514–520.

Gelman, R., & Gallistel, C. R. (1978). *The child's understanding of number.* Cambridge, MA: Harvard University Press.

Ginsburg, H. P. (1977). *Children's arithmetic: The learning process.* New York: Van Nostrand.

Ginsburg, H. P., & Russell, R. L. (1981). Social class and racial influences on early mathematical thinking. *Monographs of the Society for Research in Child Development, 46* (6, Serial No. 193).

Greeno, J. G. (1983). Forms of understanding in mathematical problem solving. In S. G. Paris, G. M. Olson, & W. H. Stevenson (Eds.), *Learning and motivation in the classroom* (pp. 83–111). Hillsdale, NJ: Lawrence Erlbaum Associates.

Greeno, J. G. (1987). Instructional representations based on research about understanding. In A. H. Schoenfeld (Ed.), *Cognitive science and mathematics education* (pp. 61–88). Hillsdale, NJ: Lawrence Erlbaum Associates.

Groen, G. J., & Parkman, J. M. (1972). A chronometric analysis of simple addition. *Psychological Review, 79,* 329–343.

Hall, J. W., Fuson, K. C., & Willis, G. B. (1985). Teaching counting on for addition and counting up for subtraction. In L. Streefland (Ed.), *Proceedings of the ninth annual meeting of the International Group for the Psychology of Mathematics Education* (pp. 322–327). Utrecht, Netherlands: Research Group on Mathematics Education and Educational Computer Center.

Hamann, M. S., & Ashcraft, M. H. (1986). Textbook presentations of the basic addition facts. *Cognition and Instruction, 3,* 173–192.

Hart, K. M. (1987). Practical work and formalisation, too great a gap. In J. C. Bergeron, N. Herscovics, & C. Kieran (Eds.), *Proceedings from the Eleventh International Conference for the Psychology of Mathematics Education* (Vol. 2, pp. 408–415). Montreal.

Hatano, G. (1982). Learning to add and subtract: A Japanese perspective. In T. P. Carpenter, J. M. Moser, & T. A. Romberg (Eds.), *Addition and subtraction: A cognitive perspective* (pp. 211–223). Hillsdale, NJ: Lawrence Erlbaum Associates.

Hedges, L., Stodolsky, S., & Mathieson, M. S. (1987). *A formative evaluation of kindergarten Everyday Mathematics.* Chicago: The University of Chicago School Mathematics Project.

Heinrichs, J., Yurko, D. S., & Hu, J. M. (1981). Two-digit number comparison: Use of place information. *Journal of Experimental Psychology: Human Perception and Performance, 7,* 890–901.

Hendrickson, D. (1983). Prevention or cure? Another look at mathematics learning problems. In *Interdisciplinary Voices in Learning Disabilities* (pp. 93–106). Austin, TX: Pro. Ed.

Hiebert, J. (1984). Children's mathematics learning: The struggle to link form and understanding. *The Elementary School Journal, 84,* 497–513.

Houlihan, D. M., & Ginsburg, H. P. (1981). The addition methods of first- and second-grade children. *Journal for Research in Mathematics Education, 12,* 95–106.

Hudson, T. (1983). Correspondences and numerical differences between joint sets. *Child Development, 54,* 84–90.

Hutchings, B. (1975). Low-stress subtraction. *Arithmetic Teacher, 22,* 226–232.

Joslyn, R. E. (1990). Using concrete models to teach large-number concepts. *Arithmetic Teacher, 38*(3), 6–9.

Kamii, C. K. (1985). *Young children reinvent arithmetic: Implications of Piaget's theory.* New York: Teachers College Press.

Kamii, C. (1986). Place value: An explanation of its difficulty and educational implications for the primary grades. *Journal of Research in Childhood Education, 1*(2), 75–85.

Kamii, C. (1989). *Young children continue to reinvent arithmetic-2nd grade: Implications of Piaget's theory.* New York: Teachers College Press.

Kamii, C., & Joseph, L. (1988). Teaching place value and double-column addition. *Arithmetic Teacher, 35*(6), 48–52.

Kamii, M. (1982). *Children's graphic representation of numerical concepts: A developmental study.* Unpublished doctoral dissertation, Harvard University, Cambridge, MA.

Kaufman, E. L., Lord, M. W., Reese, T. W., & Volkmann, J. (1949). The discrimination of visual number. *American Journal of Psychology, 62,* 498–525.

Kaye, D. B., Post, T. A., Hall, V. C., & Dineen, J. T. (1986). Emergence of information-retrieval strategies in numerical cognition: A developmental study. *Cognition and Instruction, 3,* 127–150.

Kintsch, W., & Greeno, J. G. (1985). Understanding and solving word arithmetic problems. *Psychological Review, 92,* 109–129.

Klahr, D., & Wallace, J. G. (1973). The role of quantification operators in the development of conservation of quantity. *Cognitive Psychology, 4,* 301–327.

Klahr, D., & Wallace, J. G. (1976). *Cognitive development: An information processing view.* Hillsdale, NJ: Lawrence Erlbaum Associates.

Kouba, V. L., Brown, C. A., Carpenter, T. P., Lindquist, M. M., Silver, E. A., & Swafford, J. O. (1988). Results of the fourth NAEP assessment of mathematics: Number, operations, and word problems. *Arithmetic Teacher, 35*(8), 14–19.

Labinowicz, E. (1985). *Learning from children: New beginnings for teaching numerical thinking.* Menlo Park, CA: Addison-Wesley.

Labinowicz, E. (1989, March). *Tens as numerical building blocks.* Paper presented at the annual meeting of the American Educational Research Association, San Francisco.

Leinhardt, G. (1987). The development of an expert explanation: An analysis of a sequence of subtraction lessons. *Cognition and Instruction, 4,* 225–282.

Lindvall, C. M., & Ibarra, C. G. (1980, April). *A clinical investigation of the difficulties evidenced by kindergarten children in developing "models" in the solution of arithmetic story problems.* Paper presented at the annual meeting of the American Educational Research Association, Boston.

Lorton, M. B. (1972). *Workjobs.* Menlo Park, CA: Addison-Wesley.

Lorton, M. B. (1976). *Mathematics their way.* Menlo Park, CA: Addison-Wesley.

Madell, R. (1985). Children's natural processes. *Arithmetic Teacher, 32*(7), 20–22.

Mandler, G., & Shebo, B. J. (1982). Subitizing: An analysis of its component processes. *Journal of Experimental Psychology: General, 111,* 1–22.

McCloskey, M., Sokol, S. M., & Goodman, R. A. (1986). Cognitive processes in verbal-number production: Inferences from the performance of brain-damaged subjects. *Journal of Experimental Psychology: General, 115,* 307–330.

Menninger, K. (1969). *Number words and number symbols: A cultural history of numbers* (P. Broneer, Trans.). Cambridge, MA: MIT Press. (Original work published 1958).

Michie, S. (1984a). Number understanding in preschool children. *British Journal of Educational Psychology, 54,* 245–253.

Michie, S. (1984b). Why preschoolers are reluctant to count spontaneously. *British Journal of Developmental Psychology, 2,* 347–358.

Miller, K., & Stigler, J. W. (1987). Computing in Chinese: Cultural variation in a basic cognitive skill. *Cognitive Development, 2,* 279–305.

Miura, I. T. (1987). Mathematics achievement as a function of language. *Journal of Educational Psychology, 79,* 79–82.

Miura, I., Kim, C. C., Chang, C., & Okamoto, Y. (1988). Effects of language characteristics on children's cognitive representation of number: Cross-national comparisons. *Child Development, 59,* 1445–1450.

Miura, I., & Okamoto, Y. (1989). Comparisons of American and Japanese first graders' cognitive representation of number and understanding of place value. *Journal of Educational Psychology, 81,* 109–113.

Mumme, J., & Shepherd, N. (1990). Implementing the standards: Communication in mathematics. *Arithmetic Teacher, 38*(1), 18–22.

Nesher, P. (1986, April). *Are mathematical understanding and algorithmic performance related?* Invited address for the annual meeting of the American Educational Research Association, San Francisco.

Nesher, P., & Katriel, T. (1977). A semantic analysis of addition and subtraction word problems in arithmetic. *Educational Studies in Mathematics, 8,* 251–269.

Nicholls, J. G., Cobb, P., Wood, T., Yackel, E., & Patashnick, M. (1990). Assessing students' theories of success in mathematics: Individual and classroom differences. *Journal for Research in Mathematics Education, 21,* 109–122.

Piaget, J. (1941/1965). *The child's conception of number.* New York: Norton (Trans. and published in English, New York: Humanities, 1952, from original publication with A. Szemiska, *La Genese Du Nombre Chez l'Infant,* 1941.)

Putnam, R. T. (1987). Structuring and adjusting content for students: A study of live and simulated tutoring of addition. *American Educational Research Journal, 24,* 13–48.

Putnam, R. T., deBettencourt, L. U., & Leinhardt, G. (1990). Understanding of derived-fact strategies in addition and subtraction. *Cognition and Instruction, 7,* 245–285.

Rathmell, E. C. (1978). Using thinking strategies to teach the basic facts. In M. Suydam & R. Reys (Eds.), *Developing computational skills* (1978 Yearbook of the National Council of Teachers of Mathematics, pp. 13–38), Reston, VA: NCTM.

Rathmell, E. C. (1986). Helping children learn to solve story problems. In A. Zollman, W. Speer, & J. Meyer (Eds.), *The fifth mathematics methods conference papers.* Bowling Green, OH: Bowling Green State University.

Resnick, L. B. (1982). Syntax and semantics in learning to subtract. In T. P. Carpenter, J. M. Moser, & T. A. Romberg (Eds.), *Addition and subtraction: A cognitive perspective* (pp. 136–155). Hillsdale, NJ: Lawrence Erlbaum Associates.

Resnick, L. B. (1983). A developmental theory of number understanding. In H. P. Ginsburg (Ed.), *The development of mathematical thinking* (pp. 109–151). New York: Academic.

Resnick, L. B. (1987). Constructing knowledge in school. In L. S. Liben (Ed.), *Development and learning: Conflict or congruence?* (pp. 19–50). Hillsdale, NJ: Lawrence Erlbaum Associates.

Resnick, L. B., & Ford, W. W. (1981). *The psychology of mathematics for instruction.* Hillsdale, NJ: Lawrence Erlbaum Associates.

Resnick, L. B., & Omanson, S. F. (1987). Learning to understand arithmetic. In R. Glaser (Ed.),

Advances in instructional psychology (Vol. 3, pp. 41–95). Hillsdale, NJ: Lawrence Erlbaum Associates.

Richards, J., & Carter, R. (1982). The numeration system. In S. Wagner (Ed.), *Proceedings of the fourth annual meeting of the North American chapter of the International Group for the Psychology of Mathematics Education* (pp. 57–63). Athens, GA.

Riley, M. S. (1981). *Conceptual and procedural knowledge in development.* Unpublished master's thesis, University of Pittsburgh.

Riley, M. S., & Greeno, J. G. (1988). Developmental analysis of understanding language about quantities and of solving problems. *Cognition and Instruction, 5,* 49–101.

Riley, M. S., Greeno, J. G., & Heller, J. I. (1983). Development of children's problem-solving ability in arithmetic. In H. Ginsburg (Ed.), *The development of mathematical thinking* (pp. 153–196). New York: Academic.

Ross, S. H. (1986, April). *The development of children's place-value numeration concepts in grades two through five.* Paper presented at the annual meeting of the American Educational Research Association, San Francisco.

Ross, S. H. (1988, April). *The roles of cognitive development and instruction in children's acquisition of place-value numeration concepts.* Paper presented at the annual meeting of the National Council of Teachers of Mathematics, Chicago.

Ross, S. H. (1989). Parts, wholes, and place value: A developmental view. *Arithmetic Teacher, 36*(6), 47–51.

Saxe, G. B. (1982). Culture and the development of numerical cognition: Studies among the Oksapmin of Papua New Guinea. In C. J. Brainerd (Ed.), *Progress in cognitive development research: Vol. 1. Children's logical and mathematical cognition* (pp. 157–176). New York: Springer-Verlag.

Saxe, G. B., Guberman, S. R., & Gearhart, M. (1987). Social processes in early number development. *Monographs of the Society for Research in Child Development, 52*(2, Serial No. 216).

Schaeffer, B., Eggleston, V. H., & Scott, J. L. (1974). Number development in young children. *Cognitive Psychology, 6,* 357–379.

Schoenfeld, A. H. (1986). On having and using geometric knowledge. In J. Hiebert (Ed.), *Conceptual and procedural knowledge: The case of mathematics* (pp. 225–264). Hillsdale, NJ: Lawrence Erlbaum Associates.

Secada, W. G. (1982, March). *The use of counting for subtraction.* Paper presented at the annual meeting of the American Educational Research Association, New York.

Secada, W. G. (1985). Counting in sign: The number string, accuracy and use. *Dissertation Abstracts International, 45,* 3571A–3572A.

Secada, W. G., Fuson, K. C., & Hall, J. W. (1983). The transition from counting-all to counting-on in addition. *Journal for Research in Mathematics Education, 14,* 47–57.

Siegler, R. S. (1981). Developmental sequences within and between concepts. *Monographs of the Society for Research in Child Development, 46*(2, Serial No. 189).

Siegler, R. S. (1987a). The perils of averaging data over strategies: An example from children's addition. *Journal of Experimental Psychology: General, 116,* 250–264.

Siegler, R. S. (1987b). Strategy choices in subtraction. In J. A. Sloboda & D. Rogers (Eds.), *Cognitive processes in mathematics* (pp. 81–106). New York: Oxford University Press.

Siegler, R. S. (1988). Individual differences in strategy choices: Good students, not-so-good students, and perfectionists. *Child Development, 59,* 833–851.

Siegler, R. S. (1989). The hazards of mental chronometry: An example from children's subtraction. *Journal of Education Psychology, 81,* 497–506.

Siegler, R. S., & Campbell, J. (1990). Diagnosing individual differences in strategy choice procedures. In N. Frederiksen, R. Glaser, A. Lesgold, & M. G. Shafto (Eds.), *Diagnostic monitoring of knowledge and skill acquisition* (pp. 113–140. Hillsdale, NJ: Lawrence Erlbaum Associates.

Siegler, R. S., & Jenkins, E. (1989). *How children discover new strategies.* Hillsdale, NJ: Lawrence Erlbaum Associates.

Siegler, R. S., & Robinson, M. (1982). The development of numerical understandings. In H. W. Reese & L. P. Lipsitt (Eds.), *Advances in child development and behaviour* (Vol. 16, pp. 242–312). New York: Academic.

Siegler, R. S., & Shipley, C. (1987). The role of learning in children's strategy choices. In L. S. Liben (Ed.), *Development & learning: Conflict or congruence* (pp. 71–107). Hillsdale, NJ: Lawrence Erlbaum Associates.

Siegler, R. S., & Shrager, J. (1984). Strategy choices in addition and subtraction: How do children know what to do. In C. Sophian (Ed.), *Origins of cognitive skills* (pp. 229–293). Hillsdale, NJ: Lawrence Erlbaum Associates.

Skemp, R. R. (1979). *Intelligence, learning, and action.* Chichester, England: Wiley.

Skemp, R. R. (1981). Symbolic understanding. In T. R. Post & M. P. Roberts (Eds.), *Psychology of mathematics education: Proceedings of the annual meeting of the North American chapter of the International Group for the Psychology of Mathematics Education* (Vol. 3, pp. 160–166). Minneapolis.

Song, M. J., & Ginsburg, H. P. (1987). The development of informal and formal mathematical thinking in Korean and US children. *Child Development, 58,* 1286–1296.

Starkey, P. (1987, April). *Early arithmetic competencies.* Paper presented at biennial meeting of Society for Research in Child Development, Baltimore.

Starkey, P., & Gelman, R. (1982). The development of addition and subtraction abilities prior to formal schooling in arithmetic. In T. P. Carpenter, J. M. Moser, & T. A. Romberg (Eds.), *Addition and subtraction: A cognitive perspective* (pp. 99–116). Hillsdale, NJ: Lawrence Erlbaum Associates.

Steffe, L. P., & Cobb, P. (1988). *Construction of arithmetical meanings and strategies.* New York: Springer-Verlag.

Steffe, L. P., & von Glasersfeld, E. (1983). The construction of arithmetical units. In J. C. Bergeron & N. Herscovics (Eds.), *Proceedings of the fifth annual meeting of the North American chapter of the International Group for the Psychology of Mathematics Education* (pp. 292–304). Montreal.

Steffe, L. P., von Glasersfeld, E., Richards, J., & Cobb, P. (1983). *Children's counting types: Philosophy, theory, and application.* New York: Praeger Scientific.

Steinberg, R. (1984). A teaching experiment of the learning of addition and subtraction facts. *Dissertation Abstracts International, 44,* 3313A.

Steinberg, R. M. (1985). Instruction on derived facts strategies in addition and subtraction. *Journal for Research in Mathematics Education, 16,* 337–355.

Stigler, J. W. (1988). The use of verbal explanation in Japanese and American classrooms. *Arithmetic Teacher, 36*(2), 27–29.

Stigler, J. W., Fuson, K. C., Ham, M., & Kim, M. S. (1986). An analysis of addition and subtraction word problems in American and Soviet elementary mathematics textbooks. *Cognition and Instruction, 3,* 153–171.

Stigler, J. W., Lee, S. Y., & Stevenson, H. W. (1987). Mathematics classrooms in Japan, Taiwan, and the United States. *Child Development, 58,* 1272–1285.

Stigler, J. W., Lee, S. Y., & Stevenson, H. W. (1990). *The mathematical knowledge of Japanese, Chinese, and American elementary school children.* Reston, VA: National Council of Teachers of Mathematics.

Tamburino, J. L. (1982). *The effects of knowledge-based instruction on the abilities of primary grade children in arithmetic word problem solving.* Unpublished doctoral dissertation, University of Pittsburgh.

Thompson, C., & Hendrickson, A. D. (1983). Verbal addition and subtraction problems: New research focusing on levels of difficulty of the problems and of the related number sentences. *Focus on Learning Problems in Mathematics, 5,* 33–45.

Thompson, P. (1991, April). *Representations, principles, and constraints: Contributions to the effective use of concrete manipulatives.* Paper presented at the annual meeting of the American Educational Research Association, Chicago.

Thompson, P. W. (1982). A theoretical framework for understanding young children's concepts of whole number numeration. *Dissertation Abstracts International, 43,* 1868A.

Thornton, C. A. (1978). Emphasizing thinking strategies in basic fact instruction. *Journal for Research in Mathematics Education, 9,* 214–227.

Thornton, C. A. (1990). Solution strategies: Subtraction number facts. *Education Studies in Mathematics, 21,* 241–263.

Thornton, C. A., & Smith, P. J. (1988). Action research: Strategies for learning subtraction facts. *Arithmetic Teacher, 35*(8), 8–12.

Tougher, H. E. (1981). Too many blanks! What workbooks don't teach. *Arithmetic Teacher, 28*(6), 67.

The University of Chicago School Mathematics Project (1987). *Kindergarten Everyday Mathematics.* The University of Chicago, UCSMP.

VanLehn, K. (1986). Arithmetic procedures are induced from examples. In J. Hiebert (Ed.), *Conceptual and procedural knowledge: The case of mathematics* (pp. 133–179). Hillsdale, NJ: Lawrence Erlbaum Associates.

von Glasersfeld, E. (1982). Subitizing: The role of figural patterns in the development of numerical concepts. *Archives de Psychologie, 50,* 191–218.

Wagner, S., & Walters, J. A. (1982). A longitudinal analysis of early number concepts: From numbers to number. In G. Forman (Ed.), *Action and thought* (pp. 137–161). New York: Academic.

Walters, J. A., & Wagner, S. (1981, April). *The earliest numbers.* Paper presented at the biennial meetings of the Society for Research in Child Development, Boston.

Wheeler, D. (1977). (Ed.). *Notes on mathematics for children.* London: Cambridge University Press.

Willis, G. B., & Fuson, K. C. (1985). Teaching representational schemes for the more difficult addition and subtraction verbal problems. In S. K. Damarin & M. Shelton (Eds.), *Proceedings of the North American chapter of the International Group for the Psychology of Mathematics Education* (pp. 288–293). Columbus, OH.

Willis, G. B., & Fuson, K. C. (1988). Teaching children to use schematic drawings to solve addition and subtraction word problems. *Journal of Educational Psychology, 80,* 192–201.

Wirtz, R. (1980). *New beginnings: A guide to think, talk, and read math centers for beginners.* Monterey, CA: Curriculum Development Associates.

Wolters, M. A. D. (1983). The part–whole schema and arithmetical problems. *Educational Studies in Mathematics, 14,* 127–138.

Woods, S. S., Resnick, L. B., & Groen, G. J. (1975). An experimental test of five process models for subtraction. *Journal of Educational Psychology, 67,* 17–21.

Yackel, E., Cobb, P., & Wood, T. (1991). Small-group interactions as a source of learning opportunities in second-grade mathematics. *Journal for Research in Mathematics Education Monograph, 22,* 390–408.

3

SOLVING MULTIPLICATION WORD PROBLEMS

Pearla Nesher
University of Haifa

What makes word problems so difficult? Can we teach children how to solve word problems? To answer these questions one has to understand better the processes involved in solving word problems. The emphasis here is on word problems rather than on solving problems that involve only numerical symbols. Researchers now assume that several cognitive processes are involved in solving word problems. Nathan, Kintsch, and Lewis (1988) argued, for example, that the process of solving algebra word problems has multiple layers: In reading the text, the problem solver should understand the gist of each phrase and construct a propositional representation that will serve as a *textbase* to which the solver attends during solution; the problem solver also must construct a *situation model*—a qualitative representation of the actual situation described in the text; the problem solver then must draw on problem schemata to construct a formal representation of the given problem (Kintsch, 1986; Kintsch & Greeno, 1985); and, finally, the problem solver must calculate the numeric solution from the problem's formal representation. These processes play a significant role in solving arithmetic word problems as well as in algebra; in fact, these aspects of problem solving first were studied with elementary additive word problems (Nesher, Greeno, & Riley, 1982; Riley, Greeno, & Heller, 1983).

Clearly, in solving word problems one starts with the linguistic text and ends with the numerical solution. However, the research cited previously demonstrates that the process is not a mere translation from one language into another. Rather, the problem-solving process is an elaboration under given schemata that one acquires while learning to solve different classes of word problems. The role and nature of problem schemata have been the target of extensive research on additive word problems. In this chapter, we first try to learn from the additive case, and we then move to an analysis of multiplicative situations with the intention of discovering the basic multiplicative problem types. Analyses of the types of multiplication word problems represent three major approaches to studying this domain. The first approach (Bell, Greer, Mangan, & Grimison, 1989; Fischbein, Deri, Nello, & Marino, 1985) deals with multiplication word problems from the point of view of implicit primitive psychological models; the second approach (Schwartz, 1979, 1981, 1988; Vergnaud, 1983, 1988) employs a dimensional analysis; and the third (Nesher, 1988a, 1988b; Nesher & Katriel, 1978), which is emphasized in this chapter, focuses on analysis of the text itself. Each approach regards different factors as the key in explaining categories of multiplicative word problems.

LEARNING FROM THE ADDITIVE CASE

One of the more surprising findings in the last decade of research on additive word problems in arithmetic is that word problems with the same logical structure and calling for the same mathematical operation behave differently from the point of view of the solver. Nesher et al. (1982) found subtraction word problems like the following to be very easy for students: "Dan had 10 dollars. How many dollars are left, if Dan has spent 3?" The percentage of second and third graders in four schools solving such problems correctly was: first school, 94% ($n = 967$); second school, 89% ($n = 222$); third school, 89% ($n = 256$); and fourth school, 85% ($n = 287$). However, students were much less successful on subtraction problems of the following type: "Joseph and Ronald had 7 marbles altogether. 3 of them were Joseph's. How many of them were Ronald's?" Here, the percentage of success in the same four schools was 52%, 46%, 49%, and 41%, respectively. One therefore can conclude that the kind of operation to be executed in solving the word problem—subtraction in both of the aforementioned problems—is not what determines problem difficulty. Other variables should be examined to explain this large difference in performance.

In the last decade, researchers from many countries (Belgium, France, Israel, and the United States) repeatedly have noted the same well-defined regularities in addition and subtraction word problems and have tried to seek an explanation for the phenomenon (Carpenter, Hiebert, & Moser, 1981; Carpenter & Moser, 1982, 1984; De Corte & Verschaffel, 1985, 1987; Nesher & Katriel, 1977, 1978; Nesher & Teubal, 1974; Riley et al., 1983; Vergnaud, 1982). Analysis of the additive word problems has led to their classification into three main semantic categories: (a) *combine* problems, which are static in nature and involve the combining of two or more sets; (b) *change* problems, which are dynamic in nature, describe an ongoing event, and have a clear sequentiality along time; and (c) additive *compare* problems, which compare one quantity in relation to another.

In the extensive research on how children solve additive word problems, many other structural variables that contribute to the child's level of performance have been noted. Some of these variables are semantic, some are syntactic, some deal with numerical aspects, and some concern pragmatic aspects of the problem context. All of these variables were shown to be significant in problems that involve the same mathematical operation.

A particularly significant finding was that the well-defined text of an additive word problem has a specific structure. This structure consists of three well-defined strings, each with a special role in describing the situation that calls for addition or subtraction. Two of these strings carry the given numerical information whereas the third one asks for the third missing number (i.e., the question in the text). For example:

String 1 (information): Joseph and Roland had 7 marbles altogether.

String 2 (information): 4 of them were Joseph's.

String 3 (question):   How many of them were Roland's?

Because all the information for the specific problem is given in a textual form, there are several linguistic variables to be considered. Several variables have been found to influence the difficulty of additive word problems, among them:

1. The location of the string describing the missing number, or the question string. For example, is the missing number the first, the second, or

the third number in the equation that describes the situation? In the following text, the question appears first: "How many marbles does Ron have now,
if he had 6 marbles in the morning and lost two of them during the day?"
Research findings show that the location of the question string in the text
influences problem difficulty, and, in contrast to our intuition and habits in
presenting word problems, problems in which the question is at the end
(e.g., "Ron had 6 marbles in the morning and he lost two of them during the
day. How many marbles does Ron have now?") are not necessarily the
easiest for the child.

2. The relation between the order of the text and the order of the events
described in the text (e.g., "John now has 8 marbles after he received 3
marbles from his brother. How many marbles did he have to start with?").
Note that the question here is in the third string. But, in reality, the order of
the events in this problem contradicts the order of the information given in
the text. Problems in which the order of events does not coincide with the
order of description in the text are harder for young children than problems in which the order in the text mirrors the order of the events.

3. The presence or absence of words that serve as cue words for certain
operations (such as *more* for addition and *less* for subtraction). Nesher and
Teubal (1974) demonstrated that the habit of solving word problems based
on these key words may hinder the capability of correctly solving both
word problems in which such cues do not appear, and problems in which
they appear in other roles, thus serving as distractions for some children
(for example, "Joe has 10 marbles and that is 4 marbles more than Ron has;
how many marbles does Ron have?"). In this example the appearance of the
word *more* in the text serves as a distraction rather than a hint to those
who relate the word *more* to the addition operation.

4. The familiarity of the child with the described situation (i.e., the
context). This is an obvious factor that should be taken into account in
presenting word problems to children. For example, contexts related to the
child's life, such as school life, games, or money, will be easier than more
remote situations taken from geometry or science.

To evaluate the relative impact of each variable, various researchers
have carried out well-controlled studies. It is now possible to arrange
additive word problems according to their underlying scheme and to incorporate them into the curriculum in a more consistent and meaningful
manner. From a practical point of view, this means that we can estimate
what kinds of problems can be solved successfully by a child who has
reached a certain cognitive development.

A lesson learned from studying additive word problems is that mathematical tasks cannot be studied merely according to their mathematical
structure. Word problems that share the same mathematical structure can

differ from a psychological point of view. Research on the psychological aspects and demands of the task and an understanding of the child's cognitive development is crucial for the understanding of the difficulties that children face in learning mathematics. Note that the specific mathematical tasks confronting the child are the basis for the aforementioned kind of analysis. Ideally, we need to study both the analysis of the task and the ways in which the child actually solves the problems.

THE MULTIPLICATIVE CASE: WHAT BASIC SITUATIONS ARE MODELED BY MULTIPLICATION?

Researchers studying multiplicative word problems have considered many of the same sorts of variables as those studied for additive problems. Research on multiplicative problems falls into three main approaches, each taking a slightly different perspective. In the sections that follow, I present each approach, its major research findings, and its instructional implications. Part of this analysis appeared in Nesher (1988b); it is repeated here as a general framework within which new research findings are presented.

The First Approach: Implicit Models

The first major approach to research on word problems is based on theoretical work by Fischbein et al. (1985), in which they claimed that implicitly held models account for children's performance on multiplicative tasks: "Each fundamental operation of arithmetic generally remains linked to an implicit, unconscious, and primitive intuitive model. Identification of the operation needed to solve a problem with two items of numerical data takes place not directly but as mediated by the model. The model imposes its own constraints on the search process" (p. 4).

Fischbein et al. (1985) claimed that the primitive model associated with multiplication is repeated addition. Thus, 3×7 can be viewed as $7 + 7 + 7$. In their analysis of multiplicative word problems, several researchers within this approach (Bell, Fischbein, & Greer, 1984) maintained that multiplication word problems should be divided into symmetrical and asymmetrical situations. In asymmetrical cases the two factors comprising the multiplication are assigned different roles: the *multiplier* and the *multiplicand* (e.g., liters times cost per liter). In symmetrical situations the roles of the two factors are easily interchangeable (e.g., length times width for computing area). Researchers studying multiplication problems under the assertion of repeated addition deal only with the asymmetrical cases, which are further categorized mainly according to their context. Bell et al. (1984) and Greer (1987, 1988) studied the following kinds of asymmetrical situations:

Multiple groups	3 boxes contain 4 eggs each. How many eggs are there altogether?
Iterated measures	A gardener needs 3 pieces of string each 4.6 meters long. How much string should he buy?
Rate	A man walked at an average speed of 4.6 miles per hour for 3.2 hours. How far did he walk?
Measure	A gallon is about 4.6 liters. About how many liters are there in 3.2 gallons?
Price	A carpenter buys polish which is priced at $8 per liter. If he buys 6 liters, how much does it cost?
Speed	On a trip a donkey moves at a speed of 6 miles per hour. How far does the donkey travel in 4.39 hours?
Currency conversion	If a man wants to buy a gift that is worth £0.56, how many kroners does he need? (In Denmark the rate of exchange is 14 kroner per pound.)

Symmetrical cases mentioned by Bell et al. and Greer that do not fall under the repeated addition model are area and possible combinations (e.g., How many different outfits can one arrange from 3 blouses and 2 pairs of pants?).

Fischbein et al. (1985) also argued that the asymmetry of multiplication leads children to link division to two primitive models, the *quotitive* and *partitive* models for division. In the quotitive model, the total amount and the size of the equal set are known and one is asked to find out how many sets are in question (e.g., "There are altogether 50 books in the room. On each shelf there are 10 books. How many shelves are there in the room?"). In the partitive model, the total number of objects and the number of sets are known and the child is asked to find out the number of objects in each set (e.g., "In the room there are 50 books altogether arranged on 5 shelves. How many books are there on each shelf?").

Empirical Findings for the Implicit Models

The research paradigm used by Fischbein et al. (1985) involved varying the numbers in the same word problem. Children demonstrated difficulty solving problems in which the multiplier (or operator) was a decimal number and therefore not easily interpreted as "times" (e.g., it is awkward to speak of "1.23 times of . . . "). This difficulty of children dealing with decimal operators (replacing "times") was the basis for Fischbein et al.'s theory about implicit models that determine children's performance.

Fischbein et al.'s (1985) empirical findings were replicated with children and adults several times (De Corte, Verschaffel, & Van Collie, 1988; Graeber & Tirosh, 1988; Greer, 1987; Greer & Mangan, 1984, 1986; Luke, 1988; Tirosh, Graeber, & Glover, 1986; Zeldis-Avissar, 1985). Within the Fischbein et al. paradigm researchers have examined mainly the asymmetrical cases, in which the multiplicand and multiplier are distinguished in terms of the situations described. For example, in the problem, "There are 5 desks in the room; each has 4 legs . . . ," the number of desks is the multiplier whereas the number of legs per desk is the multiplicand. Typically, researchers in this tradition presented children with several sets of such asymmetrical problems and manipulated the kinds of numbers appearing the multiplicand and multiplier positions. Children were asked to choose the correct operation; they were not asked to solve the problem numerically and therefore could not receive feedback from the numerical answer to the problem. These studies established that numbers appearing in the two distinct roles of multiplicand and multiplier affect differently a problem's difficulty, with children's ability to identify the proper operation being affected strongly by the kind of numbers appearing in the multiplier position and not in the multiplicand position (Graeber & Tirosh, 1988; Greer, 1988; Mangan, 1986; Verschaffel, De Corte, & Van Collie, 1988). Children performed significantly better on problems with an integer as the multiplier than when the multiplier was a decimal larger than 1. Problems with a multiplier smaller than 1 were the hardest. Such an effect was not observed with different numbers in the multiplicand position.

By interviewing children, Bell et al. (1984) were able to analyze the kinds of errors children made on these word-problem tasks. They found that children believe multiplication makes the result bigger and division makes it smaller, regardless of the numbers involved. Their findings also supported the claim that children look at these asymmetrical cases of multiplication as if they were repeated addition. Therefore, children could interpret situations in which the number of the multiplier was an integer. But when the multiplier was any other kind of number (e.g., a decimal or a fraction), children were unable to translate the multiplicative situation into a "times" situation resembling the repeated addition operation.

As mentioned earlier, studies in which the numbers were manipulated in the multiplicand and multiplier position were replicated several times. The last replication reported was by Verschaffel et al. (1988). Their study supports again most of the findings reported before, but they also studied symmetrical problems, in which the multiplicand and multiplier are interchangeable. Verschaffel et al. found that the effect of varying numbers holds only for asymmetrical problems, in which the multiplier and multiplicand have distinctively different roles. In the symmetrical cases they examined, such as finding an area of a rectangle, varying the type of number serving as multiplier did not affect problem difficulty. Verschaffel et al. suggested that, in addition to the repeated addition model for multiplication, there may be other primitive models of multiplication that impose constraints other than those found for the asymmetrical problems.

Instructional Implications from the Implicit
Models Approach

Graeber and Tirosh (1988) studied the effect of decimal numbers on multiplication and division with fourth and fifth graders in a study that replicated the work of Bell et al. (1984) and Greer and Mangan (1984, 1986) within this paradigm. Graeber and Tirosh studied the misconceptions, "multiplication always makes bigger," "division always makes smaller," and "the divisor must be smaller than the dividend." Based on their study, conducted in both Israel and the United States, Graeber and Tirosh recommended several instructional moves:

1. Introduce multiplication involving decimals less than 1 in a word-problem setting with a whole number multiplier. Repeated addition might even be used to justify answers perhaps using a number line to illustrate.
2. Interpret currency problems in terms of decimal notation.
3. Use the area model for multiplication with whole numbers.
4. Use the partitive model for division with whole numbers and extend it to a simple expression involving decimal divisors that allow for reasoning about the answer.
5. Contrast the results of multiplication with those of division by a decimal less than one with the results of the operation with factors greater than one.
6. Introduce word problems with decimal operators. Discuss the problem structure and estimate the anticipated answer.
7. Explore the extension of the commutative property to indicate products involving decimal and whole numbers.
8. Use both decimal notation and common fraction notation to perform the same calculation. Compare results.

(Taken from Graeber & Tirosh, 1988).

One can assume that the belief that multiplication makes bigger and division makes smaller is a natural outcome of current teaching about whole numbers. The middle-school teacher always will be in the position of having to undo part of this earlier learning. The research of Graeber and Tirosh (1988) made explicit aspects of earlier learning that cause major difficulties in further learning of multiplication and division. Future instruction that takes these recommendations into account may reduce false beliefs of students concerning multiplication and division.

The Second Approach: Dimensional Analysis

Schwartz (1979, 1981, 1988) and Vergnaud (1983, 1988) take a different approach to studying multiplication word problems. This brief description of their approach draws heavily on a previous account (Nesher, 1988b). Both Vergnaud and Schwartz (a) regard simple multiplication word problems as part of a broader multiplicative conceptual field including ratio, rational numbers, vector space, and so forth, and (b) deal with the dimensions and units structure of these kinds of problems.

Vergnaud (1983, 1988) suggested regarding a multiplicative relation not as a three-place relation or a simple binary operation but as a four-place relation. For example, consider the following problem: "Each table has four legs; how many legs would five tables have altogether?" Typically, we would treat this kind of problem as a three-place relation among "legs," "tables," and "legs per table." According to Vergnaud's analysis, this problem involves two basic dimensions, M1 (tables) and M2 (legs), each containing two numbers, as shown here:

Tables (M1)	Legs (M2)
1	4
5	?

Because one of the measures in this kind of problem always includes 1 as the basis for its ratio, it appears as though only three quantities are involved. But according to Vergnaud, the problem gives the ratio of 1 table to 4 legs and asks about the ratio of 5 tables to how many legs.

Vergnaud (1983, 1988) argued that one can see this four-place relation, which he calls *isomorphism of measures,* from two different perspectives: Within each dimension there is a scalar enlargement or decrement (between 1 & 5 or 4 & ?), and between the two dimensions M1 and M2 there is a mapping function that maintains a constant ratio (between 1 & 4 and 5 & ?, respectively).

Vergnaud (1983) also posited two other types of multiplicative problems. A *product of measures* problem consists of the Cartesian composition of two measure spaces, M1 and M2, into a third measure, M3, as in the following example: "What is the area (M3) of a room whose length (M1) is 4 meters and its width (M2) is 3 meters?" Three measures are involved here, and the problem solver must deal with double proportions, rather than with a single proportion as in isomorphism of measures problems. In a *multiple proportion* problem a measure, M3, is proportional to two different independent measures M1 and M2. For example, what is the consumption of food for 10 people for 7 days, when the consumption per one day, per one man is given? Multiple proportion problems involve magnitudes that have intrinsic meaning; none of them can be reduced to the product of the others.

Schwartz's (1979, 1981) dimensional analysis is based on the distinction between *intensive* (I) and *extensive* (E) quantities. For an extensive quantity the referent is a single entity (e.g., 6 books), whereas an intensive quantity involves a referent that is the ratio between two entities (e.g., 12 bottles per box). In a less formal language intensive quantities are "per" quantities. Based on this distinction, Schwartz defined the following categories of multiplication word problems.

Multiplication of I × E. The multiplication of an intensive quantity by an extensive quantity is the most common category of multiplicative word problems. It can be presented as repeated addition when at least one number, the E number, is an integer. This type of problem corresponds to Vergnaud's (1983, 1988) isomorphism of measures, with the intensive quantity corresponding to the function relation between the two measures. For example, in the problem about how many legs for 5 tables, the intensive quantity, 4 legs per table, corresponds to the 1 table and 4 legs in the Vergnaud mapping table. The result of an I × E multiplication is an E quantity of the same kind that originally appeared in the I quantity. For example, 3 children times 4 marbles per child results in 12 marbles. All the problems given as examples of asymmetric situations in the section describing the implicit models paradigm fall under Schwartz's (1979, 1981) I × E category.

Multiplication of E × E. This is Cartesian multiplication, in which multiplication of two extensive measures, E1 and E2, forms a third measure, E3. For example, 5 shirts (E1) can be combined with 3 pants (E2) to form 15 possible outfits (E3). Or the length of a rectangle in inches (E1) can be multiplied by its width in inches (E2) to produce its area in square inches (E3). In E × E situations, the product, E3, is a new kind of quantity (e.g., outfits or square inches) that has a different referent than either E1 or E2.

In Vergnaud's (1983) categorization, this kind of problem is a product of measures; in Fischbein et al. (1985) and Greer's (1987) analysis it would be considered symmetrical.

Multiplication of I × I. In these problems, which are common in science, one intensive quantity is multiplied by another intensive quantity to produce a third, new intensive quantity. For example, "*N* km per hour times *M* hours per day" will give a measure of (*N* × *M*) km per day. I × I problems are not addressed in this chapter, but it should be noted that the texts for these problems are more difficult than for other problem types, making them more problematic for students.

Vergnaud's (1983, 1988) and Schwartz's (1979, 1981) analyses of multiplication are both expert analyses of a certain mathematical domain. Psychological difficulties in solving various kinds of problems are a separate issue to be dealt with later. Rather, the emphasis is on the dimensional analysis as extracted from the given situations and their relations to each other. The problem text, verbally formulated, as well as the different contexts of problems are irrelevant to their analysis. Their approaches do not deal with the textual analysis a child must do to discriminate the crucial dimensions in question. For example, Mechmandarov (1987) found that understanding that the "tiles" and the "dollars," and not the wall, are the relevant dimensions in the following problem was a source of difficulty for children: "Each wall contains 12 rows of tiles. The price of each row of tiles is $2.45. How much will it cost to buy the tiles for one wall?" How a child constructs the structure of the dimensions in question from the verbal text is an important aspect of solving multiplication word problems that remains to be understood and is not treated by the dimensional approach.

Although both Vergnaud (1983, 1988) and Schwartz (1979, 1981) rely on dimensional analysis, they differ in that Vergnaud considers the multiplicative relation a four-place relation, whereas Schwartz considers it a three-place relation. Consequently, the two approaches lead to different implications for instruction.

Instructional Implications
from the Dimensional Approach

Based on his dimensional analysis, Schwartz (1988) has developed a computer program, "The Semantic Calculator," that serves as a dimensional calculator. Working within this environment to solve a multiplicative problem, one first must examine the dimensions in question and their combinations before attending to the actual calculation of numbers. For example, the child must arrange to multiply kilometers per hour times hours driven to produce kilometers traveled before carrying out the numerical calculation. To master this software, one must become aware of intensive and extensive dimensions and how one deals with these dimensions. Thompson (1988) has developed a similar piece of software, "The Word Problem Assistant," which emphasizes the dimensional analysis of word problems. Focusing on the distinction between intensive and extensive quantities, the program incorporates multiplication as a three-place relation in which a "per" quantity (or a ratio between two dimensions) is treated as a single argument. Thus "bottles per box" is one argument and does not belong to two distinct dimensions: "bottles" and "boxes." Although studies are in progress, at this time there are no empirical findings of the work done with either "The Semantic Calculator" or "The Word Problem Assistant."

Another study within the dimensional approach was reported in Nesher (1988b) and is mentioned here in short. The study, an instructional study based on Vergnaud's (1983, 1988) dimensional analysis, was conducted by Mechmandarov (1987) in Israel. It was originally intended as a kind of replication of a study conducted by a student of Fischbein (Zeldis-Avissar, 1985) on the implicit models of multiplication but with the addition of an instructional treatment. The experimental group of children underwent special instruction designed to free them from the repeated addition model by providing a pedagogical device that was neutral with respect to the specific numbers appearing in the text.

The experimental instruction employed Vergnaud's (1983, 1988) dimensional model in combination with textual analysis as a didactic device. The children were instructed when solving a problem to build a mapping table incorporating all the needed information. For example, consider the following problem:

Ruth advances .75 meters with each step.
How many steps did she walk if she had advanced 4 meters?

For such a problem the child is instructed to find out whether there is a *mapping rule* in the text. A mapping rule is the part of the verbal text that establishes the intensive quantity in Schwartz's (1979, 1981) terms, or the functional relation in Vergnaud's (1983, 1988) terms. Verbally, this rule is usually given as "each has," "per," and so forth. In the aforementioned example the mapping rule is given by the phrase, ".75 meters with each step." After identifying the mapping rule, the child is instructed to construct a mapping table with the dimensions mentioned in the text ("steps" and "meters" in this example) and complete the table according to the numerical information given in the text (see Table 3.1). For the example problem, the child writes the mapping rule in the numeric form of 1—.75,

TABLE 3.1
The Mapping Table

Steps	Meters
1	0.75
?	4.0

under "steps" and "meters," respectively. Then the child adds the additional numerical information (here, "4 meters") under the appropriate column in the mapping table (i.e., in the meters column). The child writes a question mark in the fourth position in the mapping table to represent the unknown quantity. The position of the known and the unknown information in the table defines uniquely the operation (multiplication or division) to be executed. Once the quantities are arranged in the mapping table, the decision of which operation to use with which quantities can even be taught as algorithmic rules.

The example problem is a quotitive division problem, but for the child undergoing the experimental instruction it was regarded as a multiplicative problem where the exact mathematical operation is determined after filling the table according to the position of the unknown. Filling the table, however, is a matter of understanding the written text and extracting from it the relevant dimensions. In this case, to find out the numerical solution, (after filling the table), one must divide 4 by 0.75 ($4 \div 0.75$). In Mechmandarov's (1987) study, the children did not have to find out the numerical solution, only to write down the relevant mathematical expression.

There are two reasons to assume that this specific instruction is helpful. First, the child does not have to deal with intensive quantities, but only with the more easily grasped extensive quantities. Second, the graphical scheme assists in the search for the relevant dimensions.

The main findings of the instructional study (for details see Nesher, 1988b) were:

1. Generally, the results replicated Zeldis-Avissar's (Fischbein's student) (1985) findings. In both samples problems having decimal numbers as multipliers were more difficult.

2. On average, only 10% of children voluntarily used the mapping table as a pedagogical device when not required by the examiner.

3. Children weak in mathematics tended to use the pedagogical device voluntarily more than children who were generally strong in mathematics (23% for the weak students vs. 9% for the strong students).

4. When students voluntarily used the mapping table, it was usually for

harder problems, and they were more successful than students who did not use the mapping table.

5. When required to use the mapping table as a scaffold for textual dimensional analysis, students significantly improved their performance on the same problems. The percentage of students getting three of the more difficult problems correct improved from 20% (without mapping table) to 55% (with mapping table), 29% to 71%, and 14% to 86%.

6. On average, students who were asked to use the mapping table in their solution succeeded in 70% of the problems.

Thus, instruction that emphasizes textual and dimensional analysis can improve children's performance. Using the mapping table caused students to concentrate first on qualitative relationships in the problems rather than on the quantities involved. Once the children had analyzed the dimensions qualitatively, filling the mapping table according to the given dimensions and numerical information, the question of which operation to employ became simpler. This prevented them from falling into the numerical traps described by Fischbein et al. (1985).

Mechmandarov's (1987) study also implies that the repeated addition model suggested by Fischbein et al. (1985) as a primitive model can be overcome by later instruction. Teachers can provide some device like a mapping table to help focus children's attention on the qualitative considerations rather than the quantitative. Using such devices can assist in moving the children away from using the repeated addition model for multiplication, thus gaining a broader perspective on this kind of operation.

The Third Approach: The Textual Approach

The textual approach to studying multiplicative problems (Nesher, 1988b; Nesher & Katriel, 1977) is presented here in more detail than the previous two approaches. I start with a textual analysis of three types of multiplicative problems, mention in passing empirical findings already published, expand on recent research, and conclude with instructional implications of this approach.

According to the textual approach the solution of a word problem starts with analysis of its verbal formulation. It is through the verbal formulation that a child has to discover the logical conditions and semantic relations that constitute a well-structured multiplicative problem. It is only after analyzing the text that it is possible for the child to find out what relevant dimensions should be considered in the solution. Therefore, it is important for researchers to study the textual level that is first perceived by the child, and on which the rest of the solution process rests.

In analyzing the texts of multiplicative problems, Nesher and Katriel (1977, 1978; Nesher, 1988b) distinguished three major kinds of multiplicative problems: (a) problems describing a mapping rule (referred to in the first section as repeated addition and by Schwartz (1979, 1981) as I × E problems); (b) multiplicative compare problems or enlargement (referred to as S × E by Schwartz in his early writings, and as "change of size with the same units" by Bell et al., 1989); and (c) Cartesian multiplication (referred to as E × E problems by Schwartz, and symmetrical by Bell et al., 1989). Thus, there is convergence among researchers about the types of multiplicative word problems, though they employ different criteria for categorization. In the sections that follow, I try to show how one can know from the problem text the type of problem presented and the operation to be employed.

Mapping Rule Multiplication. The major task in the textual analysis of this kind of problem is to find the mapping rule. The text of each multiplicative word problem of the I × E, or repeated addition, variety contains a description of the repeated quantity in the form of a rule, such as: "each box costs \$5," or "John earns \$20 each day." The proposition describing the mapping rule makes the connection between the two dimensions (e.g., boxes and dollars, or dollars and days) that will constitute the intensive quantity in question (cf. Schwartz, 1988). The number attached to this proposition is also the one considered to be repeated in Fischbein et al.'s (1985) terms (i.e., the multiplicand). Another proposition in this kind of text describes how many times the repetition takes place, or how many mappings occur; for example, "Jane bought 3 boxes," or "John worked for 5 days." Finally, the question is about the total of one dimension across all the repetitions. Here is an example of a mapping rule multiplication problem (from Nesher, 1988b):

There are 5 shelves of books in Dan's room.

Dan put 8 books on each shelf.

How many books are there in his room?

Like an addition problem, a minimal multiplication word problem has three propositions in its underlying structure. The logical conditions for a minimal, well-formed mapping rule multiplication problem can be formulated by the following characteristics of the three strings:

1. The first string declares in general terms that there are n_1 Xs (shelves) for which there are Ys (books) and there is a relation between the Xs and the Ys (between the books and the shelves).

2. The second string presents a general mapping rule—a functional relation, which constitutes the intensive quantity. It says that all the books in this problem fulfill the same relation between the Xs and the Ys (the books and the shelves) and that there are exactly n_2 Ys ("8 books on each shelf"). This relation constitutes a mapping rule between each shelf and 8 books, typical of this kind of problem.

3. The third string asks how many Ys (books) there are for all the Xs (shelves).

There is also an implicit assumption about the uniqueness of the mapping that the mapping of the Ys to the Xs consists of disjointed sets of Ys to each X (i.e., the books on one shelf are distinct from the books on the other shelves), but this assumption never is made explicit in the verbal formulation of the text.

Multiplication and division word problems, like addition and subtraction problems, share an underlying logical structure. We refer to this underlying structure as *multiplicative structure*. The difference between multiplication and division problem texts is in which information is presented and which is unknown. The information component of a division problem always contains the string that was the question component in the related multiplication problem. For example, a division problem related to the multiplication problem just discussed would begin, "There are 40 books in all on the shelves in the room." From here the information presented in the division problem text diverges in one of two directions. It may give the mapping rule, "Dan put 8 books on each shelf," and ask, "How many shelves are there in the room?" making it a *quotitive* problem. Or it can inform, "There are 8 shelves in Dan's room," and ask, "How many books does Dan put on each shelf?" making it a *partitive* problem. In both cases there is an implicit assumption that the books are equally distributed on the shelves.

The difference between quotitive and partitive problems is whether the question component asks about String 1 (the existential description of the x's) or String 2 (the mapping rule) as they appear in the underlying structure of the multiplication problems. Thus, according to the textual approach, quotition and partition are not implicit psychological models as described by Fischbein et al. (1985), but an explicit formulation, easily traced at the textual level.

Multiplicative Compare. A multiplicative compare problem describes one quantity in terms of another. Thus, there are always in such texts a *referent* quantity, and a *compared* quantity, as in the following example (taken from Nesher, 1988b):

Dan has 5 marbles.
Ruth has 4 times as many marbles as Dan.
How many marbles does Ruth have?

The general form of this kind of problem can be described by the following three strings:

1. The first string declares that there is a referent set containing n_1 Ys ("Dan has 5 marbles").
2. The second string declares that there is a specific function mapping each element of the referent set of Ys to a compared set of Xs (for each of Dan's marbles, there are exactly 4 of Ruth's marbles).
3. The third string, the question component, asks how many Xs there are in the compared set ("How many marbles does Ruth have?").

Central to a multiplicative compare problem is the notion of a scalar function between the number of objects in the referent set and the number of objects of the compared set. The child must distinguish that the function (under a given verbal formulation) has a direction that is not interchangeable ("Ruth has 4 times as many marbles as Dan" is different from "Dan has 4 times as many marbles as Ruth"). The compared objects need not be of the same kind. One could compare the number of Dan's marbles to the number of Ruth's stamps. A multiplicative compare problem formulates a mathematical function $[Y = f(X)]$ in ordinary language using an expression such as: "X has n times as many as Y." This verbal expression is syntactically complicated and is learned as a holistic expression denoting the multiplication operation, thus becoming a verbal cue for multiplication word problems. The distinction that X and Y are not interchangeable, and that the role of the referent and the compared are not symmetrical, as can incorrectly be thought, is usually underemphasized in instruction and therefore causes many errors.

Multiplicative compare problems also are associated with two kinds of division: (a) A problem can give the referent and the compared sets and ask about the scalar function (e.g., "Ruth has 20 marbles and Ron has 5 marbles. Ruth has how many times more marbles than Ron?"); or (b) a problem can give the compared set and the scalar function and ask about the referent set (e.g., "Ruth has 20 marbles and she has 4 times as many as Ron. How many marbles does Ron have?").

Cartesian Multiplication. This third class of problems is less known and less exercised in elementary schools. It involves multiplying two different dimensions to get a third, as in the following example (taken from Nesher, 1988b):

Ruth has 4 skirts and 3 blouses.
How many different skirt and blouse outfits can Ruth make?

Like the other types of multiplication, a Cartesian multiplication problem consists of three strings. The first two strings describe two independent sets of objects—in this example, the number of blouses that Ruth has (*X*s) and the number of skirts that Ruth has (*Y*s). The third string is the question component, which asks how many *Z*s there are, where *Z* is a cross-multiplication between each of the *X*s and each of the *Y*s. (In the example, for each blouse and skirt there is one outfit). Due to the structure of the first two strings, children sometimes believe that this type of problem is an additive word problem; there is no mapping rule or comparison function to serve as a verbal cue for multiplication. Children sometimes treat Cartesian multiplication problems as mapping-rule problems, for example, by defining a mapping rule between each skirt and the number of blouses that can combine with it.

Relative Difficulty of Problem Types. According to the textual approach, the relative difficulty of the three main types of multiplicative word problems can be predicted from their propositional structure. Mapping-rule problems should be the easiest. The child can grasp the role of the two given quantities directly, requiring no further elaboration of the text. Their structure can be viewed as a dynamic procedure in which $n2$ is repeated $n1$ times (e.g., 8 books 5 times, or 5 times 8 books), thus becoming a process of repeated addition. Teachers in early grades are inclined to treat multiplication as repeated addition in this manner, avoiding the need to talk about the mapping rule (there are 8 books on each shelf) directly. The problem then becomes a repeated addition operation rather than a binary multiplication operation with the predicates $n1$ and $n2$. Thus, the children continue to employ familiar additive procedures instead of coming to view multiplication as a distinct operation with its own constraints.

Compare problems are harder. To solve these problems successfully, one has to understand the asymmetric relation between the compared and the referent quantity. This asymmetric relation is only subtly mentioned in the structure of the second string, that is, by saying "*A* has *n* times as much as *B*." Otherwise, *A* and *B* seem symmetrical. The direction of this expression is sometimes hard to distinguish, possibly creating additional difficulty with this kind of problem. For example, compare the sentence "*A* has *n* times more than *B*" with "*B* has *n* times less than *A*." Both have the same underlying direction (that *A* has more than *B*), but it might be confusing and hard for the child to sort out the correct direction.

The third type, Cartesian multiplication, involves an assumption that is not explicitly expressed in the text of the problem but must be actively considered in solving it: Each *X* is cross-multiplied with each *Y*. Without an explicit description of this assumption, the child might think of all kinds of combinations between the *X*s and the *Y*s, including the additive combination. The similarity of this kind of problem to addition becomes even clearer when considering the first two propositions (strings), which are identical in structure to the first two propositions in additive compare problems. Both declare that there are a particular number of *X*s and a particular number of *Y*s. It can be predicted, therefore, that Cartesian problems will be the most difficult, mapping-rule problems the easiest, and compare problems in between.

As can be seen from these analyses of problem types, the textual approach focuses on the data the child first perceives in reading a word problem—the text itself. The numbers in a word problem do not determine the kind of operation to be executed; it is the verbal text of the problem that contains the information needed to make that choice. Yet, as found repeatedly by Bell et al. (1984, 1989), children usually avoid reading problem texts, trying rather to solve word problems by attending solely to the numbers in the problems (e.g., multiplying or dividing whatever numbers happen to be in the problem). To study children's knowledge of the text characteristics or word problems, researchers thus have had to use tasks other than simply having students solve the problems—tasks such as composing word problems or explaining why a particular operation should be used.

Empirical Findings Within the Textual Analysis Paradigm

The empirical data presented here are divided into two parts. The first part deals with children's comprehension of various types of multiplicative word problems and their sensitivity to the textual assumptions underlying the problems. The second considers evidence for additional variables affecting the difficulty of multiplicative word problems.

Children's Comprehension of Various Types of Multiplicative Problems. A study by Nesher (1988b; Peled & Nesher, 1988) addressed two main questions: (a) Are children aware of different kinds of multiplication, and which are best known to them? and (b) Are young children aware of the underlying assumptions of the multiplicative texts? The study considered indirectly the question of whether young children have a single implicit multiplicative model. Two tasks were given in this study: In the first task children were asked to compose a word problem that had to be solved using a multiplication operation versus a problem that had to be solved by an addition operation. In the second task children were asked to explain in their own words a word problem to a child who finds it difficult to decide which operation to choose to solve a given word problem (either addition or multiplication).

The major finding was that children do not compose only $I \times E$ problems (the repeated addition type). The distribution among the three types of multiplication word problems children composed was as follows: 34% wrote a kind of mapping-rule problem ($I \times E$); 41% wrote a special kind of multiplicative compare ($S \times E$); 2% wrote Cartesian multiplication ($E \times E$); and about 23% composed uninterpretable texts. It seems, then, that children (in Israel) have more than one multiplication model. Note that this study employed a different methodology than Fischbein et al. (1985) used and did not address differences in the type of numbers in the problems. Rather, it addressed textual variables and found them to be influential.

In Hebrew, the formulation of a compare problem is based on a very simple and short word P (read as the letter P), instead of the English phrase "n times as many as." Teachers in Israel tend to emphasize this verbal distinction between P and a similar phrase denoting an additive comparison early in their instruction. This may account for the Israeli children's responses on our tasks. The fact that a unique feature of Hebrew was incorporated into the instruction in Israel and therefore influenced the distribution of multiplication models among Israeli children should not be looked at as an esoteric phenomena to be disregarded, but should emphasize the universality of the role of schooling in introducing specific mathematical models.

Further analysis of the data showed that children were fully aware of the textual constraints upon multiplication described previously. In particular, they mentioned in their interviews the constraint that the number of objects in each set must be equal and the need for an explicit mapping rule. They were not consistent regarding the two types of multiplication and switched from one type (mapping) rule to the other (compare) by alternating their formulations from "each one has . . . " to "as many times as," noticing, when probed, that these are not the same multiplicative situations.

Because most of the children showed a good command of the $I \times E$ and $S \times E$ types of problems, we were interested in probing their knowledge of the E × E type (Cartesian multiplication). We used during the interviews, with the support of drawings, the following types of problems:

1. The area of a room: "If this room is 4m long and 3m wide what is its area?"

2. An orange grove: "If there are 4 trees on this side of the grove (showing its length) and 3 trees on the other side of the grove (showing its width), how many trees are there altogether in the grove?" (See Fig. 3.1a.) Sometimes we altered the illustration by drawing all the trees (see Fig. 3.1b).

3. A combination of outfits made out of pants and shirts: "Dan has 2 pairs of pants and 3 shirts and he complains to his mother that he does not have enough outfits to change each day without having to go twice with the same outfit." (In Israel there are 6 school days.) The interviewer then drew a rectangle with shirts drawn on its length, and pants drawn on its width (see Fig. 3.2). The intent of this drawing was to help the children arrive at multiplication as a solution to the problem. The interviewer continued: "Dan's mother insists that he has enough outfits to go each day of the week wearing a different one, but Dan still complains. Who do you think is right, Dan or his mother?"

This part of the interview revealed that E × E problems are difficult for sixth graders. Of the E × E problems, the area problem was the easiest. Many children knew they had to multiply length times width to get the area of the room (cf. Verschaffel et al., 1988). Solving area problems is a tradi-

(a)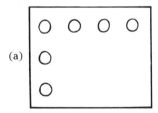

(b)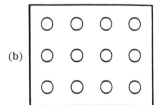

FIG. 3.1.   The grove problem.

FIG. 3.2.   Pants and shirts in combination problem.

tional school task; students who succeeded were sure about the need to
multiply, even if unable to explain why, as in the following example:

Interviewer: How did you find the area?
Zohar: I multiplied 3 by 4.
Interviewer: Is it similar to the problem you gave about bags and mar-
             bles? (The I × E problem he composed).
Zohar: No, it is not similar but I still have to multiply.

None of the children saw any resemblance between finding out the area (E
× E) and the I × E or S × E problems that were discussed with them before.
We concluded that calculating area is not a good example of E × E problems, but a special case learned in school, in isolation from other problems.

The grove problem was an easy one. The outfits problem was given to
only eight children of whom five could cope with the task. The three
children who failed could not count all the possibilities, but rather counted
the actual pants and shirts appearing in the presentation, or were occupied
with some practical matters, as in the following protocol:

Sagi: It is important that Dan make suitable outfits, and this
             depends on his taste. But if he does not care about suit-
             ability of colors, he can then, make two outfits, maybe three
             outfits if he does not care about it too much.
Interviewer: But then his mother said to him, "If you don't fuss about the
             colors you will have enough outfits."
Sagi: Even then he can make only two outfits, enough for 2 days
             and one shirt will remain for the other day, and this also
             gives only 3 days.

It seems that children's earlier experiences with disjoint sets in the I × E and S × E cases add an erroneous implicit constraint for multiplication that objects cannot be reused (as needed in the combinational case).

We have learned from this exploratory study that children understand a variety of multiplicative situations and they distinguish among them. Children, like adults, receive their cues from the verbal formulations of the multiplicative texts, focusing on the specific constraints that differentiate multiplication from addition problems as was detailed earlier. It appears that children do not analyze the texts in terms of dimensions; rather, they are sensitive to the linguistic cues appearing in the problem texts themselves. This linguistic sensitivity was especially apparent in children's distinction between I × E and S × E problems.

Additional Variables Affecting Multiplicative Word Problems. Within the textual approach, Nesher (1988a) conducted a large-scale quantitative study to examine the effects of several variables on multiplicative word problems. The first variable was the *Type* of multiplicative problem. In this experiment two types were given: (a) mapping-rule problems (I × E), and (b) compare problems (S × E). Cartesian multiplication problems (E × E) were not included because they were too difficult for the young children in the sample.

The second variable was the *Operation* required. Problems required multiplication or division, which could be partition, quotition, or a kind of compare division. The required operation was determined by which proposition in the problem text contained the unknown quantity.

The *Order* variable concerned the order of the strings describing the three components of a multiplicative problem. In an I × E problem these are (a) the description of an existential set, (b) a mapping rule, and (c) the total. In a S × E problem the three components are (a) the description of the referent, (b) the compared, and (c) the comparison function. The Order variable addressed the question of whether it matters to the solver which of these information components appears first. We included order as a variable because it was a significant one for additive word problems (Nesher & Katriel, 1978). The Order variable had six values in our study, comprising all possible orders of three propositions.

We captured several syntactic variations through a fourth variable, *Syntax,* that deals with the position of the question component; it can appear in the first, second, or third position in the text. Varying the position of the question also controlled for the number of sentences in the text. In our problems, having the question at the beginning created a text consisting of one long sentence—a question followed by a coordinated conditional sentence (e.g., "How many books are there on all the shelves, if there are *N* shelves altogether and there are *M* books on each shelf?"). With the question in the middle, the text consists of two sentences in which the second sentence is a conditional one (e.g., "There are N shelves. How many books are there on all the shelves if there are M books on each shelf?"). If the question component is at the end, the problem consists of three sentences (e.g., "There are N shelves. M books on each shelf. How many books are there on all the shelves?"). Thus, the Syntax variable captures the position of the question in the text as well as the number of the sentences in the text.

Compare problems (S × E) can be sensitive to two additional linguistic variables. First is a lexical one. The comparison function can be described in terms of an increase function or a decrease function ("John has M times more stamps than Ron" or "Ron has M times fewer stamps than John"). The use of more versus less in interaction with the operation (multiplication or division) could have a significant effect on problem difficulty (see Nesher & Teubal, 1974). This variable is not reported here because it was not studied separately and is a variable in an ongoing controlled study. Compare problems also can be sensitive to their context. In a problem that compares a big box to a small box, the direction of the comparison function becomes clear because it can usually be assumed that the big box contains more chocolates than the small one. This assumption cannot hold when comparing the amount of chocolates (or stamps) that John has versus Ron. Whether there were such context cues for the direction of the comparison was captured by the *Direction* variable.

Knowing from previous studies that the context is a significant factor, we used only one context (boxes of chocolates). We presented 36 word problems in six sets, each set fully controlled by Type, Operation, and Context, and manipulated on the textual variables Order, Syntax, and Direction. The problems were based on the following basic texts:

I × E Example: In the store they sell eight chocolates in each box. Joseph bought five boxes of chocolate. In all, how many chocolates did Joseph buy?

S × E Example: In the small box they pack eight chocolates. In the big box they pack four times as many chocolates as in the small box. How many chocolates do they pack in the big box?

Each of these problems was formulated in different ways to meet the additional textual variables, and was marked for the following variations:

Type   I × E and S × E.

Operation Multiplication and division (with division including partition, quotition and compare-division).

Order: Six different orders, I to VI.

Syntax: Position of the question (1st, 2nd, or 3rd).

Direction: Cue to the direction for the compare function provided by the context or not.

We report here data on these problems collected through a computer-assisted instruction system, TOAM, being used in about 200 varied schools in Israel. Our sample consisted of 16 of these schools selected at random ($n = 500$).

The TOAM program presented each child with a word problem individually when he or she reached the appropriate level of performance in various arithmetical skills appearing in the other strands of the program. The program accumulated in each school for each word problem the percentage of children who answered it correctly on their first attempt. The score for each problem from a given school may represent from 60 to 100 children, depending on the size of the school. The data, therefore, describe global trends rather than individual variations. Table 3.2 presents mean percent correct for each problem type.

Analysis of variance performed on the I × E problems yielded significant effects for Operation ($F = 59.53$, $df = 1$, $p < 0.001$), Order ($F = 6.52$, $df = 5$, $p < 0.001$), and Syntax ($F = 39.79$, $df = 2$, $p < 0.001$), with the three variables accounting for about 50% of the variance among I × E problems. The main effect for Type was not significant ($F = 0.14$, $df = 1$). Operation accounted for 24.8% of the variance among I × E problems, with multiplication being the easiest and quotition the most difficult.

Regarding Syntax, counter to our intuition, problems with the question in the middle with a conditional sentence as the second sentence of the text were the easiest. Having the question in the beginning, that is, all the text as one long coordinated conditional sentence, was easier than having the question in the last position and the text consisting of three separate

TABLE 3.2
Mean Percentages of Students Solving Word Problems Correctly
in 16 Schools

Set	N	Type	Operation	Direction	M	SD
(a)	6	IxE	multiplication	n.a.	87.40	5.56
(b)	6	IxE	quotition	n.a.	73.68	11.42
(c)	6	IxE	partition	n.a.	78.54	9.28
(d)	6	SxE	multiplication	+	86.16	6.77
(e)	6	SxE	multiplication	−	79.17	11.25
(f)	6	SxE	compare-div.	−	74.60	11.50

Note: n.a. (not applicable); + (there is a clear direction of the comparison).

sentences. All differences among these values were significant at the .05 level.

Order accounted for 19% of the variance among I × E problems, but this finding is harder to interpret. No clear pattern among the six different orders emerged. Additionally, there were significant two-way interactions of Order with Operation ($p < .001$), with Syntax ($p < .01$) and with Type ($p < .01$) whereas other two-way interactions were not significant.

We found no significant difference in difficulty between the I × E problems and S × E problems in which the direction of the comparison is clearly cued. But S × E problems in which the direction of the comparison must be understood on the basis of subtle linguistic cues were significantly more difficult than I × E problems. The effects of Order and Syntax also were different for S × E problems than for I × E problems, a difference we expand upon later in the discussion.

We examined three different types of division: quotition, partition (both derived from the I × E problems) and one compare-division (which asked about the comparison function; i.e., "How many more does Ron has than John?"). Problems involving partition were easiest ($m = 78.54$) and significantly different ($p < 0.05$) from quotition ($m = 73.67$) and from the compare-division problems ($m = 74.60$). Compare-division was easier than quotition but this difference was not significant. The more interesting result was that the Order and Syntax effects for division problems were highly significant, explaining 52.5% of the variance in performance.

The results of this study corroborate our previous findings regarding the importance of textual factors in solving word problems (Nesher, 1988a). Three major aspects of word problems seem especially important: The first is the mathematical operation needed for solution (the Operation variable), the second is the flow of information (the Order variable) that is decisive for selecting the needed operation, and the third is the syntactic quality of the text, its coherence and readability (the Syntax variable). The last two aspects should be regarded as being at different levels. Whereas the third is entirely syntactic, the second involves the information needed to decide that this is a multiplicative text by virtue of its components.

This last study raises some doubts regarding the theoretical distinction among types of problems (e.g., I × E vs. S × E) as the major source of problem difficulty. The distinction among types, though informative for matters of categorization of different multiplication situations and for purposes of instruction, does not seem the crucial one from the empirical point of view. Within a given problem type, other factors within the type— such as quotition in contrast to partition or compare division, or having contextual clues (Direction) within the S × E problems—are much more influential than the type of problem in determining difficulty. Although the kind of operation can explain about 25% of the variance, when the mathematical operation variable is studied in interaction with textual variables such as Order or Syntax that capture the essence of the flow of information, the explained variance increases to 57%, again supporting the importance of textual factors.

As for instructional implications, these findings suggest that, when teaching multiplicative word problems, one should pay attention not only to the general type of problem presented—whether it is an I × E or S × E problem, and whether it entails multiplication or division—but also to the linguistic characteristics of the texts that assist in making these distinctions. Because the order and the syntax are important factors, one should teach the invariance of all these surface structure variations, in the form of constraints on the entire text, as a relationship among three distinct propositions having each a special role, as was suggested in the textual analysis. Understanding at the linguistic level what makes a text a multiplicative text is a tool that can be taught explicitly (Mechmandarov, 1987) and serve the students in analyzing word problems.

DISCUSSION AND INSTRUCTIONAL IMPLICATIONS

Research on multiplicative word problems in the last decade has revealed three major categories of problems, discussed at length in this chapter. Different researchers, however, have developed somewhat different categories and terms. Table 3.3 summarizes these differences by comparing the terms used by the four major theoretical approaches to identify the main categories of elementary multiplicative word problems.

These classes of problems constitute the distinct kinds of multiplicative

TABLE 3.3
Types of Multiplicative Word Problems
from Three Theoretical Perspectives

Nesher	Fischbein et al.	Schwartz	Vergnaud
mapping rule	repeated addition (asymmetrical)	I × E	isomorphism of measures
compare enlargement		S × E	scalar
Cartesian multiplication	symmetrical	E × E	product of measures
		I × I	multiple proportion

applications that should be learned in elementary school. Of these categories the most familiar and studied are the mapping-rule (asymmetrical, I × E) problems, which deal with grouping of equal sets. Some researchers maintain that this type of problem is the easiest because the problem resembles "repeated addition," which serves as the implicit model for multiplication and division. These easy cases of I × E problems, however, do not exhaust the entire class. Rate problems, for example, are of the I × E type, but would not be considered easy problems. Moreover, research has demonstrated that some elementary school children under certain conditions of instruction can cope with others types of multiplication, such as the scalar multiplication (e.g., compare problems and enlargements where the direction is clear) or Cartesian multiplication (e.g., area problems). Thus, it appears that children can learn several models of multiplication and cope well with the easier cases within each model.

It may be beneficial to present more than one model of multiplication to children when the topic is first introduced in school. Although this will not avoid the misconception that "multiplication makes bigger," it will prevent children's closure on one type of multiplication. The misconception that multiplication makes bigger can only be clarified by performing operations with all kinds of numbers. Yet, it is important that children, even when operating with merely whole numbers, have in their repertoire problems of more than one model.

In terms of the general model of solving word problems offered by Nathan et al. (1988), it seems that there is more to problem solving than the two levels of analyses they propose, the textbase and the situation model. Each theoretical approach presented in this chapter is powerful in explaining a different process involved in the task of solving word problems. Constructing the propositional textbase calls for a prior textual analysis and distinctions like those made by Nesher and Katriel (1977) and in this chapter. Only on the basis of the textual analysis is a certain situation model called for (i.e., whether it is an I × E, S × E, or E × E situation). A dimensional analysis, the focus of Vergnaud (1988) and Schwartz (1988), must precede any meaningful numerical calculation. It might well be that these processes—the textual analysis, the selection of the situation type, the dimensional analysis, the choice of the operation, and the numerical calculations—are not sequentially ordered, but interwoven. Yet, they all must play a part in solving word problems. It should be remembered, however, that the child first faces the problem in its linguistic formulation and it is with this text that his or her problem-solving activity begins.

Although attempts to teach certain verbal cues (e.g., key words for various operations) have failed in the past, it is still necessary to deal with the linguistic aspects of problem text. But textual analysis must take the entire text and not isolated key words into consideration. Explicit knowledge about the types of multiplicative problems and their linguistic structure can assist teachers in instructing children how to recognize and distinguish among various problem texts. Too often we see children who pull numbers out of problems without reading the text, operating on them in a mindless fashion. Learning to discern a mathematical structure in a verbal text is the main task involved in solving word problems. It seems that research's contributions in the last decade can make school instruction more efficient in this respect.

Our picture of multiplicative word problems is now considerably richer than it was 10 years ago. We know that there are a limited number of problem types. Furthermore, we know the misconceptions that are relevant to each type, the effects of various variables on each category of problems, and their typical verbal formulations. In planning instruction one should consider the implicit models of multiplication that children bring with them as well as the factors that contribute to the difficulty of word problems: the dimensions involved and the order and flow of information within the problem text. It is the combination of general strategy and specific knowledge about the task that leads to successful problem-solving performance. It seems that teachers can have now a more general view on the entire complex field called *multiplicative structures* (Vergnaud, 1988), as well as more specific knowledge about important factors to guide them in improving school instruction on multiplicative word problems.

REFERENCES

Bell, A., Fischbein, E., and Greer, B. (1984). Choice of operation in verbal arithmetic problems: The effects of number size, problem structure and context. *Educational Studies in Mathematics, 15*(2), 129–147.

Bell, A., Greer, B., Mangan, C., & Grimison, L. (1989). Children's performance on multiplicative word problems: Elements of a descriptive theory. *Journal for Research in Mathematics Education, 20*(5), 434–449.

Carpenter, T., Hiebert, J., & Moser, F. (1981). The effect of problem structure on first-grader's initial solution procedures for simple addition and subtraction problems. *Journal for Research in Mathematics Education, 12*(1), 27–39.

Carpenter, T., & Moser, J. (1982). The development of addition and subtraction problem solving skills. In T. P. Carpenter, J. M. Moser, & T. A. Romberg (Eds.), *Addition and subtraction: A cognitive perspective* (pp. 9–25). Hillsdale, NJ: Lawrence Erlbaum Associates.

Carpenter, T., & Moser, J. (1984). The acquisition of addition and subtraction concepts in grades one to three. *Journal for Research in Mathematics Education, 15*(3), 179–202.

De Corte, E., & Verschaffel, L. (1985). Influence of rewording verbal problems on children's problem representations and solutions. *Journal of Educational Psychology, 77,* 460–470.

De Corte, E., & Verschaffel, L. (1987). The effects of semantic structure on first-graders' strategies for solving addition and subtraction word problems. *Journal for Research in Mathematics Education, 18*(5), 363–381.

De Corte, E., Verschaffel, L., & Van Collie, V. (1988). Influence of number size, problem structure and response mode on children's solutions of multiplication word problems. *The Journal of Mathematical Behavior, 7*(3), 197–217.

Fischbein, E., Deri, M., Nello, M., & Marino, M. (1985). The role of implicit models in solving verbal problems in multiplication and division. *Journal for Research in Mathematics Education, 16*(1), 3–17.

Graeber, A., & Tirosh, D. (1988). Multiplication and division involving decimals: Preservice elementary teachers' performance and beliefs. *The Journal of Mathematical Behavior, 7*(3), 263–280.

Greer, B. (1987). Understanding of arithmetical operations as models of situations. In J. A. Sloboda & D. Rogers (Eds.), *Cognitive processes in mathematics* (pp. 60–80). London: Oxford University Press.

Greer, B. (1988). Nonconservation of multiplication and division: Analysis of a symptom. *The Journal of Mathematical Behavior, 7*(3), 281–298.

Greer, B., & Mangan, C. (1984). Understanding multiplication and division. In T. Carpenter & J. Moser (Eds.), *Proceedings of the Wisconsin Meeting of the PME-NA* (pp. 27–32). Madison: University of Wisconsin.

Greer, B., & Mangan, C. (1986). Choice of operations: From 10-year-olds to student teachers. In *Proceedings of the Tenth International Conference of PME* (pp. 25–31). London.

Kintsch, W. (1986). Learning from text. *Cognition and Instruction, 3*(2), 87–108.

Kintsch, W., & Greeno, J. G. (1985). Understanding and solving arithmetic word problems. *Psychological Review, 92*, 109–129.

Luke, C. (1988). The repeated addition model of multiplication and children's performance on mathematical word problems. *The Journal of Mathematical Behavior, 7*(3), 217–227.

Mangan, C. (1986). *Choice of operation in multiplication and division word problems.* Unpublished doctoral dissertation, Queen's University, Belfast.

Mechmandarov, I. (1987, Draft). *The role of dimensional analysis in teaching multiplicative word problems.* Tel-Aviv: Center for Educational Technology.

Nathan, M., Kintsch, W., & Lewis, C. (1988). *Tutoring algebra word problems* (Tech. Rep. No. 88-12). Boulder: University of Colorado, Institute of Cognitive Science.

Nesher, P. (1988a, April). *Multiplication word problems: Textual variables.* Paper presented at the annual meeting of the American Educational Research Association, New Orleans.

Nesher, P. (1988b). Multiplicative school word problems: Theoretical approaches and empirical findings. In J. Hiebert & M. Behr (Eds.), *Number concepts and operations in the middle grades* (pp. 19–41). Hillsdale, NJ: Lawrence Erlbaum Associates and Reston, VA: National Council of Teachers of Mathematics.

Nesher, P., Greeno, J. G., & Riley, M. (1982). The development of semantic categories for addition and subtraction. *Educational Studies in Mathematics, 13*(4), 373–394.

Nesher, P., & Katriel, T. (1977). A semantic analysis of addition and subtraction word problems in arithmetic. *Educational Studies in Mathematics, 8*, 251–269.

Nesher, P., & Katriel, T. (1978). Two cognitive modes in arithmetic word problem solving. In E. Cohors-Fresenborg & I. Wachsmuth (Eds.), *The Proceedings of the 2nd International Conference of the PME* (pp. 226–241).

Nesher, P., & Teubal, E. (1974). Verbal cues as an interfering factor in verbal problem solving. *Educational Studies in Mathematics, 6*, 141–151.

Peled, I., & Nesher, P. (1988). What children tell us about multiplication word problems. *The Journal of Mathematical Behavior, 7*(3), 239–262.

Riley, M., Greeno, J., & Heller, J. (1983). Development of children's problem-solving ability in arithmetic. In H. Ginsburg (Ed.), *The development of mathematical thinking* (pp. 153–196). New York: Academic.

Schwartz, J. (1979). *Semantic aspects of quantity.* Unpublished manuscript. MIT, Cambridge, MA.

Schwartz, J. (1981). *The role of semantic understanding in solving multiplication and division word problems* (Final Report to NIE, Grant NIE-G-80-0144). MIT, Cambridge, MA.

Schwartz, J. (1988). Intensive quantity and referent transforming arithmetic operations. In J. Hiebert & M. Behr (Eds.), *Number concepts and operations in the middle grades* (pp. 41–53). Hillsdale, NJ: Lawrence Erlbaum Associates and Reston, VA: National Council of Teachers of Mathematics.

Thompson, P. W. (1988, Draft). *Word problem assistant (Tutorial 1).* Illinois State University.

Tirosh, D., Graeber, A., & Glover, R. (1986). Pre-service teachers choice of operation for multiplication and division word problems. In *Proceedings of the Tenth International Conference of PME* (pp. 57–62). London.

Vergnaud, G. (1982). A classification of cognitive tasks and operations of thought involved in addition and subtraction problems. In T. P. Carpenter, J. M. Moser, & T. A. Romberg (Eds.), *Addition and subtraction: A cognitive perspective* (pp. 39–59). Hillsdale, NJ: Lawrence Erlbaum Associates.

Vergnaud, G. (1983). Multiplicative structures. In R. Lesh & M. Landau (Eds.), *Acquisition of mathematics concepts and processes* (pp. 127–174). New York: Academic.

Vergnaud, G. (1988). Multiplicative structures. In J. Hiebert & M. Behr (Eds.), *Number concepts and operations in the middle grades* (pp. 141–162). Hillsdale, NJ: Lawrence Erlbaum Associates and NCTM.

Verschaffel, L., De Corte, E., and Van Collie, V. (1988, Draft). *Specifying the multiplier effect on children's solutions of simple multiplication word problems.* Center for Instructional Psychology, Leuven, Belgium.

Zeldis-Avissar, T. (1985). *Role of intuitive implicit model in solving elementary arithmetical problems.* Unpublished master's thesis, The University of Tel Aviv.

4

TEACHING AND LEARNING LONG DIVISION FOR UNDERSTANDING IN SCHOOL

Magdalene Lampert
Michigan State University

Contents

I want to get through division with two-digit numbers because then I can really go with the flow of kids' ideas, be more creative in math. Kids put a lot of math sense on finishing long division. It seems to finish arithmetic for them.

—Fifth-grade public school teacher

"Long" division is an important milestone in this teacher's work with his fifth-grade students. And he believes that the students themselves look at this topic as the culmination of their work on whole number arithmetic. Yet the topic is not associated, in his mind, with creativity or "the flow of kids' ideas." Mathematics educators who wish to reform curriculum and instruction would agree that long division, as it is now taught, has little to do with mathematical creativity, and may even get in the way of "the flow of kid's ideas." Teaching the long division algorithm often is used as an example of the misplaced emphasis on memorizing procedures in elementary arithmetic, and this emphasis is thought to be in opposition to understanding. Educators and mathematicians argue that the arithmetic procedures that dominate the school curriculum take students' and teachers' attention away from more essential mathematical ideas (Clemens, 1989; Hilton, 1989; Mathematical Sciences Education Board, 1989; National Council of Teachers of Mathematics, 1989).

What are the essential mathematical ideas underlying the long division procedure? Can the division of one large number by another be taught in ways that relate it to students' understanding of important concepts in mathematics? Is it possible to teach division in ways that support students' creative engagement with mathematical ideas? What might it look like for learners to "understand" the process of division and apply it to work with large numbers in school?

As we think about reforming the way we teach mathematics, we can decide to take the topic conventionally called "long division" out of the curriculum or we can decide to keep it in. One argument for keeping it is that it is familiar: to teachers, to parents, and to children. All of these groups consider it to be an important milestone in measuring mathematical accomplishment within the school culture. But this does not seem reason enough to teach long division, given that the technology for performing the procedure is now widely available. This chapter presents two other kinds of arguments for keeping long division in the curriculum: one derived from an analysis of the relationship between procedures for doing long division and important mathematical concepts, and the other based on the results of trying out some conceptual approaches to teaching long division in a fourth-grade classroom.[1] In making this argument, the emphasis moves away from teaching the long division algorithm and toward teaching the relationships between the operation of division and important mathematical concepts and activities.

CHANGING TEACHER AND STUDENT ROLES IN SCHOOL MATHEMATICS

Although primarily addressing the question of what it might mean to teach long division for understanding in school, the research reported in this chapter also examines more general issues of mathematical pedagogy. In the case of teaching and learning long division that is examined here, students are expected to make mathematical assertions and verify the validity of those assertions within the class as a community of discourse about mathematics. Teaching mathematics in a way that engages learners in mathematical discourse means changing the roles that teacher and students play in classroom activities. The teacher poses problems and raises questions about solutions that lead students to examine, in public discussions during lessons, the reasonability of their own assertions and those of their peers. Students test their symbolic manipulations by mapping them on to parallel operations in more familiar domains. The teacher is a source of information about mathematical conventions and provides that information to students in response to their constructions of mathematical ideas.

If lessons on arithmetic operations such as long division are to be taught within the context of a mathematical discourse, they must be constructed to emphasize learning about why a particular move in the procedure is legitimate rather than simply focusing on which moves to make in which order (Lampert, 1986a, 1986b, 1990b). The goal of such arithmetic instruction would be to have students be able to explain why they do each step in a procedure in terms of its mathematical legitimacy. In addition to being able to explain the moves in the conventional procedures for addition, subtraction, multiplication, and division, students would be encouraged to

[1]The study reported here was part of a larger study, "Teaching Mathematics for Understanding and Understanding Mathematics Teaching," which the author conducted as a Spencer Fellow with the National Academy of Education. The author would like to acknowledge the assistance of Peggy Karns in collecting data about how long division is presented in conventional texts, the support of Jackie Frese and Nancy Arnold for recording observations of teaching and learning, the editorial suggestions of Gaea Leinhardt, Lauren Resnick, Orit Zaslavsky, Jack Smith, and Vicky Kouba, and the collaboration of Thom Dye in continuing research on the teaching of long division in school.

invent their own alternative procedures and expected to be able to explain the legitimacy of their inventions (Lampert, 1990b). The content of the curriculum thus would be deeply integrated with the mode of discourse and the social structure of the class (Lampert, 1988, 1990a). This approach to teaching arithmetic procedures is derived from an examination of the nature of mathematical knowledge: Because the evidence that makes mathematical assertions true and mathematical procedures legitimate is logical argument, students are expected to legitimate their answers with mathematical arguments appropriate to their level of expertise.[2]

The discipline-derived argument for teaching students to reason about arithmetic is complimented by arguments in psychology that suggest that if students can explain and invent legitimate procedures, then they understand the mathematical concepts that underlie those procedures (Greeno, Riley, & Gelman, 1984; Putnam, Lampert, & Peterson, 1989). No claim is made here that students' capacity to explain the mathematical legitimacy of the steps in arithmetic procedures will cause them to carry out those procedures faultlessly. Indeed, research on student learning thus far has failed to establish such a connection (Nesher, 1987; Resnick & Omanson, in press). The claim that is made is both more modest and more bold: A curriculum and a method of instruction can be invented that engages students in the activity of intentionally understanding authentic mathematical ideas in school—even when the topic is something as mathematically mundane as long division.[3]

THE MATHEMATICAL CONTENT
IN LONG DIVISION

Most simply, long division could be defined as division that operates on large numbers. Because of the magnitude of the numbers, the operation requires the decomposition of the dividend and the divisor, such that the actual process of dividing occurs over several steps, and the quotient is assembled from their results. Finding the quotient in the most basic kind of division involves only one step: a simple reversal of the multiplication tables (e.g., 48 divided by 6 is 8 because 8 times 6 is 48). But these divisions become the first step in learning the symbolic routine for taking account of place value when division is carried out on large numbers. Beginning with

---

[2]See King and Brownell (1966) and Schwab (1978) for the argument that curriculum and instruction might be designed to reflect rules of discourse in a discipline.

[3]See Bereiter and Scardamalia (1989) for an explication of the notion that intentional learning might be related to school curriculum and instruction.

quotients that have only one digit, students are instructed to write the operation in its traditional form and "line up the ones" in the quotient with the "ones" in the dividend, for example:

$$\begin{array}{c} \text{tens ones} \\[4pt] \begin{array}{r} 8 \\ \hline 6\,)4\;\;8 \end{array} \end{array} \qquad (1)$$

The traditional curriculum then moves on to divisions with one-digit divisors and larger numbers in the dividend, and students are taught to divide by moving from place to place, dividing when possible, "carrying" the remainder from one place to the next, and changing the way the units are grouped; the leftover thousands become hundreds, the leftover hundreds become tens, and the leftover tens become ones, for example:

$$\begin{array}{l} 1\;\;4\;\;2\;\;3 \text{ R. } 4 \\ 6)8\;{}^{2}5\;{}^{1}4\;{}^{2}2 \end{array} \qquad (2)$$

The dividend is decomposed by place values, and each place is operated on separately.

Breaking large numbers into parts to operate on them is not unique to the division procedure. All of the familiar arithmetic procedures work on multidigit numbers place by place. The possibility of operating on the digits one or two at a time rather than operating on the whole number at once is what makes our base-ten number system usable without reference to tables of equivalences; this feature of the Arabic number system is thought to be the basis for its rapid spread through the Mediterranean trading basin in the 15th century, when it replaced the more cumbersome Roman and Greek notations and made calculation available to a large segment of the population (Swetz, 1987).

In contrast to the school-taught algorithms for other operations, division begins with work on the left-hand side of the number rather than in the "ones" place. For example, in the short division in Equation 2, above, the conventional procedure begins with the operation "8 divided by 6," then goes on to "25 divided by 6," then "14 divided by 6," then "22 divided by 6." One does not operate on the original dividend as a whole quantity (eight thousand five hundred and forty-two) but on a succession of one- or two-digit numbers (eight, twenty-five, fourteen, twenty-two). The string of numbers being divided one after the other is difficult to relate to the magnitude of the dividend because as the "leftovers" from each place are carried to the right they are transformed into different kinds of units; thousands are traded for hundreds, hundreds for tens, tens for units.

In division by a two-digit divisor, the process is made even more complex by adding yet another step that takes the focus away from the magnitude of the numbers being operated on. For example, in

$$
\begin{array}{r}
270 \text{ R. } 12 \\
18\overline{)4872} \\
\underline{36} \\
127 \\
\underline{126} \\
12 \\
\underline{0} \\
12
\end{array}
\qquad (3)
$$

the task is to divide successive numbers by eighteen, but figuring out how many times eighteen "goes into" the successive parts of 4,872 would require knowing multiples of eighteen. Instead of expecting students to know the multiples of any possible divisor, we teach "estimation": Eighteen is close to twenty, and to divide a number like forty-eight by twenty, you need to "think": "two into four" or maybe "two into five." (Cf. Fennell, Reys, Reys, & Webb, 1987, p. 376, for example.) Why does it work to do that when the original number one wants to divide by eighteen is four thousand eight hundred and seventy-two? The mathematical justification that makes this estimation procedure (as well as the step-by-step attention to the dividend) legitimate is based on the relationship between division and the concepts of ratio and proportion.

What Does Long Division Mean in the Discipline of Mathematics?

Within the discipline of mathematics, the operation of division can be given meaning by seeing it as one of many "multiplicative structures" (Vergnaud, 1983, 1988). Those areas of the conventional curriculum that fall into the domain of multiplicative structures include multiplication, division, fractions, decimals, ratio, proportion, percent, and linear and nonlinear functions (Hiebert & Behr, 1988). Multiplicative structures are mathematical ideas that are used to analyze situations that can be modeled by proportions, and multiplicative problems are those that are solved by proportional reasoning. They are differentiated from additive structures, which are modeled by counting; additive problems are solved by joining and separating quantities.[4] In proportions, a relationship between two numbers comes to be regarded as a number in and of itself; for example, the meaning of a number like $\frac{4}{5}$ is derived from the relationship between four and five. We say that the number $\frac{8}{10}$ is equivalent to the number $\frac{4}{5}$ because 8 and 10 have the same relationship to one another that 4 has to 5 and we call the equality $\frac{4}{5} = \frac{8}{10}$ a proportion. By contrast, when they are employed in additive structures, the numbers four, five, eight, and ten would be regarded as indications of quantity or size, and they would be variously grouped and counted.

To illustrate how the conventional procedure for carrying out long division instantiates the mathematical concept of multiplicative structures and engages its users in the relationships of ratio and proportion, we consider the division

$$73\overline{)1536} \tag{4}$$

In this division, the mathematical question being asked is: "What number multiplied by 73 will yield 1,536 as a product?" By the definition of multiplication, we come to be working with groups of 73 units, and we want to know how many such groups will be needed to make a total of 1,536 units: "If 73 is 1 group, 1,536 is how many groups?" Or, "What number will relate to 1,536 in the same way that 1 relates to 73?" In proportional terms, we have the relationship:

$$\frac{73}{1} = \frac{1536}{X} \tag{5}$$

where X is the quotient to be determined. This pair of equal ratios represents a linear function that maps a group of 73 units on to each single unit. Using conventional mathematical symbols, the function is written as:

$$\frac{73}{1} = \frac{f(X)}{X}$$

or

$$f(X) = 73X \tag{6}$$

Given this way of thinking about the problem, we can produce other ratios to fit the function, like

$$\frac{f(X)}{X} = \frac{146}{2} = \frac{292}{4} \tag{7}$$

---

[4]The distinction between additive and multiplicative structures is a theoretical one. There is no implication here that these types of reasoning would be easy to sort out in a particular instance of mathematical activity.

This way of thinking about the problem of division is what Vergnaud (1983) called a "dimensional model" involving proportional relationships among four terms (in the case of this division, 73:1::1536:X) and it is what Nesher (1988) called a "mapping rule"; that is, the function tells us how many times 73 will map on to a unit in the quotient.

It is this proportion or mapping rule that describes the kind of mathematical argument that is involved in justifying the first and subsequent steps of the conventional procedure for finding the answer to a long division problem. When we start to think about this division

$$73)\overline{1536} \tag{8}$$

by figuring out what multiple of 7 is close to 15, we are assuming that the quotient of

$$73)\overline{153} \tag{9}$$

will be about a tenth of the quotient of

$$73)\overline{1536} \tag{10}$$

because 153 is about a tenth of 1536, and the quotient of

$$7)\overline{15} \tag{11}$$

will be the same as the quotient of

$$73)\overline{153} \tag{12}$$

These assumptions are based on the place value and proportional relationships among these pairs of numbers.

In order to understand why 15 divided by 7 is a mathematically legitimate way to begin to find out the quotient to 1,536 divided by 73, one would need to think in terms of proportions or linear functions. That is, in order for this step in the procedure to be supported by mathematical reasoning (as opposed to being a mechanical procedure supported by a teacher's or a textbook's authority), one must consider the approximate equivalence between $\frac{153}{7}$ and $\frac{1536}{73}$, while at the same time recognizing the difference in order of magnitude between 153 and 1,536, and between 7 and 73.

In terms of functions, we have $f(X) = 73X$, and what we want to find is the value of X that will yield 1,536. This is the kind of thinking that goes into inventing a mathematically legitimate procedure for finding the quotient of these particular numbers. Reasoning proportionally, from 73 times 2,[5] one

---

[5]Doubling as a way to begin the proportional reasoning process here is somewhat arbitrary. It is productive in this case because of the particular numbers involved, but the choice of doubling as a place to begin has no particular mathematical justification.

might assert that the answer to the division is close to 20 because if 73 times 2 is 146, then 73 times 20 is 1,460:

$$\frac{73}{1} = \frac{146}{2} = \frac{1460}{20} = \frac{f(X)}{X} \tag{13}$$

The answer to the division problem will be obtained by continuing to produce equivalent fractions until one is found with a numerator of 1,536. Continuing with the process of successive approximation, 73 times 21 would be 73 more than 1,460 or 1,533, and 73 times 22 would be 73 more or 1,616. So we have

$$\frac{73}{1} = \frac{146}{2} = \frac{1460}{20} = \frac{1533}{21} = \frac{1616}{22} \tag{14}$$

from which we can conclude that the answer to the division is between 21 and 22, and very close to 21, because 1,533 is comparatively close to 1,536. This reasoning can also be represented in a function chart as follows:

X	$f(X)$
1	73
?	1536
2	146
20	1460
21	1533
22	1616

If X is doubled, $f(X)$ changes proportionally; it is also doubled. If X is multiplied by 10, so is $f(X)$. If X_1 is added to X_2 to get X_3, then $f(X_3)$ can be obtained by adding $f(X_1)$ and $f(X_2)$. Using this way of thinking, it is possible to build up to the value of X that will produce "1,536" by making combinations of known values. We get $f(22)$, for example, by adding $f(20)$ and $f(2)$. The chart illustrates that the value of X for which $f(X)$ equals 1,536 is somewhere between 21 and 22, closer to 21.

Continuing with this sort of reasoning, one could get a more and more exact answer: One-tenth multiplied by 73 would be 7.3, and so 73 × 21.1 would be 1,533 + 7.3 or 1,540.3. Too big. One-twentieth is half of one-tenth, so one-twentieth (or in decimal terms, .05) times 73 is half of 7.3 or 3.65. In chart form:

X	$f(X)$
1	73
?	1536
2	146
20	1460
21	1533
22	1616
.1	7.3
21.1	1540.3
.05	3.65

Now it is possible to figure out 21.05×73 by adding; $1{,}533 + 3.65 = 1{,}536.65$—very close to the product I was aiming for. In proportional terms, we have:

$$\frac{73}{1} = \frac{1536.65}{21.05} \tag{15}$$

Depending on the accuracy required by the situation in which the division was constructed to solve a problem in the first place, one could continue working along these lines, producing a fraction with a numerator closer to 1,536.[6] The denominator would be the "answer" to the division problem.

Working through the division in this manner illustrates how the long division process is embedded in the domain of multiplicative structures. Because of the relationship between addition and multiplication, the division could also be done by successive subtractions: taking groups of 73 away from 1,536, and then counting the number of groups taken away. This procedure does not take advantage of the multiplicative nature of the operation, however. Division procedures are used to take away groups of groups, thereby going beyond the simple operation of counting into the domain of ratio and proportion.

---

[6]This judgment is not a matter of mathematical reasoning; deciding what degree of accuracy is required depends on the situation in which mathematics is being used. Some would argue that the interface between situation and reasoning should be a constant feature of mathematical activity in school (e.g., Schwartz, 1988), but others maintain that one must put the particularities of situations aside to fully appreciate the power of mathematics (e.g., Stewart, 1987).

STUDENTS' UNDERSTANDING
OF MULTIPLICATIVE STRUCTURES

Little research has been done in psychology on the question of students' understanding of division per se (Hiebert & Behr, 1988), but the work that has been done on proportional reasoning and on students' thinking about rational numbers gives some clues about how students might think about the concepts that are involved in understanding the multiplicative concepts underlying the conventional long division procedure and why they might have difficulty with this procedure in school.

Numbers as Relationships Versus
Numbers as Quantities

The proportional reasoning required to invent or understand a mathematically legitimate procedure for doing long division requires a significant change in how children think about the concept of "number" and this change does not build directly on their knowledge of how to use numbers in counting (Kieren, 1988; Schwartz, 1988; Steffe, 1988; Vergnaud, 1983, 1988). This does not mean that one cannot do division with large numbers using counting procedures, but such procedures are tedious and prone to error, and they distract from learning about other mathematical ideas that fall in the domain of multiplicative structures. In inventing more efficient procedures used for dividing one large number by another, one works with the concept of equivalent relationships between pairs of numbers, expressed as equal ratios or equivalent fractions (Lesh, Post, & Behr, 1988). This way of using number is significantly different from the way numbers are used to represent the process of combining and separating of quantities that underlies addition, subtraction, multiplication-as-repeated-addition, or division-as-repeated-subtraction. The need for such a "cognitive reorientation" in thinking about what the numbers mean in division and in fractions leads to the speculation "that there are not smooth continuous paths from early addition and subtraction to multiplication and division, nor from whole numbers to rational numbers. . . . The new concepts are not the sums of previous ones. Competence with middle school number concepts requires a break with the past, and a reconceptualization of number itself" (Hiebert & Behr, 1988, pp. 8–9). Cognitive researchers have found that as students approach the learning of multiplication and division and the work on fractions that accompanies learning how to transform the remainder, they persist in thinking of numbers as "counters" or as names for quantities of single units. This kind of thinking gets in the way of their using numbers to count groups of groups or parts of units and using numbers to indicate a relationship between two quantities; it also hinders their ability to reason proportionally about the relationship between the dividend and the quotient (Behr, Lesh, Post, & Silver, 1983; Fischbein, Deri, Nello, & Marino, 1985; Hart, 1981; Nesher, 1986).

A large-scale survey assessment was administered in England in 1974–1979 to assess 12-year-old students' mathematical understanding (Hart, 1981). In the subsection of the test devoted to understanding addition, subtraction, multiplication, and division, it was found that the students tested and interviewed were able to solve problems and communicate about mathematical situations that involved addition and subtraction quite proficiently. They appropriately matched arithmetic symbols to problem situations that indicated addition and subtraction, and constructed procedures for solving the problems that illustrated their understanding of the operations. Many students were unable, however, to interpret the mathematical symbols associated with division in a meaningful and usable manner.

Expressions like

$$23\overline{)391}$$

and

$$391\overline{)23} \tag{16}$$

were called "the same" by about half of the students. A small but significant number of students had very little understanding of either multiplication or division as multiplicative rather than additive operations, but these students could solve multiplication and division problems to which the repeated addition or repeated subtraction strategies were appropriate (Hart, 1981).

In interviews where they were asked to relate arithmetic operations to problem contexts, many children in the British study used "divided by," "divided into," and "shared among" interchangably. When they were asked to interpret the division of a smaller number by a larger one, they often simply inverted the numbers. Correlations between these tests of understanding and a standardized test of computational skills showed that some children mastered the division algorithm without understanding the meaning of division, but those with hardly any understanding of the operation were not, in general, successful with the calculations. There were some children who performed well on the test of understanding and poorly on the test of algorithmic proficiency (Hart, 1981). Although their inability could be interpreted as a difficulty with language and symbols rather than with the concepts involved in doing division, they can also be taken more broadly as evidence for the claim that many students never move beyond the association of operations on numbers with the simple act of counting.

Research on Teaching and Learning
Long Division in School

We have known for a long time that the division algorithm is likely to cause trouble for students whose goal is to use the procedure to produce accurate answers. Buswell's (1926) research early in this century documented in great detail the nature and frequency of the sorts of errors students are likely to make in carrying out the many steps required. After documenting the habits that lead students to make errors in arithmetic procedures—not only in doing division, but in doing addition, subtraction, and multiplication as well—Buswell made two speculative suggestions for improving teaching: One was that simply drilling until answers were accurate was not going to be very effective, and the other was that teachers should try to understand the nature of our number system and how it is structured as a route toward understanding the difficulties students were having with computation (pp. 197–198). Buswell did not do research on teaching to examine the viability of practices based on these suggestions, but he certainly set the tone for more contemporary work in this area (e.g., Carpenter, Fennema, Peterson, Chiang, & Loef, 1988).

Most current instructional research on division begins from the dimensional model in Vergnaud's (1988) theory of multiplicative structures, using the sort of mapping table that was illustrated earlier (see also Nesher, 1988). The goal of these studies is to provide children with a tool that would encourage them to think multiplicatively rather than additively, that is to think of multiplication and division problems in terms of relationships among groups of groups, rather than as repeated addition. This mapping tool is thought to be useful on the basis of findings of the research on proportional reasoning in which children were found to revert to additive strategies and to use them inappropriately when the numbers in the problem did not have an obviously proportional relationship (Hart, 1988; Karplus, Pulos, & Stage, 1983). Teaching sixth-grade students to use mapping tables was found to be effective in encouraging students to think multiplicatively, even with complicated numbers. The mapping tables were also successful in guiding students in their decisions about when to multiply and when to divide. Other instructional research related to students' understanding of long division has been done beginning with problem situations in which students need to model the semantic relationships among numbers in a situation using arithmetic operations (Bell, Greer, Grimson, &

Mangan, 1989; Lesh et al., 1988; Nesher, 1987; Schwartz, 1988; Silver, 1988). This work is reviewed elsewhere in this volume in reports on "word problems" research.

TEXTBOOKS AS A CURRICULAR RESOURCE
IN TEACHING LONG DIVISION
FOR UNDERSTANDING

An analysis of the mathematical structure of long division, together with recognizing the difficulties students have in making the transition to thinking about numbers as symbols for proportional relationships, provides us with a framework for raising questions about what should be included in school curriculum and instruction if the goal is to have students appreciate the important mathematical ideas embedded in the long division procedure. In this section, we examine the extent to which textbooks take account either of the mathematical structure underlying the operation or of what researchers have argued about why the concepts behind the procedure might be difficult for children to understand.[7] Long division is introduced in most textbook series at the fourth-grade level. Students in this grade move from learning that division is the inverse of multiplication to learning about "short" divisions with remainders and then on to dividing numbers with multiple digits. The treatment of this transition in two textbook series is considered here in some detail. The two series were chosen because both are widely used in public schools and because both make claims to attend to number sense and estimation as the foundation for procedural competence (Fennell et al., 1987, pp. T10–T11, T16–T17; Willoughby, Bereiter, Hilton, & Rubenstein, 1987a, p. xviii).

Connecting Procedures and Stories,
or Not

Fig. 4.1 is a reproduction of the page in the Teachers' Guide to the Grade 4 textbook in the *Mathematics Unlimited* series (Fennell et al., 1987, p. 172), where students first meet the idea of a quotient of more than one digit. The

---

[7]The author recognizes that the curriculum as enacted by teachers and students is not isomorphic with the material found in textbooks, but that textbooks do shape the decisions teachers make about what and how to teach as well as shaping the way teachers and students think about what it means to know a subject (Freeman et al., 1983; Schmidt, Porter, Floden, Freeman & Schwille, 1987; Talmage, 1972). In mathematics, teachers seem to rely on textbooks most heavily when it comes to teaching arithmetic operations (Freeman & Porter, in press; Stodolsky, 1988).

6 | DIVISION

Objective: To divide 2-digit dividends by 1-digit divisors and obtain 2-digit quotients, with and without remainders

Warm-Up
Write these examples on the chalkboard.

8⟌640   9⟌280   4⟌330   5⟌160   2⟌150

Have students estimate each quotient. (80, 30, 80, 30, 70)

GETTING STARTED

Write *D M S C* on the chalkboard. Ask students to recall what each letter stands for in the division process. (divide, multiply, subtract, compare) Discuss each step in a division example.

TEACHING THE LESSON

The new step is the "bring down" procedure, which is a way to show regrouping. In the textbook example, 2 cannot be divided into the remainder 1 (tens) and result in a whole number. Thus it is necessary to "bring down" the 6 and divide 2 into 16 ones.
Emphasize the importance of estimating quotients to help students check on
• the number of digits that should be in the quotient.
• the reasonableness of their answers.

Checkpoint
The chart lists the common errors students make when dividing 2-digit dividends.

Correct Answers: 1b, 2c, 3d, 4c

Remediation
■ For this error, have students copy and complete these examples.

```
    1 3        □ 6 R       □ □ R
5⟌6 5      4⟌6 6       3⟌7 1
  □          4           □
  ─          ──          ──
  0 5        □ □         1 □
  □ □        □ □          9
  ───        ──          ──
   □          2           □
```

(13, 16 R2, 23 R2)
□ For this error, assign Reteach Master, p. 48.
○ For this error, assign both Follow-Up Activities on T.E. p. 173.
△ For this error, refer students to the examples on p. 170.

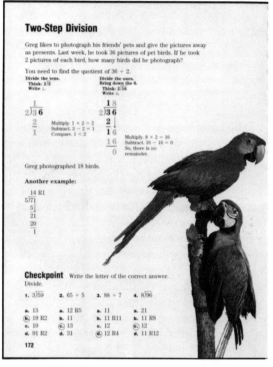

Two-Step Division

Greg likes to photograph his friends' pets and give the pictures away as presents. Last week, he took 36 pictures of pet birds. If he took 2 pictures of each bird, how many birds did he photograph?

You need to find the quotient of 36 ÷ 2.

Divide the tens.
Think: 2⟌3
Write 1.

$$\begin{array}{r} 1 \\ 2\overline{)3\ 6} \\ \underline{2} \\ 1 \end{array}$$

Multiply. 1 × 2 = 2
Subtract. 3 − 2 = 1
Compare. 1 < 2

Divide the ones.
Bring down the 6.
Think: 2⟌16
Write 8.

$$\begin{array}{r} 1\ 8 \\ 2\overline{)3\ 6} \\ \underline{2} \\ 1\ 6 \\ \underline{1\ 6} \\ 0 \end{array}$$

Multiply. 8 × 2 = 16
Subtract. 16 − 16 = 6
So, there is no remainder.

Greg photographed 18 birds.

Another example:

$$\begin{array}{r} 14\ R1 \\ 5\overline{)71} \\ \underline{5} \\ 21 \\ \underline{20} \\ 1 \end{array}$$

Checkpoint Write the letter of the correct answer.
Divide.

1. 3⟌59	2. 65 ÷ 5	3. 88 ÷ 7	4. 8⟌96
a. 13	a. 12 R5	a. 11	a. 21
b. 19 R2	b. 11	b. 11 R11	b. 11 R8
c. 19	c. 13	c. 12	c. 12
d. 91 R2	d. 31	d. 12 R4	d. 11 R12

172

COMMON ERRORS

Answer Choice	Type of Error
■ 1a, 2b, 3a	Divides tens and ones as separate examples
□ 1c, 3c	Forgets to record the remainder
○ 2a, 3b, 4b, 4d	Writes the remainder larger than or equal to the divisor
△ 1d, 2d, 4a	Records the digits of the quotient from the right to the left

RETEACH Two-Step Division

Reteach Worksheet

FIG. 4.1. Introducing long division in *Mathematics Unlimited* (from *Mathematics Unlimited*, Grade 4 by Francis Fennell, Barbara J. Reys, Robert E. Reys, and Arnold W. Webb, copyright © 1987 by Holt, Rinehart and Winston, Inc.; reprinted by permission of the publisher).

focus of this lesson is on the procedure to follow when division requires "two steps", that is, when you cannot just get the answer by reversing a multiplication fact. It is the figuring below the quotient that breaks the division into two steps and qualifies this lesson as an introduction to the procedure known as long division. At the top of the page, there is a story about dividing 36 pictures into groups of two. In the recommended procedure, the two digits in 36 are considered separately, and students are first directed to "Think 2)3" as they "Divide the tens." There is no indication that what they are doing here is figuring out how many groups there would be if they were dividing 30 pictures into groups of two. Although the story about dividing up pictures may serve in a general way to convey something about the meaning of division, it is not invoked as an aid to understanding what is happening at each step in the long division procedure, nor does it seem like a context in which it might actually make sense to go through the steps that students are directed to follow. As they consider the division of 3 by 2, students are directed to "Write 1" and the illustration shows that the "1" goes over the "3." Multiply, subtract, compare, and then on to the next digit, which is the "6" in the ones place. But what actually is now being divided is "16" because there were ten left over when thirty pictures were divided into two groups of ten. The authors of the series assert that they use stories to make topics "concrete and real—relating to students' own experience—to pave the way for future success in using estimation naturally and spontaneously in daily life" (p. T16). Although this intention addresses the understanding of the process of division as an operation, it does not illuminate the steps in the process or support their mathematical legitimacy. In actually doing the activity of dividing up the number of pictures, one might more sensibly proceed by dividing up thirty into fifteen groups of two and then dividing the other six pictures into three groups of two, making eighteen groups of two altogether. (Cf. Sowder, 1988.)

In the teachers' notes that accompany this lesson, teachers are reminded to "Emphasize the importance of estimating quotients to help students check on the number of digits that should be in the quotient [and] the reasonableness of their answers." Teachers also are informed of common errors students make when doing these kinds of divisions: "Divides tens and ones as separate examples, Forgets to record the remainder, Writes the remainder larger than or equal to the divisor, Records the digits of the quotient from the right to the left" (Fennell et al., 1987, p. 172). To help students who make the first three of these errors after being taught the lesson previously excerpted, the teacher is directed toward activities that focus on going over the mechanics of the algorithm in several different ways. For the fourth error, it is suggested that having students look back at a previous lesson on "estimating quotients" might help. That lesson also begins with a story, but like the lesson on "Two-Step Division" it only states the story and then refers back to it when stating the answer. The story is not used as a context for guiding the procedure or even for evaluating the reasonableness of the estimate (Fennell et al., 1987).

The introduction of this level of division in the fourth-grade text in the *Real Math* series (Willoughby et al., 1987a, pp. 272–279) also uses a story but makes a very explicit connection between elements of the story and the mathematical justification for the procedure (Fig. 4.2). Like the lesson in *Mathematics Unlimited,* this lesson is intended to make the transition from division using simple reversals of the multiplication facts to division that involves place-value decompositions. The *Real Math* lesson also begins with a story about a collection of something to be divided up, but it does not begin with a two-digit number divided by a one-digit number, and by contrast with the *Mathematics Unlimited* approach, the story is integrated with the algorithm at every step along the way. The teacher is directed to actually carry out the divisions and trades with play money as a class demonstration, decomposing the dividend along place-value lines and carrying out the step-by-step operation both on the numbers and in the familiar domain of money. The authors of the *Real Math* series state that the purpose of this activity is "To provide a story that shows why the algorithm works" (Willoughby et al., 1987a, p. 272TE). Several more activities of this sort are provided (four lessons) before students are asked to practice working the algorithm without reference to money.

The authors of *Real Math* intentionally introduce the algorithm using numbers larger than students would be using in their first practice in order to convey the necessity for having the algorithm in the first place. They assert that "If the dividend in the story were too small, the characters would not need an algorithm, so the development would seem artificial" (Willoughby et al., 1987a, p. 273TE). A small amount of money easily could be dealt out to one child after the other or evenly divided by trial and error. The authors do not explain why they used a story about money to develop the algorithm, but one might speculate that the sorts of bills that the children found in the story lend themselves to the kind of place-value decompositions that are characteristic of arithmetic algorithms, whereas dividing up other kinds of things (like pictures of birds) does not. The emphasis here is on explaining, both why the algorithm works and why it makes sense to have an algorithm in the first place.

In the last chapter of the fourth-grade text in the *Mathematics Unlimited* series, division by two-digit divisors is introduced, following units on fractions, mixed numbers, decimals, measurement, geometry, and multiplication with two-digit divisors. The two-digit division unit begins with a lesson on "Mental Computation: Dividing Tens and Hundreds" in which students are instructed to pay attention to the nonzero digits in divisions like $30)\overline{1,800}$. In this example, the first direction is "Think $3)\overline{18}$." The number of zeros placed after the 6 in the quotient depends on getting the 6 in the right

91

Dividing by 1-Digit Divisors (Long Form)

Student book pages 264, 265, 266, 267, 268, 269, 270, 271

Purposes

The purposes of this lesson are:

1. To introduce a division algorithm for 1-digit divisors.
2. To provide a story that shows why the algorithm works.

This is the first of 13 lessons on division with a 1-digit divisor. A checkpoint for assessing mastery is provided in lesson 94 and again in lesson 101. In this lesson, we develop a long form of the division algorithm (with the partial quotients) by showing it as a means of keeping track of a sum of money being divided equally among several people. In the next lesson (92), the students will practice using the algorithm (long form) to keep a record of how they split up a sum of play money. In lesson 93 we show a shorter form of the algorithm. By lesson 97, the students will have had many opportunities to understand, apply, and carry out the algorithm, so in that lesson we introduce the standard short form (the "shortest form"), which students may use from that point on.

By the end of the unit the students should be proficient with using some form of the algorithm to divide whole numbers by 1-digit divisors. They should also be proficient in determining when division is appropriate and in interpreting results. In addition to the checkpoints in lessons 94 and 101, ample opportunities are provided throughout the unit to assess each student's progress by observing students play the Four Cube Division Game (introduced in lesson 98) and by assessing their work on pages of division problems and on pages of mixed word problems (where only some of the answers require division).

Materials

For pages 264–269 Play money may be useful.

THE 7-WAY SPLIT

Rosa and 6 of her friends were out playing one day when they found an envelope.

Inside the envelope was money. There were eight $1000 bills, nine $100 bills, three $10 bills, and six $1 bills.

- How much money is that altogether? $8936
- What would you do if you found that much money? Answers will vary.

FIG. 4.2. Introducing long division in *Real Math*. (Reprinted from *Real Math Teacher's Guide Level 4* by Stephen S. Willoughby, Carl Bereiter, Peter Hilton, and Joseph H. Rubinstein, by permission of Open Court Publishing Company. Copyright © 1987, 1985, 1981 by Open Court Publishing Company.)

The children each took two $100 bills. Then they put that on their record.

```
      200
     1000
  7)8936
     7000
     1936
```

- How much money does each child have now? $1200
- How many $100 bills are left in the pile? 5
- How much money is left in the pile altogether? $536

The children also put on their record that they took fourteen $100 bills altogether, leaving $536 in the pile.

```
      200
     1000
  7)8936
     7000
     1936
     1400          This is how much they just took altogether.
      536          7 × 200 = 1400

                   This is how much they have left to divide.
                   1936 – 1400 = 536
```

They decided that the way to divide up the remaining five $100 bills was to exchange them for $10 bills.

- How many $10 bills should they get for five $100 bills? 50
- How many $10 bills will they have altogether? 50 from the exchange plus the 3 they had makes 53 in all.
- How many $10 bills should each child get? 7
- How many $10 bills will be left? 4

FIG. 4.2, continued

239

Mental arithmetic

Basic facts—inverse operations As in the mental arithmetic exercise in lesson 39, give the students problems with the basic facts: addition, subtraction, multiplication, and division. Focus special attention on the inverse relationship between the multiplication and division facts, as in these pairs of problems: $9 \times 7 = (63)$, $63 \div 9 = (7)$; $8 \times 7 = (56)$, $56 \div 8 = (7)$; and so on.

Student pages 264–269

Read this story with the class. It continues through page 269 and develops an algorithm for dividing a whole number by a 1-digit divisor. Stop at each question; have students give and discuss answers.

You may find it useful to actually "find" the $8936 somewhere in the classroom. Have the "bank" at your desk, or wherever play money is usually kept. You might also have 7 students play the roles of the children in the story.

When you get to page 265, begin keeping a record like the one shown on that page. (See comment for page 265.)

Note: The numbers used in the story in this lesson are intentionally larger than the numbers that the students will generally work with during the rest of this unit. There are several reasons for this:

1. If the dividend in the story were too small, the characters would not need an algorithm, so the development would seem artificial.

2. Unless the dividend were large enough, it would not be clear that the same series of steps is repeated again and again.

3. Working through a problem with large numbers (as a class, with the teacher) helps convince students that the algorithm works with any numbers, not just with simple or small ones.

Student page 265

When you get to this page, begin keeping a record like the one shown on the page. At each step, write what the figures mean. For example:

```
      1000—Amount each child has
   7)8936
     7000
     1936—Money left to be distributed
```

Make sure the students understand each transaction *before* you explain the record-keeping step.

The story continues on page 266.

The 7 children took the money to the police station and gave it to the person at the lost-and-found department.

After 30 days, nobody had claimed the money. So the police gave the $8936 back to the children.

"How shall we divide the money?" asked Marvin.

"Let's each take a $1000 bill," replied Louis. Each of the 7 children took one $1000 bill.

The children decided to keep a record of what they were doing. Because they wanted the $8936 to be divided into 7 equal amounts of money, they wrote the problem this way:

$$7)\overline{8936}$$

Each child took $1000. They kept track of this on the top of the record.

$$
\begin{array}{r}
1000 \\
7)\overline{8936}
\end{array}
$$
— This is how much each child has taken so far.

Now they had used up $7000, leaving $1936. They kept track of this at the bottom of the record.

$$
\begin{array}{r}
1000 \\
7)\overline{8936} \\
7000 \\
\hline
1936
\end{array}
$$

— This is how much they have just taken altogether.
$7 \times 1000 = 7000$

— This is how much they have left to divide.
$8936 - 7000 = 1936$

240

FIG. 4.2., continued

Each child has taken a $1000 bill.

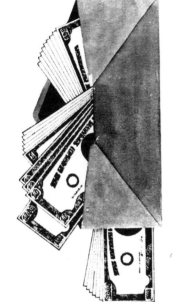

Now the 7 children have one $1000 bill, nine $100 bills, three $10 bills, and six $1 bills. "How shall we divide the rest of the money?" asked Kelli.

"We could each take a $100 bill," said Leonard.

"But what will we do with the $1000 bill?" asked Nora.

- What would you do? Answers will vary.

Kelli suggested they take the extra $1000 bill to the bank and change it for ten $100 bills.

- How many $100 bills will they have if they do this?
The ten $100 bills from the exchange plus the nine $100 bills they had makes nineteen $100 bills in all.

At the bank, they changed the $1000 bill for ten $100 bills. Now they had nineteen $100 bills.

"We can each take two $100 bills," said Elaine.

"Yes, but we're going to have some left over," Rosa said.

- How many $100 bills will be left after each child has taken two of them? 5

FIG. 4.2., continued

241

place over the dividend. There are no directions given for how to decide where to place it, however, although students are directed to check the quotient by multiplying it by the divisor to see if the product equals the dividend. In a later lesson, on "Dividing by Multiples of 10," students are directed to divide $40\overline{)286}$ by following this procedure:

Divide the hundreds.   Think $40\overline{)2}$. Not enough hundreds.
Divide the tens.   Think $40\overline{)28}$. Not enough tens.
Divide the ones.   Think $40\overline{)286}$, or $4\overline{)28}$.

Estimate 7. $\begin{array}{r} 7 \text{ R. } 6 \\ 40\overline{)286} \\ \underline{280} \\ 6 \end{array}$

(Fennell et al., 1987, p. 324).

The teacher is directed to "Point out that because the divisor is greater than the first two digits, students must place the quotient digit over the ones place in the dividend" (Fennell et al., 1987, p. 324). There is no explanation of why $4\overline{)28}$ can be exchanged for $40\overline{)286}$ as a strategy for arriving at the quotient. Earlier in the page students are instructed to

---

Think: $20\overline{)80}$ is about the same as $2\overline{)8}$.

Look at the pattern.

$2\overline{)8}$ $20\overline{)80}$ $20\overline{)800}$

(Fennell et al., 1987, p. 324).

The fact that eighty is in the same relationship to twenty as eight is to two is not explained anywhere, to teacher or student, and the use of the word "about" in the directions for thinking here is curious. The "Reteach" worksheet that is recommended for students who have difficulty doing the procedure correctly contains the same language and the same sort of example.

The explanation of the sort of proportional relationship that enables us to estimate when dividing by a two-digit quotient is not given much more attention in the *Real Math* series, but there is some mathematical justification given for the procedure. The "long division algorithm" is not introduced in this series until fifth grade, and it is not supposed to be taught until students have done considerable work on rates, ratio, equal proportions, decimal numbers, and functions.

In relation to the problem of dividing 414 by 24, the following directions are given:

First find an approximate answer.
Round 24 to 20. Then divide both numbers by ten.

$$20\overline{)414} \longrightarrow 2\overline{)41.4}$$

Now divide.

$$\frac{20}{2\overline{)41.4}}$$

So the answer is about 20.

(Willoughby, Bereiter, Hilton, & Rubenstein, 1987b, p. 230)

The process of changing divisions with large numbers into divisions with smaller numbers by considering them as equal ratios is explained in relation to a story context (analogous to the one in the fourth-grade book) in which problems need to be solved in this way (Willoughby et al., 1987b, p. 203) and teachers are told that "The material in this lesson is essential for the work in subsequent lessons. If any students are having difficulty it would be wise to extend this lesson to two or more days, using the extra teaching outlined below" (Willoughby et al., 1987b, p. 230). The extra teaching that is recommended focuses on students understanding of place-value relationships, and the use of play money, base-ten materials, and place-value charts are recommended.

These two textbooks provide an interesting contrast in the attention that is given to the connection between the mathematical structure of long division and the conventional procedure. The justification for the steps in the procedure are modeled in the *Real Math* version by using trades among different denominations of money to represent the decomposition of the dividend. In the *Mathematics Unlimited* version, the decomposition is presented as a series of mechanical steps with no justification. *Real Math* provides more resources for the teacher who wants to teach long division as a mathematical idea, but it does not give teachers much guidance about the difficulties we know students have with this idea.

HOW MIGHT WE TEACH LONG DIVISION
FOR UNDERSTANDING?

Mathematics, research on learning and thinking, and curriculum are all important considerations in examining what might be entailed in students' learning long division in a way that is related to authentic mathematical understanding. But even if taken together, they do not explicitly address the question of mathematical pedagogy. In his summary comments on the papers presented at the National Council of Teachers of Mathematics Research Agenda Project Conference on Number Concepts in the Middle Grades, Case (1988) reviewed the research on learning the number concepts that are taught at the upper elementary level, and found very little in that literature on teaching. He suggested that it would be appropriate for researchers to pursue the following questions at this time:

> How can we *teach* so that students' major conceptual errors are articulated, or at least 'headed off at the pass,' and so that partial understandings are redirected into more complete understandings?
> How can *teachers* best stay in tune with their students' mental models and processes and the changing nature of their partial understandings?
> What can *teachers* do to deal with the individual variability they encounter in examining children's mathematical representations and processes?
> (p. 269, emphasis added)

These are all questions about how teaching can be organized to pay attention to the way students think about numbers and number relationships. In their recent review of the research that has been done on mathematics education at the upper elementary and middle-school level, Hiebert and Behr (1988) also suggested that we need to find classroom-teaching strategies that will "facilitate students' constructions of meaning for written mathematical symbols [and] identify the support and development of central conceptual strategies, from their first appearance in an incomplete or intuitive form to more formal procedures that generalize to all structurally similar problems" (p. 15).

Research on Teaching
from the Teacher's Perspective

The research on the teaching of long division reported here is intended to address these questions. It looks at student thinking and curricular innovation through the lens of teaching practice, describing the teacher's actions interactively with curriculum and student cognition. It addresses such questions as what a teacher might need to do in an ordinary classroom setting to make use of such tools as mapping tables to construct lessons that are responsive to students' ways of thinking and what practices might be successful in altering the social structure of lessons to engage students in actively trying to figure out the meaning of division as an operation. The general program of research and development, of which the work on teaching long division was a part, was organized around the questions:

What sort of work is entailed in teaching that is designed to take account of how students think in the setting of ordinary classroom lessons?

What sort of work might teachers do to support the development of students' thinking in mathematically productive directions?

What constitutes mathematical understanding in the school classroom setting?

(Cf. Lampert, 1988.) This inquiry into teaching was conducted by the author from the teacher's perspective.[8] It is different from conventional instructional research in that I developed curriculum and instruction interactively with finding out about how students think about a topic, and in that it occurred as part of the regular instructional program for an entire class. It is also different from research on students' thinking that is carried out in clinical interviews by psychologists (e.g., Kieren, 1988) and research on children's mathematical competence carried out in problem-solving settings that arise outside of classrooms (e.g., Saxe, 1988) from projects that use the findings of such research to design instructional strategies (e.g. Carpenter et al., 1988).

The assumption here was that teaching practice can be designed situationally to express important mathematical principles in a way that is responsive to the particular knowledge about student thinking that can be obtained by a teacher in the course of a lesson, as well as making use of more general propositional knowledge derived from cognitive research (Lampert, 1988a). A related theoretical assumption is that students' understanding and teachers' understanding are contextual. What students can and will do in the classroom is different from what they can and will do in an interview setting and different from what they can and will do in solving a problem that arises in the course of daily living outside of either of these formats. What teachers can do and say in university settings is different from what they can do and say in classrooms. What learners and teachers can be said to "know" or "understand" in different settings is therefore functionally different. We know very little about how understanding "travels" among such different settings (Pea, 1988). Given these limitations,

---

[8]See Lampert (1988) and Lampert (1990a) for a more complete description of the relationship between research and practice that is assumed in this work and for a review of the methodological arguments for writing about teaching and learning from the teachers' perspective.

it seems problematic to define understanding based on research done outside of classrooms and then to assess whether classroom instruction is successful in producing that kind of understanding in the social setting of school activities, just as it is problematic to equate a teachers' knowledge of research with what he or she is able to do with that knowledge in a classroom context.

From some perspectives, the fact that the teacher inquires about student thinking in the classroom in the course of instruction might be considered a methodological problem. A teacher is invested in the outcomes of the interaction in a way that a researcher would not be. This problem was addressed in part by using data from many sources to document what occurred in lessons as a supplement to my own records. The decision not to use independent pre- and posttest data or interviews to examine students' thinking was based on the assumption that students' performance on tests or in interviews would not adequately measure what they were able to do during class while involved in mathematical activities with their peers and teacher. This research method is based on a definition of knowledge as a collaborative situational production of teacher and students (Greeno, 1986).

Research Methods and Setting

I have taught fourth- and fifth-grade mathematics during the past 6 years, collecting data on both teaching and learning during 3 of those years. For 1984–1985, these data included audio tapes of lessons for 6 months, video tapes of two units, records of speech and visual communication kept by an observer at least three times a week over the whole school year, notebooks in which students did their daily work including writing and drawing they do to represent their thinking, and students' homework papers. I also have kept my own detailed field notes on lessons, including descriptions of how lessons and units were planned and implemented and initial analyses of the planning process itself, the lessons as they were taught, and students' work. For this chapter, I have further analyzed the portion of these data pertaining to the teaching of division using triangulation among different data sources and constant comparison within and between lessons.

Exploratory lesson development in the area of long division was done by the author in a fourth-grade class in 1984–1985, and it is the subset of data that was collected during this period that is analyzed here. This class had been involved for several weeks in work on multidigit multiplication prior to the work on division (Lampert, 1986a, 1986b). Before any instruction took place that was directed toward learning about long division, there were a few students who were proficient in carrying out the steps of the conventional algorithm, although none of them were competent to make decisions about what to do with the remainder. Before and during the instructional sequence on division, some students were taught to carry out the conventional algorithm at home by parents, tutors, or older siblings. At the beginning of the lesson sequence, those students who knew how to perform a conventional procedure used whatever version of the procedure they had learned without regard for the problem context. Other students, presumably those not proficient in any version of the conventional algorithm, invented procedures to solve problems like "How would you share 86 cakes among 5 restaurants equally?" These solutions did not involve the use of the conventional algorithm, and the students who used them were more likely to dispose of the remainder in ways that were appropriate to the problem context. Other students simply responded to questions like this by saying, "I don't know how to do it." or "We haven't had division yet."

Lesson Architecture

Lessons were conducted as whole-class activities with me at the board and students sitting at tables in groups of four or five. The verbal interaction was conducted primarily as a large-group discussion; I posed problems and students speculated about how the problems might be solved and responded to one another's propositions. I used the blackboard to represent salient mathematical features of the students' contributions and relate them to the intended outcomes of the lesson. What was drawn or written on the blackboard was intended to be a bridge between the common language that students used for talking about their mathematical ideas, and the more formal conceptual structure represented by the conventional symbols in mathematics as an academic discipline (Vergnaud, 1988). Legitimate representations or solution strategies invented by a student became part of the lesson for the whole class as they were taken up and drawn on the board by the teacher and subsequently refined in whole-class discussion.

In order to accommodate a wide range of abilities and backgrounds among the student participants, I often acted as a coach and discussion leader while students constructed solutions to problems collaboratively with me and their classmates. The "answers" thus obtained were not the production of any one student, and students were not expected to work independently. More advanced students and the teacher provided a scaffold whereby less advanced students could develop their thinking beyond the sorts of solutions they would be competent to produce alone (Vygotsky, 1978). When students were expected to produce written solutions to problems or representations of operations, they used drawings and words as well as numerical symbols. All of these instructional strategies were designed to promote a culture of mathematical discourse in the classroom, whereby teacher and students could communicate about ideas that made sense to everyone involved. (Cf. Lampert, 1989, 1990b.)

In the fourth-grade unit on division, there were two kinds of activities, each designed to address a particular facet of the conceptual structure of division in relation to students' thinking about it. One kind of activity focused on proportional relationships among numbers, and engaged students in observing patterns and creating various kinds of groupings. In many of these activities, there was an emphasis on decomposing numbers along place-value lines. In these activities, numbers were considered as abstract symbols for quantities or groups of quantities, and no particular objects were used as representations of the operations or relationships. The other kind of activity was representing divisions with stories and pictures that referred to particular objects. Here the students were engaged in the problem of what to do with the remainder given different problem contexts. They did not begin with problem contexts, but rather created them to fit divisions that were symbolized abstractly by numbers.[9] Estimation strategies were discussed and critically evaluated in a variety of problem settings, both concrete and abstract. For large numbers, students used the multiplication capacity of their calculators to test and refine their estimates, again focusing on the proportional reasoning aspect of thinking about division. In the drawings that students produced, division was represented in many different forms. Although the issue of giving meaning to the remainder and the issue of distinguishing between partitive and quotative interpretations of division were not excluded from the series of lessons reported here, neither were they explored thoroughly. The purpose of this series of lessons was to examine whether students could become engaged, in regular mathematics lessons, in thinking about the proportional relationships within divisions of large numbers; the other topics were taken up in more detail later with this group of children in the fifth grade.

The descriptions of lessons that follow serve to document both the sort of teaching that might go on in a school classroom to engage students in

---

[9]The decision to begin in this way was not deliberate and I do not mean to suggest the starting with either numbers or story contexts is the "right" way to teach. The purpose of the description and analysis in this chapter is to examine what happened rather than to justify it on the basis of research on learning. In the case of this lesson segment, as with all the others described here, the intention is to conduct an investigation into teaching and learning processes, not to portray the direct translation of research into practice; teaching is not the sort of practice in which such translations are possible (Lampert, 1985). Where justifications for teaching decisions do appear, they are based on the teachers' understanding of the mathematical terrain.

understanding long division and how a particular group of fourth graders responded to this sort of teaching. In their responses, there is evidence that they have the capacity to reason proportionally about relationships among numbers. There is also some informal evidence that suggests that they can connect this reasoning with conventional computational activity, but the research was not designed to examine this connection using conventional methods.

THE LESSONS

The lessons that are described in this section of the chapter are not meant to represent a script for how to teach long division. They were constructed on the foundation of the mathematical concepts described earlier, and they might be conceived as a journey through the "long division region" in the territory of multiplicative structures. Many alternative journeys through this region are possible, and if teaching is constructed interactively with students, it is likely that a different class would take a different journey.[10]

An Exploration of Students' Thinking About Grouping and Counting

The first activity in the fourth-grade division unit that I taught in 1984–1985 was designed to engage students in thinking about the patterns and relationships that would emerge if a given number of units were partitioned into groups of different sizes. The major purpose of this lesson was for me to gather information about how the members of the class would think about some of the ideas underlying the operation of division when it was not presented in its conventional curricular form. The activity could be done using several different procedures ranging from simple counting to conventional long division. The activity was set up in such a way as to emphasize the "mapping rule" that would relate the divisor and the quotient, thereby giving students a tool for thinking about division as a proportional relationship. What I was looking for was the extent to which students would be able to recognize relevant patterns and relationships, and the

---

[10]See Spiro, Vispoel, Schmitz, Samarapungavan, & Boerger (1987) and Greeno (1990) for a theoretical exposition of this way of thinking about curriculum and instruction. See also Resnick (1989).

language they used to describe them. The observations made by the students after they did several "divisions" of the given number into different size groups established a way of talking about the concepts underlying division. More conventional terms and symbols could be introduced gradually in direct connection with the students' own expressions.

This lesson was the first in a series in which the mathematical structure underlying long division was constructed collaboratively and interactively by teachers and students. As the more knowledgeable adult in these discussions, I interjected new ideas and information when they seemed related to the students' thinking and questions. I provided representations of elements in the discussions that focused the activity on elements relevant to understanding division by being somewhat symbolic, but they also made use of the ordinary language that fourth graders use to talk about the operation of division. This practice was designed to establish a system of communication midway between students' informal language for expressing their understanding of mathematical relationships and the formalities of mathematics that I wanted them to learn.[11]

In the lesson, I used two visual representations to begin to make connections between student thinking and the mathematics I wanted them to learn. The first was groups of units represented by rows of Xs on the blackboard, and the second was a chart in which the patterns and relationships in divisions of different quantities would be more transparent than they are in ordinary language. The groups of Xs on the board were intended to illustrate the relationship between multiplication and division in situations with large numbers and "leftovers." The first lesson described here is comparable in scope and sequence to the first set of textbook lessons described earlier in that it turned the class's agenda toward divisions that were more complex than reversals of the "multiplication facts."

In the introduction to the activity, a class volunteer was asked to pick a number between 25 and 50 to indicate the number of objects to be divided into groups; she picked "45." Then other volunteers were asked to suggest numbers that might be tried in the experiment to see what would happen if 45 were divided into groups of that magnitude. The first student suggested we try groups of five. Another student said that would make fifty groups. A third student said, "No, you don't add, you multiply. Nine times five is forty-five, so it's nine in a group." Another concurred, "It's five things in every group with none left over."

---

[11]Vergnaud (1988) called the mathematical relationships that are taken into account in students' informal reasoning "theorems in action." These relationships are not formally asserted by students in discussion, but Vergnaud asserted that they "underlie students' behavior" and can be expressed in formal mathematical terms by the teacher as a way to make a bridge between students' thinking and the mathematics the teacher wants them to learn.

We were well on our way to figuring out how to communicate about what division might mean. To represent the results of this discussion, I drew on the board:

XXXXXXXXX
XXXXXXXXX
XXXXXXXXX
XXXXXXXXX
XXXXXXXXX

calling the drawing "five groups of nine." Then I asked, "What would happen if I took the same forty-five things and made them into groups of two?" Two was chosen because students have a variety of techniques for dividing by two, and it would be an example of what it would mean for something to be left over. A student answered, "Twenty-two groups altogether. I counted by two's and kept going up to numbers close to forty-five, and got forty-four with one left over." Another student said simultaneously, "The leftover will be one." The groups of two were shown on the aforementioned drawing by ringing pairs of Xs.

At this point I proposed making 45 into groups of eight. Groups of eight is more challenging because the eight times tables are less likely to be mastered by fourth graders. But thinking about groups of eight can build proportionately on thinking about groups of two because the groups of eight can be composed of four groups of two. An activity like this has the potential, therefore, to help students bridge between additive and multiplicative ways of understanding the operation of division. Several students worked on the question by drawing groups of eight Xs and adding or counting until they came to a number close to 45. The first student to respond said, "Five groups of eight." To elicit the student's thinking about leftovers without asking the question directly, I asked "And?" in a questioning tone of voice. Another student responded: "Five left." This was recorded in the chart on the blackboard, as another student asserted, "You could also put six groups of eight and three left over." In response to this assertion, I asked the class, "Can we make another group of eight?" Although it was unconventional, the student's thinking was treated as a serious speculation, reflecting the way he thought about dividing a large quantity up into groups.[12] I asked the student and the

---

[12]This sort of teacher thinking has been referred to as "giving a child reason"; it evolved as part of the culture of the Teacher Development Project at the Massachusetts Institute of Technology as the teacher and researcher participants sought to find ways of making connections between children's informal understanding and the formal knowledge they are expected to acquire in school (Duckworth, 1988; Lampert, 1984).

rest of the class to think about this solution while drawing

XXXXXXXX
XXXXXXXX
XXXXXXXX
XXXXXXXX
XXXXXXXX
XXXXX

on the board. The visual portrayal of the data was intended to help the students think about the difference between what was being assumed in the proposed solution, and the assumptions behind the solution "five groups of eight with five left over." I counted the Xs in the bottom row aloud, and asked, "How many more would we need?" The student who had proposed six groups said, "Three more. We could make six groups if we had three more."

This kind of discourse leaves the reasoning about mathematical legitimacy to the student, and removes the teacher from the role of judging whether answers are right or wrong. What the teacher does do here is to surface the differences in the assumptions behind different answers and make them part of the public conversation. The teacher makes explicit some of the reasoning processes that students are using to arrive at their conclusions, and builds instruction on the basis of what can be learned about these processes.

I then asked, "Any more ideas about groups of eight?" And then, "What about groups of ten?" Ten is an "easy number" to divide and multiply by, and it would serve to assess whether anyone would make the same kind of assertion as the student had made about groups of eight; that is, going higher than the number, and identifying the "leftovers" with how many you would need to get complete groups. No one did. There seemed to be a consensus in the group that the assumption that one could make the division "come out even" by adding more to the dividend was inappropriate, or at least unconventional.

I assumed that the student who responded early in the discussion by adding 45 and 5 to get fifty, and the student who asserted that you could get six groups of eight by adding three more were revealing connections in their thinking between the concepts of division and arithmetic. I did not take the role in either of these instances of judging their thinking against a formal standard. The purpose here was to find out what students thought rather than to make an assessment of whether they were thinking in a conventionally correct manner. I did not simply elicit and accept assertions, however. In the process of listening to and interpreting what the students were saying, I also guided the conversation so that students had the opportunity to test their ideas in mathematical discussions with their peers. The students' assertions were revised in the process of discussion with me and other students, not because I told them they were "wrong." (Cf. Lampert, 1990a.)

During the discussion, I had begun to fill in a chart on the blackboard, at first without any comment. At the beginning of the discussion, the chart looked like this:

NUMBER OF OBJECTS TO BE DIVIDED INTO GROUPS: _____

If you make groups of:	How many will be in each group?	How many left over?

After the discussion of different groupings of 45 objects, the chart looked like this:

NUMBER OF OBJECTS TO BE DIVIDED INTO GROUPS: _____45_____

If you make groups of:	How many will be in each group?	How many left over?
5	9	0
2	22	1
8	5	5
10	4	5

The numbers 5, 2, 8, and 10 had been chosen by the teacher to introduce the different sorts of relationships that might exist among number in a group, number of groups, and number of leftovers. What is important here is that the visual representation of the activity was constructed collaboratively by students and teacher. Such an approach requires a more active role in sense making on the part of students than simply looking at a diagram that has already been constructed in a book.

Next I invited students to choose the number that would go in the first column of the chart, given the same 45 objects to be divided up. This gave the students more opportunities to try their own hypotheses about what might happen when a given quantity was divided into groups. The first student to volunteer a number picked "30" and I asked the class, "How many groups of 30 are in 45?" There was a long pause, after which a student responded, "One. There's only one because you would have to have 60 to make two." Another student added, "There's a remainder of fifteen left over." This was the first time the conventional language usually used to talk about division in school had been used. The first student probably arrived at this assertion by adding 30 and 30, but his thinking provides a foundation for the teacher's expanding his thinking into other, more complex proportional relationships. The second student was making a verbal, and perhaps a conceptual, connection between the activity of finding groups and the formal arithmetic of division. The students' language for referring to the conceptual relationships in division—both formal and informal—set the tone for that way teacher and students would continue to talk about the operation. This talk evolved out of students' individual ways of making sense of the operation, the ways they had been taught to talk about it in school and at home, and the teacher's insertion of formal mathematical language into the conversation. Another student volunteered, "You could make 45 groups of one, and there would be none left over." And another added, quickly and playfully, "Or one group of 45." The legitimacy of the idea of "groups" of one, or one group, was being tested by these students. They were pleased to get their contributions registered on the chart, and they had made a discovery that was rehearsed by other students as part of this activity when it was done with different numbers on subsequent occasions.

The next student to speak said, "What about groups of 40?" I asked in return, "What about it?" and the student responded, "Ten, twenty, thirty, forty, four." Another said, "No, there's only one group of forty." Then I asked the student who had speculated that there might be four groups, "If I take forty away from forty-five once, how many are left?" He responded, "There's only five left." "So how many groups of forty in forty-five?" "Only one." This exchange allowed the student to rethink and revise his initial conjecture with help from me and from another student. It was also meant to make the relationship between division and subtraction that he was using explicit. His initial assertion may have come from a mismatch between his thinking and the language he was using to express it. He may have been thinking "four groups of ten in forty five," that is, groups that would add up to forty, rather than one group of forty.

So far, twelve of the twenty-one students present had made a verbal contribution to this discussion. With the chart still up on the board, I passed out a similarly constructed worksheet and directed the students to "Pick your own number, and divide it into different sized groups." Most students, after working for about 10 minutes, filled the front with groupings and were working on the back of the page. (See Fig. 4.3.) Near the end of the class period, I asked the students what they had noticed from their work.

Michael: The number of leftovers is always less than the number in the group.

Carl: When it comes out even you can switch the numbers around. Like 3 groups of 15 or 15 groups of 3.

Sally: If you pick a number close to the number you are working with you'll always have one group, and you can count the remainder.

Charles: As you make the size of the groups bigger, the number of groups you can get gets smaller.

Alice: If you double the size of the group, you get half as many.

These statements indicate that the students who spoke were beginning to use proportional reasoning to analyse their list of groupings and produce more groupings. They did not work out each item separately, but they looked for patterns and constructed mathematical relationships appropriate to the concept of division to find solutions. Although many had begun with the primitive strategy of repeated subtraction to arrive at their construction of the quotient, their work evolved into looking for patterns in the results that carried them into the domain of multiplicative reasoning.

Extending Students' Thinking About Grouping into New Domains and Making Connections with Conventional Symbols

Variations on this activity of making groups continued for the rest of the week with teacher and students choosing different numbers to divide into groups, and students sharing and refining their observations of patterns and relationships. By the end of the week, there was general consensus in the class that if you wanted to make a group that was more than half of the original number, the number of groups would always be one, and you could subtract to get the leftovers. Several students also noted that if the size of the group doubled, the number of groups would be halved, and some extended this reasoning to tripling and quadrupling. Numbers were identi-

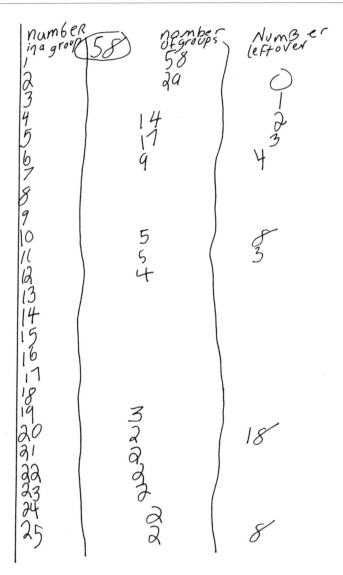

FIG. 4.3.   Dividing a number into different sized groups.

fied that could be divided evenly in many ways (like 60 and 144) and these were contrasted with numbers that "never came out evenly, except if you used the whole thing as one group, or you made groups of one" (like 79 and 43). Some students proposed "breaking things in half to make the groups come out even" so that 13 for example could be made into two groups of $6\frac{1}{2}$.

This line of thinking did not extend much beyond simple fractions, but it was a beginning for reasoning about what to do with the remainder. I chose not to take the journey off along that track at this time, however, and instead turned the agenda toward using the framework we had developed to work with larger numbers. This decision was driven in part by my intention to focus on place-value decomposition that would lead students toward an understanding of the steps in the conventional algorithm.

To begin the transition toward working with the conventional algorithm, the final class in this series was devoted to dividing up three, four, and five digit numbers into groups of 100, 1,000, or 10,000. The chart that was produced in this class looked like this:

How many units?	How many in a group?	How many groups?	How many left over?
43	100	0	43
98,999	100	989	99
999	100	9	99
8,632	100	86	32
7,591	100	75	91
7,591	1,000	7	591

Students defended their assertions using multiplication, with particular attention to the patterns that are evident in working with powers of ten. At the end of this work, students were asked to make speculations about what would happen to "any number" if it were made into groups of 100, 1,000, or 10,000. They made assertions and asked questions like:

The more zeros you add in the second column, the less places there will be in the third column.

I wonder what would happen if you just added zeros to the numbers in the first column, after the other digits.

If it was a ten [for how many in a group], the number left over was always less than ten. When it was a hundred [in a group], it was always less than 100 [left over], and when it was a thousand, what was left was less than 1,000. There was no way you could get bigger leftovers.

The chart that was used throughout these activities again provided a bridge between the students' natural language for talking about division and the proportional character of multiplicative structures. It made use of enough common words to identify the relationships among the numbers in terms that suggest operations, but it also may have functioned to help students "'forget' non-essential features of the situation and concentrate on the relevant elements and relationships" of multiplicative structures (Vergnaud, 1988, p. 148).

The next step in the unit was to take three-digit numbers and divide them into a small number of groups, and to focus the discussion on what might be "done" with the leftovers to make the groups "come out even." The independent variable now would be the number of groups, and the problem would be to think about how the number of groups would affect the size of the groups and the leftovers. Ordinarily, this question is associated with the problem of what to do with the remainder after the division of the whole numbers is completed. But where we start thinking in terms of a remainder is arbitrary, determined by the level of accuracy required by the problem context. Do you need an answer to the nearest hundred, the nearest ten, unit, tenth, hundredth? In

$$5\overline{)765} \qquad\qquad (17)$$

for example, the division does not come out even if you just consider hundreds. If we were talking about dividing up 765 dollars, for example, in the form of 7 hundred dollar bills, 6 tens, and 5 ones, the "answer" to 7 hundreds divided by 5 would be "one remainder two." If we change the remainder (2) into tens, however, the division does come out evenly because five divides 20 (tens) evenly. When we add a decimal point and zeros to a whole number quotient, we are carrying out this process in terms of smaller units; for example, changing one dollar bills to dimes, or in more abstract terms, changing units to tenths. The concept is the same—that is, taking one kind of unit and transforming it into an equivalent quantity in different size units—whether we are changing hundreds to tens or units to tenths. So learning to deal with the remainder needs to begin with the very first step, even when the division "comes out even" in terms of whole numbers.

The language of classroom discourse in this part of the lesson sequence connected abstract talk about units and groups and parts of units, and talk about what special constraints needed to be considered when dividing up concrete objects like pennies or cookies or people. Students made up their own division stories to go with the symbols that they would then manipulate to find the quotient, giving them some ownership over the meaning of the outcome. A more visually rich sort of representation was used to help students think about how to divide up the remainder when there were no longer enough units to go around, and it incorporated the place-value decompositions that were part of the earlier lessons.

The first problem in this section of the unit was to figure out how to represent the division of 765 into 5 equal groups. One student argued that if you "counted by fives" you would get to 765 eventually, so there would be no leftovers. Others concurred, making the assertion that "anything that ended in a five or a zero would come out evenly in groups of five." These arguments helped to solidify the relationship between multiplication and addition, and division and subtraction as part of the reasoning process and suggested the question of what to do with the "remainder." (A later series of lessons taught to this group of students in the fifth grade would be more focused on the question of how to give meaning to the remainder that is left when all of the whole units have been distributed.)

In order to keep the value of each place prominent while at the same time decomposing the number, I suggested that the class, "Think of 765 as 7 hundred dollar bills, 6 ten dollar bills, and 5 one dollar bills." This decomposition deflects students from the procedural first step ("How many times does five go into seven?") which loses the meaning of the numbers being considered and may make it more difficult to reason about the remainder at each step of the decomposition. Associating the digits with amounts of money has the potential to represent the magnitude of the "7" while at the same time breaking it off from the other digits for consideration. It is similar to the approach taken in the fourth-grade book in the *Real Math* series described earlier. The five groups were represented by five circles on the blackboard, and the problem was to get an equal amount of money into each circle. Each of the paper money denominations were distributed, which resulted in:

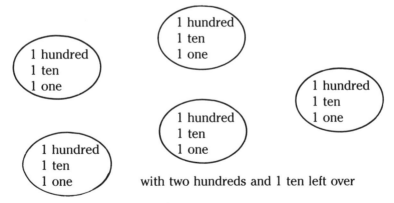

with two hundreds and 1 ten left over

This representation, unlike the conventional answer to the division problem, retains the idea of five groups; that is, it shows how many are in each group if there are five groups. The two hundreds and the one ten are "remainders" that are now left to be traded so that they can be distributed among the groups.

Once this representation was up on the board, I referred back to an assertion made earlier by a member of the class, saying, "I thought you said it was going to come out even." This challenged students to work with place value to resolve the discrepancy. It gave them a reason for changing hundreds to tens and tens to ones, rather than just doing it as the next step in a formal procedure. The discussion resulted in the following revision to the aforementioned grouping:

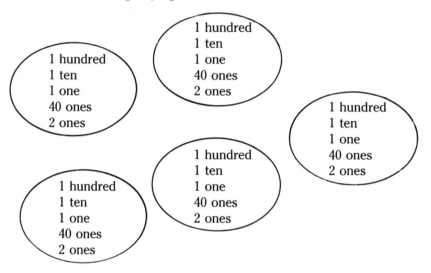

because the initial suggestion was to change 2 hundreds to 200 ones and give each group 40. Now the "contents" of each group could be added up, to yield "153" dollars in each.

Now I asked students to think about "What else it could mean to divide 765 into 5 groups," beginning the story-telling activity that would provide a basis for thinking about different ways to dispose of the remainder. Some of their stories included:

765 transformers were sold in five stores. How many did each store sell?

There were 765 reading books in the whole school and each child is supposed to get five books. How many children can get books?

You had 765 people you wanted to invite to five parties. How many would you invite to each party?

The second story is not isomorphic, either to the money story, or to the other two, about stores and parties, even though the procedure for obtaining the numerical answer would be the same. I noted this difference, using a drawing to illustrate, and the contrast became the focus for another day's lesson. We did not spend much time on the two possible interpretations of division, but students made drawings (e.g., Fig. 4.4) to explore what each might mean.

The purpose of these stories is not to "motivate" students (as stories are reputed to do in the *Addison-Wesley Mathematics* textbook series [Eicholz et al., 1985]) nor to help them see that long division is "useful" for solving real-world problems (as they are intended to do in *Mathematics Unlimited*). My intention in using the stories was to have students construct an expression of the meaning of the operation of division in terms of an activity whose elements they understood, like giving out books or planning parties. (cf. Lampert, 1986a, 1986b.) I did not assume that I was teaching students how to use long division when confronted with such problems in life outside of school; my intention was to teach them to create connections between concrete and familiar situations and the abstractions of mathematical operations and relationships.

Making Connections Between Reasoning
About Relationships and Conventional
Expressions of Long Division Problems

After discussing and representing the distinction between the two interpretations of the symbols that are used to indicate division (finding the number in each group and finding the number of groups), I turned the unit back toward the place-value decompositions involved in "long" division. The first problem to be tackled was:

$$65\overline{)787} \tag{18}$$

After writing these symbols on the board, I assigned the class the task of writing stories that would fit these symbols. (I deliberately began the lesson with a division of a three-digit number by a two-digit number that would not "come out even.") When all of the students had stories in their notebooks, I chose one for discussion: "Seven hundred and eighty-seven kids were in school and they have to be divided up into different classrooms. How many in each classroom? How many won't be put in classrooms?" The first part of the discussion was an interpretation of the story that was directed toward an estimation of how many students would be in each classroom if they were divided up evenly. (I regularly added conditions to the students' stories in discussions to make explicit that division implied making equal groups. The fact that the students' story does not mention equal groups should not be taken to mean that she did not have equal groups in mind. Within the framework of the conversation, that

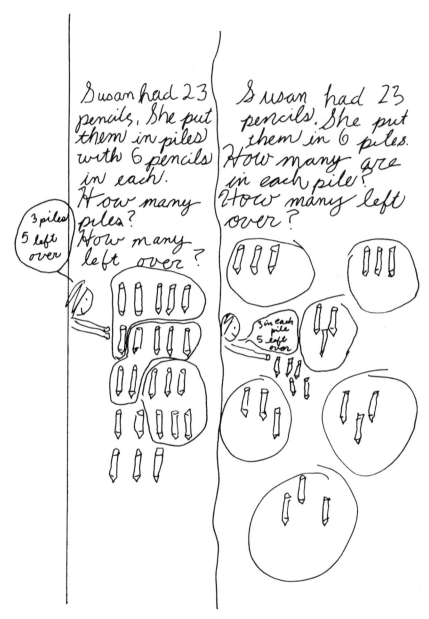

FIG. 4.4. Two interpretations of division.

262

condition may be assumed, as well as that the students were to be divided into sixty-five classrooms. The story chosen is printed as it was written in the student's notebook.)

To begin the estimation process in a way that would deliberately deflect students away from attempts to use a procedure they did not understand, I asked the class: "Do you think the number of kids in a class is going to be more or less than a hundred? More or less than ten? Twenty?" Following a familiar class routine, the students were expected not only to give an estimate, but to explain why their assertion was mathematically reasonable. The student who answered said that he was sure that it would be more than ten because ten times sixty-five is six hundred and fifty, and that is less than the total number of kids. His reasoning could be expressed in terms of the unequal proportional relationship:

$$\frac{10}{787} < \frac{10}{650} \tag{19}$$

The next student who spoke said he was sure it had to be less than twenty "Because two times 65 is 130, and if you do twenty times 65 you get 1,300, which is way too much." His thinking expressed another unequal proportional relationship:

$$\frac{20}{1300} < \frac{20}{787} \tag{20}$$

The symbolic expression of these proportions was not made an explicit part of the lesson. They are indicated here to illustrate the relationship between the way long division was approached in these lessons and the students' understanding of the concept of multiplicative structures. I asked if another student could give a reason why the number of students would be less than twenty, and he said, "If you doubled what you had for ten, it would be over a thousand." In terms of functions, these students are trying to find X such that $f(X) = 787$. The value of $f(10)$ is too small, and the value of $f(20)$ is too large. The last student to speak was reasoning that $f(20)$ would be double $f(10)$. As in earlier lessons, the students' answers suggest that they have theories (or "theorems in action") about how numbers are related in the operation of division that could be mapped onto the conceptual web that defines the mathematical structure of division. The teacher's work in this circumstance is encouraging students to articulate and use their theories rather than guessing mindlessly or relying on the teacher to give them a procedure.

At this point, one member of the class asked if he could "guess" a number between 10 and 20. I asked him, "How would you know whether your guess was a good guess?" The student answered that he would multiply it by 65, and see if it came out to 787. There followed some discussion of the assertion, made by another class member, that no number multiplied by 65 was going to result in 787, and various students gave reasons for why this was true. One student suggested that it would be a good idea to try 15 × 65. She thought that this multiplication would help figure out the answer because it was "right in between ten and twenty, and so we would know right away whether there were more or less than 15 students." I then wrote on the board:

$$
\begin{array}{r}
65 \\
\times 15 \\
\hline
325 \\
650 \\
\hline
975
\end{array}
$$

(21)

and a student said, "That's too high. 15 is too high." She was reasoning on the basis of the relationship between 15 and 975 and comparing it with the relationship between some unknown number and 787. At this point, another girl in the class said she knew it was 12, because she "did it" herself. Upon being queried, she explained that what she "did" was multiply 12 × 65 using the conventional algorithm. What was going on in this conversation was the collaborative construction of a mapping table to figure out the proportional relationship between 65 and 787.

The conversation that followed illustrates how students used the story context to help them think about how to interpret the remainder:

Candice: I multiplied 12 times 65 and it's 780.

Teacher: But there were 787 kids all together.

Janet: Seven had to go to another school.

Juan: They went to chapter one.

These students were figuring out what to do with the remainder, while another student entered the discussion to explain his reasoning about the relationship between 787 and 65:

Ralph: If you take away 200 from 975, you get 775.

Teacher: What does that have to do with the problem?

Ralph: Well here's what I did. You keep taking sixty-five away from 975 until you get close to the number of kids.

Then I wrote on the board as he spoke, relating the subtraction to multiplication and the multiplicative structure of this particular division problem:

$$
\begin{array}{ll}
975 & 15 \times 65 \\
-65 & \\
\hline
910 & 14 \times 65 \\
-65 & \\
\hline
845 & 13 \times 65 \\
-65 & \\
\hline
780 & 12 \times 65 \qquad\qquad (22)
\end{array}
$$

It is not clear from what he said what this successive subtraction had to do with taking 200 away from 975; he may have reasoned that he would have to take away 65 about four times (because 65 doubled is 130 and 130 doubled is 260) to get near 787. At this point, the student said, "That is as close as you are going to get to 787, and it's under." He was using successive subtractions of groups of 65 to arrive at his answer: 65 was a unit, and every time he took away one such group-unit from the total, he took away a single unit from the multiplier. His subtraction could be written as a proportion, as well:

$$
\frac{975}{15} = \frac{910}{14} = \frac{845}{13} = \frac{780}{12} \qquad\qquad (23)
$$

where what he was aiming for was the denominator that would have a numerator close to 787.

Being able to make the sorts of estimates that make it possible to get started on a long division problem is a matter of compressing this kind of "additive" thinking into a multiplicative structure, thinking in terms of groups of groups and their relationship rather than in terms of one group at a time.[13] In this lesson, the class went through a similar discussion with the divisions

$$
79)\overline{1584}
$$

and

$$
89)\overline{2567} \qquad\qquad (24)
$$

The numbers for these problems were proposed by students, within the teacher's constraint that a four-digit number be divided by a two-digit

---

[13]The approach that is taken to long division in *Mathematics Around Us* (Bolster et al., 1978, pp. 230–238) begins with the process of taking groups the size of the divisor away from the quotient and counting how many you have taken away, then progressing to taking more than one group away at a time, and finally taking away tens or hundreds of groups away. This approach retains the meaning of the operation, but it does not make explicit the proportional relationship entailed in the more efficient process. This point is important to note because *Mathematics Around Us* was the series used in other classes in the school where the author taught at the time the research reported here was conducted.

number. I focused the discussion of these two problems on successively closer estimations of the quotient; students refined their estimates using information derived from multiplying an earlier estimation by the divisor. Particular attention was paid to strategies for estimating that made careful use of the data. The estimates could be refined using proportional reasoning, and this is what I encouraged students to do, not by formalizing the process, but by responding to its informal use by some members of the class. By the end of working through the third problem, the class had expressed the goal of "getting close to the answer with the fewest estimates," and so proportional reasoning became a tool for accomplishing their ends.

Students' Independent Use
of Proportional Reasoning to Do
Division

In order to assess the extent to which students would independently connect proportional reasoning to doing division, and concurrently, to encourage them to do so, the next few lessons in my fourth-grade class were organized around students working in pairs with a calculator. Each pair of students was given a division of a four-digit number by a two-digit number written on an index card, a sheet on which to record their estimates (Fig. 4.5), and a calculator. The divisions all involved numbers that would not produce remainders because the class had not yet had the opportunity to explore what it might mean to represent a remainder as a decimal number and this background would have been required to make their work with the calculator meaningful. (At this point a teacher could take the journey off into the territory of figuring out what the decimal numbers that appear on the calculator mean, but I decided not to do that with this group at this time.)

In each lesson in this part of the unit, I first conducted a whole-class demonstration to illustrate to students the kind of thinking they might do to pursue these progressive estimations. Before students started working in pairs, I did a problem at the board (I with calculator, students making estimates) and commented on those guesses that were particularly good examples of proportional reasoning strategies. I asked those students who made assertions to explain their thinking so that other students would have examples of how one might go about using number relationships to reason through a division problem. When students worked together in pairs, they were observed to mimic the language I had used to direct one another's thinking about these problems.

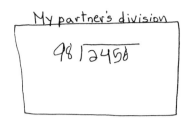

First guess: 10	Multiplication: 10 X 98	Answer: 980
Second guess: 60	Multiplication: 60 X 98	Answer: 5880
Next guess: 45	Multiplication: 45 x 98	Answer: 4410
Next guess: 27	Multiplication: 27 x 98	Answer: 2646
Next guess: 23	Multiplication: 23 x 98	Answer: 2254
25	25 x 98	2450

FIG. 4.5. Estimation game with a partner.

The whole-class discussions began with stories to set a context for making sense of the number manipulations:

Teacher: Before we start working on guesses, I want some stories for:

$$96\overline{)5184}$$ (25)

(on blackboard)

Barbara: 5,184 kids in school and 96 classrooms. How many kids in each classroom?

Matthew: 5,184 ships divided into 96 in each group. How many groups?

Sally: 5,184 potato chips in a bag and 96 bags. How many chips in all?

After this contribution, I wrote on the board:

$$\begin{array}{r} 5184 \\ \times\, 96 \\ \hline \end{array} \qquad (26)$$

and said: That's the problem she told me."

No other judgment was expressed. The stories continued, and Sally eventually revised hers.

Joshua: 5,184 mice in a laboratory and divide into 96 different cages. How many in a cage?

Carl: 5,184 transformers put in piles of 96. How many piles? How many left over?

Eylie: 5,184 pizzas—put in 96 groups. How many in each group? How many groups?

Sally: I want to change mine. 5,184 potatoes chips put into 96 bags. How many in each bag?

Peter: 5,184 fultrons divided into 96 groups. Put 96 fultrons on each planet. How many fultrons on each planet?

Allison: 5,184 roses had to put them into 96 groups. How many roses in each group?

Teacher: You could use vases to divide them into.

The students who contributed these stories were a diverse group, and for some this was the first occasion on which they had done any "public" thinking about division. Although the language of Peter's story did not represent the division appropriately, I did not call attention to it; I decided to focus this lesson on estimation. The focus of discussion was on what makes a good estimate, and why, and thus proportional reasoning was made part of the public discourse about this operation. The conceptual content was similar to work we had done with smaller numbers, but the calculator enabled us to extend that thinking into the domain of large numbers.

Teacher: I want you to start guessing for the problem $96\overline{)5184}$.

Sally: 51.

Teacher: (To the whole class) Why do you think she picked 51?

Alfred: If you started out with a hundred, $100 \times 96 = 9,600$—is close to 10,000. Half of 10,000 is 5,000. Need a little over half of one hundred.

Teacher: (Using calculator, writes on the board: $96 \times 51 = 4,896$.) Sally and Alfred have come up with a good first guess.

Matthew: I would pick 53 because if you add 96 to 4,896 you come close, and then I added another 96.

Teacher: What multiplication problem is 4,992 the answer to? (Writing on the board:)

$$\begin{array}{r} 4896 \\ +\ 96 \\ \hline 4992 \end{array} \qquad (27)$$

Ana: 96×52.

Teacher: Then Matthew added another 96 that's 96×53. (Writing on the board:)

$$\begin{array}{r} 4892 \\ +\ 96 \\ \hline 5088 \end{array} \qquad (28)$$

At this point, a chorus of students asserted with certainty: "It's fifty-four!" and I wrote on the board, as I did the computation on the calculator:

$$96 \times 54 = 5184 \qquad (29)$$

There was some discussion of why so many people were sure that fifty-four was going to work, integrating the addition and subtraction of groups that go into creating a mapping table like this:

X	$f(X)$
100	9600
50	4800
51	4896
52	5088
54	5184

with the operations of multiplication and division whose relationship enables the use of the "multiplying calculator" as a tool in developing a strategic approach to estimating the answer.

The teacher's contributions here were articulations (or explanations) that linked what a student said he or she was thinking to the web of conceptual relationships in mathematics that structures the operation of long division and to the conventions of mathematics that characterize school discourse about division and related topics. All three—proportional reasoning, mathematical concepts, and conventional terms and symbols—combine to define what students might come to know from participating in these lessons. The lessons are constructed so that students operating at different levels of skill and knowledge can be challenged to think about the topic at hand at an appropriate level.

After the whole-group discussion, the students worked in pairs, taking turns in the role of estimator and multiplier, with the multiplier using the calculator to tell the estimator the product of his or her estimate and the divisor. As with the other activities in the unit, the emphasis here was on thinking of the numbers as quantities and thinking about the relationship between multiplication and division. By using the calculator to work with the numbers without decomposing them into place-value related parts, students were encouraged to bring the structure that relates division "facts" to multiplication "facts" to bear on large numbers.

An example of the sort of conversation that occurred between pairs of students as they worked with the calculator follows. Nancy and Janice were working on the division $98\overline{)2450}$.

Nancy: Try ten.

Janet: Nine hundred and eighty [i.e., $98 \times 10 = 980$]. Take your time! Think, you know, anything times a number is going to make it hundred if you use ten.

Nancy: Um; sixty.

Janet: (Using calculator) Five thousand six hundred and eighty [i.e., $98 \times 60 = 5,680$]. Why don't you try something lower. That's about twice as much.

Nancy: Forty-five.

Janet: Four thousand four hundred and ten [i.e., $98 \times 45 = 4,410$]. I think you can try something lower. Try twenty-seven.

Nancy: Okay, twenty-seven.

Janet: Two thousand—a little too high—two thousand six hundred and forty-six [i.e., $98 \times 27 = 2,646$].

Nancy: Twenty-three.

Janet: Two thousand two hundred and fifty-four [i.e., 98 × 32 = 2,254]. Too low.

Nancy: Twenty-five.

Janet: You got it on your sixth guess. That's better than me.

At first, it seemed as if Nancy was not making strategic guesses, although she was not wildly off the mark. Toward the end of working on this problem, Nancy seemed more thoughtful, raising or lowering her guesses in a range that got her closer to the target.

On the first occasion of doing this activity, many students had long lists of somewhat random guesses as to what the quotient might be. After several trials, in which there was considerable discussion between pairs about how to make a good guess, as well as some conversation along these lines between pairs and the teacher, the number of guesses required to get close to the quotient diminished considerably. One incentive that the pairs invented to get one another to make better guesses was a competition for how many problems a given pair could conquer in the course of one class period.

Putting It All Together

In the final lesson of the unit on division, I attempted to bring together the various themes of each of the unit segments: place value, stories, proportional reasoning, estimation, and interpreting the conventional symbols. In this final lesson, as in each lesson in the unit, I tried to portray the "coherence" of the mathematical activities in which we were engaged so that students would be able to make sensible relationships among mathematical ideas in their own thinking. (Cf. Stigler & Baranes, 1988.) The discussion in the last lesson suggests that students were able to make productive connections among ideas in the conceptual web that constitutes the mathematical meaning of long division. There were, at the same time, several instances during the discussion when students acted in ways that did not express attempts to make sense of this procedure—they focused instead on mechanical processes for getting the answer.

The task that I gave students at this point is very similar to tasks that constitute conventional textbook lessons on long division. Part of what I wanted to assess was whether students would take an active role in making sense of problems that were posed in that form. I began the lesson by putting these divisions on the board:

$$6\overline{)49} \qquad 63\overline{)495} \qquad 63\overline{)4956} \qquad 635\overline{)4956} \qquad (30)$$

and I directed the students to "Think about how you would estimate the answers." and "Think about what the relationship might be among the answers to these problems." To focus students on exploring the proportional relationship among the problems, I asked: "How many groups of 6 in 49?" The class chorused "Eight" and then I asked "How many groups of 63 in 495?" and raised similar questions about the other divisions. A major portion of the dialogue that ensued is presented here to communicate the diversity, scope, and content of student thinking that went into the discussion.

Teacher: What about this one? (pointing to $63\overline{)495}$.)

Rose: [The groups of 63 in 495 is] Less than 10, not bigger.

Candice: Check 5 because it's in the middle of 1 and 10.

Teacher: What about this one: $63\overline{)4,956}$ (pointing to it on the board). Is it less than ten or more than ten?

Janet: Bigger than 10. Because 10×63 is 630.

Teacher: Is it bigger than a hundred?

Students: (in chorus) No.

Teacher: Nancy, what's 100×63?

Nancy: 6,300.

Teacher: So is the answer to this (pointing to $63\overline{)4,956}$) as big as 100?

Peter: I think it should be 15.

Teacher: Other ideas on that one? (No response)

Teacher: What about (pointing to it on the board) $635\overline{)4,956}$. Let's think about this problem.

Eylie: I think it's smaller than 10 because 6,350 is too big.

Matthew: I think it's seven.

Teacher: Those guesses are kind of different from one another. One is an estimate based on thinking about the number relationships, and the other is an exact guess.

Candice: I want to change 5 to 6 because I worked it out on paper.

Teacher: We're trying to think right now. Not working it out on paper. What else do you think about $63\overline{)495}$?

Janet: 6. Kara said it and I thought it over, and though 6×63. Because I figured out five times 63 is 315 and six times 63 is 378.

Teacher: How much bigger will that be than 315? (No response). How much am I adding on?

Janet: 63. But I was thinking about it different. I was multiplying not adding.

Juan: Try 9.
Teacher: 9 × 63 = 567, too high.
Barbara: 8.
Teacher: 8 × 63 = 504. Do you think it's closer to 8 or 7?
Eylie: $7\frac{1}{2}$.
Matthew: It's more than that. It's pretty close to 8.

Collectively, these students had worked out the proportional relationship that would get them close to finding out $63\overline{)495}$. They had built on one another's thinking to come up with the progressive proportional estimation:

$$\frac{5}{315} = \frac{6}{378} = \frac{9}{567} = \frac{8}{504} = \frac{7\frac{1}{2}}{487.5} = \frac{\text{``almost eight''}}{495} \qquad (31)$$

Except for Janet and Candice, students used proportional reasoning to refine their estimate. Candice used the conventional algorithm (which she had been taught at home) to get the "answer" and Janet did not build directly on an earlier estimate to get a better one. Eylie did not compute $f(7\frac{1}{2})$, but Matthew thought that taking half a group of 65 away from 504 would be taking away too much. The distinction between students who "added on" (i.e., used additive strategies) and those who thought in multiplicative terms is interesting, especially because the students themselves thought it important to make the distinction. They were progressively multiplying one digit after another, but they were using multiplication.

I did not press for a more precise answer than "almost eight" but moved the discussion toward the next division:

$$63\overline{)4956} \qquad (32)$$

The first student to give an estimate said "Try forty." He did not seem to derive any information from the discussion on the previous problem. He did have the order of magnitude correct, but he did not seem to be considering the multiplication of 40 × 63 in making his guess. I gave the results of 40 × 63 = 2,520 using the calculator, and then the same student (Peter) called out: "Try 85 × 63." He may have been reasoning proportionally to arrive at the idea that the estimate should be a little more than double forty. I did not inquire about his thinking, however, because several other students were now anxious to contribute an estimate.

Teacher: 85 × 63 = 5,355. Now there was some good thinking, very
          close!
Students: (in chorus) Try 83.

Teacher: $83 \times 63 = 5{,}229$. I would like to take estimates from people who can convince me they've been thinking, and have thought it through.

Matthew: I think it should be 78 because it needs to be a little lower than 80, and I don't think 79 is lower enough.

Peter: I still think it will be 77 because I'm narrowing the problem down.

Teacher: $78 \times 63 = 4{,}914$.

Peter: 77.

Teacher: Peter, when I used 78 I got 4,914.

Peter: Oh, then it should be 79.

Teacher: $79 \times 63 = 4{,}977$. Which is better, 78 or 79?

Students: (in chorus) 79.

Teacher: Why?

Candice: If you have 14 and you try 50, if you have 77 it's only about 20 away.

At this point I turned the discussion toward general observations of the relationships among the four division problems with which the lesson began:

$$6\overline{)49} \qquad 63\overline{)495} \qquad 63\overline{)4956} \qquad 635\overline{)4956} \qquad (33)$$

Students made observations about the similarities and differences among the answers to these problems, all of which were expressed in approximate, whole-number form. Their observations included talk about place-value relationships, and comments about how such different problems could have such similar answers.

Getting students to the point where they are able to move back and forth between confidently using their own sense-making strategies and working productively on problems of the sort that are posed in school is a step along the way toward their being able to participate in the culture of mathematics. Although finding the "answer" to a division like

$$63\overline{)4956} \qquad (34)$$

is an academic rather than a practical task, learning to approach this task as a process of mathematical sense making rather than as a process of following mechanical rules seems to have the potential to move students toward more meaningful and satisfying engagement in mathematical activity both in school and out.

CONCLUSIONS AND IMPLICATIONS

The lessons described here could be counted as successful on two counts. First of all, they resulted in fourth-grade students thinking and talking about the multiplicative structure that underlies division in terms of their own "theorems in action." Second, they demonstrated that the teaching of long division lessons could be coherently organized and at the same time move around flexibly in the web of concepts that justify the mathematical legitimacy of procedures. There is also evidence that a third goal, that of having students tie their understandings of the mathematical structure of division to the conventional symbols and procedures, was accomplished for at least some of the students. In Case's (1988) terms, the design of these lessons worked to enable the teacher to "stay in tune with" students' mental models and the changing nature of their partial understandings; what was described here is teaching that produced the articulation of students "major conceptual errors" and attempted to "head them off at the pass" (cf. Case, 1988, p. 269). In terms used by Hiebert and Behr (1988), the lessons served to "facilitate students' constructions of meaning for written mathematical symbols" (p. 15); their meanings were expressed in the class discussions of relationships among numbers and the representation of these relationships using conventional symbols.

Implications for Teaching Practice

In contemporary classroom practice it is problematic to have students work on the sorts of problems that take them into the web of concepts related to division if this sort of work is simply laid on top of the straight and narrow path through whole number and fraction arithmetic. The conceptual approach is problematic in this context because some students will have mastered the mechanics of the algorithm (having been taught it by another teacher or at home) and some believe they should not yet be "on" division because they have not even mastered their times tables. At all of these levels, students give some meaning to symbolic expressions like $56\overline{)693}$, even if it is only to see this as a representation of something yet to be studied or as a signal to start by figuring out "how many times 56 goes into 69." Rarely do students treat these symbols as a meaningful expression that asks a question about relationships among quantities. In order to teach long division or any other mathematical procedure for understanding, a teacher needs to intervene in the classroom culture that shapes these attitudes. This sometimes means countering resistance from students who would prefer "just to be told how to get the answers" (Cooney, 1987; Stephens & Romberg, 1985).

Classroom practices shape what teachers and students think it means to know and learn mathematics, and what teachers and students think shapes classroom practices. Given this circle of beliefs and expectations, treating division as a concept about which one can reason and communicate requires the teacher to aggressively challenge both students' expectations about what is going to occur in lessons and the framework they have been using to assess their own progress as learners of mathematics. Getting students to reveal their "theorems in action" in the course of a classroom lesson requires convincing students that their own reasoning processes are relevant to the activity of learning mathematics in school. But even more challenging for the teacher is the implication of treating division as a concept related to other important pieces of mathematics and to students' thinking in the process of designing instruction. If this view of the subject matter and the student is taken seriously, the teacher must be prepared to move around in the conceptual territory of multiplicative structures in response to what he or she can find out about what students already know about these structures. Given what we know about teachers' beliefs about mathematics, and the argument that their classroom practices are intimately related to their beliefs, changing instruction in the direction of attention to students' reasoning processes is not going to be a simple matter.

Implications for Curriculum

Although the lessons described here were constructed by the author, a similar approach to making sense of long division could be undertaken in conjunction with activities in textbooks, carefully chosen. The important issue is how the operation is interpreted, not whether it is or is not taught. For example, the kinds of discussions that are described here could be constructed around the sort of long division lessons that are included in the *Real Math* unit (Willoughby et al., 1987a). The way in which problems are posed in *Real Math* suggests that proportional reasoning, with place-value considerations in mind, is an appropriate way to go about working on long division. Activities that would promote the kind of discourse reported here are actually available in several other textbooks as well, but they are rarely part of the main lessons. For example, *Mathematics Unlimited* includes an "Enrich" activity in which students are introduced to the "Egyptian Method" of dividing by doubling: a procedure that follows the proportional relationships in the numbers and is recorded in a way that makes the meaning of the procedure explicit (Fennell et al., 1987, p. 173). In *Silver Burdett Mathematics* students are directed in "resource activities" to use patterns to make relationships and find missing quotients (Orfan, Vogeli, Krulik, & Rudnick, 1987), and *Harper & Row Mathematics* includes activities like those described here in "Challenge" and "Super Challenge" sections (Payne et al., 1985).

None of these textbooks suggests discussing the patterns and relationships that underlie reasoning about division, however. And the activities that might lead to students' noticing such ideas and thinking that they are important are not included in the main lessons; often they are suggested only for those students who finish more conventional assignments. They are not generally part of "reteaching" or "extra practice" activities that are suggested for students who have difficulty with the conventional arithmetic procedures. The research reported here suggests that a wider range of students can participate in both doing and discussing such activities and relating them to the more conventional aspects of work on long division.

Implications for a Theory
of Teaching and Learning Mathematics
for Understanding

Teaching division—and expecting students to understand it as a procedure connected to a set of related mathematical concepts that go substantially beyond counting—requires a serious intervention in the procedure-oriented culture of mathematical knowing in the classroom. It is not a matter of enrichment or supplementary activities. In the currently typical scenario for teaching and learning arithmetic in elementary school, long division is the capstone of whole number procedures. If a student can do long division successfully, it often is taken as an indication that he or she can do all of the other whole number procedures as well and is ready to move on to fractions. This perspective on long division is consonant with the common belief that elementary mathematics is a collection of procedures that need to be learned in order, and that any tampering with that order will be confusing rather than meaningful to learners. If students believe they cannot know division unless their teachers have done lessons on division, or unless they have gotten to it in the textbook, they will be unlikely to bring their understandings of proportional relationships—undeveloped as they may be—to the task of understanding division. If, in contrast, the goal of mathematics curriculum and instruction is to have students learn to become confident in their capacity to reason about mathematical entities, the research reported here suggests that it may be worth trying to develop instruction interactively with their "theorems in action" rather than following a straight and narrow path through the subject.

What has been portrayed here is not a collection of lessons to be reproduced so that students will predictably learn the meaning of divisions with large numbers. It is a description and analysis of an exerpt from a year's work with a particular class, in which every teaching and learning interaction was organized to give meaning to the activity that was being carried out in the social setting of the classroom. The purpose of the research reported here was to explicate further what might be meant by mathematical pedagogy (Lampert, 1988) in a domain that often is regarded as antithetical to promoting mathematical understanding. Teaching decisions were made with this basic principle in mind: Mathematical knowledge is warranted by establishing the legitimacy of procedures in the domain of number and examining the appropriateness of those procedures for modeling processes in other domains. This principle has several implications for developing a theory of mathematical pedagogy. In the classroom setting, the culture determines the way in which knowledge is regarded and acquired, and the teacher has a leading role in shaping that culture toward students taking responsibility for warranting the procedures they use. Communication is a tool that the teacher can use to shape the classroom culture. The meaning of knowledge is created as students and teacher talk about their common activities and visually represent mathematical concepts. And these concepts form the emerging curriculum of the mathematics class, as the teacher investigates students' ways of thinking about problems and constructs connections among these ideas and important ideas in a mathematical domain. All of these elements of mathematical pedagogy can be represented in lessons on long division as they are in other mathematical arenas if teacher and students are working together to investigate the ideas in their midst.

REFERENCES

Behr, M., Lesh, R., Post, T., & Silver, E. (1983). Rational number concepts. In R. Lesh & M. Landau (Eds.), *Acquisition of mathematical concepts and processes* (pp. 92–127). New York: Academic.

Bell, A., Greer, B., Grimison, L., & Mangan, C. (1989). Children's performance on multiplicative word problems. *Journal for Research in Mathematics Education, 20,* 434–449.

Bereiter, C., & Scardamalia, M. (1989). Intentional learning as a goal of instruction. In L. B. Resnick (Ed.), *Knowing, learning, and instruction: Essays in honor of Robert Glaser* (pp. 361–392). Hillsdale, NJ: Lawrence Erlbaum Associates.

Bolster, L. C., Cox, G. F., Gibb, E. G., Hansen, V. P., Kirkpatrick, J. E., Robitaille, D. F., Trimble, H.

C., Vance, I. E., Walch, R., & Wisner, R. J. (1978). *Mathematics around us: Skills and applications* (Grade 4). Glenview, IL: Scott, Foresman.

Buswell, G. T. (1926). *Diagnostic studies in arithmetic.* Chicago: University of Chicago Press.

Carpenter, T. P., Fennema, E., Peterson, P. L., Chiang, C. P., & Loef, M. (1988, April). *Using knowledge of children's mathematical thinking in classroom teaching: An experimental study.* Paper presented at the annual meeting of the American Educational Research Association, New Orleans.

Case, R. (1988). Summary comments: Developing a research agenda for mathematics in the middle grades. In J. Heibert & M. Behr (Eds.), *Number concepts and operations in the middle grades* (pp. 265–270). Reston, VA: Lawrence Erlbaum Associates & National Council of Teachers of Mathematics.

Clemens, H. (1989). What do math teachers need to be. In *Competing visions of teacher knowledge: Procedings from an NCRTE seminar for education policy makers* (Vol. 1: Academic subjects pp. 123–135). E. Lansing: National Center for Research on Teacher Education, Michigan State University.

Cooney, T. (1987, October). The issue of reform: What have we learned from yesteryear? In Mathematical Sciences Education Board, *The teacher of mathematics: Issues for today and tomorrow* (pp. 17–36). Washington, DC: National Research Council.

Duckworth, E. (1988). *The having of wonderful ideas.* New York: Teachers College Press.

Eicholz, R. E., O'Dafer, P. G., Fleenor, C. R., Charles, R. I., Young, S., & Barnett, C. S. (1985). *Addison-Wesley mathematics* (Teacher's edition, Book 4). Menlo Park, CA: Addison-Wesley.

Fennell, F. S., Reys, B. J., Reys, R. E., & Webb, A. W. (1987). *Mathematics unlimited* (Teacher's guide, grade 4). New York: Holt, Rinehart & Winston.

Fischbein, E., Deri, M., Nello, M., & Marino, M. (1985). The role of implicit models in solving verbal problems in multiplication and division. *Journal for Research in Mathematics Education, 16,* 3–17.

Freeman, D. J., Kuhs, T. M., Porter, A. C., Floden, R. E., Schmidt, W. H., & Schwille, J. R. (1983). Do textbooks and tests define a national curriculum in elementary school mathematics? *Elementary School Journal, 83,* 501–513.

Freeman, D. J., & Porter, A. C. (in press). Do textbooks dictate the content of mathematics instruction in elementary schools? *American Educational Research Journal.*

Greeno, J. G. (1986). Collaborative teaching and making sense of symbols: Comments on Lampert's "Knowing, doing, and teaching multiplication." *Cognition and Instruction, 3,* 343–348.

Greeno, J. G. (1990). *Number sense as situated knowledge in a conceptual domain* (Report No. IRL90–0014). Palo Alto, CA: Institute for Research on Learning.

Greeno, J. G., Riley, M., & Gelman, R. (1984). Conceptual competence and children's counting. *Cognitive Psychology, 16,* 94–143.

Hart, K. (1981). Ratio and proportion. In K. M. Hart, M. L. Brown, D. E. Kuchemann, D. Kerslake, G. Ruddock, & M. McCartney (Eds.), *Children's understanding of mathematics: 11–16* (pp. 88–101). London: John Murray.

Hart, K. (1988). Ratio and proportion. In J. Heibert & M. Behr (Eds.), *Number concepts and operations in the middle grades* (pp. 198–219). Reston, VA: Lawrence Erlbaum Associates & National Council of Teachers of Mathematics.

Hiebert, J., & Behr, M. (1988). Introduction: Capturing the major themes. In J. Heibert & M. Behr (Eds.), *Number concepts and operations in the middle grades* (pp. 1–18). Reston, VA: Lawrence Erlbaum Associates & National Council of Teachers of Mathematics.

Hilton, P. (1989, December). The joy of mathematics or down with arithmetic. Address to the Asilomar Conference, California Mathematics Council, Northern Section, Monterey.

Karplus, R., Pulos, S., & Stage, E. (1983). Proportional reasoning of early adolescents. In R. Lesh & M. Landau (Eds.), *Acquisition of mathematical concepts and processes* (pp. 45–91). New York: Academic.

Kieren, T. (1988). Personal knowledge of rational numbers: Its intuitive and formal development. In J. Heibert & M. Behr (Eds.), *Number concepts and operations in the middle grades* (pp. 162–181). Hillsdale, NJ and Reston, VA: Lawrence Erlbaum Associates & National Council of Teachers of Mathematics.

King, A. R., & Brownell, J. A. (1966). *The curriculum and the disciplines of knowledge: A theory of curriculum practice.* New York: Wiley.

Lampert, M. (1984). Teaching about thinking and thinking about teaching. *Journal of Curriculum Studies, 16,* 1–18.

Lampert, M. (1985). How do teachers manage to teach? Perspectives on problems in practice. *Harvard Educational Review, 55,* 178–194.

Lampert, M. (1986a). Knowing, doing, and teaching multiplication. *Cognition and Instruction, 3,* 305–342.

Lampert, M. (1986b). Teaching multiplication. *Journal of Mathematical Behavior, 4,* 157–168.

Lampert, M. (1988). Connecting mathematical teaching and learning. In E. Fennema, T. Carpenter, & S. Lamon (Eds.), *Integrating research on teaching and learning mathematics* (pp. 132–167). Madison: Wisconsin Center for Educational Research.

Lampert, M. (1989). Choosing and using mathematical tools in classroom discourse. In J. Brophy (Ed.), *Advances in research on teaching* (Vol. 1, pp. 223–265). Greenwich, CT: JAI.

Lampert, M. (1990a). When the problem is not the question and the solution is not the answer: Mathematical knowing and teaching. *American Educational Research Journal, 27,* 29–63.

Lampert, M. (1990b). Connecting inventions with conventions: The teacher's role in classroom communication about mathematics. In L. Steffe (Ed.), *Transforming early childhood education* (pp. 253–265). Hillsdale, NJ: Lawrence Erlbaum Associates.

Lesh, R., Post, T., & Behr, M. (1988). Proportional reasoning. In J. Heibert & M. Behr (Eds.), *Number concepts and operations in the middle grades* (pp. 93–118). Reston, VA: Lawrence Erlbaum Associates & National Council of Teachers of Mathematics.

Mathematical Sciences Education Board (1989). *Everybody counts: A report to the nation on the future of mathematics education.* Washington, DC: National Academy Press.

National Council of Teachers of Mathematics (1989). *Curriculum and evaluation standards for school mathematics.* Reston, VA: National Council of Teachers of Mathematics.

Nesher, P. (1986). Learning mathematics: A cognitive perspective. *American Psychologist, 41,* 1114–1122.

Nesher, P. (1987). Are mathematical understanding and algorithmic performance related? *For the Learning of Mathematics, 6*(3), 2–9.

Nesher, P. (1988). Multiplicative school word problems: Theoretical approaches and empirical findings. In J. Heibert & M. Behr (Eds.), *Number concepts and operations in the middle grades* (pp. 19–40). Reston, VA: Lawrence Erlbaum Associates & National Council of Teachers of Mathematics.

Orfan, L. J., Vogeli, B. J., Krulik, S., & Rudnick, J. A. (1987). *Silver Burdett mathematics* (Teacher edition, grade 4). New York: Silver Burdett & Ginn.

Payne, J. N., Beardsley, L. M., Bunch, B. H., Carter, B. B., Coburn, T. G., Edmonds, G. F., Payne, R. C., Rathmell, E. C., & Trafton, P. R. (1985). *Harper & Row mathematics* (Teacher's edition, grade 4). New York: Harper & Row.

Pea, R. (1988). Putting knowledge to use. In R. S. Nickerson & P. P. Zodhiates, *Technology and education: Looking toward 2020* (pp. 169–212). Hillsdale, NJ: Lawrence Erlbaum Associates.

Putnam, R., Lampert, M., & Peterson, P. L. (1989). Alternative perspectives on knowing mathematics in elementary schools. In C. Cazden (Ed.), *Review of research in education* (Vol. 16, pp. 57–152). Washington, DC: American Educational Research Association.

Resnick, L. B. (1989). Teaching mathematics as an ill-structured discipline. In R. Charles & E. A. Silver (Eds.), *Research agenda for mathematics education: Teaching and assessment of mathematical problem solving* (pp. 32–60). Hillsdale, NJ: Lawrence Erlbaum Associates.

Resnick, L. B., & Omanson, S. F. (in press). Learning to understand arithmetic. In R. Glaser (Ed.), *Advances in instructional psychology* (Vol. 3). Hillsdale, NJ: Lawrence Erlbaum Associates.

Saxe, G. (1988). Candy selling and math learning. *Educational Researcher, 17*(6), 14–21.

Schmidt, W. H., Porter, A. C., Floden, R. E., Freeman, D. J., & Schwille, J. R. (1987). Four patterns of teacher content decision making. *Journal of Curriculum Studies, 19*(5), 439–455.

Schwab, J. J. (1978). Education and the structure of the disciplines. In I. Westbury & N. J. Wilkof (Eds.), *Science, curriculum, and liberal education: Selected essays* (pp. 229–272). Chicago: University of Chicago Press.

Schwartz, J. (1988). Intensive quantity and referent transforming arithmetic operations. In J. Heibert & M. Behr (Eds.), *Number concepts and operations in the middle grades* (pp. 41–52). Hillsdale, NJ: Lawrence Erlbaum Associates and Reston, VA: National Council of Teachers of Mathematics.

Silver, E. (1988). Solving story problems involving division with remainders: The importance of semantic processing and referential mapping. In M. Behr, C. Lacampagne, & M. Wheeler (Eds.), *Proceedings of the tenth annual meeting, PME-NA* (pp. 127–133). DeKalb: Northern Illinois University.

Sowder, J. T. (1988). Mental computation and number comparison: Their roles in the development of number sense and computational estimation. In J. Heibert & M. Behr (Eds.), *Number concepts and operations in the middle grades* (pp. 182–197). Reston, VA: Lawrence Erlbaum Associates & National Council of Teachers of Mathematics.

Spiro, R. J., Vispoel, W. L., Schmitz, J. G. Samarapungavan, A., & Boerger, A. E. (1987). *Knowledge acquisition for application: Cognitive flexibility and transfer in complex content domains* (Technical Rep. No. 409). Champaign: University of Illinois, Center for the Study of Reading.

Steffe, L. (1988). Children's construction of number sequences and multiplying schemes. In J. Heibert & M. Behr (Eds.), *Number concepts and operations in the middle grades* (pp. 191–141). Hillsdale, NJ and Reston, VA: Lawrence Erlbaum Associates & National Council of Teachers of Mathematics.

Stephens, M., & Romberg, T. A. (1985, April). *Reconceptualizing the role of the mathematics teacher.* Paper presented at the annual meeting of the American Educational Research Association, Chicago.

Stewart, I. (1987). *The problems of mathematics.* Oxford, England: Oxford University Press.

Stigler, J. W., & Baranes, R. (1988). Culture and mathematics learning. *Review of Research in Education, 15,* 253–306.

Stodolsky, S. (1988). *The subject matters: Classroom activity in math and social studies.* Chicago: University of Chicago Press.

Swetz, F. J. (1987). *Capitalism and arithmetic: The new math of the 15th century.* LaSalle, IL: Open Court.

Talmage, H. (1972). The textbook as arbiter of curriculum and instruction. *The Elementary School Journal, 73,* 20–25.

Vergnaud, G. (1983). Multiplicative structures. In R. Lesh & M. Landau (Eds.), *Acquisition of mathematical concepts and processes* (pp. 128–175). New York: Academic.

Vergnaud, G. (1988). Multiplicative structures. In J. Heibert & M. Behr (Eds.), *Number concepts and operations in the middle grades* (pp. 141–161). Reston, VA: Lawrence Erlbaum Associates & National Council of Teachers of Mathematics.

Vygotsky, L. S. (1978). *Mind in society: The development of higher psychological processes* (M. Cole, V. John-Steiner, S. Scribner, & E. Souberman, Eds.). Cambridge, MA: Harvard University Press.

Willoughby, S. S., Bereiter, C., Hilton, P., & Rubenstein, J. H. (1987a). *Real math* (Teachers guide, level 4). LaSalle, IL: Open Court.

Willoughby, S. S., Bereiter, C., Hilton, P., & Rubenstein, J. H. (1987b). *Real math* (Teachers guide, level 5). LaSalle, IL: Open Court.

5

MATHEMATICAL, COGNITIVE, AND INSTRUCTIONAL ANALYSES OF DECIMAL FRACTIONS

James Hiebert
University of Delaware

Contents

Decimal fractions form a deceptively complex mathematical system. On the surface, they appear to involve a simple extension of the whole number system. A decimal point is inserted after the ones position and values of positions to the right are defined by partitioning by 10, just as values to the left were defined earlier for students by grouping by 10. The values of the new positions simply extend the pattern already established with whole numbers and the pattern is so consistent that, presumably, it should be easy to detect and easy to understand.

If decimal fractions are straightforward extensions of whole numbers, why do students have trouble mastering them? Why does a junior high school student interpret 11.9 miles per hour as "11 miles 9 minutes per hour" (Bell, Swan, & Taylor, 1981, p. 405) or why does a ninth grader explain writing 5.1 directly underneath .36 to add them (getting .87) by saying "If you're adding .36 and 5.1 it would make a lot more sense if it came out to .8 or so" (Hiebert & Wearne, 1986, p. 218). Why are more than half of 13-year-olds in the United States unable to choose the largest of .19, .036, .195, and .2 (Carpenter, Corbitt, Kepner, Lindquist, & Reys, 1981) and why do many entering college freshmen still have trouble ordering decimals (Grossman, 1983)? Classroom teachers of students in Grade 4 and beyond could add many of their own stories about the difficulties students have with decimals. The reason for these difficulties, simply put, is that decimals are harder than they look. There are more complexities wrapped up in decimals than might appear at first glance.

The goal of this chapter is to unravel some of the complexities of decimal numbers. The complexities that may be responsible for students' difficulties are likely to lie in one of three overlapping domains. First, the mathematics that is represented by decimal notation is considerably more complex than the mathematics of whole numbers. A conclusion that is drawn from the analysis of mathematical complexities is that the similarities in the symbol notation that are retained as students move from whole numbers to decimals mask a dramatic shift in the kinds of quantities that can be represented—a shift from discrete quantities to continuous quantities. Symbols that look like whole numbers represent quantities that are fractions. A second source of potential difficulties for students can be described as cognitive complexities. It is more difficult for students to think about decimals than previously encountered systems because the connections between symbols and the quantities they represent are more subtle, the language used to talk about decimals provides little support for establishing these connections, and the habit of thinking about whole numbers may interfere with thinking about decimals. The discussion of cognitive complexities focuses on the development of meaning for decimal notation and reviews whether and in what ways students ordinarily construct meaning for decimals. A final source of potential difficulties for students is the instruction they receive. Of course, instruction has the potential to relieve the difficulties and support students' efforts to master decimals but it also can compound the difficulties that the mathematical and cognitive complexities generate. The analysis of instruction focuses on the ways in which conventional textbooks help and hinder students' construction of meaning for decimals and describes the types of instructional activities that seem likely to encourage the development of meaning. The purpose of examining the mathematical, cognitive, and instructional aspects of decimals is to understand why students have trouble mastering them and how instruction might be improved to help students make sense of them.

MATHEMATICAL ANALYSIS OF DECIMALS— WHAT ARE THEY?

By "decimal fractions" or "decimal numbers" or just "decimals," I mean numbers that can be represented by base-10 numerals with digits to the right as well as the left of the decimal point. There are two essential aspects of the decimal system: (a) the quantities that are being represented and (b) the written symbols or notation system that is representing the quantities. Sometimes the distinction between these aspects is made explicit and sometimes the distinction is only implicit, but the reader is encouraged to keep the distinction in mind throughout the chapter.

Principles of the Notation System

A notation system is a set of written symbols and some principles or rules that prescribe how the symbols will be written to represent something. The decimal notation system is designed to represent quantities that have been measured with units and parts of units. In contrast to common fractions, decimal fractions require that the parts of units have a specified size relationship to the unit: tenth of a unit, hundredth of a unit, thousandth of a unit, and so on.

The decimal system that we use today developed over a long period of time (Boyer, 1968). The beginning of the system dates back to about 2400 B.C. when the Babylonians introduced the idea of place value into the notation for their base-60 system. A form of place value was used to represent both whole number and fraction values. However, their system looked much different from ours. One difference is that the Babylonians did not use a zero until about 300 B.C., when a placeholder appears in their notation. It was not until about 850 that the base-10 place-value system, as we know it, was developed by Hindu mathematicians in India. But the Hindu mathematicians used the notation for whole numbers only and did not follow the early Babylonians in using the place-value idea to represent fractions as well. The decimal fraction system took on its current form by about 1500. Several Arab mathematicians demonstrated the power and elegance of the system and promoted its use. Their developments perhaps were based on records of much earlier Chinese efforts to apply a base-10 system to describe fraction quantities. As this brief review indicates, the development of decimal fractions was a worldwide event, covering thousands of years.

After the lengthy, involved evolution, it is quite remarkable that all of the important properties of the decimal system notation we have inherited can be captured in three principles.

Principle 1. The value of a digit is a function of its position or place in the numeral. The value of a particular position is determined by beginning with the unit (the "ones") and, if moving to the right, dividing the previous value by 10 and, if moving to the left, multiplying the previous value by 10. The ones position is marked with a decimal point on its immediate right. One consequence of this principle is that the relationship between any two adjacent places is that the one on the left is worth 10 times as much as the one on the right or, alternatively, the one on the right is worth one tenth as much as the one on the left. It is important to notice that the pattern of place values is based on multiplication by a common factor rather than addition of a common addend.

Principle 2. The value of a digit (the amount of quantity that it represents) is the product of its face value and its place value. The face value is the value of a digit without regard to its position in the numeral. For example, in the numeral 300.60, the value of the 3 is 3×100 because its face value is 3 and, using Principle 1, the value of the place that 3 occupies is 100. Similarly, moving left to right, the value of 0 is 0×10, the value of the next 0 is 0×1, the value of 6 is $6 \times \frac{1}{10}$, and the value of the rightmost 0 is $0 \times \frac{1}{100}$. The values of the digits also can be illustrated by writing the place values as powers of 10. Moving left to right, the values of the digits in 300.60 are $3 \times 10^2, 0 \times 10^1, 0 \times 10^0, 6 \times 10^{-1}, 0 \times 10^{-2}$. The advantage of this form is that the pattern of the exponents—$2, 1, 0, -1, -2$—shows the symmetry around the ones position (10^0). The notion of symmetry arises again later in the discussion of the language used to talk about decimals.

Multiplying the face value of a digit times its place value gives the *canonical* value of the digit, the value in terms of the number of units of quantity. This value is usually the most useful. But the value of a digit can be expressed in an endless variety of ways. For example, consider the 3 in the numeral 3.1. The canonical value of 3 is 3×1. But the 3 also could represent 30 tenths of one, 3 tenths of a group of ten ones, or even 18 sixths of one. Because the notation system is based on a factor of 10, the most useful alternate ways of treating the value of a digit are those in which the unit is partitioned or grouped in powers of 10. For example, it may be useful on occasion to think of the 3 in 3.1 as representing 30 tenths so that 3.1 can be treated as 31 tenths.

Principle 3. The value of a numeral is the sum of the values of the individual digits. For example, the value of 46.07 is $(4 \times 10) + (6 \times 1) + (0 \times \frac{1}{10}) + (7 \times \frac{1}{100})$ or "forty-six and seven hundredths." The canonical value describes the number of units or ones that the quantity being represented by the numeral has measured.

The three rather simple looking and familiar principles generate a notation system that is powerful—a notation system that provides a remarkable amount of information about the quantities represented. Much of the information is not immediately apparent. For example, consider the numeral 23.48. Its canonical value is "twenty-three ones and forty-eight hundredths of one." But 23.48 also tells us that the same quantity could be described as (a) 234 tenths of one and 8 hundredths of one, (b) 2,348 hundredths of one, (c) 2 groups of 10 ones and 348 thousandths of a group of 10, and so on. A common alternate description that is cumbersome but instructionally useful is 2 groups of 10 ones and 3 ones and 4 tenths of one and 8 hundredths of one or, in briefer form, 23 and 4 tenths, 8 hundredths.

Summary. Three principles capture the essentials of the notation system of decimal fractions. The principles describe how the written numerals are to be interpreted in terms of the quantities that they represent. In other words, the principles describe the links between the written symbols and physical quantities.

The principles probably are familiar to most readers, in part because they are nearly identical to the principles of the whole number notation system. The only difference is in Principle 1. For whole numbers, the units or ones position is marked by the rightmost digit whereas, for decimal fractions, the ones position is marked by a decimal point. Corresponding to this notational difference is an important conceptual difference: Whole numbers are conceived as beginning with 1 and building up through grouping by 10 whereas decimal fractions are conceived as beginning with 1 and both building up through grouping by 10 and breaking down through partitioning into 10.

The genius in the evolution of the decimal fraction notation system was the recognition that, in the familiar whole number system, the building-up conception is only half the story. Inherent in the system also is a partitioning down property—partition 100 into 10 equal groups and each has a value of 10; partition 10 into 10 equal groups and each has a value of 1 (unit). If one simply continues this partitioning process new positions are created and the values of these positions are clear (tenths, hundredths, etc.). With this reconceptualization, one has a notation system that can be conceived as building up or partitioning down (depending on the direction in which the digits are read) and a system that can represent quantities measured with parts of units as well as whole units. The only difference in the principles of the notation is the convention used to mark the units position.

Quantities Represented
by the Notation System

A notation system that includes position values generated by successive division (as well as multiplication) is a system that can represent a new kind of quantity. Decimal notation is not limited to representing quantity measured with whole units (quantity that is countable) but can represent continuous quantity as well, and can represent it to any degree of accuracy. Suppose a board in a squeaky floor needs to be replaced. Before cutting a new one, the old board is measured to ensure a tight fit. The old board measures 2 meters and a little more. That is not accurate enough so the unit (meter) is partitioned into tenths and the "little more" is measured with these parts of units. The additional length is 3 tenths of a meter with a little left over. The tenth meter is partitioned into tenths and the leftover portion is measured with tenth of tenth meters or hundredth meters. From 0–9 of these smaller parts of the unit will be sufficient to cover the remaining portion (suppose 6 will do it), possibly with a very little left over. So far, the length of the board can be described as 2.36 meters. If further accuracy is needed, a hundredth meter part can be partitioned into tenths, and some of these thousandth meters can be used. Then a tenth of a thousandth can be partitioned into tenths, and so on. Of course, a common meter stick already has several iterations of this partitioning process indicated on the stick. The points are that (a) a continuous quantity can be measured to any degree of accuracy by beginning with a unit and partitioning by 10 as many times as needed and (b) the decimal fraction notation system can represent this measure of the quantity (the notation can handle any number of partitions by 10).

There are two features of the notation system that follow from the fact that the notation represents continuous quantity. One feature of the decimal notation system is that, given any two decimal fractions, one can always write a third decimal fraction between the two. For example, a decimal that would fall between 0.317 and 0.318 is 0.3172. It is not hard to see that there is more than one decimal between the two (0.3176 and 0.317119 are others). Indeed, there are an infinite number of them. This property is commonly known as the property of being dense and usually is highlighted in discussions of how rational numbers are different than whole numbers.

A second feature of decimal notation that results from representing continuous quantity is the decreasing rate of increase in the size of the number as digits are adjoined to the right. The feature of decreasing rate of increase is not new with decimal fractions. Consider the size of the whole number 487. The leftmost digit (the 4) contains the most information; it contributes the largest portion. As one moves to the right, each digit adds to the total but each digit adds less. The 8 adds 80 and the 7 adds 7. What is different about decimal fractions is that this decreasing contribution can continue forever. Digits can be adjoined to the right without end, as in 26.343434 . . . , and each digit contributes something to the size of the number but each contributes less than the digit to its left (excluding, of course, the case of a 0 digit).

It is interesting to note that, although this decreasing rate of increase can continue without end, the size of the number is bounded. For example, by looking only at the 2 in 26.343434 . . . it is clear that the number will not be larger than 30. In fact, it will not be larger than 27, than 27.4, than 27.35, and so on. What is remarkable about this feature of boundedness is that the number can be written to be as close to the bound or limit as one would like. Because this feature of the notation is linked to the fact that the notation represents continuous quantity, it should come as no surprise that this is equivalent to saying that one can represent a quantity measured as accurately as one would like.

To summarize, a fundamental consequence of the three principles of the notation system of decimals is that decimal fraction numerals can represent the measures of continuous as well as discrete quantities. This is equivalent to observing that: (a) Decimals can represent quantities measured with parts of units as well as whole units, and can represent quantities measured as accurately as needed, (b) it is always possible to write a third decimal fraction between any two, and (c) digits can be adjoined to the right of a numeral without end (and that they add less and less to the size of the number). Although these statements may sound quite different, they reflect the same essential feature of the decimal system. They all result from representing the measure of continuous quantity. The consequences for students of using a whole-number-looking system to represent continuous quantity is considered in the next section.

COGNITIVE ANALYSIS OF DECIMALS—
HOW ARE THEY LEARNED?

The analysis of how students learn decimals is based on the assumption that learning about decimals, just as learning about any mathematical topic, involves learning a variety of different things about decimals and connecting these things together. In this section, the discussion focuses first on the different kinds of knowledge that students need to acquire about decimals and then considers the connections between them. Because understanding decimals depends on making connections between different kinds of decimal knowledge, a major part of the discussion is devoted to examining connections: potential impediments to making connections, places where connections might be made, and how well students ordinarily make such connections.

Different Kinds of Knowledge

When studying school learning of mathematics it is useful to distinguish among different kinds of knowledge that students may acquire. Knowledge is not all of one kind, and by identifying different types of knowledge and their potential relationships it is possible to uncover the reasons for many learning successes and failures. Three kinds of knowledge are distinguished here: (a) knowledge of the notation system, (b) knowledge of the rules for manipulating the notation, and (c) knowledge of the quantities that are represented by the notation. There are other ways to classify the components of knowledge about decimals but these three categories are especially useful for considering the relationships between knowledge of decimals and knowledge of related topics, such as whole numbers and common fractions.

Knowledge of the Notation. Perhaps the first knowledge about decimal fractions that students traditionally acquire in most classrooms is knowledge of the notation. This is knowledge of the symbols that are used to write decimal fractions and knowledge of the form that constrains how the symbols are positioned on paper. This does not necessarily include knowledge of what the symbols mean, what quantities they represent. Rather, as defined here, it is knowledge about the form in which symbols are written to represent decimal fractions. This knowledge would enable students to recognize 3.08 as a decimal fraction and to recognize that 3.0.8 or $\frac{3.8}{100}$ are inappropriate forms.

Knowledge of the Symbol Rules. Much of what students learn about decimal fractions from textbooks (see the discussion later in the chapter) is knowledge of the rules that prescribe how to manipulate the written symbols to produce correct answers. The problems usually are computation exercises or rewriting decimal fractions in equivalent forms. Examples of the rules are: (a) Line up the decimal points before adding or subtracting, (b) adjoin zeros on the right to "even out" ragged decimals, and (c) divide the denominator into the numerator to write a common fraction as a decimal. The rules usually are step-by-step prescriptions which, if followed precisely, will produce correct responses. Textbooks encourage a great deal of practice in using rules.

Knowledge of Quantities. Knowledge of the quantities that are represented by decimal fraction notation can be thought of as knowledge of the real world that provides referents for decimal fraction symbols. To be more specific, knowledge of quantities is knowledge of concrete or visual objects that can be measured by units, tenths of units, hundredths of units, and so on. For example, this might be knowledge that a jar of punch can be measured by dipping out full liter containers first, then dipping out smaller deciliter containers for the rest, then dipping out centiliter containers if any is left. Or this might be knowledge that the amount of wood in a pile of Dienes base-10 blocks could be described by assigning the large block the unit value and counting the number of units, tenths, hundredths, and thousandths.

Knowledge of the quantities includes knowledge of what happens when the quantities are moved, partitioned, combined, or acted upon in other ways. For example, suppose there are two piles of base-10 blocks and, in both piles, the flat has been assigned the unit value. The total amount of wood can be described in a natural way by combining the blocks of the same size. To anticipate the discussion to come, knowledge of quantities and actions on quantities provide the meaning for the symbol notation and provide the "reasons" for the rules. In other words, there is an intended relationship among the three kinds of knowledge.

Comparing Knowledge of Decimal Fractions, Whole Numbers, and Common Fractions

To set the stage for thinking about connections among the different kinds of knowledge, it is useful to consider the differences and similarities of decimals compared with whole numbers and fractions. In some sense, decimal fractions represent a confluence of whole numbers and common fractions. Fundamental concepts, principles of the notation system, and written and spoken conventions of the decimal system are drawn largely from one or the other of these two prior systems. Whole numbers and common fractions often are prior systems for students in that they are introduced before decimals in most curricula. Thus, many students already have acquired considerable knowledge of whole numbers and limited knowledge of common fractions by the time they encounter decimal fractions. An analysis of the relationships between the systems along with considerations of students' prior knowledge provide some important clues about the difficulties students can have in making connections between pieces of decimal knowledge.

The three kinds of knowledge identified earlier provide a framework for comparing the systems of whole numbers, common fractions, and decimal fractions. Table 5.1 summarizes the comparisons among the three systems for each kind of knowledge—knowledge of the notation, knowledge of the rules for manipulating the notation, and knowledge of the quantities. These comparisons are elaborated a little further in each case. First, however, it should be noted that there are many different interpretations of "fraction" (Kieren, 1976, 1980; Lesh, Post, & Behr, 1988; Ohlsson, 1988) and different interpretations would yield different relationships between common fractions and the other systems. Most students are introduced to fraction as part of a whole (part of a region or part of a set) so their knowledge of common fractions prior to decimals is tied mostly to this interpretation. Consequently, the interpretation that is used for common fractions to compare systems is part of a whole.

Comparing Notation Systems. As stated earlier, the principles of the decimal fraction notation are nearly identical to those for whole number notation. These similarities are reflected in Table 5.1. Items 1 and 2 identified for whole numbers and decimal fractions are nearly the same and Items 3 and 4 are identical. There is a difference in the form of the numerals as indicated in Item 1, a difference that appears to be minor, and a corresponding difference in how the units position is marked (Item 2). Otherwise, the number systems use the same notation. In contrast, there are few similarities between decimal and common fraction notation. The items for knowledge of common fraction notation sound very different than the items for whole numbers or decimal fractions. Any similarities that could be drawn are overwhelmed by the striking difference in form.

Comparing Rules. Rules are prescriptions for the ways in which written symbols can be manipulated to produce correct answers. Often there are several rules or algorithms that work. The rules identified in Table 5.1 are abbreviated descriptions of those that ordinarily are taught in the United States. For purposes of comparison, only the core procedural aspects are identified. The descriptions do not include the conceptual ideas that might accompany their actual presentation during instruction.

Note the great similarity between the rules for decimals and for whole numbers. This is a direct consequence of the similarity of notation. Note

TABLE 5.1
Comparison of three numeration systems

Whole numbers	Common fractions	Decimal fractions
	Notation system	
1. Numerals take the form abc	1. Numerals take the form $\frac{a}{b}$	1. Numerals take the form ab.c
2. Place value in base 10; unit position marked by last digit on right	2. Bottom numeral describes the number of equal parts into which the unit has been partitioned. The unit is implicit.	2. Place value in base 10; unit position marked by digit to left of decimal point
3. Value of digit is product of face value and place value	3. Top numeral identifies the number of parts being considered	3. Value of digit is product of face value and place value
4. Value of numeral is sum of value of digits		4. Value of numeral is sum of value of digits
	Symbol manipulation rules	
1. Add and subtract by combining digits with same place value, regroup using 10 for 1 or 1 for 10 exchange when necessary.	1. Add and subtract by finding a common denominator; substituting equivalent fractions, and combining numerators	1. Add and subtract by combining digits with same place value, regroup using 10 for 1 and 1 for 10 exchange when necessary
2. Multiply using multistep algorithm	2. Multiply by multiplying numerators and multiplying denominators	2. Multiply using multistep algorithm (same as for whole numbers); place decimal point
3. Divide using multistep algorithm	3. Divide by inverting second fraction (divisor) and then multiplying	3. Place decimal point(s); divide using multistep algorithm (same as for whole numbers); place decimal point
4. Order numerals from largest to smallest by comparing digits with largest place value first	4. Order fractions from largest to smallest by finding a common denominator, substituting equivalent fractions, and comparing numerators (as whole numbers)	4. Order numerals from largest to smallest by comparing digits with largest place value first
	Quantities	
1. Discrete quantities; countable sets of individual units	1. Discrete and continuous quantities; measurable to any degree of accuracy	1. Discrete and continuous quantities; measurable to any degree of accuracy

also, however, that rules can be described at many different levels and the similarity of description depends, in part, on the level of description. For example, at the surface or form level, the rule for adding or subtracting decimals can be described in terms of lining up decimal points and that for whole numbers in terms of lining up digits on the right. However, a description at a little deeper level talks about combining digits with the same place value. This level of description, as shown in Table 5.1, reveals the similarity of procedures with whole numbers and decimals. At a still deeper level, the description would talk about combining items (numerals) that had been measured with the same unit. This description reveals the similarity in addition or subtraction across all number systems, indeed, across all mathematical systems. So, the level of description is important. Surface level descriptions may mask similarities of procedures, similarities that are revealed by deeper level descriptions.

In contrast to the similarity of whole number and decimal rules, the rules for manipulating fraction symbols shown in Table 5.1 are entirely different. Again, this is a direct consequence of the differences in notation. The written symbols for common fractions have a very different form than whole numbers or decimals. Consequently, the rules for manipulating these symbols are very different. At least they are very different as described in Table 5.1. At a more general level of description the procedures show striking similarities, but traditional instruction describes them (as in Table 5.1) at a level that highlights their differences.

Comparing Quantities. Table 5.1 shows that the quantities represented by decimals and common fractions have the same character and that the quantities represented by whole numbers are different. In other words, when moving from symbols and rules to quantities there is a realignment of systems that are similar and different. Whole numbers represent the measure of discrete quantities whereas decimals and common fractions represent the measure of discrete and continuous quantities.

The important conclusion from Table 5.1 reiterates an earlier point: The decimal system uses notation and rules like those for whole numbers to represent quantities like those of fractions. For most students, this means building new kinds of connections. Connections must be made between whole-number-looking symbols, previously connected to whole number quantities, and fractional quantities, previously connected to common fraction symbols. Given the usual instructional sequence, decimal fractions use the symbols and rules first introduced for whole numbers to represent quantities first introduced for fractions. This means that students may need to suppress old connections and not allow them to interfere. At the least, students must recognize the change in the nature of the quantities that are represented by the whole-number-looking symbols.

Language Conventions That Reveal and Hide Comparisons. The connections that must be made between whole-number-looking symbols and fractional quantities are more complicated than one might expect. The complications are both revealed and hidden in the common language used to talk about decimals. An examination of language conventions also suggests new clues about the causes of students' difficulties with decimals.

The language used for decimal fractions is different from the language used for whole numbers in several important ways. In order to clarify the differences, it is necessary to examine the meaning of the word *unit.* Unit can be used to convey two different meanings and it is helpful at this point to distinguish between what I call a counting unit and a referent unit. A referent unit is defined as a single entity that is used in a particular context as a basis for all measurements in that context. It is 1 of something. It might be an inch, a cubic meter, a shaded circle, or any other entity. When counting or measuring, however, we might not use the referent unit. A fractional part of the referent unit might be used rather than the entire unit. For example, .7 m can indicate that tenths of a meter were used to measure or count. I use the term counting unit to refer to the tenth of a meter in this case because it was the unit that was counted. Similarly, a composite of referent units might be used to count. For example, in a description of 23 dozens of eggs, the counting unit is 12 eggs. It is important to note that the counting unit takes on meaning only in relation to the referent unit. The number .7 indicates that the counting unit is tenth, but tenth of what? The referent unit is needed to answer the question and give meaning to tenth (cf. Schwartz, 1988).

With this distinction it is possible to examine the language of decimal fractions and contrast it with the language of whole numbers. An initial difference is that the language used most commonly for the fraction portion of decimal numbers uses the position value of the rightmost digit as the counting unit and states it explicitly. For example, .38 is "thirty-eight hundredths." This matches the language for common fractions with a denominator of 100 implied in the written decimal form. Similarly, .7 is "seven tenths," and .154 is "one-hundred fifty-four thousandths." In contrast, the language for reading whole numbers emphasizes periods of three digits by stating the rightmost position value in the period as the counting unit. For example, 2,526,817 is "two million, five hundred twenty-six thousand, eight hundred seventeen"; the counting unit for the rightmost period ("ones") is not stated explicitly.

Whole number language uses the counting unit for the rightmost period (ones) as the referent unit, unless there is information to the contrary. So, 28 is "twenty-eight ones" and we presumably have counted 28 referent units. But with decimal fractions, the counting unit is never the referent unit; the counting unit is always a fractional part of the referent unit (tenths, hundredths, etc.). This means that when the language used to express the number of units counted is imported from whole numbers to decimals, the assumptions about what serves as the counting unit must be changed. To make matters worse, we end up with two levels of counting units. Consider the number .52341, "fifty-two thousand, three hundred forty-one hundred-thousandths." Because the language of 3-digit periods is imported from whole numbers, "thousand" is a counting unit. But thousand is a second-level counting unit because it describes how many first-level counting units (hundred-thousandths) have been counted. The referent unit, as before, is a single entity that is not explicit in the numeral but must be made explicit by the reader to give hundred-thousandth a meaning. Although the difference in language for whole numbers and decimal fractions may appear at first glance to be a simple addition of one fraction word at the end of decimal numbers, this addition signifies a fundamental change in the units being counted, and many of the corresponding changes in the meaning of the language are implicit rather than explicit.

Another contrast in whole number and decimal language arises from the fact that there are a variety of acceptable ways of saying decimal numbers. For example, there are two common ways of saying 2.38, "two and thirty-eight hundredths" and "two and three tenths, eight hundredths." Note that the first form implies two counting units (ones and hundredths) and the second form implies three counting units (ones, tenths, and hundredths). Whole numbers, on the other hand, are usually said in only one way. The number 47 could be said "four tens, seven ones" but it is almost always said "forty seven."

A final contrast between whole number and decimal language concerns the match between the words used to express each digit and its position value. Consider the number 273, "two hundred seventy-three." The word hundred correctly labels the position value of the 2, using "ty" for "ten" the word seventy correctly labels the position value of 7, and the implied "ones" labels the position value of 3. For larger numbers, the match is not as straightforward but it still exists. Consider the number 521,846, "five hundred twenty-one thousand, eight hundred forty six." For the digits in the left period, the position value is the product of the digit word (e.g., five hundred) and the counting unit (thousand). Thus, the position value is easily reconstructible from the language. But for decimal fractions, no such match exists. The number .273 is "two-hundred, seventy-three thousandths." The word *hundred* is used with a digit in the tenths position. The other words are equally mismatched with position value. What is more, the match between words and positions is not stable but changes with changes in the number of digits in the fraction part of the decimal.

Not only is there a mismatch between the values represented by the words and the position values in decimal fraction language, there also is a mismatch between the words and the counting unit. In this case the mismatch is consistent. The number .273 has a counting unit of thousandths and the word associated with two is hundred. Because the position values are symmetric around the ones position rather than the decimal point, the word associated with the first digit to the right of the decimal point always will be "off by one" from the symmetric whole number word in identifying the counting unit. As another example, the digit 7 in .7435 has "thousand" associated with it, and the counting unit is ten-thousandths.

As indicated earlier, the changes in the features of the notation and the language as one moves from whole numbers to decimals signify deeper changes in the nature of the quantities that are represented with the notation. But these surface changes are potentially confusing for anyone first encountering decimal fractions, especially because many of the changes are implicit. The changes may inhibit students in making appropriate connections between symbols and quantities. Consequently, their significance when thinking about effective instruction should not be underestimated.

Building Connections Between
Different Kinds of Knowledge

It can be argued that the major task for students in acquiring meaningful knowledge of decimals is to connect the written symbols and rules of decimal fractions with the quantities they represent (Hiebert & Wearne, 1986; Wearne & Hiebert, 1988a, 1988b). For most students in fourth and fifth grades, this means connecting symbols and rules that look very familiar with quantities that are much less familiar. It is argued here that many textbooks (see the last section of the chapter) devote too much time and attention to perfecting the rules for symbols (many of which are already familiar) at the expense of providing experience with the quantities being represented and supporting the construction of connections between quantities and the symbols and rules that represent them.

The importance of connecting the written symbols and rules of mathematics with concrete and familiar referents is based on the argument that meaning is derived from connecting abstract mathematical representations of quantity with concrete real-world representations of quantity (Kaput, 1987; Van Engen, 1949). When a written symbol is connected with concrete objects the written symbol re-presents the object in the mind's eye. Thus, the learner can think with the object rather than only with the symbol (Mason, 1987). The underlying idea is that recognizing (or constructing) correspondences between different representational systems is at the heart of knowing or understanding mathematics (Hiebert & Carpenter, in press; Lesh, Post, & Behr, 1987).

What it means to know or to understand mathematics is a question that is not easily answered (e.g., Kitcher, 1983; Lakatos, 1978). For example, there are a variety of ways to characterize what it means to learn and understand mathematics in school (e.g., Brownell, 1935; Davis, 1984; Hiebert & Carpenter, in press; Lampert, 1986, 1989; Leinhardt, 1988; McLellan & Dewey, 1985; Noddings, 1985; Putnam, Lampert, & Peterson, 1990). One alternate position to that presented earlier is that meaning can be derived by observing the patterns and behaviors of symbols entirely within the symbol system, without considering the connections to referents outside the system (Hiebert, 1990; Kaput, 1987; Lampert, 1989). However, it is argued here that because students often bring with them a good deal of knowledge about quantities in the real world, it is likely that the initial meanings for decimal symbols and rules are developed best by emphasizing connections between written symbols and familiar quantitative referents (Hiebert, 1988).

To examine the kind of connections that students might make between symbols and quantities, to review whether students ordinarily make the connections, and to support instruction that might help students with the connecting process, it is useful to consider three sites where connections can be made between symbols and rules on the one hand, and quantitative referents on the other (Hiebert, 1984). The sites are specified as points in real time during the process of doing mathematics and solving problems. From a mathematical point of view the sites represent three distinguishable phases in solving mathematical problems. The sites provide a useful way of thinking about building connections because they represent places where potential connections are especially productive and the absence of connections are especially damaging. The following discussion describes the three sites and, in each case, summarizes the evidence on the connections that students ordinarily make. The next section of the chapter examines instructional conditions that promote connections at each site.

Site 1: Connecting Individual Symbols with Meaningful Referents. Site 1 is the initial point in the problem-solving process when the problem statement is interpreted. I limit my discussion to problems that are presented with written symbols, not an overly restrictive limitation for dealing with decimal fractions in school. Site 1, then, is the point at which the symbols of the problem are given some meaning. Two kinds of symbols must be interpreted—numerical symbols (e.g., 3, 1.7) and operational symbols (e.g., $+$, $-$). Meanings are established for numerical symbols by connecting the symbols with quantitative referents. For example, 1.7 takes on meaning if it is connected to a quantity that measures one unit and seven tenths more of the unit (e.g., one and seven-tenths liters of fruit punch).

Meanings for operation symbols are constructed as connections are made between the symbol and an appropriate action on quantities. For example, the $-$ symbol takes on meaning when it is connected to the action of comparing the heights of two students, John (1.54 m) and Carlos (1.61 m), and finding how much taller Carlos is than John (this, of course, is only one of the meanings of $-$). As another example, the symbol $\div$ takes on meaning when it is connected to the action of repeatedly measuring out .3 liters of fruit punch from a bowl holding 6.2 liters of punch to find how many glasses can be served. It is important to notice that the meaning that is derived for the symbols $-$ and $\div$ does not include knowledge of how to manipulate the symbols to produce the "answer." The meaning for the symbol does not include knowledge of the algorithm to carry out the operation. Rather, the meaning provides (a) knowledge of what the problem is about, (b) knowledge of what the algorithm will do for you if and when it is carried out, and (c) knowledge of what the answer stands for. The meaning derived from connecting the operation symbol clearly is important for interpreting the problem and the answer, but it does not tell you how to operate on the symbols to produce the answer.

Do Students Ordinarily Make Connections at Site 1? The available evidence suggests that most students do not connect decimal fraction symbols with appropriate quantitative referents. For example, data from the National Assessment of Educational Progress (NAEP) show that only about one half of 13-year-olds can translate between decimals and fractions in the easiest situations—when the denominators are powers of 10 (Carpenter et al., 1981). A number of students simply convert the numerals of the given number to the alternate form (e.g., $.09 = \frac{9}{9}$) (Hiebert & Wearne, 1986). Of course, this kind of task may not be getting at the connections students have established between decimal symbols and fraction quantities because, on one hand, failures may result from lack of connections between fraction symbols and quantities (a likely situation [Behr, Wachsmuth, Post, & Lesh, 1984]) and, on the other hand, successes may result from memorized but little-understood rules for converting form.

Perhaps a better task is to ask students to write decimals for visual fraction quantities. Hiebert and Wearne (1986) presented shaded parts of unit rectangular regions to students in Grades 5, 6, 7, and 9. One region was divided into 10 equal parts with 3 shaded, a second was divided into 100 equal parts with 4 shaded, and a third was divided into 5 equal parts with 1 shaded. Not more than one half of the students, even in Grade 9, responded correctly to any of these items. The most frequent errors on the three tasks in all grades were 3.10, 4.100, and 1.5 respectively. A plausible explanation for these responses is that students called up a common fraction response ($\frac{3}{10}, \frac{4}{100}, \frac{1}{5}$, respectively) and then manipulated the symbols into a decimal form.

The most commonly administered item to assess students' knowledge of decimal fractions is one in which students are asked to order a number of decimals by size, or to choose the largest or smallest in a set of decimals. Such items are useful for this discussion because students' responses provide additional information on the meaning they assign to decimal symbols. That is, students' responses on the items provide some insight into whether or not students think of quantities when they see decimal symbols. Many students perform poorly on any item involving "ragged" decimals (different numbers of digits to the right of the decimal points). This includes students who are just beginning work with decimals (Hiebert & Wearne, 1986; Hiebert, Wearne, & Taber, 1991), students who have studied decimals for several years (Carpenter et al., 1981), students who are entering college (Grossman, 1983), and students from countries in addition to those in the United States—such as France (Sackur-Grisvard & Leonard, 1985), England (Brown, 1981), Israel (Resnick et al., 1989), and Sweden (Ekenstam, 1977). Typical of the level of performance is the NAEP data cited at the beginning of the chapter showing that 45% of 13-year-olds correctly chose the largest of .19, .036, .195, and .2 (Carpenter et al., 1981). Clearly, students who are unable to complete this task have little if any idea of the size of quantities represented by the symbols—at least, they do not think of quantities when performing the task. They seem to have little understanding of the value represented by each of the digits and/or little understanding that the value of the numeral is the sum of the values of its digits (Bell et al., 1981; Carr, 1983). Note the match between the knowledge that is lacking and the principles of the notation system. That is, the missing knowledge appears to be of a fundamental kind.

To deal with the ordering task, it appears that many students initially fall back on familiar rules (from whole numbers) to perform the task and then gradually invent or adopt new rules that incorporate some features of decimal fractions (Nesher & Peled, 1986; Resnick & Nesher, 1983; Resnick et al., 1989; Sackur-Grisvard & Leonard, 1985). More specifically, some students move from (a) ignoring the decimal point entirely and treating the numeral as a whole number to (b) recognizing the decimal point but treating the decimal portion as a whole number to (c) recognizing that digits further to the right are smaller and (d) recognizing that zeros to the left of decimal digits affect the value of the numeral but those to the right do not (Sackur-Grisvard & Leonard, 1985). Awareness of these features of the notation yield three incorrect rules that some students seem to acquire, in sequence. First, the number with more digits is larger. Second, the number with fewest decimal digits is larger. Third, the number without 0 in the tenths place is larger (Nesher & Peled, 1986; Resnick et al., 1989; Sackur-Grisvard & Leonard, 1985).

It is important to notice that the knowledge students are acquiring as they adopt and execute these rules may be knowledge only about the form of the notation; the knowledge does not necessarily include connections between the written symbols and the quantities they represent. Even when students acquire a rule that generates the correct answer, there is no assurance that students know what the symbols mean. The importance of this concern rests on the point of view taken here: To do mathematics, one must, at least, know what the symbols mean. Performing mathematical tasks by executing a series of rules rather than considering mathematical relationships (in this case, comparing the sizes of quantities represented by written numerals) is not productive in the long run (Hiebert, 1988; Wearne, 1990). Indeed, it could hardly be considered doing mathematics at all (Brownell, 1935).

To summarize the evidence to this point, it appears that many students fail to connect decimal numerals with quantitative referents. Are students any more successful connecting operation symbols with actions on referents? Two kinds of tasks provide some measure of these connections. One is estimation in which students are asked to produce an approximate answer to a computation problem without using a conventional algorithm. For example, what would be a good guess for $3.012 \div .96$? A second type of task is one in which students are asked to relate a computation expression to a story problem. The assumption here is that if students know the meaning of, for example, "$\div$," they would be able to relate the expression $3.012 \div .96$ to a story that describes such a situation. The estimation tasks assess connections at Site 3 as well as Site 1 and consequently are discussed later; what follows is a description of students' facility with computation story problems involving decimals.

By the time students reach upper elementary school, the symbols $+$ and $-$ are quite familiar, and primitive notions that often accompany these symbols, such as "$+$ makes bigger" and "$-$ makes smaller," can be brought to decimal numbers with no adverse effects (as long as the numbers are positive). In other words, the meanings of $+$ and $-$ can be generalized from whole numbers to positive decimal numbers without extension or modification. Because most students in upper elementary school can interpret stories involving one-step addition and subtraction with whole numbers (NAEP, 1983), they should be able to interpret simple stories involving addition and subtraction with decimals as well. This expectation is generally confirmed (Hiebert & Wearne, 1986). Of course, this does not mean that students always add and subtract correctly. There is still the matter of deciding which digits to combine. The claim here is only that most students seem to recognize the general adding and subtracting actions conveyed by $+$ and $-$ in decimal contexts.

Students' performance in multiplication and division situations presents a different picture. Unlike the case for addition and subtraction, primitive notions of multiplication and division cannot be transferred wholesale from whole numbers to decimals. Decimal fractions may be (and often are in students' experience) less than 1. Thus, multiplication does not always "make the second number bigger" and division does not always involve "taking a smaller number into a bigger number." Students must extend the meanings of "×" and "÷" and suppress certain primitive notions that may have developed in whole number contexts. Performance data suggest that many students do neither.

Students apparently perform quite well on story problems in which the numerical values support the primitive notions that multiplication makes the second number bigger and that division involves taking a smaller number into a bigger number (Bell et al., 1981; Fischbein, Deri, Nello, & Marino, 1985; Hiebert & Wearne, 1986). For example, Fischbein et al. (1985) reported that most students (ages 10–15 years) identified multiplication as the operation needed to solve a story involving 15 groups of .75. However, in all studies performance drops dramatically on problems where the numerical values conflict with students' primitive meanings. The most striking example of this is reported by Bell et al. (1981). Many students (ages 12–15 years) correctly selected multiplication as the operation needed to solve a problem with m gallons of gasoline at n per gallon when m and n were whole numbers, but selected division for the same problem when m and n were decimal numbers with m less than 1. Of course, many factors in addition to the size of the numbers influence students' behavior on multiplication and division problems (Bell, Fischbein, & Greer, 1984; Nesher, 1988). The important point for this discussion is that many students do not establish sound meanings for operation symbols.

As with numeric symbols, it appears that students fall back on whole number rules to deal with operation symbols. Primitive meanings of multiplication and division are inappropriately transferred from whole number to decimal contexts. Actions on quantities that would give a more complete meaning to the operation symbols may not have been experienced by many students. At the least, they remain unconnected to the written symbols.

One final distinction should be reiterated. Whether or not students execute a computation rule accurately when they encounter an operation symbol is a different question than whether they have established an appropriate meaning for the symbol. Accurate execution of an appropriate rule is important, but the connection between the operation symbols and actions on quantities is a separate issue. The meaning of the symbol derived from its connection with actions on quantities provides an entirely different kind of knowledge. The meaning of the symbol tells you, in very general terms, what the rule is doing for you.

Site 2: Connecting Rules with Actions on Referents. After the problem has been interpreted, procedures are selected and applied to solve the problem. The execution of procedures is the domain of Site 2. Most of the procedures that students learn in school are rules that prescribe how to manipulate written symbols. Many of the rules are motivated by actions on quantities. In fact, many of the manipulations of symbols parallel actions on quantities. For example, when adding decimal fractions each of the decimal numbers represents a quantity that can be concretized with objects, say base-10 blocks. To add the quantities, the blocks can be added by combining blocks of the same size. This action on the blocks corresponds to combining the digits with the same positional value. Hence the rule "Line up the decimal points." When combining blocks of the same size, the act of trading 10 blocks for 1 block of the next bigger size corresponds to the manipulations of symbols involved in regrouping. Thus, the rules for adding decimal fraction symbols can be paralleled with actions on objects. If students construct a correspondence between the actions on symbols and the actions on objects, then they can begin to understand what the rules mean and why the rules work.

Unfortunately, the process of connecting rules for decimal symbols with actions on quantities is not as easy as the addition example indicates. There are two facts that complicate the process. First, the concrete objects are themselves, in a real sense, representations of quantity just as written symbols are representations of quantity. They are useful representations because they display many relevant features of quantity (e.g., size, weight, etc.) in a salient way. But as representations, they also contain many features that are not relevant and even may confuse the correspondence with symbol rules.

For example, base-10 blocks can be arranged in any order on the table (rather than in positions ordered by size) and two sets can be combined by beginning with any size block and moving back and forth to trade for another size when necessary. Such back and forth movement does not correspond well with our traditional algorithm.

A second difficulty in connecting rules for decimal symbols with actions on quantities is that some of the rules (e.g., the multiplication and division algorithms) are quite complex and it is not easy to parallel all the moves with symbols by actions on quantities. At least, it is not easy to do in a way that the actions on quantities can be easily interpreted.

In spite of the difficulties, it is worth considering connections at Site 2. Connections at Site 2 provide a way of linking procedural rules with their conceptual rationales. Although students can memorize rules and get correct answers without connecting the rules with actions on quantities that would give them meaning (and show why they work), it is likely that such connections would contribute to success in the long run (Byers & Erlwanger, 1984; Lampert, 1989; Wearne, 1990).

The discussion of whether students ordinarily make connections at Site

2 focuses on addition and subtraction and considers whether students have connected the rules they use to compute with the actions on quantities that motivate them. Unfortunately, no research evidence is available on students' connections between multiplication or division rules and actions on quantities.

One of the rules that students first encounter when learning to add and subtract with decimals is "line up the decimal points." The rationale for the rule is that one can make sense of the answer when things are combined that have been measured with the same counting unit. Thus, decimal points are aligned so tenths are combined with tenths, hundredths with hundredths, and so on. There is precedent for this idea in students' previous work (like quantities are combined when working with whole numbers and fractions), it is a rather simple (and powerful) idea, and students spend time practicing it. The question is whether students understand why it "works."

During individual interviews, Hiebert and Wearne (1986) asked students to explain their procedures on simple addition and subtraction problems with ragged decimals (e.g., 4.2 + .36). If they described lining up decimal points on the addition and subtraction problems, they were asked why they used the rule. Students were pressed quite hard to describe all possible reasons for the rule. Later in the interview they were asked to "teach" addition or subtraction to their friends who supposedly had missed class and again were asked to justify lining up the decimal points. The following percentages of students in each grade referred at any time during the interview, even vaguely, to the values of the numbers or other conceptual bases for the rule: 0%, 12%, 33%, 60% in Grades 5, 6, 7, and 9, respectively. It appears that if the link between rule and notions of quantitative value is established at all, it is a late rather than an early development.

Another expression of the lack of connection between rules and actions on quantities is the belief that actions in the symbol and quantity worlds can be contradictory. Students were asked by Hiebert and Wearne (1986) to compute the answers to four addition and subtraction problems with paper and pencil and then with base-10 blocks. When students got different answers the results were compared and the students were asked whether it was acceptable to get different answers to the same problem. Many fifth and sixth graders believed it was permissible to get different answers to the same problem. Most often the justification for this belief was that they had used "different methods." In Grade five, 6 of the 10 students who got different answers accepted both answers. In Grade six, 6 of 11 students who found themselves in this situation accepted both answers as correct.

These data suggest that students learn procedures within particular contexts. If the contexts are different, the procedures are believed to be different and, naturally, may have different results. Symbolic contexts are different than block contexts. So, actions on blocks do not influence actions on symbols. The separation between rules with symbols and actions on referents is not unique for decimal fractions. The same kind of separation has been reported in other topic areas, by younger and older students (Davis & McKnight, 1980; Kaput, 1982; Resnick, 1982; Resnick & Omanson, 1987; Schoenfeld, 1986; Silver, 1986). But the separation certainly is prevalent with decimal fractions, even on the simple rules such as line up the decimal points to add or subtract. Although no data are available on the extent of separation with the more complex rules such as those for multiplication and division, it is reasonable to speculate that such rules would have no more meaning for students than the simpler rules.

Site 3: Connecting Answers with Real-World Solutions. Site 3 hosts the third point in the problem-solving process where connections between symbols and quantities could be especially beneficial. Assuming the rules have been executed, a response is produced that represents the student's answer to the problem. Site 3 focuses on the connections between the answers produced by manipulating symbols and the outcomes when acting on quantities. If these connections are made, then the answer "makes sense" or is "reasonable."

Imagined actions on quantities, although not always generating exact answers, do provide some clues about the reasonableness of solutions. As an example, consider the problem 3.1×4.98. Assuming that meanings have been established for the symbols, one can imagine forming about 3 groups of 5 objects. So, the answer obtained on paper (or with the calculator) should be about 15. It is this sort of estimation process that encourages the connections at Site 3. Knowledge about the meaning of the symbols and about corresponding actions on quantities are used to evaluate the reasonableness of answers (Davis, 1984).

Connections at Site 3 require connections at Site 1, connections between both the numeric and operation symbols and appropriate quantitative referents. However, connections at Site 2 (between procedural rules and actions on quantities) are not required. As an example, consider the problem 3.152×24.98. Judging that an answer close to 75 is reasonable depends on possessing some appropriate meaning for the numerical symbols 3.152 and 24.98, and some intuitive notion of "$\times$," such as repeated addition or multiple groupings. The actions on quantities can be carried out mentally using approximate values (3 and 25) for the numerals. For connections at Site 3, it is not necessary to know why the conventional algorithm for decimal multiplication "works." In other words, it is not necessary to have established connections at Site 2. In a sense, connections at Site 3 represent an application of connections at Site 1.

Considering that many students lack connections at Site 1, it is not surprising that connections at Site 3 seem to be largely missing. A first indication that many students do not check the reasonableness of their answers comes from error analyses on written computation items. Many investigators have reported large numbers of students that produce answers that are in many ways unreasonable, that are not close to an estimate that would be generated working with actual quantities (Bell et al., 1981; Brown, 1981; Carpenter et al., 1981; Ekenstam, 1977; Hiebert & Wearne, 1985, 1986). Consider an example from Hiebert and Wearne (1986). During individual interviews, students were asked to focus directly on the reasonableness of answers. They were shown two problems, $3.51023 + .4625$ and $.92 \times 2.156$, and asked to pick from several choices $(.7, 3, 4, 6, 7, 8$ and $18, 180, 2, .00018, .21$, respectively) the number that would be the closest to the actual answer. The percentage of students who correctly chose 4 for the addition item were 8, 9, 33, and 60 in Grades 5, 6, 7, and 9 respectively. Fewer students were able to pick the most reasonable estimate for the multiplication product. Percentages of students correct were 8, 18, 33, and 30 in Grades 5, 6, 7, and 9 respectively.

A common explanation for the frequency of unreasonable responses is that students simply do not think to check the reasonableness of their answers. If students remembered to "look back" and check their answers they may recognize the implausibility of the responses and correct the errors. Remembering to look back and check the reasonableness of answers certainly is good advice and undoubtedly would eliminate some errors. But it is not enough. Consider the explanation of a ninth-grade student described earlier for writing 5.1 directly underneath .36 when adding and getting .87 for the answer: "If you're adding .36 and 5.1 it would make a lot more sense if it came out to .8 or so" (Hiebert & Wearne, 1986, p. 218). In order to check whether an answer makes sense, one also must know what the numerals mean.

In summary, the separation between symbols and quantities culminates at Site 3. If connections are absent at Site 1, students have no chance of evaluating the reasonableness of answers at Site 3. Why do so many students fail to connect symbols and rules with quantities? The next section considers sources that are influential in the connecting process.

INSTRUCTIONAL ANALYSIS OF DECIMALS— HOW ARE THEY TAUGHT?

Given the mathematical complexities of decimal fractions and the accompanying cognitive complexities, it may not be surprising that many students fail to connect their knowledge of decimal symbols and rules with meaningful referents. Indeed, constructing relationships between symbols and referents is an intellectually demanding task with any symbol system (Hofstadter, 1979; Werner & Kaplan, 1963) and certainly with the formal symbols of mathematics (Janvier, 1987; Skemp, 1982).

The evidence on students' failure to connect symbols with referents suggests that instruction will succeed in helping students build appropriate connections only if it is intentionally designed to do so. Although the exact nature of the "best" instruction is not yet clear, several features that are sure to be included in effective instruction are (a) explicit attention to connections between meaningful, familiar referents and symbols that represent them, (b) reflection on the semantic characteristics of written symbols, and (c) the development of a rich language that can be used to talk about the symbols (Carpenter, 1986; Davis, 1984; Hiebert, 1984, 1988; Lampert, 1986, 1989; Resnick & Omanson, 1987; Wearne & Hiebert, 1988a, 1988b, 1989).

Because instruction varies significantly from classroom to classroom, it is impossible to make blanket statements about how instruction in every classroom measures up against these standards. It is impossible to say how many teachers are assisting students in making sense of decimal fractions, in connecting decimal fraction symbols and rules with meaningful referents. But it is possible to approximate a general description by looking at widely used textbook series. Many teachers depend heavily on textbooks for their mathematics instruction (Freeman & Porter, 1989; McKnight, Travers, Crosswhite, & Swafford, 1985) so an analysis of texts provides some clues about the instruction students are receiving. In many cases, the analyses show that supplementary activities are needed to help students make connections.

Two textbook series were selected for this discussion. The series were selected because both have released recent editions, both are widely used in elementary schools across the United States, and both appear to represent many of the textbooks currently available. The analysis of the texts are organized around the three Sites: developing meaning for the symbols, making sense of the rules, and judging the reasonableness of answers. After analyzing textbook support for making connections at each Site, supplementary activities are described that teachers could use to encourage students to make appropriate connections.

Developing Meaning for Written Symbols

Analysis of Textbooks. Based on the earlier discussion, there are two kinds of written symbols for which meaning must be established—numerals and operation signs. The initial question concerns the way in which students are assisted in connecting decimal fraction numerals with familiar and meaningful referents. The two text series (A and B) differ somewhat here but neither provides the intensive and extended experience that students need early on in order to make sense of later instruction (Wearne, 1990; Wearne & Hiebert, 1988b, 1989). This is perhaps the most telling observation that is made about the textbooks and its significance cannot be overstated. Series A helps students begin the connecting process by asking them to use a unit square and tenth strips as a model to show decimal fractions written with symbols and with words. However, these activities are limited to several pages at the beginning of Grades 3 and 4. Series B provides only a few pictures of a unit square partitioned into tenths.

Although both series use the partitioned unit square as the primary referent for decimal numerals, other models are shown. These include an odometer, a meter stick, a number line, and money. Unfortunately, the models are shown only in a few cases and used for only a few problems. It is difficult to imagine students making lasting connections with a handful of activities devoted to connecting symbols and referents. Furthermore, some of the models are not presented in a way that would reinforce appropriate connections. For example, on the first page of decimals (Grade 3) Series A presents a picture of a dollar bill partitioned into tenths. It is not clear that one tenth of a paper bill has a value of one tenth of a dollar so this model may not be helpful. Then in Grade 4, money is used again as a model. But this time 100 pennies are shown and students are asked to write given amounts by using both the ¢ and $ notation. The ¢ symbol reinforces the conception of a penny as the referent unit along with the idea of building up by 10 rather than partitioning by 10. This decreases the usefulness of this model as a referent for decimals.

An analysis of the assistance provided students in developing meaning for numerals should consider whether the models or referents reveal the properties of the decimal notation system. First, place-value charts are used by both series as a way to show that the value of the digit depends on its position in the numeral. This certainly is an appropriate visual, but it is treated in a way that limits its effectiveness. It is used primarily as a way to introduce the name of the place value and usually appears only on the page where a new "place" is introduced. No mention is made by either series in Grades 3 and 4 of the relative value of positions, of the fact that each position is worth one-tenth as much as the position on the left. Such an important feature of decimals is first hinted at in Grade 5, Series A, when hundredths are discussed as tenths of tenths and in Grade 5, Series B, when thousandths are discussed as tenths of hundredths.

There is no explicit attention given in either series (Grades 3–6) to the remaining two properties: The value of a digit is its face value times its place value and the value of the numeral is the sum of the value of the digits. Of course, the authors may assume that such properties will generalize automatically from whole number notation, but no help is given students in recognizing the similarities between whole number and decimal notation. An even more serious deficiency is that students' attention is never drawn to the power provided by these properties. The quantity represented by 2.16 can be described in many ways—two hundred sixteen hundredths, or twenty-one tenths six hundredths, or one and eleven tenths six hundredths, and so on. None of these noncanonical forms are explored; only the canonical form, two and sixteen hundredths, is presented.

The mathematical analysis presented earlier suggested that a far-reaching consequence of these properties of the notation is that decimal fractions can be used to represent continuous quantity measured to any degree of accuracy. Although both series include measurement with the metric system and such activities could provide the context for developing this notion, neither series considers this aspect of decimal fractions. Exercises in converting between metric units contain several important features of decimal fractions, but the emphasis is on developing proficiency in moving the decimal point rather than on reflecting on properties of decimal notation as a system capable of representing continuous quantity.

Saying that decimal fractions can represent continuous quantity is equivalent, at a fundamental level, to saying that the decreasing value of each position, as one moves to the right, can continue indefinitely. Series B hints at this fact when the authors recommend that decimal fractions can be arranged from smallest to largest by looking at the value of digits in the same positions, moving left to right. However, this recommendation is presented as an algorithm for performing tasks and not reflected upon as an important feature of the notation.

As noted earlier, students enter decimal instruction with important prior knowledge. They probably are familiar with many of the features of whole number notation and may be familiar with some features of fraction quantities. Do the texts help students make the links to prior knowledge, to recognize what is similar and what is different about decimals? The answer is no. As indicated earlier, the similarities to whole number notation are not drawn explicitly; neither are the differences. The confusing mix of similarities and differences with whole number language conventions are never addressed directly. Students are told the correct way of saying decimal fractions (only one alternative is presented) but the expression is not analyzed for its meaning or its similarity and difference with a whole number expression.

Quantities that are referents for decimal numerals are fractional quantities (see Table 5.1). But the links between fractions and decimals in the texts are made at the symbol level rather than the referential level. Students are shown very early (on the first page, Grade 3) that, for example, $\frac{3}{10}$

= 0.3. But there are no discussions of the similarity of quantities. Series B hopes students will make the link themselves by presenting unit squares partitioned into tenths and hundredths and shaded portions written with common fractions on the two pages immediately preceding the introduction of decimals (Grade 3). But the fact that decimal notation is another way of representing the same quantities previously represented with common fractions is never discussed.

In summary, neither text series provides the support needed to develop meaning for decimal fraction numerals. One could not expect students to connect numerals with meaningful referents unless the teacher supplemented the textbook with many additional activities. Series A presents a few activities that will help students begin the connecting process. But the teacher must add more activities if students are to have a chance of connecting symbols and referents, and the teacher must encourage students to reflect on the nature of the quantities and the written symbols if they are to recognize the properties of decimal fraction notation.

Both textbook series spend very little time developing meaning for the operation symbols. The meanings for $+$ and $-$ carry over nicely from whole numbers and both series assume the generalization will be automatic. Neither discusses the meaning of these operation symbols.

Previous and current research (Bell et al., 1984; Bell et al., 1981; Fischbein et al., 1985; Nesher, 1988; Schwartz, 1988) suggests that the meaning of $\times$ and $\div$ is a much more complex issue. Indeed, the interpretations of these operations and the outcomes when performing them change dramatically as one moves from discrete quantities to continuous quantities, from whole numbers to fractions and decimals. Neither text series provides much information about these changes. Series A begins to address the issue by using the repeated addition interpretation of $\times$ for whole numbers times decimals, and then shifts to an area model with the unit square partitioned vertically and horizontally to show tenths times tenths. But the focus soon shifts to getting the procedural steps in place; reflection on the nature of multiplication (e.g., the product is smaller than the multiplier or the multiplicand) is not encouraged. Series B does not deal with the issue at all. The whole number form is imported from the beginning and attention is directed toward developing the procedure.

Observations about the treatment of $\div$ are much like those for $\times$. Series A addresses the meaning for the operation but stops short of developing it fully whereas Series B moves directly to procedures.

Recommended Supplementary Activities. Perhaps the most important conclusion that can be derived from reviewing previous research and analyzing current textbooks is that instruction must spend more time and attention helping students establish rich meanings for decimal symbols.

Teachers will need to supplement the textbooks heavily to provide enough appropriate activities for students to construct connections between decimal numerals and fraction quantities and between operation symbols and actions on quantities.

A first useful activity, in third or fourth grade, involves base-10 blocks where the large block is assigned the unit. The class then can discuss what a tenth would look like, with the flat becoming a tenth. (If base-10 blocks are not available, a square cardboard piece can be the unit with strips representing tenths.) A day of activities would include building concrete representations of spoken decimals (e.g., "two and seven tenths") and verbalizing the number represented with concrete materials (e.g., 1 large block and 3 flats). Regrouping can be introduced easily by (a) laying out, for example, 2 large blocks and 13 flats, and talking about the different ways to say this number and (b) asking students to show, for example, "four and one tenth" in as many different ways as possible. The language used to describe the representations helps demonstrate for students the relationships between the (positional) values of ones and tenths.

As part of the first day or two of activities, the block representing the unit should be changed. This is to encourage students to see that the value of tenth is relative to the referent unit rather than linked permanently to a particular block. So the flat might be assigned the unit value and the students asked to determine that the stick is now a tenth.

After numerous oral activities, the written notation can be introduced. Activities then can include building concrete representations for numerals and writing numerals for concrete representations. It is only at this point that the textbook activities will have some meaning for the students. The common picture of a square partitioned into tenths now matches the concrete materials they have been using.

After several days with tenths, and before beginning addition or subtraction, hundredths can be introduced with the concrete materials as both tenths of tenths and hundredths of the unit. The same sequence of activities can be followed as with tenths: (a) using verbalizations and concrete representations only, (b) changing the unit block, and (c) eventually introducing the written symbol and showing connections between concrete and written representations.

The research evidence suggests that the extra time spent up front helping students establish meaning for decimal symbols allows them to progress easily to adding and subtracting decimals, and to perform well on a variety of decimal tasks, such as ordering decimals (Wearne & Hiebert, 1988a, 1989). It also appears that one well-chosen concrete model is sufficient for many students to develop sound meanings for decimal symbols.

The research evidence that exists on the effect of using multiple models (Hiebert et al., 1991) does not point to one model as the best. It is clear that base-ten blocks can be quite effective (Wearne & Hiebert, 1988a, 1989) and that the number line model is quite difficult (Behr, Lesh, Post, & Silver, 1983; Lampert, 1989). This is not to say that number line models are inappropriate; they are the models that carry the continuous nature of quantity that can be represented by decimal notation. But perhaps the number line models should follow base-10 block type of models. This is still an open question.

Research evidence is very sketchy on how students can be helped to make connections between operation symbols and actions on quantities. It is possible to speculate that a useful activity for developing meaning for the operation symbols is the construction or interpretation of story problems. This may be especially important for × and ÷ because students often carry over inappropriate meanings for these symbols. Furthermore, the textbooks provide little help here. Students might be asked, for example, to write a number sentence for the story, "Carlos was baking a cake for his mother's birthday. The recipe called for .75 liters of milk and he had .50 liters of milk left. How many cakes (or how much of a cake) could he make?" Conversely, students might be asked to write a story for number sentences such as $1.45 \div .3$ and $1.45 \div 2.9$. These activities are not easy but until students are comfortable in completing them it is difficult to imagine that they understand what the symbols really mean. Classroom discussions, group work, and concrete materials can provide important support for students as they engage in these activities.

Developing Meaning for Rules

Analysis of Textbooks. Decimal fractions use the same core features as whole numbers for computation algorithms (see Table 5.1). This is a direct consequence of the similarities in notation. But the referents for decimal numerals are fractional quantities, so the actions on these referents may appear somewhat different to students than actions on whole-unit quantities. Do the textbooks help students connect the manipulations on symbols prescribed by the procedures with parallel actions on referents? As before, the answer is no. But there are some important differences between the series.

For addition and subtraction, Series A uses the partitioned unit square models and asks students to combine the quantities (for addition) or take away one quantity from another (for subtraction) and write the result. Such activities certainly provide a source for actions on referents, but these are not connected explicitly with steps in the symbol procedure. Students are asked "Why do you think you line up the decimal points?" and class discussions here may help some students connect actions and rules. But the text does not provide the explicit support that many students may need. As presented, the actions with referents probably serve more as a support for Site 3 than for Site 2.

Series B provides students with no help in developing meaning for addition and subtraction rules, in connecting the rules with actions on referents. Rules for manipulating symbols are presented from the outset, usually with no rationale or meaningful (referential) justification. In Grade 4, students are told "Because you must add hundredths to hundredths, tenths to tenths, and ones to ones, it is important to keep the decimal points in line." This is certainly true. But there is no indication of why one should add hundredths to hundredths, and the cryptic rationale does not accompany the rule when it is first introduced in Grade 3, or later in Grades 5 and 6.

It is more difficult to design instructional activities that reveal the connections between the steps in multiplication and division algorithms and actions on referents than to design such activities for addition and subtraction. The multiplication and division algorithms are considerably more complex than those for addition and subtraction. It comes as no surprise, then, that neither series attempts to connect the steps in the multiplication and division algorithms with actions on referents.

Series A presents an example of tenths times tenths, as noted earlier, that shows a unit square partitioned into tenths twice. This may help students see that it is reasonable to get hundredths in the product but no explicit attempt is made to connect this action with the algorithm and the example is not pursued further. The series rather uses an approach of asking students to work initial problems on a calculator and notice the patterns, and then presents the algorithmic rules as statements of the patterns (multiply as for whole numbers, count the decimal places, etc.). Such activities certainly seem preferable to simply stating the rules because they may soften the perception that mathematics is an arbitrary set of rules handed down from the teacher (of course, students may perceive that these rules are handed down from the calculator in which case there is no real gain). But it is important to notice that discovering patterns in the symbols is an activity contained entirely within the symbol world. Whatever meaning is derived from such activities is meaning carried in the syntax of the system, not meaning that comes from the outside world. Such internal meaning is important in mathematics, but it may be useful to those just becoming competent only if it builds on meaning that it is carried over from the real world, the world of objects and ideas with which students are familiar (Hiebert, 1988).

Series B includes no demonstrations using visual models when multiplication and division are first introduced (Grade 5) and does not try to motivate the rules by looking for patterns. Rather, the approach is to present a new kind of problem (e.g., tenths times tenths), present the rule and show an example, and then ask students to practice the rule. Some exercises are included on rounding the decimal fractions to whole numbers, multiplying the whole numbers, and then noticing that the two answers are reasonably close. But there is no help in connecting the new rules for decimals with other things the students may know.

In summary, it is unlikely that students using either series will connect the computational rules for decimal fractions with actions on decimal fraction quantities. In other words, it is unlikely that students will understand why the rules work.

Recommended Supplementary Activities. The computational rules for addition and subtraction are much simpler than those for multiplication and division so they are discussed separately. If students have engaged in the kinds of supplementary activities described for Site 1, they are in a good position to connect the rules for adding and subtracting decimal symbols with joining and separating actions on concrete referents. The research evidence suggests that most fourth-graders can combine base-10 blocks, for example, and then recognize how their actions with the blocks are reflected in the steps for adding or subtracting the symbols (Wearne & Hiebert, 1988a, 1989). The common errors students make (e.g., $3 + .4 = .7$) largely disappear and most students can explain why they do what they do with the symbols.

Some of the activities in the Series A textbooks (mentioned earlier) fit well with this development and could be used effectively after students have had experience in joining and separating concrete materials representing ones, tenths, hundredths, and so on. The activities in the Series B textbooks do not connect easily with the suggested supplementary activities. If students using this series are expected to make sense of the rules, all of the activities would need to be supplemented by the teacher.

Supplementary activities for multiplication and division are more difficult to suggest for two reasons. First, the algorithms are more complex and it is difficult to create a sequence of actions on objects that mirrors the steps in the algorithm in an easily interpretable way. Second, there is no research evidence that points to effective activities. In spite of these problems, a few general suggestions can be made. First, students have no chance of making connections at Site 2 unless connections have already been made at Site 1. Second, if students have made connections at Site 1 and they know what the symbols mean (numeric and operation symbols), then it may be possible to help students recognize that the algorithmic rules are, at least, reasonable. For example, there are three kinds of activities that may help students see that $.2 \times .3 = .06$. One activity, included in Series A, uses an area model and partitions a square vertically (for .2) and horizontally (for .3) and focuses on the intersection (on .2 "of" .3). Another activity would consider the common fraction form of .2 ($\frac{2}{10}$) and .3

($\frac{3}{10}$) and reflect on what happens with this notation (this depends, of course, on prior experience in multiplying fractions). A third activity would look at patterns, reason by analogy, and encourage conjectures. For example 2 × 3 might be discussed and modeled, then 2 × .3, and then .2 × .3. The discussion should emphasize both the real-world situations represented by these expressions and the patterns evident within the symbol system.

Division is even more difficult because the first two kinds of activities are less helpful. The third activity—looking for patterns, reasoning by analogy, making conjectures—may be the most helpful. As an example, consider the problem 2.5 ÷ .5. Connections at Site 1 ensure that students know that we can think of this problem as finding the number of five-tenths that are in two and five-tenths. This, of course, can be worked out with quantities to find the solution 5. Now compare this with the solutions for 25 ÷ 5 and 250 ÷ 50 and notice the pattern in the symbols. Now guess at the answer for .25 ÷ .5, or 2.5 ÷ .05, or .25 ÷ .5. These are not easy activities but, again, classroom discussions can provide supportive environments for these explorations (Lampert, 1989).

Judging the Reasonableness of Answers

An answer is "reasonable" if it matches something else one knows about the situation. One's confidence in the reasonableness of an answer rises the more familiar one is with the "something else." For example, I believe 0.09 is a reasonable answer for 0.1 × 0.9 because I know that if I have a board that is nine-tenths of a meter long and I want to cut a piece that is one-tenth of that, the piece I cut will be slightly less than one-tenth of a meter. Knowledge about real-world situations is used here to check the reasonableness of answers with symbols. Of course, connections between symbols (numeric and operation) and referents must be in place already for such monitoring to occur.

Analysis of Textbooks. Although both textbook series do attend periodically to the reasonableness of answers, they do so within the symbol system rather than by appealing to knowledge outside the system. Students are asked to round the decimal fractions to whole numbers, operate on the whole numbers, and then compare the answers. Such activities are not inappropriate, but it is likely that the rules taught for rounding are applied with as little meaning as the computational procedures, so that students end up comparing two answers that are equally meaningless. If the answers match, students' confidence may rise. But the increased confidence comes from feeling that the rules have been recalled and executed without error rather than from recognizing that the answer matches reality in some way.

Series A includes activities that could be used by students to judge the reasonableness of answers, but the authors do not exploit their potential. The models suggested to students when introducing the arithmetic operations are perhaps most useful for checking whether symbol rules are producing appropriate answers. But after the models are presented to motivate the rules they are dropped. Students are not asked later to return to these concrete models as a way of validating or checking the reasonableness of their answers.

Recommended Supplementary Activities. The reasonableness of answers can be evaluated both within the symbol system and by comparing the symbol answer to a solution for a parallel real-world problem. The textbooks contain some activities of the first kind but not of the second. The textbook activities ask students to round the numbers, compute with the simpler numbers, and compare the answers. These are useful activities but their benefit depends on how they are implemented (Sowder, 1988). If the rules for rounding are applied blindly, they lose their meaning and their power. Consider, for example, the problem $24.83 \div 7.3$. Rounding to the nearest whole number would leave $25 \div 7$. This problem then could be computed and, although it is somewhat simpler than $24.83 \div 7.3$, the real advantage of the process is lost. A more useful approximation, for most purposes, is $24 \div 8$, with the actual answer recognized to be slightly larger. It is more useful because it can be carried out mentally and used as a quick check on the actual calculation. Of course, the process used to estimate the answer and the degree of accuracy required depends on the purpose of the estimate. But the little research evidence that exists on the topic suggests that the benefit for students of estimating does not come from memorizing rounding rules but rather from reflecting on the meaning of the numerals and the operation and, from these meanings, developing strategies for estimating the solution (Sowder, 1988). These kinds of activities are not prevalent in most current textbooks.

The second kind of activity mentioned previously, that of comparing the symbol answer with a real-world solution, may be useful to support the development of the meanings and skills needed to estimate with symbols alone. There is no research evidence on this issue so the claim is only plausible speculation. But consider the problem $2.3 + .84$. If a story was constructed for the problem, students could compare the symbol answer with the solution to the story problem. The story might be "Marie and Jason were building a train track for their train. Marie had 1.3 meters of track and Jason had .83 meters of track. How long of a track could they make." Students actually could measure out the track or, if they have had experience with these problems, they might just envision the solution. In either case, the very common error responses for this problem, .97 and 9.7 (Hiebert & Wearne, 1985), would be ruled out as unreasonable. The idea of adding a little more than 1 to a little less than 1 and getting about 2 (in the symbol world) would receive real-world instantiation.

Conclusions

It has been proposed that the major learning task for students with regard to decimals is to build connections between the written symbols and appropriate real-world referents. Three sites have been identified where such connections would have important benefits. These sites can be used as a framework for analyzing existing instruction and for suggesting more effective instructional activities. Analyses of two popular textbook series suggested that students do not receive much help from textbook instruction in building the essential connections. Activities are designed primarily to increase the proficiency with which they can execute symbol manipulation rules. Relatively little, and sometimes no, attention is paid to revealing connections between symbols and meaningful referents.

Suggestions for improving instruction can be summarized as follows. The instructional priority should be to help students create meaning for written symbols. The suggestion connotes more than its simplicity conveys. Creating meanings for symbols first requires establishing or reviving a rich store of knowledge about appropriate quantitative referents. This means designing instruction to promote meaningful experiences with quantitative referents (to hook with numerical symbols) and actions on referents (to hook with operation symbols). A second recommendation is that, at least for the simple rules (e.g., addition and subtraction, ordering), time should be devoted to connecting the symbol procedure with actions on quantities. Such connections are not difficult to make, and if connections have been made at Site 1, some students spontaneously create their own connections between rules and actions on referents. Finally, instructional time should be devoted to helping students judge the reasonableness of answers. This is not a burdensome task because it simply involves encouraging students to apply the connections they have already established at Site 1.

SUMMARY

The decimal fraction system has been analyzed from a mathematical, a cognitive, and an instructional point of view. The aim of the analyses was to understand why students have so much trouble mastering a system that looks like a rather straightforward extension of whole numbers.

The mathematical analysis revealed that decimals are much more complex than they appear at first glance. They are not a simple extension of whole numbers because they can represent the measure of continuous as well as discrete quantity. In fact, they are a very complicated and often confusing extension of whole numbers because they use nearly the same notation to represent the measure of very different quantities. A comparison of the knowledge required to deal proficiently with whole numbers, fractions, and decimals confirmed the complex relationships that exist between these systems.

The cognitive analysis proposed that understanding decimals depends on making connections—connections between the different number systems and between the decimal symbols and appropriate quantitative referents. Unfortunately, the language we use to talk about decimals may hide rather than reveal important similarities and differences between the number systems. In order to think about the way in which connections might be made, three sites were suggested as locations for building connections. The sites are places that written symbols and rules can connect with quantitative referents. A brief review of the literature indicated that many students fail to make connections at all of the sites.

Analyses of current instruction focused on two textbook series and on recommended instructional activities. The primary recommendations called for increased opportunities for students to build connections at all three of the sites but especially at sites 1 and 3. It should be noted that the recommendations require a significant shift in our thinking. They require moving away from developing symbol manipulation proficiency with decimals in the short run toward competency with all facets of using decimals in the long run. A greater investment of time would be required to develop meaning for the symbols at the outset and less emphasis would be placed on immediate computational proficiency. The payoff would be long-term: using decimal fractions meaningfully and flexibly to solve real problems. Such a shift in thinking and in instructional design is consistent with the analyses presented here and also with analyses contained in many recent calls for school mathematics change (Conference Board of the Mathematical Sciences, 1982; National Council of Teachers of Mathematics, 1989; National Research Council, 1989).

ACKNOWLEDGMENTS

Acknowledgments are gratefully extended to Barbara Grover, Gaea Leinhardt, Ralph Putnam, Ed Silver, and Orit Zaslavsky for their comments on the first draft of this chapter, to Merlyn Behr and Stellan Ohlsson for their extensive comments on a revised version, and to the National Science Foundation (MDR 8651552 and TPE 8751494) for its support while writing the chapter. However, the author, rather than the reviewers or the Foundation, is responsible for the opinions and conclusions expressed in the chapter.

REFERENCES

Behr, M. J., Lesh, R., Post, T. R., & Silver, E. A. (1983). Rational-number concepts. In R. Lesh & M. Landau (Eds.), *Acquisitions of mathematics concepts and processes* (pp. 91–126). New York: Academic.

Behr, M. J., Wachsmuth, I., Post, T. R., & Lesh, R. (1984). Order and equivalence of rational numbers: A clinical teaching experiment. *Journal for Research in Mathematics Education, 15,* 323–341.

Bell, A., Fischbein, E., & Greer, B. (1984). Choice of operation in verbal arithmetic problems: The effects of number size, problem structure, and context. *Educational Studies in Mathematics, 15,* 129–147.

Bell, A., Swan, M., & Taylor, G. (1981). Choice of operation in verbal problems with decimal numbers. *Educational Studies in Mathematics, 12,* 399–420.

Boyer, C. B. (1968). *A history of mathematics.* New York: Wiley.

Brown, M. (1981). Place value and decimals. In K. M. Hart (Ed.), *Children's understanding of mathematics: 11–16* (pp. 48–65). London: John Murray.

Brownell, W. A. (1935). Psychological considerations in the learning and teaching of arithmetic. In *The teaching of arithmetic. Tenth yearbook of the National Council of Teachers of Mathematics.* New York: Teachers College, Columbia University.

Byers, V., & Erlwanger, S. (1984). Content and form in mathematics *Educational Studies in Mathematics, 15,* 259–275.

Carpenter, T. P. (1986). Conceptual knowledge as a foundation for procedural knowledge: Implications from research on the initial learning of arithmetic. In J. Hiebert (Ed.), *Conceptual and procedural knowledge: The case of mathematics* (pp. 113–132). Hillsdale, NJ: Lawrence Erlbaum Associates.

Carpenter, T. P., Corbitt, M. K., Kepner, H. S., Lindquist, M. M., & Reys, R. E. (1981). Decimals: Results and implications from the second NAEP mathematics assessment. *Arithmetic Teacher, 28*(8), 34–37.

Carr, K. (1983). Student beliefs about place value and decimals: Any relevance for science education? *Research in Science Education, 13,* 105–109.

Conference Board of the Mathematical Sciences. (1982). *The mathematical sciences curriculum K–12: What is still fundamental and what is not.* Washington, DC: National Science Foundation.

Davis, R. B. (1984). *Learning mathematics: The cognitive science approach to mathematics education.* Norwood, NJ: Ablex.

Davis, R. B., & McKnight, C. (1980). The influence of semantic content on algorithmic behavior. *Journal of Mathematical Behavior, 3*(1), 39–87.

Ekenstam, A. (1977). On children's quantitative understanding of numbers. *Educational Studies in Mathematics, 8,* 317–332.

Fischbein, E., Deri, M., Nello, M. S., & Marino, M. S. (1985). The role of implicit models in solving verbal problems in multiplication and division. *Journal for Research in Mathematics Education, 16,* 3–17.

Freeman, D. J., & Porter, A. C. (1989). *Do textbooks dictate the content of mathematics instruction in elementary schools?* (Research Series No. 189). East Lansing: Michigan State University, Institute for Research on Teaching.

Grossman, A. S. (1983). Decimal notation: An important research finding. *Arithmetic Teacher, 39*(9), 32–33.

Hiebert, J. (1984). Children's mathematics learning: The struggle to link form and understanding. *Elementary School Journal, 84,* 497–513.

Hiebert, J. (1988). A theory of developing competence with written mathematical symbols. *Educational Studies in Mathematics, 19,* 333–355.

Hiebert, J. (1990). The role of routine procedures in the development of mathematical competence. In T. J. Cooney (Ed.), *Teaching and learning mathematics in the 1990's: 1990 NCTM yearbook* (pp. 31–40). Reston, VA: National Council of Teachers of Mathematics.

Hiebert, J., & Carpenter, T. P. (in press). Learning and teaching with understanding. In D. A. Grouws (Ed.), *Handbook of research on mathematics teaching and learning.* New York: Macmillan.

Hiebert, J., & Wearne, D. (1985). A model of students' decimal computation procedures. *Cognition & Instruction, 2,* 175–205.

Hiebert, J., & Wearne, D. (1986). Procedures over concepts: The acquisition of decimal number knowledge. In J. Hiebert (Ed.), *Conceptual and procedural knowledge: The case of mathematics* (pp. 199–223). Hillsdale, NJ: Lawrence Erlbaum Associates.

Hiebert, J., Wearne, D., & Taber, S. (1991). Fourth graders' gradual construction of decimal fractions during instruction using different physical representations. *Elementary School Journal, 91,* 321–341.

Hofstadter, D. R. (1979). *Godel, Escher, Bach: An eternal golden braid.* New York: Vintage.

Janvier, C. (Ed.) (1987). *Problems of representation in the teaching and learning of mathematics.* Hillsdale, NJ: Lawrence Erlbaum Associates.

Kaput, J. (1982, March). *Intuitive attempts at algebraic representation of quantitative relationships.* Paper presented at the annual meeting of the American Educational Research Association, New York.

Kaput, J. J. (1987). Toward a theory of symbol use in mathematics. In C. Janvier (Ed.), *Problems of representation in the teaching and learning of mathematics* (pp. 159–195). Hillsdale, NJ: Lawrence Erlbaum Associates.

Kieren, T. E. (1976). On the mathematical, cognitive, and instructional foundations of rational numbers. In R. A. Lesh (Ed.), *Number and measurement.* Columbus, OH: ERIC/SMEAC.

Kieren, T. E. (1980). The rational number construct—Its elements and mechanisms. In T. E. Kieren (Ed.), *Recent research on number learning* (pp. 125–149). Columbus, OH: ERIC/SMEAC.

Kitcher, P. (1983). *The nature of mathematical knowledge.* New York: Oxford University Press.

Lakatos, I. (1978). *Mathematics, science, and epistemology* (J. Worrall & G. Currie, Eds.). New York: Cambridge University Press.

Lampert, M. (1986). Knowing, doing, and teaching multiplication. *Cognition and Instruction, 3,* 305–342.

Lampert, M. (1989). Choosing and using mathematical tools in classroom discourse. In J. Brophy (Ed.), *Advances in research on learning* (Vol. 1, pp. 223–264). Greenwich, CT: JAI.

Leinhardt, G. (1988). Getting to know: Tracing students' mathematical knowledge from intuition to competence. *Educational Psychologist, 23,* 119–144.

Lesh, R., Post, T., & Behr, M. (1987). Representations and translations among representations in mathematics learning and problem solving. In C. Janvier (Ed.), *Problems of representation in the teaching and learning of mathematics* (pp. 33–40). Hillsdale, NJ: Lawrence Erlbaum Associates.

Lesh, R., Post, T., & Behr, M. (1988). Proportional reasoning. In J. Hiebert & M. Behr (Eds.), *Research agenda in mathematics education: Number concepts and operations in the middle grades* (pp. 93–118). Reston, VA: National Council of Teachers of Mathematics.

Mason, J. H. (1987). What do symbols represent? In C. Janvier (Ed.), *Problems of representation in the teaching and learning of mathematics* (pp. 73–81). Hillsdale, NJ: Lawrence Erlbaum Associates.

McKnight, C. C., Travers, K. J., Crosswhite, F. J., & Swafford, J. O. (1985). Eighth-grade mathematics in U.S. schools: A report from the Second International Mathematics Study. *Arithmetic Teacher, 32*(8), 20–26.

McLellan, J. A., & Dewey, J. (1895). *The psychology of number and its applications to methods of teaching arithmetic.* New York: Appleton-Century-Crofts.

National Assessment of Educational Progress. (1983). *The Third National Mathematics Assessment: Results, trends and issues.* Denver: Education Commission of the States.

National Council of Teachers of Mathematics. (1989). *Curriculum and evaluation standards for school mathematics.* Reston, VA: Author.

National Research Council. (1989). *Everybody counts: A report to the nation on the future of mathematics education.* Washington, D.C.: National Academy of Sciences.

Nesher, P. (1988). Multiplicative school word problems: Theoretical approaches and empirical findings. In J. Hiebert & M. Behr (Eds.), *Number concepts and operations in the middle grades* (pp. 19–40). Reston, VA: National Council of Teachers of Mathematics.

Nesher, P., & Peled, I. (1986). Shifts in reasoning. *Educational Studies in Mathematics, 17,* 67–79.

Noddings, N. (1985). Formal modes of knowing. In E. Eisner (Ed.), *Learning and teaching the ways of knowing: Eighty-fourth yearbook of the National Society for the Study of Education, Part II.* Chicago: University of Chicago Press.

Ohlsson, S. (1988). Mathematical meaning and applicational meaning in the semantics of fractions and related concepts. In J. Hiebert & M. Behr (Eds.), *Number concepts and operations in the middle grades* (pp. 53–92). Reston, VA: National Council of Teachers of Mathematics.

Putnam, R. T., Lampert, M., & Peterson, P. L. (1990). Alternative perspectives on knowing mathematics in elementary schools. In C. Cazden (Ed.), *Review of research in education* (Vol. 16, pp. 57–150). Washington, DC: American Educational Research Association.

Resnick, L. B. (1982). Syntax and semantics in learning to subtract. In T. P. Carpenter, J. M. Moser, & T. A. Romberg (Eds.). *Addition and subtraction: A cognitive perspective* (pp. 136–155). Hillsdale, NJ: Lawrence Erlbaum Associates.

Resnick, L. B., & Nesher, P. (1983, November). *Learning complex concepts: The case of decimal fractions.* Paper presented at the 24th annual meeting of the Psychonomics Society, San Diego.

Resnick, L. B., Nesher, P., Leonard, F., Magone, M., Omanson, S., & Peled, I. (1989). Conceptual bases of arithmetic errors: The case of decimal fractions. *Journal for Research in Mathematics Education, 20,* 8–27.

Resnick, L. B., & Omanson, S. F. (1987). Learning to understand arithmetic. In R. Glaser (Ed.), *Advances in instructional psychology* (Vol. 3, pp. 41–95). Hillsdale, NJ: Lawrence Erlbaum Associates.

Sackur-Grisvard, C., & Leonard, F. (1985). Intermediate cognitive organizations in the process of learning a mathematical concept: The order of positive decimal numbers. *Cognition and Instruction, 2,* 157–174.

Schoenfeld, A. H. (1986). On having and using geometric knowledge. In J. Hiebert (Ed.), *Conceptual and procedural knowledge: The case of mathematics* (pp. 225–264). Hillsdale, NJ: Lawrence Erlbaum Associates.

Schwartz, J. (1988). Intensive quantity and referent transforming arithmetic operations. In J. Hiebert & M. Behr (Eds.), *Number concepts and operations in the middle grades* (pp. 41–52). Reston, VA: National Council of Teachers of Mathematics and Hillsdale, NJ: Lawrence Erlbaum Associates.

Silver, E. A. (1986). Using conceptual and procedural knowledge: A focus on relationships. In J. Hiebert (Ed.), *Conceptual and procedural knowledge: The case of mathematics* (pp. 181–198). Hillsdale, NJ: Lawrence Erlbaum Associates.

Skemp, R. R. (Ed.). (1982). Understanding the symbolism of mathematics [Special issue]. *Visible Language, 16*(3).

Sowder, J. T. (1988). Mental computation and number comparison: Their roles in the development of number sense and computational estimation. In J. Hiebert & M. Behr (Eds.), *Number concepts and operations in the middle grades* (pp. 182–197). Reston, VA: National Council of Teachers of Mathematics and Hillsdale, NJ: Lawrence Erlbaum Associates.

Van Engen, H. (1949). An analysis of meaning in arithmetic, *Elementary School Journal, 49,* 321–329, 395–400.

Wearne, D. (1990). Acquiring meaning for decimal fraction symbols: A one year follow-up. *Educational Studies in Mathematics, 21,* 545–564.

Wearne, D., & Hiebert, J. (1988a). A cognitive approach to meaningful mathematics instruction: Testing a local theory using decimal numbers. *Journal for Research in Mathematics Education, 19,* 371–384.

Wearne, D., & Hiebert, J. (1988b). Constructing and using meaning for mathematical symbols: The case of decimal fractions. In J. Hiebert & M. Behr (Eds.), *Number concepts and operations in the middle grades* (pp. 220–235). Reston, VA: National Council of Teachers of Mathematics and Hillsdale, NJ: Lawrence Erlbaum Associates.

Wearne, D., & Hiebert, J. (1989). Cognitive changes during conceptually based instruction on decimal fractions. *Journal of Educational Psychology, 81,* 507–513.

Werner, H., & Kaplan, B. (1963). *Symbol formation.* New York: Wiley.

6

RATIONAL AND FRACTIONAL NUMBERS AS MATHEMATICAL AND PERSONAL KNOWLEDGE: IMPLICATIONS FOR CURRICULUM AND INSTRUCTION

Thomas E. Kieren
University of Alberta

Contents

What is number, that a man may know it, and a man that he may know number?

—W. McCulloch, 1963, p. 1

When, as a young man, Warren McCulloch was asked by his master, Rufus Jones at Haverford College in 1917, "Warren, what is thee going to do?" McCulloch, who became one of the patriarchs of information science, re-

323

plied with the now quaint-sounding though profound question quoted
above. In reply, Jones said, "Friend, thee will be busy as long as thee lives."

It would seem that both McCulloch's question and Jones's reply would
be continuously pertinent to anyone—theorist, researcher, curriculum de-
veloper, teacher, student—interested in fractional numbers or, more generally, rational numbers and how persons come to know/understand them.

WHAT WE ALL KNOW ABOUT PERFORMANCE
ON FRACTION ITEMS—AGAIN

Kouba et al. (1988) and Brown et al. (1988) gave and discussed the following results from the most recent National Assessment of Educational Programs (NAEP) testing in the United States:

Item	Percent Correct	
	Grade 7	*Grade 11*
1. $3\frac{1}{2} - 3\frac{1}{3}$	53	71
2. $7\frac{1}{6} - 3\frac{1}{2}$	32	45
3. $9 \times \frac{2}{3}$	60	76
4. Which is one way to find $\frac{3}{4}$ of a number (students selected from among given alternatives)?	26	38
5. $4 \times 2\frac{1}{4}$	56	70
6. 30 is what percent of 60	43	70

There are several things worth noting about these results. Compared with
related whole number results, performance on fractional number items
was low. The results suggest that the students proceed in an algorithmic
manner. The dependence on a "rule" or remembered algorithm can be seen
in the comparison of items 1 and 2. In some sense, the second item should
be easier to "figure out" using fractional number sense—"three and a half
or three and three sixths takes you up from $3\frac{1}{2}$ to 7, then a sixth more so the
difference is $3\frac{4}{6}$." The first item is easier to compute using a rule because
the 3s can be ignored, leaving $\frac{1}{2} - \frac{1}{3}$. Performance is much higher on the
item where a known algorithm can most easily be applied. Brown et al.
(1988) made a similar contrast between results here given as 3 and 4. They
noted that "less than half the eleventh grade students who had completed
two years of algebra correctly [selected the procedure for finding $\frac{3}{4}$ of 60]"
(p. 343), although most could do the related routine computation. It should

be noted that the procedural item required students to discriminate among several given procedures instead of executing one. Yet it would seem that although students could perform particular algorithms with fractions, they did not exhibit fractional number or algorithmic sense nor what the NAEP testers called "understanding" to the same degree.

This is even more vividly observable in the following discussion from Kouba et al. (1988): "About 80 percent of seventh graders could change a mixed fraction to an improper fraction, but fewer than one-half recognized that $5\frac{1}{4}$ was the same as $5 + \frac{1}{4}$" (p. 16). It would appear that fractions form a symbolic domain in which students learn to operate with the syntax and certain rules of combination. Such performances do not appear to be linked to the idea that fractions represent numbers or that fractional numbers allow one to operate in the world of quantity.

In a more clinical study, Peck and Jencks (1981) discussed in detail the work of a Grade 6 girl. In working with the sum of two fractions, she used a wrong procedure. Later, while working on the product $\frac{5}{2} \times \frac{5}{2}$, she stopped and seemed to remember her "sum rule." She returned to the prior exercise and correctly and confidently executed the algorithm. Now coming back to the product, she wrote $\frac{5}{2} \times \frac{5}{2} = \frac{25}{2}$ —"Since the denominators are the same you can leave them." Again we see that, for this girl, computation with fractions was tied up in a series of nonvalidatable rules. That is, these rules exist simply in a domain of symbolic activity. The "truth" of the "results" of such activity does not seem to be related to other aspects of the child's thinking. In a summary of performance of 20 Grade 6 students, Peck and Jencks found only 2 who both had a concept and algorithms for fractional addition and comparisons and only 5 who had a concept of both. On the other hand, 10 of the 20 could use algorithms for adding fractions. Peck and Jencks concluded that very few Grade 6 students can justify fraction rule execution in a meaningful way.

Hasemann (1985) found that with 100 Hauptschuler in Germany (Grade 7), whereas 52% of the students could compute $\frac{1}{6} \times \frac{3}{4}$, only 30% could shade in one sixth of the shaded portion of a circle representing $\frac{3}{4}$. In fact, he suggested that their responses showed that although particular individuals could perform the algorithm flawlessly, their shading and drawing showed no understanding of the task or its multiplicative nature. It appears that students could not use a fraction as an operator on a fractional quantity. Hasemann contrasted this performance with that of similar British children (see Hart, 1981). Hart found that on the identical items from the Concepts in Mathematics and Science Project 53% could do the shading, whereas only 23% could perform the computation. Interviews and extensive classroom observations have led Hart (1988) to question the way in which manipulative materials are used in British schools, suggesting that the bridge or connection was lacking between children's work on conceptual models of fractional numbers and the related symbolic tasks—"That's the way it is with bricks, but this is the way it is with math."

As reported by Kieren and Behr (1986) in a discussion on the work of the theme group "Research on Fractions" at the 1984 International Congress on Mathematics Education, there appeared to be a worldwide concern with the learning of fractions in general and with the apparent detachment of algorithmic behavior from meaningful representations of it by children. This concern also is seen in the work of Vinner, Hershkowitz, and Bruckheimer (1981), who found the typical "add numerators—add denominators" errors still common in Israeli children even after several years of instruction. Similarly, Wearne and Hiebert (1983) studied student difficulties with fractions in Grades 6 and 8 students. They noted a lack of substantial improvement in performance of the Grade 8 students over the Grade 6 students despite instruction. It seems that in various places in the world, the problem with student knowledge/understanding of fractions is a persistent one. As Hasemann (1985) suggested, students seemed undisturbed by the nonsense of their work and seemed to have "fragments of fraction concepts and misunderstood rules superimposed."

The philosopher of mathematics Detlefsen (1986) suggested that there are two ways one can make a knowledge claim in mathematics. One can either validate one's claim (for example, that $1\frac{3}{4} + 5\frac{1}{2} = 7\frac{1}{4}$) by tracing it back to a piece of mathematics that is "real" (e.g., constructions for Euclid; concrete or meaningful experiences for a child) or one can evaluate the logic of the set of formal steps one used in formally producing one's result. If one can do neither of these, then one's knowledge is knowledge in name only and is likely fragile, subject to forgetting and deterioration. One might speculate that many recent practices, perhaps through premature or unattached symbolic work, have left children unable to relate symbolic work to other fractional experiences and unable to judge for themselves the truth of symbolic statements. One also might argue developmentally or experimentally that in the first eight grades most children are unlikely to be able to use formal logic to evaluate their formal procedures. Hence, children are left with fractional knowledge that is nominal, such as it is. The question is what to do about it. The answers to that question are not obvious or simple.

It is the purpose of the rest of this chapter to consider alternatives that have been and are being raised as bases for fractional and rational number instruction. The second section of this chapter considers approaches in which an analysis of the mathematics of fractional numbers serves as a basis for the development of experience for children. Fraction number knowledge is seen as a body of knowledge that can be acquired with understanding through experiences whereby the critical features of the mathematics are translated into experiences accessible to children and young adults. The third section considers approaches that look at the problem of curriculum development from the point of view of the child or young adult as fraction knower. The models used and the research reviewed at least implicitly view mathematics as constructed by the person and view the roles of teacher or text or curriculum experience as orienting rather than information transmitting. The final section provides a review of text series that are typical of those used in the 1980s with respect to fractions. This review reflects both the evaluation results presented earlier and the analyses of the second and third sections.

MATHEMATICAL APPROACHES
TO THE FRACTIONAL NUMBER EXPERIENCE
OF LEARNERS

If one takes fractional and rational number knowledge as a body of knowledge to be known or acquired by a person, in light of the aforementioned evaluation data, one might ask why it is important that this knowledge be taught. A simple answer to that question is that rational number knowledge is a rich part of mathematics which takes a person's idea of number well beyond that of whole numbers and is a vehicle for relating such number knowledge to many aspects of mathematics and its applications.

Because the rational numbers are the most familiar example of quotient fields, one could look at the axioms of that system (Birkhoff & MacLane, 1953) as a defining source of the richness of rational numbers. First, the elements of such a field are numbers of the form $\frac{a}{b}$ (a, b integers and $b \neq 0$) such that they are *quotients,* that is solutions to the equation $bx = a$. Second, these rational numbers are ratios in that $\frac{a}{b} = \frac{c}{d}$ if and only if $a \times d = b \times c$. Thus, as elements of a quotient field, both rational and fractional numbers are simultaneously quotients and ratios. In the more contemporary terms of Schwartz (1988), they are simultaneously extensive and intensive quantities.

Because the rational numbers (the nonnegative rationals or fractional numbers and the negative rationals) are an example of a field, they obey the group properties for "addition," $+$, and "multiplication," $\times$, these two operations defined independently from one another. In studying whole numbers, one can learn of multiplication as repeated addition. But in learning fractional numbers, a learner must see addition and multiplication and their interaction in a different light. Because multiplication by a fractional number is not repeated addition or replicative in nature, such rules of thumb as "multiplication makes bigger" no longer necessarily hold true.

Multiplication of fractions has a compositional quality. Multiplying $\frac{3}{4} \times \frac{2}{3}$ means taking $\frac{2}{3}$ of one and then $\frac{3}{4}$ of that result. Similarly, addition does not grow out of "counting on" or the use of successors, but it means combining quantities in a "put together" fashion.

One other characteristic of rationals as elements of a field worth mentioning is the role of one. Like one in the whole numbers, the fractional or rational "one" is the unit on which the system is based. Yet this unit is different. In the whole numbers, this unit is replicable, countable, and groupable (in tens, etc.). These roles continue for fractions. But the unit in fractional numbers is a measuring unit that can be divided up. Behr, Wachsmuth, Post, and Lesh (1984) saw the fractional number $\frac{m}{n}$ as based on the idea of m "$\frac{1}{n}$ elements." The creation of such "$\frac{1}{n}$ elements" or "$\frac{1}{n}$ units' is a critical developmental task for a knower in developing fractional knowledge. Further, "one" as a rational number plays the role of the multiplicative identity element. This property is basic in defining the relationship between a fractional number and the unit. It is obvious that a person not only must be able to create a meaning for $\frac{1}{5}$ as the unit divided into 5 equal parts, but also must see the unit as made up of five fifths. Further, the knower of fractional numbers must eventually see $\frac{5}{2}$ not only as $2\frac{1}{2}$ units but also realize that two fifths of $\frac{5}{2}$ is one.

But it is not only this field structure that gives the fractional and rational numbers their richness. Rational number knowledge can be related to many elements of mathematical knowledge in general. In his creative analysis of ways of mathematical thinking, Rucker (1987) in Fig. 6.1 portrays classical mathematics as a whole interrelating the ideas of number, space, logic/algebra, and infinity. How and where does rational number thinking/knowing/understanding fit into this "picture"? The numerals inserted in the diagram in Fig. 6.1 suggest different approaches to rational numbers and give a perception of the variety of the mathematical ideas entailed by fractions or rationals. Numeral 1 is located very close to "number" and indicates various efforts, including many of those in modern school texts,

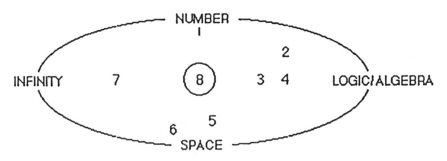

FIG. 6.1.   Location of rational number thinking.

to build from and connect fraction knowledge to whole number knowledge. An extension of this is "2" where fractions are considered ordered pairs of whole numbers (or integers) obeying the field structure. As suggested in the aforementioned argument, "2" reminds us that in facing fractions the child is faced with such algebraic notions as inverse (not just the psychological "reverse"), operations that are independent (multiplication is not repeated addition), and a double meaning for 1 (as the unit of comparison and the identity element).

The numeral "3" indicates that fractional numbers are ratio numbers. Fractions are equivalent in the sense of ratios, an idea that is central to much of the standard algorithmic work with fractions. As suggested by Behr et al. (1984), the fractions $\frac{3}{4}$ and $\frac{6}{8}$ can represent both an absolute (extensive quantity) equality and a relative (proportional) equality. Even from beginning work with sharing or dividing up, a person or a child is faced with a result that is at once an amount ($\frac{1}{2}$ of a pizza as one's share or quotient result) and a ratio (2 pizzas for 4 persons or 1 for 2).

The numeral "4" indicates with Dienes (1971), that fractions are operators. Whether one takes this notion algebraically (in the group sense) or actively ("he took three fourths of the pizza"), it is part of the fractional experience. This emphasis suggests the connection between fractions and transformation groups under composition and is thus a natural setting for the notion of multiplicative inverse. This can be considered in a machine setting: "Punching $\frac{3}{4}$ on a photocopier reduces a particular image. What would you use to enlarge the reduced image to its original size?" In simpler terms, if $\frac{3}{4}$ is a multiplicative comparison or mapping between measures— "Peter has $\frac{3}{4}$ as much as Joan"—this has a natural inverse "Joan has $\frac{4}{3}$ as much as Peter." Such fractional language use and the algebraic interrelationship between inverses and identities are not sponsored by a fraction curriculum based on a static part–whole definition of fractions.

The numeral "5" suggests that fractions or rationals have a geometric character (Piaget, Inhelder, & Szeminska, 1960). This is reflected in linear or regional models or of the fractured whole (Freudenthal, 1983). For Piaget, the idea of fractions was geometric in character, requiring the ability to partition wholes (or units of various types), to reconstruct wholes from parts (one psychological basis for the notion of inverse), and to subdivide a part and consider the relationship between subpart with the part but also with the original whole (a geomatric basis for composite operations). This geometric notion can be given a metric interpretation. That is, the set of rationals or positive rationals can be seen as isomorphic to a set of linear measures (Blakers, 1967). Freudenthal (1983) and Vergnaud (1983) saw a measurement construct of fraction as related to a dynamic "comparison to a unit" concept rather than a simplistic part–whole comparison. For Vergnaud, this comparison can arise in a functional fashion in a quotient relationship between 2 measure spaces: 4 pizzas divided among 7 persons; $\frac{4}{7}$ as a functional relationship; or in a scalar fashion within measure spaces; $\frac{3}{4}$ denoting a mixture of 3 portions of one type with one of another. That is, $\frac{3}{4}$ is not simply 3 equal parts out of 4, but is a quantity related to one that can be added, doubled, and so forth. Although most curricula use the number line with fractional and rational numbers, the character of rational numbers as measures often is missed.

The location of "6" in the left half of the space indicates the "infinite" notions of infinitely small and infinitely close together (denseness) inherent in rational numbers. In addition, the fractional numbers through their archmedean and order properties allow one to think of the infinitely large as well as infinitely many. For any number q and fraction $\frac{1}{n}$, there is an m such that $\frac{m}{n} > q$.

The move from common fractions to decimal fractions is indicated by "7." Decimals, particularly those whose common fractional denominators have factors other than 2 or 5, lead one immediately to the infinite (infinite series). Under the decimal representation, it is also important to note that there is no standard smallest place value, so the "action" of building up fractions cannot be grouping but is the action of iterative dividing up. Thus, decimal fractions borrow a notation from and are an extension of the decimal system of numeration; yet they are different in substance from that aspect of whole number knowledge, because they are defined from a different notion of unit and a different generating action.

Rucker (1987) identified a the fifth and modern element of mathematical thought interrelating the other four elements in Fig. 6.1—information. In an age of computers and calculators, rational numbers have finite decimal (or other base) representations and can be used to represent the world in a finite computable manner. The numeral 8 reminds us that all real numbers, including irrationals such as the square root of 2 and pi, have finite rational approximations. Such approximations are the basis of digital computer arithmetic, but on a more concrete level allow us to measure with fractional numbers a board to be a diagonal brace on a square gate (the length of which could be an irrational number).

Situating fractional knowledge in the broad realm of mathematical knowledge is done to suggest that fraction concepts are inherently multifaceted. It is commonplace in school curricula to focus on the connections between the algorithms for rational numbers and their whole number components. These connections are sponsored by a static "already divided up" notion of part–whole, with emphasis on numerator and denominator as separate numbers. This emphasis or attachment to "1" in the diagram allows a child to use already acquired whole number language to discuss fractional situations with all its attendant benefits and problems. But this approach tends to mask fractions as denoters of quantity. Under static part–whole presentations, three fourths is a double count and not an amount—seven fourths is a conceptual anomaly and even "improper." Although 3 out of 4 equal parts suggests the ratio (numeral 2) notion, this is a limited inclusive notion (Vergnaud, 1983). The notion of equivalence of ratios is used primarily for algorithmic purposes. Fractional and rational numbers are not seen as multiplicative in nature as seen by Vergnaud. Thus, the situating of fractions in the Rucker tetrad highlights the limited nature of a whole-number-based approach to fractions. At the same time, it highlights the potential of the study of fractions as a true window into the whole world of mathematics. It also suggests that there are numerous alternative approaches to instruction in fractions open to the curriculum maker or teacher. One can build fraction curricula from many alternative vistas.

Another way of seeing the power of mathematical ideas, in this case rational number ideas, is to trace the relationship between the theory of mathematical elements and operations and the situations in which they are applied by persons. Ohlsson (1988) developed a semantic theory which tries to explicate why different mathematical constructs with distinct theories have become associated with one symbol $\frac{x}{y}$ and its myriad applications. As has been suggested previously, Birkhoff and MacLane (1953) saw the rational numbers as a specific example of a quotient field with all its attendant ideas. Ohlsson, on the other hand, defined rational numbers in such a way that he observed them arising out of a whole-number-based quotient function. Although this analysis ignores such important ideas as unit and multiplicative inverse, it does see the applications situations of fraction and measurement as critically based on the mathematical idea of quotient. Thus, whereas in the fraction $\frac{n}{d}$ the numerator and denominator are counts of objects, these objects themselves arise as quotients. The quantity x is compared to a reference quantity y by dividing y into parts of size z where $d \times z = y$ and $n \times z = x$, with n and d both being whole numbers. Thus, $\frac{n}{d}$ can describe and correspond to a fractional quantity or a measure, although in both constructs the action of dividing up and the comparison to a unit may be hidden.

Ohlsson (1988) also showed how $\frac{x}{y}$ is related to the mathematics of composite functions and the application of counteracting multiplicative processes. Six percent interest on $50 can be seen as taking one hundredth of 50 or dividing 50 by 100 and then multiplying the result by 6. The rational number idea could be seen in the equation $I = \frac{r}{100} \times P$. More generally, rational numbers as operators can be seen as relating two quantities q_1, and q_2; $q_2 = \frac{x}{y} \times q_1$. Although Ohlsson did not do this, Dienes (1971) showed how the mathematics of composite functions as a multiplicative group corresponds to the applications of fractions as multiplicative operators, bringing into play critical rational number ideas such as multiplicative inverse and identity.

Regardless of the mathematical theory or the applicational situations, one aspect that Ohlsson (1988) highlighted is the equivalence of $\frac{2}{3}$ and $\frac{4}{6}$. What is critical to note is that because a reference quantity or unit can be divided into parts in many ways or because fractional operators with different names—for example, $\frac{4}{6}$, $\frac{6}{9}$—yield the same quantity when applied to a given quantity, different fractions or ordered pairs can be associated with the same fractional quantity, quotient, or operator. As mentioned earlier in making correspondences between mathematical theories and applications, this equivalence is as ratio equivalence.

The mathematical-applicational analyses described here have implications for curriculum development in mathematics. Once again, these analyses suggest that rational numbers can arise in a myriad of mathematical or applicational settings. This has a positive side in that there are many roads into fractions, although Ohlsson (1988) noted the critical role of quotient and division. Further, one can build mathematics from the domain of application rather than from mathematics to its application. However, the fact that rational and fractional numbers have these many facets means that curriculum must allow a child to attend to critical distinctions that arise in different mathematical interpretations. For example, one adds measures or fractional quantities one way, but ratios another. But the same terms, for example $\frac{3}{4}$ or 40%, can arise both as measures and ratios. The mathematical and semantic analyses previously discussed highlight the problem in providing experiences for children that help them learn rational numbers. Because of the ratio idea of equivalence and the diversity of applicational situations, a particular quantity may be referred to using a number of different terms: $\frac{3}{4}$, $\frac{15}{20}$, $\frac{75}{100}$, 75%, 3 for 4, 0.750, and so on. This means there is a rich diverse language available for discussing fractional situations which needs to be learned. On the other hand, as Ohlsson pointed out any particular fractional term $\frac{x}{y}$ is a two-part entity that is applied in diverse situations, the connections and distinctions between which are by no means obvious.

Mathematically Based Curriculum and Instruction Developments

The particular fractional number elaborations discussed earlier seem to represent a set of propositional truths "out there" to be known. If one takes that to be the case, then one might ask how this knowing can be done in an efficient manner. For example, if one were to consider fractional number knowledge fundamentally to involve procedures based on whole number arithmetic, one might see a piece of the curriculum and student learning guided by the following traditional sequence for adding fractions.

Level TAF0: A fraction is assumed to be a part of a whole.

Level TAF1: A fraction arises from counting parts in a single predivided whole.

Level TAF2: Fractions in general are double counts.

Level TAF3: Fractions with like denominators are added by counting like "parts."

Level TAF4: Fractions in general are added by number theoretically finding common denominators, using equivalence.

Level TAF5: Standard symbolic addition of fractions.

Although the aforementioned sequence does represent a hierarchical ordering, there are serious "disconnections" in it. Knowledge from the "lower" level is used only in a nominal way at the "higher" level. For example, the concept of fraction in TAF1 and TAF2 arises from counting all of the (equal) parts in a predivided whole and then counting the indicated parts (perhaps shaded). Thus, fraction here is not a quantity but a double count or an inclusive ratio. TAF3 involves counting but not ratios. Here, one is counting together the like parts in two different sets. In TAF2, the double count is usually such that the count of indicated parts never exceeds the total parts. Of course, Ohlsson (1988) also pointed out that fractions arise as double counts. But the traditional sequence in TAF1 and TAF2 misses the essential connection of such counts to the act of dividing up a reference quantity as suggested by Ohlsson. This leads to adding fractions with like denominators being disconnected from TAF2 because of a different kind of counting and from TAF0 because the part of a whole model breaks down when the sum is greater than one. There is another serious break between Level TAF3 and Level TAF4. In TAF4, equivalence and number theory form the basis for "adding." Adding can be posed partly as a problem of finding common denominators and hence nominally linked to TAF3. But in TAF4 this has not been related to finding a common dividing piece of a common unit for the two fractions that would provide this link. Addition, for example $\frac{1}{3} + \frac{1}{2}$, is not seen as a combining of quantities but as a symbol transformation exercise. It should not be surprising that children learning addition of fractional numbers under such a scheme would have "fragmented knowledge and misunderstood rules."

There was a major attempt to redress the problems indicated in TAF during the late 1960s and early 1970s in a series of research projects at the University of Michigan (Payne, 1976). Hunting (1987), in carefully reviewing this work, noted the following: To develop initial fraction concepts children were to (a) make equal size parts (partitioning) using concrete material, (b) associate oral names with such parts as well as those in drawn diagrams, and (c) build from this concrete-oral background to the writing of fraction symbols.

There are two critical things to notice about this strategy. First, it involves partitioning as student action and, second, there is a careful association of fractional language with objects or actions. Hunting (1987) noted that, for example, addition is developed then through consideration of common denominators with an attention to the size of the parts or pieces. Such attention to size also is a base for the equivalence notion; equivalent fractions are attached to the same fractional quantity. From this base, equivalent fractions are generated through multiplying numerator and denominator of a fraction by the same number. Once one can do this, adding "unlike" fractions is reduced to adding like fractions.

Two things make this sequence reported by Payne (1976) different from the TAF sequence previously outlined. The first is that the sequence is such that there are many more steps that are hopefully closer together. This sequence would more likely have the quality of a necessary hierarchy even though it maintains adding like terms (or counting) as a basis. Further, a deliberate attempt is made to capitalize on the geometric/measurement aspects of fractions.

This research, although whole-number-based, did not directly relate fractions to a whole number quotient function idea. Yet it did suggest giving meaning to fractions language through the act of dividing concrete reference units and building meanings for equivalence in this environment. Equivalence of fractional subunits provides the foundation for operations, particularly addition. Thus, the Initial Fraction Sequence research at Michigan provides an instructional approach to whole-number-related fractional mathematics.

One can use the multifaceted mathematical connections of rational numbers in the diversity of applicational situations to build microworlds in which fractional numbers could be studied by children. For example, Trivett (1980) built such an environment around the algebraic notions of rationals as equivalent classes of ordered pairs. He used pairs of colored rods as embodiments for pairs of whole numbers and defined and provided fraction activities for children in this fractional environment. Such an approach inherently focuses on rationals as ratio numbers and provides an explicit intuitive model for fraction equivalence: $\frac{6}{9}$ is equivalent to $\frac{2}{3}$ because $\frac{6}{9}$ can be made by 3 replicates of the $\frac{2}{3}$ pair or because $\frac{6}{9}$ and $\frac{2}{3}$ have the same "shape" as pairs of rods. Although equivalence is easily developed, operations are complex even if concrete.

Sambo (1980) observed that Blakers (1967) had shown an isomorphism between the mathematics of linear (or region) measure and rational numbers. Sambo developed a scheme in which children entering Grade 7 (12-year-olds) in three Nigerian schools were deliberately taught a unit on the mathematics of measure followed by a special measure-oriented approach to additive fractional knowledge and equivalence. Fraction concepts were developed in a manner similar to that suggested by Ohlsson (1988) using a continuous unit to measure continuous objects (e.g., a paper strip or a meter stick for length). In a classic research design, Sambo studied three replications of a Measure/Fractions (MF) approach compared with teaching measurement only (MO) and these two with a traditional algorithmic approach of textbooks. He also had a control group in each school that did no mathematics during the experiment. Although the children had had a little background in fractions prior to Grade 7, only the MF group showed significant growth from pretest to posttest. On a retention test some months later, the MF group was significantly better than the MO group, which in turn scored higher than either the traditional or the control group. Thus, there is some evidence to conclude that one can successfully build a measurement/fraction microworld and use it to provide fractional number instruction.

There are other alternative microworlds that might form a basis for the building of fractional knowledge. For example, Dienes (1971) used the notion of multiplicative operator as a basis for developing fractional and rational number concepts. Under this model a fractional number acts as a function to map one set or quantity onto another. For example, the fraction $\frac{2}{3}$ maps 30 to 20, 15 to 10, 9 to 6, and so on. Dienes gave detailed analyses of the multiplicative operator and gave examples for composition (multiplication) of such fractions as well as addition. Dienes argued that fractional numbers are naturally multiplicative and that multiplying fractional numbers is simple. The action and algorithm for addition requires a judicious choice of what Ohlsson (1988) referred to as a reference quantity unit. Thus, $\frac{2}{3} + \frac{3}{8}$ could only be added using a reference quantity such as 24: $24 \times \frac{2}{3} = 16$; $24 \times \frac{3}{8} = 9$; $24 \times (\frac{2}{3} + \frac{3}{8}) = 25$, so $\frac{2}{3} + \frac{3}{8} = \frac{25}{24}$. This is a conceptually sophisticated way of looking at common denominators and hence addition.

A fraction curriculum for upper middle-school children in Germany was based on an operator approach (Griesel, 1973). As suggested by Hasemann (1985) and Padberg (1978), this approach was rather formal in character (children learned that $\frac{2}{3}$ resulted from the combination of a $\times 2$ operator and a divide-by-3 operator), but was relatively successful in terms of algorithmic skill performance (children's ability to connect fraction algorithms to any common model seemed relatively poor, however). Padberg (1985) reported that, under this model, if the algorithm for multiplication of fractions was taught prior to the addition algorithm, then the common negative transfer from multiplication to addition of fractions was evident, whereas teaching the algorithms in the opposite order reduced this effect. Thus, as suggested theoretically by Dienes (1971), it would appear that the use of an operator approach to fractional numbers does have implications for the ease of learning the operations on fractions. Ironically, it would appear that teaching the "easy" algorithm first has negative consequence in this operator context.

Because fractional number knowledge can be interpreted in the mathematics of ratios, measures, or operators, curricula have been designed that attempt to have children learn the given propositions and procedures using a single mathematical embodiment (fractions as measures or operators, for example). This has been done with some success theoretically and practically. The limitations arise because of the embodiment chosen— fractions as measures seem naturally additive, fractions as operators multiplicative. Thus, although it is possible, it does not seem that basing an entire fraction curriculum on any single aspect of mathematics or one applicational situation is entirely fruitful.

Developing Situation-Based
Instruction

In planning for instruction based on any construct from any applicational situation, one might consider a model developed by Hiebert and Wearne (1987) in response to what they saw as a divorce between procedural and conceptual knowledge of decimals not unlike that discussed for fraction knowledge earlier. They indicated three "sites" in the process of computing with decimals that mark primary sources of student difficulty. Children could not connect decimal symbols to meaningful referents. Children could not validate computational procedures. Children were not aware that results of algorithmic processing should be reasonable or connected to an intuitive idea of decimal numbers.

Hiebert and Wearne (1987) developed and tested a four-stage model accounting for the semantics and the syntactics of symbolic knowledge (in their case decimals). The first two stages deal with establishment of meaning:

1. Create meaning for individual symbols by connecting them with familiar or meaningful referents.
2. Develop symbol manipulation procedures that are based on the meaning of the symbols and thus reflect actions on the referents.

The third stage aims at the fluency with this symbolic algorithm:

3. Elaborate and routinize the procedures and rules for symbols.

The final stage appears to reflect the fact that in mathematics one can use formal knowledge at one level as a base for new knowledge:

4. Use symbols and rules as referents for building more abstract systems.

Hiebert and Wearne (1987) tested at least the first two stages of this model on early middle-school children. The particular referent system used was base-10 blocks, which can model the relative size of the place values in decimal fractions as well as whole numbers. Experience with instruction based on this model proved positive for children without prior decimal fraction experience. They were able to learn to add and order decimal fractions and to transfer their knowledge beyond the tenths and hundredths upon which instruction was based.

This sequential model could be used in examining and generating fractional number instructional sequences as well, and in fact can be seen as a formalization of the Initial Fraction Sequence work reported by Payne (1976). The fact that the instruction under this model starts with referents suggests that instruction would tend to build from the field of application to formal symbolic work within a particular mathematical theory. The choice or, in the case of fractional number, choices of referents would be critical. The referent system must (a) allow for the unambiguous attachment of fractional symbols to referents and (b) reflect in a clear way the critical features of the mathematical concept system (for fractional numbers these would include the identification of dividable units: fractions as quantities and ratios, equivalence, order, independent operations, and the double role of one).

From the work of Hiebert and Wearne (1986, 1987), it would appear that students who build decimal ideas through a multitude of active and linguistic experiences in such a reference environment build sound decimal concepts that they can extend and elaborate. Students make sense of decimals instead of nonsense. The question still remains as to what it is about the referent system that allows for the building of sensible knowledge. Might a particular choice of a referent systems actually inhibit some aspects of fractional number knowledge as well as enhance others? In using the model, a researcher or a teacher would need to develop ways of getting from using fractional language within the referent system to formal use of the language. One also would have to consider how to connect various fractional knowledge systems that a child might develop.

Summary

Rational or fractional number knowledge has been portrayed as a complex of interrelated systems. Within the context of mathematics, this knowledge extends beyond the traditional realm of number and relates to algebra and measurement, as well as providing different experiences with infinite quantities and processes. This complex of systems also is seen to relate to a variety of applicational situations—if people knew rational numbers they would be enabled to take effective action in a wide variety of situations.

Previous research and curriculum developments show that one can build successful experiences for children that reflect one of the mathematical constructs of fractions, for example, measurement or operator. If one is trying to build such instruction, there exists at least one theory that would be useful in building systematic instruction. What is not yet clear is how, given the complexity of the mathematical knowledge to be acquired, one should systematically provide experiences for children that would cover all aspects.

PERSON-CENTERED APPROACHES

The fractional number knowledge discussed to this point assumes that it is a complex interrelated body of propositions found in a wide variety of mathematical and applicational circumstances. One might get the sense that there is a coherent body of knowledge that, under inappropriate circumstances, children and adults come to acquire in an incomplete, fragmented, and disconnected way. Under more appropriate circumstance, however, children's knowledge could be more complete and transferable. This view represents a classical view of mathematics instruction as a topical search for knowledge "out there." In contrast to a position that identifies knowing and doing, it might represent mathematics knowing for children not as doing, but as mathematically doing what they are told (ideally, doing this effectively under the tutelage of benevolent adults in a coherent manner, using appropriate referents).

Davis and Hersh (1986) argued for a different view of mathematics. Under the apparent timelessness of formal symbolic mathematical propositions lies its meaning, which "requires full association with all types of human activity, mental and physical" (p. 304). To Davis and Hersh, treating mathematics as propositions dissociated with the knower is to separate mathematics from its meaning, whether this meaning be made through validation against personal models of reality, which could be mental in nature as well as physical, or through personal logical evaluation.

Steen (personal communication, April 15, 1988) suggested that a contemporary view of mathematics itself is the study of all the patterns that exist in number, space, science, computers, and the imagination. Mathematics thus is the building up of patterns and involves for the person distinguishing, modifying, and using patterns and particularly forming patterns on patterns and patterns of patterns. As suggested by the analysis and literature reviewed earlier in the second section of this chapter, the study of fractions presents an opportunity to build and use a wide variety of such patterns.

These two points of view consider mathematics as closely related to the knower or pattern maker. Mathematics is a personal activity more than simply a collection of propositions "out there." What is this human activity like, particularly for children and particularly with respect to fractional number knowledge? Freudenthal (1983) suggested that human beings, especially children, grasp mathematical ideas as mental objects and carry out mathematics as mental activities. Freudenthal saw fractions as the phenomenal basis for the mathematical mental objects that are fractional or rational numbers. A person's use of even formal rational number thinking should be rooted in the objects, actions, and language of fractions. This view seems close to that of the philosopher Cassirer (1953), who claimed that even our most abstract (personal) thoughts are rooted in intuitions. It is also congruent with the personal referential mapping between a mathematical construct and its applications which Ohlsson (1988) would typify as understanding.

What kinds of patterns are fraction patterns? Freudenthal (1983) saw fractions and thus rational numbers as organizing breaking up, or "fracturing" activities. Playing with the mental objects related to sharing or dividing up equally can form one base for building up rational number knowledge. In building up personal knowledge of mathematics, Freudenthal (1983) would see a child as acting out the mathematics in situations: measuring and ordering quantities, treating ratios as numbers, and transforming quantities fractionally as well as the quotient activities noted earlier. These activities are consistent with the analysis of rational numbers as personal knowledge done earlier by Kieren (1976) and the analysis of rational numbers as a personal multiplicative structure by Vergnaud (1983), as well as the analysis that supported the early work of the Rational Number Project (Behr, Lesh, Post, & Silver, 1983). To know something means to be able to take effective action in a situation. Personal knowledge of rational or fractional numbers should enable a person to take effective action in the domains of measurement, quotients, ratio treated as number including part/whole, and quantitative transformation or operators.

Because Ohlsson (1988) was making a theoretical response to some of the work cited earlier, it is not surprising that there is a relationship between the constructs of rational number as mathematics and rational number as personal knowledge. But there is even a stronger reason for this connection. Because the axiom system represents the foundation of assumptions on which the rational numbers are built, these assumptions should be related to fundamental problems in the building of that knowledge. Thus, key elements of the mathematical structure should be apparent in the personal knowledge of rationals.

However, the effective actions in the four domains or the four subconstructs of personal rational number knowledge are intuitive. The language in use, though perhaps looking and sounding like formal mathematics, is informal in character. Adopting the ideas from Frye (1981), one might argue that language for younger children (and probably for novices in a field at any age) is used in conjunction with objects and actions or "put for" them. Even when language or symbolism is used independently from objects and actions by young persons, its development and use should be such that it can be seen as an analog for objects or actions. This allows the child to validate any symbolic statement made or to map it to elements in a domain of application. With reference to fraction knowledge, this suggests that symbolic statements be presented not just in conjunction with, but be connectable by the child to, objects, actions, or some domain with which he or she is familiar. This connection should have several effects. In Ohlsson's (1988) terms, it is part of a program of developing meaning for fraction language. Further, it allows for personal validation of symbolic sentences and hence is knowledge developing. Finally, it prevents the symbols themselves from having an incorrect level of concreteness—symbolic language becomes a part of a child's construction rather than a set of "concrete" objects in the environment from which a child draws inappropriate concrete patterns—for example, "add numerators—add denominators"; "fractions do not represent single numbers."

One final comment needs to be made on the development of children's thinking. It appears that children move from sequential, additive, and replicative thinking structures to composite coordinated multiplicative structures (Vergnaud, 1983). Because fractional numbers have a multiplicative, composite essence (Dienes, 1971), because full knowledge of fractions demands control of aspects of proportional reasoning (rational numbers are ratios under equivalence), and because reasoning with and about rationals requires coordinated thinking (Noelting & Gagne, 1980), curriculum decisions and demands should be informed by the state and growth of the learner. Thus, children's knowledge of rational numbers and not simply the mathematics itself would form a basis for assessing and building mathematics curriculum.

Children's Fractional Schemes

What is the nature of fractional number pattern making in children? There has been considerable research on the mental schemes children could bring to bear in building fractional knowledge. Most of these studies faced children with a fractional task that allowed for physical action either on objects or drawings in some context. Most also allowed the researcher to observe the (mathematical) language used by children.

Partitioning Schemes. If a response to "how many" or "manyness" can be thought of as the social personal beginning of natural number, then a response to the question of "how much" or "muchness" can be thought of as the beginning of fractional numbers. A natural situation in which "how much" arises is in the act of sharing or determining a fair share. A fair share can mean many things, but one critical social meaning is that the given quantity is divided to yield equal portions for all. Thus, the questions "How much did I get?" and "Is it the same amount as others?" are pertinent questions.

It is clear that even young children can understand and respond to such questions at least in a concrete way (Bana & Nelson, 1977). If the quantity to be divided up consists of discrete objects (e.g., a bag of cookies, a dozen eggs), then the question of sharing allows for the use of corresponding in a repetitive, sequential one-to-one manner. Hunting and Sharpley (in press) reported a study in which 60% of a sample of 206 preschoolers were able to share 12 biscuits equally among three dolls. Of course, such partitioning was a completely physical act for them. They could not predict what the share would be. A check on the veracity of their process would involve repeating the process. What is clear is that whereas young children can deal with discrete partitioning tasks, their solutions are clearly pre-mathematical. They represent children acting on the environment, but not likely having language or language use that allows them to abstract from it.

However, studying the behavior of even young children does give us insights into the perceptual/geometric problems associated with fractions. Piaget, Inhelder, and Szeminska (1960) associated fractions with geometry and not number. They saw the primary facets of fractions to be the dividing of the whole (continuous) into equal parts, the reconstruction of the whole given a part, and the importance of the part as an object for combination or further subdivision in its own right. These features clearly entail conservation, reversibility in a sophisticated way, and the use of a part as an abstracted object, all of which would be considered features of the dimensional stage of intellectual development (Case & Sandieson, 1988) and particularly the substages of more coordinated actions occurring from the age of 7 years on.

Partitioning, which might be thought of as a cognitive precursor to fractional number, has discrete (corresponding-number) as well as continuous aspects. The effect of this was vividly perceived by Pothier (1981). While interviewing 5-year-olds on the task of dividing sets of cookies between two dolls, she found that they could easily do a "dealing" solution for even numbers of cookies. However, when the task involved five cookies, seven cookies, or three cookies, the response was that it could not be done—there was always a leftover cookie. When the task was the sharing of one cookie, the response was "Oh, that's easy; they get half." Thus, even at an early age, fractioning exhibits distinct actions that later have to be coordinated by the child. This coordination may be fostered through instruction, but it surely cannot be ignored.

Pothier (1981) and Pothier and Sawada (1983) reported a detailed study of the partitioning behavior in children from kindergarten to Grade 3 (approximately 5–8 years old). They reported four levels of partitioning behaviors:

Level 1 Sharing: Here the concern is for breaking and sharing, with a major concern that there be at least a piece for each. The exhaustion of the whole or the quality of the shares are a secondary concern.

Level 2 Algorithmic Halving: This notion involves systematic and replicative partitioning in two. This allows children to control unit fractions whose denominator is a power of two. As with the "dealing" of sets of discrete objects, the child is not necessarily aware of either the outcome or the size of the partitions.

These two levels fit with a theoretical development of Kieren (1980) and are supported by work in a different context by Hunting (1987). Level 2 in particular provides one prenumerical basis for early quantitative work with fractions and fraction numbers, their quantitative equivalence as the same amount, their combination under actions analogous to the arithmetic operations, as well as primitive ideas of denseness. For example, children in the early school grades can easily partition continuous regions into two parts, four parts, eight parts, and so on and usually do so in a multiplicative manner (they halve the halves). They can relate combinations of parts to larger parts (e.g., "an eighth and an eighth make a quarter"). Early school-age children can compare fractional quantities in concrete situations where at least one fraction is a half fraction. For example, a person in a group of four sharing two pizzas gets less than a person in a group of seven sharing four pizzas because the second person gets "a half plus a bite" (Kieren, 1986; Wales, 1984). In fact, one could develop a completely satisfactory fractional system in base-2. The problem would be its combination with a base-10 representation of whole numbers, as well as the everyday practical problem that some quotients call for three parts, five parts, six parts, and so forth.

The third level of partitioning deliberately involves a consciousness of the coordination of the n in $\frac{1}{n}$ part. Pothier and Sawada (1983) called this:

Level 3 Evenness: This kind of partitioning involves repeated halving or other breaking methods followed by geometric transformations. For example, sharing among six might be accomplished in two steps.

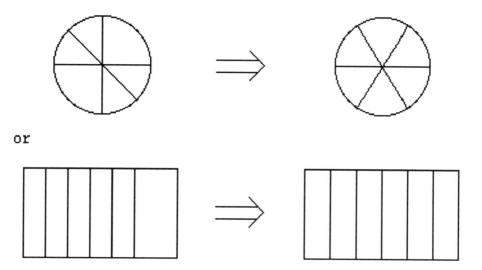

or

Level 4 Oddness: This is the first general partitioning. It is a break from any reliance on halving. In work on circles, it requires realization that a new first move (using the radius instead of diameter) is critical. In work on rectangular regions, it is the realization that halving a previous portion with an orthogonal cut may not be appropriate.

What should be noticed in considering partitioning as a basis for fractions and hence fractional and rational numbers is the multiplicative nature of the act in the sense that it can be repeated on its product. Pothier and Sawada (1983) argued that the older children in their sample acted as if they were using number theoretic thinking. For example, a partition into tenths was thought of indirectly as a partition in fifths, each result of which was halved. This latter level seems to involve the use of internally represented actions by children. This would relate to Hunting's (1987) discussion of discrete set partitioning where a 9-year-old girl Rachel moves from actions on external objects, to actions on internally referenced objects, to partitioning based on known number relationships, particularly useful in discrete object set partitioning, itself a base for Ohlsson's (1988) whole number quotient function.

The purpose of the previous discussion of partitioning has been to establish its potential as a foundation in children's actions and everyday knowledge for the development of fractional number ideas. It would appear that dividing up equally provides an intuitive basis for solutions to problems that could be more formally thought of as fractional number problems. Further, children formalize the activity through the internalization of actions and then through their replacement with symbolic schemes (Hunting, 1987; Kieren, Nelson, & Smith, 1985; Pothier & Sawada, 1983). This activity seems to be an early way into the quotient or quotient function, and the fraction and measurement constructs of fractional number. As observed in the actions of young children, partitioning is a process with a multiplicative character yielding results that children treat as addition quantities.

Equivalence. Partitioning is a child scheme which can be observed as a basis for fractional number as quantity. However, that fractional numbers are also ratios and equivalence is critical to the understanding of the concept of fractional number itself as well as of the ordering of such numbers and any of the operations on fractional numbers. As discussed by Behr et al. (1984) in terms of actions by children and as seen in the axioms and basic theorems of a quotient field, equivalence for rational numbers involves three ideas: absolute equality ($\frac{1}{2} = \frac{2}{4}$ because $\frac{1}{4} + \frac{1}{4}$ make $\frac{1}{2}$); relative equality ($\frac{2}{3} = \frac{6}{9}$ because either there is the same within fraction relationship between 2 and 3 as 6 and 9 or because $\frac{6}{9} = 2 \times 3/3 \times 3$ or $\frac{6}{9} = \frac{2}{3} \times \frac{3}{3}$); or deductive equality ($\frac{2}{3} = \frac{6}{9}$; $[9 \times 3] \times \frac{2}{3} = [3 \times 9] \times \frac{6}{9}$; $9 \times 2 = 3 \times 6$).

The relative or multiplicative notion of equivalence has been studied in terms of equilibration theory in developmental psychology by Noelting (1978) and Noelting and Gagne (1980). Noelting and his colleagues tested over 300 suburban children age 6–16 years with what proved to be a scale of 25 tasks asking children to compare two ratios in a problem setting involving mixtures of orange drink—for example, a mixture of 1 cup of orange concentrate with 3 cups of water (a $\frac{1}{4}$ mixture) to a mixture of 2 cups of orange with 5 cups of water (a $\frac{2}{7}$ mixture). Noelting identified three main stages and several substages as indicated in Table 6.1. In general, the transition from Stage I to II (Stages IC and IIA) represents a change from a

TABLE 6.1
Acquisition of Ratio Comparison Thinking

Stage	Name	Age of Accession (50% Sg)	Typical Item	Characteristics of Stage
0	Symbolic	(2;0)	(1,0) vs (0,1)	Identification of elements.
IA	Lower Intuitive	(3;6)	(4,1) vs (1,4)	Comparison of first terms only.
IB	Middle Intuitive	(6;4)	(1,2) vs (1,5)	Like first terms, comparison of second terms.
IC	Higher Intuitive	(7;0)	(3,4) vs (2,1)	Inverse relationship between terms in the ordered pairs.
IIA	Lower Concrete Operational	(8;1)	(1,1) vs (2,2)	Equivalence class of (1,1) ratio.
IIB	Higher Concrete Operational	(10;5)	(2,3) vs (4,6)	Equivalence class of any ratio.
IIIA	Lower Formal Operational	(12;2)	(1,3) vs (2,5)	Ratios with two corresponding terms multiple of one another.
IIIB	Higher Formal Operational	(15;10)	(3,5) vs (5,3)	Any ratio.

comparison of absolute quantities to relative or intrinsic quantities. The transition from Stage II to III (although one might argue that this is partly due to the nature of Noelting's test) appears to be due to a change from a simple multiplicative comparison to a coordinated multistep comparison, with Stage III involving what Noelting would term full "common denominator thinking."

Vergnaud (1983) offered the most detailed and penetrating analysis of this kind of multiplicative thinking. He used the concepts of two measure spaces and suggested that one could have ratios and hence rational numbers that represented pairs of elements in the same measure space or elements in two distinct measure spaces. Thus, equivalence meant either the same scaler relationship held between elements in the same measure space or the same functional relationship held between elements of the two measure spaces. For example, in seeing that 2 pizzas for 5 eaters is the same as 6 for 15, one could observe that $\frac{2}{5}$ and $\frac{6}{15}$ are members of the same function or class ($\frac{a}{b}$ such that $b = 2\frac{1}{2} \times a$). Or one could observe that there is the same scaler relationship ($\times 3$) between persons and pizzas.

What is common to all of these researchers' considerations of equivalence and the related reasoning involved is that this kind of thinking grows slowly in young persons. Noelting and Gagne (1980) identified the age of 8 as the age at which at least half of the age group first reaches the capacity to think in terms of relative equality. It is not until age $10\frac{1}{2}$ that half of the age group can handle simple multiplicative equivalence. (Given the research of Vergnaud [1983], and Hunting [1987], the particular items on which Noelting based this classification are very simple. Hence, $10\frac{1}{2}$ years may actually underestimate this age.) Using equivalence in an internalized way as a step in a judgment does not occur for half of the age cohort until age 12 with full common denominator reasoning occurring later.

One can contrast this information on child schemes with the cognitive demands suggested by text and teacher semantic networks for lessons on reducing fractions to lowest terms taught to Grade 4 students (Leinhardt & Smith, 1985). Even with the use of representations (which might even confuse matters), the equivalence thinking demanded seems sophisticated when compared with the schemes of children in the work discussed earlier. It is likely no wonder that student performance or achievement in this curriculum is related to the clarity and power of teacher exposition and that such performances might reflect procedural rather than conceptual knowledge or understanding.

This is not to say that making equivalence judgments and even internalizing such judgments is out of the range of younger elementary school children. In a study of problem-solving communication, children age 7–9 years working individually and in groups were studied while working on pizza problems which were similar to but that differed in significant ways from Noelting's (1978; Noelting & Gagne, 1980) orange juice problems (Wales, 1984). A sequence of questions prompted children to think of the quantity or amount a person would get in each of the two situations being compared; these questions also prompted students to bring ideas of sharing and partitioning to bear. The order of questions allowed children to make the equivalence or order comparison between situations based on information they had already determined. Although the items ranged across what Noelting would call Stages II and III, these younger children now were able to answer a median of four of eight questions with, for example, all but one child successfully able to compare four pizzas for seven children with two pizzas for four children. In this setting, almost all children immediately recognized two for four as "half each." They then divided the four pizzas in halves and said things like "*A* gets more—he gets half and a bite" or "*A* gets more—he gets one half plus a quarter of a half." Although children had only limited fraction language and learned procedures, they were able to solve the problem successfully. Of course, such reasoning is limited in the face of questions like (5,3) versus 8,5), where even comparing partitions in terms of physical size is difficult and not useful. Nonetheless, it does illustrate that a sequence of actions and reasoning on them can be done on fractional information by young school-age children.

If one thinks of a child building up his or her fractional knowledge by building and modifying patterns in fractional situations, then the results from the studies previously discussed are of use in thinking about fraction learning and instruction. The ability to use, internalize, and reason about partitioning is available to early school-age children. These abilities grow, become more sophisticated, and change positively with instruction. Although full multiplicative thinking and reasoning proportionally develops only slowly over the school years, children exhibit many schemes or "theorems in action" (Vergnaud, 1988) that allow for a more concrete equivalence reasoning. This seems particularly evident when equivalence or order judgments are based on absolute quantities rather than relative values.

Personal Knowledge of Rational Numbers

How does a child build from the partitioning and equivalence schemes to mature fractional or rational number knowledge? Links obviously could be made to the personal constructs of quotient number, measure number, multiplicative operator number, and ratio number, the first and last of which include part–whole and fractional conceptions. Of course, as Vergnaud (1983) cogently argued, these four subconstructs do not constitute rational number knowledge for a person—it is a synthesis that occurs only if "measures, scaler operators and function operators lose their dimensional aspects and the distinction between [fractional number as] element and relationship, and if the concept of rational number as pure numbers is built up. But this concept is inherent in all three aspects" (p. 165). Thus, Vergnaud appears to argue for a leveled, but interrelated scheme for personal knowledge of rational number.

Kieren (1988) attempted to provide one view of what such a scheme might look like. This ideal model, shown in Fig. 6.2, uses Margenau's (1987) idea of the cognitive domain as a set of interrelated constructs (c) that relate more or less closely to and that give one more or less extensive control of the environment in which one exists. The intent of the model is not to provide a map of any person's rational number thinking, but to point to features that might govern our study of the growth of rational number knowledge and also to features of a curriculum that could foster such growth.

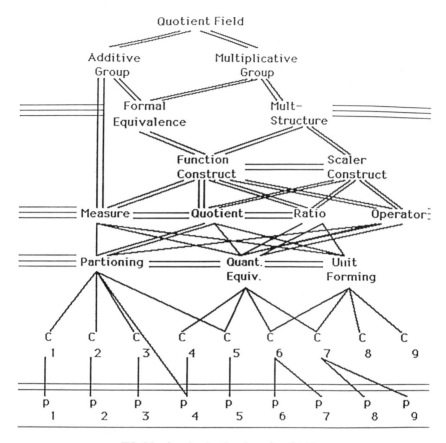

FIG. 6.2. Levels of rational number thinking.

Ideal personal knowledge or understanding of fractions is seen as a structured whole. This whole is based on mental constructs that represent very local knowledge. These are labeled $C_1, C_2, C_3 \ldots Cn$ and are directly based on and related to the cognitive events that form an interface with any environmental niche. These events are the percepts, prehensions, or protocols, the connectors to the environment itself, and are labelled P_1, $P_2 \ldots Pn$.

The structure as a whole is extensive. It would allow a person to relate to all of the wide variety of events in one's environment that might entail rational numbers. As one moves "away" from the level of percepts (P-level), the constructs become ever more extensive and hence ever more potentially applicable in a person's living and doing. Like Skemp (1987) and Maturana and Varela (1980), the model indicates that one's own mental activities or constructs themselves are elements in the "environment" for "higher level" constructs. Rather than having a two-state mental system as suggested by Skemp, constructs "above" integrate and entail lower level constructs. How this occurs is not discussed here but surely would be congruent with the processes of reflective abstraction (Steffe & von Glasersfeld, 1988) and would likely represent a continuing if not continuous growth from exogenously determined thinking, mental activities that the knower would see as driven by the environment, whether this is so or not, to endogenous thought based on a person's own thinking (Piaget, 1980).

Pieces of fractional number knowledge should not be thought of as isolated, but should be interconnected not just vertically but horizontally as well. Although by definition the low-level constructs $C_1, C_2, \ldots Cn$ are directly connected vertically to events at the p level, they are local in the sense that they are unconnected and not extensive. The constructs that indicate proto-mathematical knowledge, such as partitioning and quantitative equivalence, are seen as interconnected. This is surely so of the higher level constructs. For example, rationals as an additive group are connected with rationals as a multiplicative group through the higher level field concept and the distributive property.

A second set of connections is indicated by the triple segments at the side. They suggest that fractional knowledge above the $C_1, C_2 : \ldots Cn$ level is connected to other mathematical ideas. For example, rational numbers as partitive quotients is connected to quotitive notions not shown here. This connection comes through the form or symbolic representation for action, rather than as a direct relationship between processes. Fractions as multiplicative operators are connected as an instance of the notion of composite functions and as an example of groups of transformations. Vergnaud (1983) has carefully developed the connections between rationals as a personal multiplicative structure and multiplicative notions in general (e.g., proportionality, area).

The triple segments also represent connections between the constructs held by an individual and those with whom he or she has significant mathematical relationship, for example, the fractional number ideas of the teacher. Leinhardt and Smith (1985) have given explicit diagrams of such teachers' mathematics, at least as indicated by lesson plans. These personal connections in Fig. 6.2 indicate that a teacher's rational number knowledge can relate to that of the student.

Obviously, such a total knowledge structure does not arise as one complete piece for the learner. Under ideal circumstances it is a growing phenomenon. What are some of the critical elements of this ideal growing phenomenon? First, it contains different kinds of knowledge elements. Some of this knowledge is intuitive. That is, its use involves imagery (physical or mental), premathematical thinking tools (e.g., counting, extracting, dividing up), and informal use of language—language used in reference to activities or objects. Some examples of such knowledge that can see a child using correct fractional language or fractionlike language in its expression are partitioning knowledge, discussed in detail earlier, or operator knowledge: "12 goes to 9 because you divide by 4 and subtract" or "you divide by 4 then multiply by 3" (Kieren & Southwell, 1979). The main constituents of this intuitive knowledge are the four subconstructs (a) fractions as measures, (b) quotients (usually between measure spaces), (c) ratios (usually within measure spaces), and (d) operators. This type of knowledge, which directly or indirectly references actions and objects, also contains the more sophisticated constructs, the scaler and functional operators of Vergnaud (1983). It contains less sophisticated constructs, such as forming dividable units (related to, but very distinct from whole number units) and quantitive equivalence ("as much as" distinct from but related to "as many as").

The structure also contains knowledge that generates pure number relationships, that of equivalence, multiplicative structures, and the multiplicative and additive groups of rational numbers. This is knowledge that is represented symbolically and can be developed through symbol manipulations, as well as through local logical analyses. The structure also contains knowledge that is axiomatic deductive in its character. For example, one can deduce that there is a unique identity element or that a set isomorphic to the domain of integers is embedded in the rationals. Such knowing is indicated by the label "rationals as a quotient field."

There are a number of curricular and instructional implications of the model. Eventually, one would wish a person to be able to function at a symbolic or even a deductive level with rational numbers as pure numbers. But in teaching for these upper level constructs, a teacher needs to be aware of the influence of his or her knowledge and that of "the textbook." If the teacher (or text author) thinks of fractions as an easy extension of whole numbers and instruction begins at or moves quickly for a Grade 3 or Grade 4 child from a static diagram to a symbolic level, this action may ignore the need of the child to build up the underlying intuitive knowledge constructs. A consequence may be the fragmented and seemingly nonsensical fraction number performance seen in the evaluation literature. Or it may mean that knowing fractional numbers means only taking specific algorithmic actions.

In trying to provide instruction for a semantically or personally complex field such as the rational numbers, one could try to effect some simplifications. For example, one could assume that knowledge of one intuitive construct such as measure number would lead directly, with only limited extra instructions to the other intuitive constructs of quotient, ratio, or operator. Can one make such a simplifying assumption? The answer at present is that we do not know. However, research using the Rational Number Thinking Test (Kieren, 1984) has indicated that whereas performance on quotient comparison items (dividing pizzas among persons), ratio comparison items (drink mixtures), and operator recognition items (fractional machine) were significantly correlated, such items still form unique factors under a factor analysis of the correlation matrix (Rahim & Kieren, 1988). Thus, in building personal knowledge it may be necessary to treat the constructs separately. The interrelationships of constructs could arise at the level of persons comparing their formalizations of each intuitive construct.

It should not be assumed that the lower level constructs do not deal with complex phenomena in complex ways. Movement "up" this knowledge model is more like the "growth" in the van Hiele levels (Hoffer, 1983). Because of the connection to both geometry and number, one might expect the constructs at the lower levels to be about fractional situations in some holistic sense, middle-level constructs to be about quantitative and relational properties and local logical relationships, whereas the highest level represents the axiomatic deductive knowledge of rationals. Yet, for a person, knowledge should be a connected historical whole.

Of course, this model of personal rational number knowledge, as complex as it is, still does not portray all the facets that might be part of coming to know rational numbers. For example, this model does not explicitly include either the informal, formal, or axiomatic notions of order. Nor does it consider at its lower levels the distinctions between discrete and continuous representations of rational or fractional numbers. Although the latter distinction may not be critical mathematically, it may be important in the way in which and level to which children come to know each of the four intuitive constructs, in the way in which partitioning is done and understood, in the distinction of the whole or the unit, and in the devices—for example, counting versus measuring—used in developing a sense of quantitative equivalence (Bigelow, Davis, & Hunting, 1989).

Kinds and Validity of Rational Number Knowledge. The kinds of knowledge seen in Fig. 6.2 also can be observed in the structure embodying the four kinds of (rational number) knowledge in Fig. 6.3. The qualities of such knowledge types have been described in detail elsewhere (Kieren, 1986, 1988) as well as by Leinhardt (1988) in a slightly different way. What is salient for the discussion here is the embeddedness of the levels. In such a structure, the more formal language use and knowledge of the outer two layers is seen to grow from less formal more everyday knowledge and informal use of fractional language. If one thinks of rational number knowledge as built up through experiences in building and studying patterns in situations, then these four knowledge types represent four kinds of experi-

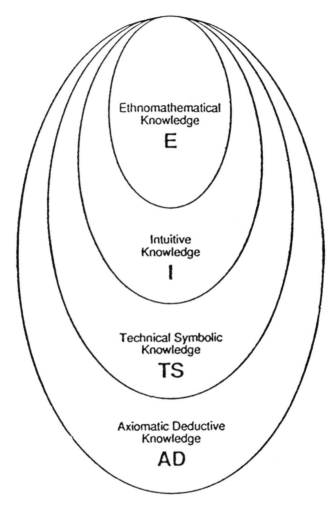

FIG. 6.3.   Ideal elements of mathematical knowledge building.

ences of fractional number or rational number pattern making: that is, everyday experience, experiences in designed but informal fractional situations, symbolic experiences, and axiomatic structuring and proving experiences.

This embedded model also has implications for how a child can validate his or her own rational number knowledge. The philosopher Bateson (1979) contended that personally useful knowledge is knowledge that connects or is about something. What of children's fractional knowledge and its building? Knowledge of one kind or level should be about prior experience either at that level or an inner level. In particular, given the evaluation data cited in the first part of this chapter, it is critical that a child be able in some way to validate technical symbolic expressions against what is for them intuitive experience. For example, for one child knowing that $5\frac{1}{4}$ is $5 + \frac{1}{4}$ might come from the experience of jumps on a number line. This should not be thought of as a universal intuitive base. As Larson (1987) pointed out for her sample of "average" urban upper elementary students, fractions are not easily recognized by children on a number line—it itself is a technical-symbolic device. In fact, Streefland (1984b), although seeing the number line as a critical device for making coherent much of students' fractional knowledge, sees it used after other experiences to formalize and organize results known from more action-oriented or ethnomathematical contexts. Larson pointed out that fractions were more easily identified by her sample on a ruler than a number line. This may be because the ruler is a familiar everyday object in the lives of children (at least in school and probably out of school as well). Mellin-Olsen (1987) forceably argued the value of folk mathematics or what is here called ethnomathematics for exactly this reason of more universal familiarity. Thus, fractional knowledge could and should be attached to a variety of informal experiences, at least some of which should pertain to a child's everyday life.

In Fig. 6.3, ethnomathematical and intuitive mathematics are illustrated as cores for technical symbolic mathematics. This implies that everyday life or intuitive actions are not simply used to illustrate or provide a context for episodal memory of symbolic algorithms to be learned. Mathematics in its own right exists at these levels and can serve as a powerful base for more formal knowing. Using standard mathematical language informally to build such knowledge allows technical symbolic knowledge to formalize it. Further, if systematic but informal mathematical knowledge exists, a child can validate knowledge they build using the power and efficiency of symbolic manipulation.

Examples of Person Based-Approaches. Just as there is no research that tests in practice the semantic-mathematical analysis of rational numbers discussed earlier in the second section, similarly there are no practical curricula that follow the aforementioned personal knowledge theories as yet. There have been research and curriculum work with children in which it was assumed that the child built up or constructed his or her own mathematics from given experiences that can be taken to relate to the aforementioned personal knowledge theories. Of the five studies discussed next, one presents a detailed description of one child, two are studies of one or a small number of classes, and two entailed the study of a large number of classes. All five in one way or another based instructional or curricular actions on the perceived knowledge and knowledge building of children.

Pirie (1988) recorded the interactions of pairs of 11- to 12-year-old students working on division of fractions over a period of days. She excerpted a detail case of one child, Katie. The class had developed the idea that $1 \div \frac{1}{n} = n$. Katie, like her classmates, had then concluded that $1 \div \frac{2}{3} = 1$ (one two-thirds piece fits one time into 1), a reasonable quotitive conclusion. Rather than developing an exposition that would clarify the student error, the teacher asked them to study the situations $2 \div \frac{2}{3}$, $3 \div \frac{2}{3}$, $4 \div \frac{2}{3}$ . . . as they wished. Pirie then showed that Katie first developed a physical theory—in $3 \div \frac{2}{3}$, there are other "bits" that could make up $\frac{2}{3}$ pieces and $3 \div \frac{2}{3} = 4\frac{1}{2}$ (two-thirds pieces). After the teacher challenged Katie to work on her own harder problems, Pirie observed Katie moving to an action-related but numerical approach: $6\frac{1}{3} \div \frac{2}{3}$ can be analyzed as follows: There are 18 one-thirds in 6, so $6\frac{1}{3}$ contains 19 one-thirds and half that many two-thirds. She now used this strategy in several self-invented fraction division situations.

Some weeks later, Pirie (1988) interviewed Katie and asked what she and her partner knew about division of fractions, and they gave the standard turnover and multiply algorithm. This algorithm had not been taught by the teacher, and Katie at first seemed to only know it in a way detached from her experience. Pirie then changed to questions of order: "Will $50 \div \frac{1}{3}$ be more or less than 50?" Now Pirie observed Katie use and elaborate upon her more intuitive and concrete reasoning in response to this and other more complex order questions. In the Katie example, we see one student working in an environment that allowed her to explore division of fractions as intuitive mathematics which she formalized into technical symbolic mathematics. She could efficiently use symbolic knowledge and appears to have embedded in it meaningful and complex informal intuitive mathematics.

Streefland (1984a, 1987) provided numerous curricular and instructional examples of intuitive fractional knowledge building. His basic strategy is to take everyday examples and provide children with mathematical language and ideas for analyzing them. Students act out and record their activities using fractional language in an informal way connecting it to everyday or intuitive events in descriptive and controlling ways. As an example one might present a Streefland growth sequence for addition of fractions as in Fig. 6.4.

In looking at Streefland's (1984a, 1984b, 1987) work with upper elementary school children there is a conscious effort to put children in intuitive mathematical situations through analyzing and writing mathematically about ethnomathematical situations. There is also an effort to give children the opportunity for image-action-language experiences for developing and writing about intuitive fractional mathematics. Finally, such mathematics is formalized using the number line and informal and stan-

Sharing, muchness, fraction names	Make fractional sentences about dividing up.	Relationship between fractional quantities and ratios. (See Fig. A below)	Addition using quantity and ratio. (See Fig. B below)	Activities are given symbolic form; fraction monographs.

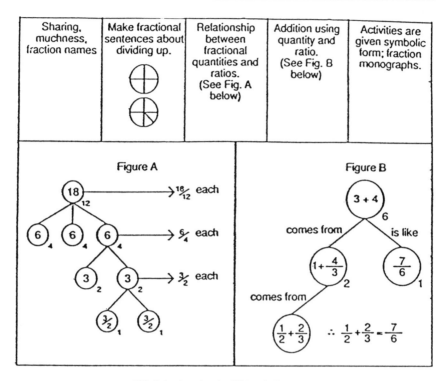

FIG. 6.4. Levels of addition behaviors.

dard symbolic representations. This latter work is highlighted in students' writing fraction monographs giving and validating what they see as formal true statements about various fractional numbers.

Harrison, Bye, and Brindley (1981) were concerned with the fact that the cognitive demands made by texts and teacher instruction in fractions (at the Grade 7 level) did not match student thinking. They used a test by Kieren (Rational Number Thinking Test) to assess the cognitive level of children whom they classified as concrete, transitional, and formal with respect to fraction knowledge using neo-Piagetian terminology. Along with a group of teachers, they developed a sequence of investigations that matched the topics in the provincial curriculum but had children investigating fraction equivalence, operations, and order in intuitive settings and writing about their experiences. This curriculum was used with several hundred children in urban classrooms. Student performances on standard fraction understanding and computation tests (Hart, 1981) were contrasted with those of a like number of students receiving the traditional algorithm-oriented instruction based on text material very similar to that analyzed later in this chapter. Although doing as well as the traditional students (and adequately) on computation, the experimental group was systematically better than the traditional group in understanding. The bulk of both groups were classified as concrete or transitional thinkers. In the traditional class, performance on the understanding test was linear: concrete-low, transitional-middle, formal-high. But under the experimental intuitive treatment, transitional students performed as well as the formal students on the measure of understanding. It would appear that, at least for students who had some basis for learning the ideas presented but who did not yet exhibit formal knowledge, an intuitive environment that stresses language use with actions, thinking tools, and images is facilitating of fraction understanding and provides a better cognitive match than an algorithm-oriented traditional setting.

Behr and others (Behr, Wachsmuth, Post, & Lesh, 1984; Behr, Wachsmuth, & Post, 1985) did extensive teaching experiments over 2 years with fourth- and fifth-grade students learning fractions. They used what they called part–whole activities to base a curriculum that tried to use the four constructs—measure, quotient, ratio, and operator—as sources of representations for children's thinking. They found that fractional knowledge building was a slow process in this rich environment, but that children in fact could come to an understanding of such things as the compensatory relationship between the size of $(\frac{1}{n})$ and the number n. They also verified the fact that using concrete representations for fraction ideas has its difficulties. For example, a child could show one and one-half units or $\frac{3}{2}$ unit with 6 as a unit divided into two sets of 3. Simply transforming the unit in the view of the child into 3 sets of 2 inhibited showing $\frac{3}{2}$ or one-and-a-half units. This research group also developed a large number of interesting tasks for assessing fractional knowledge in concrete, semiconcrete, and symbolic ways and for assessing abilities to translate between representations.

Kerslake (1986) conducted an extensive interview, instructional development and design, and curriculum testing study with low-achieving 13- and 14-year-olds in England. She found that although such students had a good idea of fractions as parts of a whole, they had fragile ideas of equivalence, confusing quantity and proportion, very limited ideas of fractions as number, and limited knowledge of the relationship of fractions to division. Based on the interview study, Kerslake developed a set of 15 experiences that allowed students to relate fractional number expressions and computations to physical, image, or gamelike real situations. Five of these experiences were directed respectively toward quotient, equivalence, and number notions of fraction. In a detailed testing of these experiences, Kerslake worked with three classes of 13- and 14-year-olds (59 actually were tested). Significant improvement in all three areas occurred, with children with initial low scores showing the least benefit from the experience, a result not unlike that of Harrison et al. (1981). Kerslake concluded that although division scores showed a strong gain on the immediate post-test (29 = 64%), they fell to 51% on the delayed posttest, whereas scores on the others actually increased slightly from the posttest to the delayed posttest. Kerslake suggested in light of the delayed posttest performance that the division experiences did not "enable the children to restructure their view of fractions . . . to accommodate . . . the aspect of fraction as quotient" (p. 50). Thus, although this student-knowledge-based curriculum proved successful, it was not uniformly successful across topics.

The experimental worksheets on division, equivalence, and number were then tested by six teachers in comprehensive schools in different parts of England. With relatively little teacher training and supervision of the teaching, results similar to those previously outlined were obtained in the six trial schools, leading one to believe that even modest instructional intervention based on intuitive fraction number building can be useful.

It is important to note that the basis of the intuitive instruction in the studies described earlier was carefully developed to avoid a static part–whole interpretation of fractions. Like Kieren (1981) and Vergnaud (1983) for theoretical reasons, Kerslake (1986) on the empirical basis of her inter-views and teaching experiments suggested that "it is the part of a whole view of fractions which inhibits other aspects of the work with fractions" (p. 95). Even though Behr et al. (1983) identified part–whole as critical in their experiments, theirs was not a static double count meaning.

In providing student-knowledge-based instruction, a question arises, for individuals or for classes, as to when to move from the informal to the more formal levels of activity. The knowledge-building models previously described imply a matching of children's mathematics and mathematics for children. Although Lampert (1985), using contexts with which children identify and in which they proceed naturally on their own, provided one answer to this question, one might still wish means of identifying and assessing a child's mathematics. The recent research described earlier provided some instrumentation for studying the intuitive rational number knowledge of children individually (Kerslake, 1986) or in classroom groups (Behr et al., 1984; Figueras, Filloy, & Valdemoros, 1987; Harrison et al., 1981; Lesh, Landau, & Hamilton, 1983; Noelting & Gagne, 1980). The transition from intuitive to technical symbolic knowledge might well be studied using the "construct a sum" task where children are asked to select from a given set of digits four values for numerators and denominators such that the sum of two fractions is as close as possible to but not equal to one (Behr et al., 1985).

The five studies cited earlier show that work with children consistent with the models of personal rational number knowledge and knowing has been done. All of the work was done in real school settings, but in some cases with special materials. One can see obvious differences between knowledge structure of Katie or the addition sequence of Streefland (1984a, 1987) and that represented by the traditional sequence for adding fractions shown in the second section. One would also imagine semantic networks describing instruction in these classes and materials used in these classes to differ, not in basic mathematical content, but in the role and use of representations from those described by Leinhardt and Smith (1985) and Leinhardt and Greeno (1986).

A STUDY OF TWO TEXT SERIES

It is the purpose of this section to review the discussion of fractions and rational numbers in two Canadian text series—*Holt Mathematics Systems* (Bye & Sauer, 1980), and *Houghton Mifflin Mathematics* (Burbank, Holmes, & Poce, 1982)—in light of the discussion of mathematical and personal knowledge-based analyses of relational and fractional number knowledge building.

The models for rational number knowing and the research with children building up their own fraction ideas represent a call for meaningful teaching that serves as a reaction to the evaluation data presented in the forepart of this chapter. One might ask about the contributions of textbooks to meaningful teaching of mathematics. But first one must ask what might be reasonably expected from mathematics textbooks and their presentations related to fractional numbers. Leinhardt and Smith (1985) have illustrated that, at least for some expert teachers, there was a relationship between the semantic network of their lesson on a topic in fractions and that of the development in the text used. However, in the cases detailed, the teacher lesson was an extensive elaboration on what was presented in the text both mathematically and instructionally. It is easy to criticize both series of texts (and, in fact, any other text I have looked at) as presenting fractional number ideas in small chunks or two-page lessons. It was a pattern in both text series, from the Grade 4 versions on, to devote a few lessons to equivalence and operations on fractions at each grade level, with the actual exercises and explanations at each grade level becoming more symbolic and involving more fractions. One might get the impression that fractions should be taught by quick repeated passes through the canon of knowledge of fractions once a year for 4 or 5 years. Thus teaching, to be effective, would have to elaborate the text.

But perhaps it is wrong to analyze the situation in this way. One could think of a text development as giving what a good experienced teacher or mathematics educator thinks of as an exemplar of a particular idea. This exemplar could be used after (or during) much more elaborate teacher development or learner experience as signal or reminder of the whole complex idea taught or learned. Under such an analysis, the texts analyzed would only be seen as source books of fraction idea exemplars for teachers and particularly for students. Unfortunately, the teacher guides for these books only give more of the same kind of examples as the texts, and in general do not give alternative or elaborative learning suggestions beyond practice games. Thus for both of the following series, with respect to fractions, what you see in the texts is what you get.

How might one proceed to analyze such texts? One might develop the semantic nets for the fraction chapters or lessons and examine the explicit and implicit ideas and assumptions used (Leinhardt & Smith, 1985). It is beyond the scope of this brief analysis to do that. One might count the items (or lessons) that develop fraction ideas concretely, or formal/symbolically or at some transition levels as did Harrison et al. (1981). They found that in prior versions of one of the Grade 7 texts studied here 72% of the learning items were at the symbolic formal level. The texts made cognitive demands at a formal level that went beyond those suggested in the provincial curriculum guide at the Grade 7 level. Rather than providing a less formal basis for fraction number development in classes, the teachers using these texts had lesson presentations and class work that contained 77% formal symbolic elements of items at Grade 7. Thus, such an analysis would not truly get at the approaches used for fractions and at any rate would play only a limited role in determining an understanding of formality in fraction instruction.

What is done instead is to ask a series of questions based on the discussion in the previous parts of this chapter. How do these text series appear to treat the concepts of fractional numbers? A related question is: How is what is done related to the research and theory discussed earlier?

A more elaborate set of questions can be generated based on the portrayal of ideal rational number knowledge in Fig. 6.2. In that network of constructs there are four kinds of legitimate mathematical knowledge. There is the fractional number knowledge about actions based on the constructs of partitioning or dividing up equally, of comparing quantities to dividable units, and of a quantitative sense of equivalence. There is fractional number knowledge of intuitive settings: measurement of continuous and unit-bound discrete quantities, quotients, operators, and ratio numbers. There is knowledge of fractions "stripped" of situational trappings and generated through the study and use of symbolic patterns. And finally there is logical algebraic knowledge. As has been mentioned previously, mathematical knowledge at all the aforementioned levels could and should involve fractional and rational number language. It might well involve operations, ordering, patterns, and properties at any level as well. The question is what is the personal basis for the knowledge? How can it be validated by a person? Are these various levels of fractional number knowledge apparent in what is done in these texts? In answering any of these questions it is fair to say that, in their treatment of fractions, the Grades 1–3 texts are informal in nature, the Grade 4 more transitional, and the Grades 5–8 texts more symbolic in their orientation. Thus the comments that follow should be interpreted in this light.

How do the texts treat fractional number knowledge? In general, from Grade 1 through Grade 8 both text series treat fractions as parts of wholes. Generally they call continuous wholes "wholes" and discrete wholes "sets" and make a distinction between them. It would seem to this observer that the main general objective is to develop elements in a certain fractional language and sentences, comparisons, and computations in that language. The treatment in Grades 1–3 in both texts basically is used to provide students with language for particular fractions moving from a limited set of unit fractions to a similarly limited set of nonunit fractions. The emphasis in both texts is on counting, or indicating to establish the use of the fraction symbol. There is limited attention to using spoken or written-out words in place of numerical symbols. There seems to be an emphasis on the early use of the standard fraction symbols. All of the illustrations (Grades 1–8 in both texts) use predivided regions, emphasize the congruence of the shown parts, and explicitly or implicitly indicate counting as the way of establishing meaning for fraction symbols.

There is emphasis on the concepts of numerator and denominator. However, all of this is syntactic ("2 parts are shaded, 3 parts same size," Burbank et al., 1982, Book 3, p. 252). There is no explicit use of a semantic analysis (Ohlsson, 1988) of different meanings for numerator and denominator nor of the different quantities from which the numerator and denominator numbers might be developed. In the case of parts of sets, there is a deliberate attempt to use discrete objects of the same size in a set. Thus there is an implicit agenda that one eighth of a set should be a "muchness." But this is never made explicit, even in the teacher's guide. Such attention to identically sized objects might, in fact, hinder a child's development of the concept of ratio number as exemplified by the statement "three fourths of the vehicles going by the school were trucks." With respect to discrete quantities there is no attempt to explicitly define a unit to which the number of objects in a subset or superset might be compared.

In terms of the Grades 4–8 materials, there is a repeating of the double count models of fractions. There is a limited development, using region models, of equivalence as showing the same amount. This and some implicit work with "mixed numbers," only started in Grade 4 in each series, are the only indications in the series that fractions are numbers which can indicate quantity or "muchness." This leads to side-by-side exercises

(Houghton Mifflin 4, p. 149) where the "answer" to two parts shaded out of four equal parts is "$\frac{2}{4}$" (not $\frac{1}{2}$ or . . .), whereas in the next exercise $\frac{2}{3} = \frac{4}{6}$. Thus the meaning of fractions seems tied to the way the illustration looks or to ways in which items can be counted. In terms of equivalence both series defer the actual creation of equivalent fractions symbolically or "mentally" until Grade 5. They do not show this as using multiplication by $\frac{n}{n}$ until Grade 7. Such a deferral may be reasonable. For example, in building up the quotient meaning of fraction, it is reasonable to "see" that 1 pizza for 3 gives the same amount as 3 pizzas for 9. But it is difficult to "see" how multiplying by 1 in the form of $\frac{3}{3}$ relates to this applicational situation. Similarly, in looking at a ruler one can see that $\frac{3}{4}$ and $\frac{6}{8}$ describe the same length, but the multiplication by $\frac{2}{2}$ is obscure. Justifying equivalence in terms of multiplying by $\frac{n}{n}$ arises at a more formal mathematical level and should follow less formal developments that are logical or defensible to the child on other grounds. Whether one uses $\frac{n}{n}$ in this way depends on prior experience of the child. There is evidence that could support waiting to use the $\frac{n}{n}$ strategy on developmental grounds.

The same kind of instruction on fractional operations is repeated over Grades 4–8 in both series with a gradual change in fractional numbers used. Operations became more symbolic and a wider variety of fractions are considered. This culminates in both Grade 8 books as identifying rational numbers as the set of positive and negative fractions and zero. In the Houghton Mifflin series the change from Grades 4–8, let us say in addition, is from work with like terms, to work with simple common proper fractions with proper fraction results, to work with mixed numbers, to work with positive and negative fractions. A similar pattern is observed in the Holt series. However, the Holt series contains a number of sections from Grade 5 in which properties of the operations are considered as well.

In terms of multiplication, both series show multiplication of a fraction by a whole number and vice versa using set models and fraction times a fraction using region model. In both cases the model is not studied in detail by the child, but is used only to illustrate the algorithm. For example, the diagram sequence for $\frac{2}{3} \times \frac{3}{4}$ might be as follows.

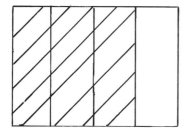 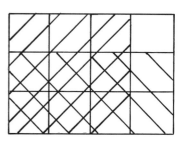

In the second diagram, the double-shaded region represents $\frac{2}{3} \times \frac{3}{4}$ and can be read as $\frac{6}{12}$. Thus the diagram supports the computation. But it can inhibit meaning. For example, it does not allow a child to see that $\frac{3}{4}$ has 3 ($\frac{1}{4}$ units) and that hence $\frac{2}{3} \times \frac{3}{4}$ would be 2 of the 3 ($\frac{1}{4}$ units) or $\frac{1}{2}$. The orthagonal partitioning, double shading model simply cannot be extended to $\frac{1}{2} \times \frac{2}{3} \times \frac{3}{4}$, for example, as might a more active, operator-oriented, region-folding approach. In multiplying "mixed numerals," the Holt series chooses to give an algorithm (Book 6, p. 213; Book 7, p. 174), whereas the Houghton Mifflin series starts with an algorithmic approach in Grade 6 but uses confusing diagrams in Grades 7 (Book 7, p. 226) and 8 (Book 8, p. 166).

Although both series quickly give the rule—multiply by the reciprocal—for division of fractions, the Houghton Mifflin 6 (pp. 267–275) attempts to attach this to the quotitive meaning of division in more detail. However, as with other parts of fractional knowing, if a teacher wished to allow and foster the personal development of division ideas with respect to fractional numbers such as that illustrated earlier from Pirie (1988), the material in the text would serve to reflect and summarize such development rather than lead it.

Perhaps because of the fact that Canada is officially a "metric" country, both series provide early and extensive emphases on decimal fractions from Grade 2 onward. Pictures indicate that decimal words and symbols are attached to the base-10 blocks, but in some places a strip is 1, then a "flat," then a large block. Although it might be argued that such variation builds a more robust concept, there is not the uniform attachment of symbol and object/action suggested by the Hiebert–Wearne theory (Wearne & Hiebert, 1988). The images or materials are not used in developing the algorithms. Instead, decimal place rules are given in "practical" illustrative settings. The inferred instructional practice is "give a rule or algorithm in a clear manner; illustrate the rule where practical; provide practice; provide meaning through practical examples and exercises."

From Grade 5 on both series provide extensive work in building up the facility in changing from one notation system to another (e.g., fractions to decimals, fractions to percents). This language translation activity might be seen as a capstone for years of building fractions (or decimals) as a kind of computational language rather than considering rational numbers as numbers, quantities, or mathematical entities in their own right. One can rightly think of fractions as a symbol system useful in many settings. The problem is that in developing this language as central, the knowledge of fractional number can be lost. Further, fractional language can be used in many different meaning settings. Thus, as in these texts when ratio instruction closely follows fraction instruction, ratios are seen as fraction ideas. Language use here can lead to conceptual confusion. Rather than correctly seeing fractional or *ratio*-nal numbers as a restricted subidea of ratios considered as extensive quantities or numbers, students often incorrectly use concepts (addition) or syntax (lowest terms) of the fractional number system in the ratio system, potentially causing confusion.

In what sense do the developments of fractional number knowledge in these text series relate to the research previously discussed? In the teacher materials for the Grades 1–3 books, both series make reference to cognitive development. The Houghton Mifflin series advises that the concepts develop slowly in young children. These guides do not suggest how teachers might select sequences of instruction, or child activities that reflect different paces of idea development. In fact, there are very few ideas given for helping students at different levels. There is very little information on childrens' knowledge or thinking with respect to fractional numbers. There are not suggestions of questions teachers might ask to ascertain such thinking or knowledge.

One might say that both series take equivalence to be a significant concept. Although neither probably gives it the mathematical flavor or the conceptual development suggested by Payne (1976) and his students, both carefully develop additive computations on the basis of equivalence. In particular, Holt from Grade 5 onward has some nice symbolic developments of equivalence using multiplication tables as a basis. Fractional equivalence is related to student knowledge of whole number multiplication.

The Houghton Mifflin series also uses region models exclusively in early work on fractions and equivalence. This seems to square with some of the work of Behr et al. (1984). However, Hunting (1987) has suggested that set models can be used more easily by young children. The use of the region model could be seen as related to the work of Piaget, Inhelder, and Szeminska (1960) in that fractions are seen and labeled as parts of a geometric whole. However, except in passing, there is no work at any grade-level year on constructing the whole or unit from one given part of a fractional number, or seeing a part itself as an object to be divided into two parts, two other central features of the Piagetian notion. These activities can be done by young children (Grade 3 or 4) as seen in the work of Bergeron and Herscovics (1987), but such work is not developed in either text series.

In particular, the mathematics of actions, the actual dividing up of quantities, the comparing a quantity with a unit or one, and the careful consideration of quantitative (connected to ratio) equivalence, is simply absent. There are programs of activities for young children that involve them in pre-fractional actions of partitioning units and comparing the resulting parts. Such activities include the ongoing use of appropriate language to describe results of actions (Behr & Post, 1988). But in the text series studied, the actions of dividing up and the writing about these actions using fractional words and later symbols is not done. In working with equivalence, although pictures are used, the validating of symbolic work back to personal actions on images or objects is not done. In almost every lesson there is the appearance to move the child's thinking from the concrete to the symbolic. However, the formal mathematical language does not grow out of or describe action. Algorithms and concepts do not grow out of actions, explorations, or images. Instead, the model or visual image simply but carefully "illustrates" the language or algorithm presented. As suggested earlier, the text materials could be used to summarize or remind students of previous learning, rather than lead it.

If one looks at the constructs of fractional numbers as measures, operators, ratios, or quotients, one might say that these constructs are ignored in these series. In particular, the only time one sees a fraction as the result of a division is in changing improper fractions to mixed numerals. Fractional numbers as quotient numbers are not seen in any informal way. The notion of $\frac{3}{4}$ as 3 replications of a quantity of $\frac{1}{4}$ yielding the same quantity as 3 divided into by 4 is unaddressed. The other three constructs, measure, ratio, or operator, never arise in consideration of common fractional numbers. There is some reference to decimal numbers as measures in both series. Decimal fractions are illustrated in terms of metric measures, but mathematical actions, such as operations, are not developed in this context.

It would not be expected that Grades 1–8 texts would develop the mathematics of rational numbers as a deductive logical system, although both series discuss this idea at the Grade 8 level. The Holt series does consider properties of fractional number sentences that could form a basis for the rational number system. Both also consider equation solving, particularly at Grades 7 and 8, in which fractional numbers are both solutions and coefficients in linear equations. Thus fractions as quotients, if not as elements of a quotient field, appear in symbolic form here.

In summary, it seems fair to characterize the focus of these text series to be on the technical symbolic knowledge or particularly the computational language of fractions. To the extent that intuitive means are used, images mainly illustrate a particular use of language, which itself is mainly standard mathematical symbolism. Both series attempt to give children lots of problems, some of which involve use of fractions. Especially as they involve symbolic patterns with fractions, these problems are imaginative and good.

The opening quote in this essay from McCulloch orients one to the mathematical and personal characteristics of mathematical knowing. To this one might add the role of the world on and in personal mathematics and a person's mathematical stance in the world. A mathematics curriculum should account for all of these things.

In terms of the mathematics of rational numbers, these text series take a narrow view—mathematics as a computational language based on whole numbers. Although it is unquestionably conservative to use old (whole number) language in new ways, if this is to be effective the user must have broad conceptual knowledge not emphasized here. There is a very limited interpretation or use of knowledge of persons as mathematical knowers. The relationship of this mathematics to the world is also taken narrowly— the world is mainly seen in a contrived way as an illustration of fractional number language and its use.

To experience the full power of rational number knowledge one must be able to operate with its symbols. Thus the fluent use of fractional language is a reasonable goal toward which these text series are striving. However, such language must be about something, in fact in light of the arguments of this chapter about a complex of things. Teachers who slavishly follow the content and methods of these texts might find their students exhibiting computational fluency at the expense of conceptual richness.

CONCLUDING REMARKS

There are three approaches to providing curriculum and instruction in fractional numbers for children, which go beyond the traditional disconnected fractional number sequence that sees the elements primarily as individual pieces of information or language or procedures to learn. The first approach is to reorganize and rebase such a traditional approach to fractional number instruction. In particular, curriculum and instruction should provide experience with dividable units and a nonstatic representation of $\frac{1}{n}$ through partitioning activities. This would be followed by a detailed sequence, centered on equivalence, for the various operations on fractions. Such an approach has been developed in detail in the Initial Fraction Sequence work described earlier. This approach has the advantage of not calling for a radical change in curriculum or instruction. But this approach also runs the risk of knowledge being reduced to a set of syntactic rules. Further, it treats fractions, for learning purposes, as almost a direct extension of whole number ideas. Such an approach has limited interconnectedness with other mathematics and with applications of fractions as measures or operators.

A second approach is to select a particular mathematical theory related to fractional number knowledge, to base instruction on this mathematical theory and in particular on its related applicational situations. Fractional numbers could be treated as measures or operators for instance. This approach sees mathematical knowledge as existing "out there," but prescribes a single coherent model as best for instructing children. This could also be related to the Hiebert–Wearne (Wearne & Hiebert, 1988) instruc-

tional scheme of attaching fraction symbols to particular object/actions
and building intuitive mathematical knowledge in such a setting. Although
evidence suggests learning with understanding can occur under such circumstances, children get a limited interpretation of fractional or rational
number knowledge. Measure interpretations are useful for quantitative
equivalence, addition, and a meaning of unit as one; on the other hand,
operators interpretations emphasize multiplicative equivalence, multiplication, and inverse/identity operators But curricularly, one approach is
weak where the other is strong.

The third approach is to see mathematics as the science of patterns
made by persons themselves. Fractional knowledge has complementary
pattern fields of measure, quotient, ratio, and operator. Children under this
approach need experience in using fractional language for all four intuitive
pattern settings and then in more formal pattern settings of rational number and quotient fields. There are four types of personal knowledge of
mathematical and fractional patterns: two informal, ethnomathematical
and intuitive mathematical patterns, and two more formal, technical symbolic and deductive patterns. In personal knowledge one's informal knowledge related to actions and objects would be embedded in one's formal
knowledge. This approach is deliberately congruent with a child moving
with any aspect of fractional number knowledge from exogenously driven
to endogenously created patterns of knowledge and understanding. There
is some research support that this approach does provide fractional number knowledge/understanding that is whole and connected in nature.

These three curriculum approaches previously described are related to
two general philosophical perspectives for mathematics and its curriculum
and instruction. One could consider fraction knowledge as existing "out
there" to be acquired by students. If so, the curriculum would be considered an ordered set of experiences for children with a wide variety of
aspects of fractions. Although such experiences would involve and relate to
whole number knowledge, fraction knowledge would be a separate domain
offering a child an opportunity to experience geometric, algebraic, and
infinite aspects of mathematics. One problem with this approach is that
knowledge could appear to the child as discrete and disconnected. Thus
instructional efforts would have to be made to provide settings in which a
child would connect fractional symbols to meaningful objects. Beyond that
the teacher and the curriculum would have to provide the opportunity for
the child to see that the alternative meanings of fractions are connected
through operations and properties of fractional numbers.

One could also consider fractional number knowledge as personal, built
up or constructed by the person. This approach would seem to suggest
fractional and later rational number knowledge as an organizing phenomenon in the world of the child or person. One problem with such a view is

that it, like the traditional view, could miss the variety of meanings and the semantic complexity of fraction knowledge. Fortunately, the "natural" activities of dividing up, and comparing and generating multiplicatively related quantities can be seen, and appear in the study of the actions of children doing them, to provide a basis for semantically rich and varied fractional knowledge. It would be necessary for a teacher to understand the patterns of growth from "natural" experiences to a semantically rich rational number knowledge. The teacher could not give such knowledge to students, but could point to rich experiences ahead for the student.

There has been extensive curriculum and instructional research that reflects both philosophical approaches. However, we still do not have a complete picture of rational number knowledge or how such knowledge is developed by young persons. Research, curriculum development, and instructional analysis to help provide this whole picture remain before us as researchers and teachers. Such work is critical, for it is only as a growing and consistently organized or organizing whole that fractional knowledge, like any other, becomes fully useful and powerful for a person.

REFERENCES

Bana, J. P., & Nelson, D. (1977). Some effects of distractions in nonverbal mathematics problems. *Alberta Journal of Educational Research, 23*(4), 268–279.

Bateson, G. (1979). *Mind and nature.* New York: Dutton.

Behr, M., Lesh, R., Post, T., & Silver, E. (1983). Rational number concepts. In R. Lesh & M. Landau (Eds.), *Acquisition of mathematics concepts and processes* (pp. 92–126). New York: Academic.

Behr, M., & Post, T. (1988). Teaching rational number and decimal concepts. In T. Post (Ed.), *Teaching mathematics in Grades K–8* (pp. 190–229). Boston: Allyn and Bacon.

Behr, M., Wachsmuth, I., Post, T., & Lesh, R. (1984). Order and equivalence of rational numbers: A clinical teaching experiment. *Journal for Research in Mathematics Education, 15*(4), 323–341.

Behr, M., Wachsmuth, I., & Post, T. (1985). Construct a sum: A measure of children's understanding of fraction size. *Journal for Research in Mathematics Education, 16*(2), 120–131.

Bergeron, J., & Herscovics, N. (1987). Unit fractions of a continuous whole. In J. Bergeron, N. Herscovics, & C. Kieren (Eds.), *Psychology of mathematics education, Psychology of Math Education, 11,*(1), 357–365.

Bigelow, J., Davis, G., & Hunting, R. (1989, April). *Some remarks on the homology and dynamics of rational number learning.* Paper presented at the research presession of the National Council of Teachers of Mathematics annual meeting, Orlando, FL.

Birkhoff, G., & MacLane, S. (1953). *A survey of modern algebra* (rev. ed.). New York: Macmillon.

Blakers, A. (1967). *Mathematical concepts of elementary measurement: Studies in mathematics* (Vol. 17). Palo Alto: School of Mathematics Study Group.

Brown, C., Carpenter, T., Kouba, V., Lindquist, M., Silver, E., & Swafford, J. (1988). Secondary school results for the fourth NAEP mathematics assessment: Algebra, geometry, mathematical methods and attitudes. *Mathematics Teacher, 81*(5), 337–347.

Burbank, I. K., Holmes, R., & Poce, C. (1982). *Houghton Mifflin mathematics* (Books 1–6). Markham, Ontario: Houghton Mifflin Canada.

Bye, M., & Sauer, R. (1980). *Holt mathematics system* (Books 1–8). Toronto: Holt, Rinehart, & Winston Canada.

Case, R., & Sandieson, R. (1988). A developmental approach to the identification and teaching of the central conceptual structures in mathematics and science in the the middle grades. In J. Hiebert & M. Behr (Eds.), *Number concepts and operations in the middle grades* (pp. 236–259). Reston, VA: The National Council of Teachers of Mathematics and Hillsdale, NJ: Lawrence Erlbaum Associates.

Cassirer, E. (1953). *The philosophy of symbolic forms: Language* (Vol. 1). New Haven, CT: Yale University Press.

Davis, P. J., & Hersh, R. (1986). *Descartes' dream: The world according to mathematics.* Boston: Harcourt Brace Jovanovich.

Detlefsen, M. (1986). *Hilbert's program: An essay on mathematical instrumentalism.* Dordrecht, Netherlands: D. Riedel.

Dienes, Z. (1971). *The elements of mathematics.* New York: Herder & Herder.

Figueras, O., Filloy, E., & Valdemoros, M. (1987). Some difficulties which observe the appropriation of the fraction concept. In J. Bergeron, N. Herscovics, & C. Kieren (Eds.), *Psychology of Mathematics Education, 11*(1), 366–372.

Freudenthal, H. (1983). *A didactical phenomenology of mathematics.* Dordrecht, Netherlands: D. Riedel.

Frye, N. (1981). *The great code.* Toronto: Academic Press.

Griesel, H. (1973). *Die neue mathematik fur lehrer und studenten.* [The new mathematics for teachers and students.] Hannover, W. Germany: Schroedel Verlag.

Harrison, D., Bye, M., & Brindley, S. (1981). *The Calgary junior high school mathematics project.* Edmonton: Government of Alberta.

Hart, K. (Ed.). (1981). *Children's understanding of mathematics.* London: John Murray.

Hart, K. (1988). Ratio and proportion. In J. Hiebert & M. Behr (Eds.), *Number concepts and operations in the middle grades* (pp. 198–219). Reston, VA: The National Council of Teachers of Mathematics and Hillsdale, NJ: Lawrence Erlbaum Associates.

Hasemann, K. (1985). On difficulties with fractions in German schools. In A. Bell, S. Kilpatrick, & R. Lowe (Eds.), *Research and theory in mathematics education* (pp. 31–38). Nottingham: Shell Centre for Mathematics Education/International Congress on Mathematics Education.

Hiebert, J., & Wearne, D. (1987). Cognitive effects of instruction designed to promote meaning for written mathematical sumbols. In J. Bergeron, N. Herscovics, & C. Kieran (Eds.), *Psychology of Mathematics Education, 11*(1), 391–398.

Hiebert, J., & Wearne, D. (1986). Procedures over concepts: The acquisition of decimal number knowledge. In J. Hiebert (Ed.), *Conceptual and procedural knowledge: The case of mathematics* (pp. 199–223). Hillsdale, NJ: Lawrence Erlbaum Associates.

Hoffer, A. (1983) Van Hiele-based research. In R. Lesh & M. Landau (Eds.), *Acquisition of Mathematics concepts and processes* (pp. 205–227). New York: Academic Press.

Hunting, R., & Sharpley, C. (in press). The fraction knowledge of preschool children. *Journal for Research in Mathematics Education.*

Hunting, R. (1987, April). *What does the last decade of rational number research offer the elementary teacher?* Paper presented at the annual meeting of the National Council of Teachers of Mathematics, Anaheim, CA.

Kerslake, D. (1986). *Fractions: Children's errors and strategies.* Windsor, England: National Foundation for Education Research, Nelson.

Kieren, T. E. (1976). On the mathematical, cognitive, and instructional foundations of rational numbers. In R. Lesh (Ed.), *Number and measurement* (pp. 101–144). Columbus, OH: ERIC/SMEAC.

Kieren, T. E., & Southwell, B. (1979). The development of children and adolescents of the construct of rational numbers as operators. *The Alberta Journal of Educational Research, 25*(4), pp. 22–30.

Kieren, T. E. (1980). The rational number construct—Its elements and mechanisms. In T. Kieren (Ed.), *Recent research on number learning* (pp. 32–55). Columbus, OH: ERIC/SMEAC.

Kieren, T. E. (1981). *The five faces of mathematical knowledge building.* Edmonton: Faculty of Education, University of Alberta.

Kieren, T. E. (1984). *The rational number thinking test* (1984 version). Edmonton: University of Alberta.

Kieren, T. E., Nelson, D., & Smith, G. (1985). Graphical algorithms in partitioning tasks. *The Journal of Mathematical Behavior, 4,* 25–36.

Kieren, T. (1986). Mathematical knowledge building: The contributions of ethnomathematical and intuitive knowledge. In G. Lappan & R. Evan (Eds.), *Proceedings of the eighth annual meeting of the North American chapter of the International Group for the Psychology of Mathematics Education* (pp. 14–20). East Lansing: PME-NA.

Kieren, T. E., & Behr, M. (1986). Fractions—rational numbers. In M. Carss (Ed.), *Proceedings of the Fifth International Congress on Mathematical Education* (pp. 179–180). Boston: Birkhauser.

Kieren, T. (1988). Personal knowledge of rational numbers: Its intuitive and formal development. In J. Hiebert & M. Behr (Eds.), *Number concepts and operations in the middle grades* (pp. 162–181). Reston, VA: The National Council of Teachers of Mathematics.

Kouba, V., Brown, C., Carpenter, T., Lindquist, M., Silver, E., & Swafford, J. (1988). Results of the fourth NAEP assessment of mathematics: Number, operations, and word problems. *Arithmetic Teacher, 35*(8), pp. 14–19.

Lampert, M. (1985). Mathematics learning in context: The voyage of the Mimi. *The Journal of Mathematical Behavior, 4*(2), 157–167.

Larson, C. N. (1987). Regions, number lines, and rulers as models for fractions. In J. C. Bergeron, N. Herscovics, & C. Kieran (Eds.), *Proceedings of the eleventh annual meeting of the International Group for the Psychology of Mathematics Education* (Vol. 1, pp. 398–404). Montreal: Psychology of Mathematics Education.

Leinhardt, G. (1988). Getting to know: Tracing students' mathematical knowledge from intuition to competence. *Educational Psychologist, 23*(2), 119–144.

Leinhardt, G., & Smith, D. (1985). Expertise in mathematics instruction: Subject matter knowledge. *Journal of Educational Psychology, 77*(3), 247.

Leinhardt, G., & Greeno, J. (1986). The cognitive skill of teaching. *Journal of Educational Psychology, 78*(2), pp. 75–95.

Lesh, R., Landau, M., & Hamilton, E. (1983). Conceptual models and applied problem solving research. In R. Lesh & M. Landau (Eds.), *Acquisition of mathematics concepts and processes* (pp. 264–344). New York: Academic Press.

Margenau, H. (1987). *The miracle of existance.* Boston and London: New Science Library, Shambhala.

Maturana, H., & Varela, F. (1980). *Autopoesis and cognition* (Boston University, Philosophy of Science Series, Vol. 42). Dordrect, Netherlands: D. Reidel.

McCulloch, W. (1963). *Embodiments of mind.* Cambridge: MIT Press.

Mellin-Olsen, S. (1987). *The politics of mathematics education.* Dordrect, Netherlands: D. Riedel.

Noelting, G. (1978). *Constructivism as a model for cognitive development and (eventually) learning.* Unpublished manuscript, University Laval, Quebec.

Noelting, G., & Gagne, L. (1980). The development and proportional reasoning and the ratio concept: Part I. Determination of stages. *Educational Studies in Mathematics, 11*(2), pp. 217–253.

Ohlsson, S. (1988). Mathematical meaning and applicational meaning in the semantics of fractions and related concepts. In J. Hiebert & M. Behr (Eds.), *Number concepts and operations in the middle grades* (pp. 55–92). Reston, VA: The National Council of Teachers of Mathematics and Hillsdale, NJ: Lawrence Erlbaum Associates.

Padberg, F. (1978). *Didaktek der bruchrechnung,* [Didactics of fractions]. Freiburg: Herder.

Padberg, F. (1985). What first—addition or multiplication of fractions? In A. Bell, J. Kilpatrick, & R. Lowe (Eds.), *Research and theory in maths education* (pp. 39–47). Nottingham, England: Shell Centre for Mathematics Education and International Congress on Mathematics Education.

Payne, J. (1976). Research on rational number learning. In R. Lesh (Ed.), *Number and measurement: Papers from a research conference* (pp. 145–188). Columbus, OH: ERIC/SMEAC.

Peck, D. M., & Jencks, S. M. (1981). Conceptual issues in the teaching and learning of fractions. *Journal for Research in Mathematics Education, 12*(5), 339–348.

Piaget, J. (1980). *Adaption and intelligence: Organic selection and phenocopy.* Chicago: University of Chicago Press.

Piaget, J., Inhelder, B., & Szeminska, A. (1960). *The child's conception of geometry.* New York: Basic.

Pirie, S. (1988). Understanding—Instrumental, relational, formal, intuitive. How do we know? *For the Learning of Mathematics, 8* (November), pp. 2–6.

Pothier, Y. (1981). *Partitioning: Construction of rational number in young children.* Unpublished doctoral dissertation, University of Alberta, Edmonton.

Pothier, Y., & Sawada, D. (1983). Partitioning: The emergence of rational number ideas in young children. *Journal for Research in Mathematics Education, 14,* 307–317.

Rahim, M., & Kieren, T. (1988). A preliminary report on the reliability and factorial validity of the rational number thinking test in the Republic of Trinidad and Tobago. In M. Behr, C. Lacampagne, & M. Wheeler (Eds.), *Proceedings of the tenth annual conference of the International Group for the Psychology of Mathematics Education—North American chapter* (pp. 114–120). De Kalb, IL: Northern Illinois University.

Rucker, R. (1987). *Mind tools.* Boston: Houghton Mifflin.

Sambo, A. (1980). *Transfer effects of measure concepts on the learning of fractional numbers.* Unpublished doctoral dissertation, University of Alberta, Edmonton.

Schwartz, J. L. (1988). Intensive quantity and referent transforming arithmetic operations. In J. Hiebert & M. Behr (Eds.), *Number concepts and operations in the middle grades* (pp. 41–52). Reston, VA: The National Council of Teachers of Mathematics and Hillsdale, NJ: Lawrence Erlbaum Associates.

Skemp, R. (1987). *The psychology of learning mathematics* (expanded American ed.). Hillsdale, NJ: Lawrence Erlbaum Associates.

Steffe, L., & von Glasersfeld, E. (1988). On the construction of the counting scheme. In L. Steffe & P. Cobb (Eds.), *Construction of arithmetical meanings and strategies* (pp. 10–31). New York: Springer-Verlag.

Streefland, L. (1984a). *How to teach fractions so as to be useful.* Utrecht, Netherlands: OW & OC.

Streefland, L. (1984b). *N*-Distractors as a source of failures in learning fractions. In B. Southwell, R. Eyland, M. Cooper, & K. Collis (Eds.), *Proceedings of the Eighth Annual International Conference for the Psychology of Mathematics Education* (pp. 142–152). Sydney: Mathematical Association of New South Wales.

Streefland, L. (1987). Free production of fraction monographs. In J. Bergeron, N. Herscovics, & C. Kieren (Eds.), *Psychology of Mathematics Education, 11*(1), 405–410.

Trivett, J. (1980). *And so on: New designs for teaching mathematics.* Calgary, Alberta, Canada: Detselig Enterprises Limited.

Vergnaud, G. (1983). Multiplicative structures. In R. Lesh & M. Landau (Eds.), *Acquisition of mathematics concepts and processes* (pp. 127–174). New York: Academic Press.

Vergnaud, G. (1988). Multiplicative structures. In J. Hiebert & M. Behr (Eds.), *Number concepts and operators in the middle grades* (pp. 141–161). Reston, VA: The National Council of Teachers of Mathematics and Hillsdale, NJ: Lawrence Erlbaum Associates.

Vinner, S., Hershkowitz, R., & Bruckheimer, M. (1981). Some cognitive factors as causes of mistakes in the addition of fractions. *Journal for Research in Mathematics Education, 12*(1), pp. 70–76.

Wales, B. (1984). *A study of children language use when solving partitioning problems: Grades two through four.* Unpublished master's thesis, University of Alberta, Edmonton.

Wearne, D., & Hiebert, J. (1983). Junior high school students' understanding of fractions. *School Science and Mathematics, 83,* 96–106.

Wearne, D., & Hiebert, J. (1988). Constructing and using meaning for mathematical symbols: The case of decimal fractions. In J. Hiebert & M. Behr (Eds.), *Number concepts and operations in the middle grades* (pp. 220–235). Reston, VA: The National Council of Teachers of Mathematics and Hillsdale, NJ: Lawrence Erlbaum Associates.

7

FROM PROTOQUANTITIES TO OPERATORS: BUILDING MATHEMATICAL COMPETENCE ON A FOUNDATION OF EVERYDAY KNOWLEDGE

Lauren B. Resnick
Learning Research and Development Center
University of Pittsburgh

Contents

Over the past decade, two lines of research on mathematics learning have produced apparently contradictory results. One has documented substantial amounts of mathematical knowledge on the part of young children and minimally schooled adults. The other has documented persistent and systematic difficulties that many children have in learning school mathematics. Both lines of work are independently convincing. Taken together, however, they seem to constitute a paradox. How can it be that mathematics is simultaneously so ubiquitous and fundamental that everyone seems to learn it, and so difficult that many seem never to master it? What kinds of discontinuities could be producing this misfit?

One possibility is that school mathematics teaching is failing to capture what children already know. By teaching a primarily symbolic form of mathematics detached from physical material and everyday experience, schools deprive children of the chance to use what they have learned informally to ground and constrain the new rules and procedures they are asked to master. This hypothesis underlies many proposals for using familiar problems and manipulatives in the elementary math classroom.

A quite different possibility is that the formal mathematics to be learned in school in fact requires concepts and ways of reasoning that do not develop informally. This hypothesis, less extensively explored up to now, suggests that explicit attention to developing concepts and ways of reasoning that are specifically mathematical is necessary. In fact, helping students develop forms of reasoning that do not occur in everyday life may be the primary *raison d'etre* of institutionalized schooling (cf. Scribner & Cole, 1981, for a parallel argument with respect to literacy).

Both hypotheses are plausible. Indeed, they are not mutually exclusive. If some aspects of mathematics learning proceed effectively in nonschool environments, surely it is a worthwhile venture to try to figure out what makes those environments so effective and even, perhaps, to mimic aspects of them in school. At the same time, it is important to ask what is *not* learned well in informal settings and to try to identify those aspects of mathematics learning that might proceed best in environments designed specifically for the purpose.

In this chapter, I first lay out the nature of informal, everyday mathematics knowledge and then develop in more detail the two hypotheses just mentioned concerning the sources of persistent difficulty in learning school mathematics. With these as background, I then develop an empirically grounded epistemological theory that I believe can account for differences between everyday and formal mathematics knowledge and describe a set of processes by which informal knowledge is transformed into formal mathematics. Finally, I consider what my analysis suggests for how elementary mathematics education might proceed. The arguments I develop are based on a multiyear program of research on the nature of children's informal mathematics knowledge and on a more recent project, developed in collaboration with Victoria Bill, a primary school teacher, that uses these research findings to design a radically changed classroom instructional program. This instructional program has also been heavily influenced by recent research and theory that challenge traditional views of knowledge, learning, and teaching and call for a reconceptualization of learning as apprenticeship (see Collins, Brown, & Newman, 1989; Lave, 1988, 1991) in a particular environment of practice.

ADDITIVE COMPOSITION: EARLY
AND UNIVERSAL MATHEMATICS KNOWLEDGE

Much of elementary arithmetic has as its conceptual base the fact that all numbers are additive compositions of other numbers. This compositional character of numbers provides an intuitive basis for understanding fundamental properties of the number system. These properties include commutativity and associativity of addition, equivalence classes of addition pairs, and complementarity of addition and subtraction (additive inverse). Children appreciate these properties at a surprisingly young age, as I document in this chapter. My evidence is drawn primarily from a series of studies of invented arithmetic performances by children. Challenged to solve problems for which they have no ready algorithms, children invent procedures that can be shown to apply implicitly the additive composition principle. Others have shown that similar reasoning takes place among minimally schooled adults carrying out arithmetic tasks as part of their daily work. Taken together, these two lines of research point to a body of mathematical knowledge that appears to be easily and, probably, universally acquired.

Permissions and Constraints in Arithmetic Procedures

The cases presented here are analyzed in terms of the permissions and constraints on number operations that the additive composition principle embodies. I can best illustrate the ways in which permissions and constraints interact to define a rule system, and the ways in which they derive from additive composition, by developing a justification for the standard subtraction-with-borrowing algorithm taught in American schools.

In multidigit subtraction, the goal of the entire process is to find a difference between two quantities, each of which is symbolized by a string of digits that conforms to the conventions of place value notation. Place value notation uses the additive composition principle to permit us to write an infinite set of natural numbers without needing an infinite number of distinguishable symbols. It does this by assigning a value to each position in an ordered string, so that an individual digit's values are determined by its position. This means that 324, for example, must be interpreted as a composition of 300 (itself a composition of 100 plus 100 plus 100) plus 20 (10 plus 10) plus 4 (1 plus 1 plus 1 plus 1) (see also Hiebert, this volume). Additive composition also justifies another permission that is central to the subtraction algorithm: the permission to calculate by partition. In doing a calculation, it is permissible to divide the quantities being operated on into any convenient parts, to operate on the parts, and to accumulate partial results. This allows subtraction to proceed column-by-column.

Calculation by partitioning is, however, subject to several constraints. In the case of subtraction, these constraints specify that (a) each part of the subtrahend (the bottom number) must be subtracted from a part of the minuend (the top number); (b) each part of the subtrahend may be subtracted only once (thus, each subtrahend part may be "touched" only once); (c) all of the subtrahend parts may be removed sequentially from the same minuend part (thus, some minuend parts may be touched several times, and others may not be touched at all); and (d) in summing the partial results, any minuend part that has not been touched must be treated as the result of a subtraction.[1]

In the course of calculating by partitioning, it may be convenient to recompose the parts. In the case of subtraction, such recomposing is done to avoid accumulating negative partial results. Thus, when the top number in a column is smaller than the bottom number in that column, one adds to the top number to make it larger. This is called *borrowing* or, in more modern school parlance, *regrouping*. Regrouping is permitted by the additive composition principle but is subject to an essential constraint: Addition in one column must be compensated by subtraction in another column, so that the total quantity in the top number is conserved. The constraint of conservation via compensation is necessary because the original goal of the algorithm is to find a difference. If either number is allowed to change in the course of calculation, the difference between the numbers would also change.

This kind of analysis of algorithms as interacting permissions and constraints allows us to give a new and more specific meaning to the idea of understanding rules and procedures. One understands a rule or procedure

---

[1]This is what children are taught in school as "bringing down" the top number in a column when the bottom of the column is empty; it is equivalent to subtracting 0 from each minuend part that has not otherwise been touched.

when one knows all constraints and permissions governing it. Greeno, Riley, and Gelman (1984) have shown that such analysis allows strong inferences about children's understanding of counting, even when the children are unable to verbalize explicitly their knowledge of constraints and permissions. Particularly strong inferences about understanding can be made when children construct variants of a standard procedure. In such cases, we can analyze the newly constructed procedures to see which constraints have been violated and which have been respected. If a constraint is violated, we can infer that the child either does not know the principle justifying the constraint or has failed to recognize its appropriateness to the procedure under construction. I analyze here several examples of such invented procedures.

Partitioning and Recombining in Calculation

A particularly rich set of examples of principle-based informal mathematical reasoning comes from a longitudinal case study we conducted of a single child's invented arithmetic (Resnick, 1986). We began to study Pitt's mathematical knowledge when he was 7 years, 5 months old.[2] At the time, he had just finished first grade. As will become clear, Pitt was unusually flexible in his arithmetic procedures. He enjoyed arithmetic and participated eagerly in our interviews. His value to us lay in the great variety of invented procedures that he used (because he was working somewhat ahead of his school instruction) and in the exceptionally articulate explanations and justifications he gave for what he was doing.

A first sign of Pitt's command of additive composition came when he was faced with the task of counting a large disorderly pile of monopoly money. (He was 7 years, 5 months old at the time.) After being shown the pile and told to count it any way he wanted, he was asked to say how he planned to do it. He responded:

> Well, I'm going to get the most first, then the second most. Like I'm going to get the five hundreds first . . . take out all the 500s and count those. Then take out all the 100s and count those. And add those two up. Then I'm going to go to the 50s, and the 20s, then the 5s, and the ones. . . .

Here, we see that Pitt knew that it was permissible to partition the task of counting, to count some portion of the money, then another portion, then combine his partial counts. This simple and primitive permission derives from the composite nature of numbers.

---

[2]This work was conducted in collaboration with Mary Means.

Pitt worked for awhile with his largest-first strategy but lost track of his counts somewhere in the 7000s. To help him remember (he was explicit about the reason), he did two things: wrote down some partial amounts and began to group the bills into round amounts before counting. He said:

> I'm going to put all the 500s in 5000s; then I'll add up all the 5000s. [Pitt put the $500 bills together in groups of ten and counted them by five thousands; he put $50 bills together in pairs and counted them by hundreds] . . . I'm making up all the 20s and trying to make 100 so I can just have 7200 . . . I'm doing it differently 'cause I have two twenties and a ten, makes fifty. Then I have fifty here. And adding that up makes one hundred. So now . . . 7300. . . . Well, 4 twenties. Now I'm going to get 2 tens since there's no more twenties, and that'll make one hundred . . . 7400.

In this sequence, Pitt showed great flexibility in composing his round groupings. This is evidence of his understanding that a number can be composed in many different ways and still be the same number. At the same age, Pitt's invented addition and subtraction procedures demonstrated additional aspects of his understanding of the compositional structure of numbers. In the following example, he is adding 152 and 149, which were stated to him orally:

> I would have the two 100s, which equals 200. Then I would have 50 and the 40, which equals 90. So I have 290. Then plus the 9 from the 49, and the 2 from the 52 equals 11. And then I add the 90 plus the 11 . . . equals 102. 102? 101. So I put 200 and the 101, which equals 301.

Here we see Pitt using the key permission, derived from the additive composition of number principle, of computation by partitioning. In this case, Pitt broke each of the numbers into three components. The three components were not a random choice but responded to the decimal structure of our system for naming and notating number. He then added convenient components and accumulated everything at the end.

The unorthodoxy of Pitt's methods with respect to what would be taught in school a year or so later can best be conveyed by the written work he did when asked to explain his method of adding 60 and 35. Pitt's writing appears in Fig. 7.1. His accompanying verbal description was:

> I would take away the 5 from the 35. Then I'd add the 60 and the 30, which equals 90. Then I'd bring back the 5 and put it on the 90, and it equals 95.

Here Pitt temporarily removed a component from one of the numbers in order to allow him to use a known "number fact" (60 + 30 = 90) but then brought back the removed component at the end. Thus, he knew that it is

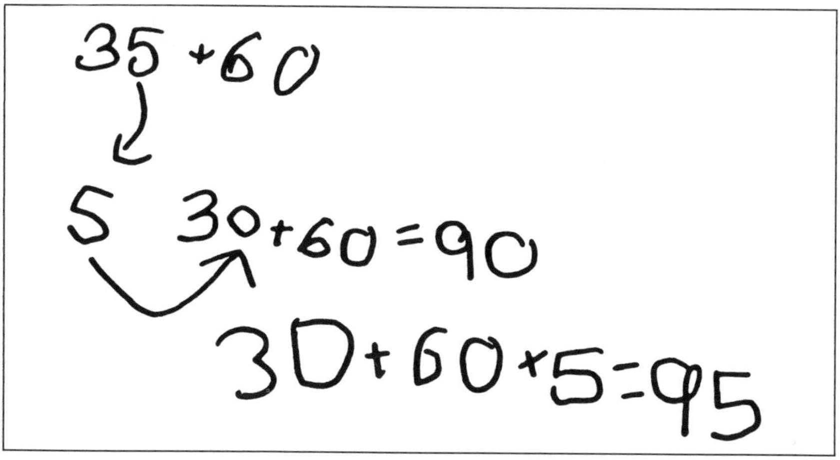

FIG. 7.1. Pitt's written display of his method for adding 60 and 35. From "The Development of Mathematical Intuition" by L. B. Resnick, 1986, *Perspectives on Intellectual Development: The Minnesota Symposium on Child Psychology* (p. 165) by M. Perlmutter (Ed.), Hillsdale, NJ: Lawrence Erlbaum Associates. Copyright 1986 by Lawrence Erlbaum Associates. Reprinted by permission.

permissible to change a number in the course of calculation, as long as a compensating change is made at another point, so that the total quantity is preserved.

Other examples of invented procedures that depend on the permission to decompose numbers, and of the accompanying compensation constraint, come from the work of children in a mathematics program in which there is no teaching of standard algorithms. Instead, children invent and discuss multiple solutions to problems (Resnick, Bill, & Lesgold, in press). Figure 7.2 shows several solutions developed by children for a single story problem. The notations are copied from notebooks kept by the children to record the procedures proposed and explained by each of several working groups in the classroom. The class first developed an estimated answer— not enough barrettes. They were then asked by the teacher exactly how many more barrettes would be needed. The additive composition principle came into play in the different ways in which the children interpreted the problem. Group 1 interpreted the problem as a missing addend addition problem, $36 + \_ = 95$. Groups 2 and 4 interpreted it as a subtraction problem, $95 - 36 = \_$, in Groups 2's notation. The children's ability to accept the two interpretations as equivalent depends on their appreciation of the property of complementarity of addition and subtraction. This property, as I show later, derives from an interpretation of numbers as parts (additive compositions) of other numbers.

The additive composition principle also came into play in the way chil-

> **Mary told her friend Tonya that she would give her 95 barrettes. Mary had 4 bags of barrettes and each bag had 9 barrettes. Does Mary have enough barrettes?**

The class first developed an estimated answer. Then they were asked, "How many more does she need?" The solutions below were generated by different class groups.

Group 1 first solved for the number of barrettes by repeated addition. Then they decomposed 4 x 9 into 2 x 9 plus 2 x 9. Then they set up a missing addend problem, 36 + 59, which they solved by a combination of estimation and correction.

Group 2 set up a subtraction equation and then developed a solution that used a negative partial result.

Group 4 began with total number of barrettes needed and subtracted out the successive bags of 9.

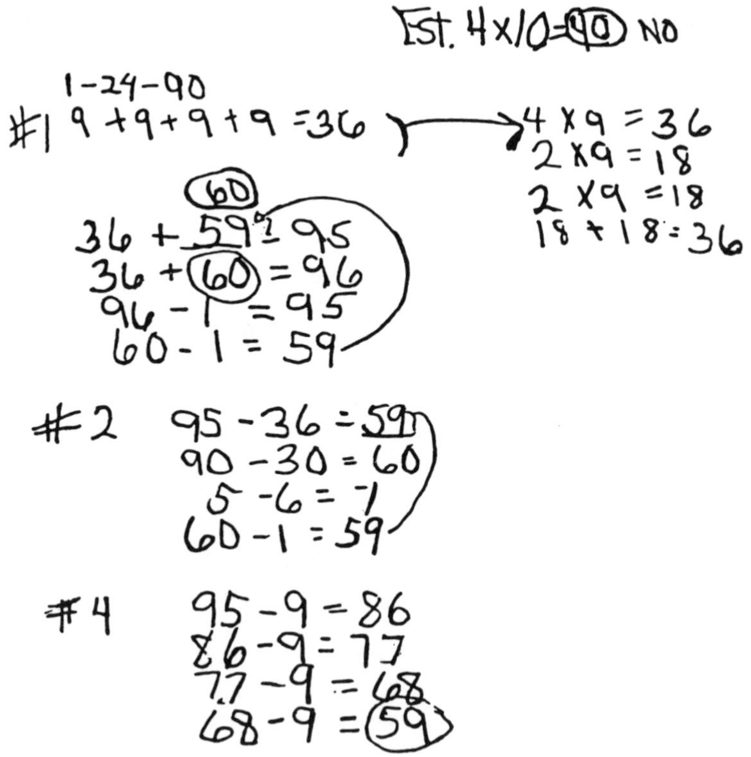

Est. 4 x 10 = 90 NO

1-24-90

#1 9 + 9 + 9 + 9 = 36 ⟶ 4 x 9 = 36
2 x 9 = 18
2 x 9 = 18
18 + 18 = 36

60
36 + 59 = 95
36 + 60 = 96
96 - 1 = 95
60 - 1 = 59

#2 95 - 36 = 59
90 - 30 = 60
5 - 6 = -1
60 - 1 = 59

#4 95 - 9 = 86
86 - 9 = 77
77 - 9 = 68
68 - 9 = 59

FIG. 7.2. A second-grade problem and several solutions. From "Developing Thinking Abilities in Arithmetic Class" by L. B. Resnick, with V. Bill and S. Lesgold, in A. Demetriou, M. Shayer, and A. Efklides (Eds.), *The Modern Theories of Cognitive Development Go to School* (in press), London: Routledge. Copyright by Routledge. Reprinted by permission.

dren performed the computations. Group 1 first found the number of bar-rettes by repeated addition and then checked this result by a decomposi-tion of 4×9 into $(2 \times 9) + (2 \times 9)$. This decomposition depends on an implicit understanding of the property of distribution. We also see the compensation constraint at work in Group 1's solution. They solved their missing addend problem using an estimation procedure in which they tried adding a round amount, 60, to 36. This yielded 96, 1 more than the 95 specified in the equation they had written. They therefore subtracted 1 from 60, yielding their final answer of 59. Group 2 showed an even more sophisticated understanding of decomposition, for they included a nega-tive partial amount in their computation. Using a place value decomposi-tion permission, they avoided regrouping by noting -1 as the result of $5 - 6$. They then combined the two partial results, 60 and -1, to yield the answer of 59.

Ginsburg and his colleagues (Ginsburg, 1982; Ginsburg & Allardice, 1984; Ginsburg & Russell, 1981) have documented similar decomposition methods of doing computation—all involving procedures quite different from school-taught algorithms—in American children, including many from socially disfavored families or labeled in school as mathematically delayed. Furthermore, the same kinds of procedures dominate in the per-formances of minimally schooled children and adults carrying out the arithmetic computations associated with their everyday work (e.g., Car-raher, 1990; Carraher, Carraher, & Schliemann, 1985; Ginsburg & Allardice, 1984; Ginsburg, Posner, & Russell, 1981). For example, Schliemann and Acioly (1989) studied the methods used by lottery ticket vendors in north-eastern Brazil. They found that the vendors often calculated amounts owed for particular bets by methods of partitioning and grouping. Partitioning methods were similar to those used by Group 2 in Fig. 7.2, except that the partitions were not always based on place value decomposition. That is, the quantities involved were partitioned into subtotals, necessary opera-tions were performed on these subtotals, and the partial results were then reunited. For example, a bookie with 5 years of school experience arrived at the price for a complex bet as follows:

> Because I know that [the bet] for 1 cruzeiro . . . makes 240. [The bet requires accumulating individual bets on 240 different digits.] Since it was 1 and 50 [The customer wanted to bet 1 cruzeiro 50 on each digit], and 50 is half of 1, this makes 120 more. Then you add. This makes 360.

Grouping methods observed were more like those of Group 4 in Fig. 7.2. That is, quantities were operated on iteratively until the desired result was reached. For example, here is a bookie's calculation of the price of a two-part bet:

On the thousands [one part of the bet] you have 16, because 4, 8, 12, 16. On the hundred [the second part of the bet] you have [pause] 28 + 28 makes 56, and 56 plus 56 makes 112. 112 plus 16 makes 128.

Similar partitioning and grouping procedures have been reported by Scribner (1984) for delivery and warehouse workers in an American dairy and by Carraher et al. (1985) for street vendors.

Commutativity and Associativity

Many of the partitioning solutions discussed above involved implicit appreciation of the properties of commutativity and associativity of addition. Commutativity and associativity are distinct properties in number theory, but children appear to understand them as a single permission to combine numbers in any order. Again we can turn to Pitt, our enthusiastic longitudinal participant, for an explicit verbalization. For Pitt, commutativity and associativity of addition were permissions, rooted in additive composition, that seemed self-evident. When (at 7 years, 7 months) he was asked to add 45 and 11, and then immediately afterward 11 and 45, he simply repeated his first answer and said, "They're the same numbers, so they have to equal the same thing." Commutativity, in other words, was not a special law for Pitt. It derived from the same principle that allowed him to partition addition problems in different ways but still get the same answer, because, in his words, he "used all the numbers . . . that were in the adding problem but not in the same order."

Children much younger than Pitt, preschoolers who still perform addition by counting, show evidence of implicitly understanding the permission to commute when adding. When given addition problems to solve, preschoolers and kindergarten children know that they should combine the objects in two sets and then count the combined sets. If problems are given verbally, they will first count out the number of objects in each of the sets separately and then recount the combined set. Fuson (1988, this volume) and Carpenter and Moser (1984) provide a nice description of this process, called *count-all.* A more sophisticated procedure, *count-on,* starts with the number in the first set and counts on from there, with the number of counts equal to the number in the second set. In this procedure, 3 and 5 would be added by saying, "three . . . four, five, six, seven, eight." Counting on requires some way of mentally keeping track of how many counts have been made. The number of counts needed and, thus, the difficulty of keeping track of counts can be reduced by applying the commutativity permission. Using this procedure, known as the MIN procedure because the number of counts is equal to the smaller of the two addends, 3 and 5 would be added by saying, "five . . . six, seven eight." Groen and Resnick (1977) showed that children as young as kindergarten age invented the MIN procedure, thus providing evidence that children implicitly appreciate the commutativity permission.

Resnick and Omanson (1987) reported a sophisticated implicit application of the associativity property by second and third graders in the context of another invented procedure for mental addition. Using a mixture of reaction time and interview data, we showed that several children added problems such as 23 + 8 by decomposing 23, yielding (20 + 3) + 8, and then reconfiguring the problem to (20 + 8) + 3. Because (20 + 8) could be recombined to 28 very quickly on the basis of place value knowledge, this allowed them to apply a simple counting-on solution: "twenty-eight . . . twenty-nine, thirty, thirty-one."

Equivalence Classes of Addition Pairs

Compensation, which children initially understand as a constraint on the decompositions and recompositions permitted by the additive composition principle, plays a special role in developing concepts of equivalence. Once again, Pitt provides a particularly articulate expression of children's early thinking about equivalence classes. At 7 years, 7 months, he was asked how 23 + 41 (written vertically on paper) could be rewritten so that it would still equal 64. He first said 24 + 40 and then continued:

> *I'm going one less than 40 and this one more . . . 25 plus 39.* Tell me what you're doing now to get that. *I'm just having one go lower; take one away and put it on the other. . . . I'm taking the 3* [from 23] *away and making that 2, and putting it on the 41 to make it 42. Like that, I was going lower, lower, higher, higher.* Okay, you gave me three examples of how you could change the numbers. Now why do all those numbers equal the same amount? *Because this is taking some away from one number and putting it on the other number.* And that's okay to do? *Yes.* Why is that okay to do? *Why not?* Well, can you give me a reason? *No, anyone can do that. . . . Because you still have the same amount. You're keeping that but putting that on something else. . . . You're not just taking it away.*

Here Pitt demonstrated his understanding that one can think of the original numbers, 23 and 41, as composite parts of the larger number, 64, and that one is free to recompose the 64. Furthermore, he showed that he knew that one can conserve the whole by compensating a reduction in one of the parts with an increase in the other part. He also expressed verbally a critical constraint on recompositions: It is permissible to move part of a number to another number but not simply to "[take] it away." This is the heart of the compensation constraint on recompositions: To maintain equivalence, one must compensate changes made in one part of a number with equal changes in another part.

At an even younger age, another child we have studied extensively used his knowledge of compensation and equivalence to invent an efficient procedure for solving problems of the form, "If you have six marbles and I have four, what could we do to each have the same number?" (Resnick, 1986).[3] There are three basic methods for solving this problem. In the simplest method, which we called *buy/sell,* following David's (our case study child's) language, the larger set is diminished or the smaller increased by the difference between the two sets. In the second method, *share,* the objects in the two sets are (mentally) "put in the middle" and then each person takes half. In the third method, the most complex and the object of our microgenetic study, enough objects are transferred from the larger to the smaller set to make the two sets equivalent. This is called *transfer.*

David, first interviewed at 6 years, 2 months, had full mastery of buy/sell and share, even when the problems involved rather large numbers. Transfer was demonstrated to him by the interviewer in a second interview a few weeks later. He clearly understood the goal of direct transfer. Further, if a number to be transferred was proposed to him, he could calculate its consequences for both sets and decide whether or not it met the goal of equalizing the sets. However, he could not himself generate the number of objects to be transferred. David's early ability to grasp the *goal* of directly transferring objects from one set to another, together with his ability to evaluate the effects of a proposed transfer, allows us to attribute to him a basic schema for transfer that might be represented graphically as shown in Fig. 7.3. This schema includes knowledge that one can think of the two initial sets as parts of a whole superset and that one can repartition the superset so that each part contains the same number. It also includes knowledge that one can move elements of the larger set into the smaller set and that this movement will make the large set smaller and the small set larger. Thus, although David could not yet do all of the numerical arithmetic necessary, he understood both the permission to repartition and the constraint of maintaining equivalence.

David's gradual acquisition of the full transfer strategy over a 10-month period constituted the main focus of the case study. Initially, David could only guess at what number to move from the large to the small set. However, his guesses never exceeded the difference between the two sets. We can conclude, therefore, that David understood that he must move the

---

[3]This work was done in collaboration with Terry Greene.

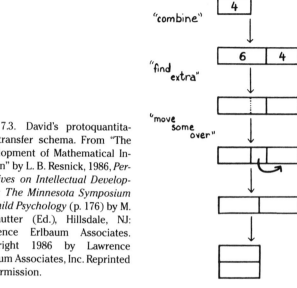

FIG. 7.3. David's protoquantitative transfer schema. From "The
Development of Mathematical Intuition" by L. B. Resnick, 1986, *Perspectives on Intellectual Development: The Minnesota Symposium
on Child Psychology* (p. 176) by M.
Perlmutter (Ed.), Hillsdale, NJ:
Lawrence Erlbaum Associates.
Copyright 1986 by Lawrence
Erlbaum Associates, Inc. Reprinted
by permission.

difference amount or some part of it over to the smaller set. During the 10
months, David gradually quantified his transfer schema, eventually arriving
at a systematic rule of transferring half the difference between the two sets.

Many other examples of children's appreciation of the compensation
constraint have appeared in our studies. I have already mentioned its role in
the estimation-based solution of Group 2 in Fig. 7.2 and in the justification
for regrouping in conventional multidigit addition and subtraction algorithms. In an instructional experiment aimed at helping children overcome the tendency to interpret the rules of written subtraction entirely in
terms of rules for manipulating symbols, without reference to the quantities
exchanged in the course of borrowing, Resnick and Omanson (1987) focused
children's attention on the quantities removed from or added to columns by
decrement and increment marks. After such instruction, many children
constructed explanations of the subtraction algorithm in terms of compensating additions to one column and subtractions from another. For example,
one child described what she had done when she produced the notation,
$^2\!3\ ^9\!0\ ^9\!0\ ^1\!2$, as taking 1000 from the 3 and distributing it to the other columns:
900 to the hundreds column, and 100 to the tens plus the ones columns,
broken up into 90 and 10. Because the instruction never directly discussed
parts and wholes or the idea of conserving a quantity while redistributing its
parts, it seems appropriate to conclude that the children who constructed

these explanations already had a compensation constraint available that they used to interpret the scratch marks of written borrowing as soon as their attention was focused on the quantities to which the marks referred.

Perhaps the most systematic study to date of children's understanding of equivalence and compensation constraints is that of Putnam, deBettencourt, and Leinhardt (1990). They asked third-grade students to watch puppets demonstrate "derived fact strategies" for addition and subtraction, to complete the calculations, and then to justify them. Derived fact strategies transform presented problems into problems that are easy to solve, because they use well-known addition and subtraction facts. The transformations in one number require compensating transformations in another. For example, 3 + 4 can be transformed to (3 + 3) + 1 to allow use of the familiar doubles fact. In the transformation, 1 is subtracted from the 4 but then added back to the result. In another case, 7 + 9 can be transformed to 8 + 8. In this case, 1 is subtracted from 9 and added to 7 in order to preserve the whole. Table 7.1 shows the full set of transformation and compensation rules that could be used to justify the derived fact strategies they studied. They found that 50% to 60% of the third graders interviewed could explicitly justify addition-derived fact strategies with verbalizations expressing these rules. Many more could complete the strategies and give partial explanations, perhaps indicating a more implicit appreciation of the rules. Subtraction-derived fact strategies were much more difficult for the children to justify, with only 10% to 20% providing complete, explicit justifications.

Additive Inverse: Complementarity
of Addition and Subtraction

The examples already considered include several cases in which the additive inverse property was implicitly applied. For example, the second-grade class whose work is shown in Fig. 7.2 recognized as equivalent two different interpretations of the same story problem: one an unknown addend addition interpretation, the other a subtraction interpretation. More systematic evidence of children's understanding of the additive inverse principle comes from research on the mental counting procedures young children use to solve problems presented as numerical subtraction problems. Several studies (e.g., Svenson & Hedenborg, 1979; Woods, Resnick, & Groen, 1975) have shown that, starting at about age 7, children figure out the answer to these problems by either counting down from the larger number or counting up from the smaller number, whichever requires the fewest counts. Thus, children do the problem "9 − 2" by counting down: "nine . . .

TABLE 7.1
Constraint/Transformation Productions

Transformation	Both Parts Known (Addition)		Whole and One Part Known (Subtraction)	
Change-part-and-part				
Increase in PART-X	CT1	IF PART-X → PART-X + n PART-Y → PART-Y − n THEN WHOLE → WHOLE	CT2	IF PART-X → PART-X + n WHOLE → WHOLE THEN PART-Y → PART-Y − n
Decrease in PART-X	CT3	IF PART-X → PART-X − n PART-Y → PART-Y + n THEN WHOLE → WHOLE	CT4	IF PART-X → PART-X − n WHOLE → WHOLE THEN PART-Y → PART-Y + n
Change-part-and-whole				
Increase in PART-X	CT5	IF PART-X → PART-X + n PART-Y → PART-Y THEN WHOLE → WHOLE + n	CT6	IF PART-X → PART-X + n WHOLE → WHOLE + n THEN PART-Y → PART-Y
Decrease in PART-X	CT7	IF PART-X → PART-X − n PART-Y → PART-Y THEN WHOLE → WHOLE − n	CT8	IF PART-X → PART-X − n WHOLE → WHOLE − n THEN PART-Y → PART-Y
No change in PART-X		—	CT9	IF PART-X → PART-X WHOLE → WHOLE + n THEN PART-Y → PART-Y + n
		—	CT10	IF PART-X → PART-X WHOLE → WHOLE − n THEN PART-Y → PART-Y − n

Note. From "Understanding of derived-fact strategies by addition and subtraction" by R. T. Putnam, L. U. deBettencourt, and G. Leinhardt, 1990, *Cognition and Instruction, 7*(3), p. 276. Copyright 1990 by Lawrence Erlbaum Associates, Inc. Reprinted by permission.

eight, seven . . . the answer is seven"; but they will do the problem, 9 − 7, by counting up: "seven . . . eight, nine . . . the answer is two." This *choice* procedure, as it has become known, has been inferred from a combination of interview protocols and the pattern of reaction times for subtraction problems with different numbers.

Applying the choice procedure means that children must convert some subtraction problems into addend-unknown addition problems; for example, 9 − 7 = _ converts to 7 + _ = 9. Children's willingness to treat these two problems as equivalent means that, at least implicitly, they understand the additive inverse property. This property, in turn, depends on an additive composition interpretation of the problem in which 9 is understood to be a whole that is decomposed into two parts, one of which is 7. In this interpretation, the problem becomes finding the other part, and it does not matter whether one subtracts a known part from the whole to find it or starts with the part and determines how much more is needed to make up the whole.

Multiplication and Division Interpreted Additively

One further point is needed to complete the story of the primacy of additive composition in children's early understanding of arithmetic. This is the tendency of children to prefer additive composition interpretations even of situations that adults might understand in terms of multiplicative relations between numbers. Again, Pitt provides a particularly compelling example. Remember that he thought commutativity of addition so self-evident that he found it somewhat difficult to provide a justification. Commutativity of *multiplication*, however, was not so self-evident for him; it required an explanation. Although he freely used the commutativity property in his multiplication calculations, he did not claim that multiplier and multiplicand could be inverted just because they are the same numbers. Instead, he justified the commutativity of multiplication in terms of *additive* compositions:

What's two times three? *Six.* How did you get that? *Well, two threes . . . one three is three; one more equals six.* Okay, what's three times two? *Six.* Anything interesting about that? *They each equal six, and they're different numbers. . . . I'll tell you why that happens. . . . Two has more ways; well, it has more adds . . . like two has more twos, but it's a lower number. Three has less threes but it's a higher number. . . .* Alright, when you multiply three times two, how many adds are there? *Three . . . And in the other one there's two. But the two—that's two threes—but the other one is three twos, 'cause twos are littler than threes but two has more . . . more adds, and then the three has less adds but it's a higher number.*

Ginsburg (1977) provided a number of examples of children's invented solutions to problems involving multiplication, division, and fractions. In virtually every case, children relied on knowledge of *additive* properties of number to find solutions, as they did in the following:

6×8. Okay why don't you write that down? 6×8 is . . . [wrote down $6 + 6 + 6 + 6 + 6 + 6 + 6 + 6$]. O.K. Do you expect to get the same answer from this problem [referring to the $6 + 6$, etc.] as this problem [referring to the 6×8]? *48.* O.K. How did you get 48? *Well I did four sixes . . . I mean I added them together. And then I added; the answer was 24 . . . so I added them together, and that was 48* [wrote down $24 + 24 = 48$]. (Ginsburg, 1977, p. 99)

How many are half of these? *15.* Can you prove that? Can you convince me it's true. *I don't think so.* O.K. How many is a quarter of these blocks? One fourth? That might be too tough. I won't ask you that. *Wait . . . 5 and $\frac{1}{2}$ . . . 7 and $\frac{1}{2}$.* Very good. Now tell me how you got 7 and $\frac{1}{2}$. *I did 8 and 8 is 16, and so that's just one more, so it would be $7\frac{1}{2}$.* (Ginsburg, 1977, p. 102.)

A further example of the tendency to prefer additive over multiplicative solutions comes from a study of children who work as street vendors in Recife, Brazil:

How much is one coconut? 35. I'd like ten. How much is that? [Pause] *Three will be 105; with three more, that will be 210.* [Pause] *I need four more. That is* . . . [Pause] *315.* . . . I think it is 350. (Carraher et al., 1985, p. 23).

EVIDENCE OF SYSTEMATIC DIFFICULTY IN LEARNING SCHOOL MATHEMATICS

The evidence just assembled seems to fly in the face of common experience with the difficulties of mathematics learning. It suggests that mathematical ideas based on additive composition are accessible to children and may be universally mastered, even by people with little or no schooling. Yet many children have a great deal of difficulty learning school mathematics. The phenomenon of math anxiety—extreme lack of confidence in one's ability to cope with mathematics—is familiar in virtually all highly educated societies. Further, many who proceed at accepted rates in standard mathematics instruction have little taste for it and seem unable to use their knowledge flexibly and creatively. Why should strong and reliable intuitions of the kind documented for young children and unschooled people not be sustained in school mathematics learning?

I explore here the two hypotheses mentioned in my introduction. One is that the focus in school on formal symbol manipulation discourages children from bringing their developed intuitions to bear on school mathematics learning. I call this the *syntax-semantics* hypothesis. The second hypothesis is that there is an epistemological discontinuity between informal mathematics rooted in everyday behavior and the kind of mathematical reasoning sought in school. That is, because formal school mathematics calls for reasoning about abstract entities—for example, numbers, operators, functions—that cannot be directly experienced in the physical world, mathematical competence "on the streets" may do little to prepare children for formal mathematics participation. I call this the *abstract entities* hypothesis.

The Syntax-Semantics Hypothesis

A recurrent finding in studies of arithmetic learning is that children who are having difficulty with arithmetic often use systematic routines that produce wrong answers. This observation has been made repeatedly over the years by researchers concerned with mathematics education, and several studies have attempted to describe the most common errors. Systematic procedural errors have been documented for many topics in school arithmetic (e.g., Brown & Burton, 1978; Buswell, 1926; Cox, 1975; Hiebert & Wearne, 1985; Sackur-Grisvard & Leonard, 1985; Young & O'Shea, 1981) and for algebra (e.g., Matz, 1982; Sleeman, 1984). Investigation of *buggy algorithms* and *malrules* by cognitive scientists has yielded automated diagnostic programs capable of reliably detecting the particular errorful algorithms used by a child on the basis of responses to a very small but carefully selected set of problems (e.g., Brown & Burton, 1978; Burton, 1982). Formal theories of the reasoning processes by which children invent incorrect procedures have also been constructed (e.g., Brown & VanLehn, 1980, 1982; VanLehn, 1990). All of these studies point to the conclusion that systematic errors result from applying intelligent forms of reasoning, such as generate-and-test problem solving heuristics, to a knowledge base devoid of representations of quantity and filled only with rules for operating on symbols. Because reasoners do not represent quantities, they often cannot recognize and do not apply mathematical principles derived from knowledge of the additive composition of quantities when doing school mathematics.

Some examples of buggy procedures and their analyses will help to make clear what is meant. The domain that has received the most careful analysis is written subtraction with borrowing (Brown & VanLehn, 1982; Burton, 1982; VanLehn 1990). A finite number of bugs, which in various combinations make up several dozen buggy algorithms, has been identified for subtraction. Here are two of the most common bugs:

Borrow-From-Zero. When borrowing from a column whose top digit is 0, the student writes 9 but does not continue borrowing from the column to the left of the zero.

$$
\begin{array}{r}
6\,^9\!\emptyset_1 2 \\
-4\ 3\ 7 \\
\hline
2\ 6\ 5
\end{array}
\qquad
\begin{array}{r}
8\,^9\!\emptyset_1 2 \\
-3\ 9\ 6 \\
\hline
5\ 0\ 6
\end{array}
$$

Borrow-Across-Zero. When the student needs to borrow from a column whose top digit is 0, he skips that column and borrows from the next one. (This bug requires a special "rule" for subtracting from 0: either $0 - N = N$ or $0 - N = 0$.)

$$
\begin{array}{r}
^5\!\emptyset\ 0\ 2 \\
-3\ 2\ 7 \\
\hline
2\ 2\ 5
\end{array}
\qquad
\begin{array}{r}
^7\!\emptyset\ 0_1 4 \\
-4\ 5\ 6 \\
\hline
3\ 0\ 8
\end{array}
$$

These examples show that the results of buggy calculations tend to look right (cf. Davis, 1984, on "visually moderated sequences"). They also tend to obey a large number of the important rules for manipulating symbols in written calculation: There is only one digit per column; all columns are filled; there are increment marks in some columns with (usually) decrements to their left, and so forth. The buggy algorithms seem to be orderly and reasonable responses to problem situations. On the other hand, if we look beyond the symbol manipulation rules to what the symbols represent, the buggy algorithms look much less sensible. Each of the bugs violates fundamental mathematical principles (Resnick, 1982).

For example, *Borrow-From-Zero* looks reasonable at first glance, because it respects the requirement that in a borrow there must be a crossed-out and rewritten numeral to the left of the column that is incremented. It also respects the surface rules for the special case of zero, where the rewritten number is always 9. However, the bug violates the fundamental constraint that the total quantity in the top number must be conserved during a borrow. Interpreted semantically (that is, in terms of quantities rather than simply as manipulations on symbols), a total of 100 has been added: 10 to the tens column and 90 to the hundreds column. Similarly, *Borrow-Across-Zero* respects the syntactic rules for symbol manipulation requiring that a small 1 be written in the column that is incremented and that a nonzero column to the left be decremented. Like the previous bug, however, it violates the constraint of conserving the top quantity. In this case, 100 is removed from the hundreds column, but only 10 is returned to the units column.

In these two bugs, as in all of the others observed for subtraction, constraints imposed by the quantitative meaning of the symbols (the semantics) are dropped, but constraints derived from the rules of symbol manipulation (the syntax) are retained. The same separation of syntax from its underlying semantics seems to be the case for systematic errors in other parts of mathematics, although the particular forms, of course, vary. For example, Matz (1982) has argued that many algebra errors can be attributed to a process of extrapolating new rules from "prototype rules." An example appears in Fig. 7.4. The initial rule is the distribution law as it is typically taught in beginners' algebra courses. From this correct rule a prototype is created by generalizing over the operator signs. From this prototype, new, incorrect distribution rules can be constructed by substituting specific operations for the operator placeholders in the prototype. As for the buggy subtraction rules, there is no representation of the quantities and relationships involved in the algebra expression or its transformation. Instead, the malrule results from deformation of rules of symbol manipulation.

Resnick, Cauzinille-Marmeche, and Mathieu (1987) explicitly pitted syntactic versus semantic interpretations of algebra expressions in a study in which French children between 11 and 14 years of age made judgments about the equivalence of algebraic and numerical expressions. For exam-

1. The correct rule as taught:

$$a \times (b + c) = (a \times b) + (a \times c)$$

2. Prototype created by generalizing over operator signs:

$$a \,\square\, (b \,\triangle\, c) = (a \,\square\, b) \,\triangle\, (a \,\square\, c)$$

3. Incorrect rules created from the prototype:

$$a + (b \times c) = (a + b) \times (a + c)$$
$$\sqrt{b + c} = \sqrt{b} + \sqrt{c}$$

FIG. 7.4.   The invention of an algebra malrule. From "Understanding Algebra" by L. B. Resnick, E. Cauzinille-Marmeche, and J. Mathieu, 1987, *Cognitive Processes in Mathematics* (p. 175), by J. A. Sloboda and D. Rogers (Eds.), Oxford: Clarendon Press. Copyright 1987 by Clarendon Press. Reprinted by permission.

ple, several types of items provided opportunities for children to express knowledge of a principle termed *composition of quantity inside parentheses*. This principle expresses the fact that the two terms inside parentheses in an expression such as $a - (b + c)$ are the parts of a single whole quantity and that this whole quantity is to be subtracted from the starting quantity, a. This principle can be used to explain the sign-change rules for removing parentheses. We asked children whether pairs of expressions such as $a - (b + c)/(a - b) + c$; $a + (b - c)/(a + b) - c$; and $(a - b) - c/a - (b - c)$ were equivalent or not, and why. Children predominantly used rules they had learned in school, or deformations of these rules, to make the judgments. One common error was to focus preemptively on parentheses, claiming that, if the material inside parentheses was different, two expressions could not be the same. This led to judgments such as $a + (b - c) \neq (a + b) - c$. This malrule probably results from an intrusion into the algebraic system of a rule for numerical expressions that calls for operating inside parentheses first.

A second common parentheses error seemed to derive from deformation of an algebraic transformation rule rather than from an intrusion of a calculation rule. This malrule claimed that the placement of parentheses was irrelevant, as long as the letters and signs retained their positions. Thus, $a - (b - c)$ was judged equivalent to $(a - b) - c$. Some children justified this equivalence by calling on the formal rule of associativity, misapplying it to subtraction. Another purely formal error was to apply the law of commutativity to subparts of an expression that were not enclosed in parentheses and thus did not warrant being treated as a separate quantity. For example, $a - b + c$ and $a - c + b$ were judged equivalent because $b + c$ commutes to $c + b$.

Another domain in which systematic errors have been documented and analyzed is decimal fractions (Hiebert & Wearne, 1985; Sackur-Grisvard & Leonard, 1985; see also Hiebert, this volume). Following up on that earlier work, Resnick and colleagues (1989) showed that the errorful rules for comparing decimal fractions could be classified into two basic categories. One class of errors applied a whole-number rule in which rules for comparing whole numbers were incorrectly applied to the fractional part of a number. Children applying this rule would consistently judge as larger the decimal number with more digits. Thus, they judged 4.63 to be greater than 4.8, 0.36 to be greater than 0.5, and 0.100 to be greater than 0.25, giving reasons such as, "63 is bigger than 8." Children making the second class of errors consistently judged as larger the decimal number with *less* digits, yielding judgments such as 4.45 > 4.4502 and 2.35 > 2.305. We called this the *fraction rule* error, because it resulted from children's efforts to integrate knowledge about fractional parts and ordinary fraction notation with their incomplete knowledge of the decimal notation system. These children knew that if a number is divided into more parts, the parts are smaller—correct semantic knowledge about quantities. They also knew another correct piece of semantic knowledge: that a number cut into thousandths has more parts than one cut into hundredths, which in turn has more parts than one cut into tenths. So they judged a number that had thousandths or ten thousandths in it to be smaller than one that had only hundredths.

The tendency to separate quantitative and symbolic representations seems to be a major stumbling block in school mathematics learning. When working with mathematical notation, one does not automatically think about the quantities and relationships that are referenced. Furthermore, school instruction probably tends to aggravate this tendency for the formal notation of mathematics to function independently of its referents. The focus in elementary school is on correct ways to perform procedures, a focus largely detached from reflection on the quantities and relationships to which symbolic expressions refer. This probably encourages children to attend to formal notations and rules for manipulating them without relating these rules to the semantics—that is, to the external referents—of the notations. This separation of syntax and semantics does not occur in the work-contextualized mathematical performances observed among minimally schooled children and adults (Carraher, 1990; Carraher, Carraher, & Schliemann, 1985; Ginsburg & Allardice, 1984; Saxe, 1988; Schliemann, & Acioly, 1989).

The pervasiveness of semantically unconstrained syntactic ways of thinking about school mathematics and of the systematic errors that this way of thinking appears to induce suggests that a major revision of school mathematics instruction, in the direction of rooting it in the kinds of semantic knowledge that children seem to have when they first come to school, would do much to limit errors and enhance mathematical understanding. This is a widely promoted idea among mathematics educators and psychologists. It is at the heart of many proposals to use manipulatives and graphic models in early mathematics teaching. Fuson (1988, 1990, this volume), Nesher (1989), Ohlsson (1987), and Resnick (1982) are examples of investigators who have proposed that procedures for multidigit arithmetic be taught by linking written notations to manipulations of concrete embodiments of place value relations. Leinhardt (1987) provided a careful analysis of how an effective classroom teacher tied concrete and graphic representations to symbolic notation in teaching subtraction. There is also evidence, however, that even very carefully crafted lessons that use manipulatives to establish the semantic principles underlying calculation procedures do not, by themselves, succeed in establishing a propensity for attending to the semantics of procedures (cf. Lampert, 1989; Nesher, 1986). Resnick and Omanson (1987) used a *mapping* procedure to teach the semantics of multidigit subtraction to children who had used buggy procedures on two different tests. In mapping instruction conducted in individual tutorials, children used Dienes blocks (which physically represent the value of numerals in the columns) to perform the various steps of exchange involved in subtraction with regrouping and recorded each step. In this way, the actions on the physical quantities—well constrained by the principles of additive composition—would, we thought, generate and thereby give meaning to the written notations of the algorithm. Despite the intensive personal instruction, however, only half the children taught learned the underlying semantics well enough to construct an explanation of why the algorithm worked and what the marks represented. More surprising, even children who did give evidence of good understanding of the semantics often reverted to their buggy calculation procedures once the instructional sessions were over.

This result does not, of course, suggest that there is no value in using manipulatives to teach the meaning of algorithms. In particular, because our study involved children who had already established buggy patterns, it does not tell us what to expect from instruction that initially introduces computational procedures on the basis of manipulatives and other semantic aids. It does, however, suggest that simple reliance on manipulatives to teach algorithms does not go far enough in capturing and building on children's informal mathematics knowledge. Instead, instruction that develops a fundamental *attitude* toward arithmetic as grounded in meaningful relationships is probably needed. This would require far more than occasional lessons using manipulatives or explaining an algorithm. It would mean grounding the entire learning program in problems that treat numbers as representations of real-world quantities. This is what some successful early mathematics programs have done (see e.g., Carpenter, Fennema, & Peterson, 1987; Carpenter, Fennema, Peterson, Chiang, & Loef, 1989; Cobb et al., 1991; Resnick, Bill, & Lesgold, in press).

The Abstract Entities Hypothesis

At some point, however, we must expect an instructional program focused entirely on relations among physical quantities to founder. This is because of three features that distinguish mathematical knowledge from most other forms of knowledge. First, mathematics is concerned not just with physical quantities, but also with abstract entities—numbers, operators, functions—that cannot be directly observed in the world. Second, mathematical knowledge is intimately linked to a specialized formal language that both imposes constraints on mathematical reasoning and confers extraordinary power. Third, the formal language of mathematics plays a dual role as *signifier* and *signified,* as both the instrument of reasoning and the object of reasoning. (Putnam, Lampert, & Peterson, 1990, provide an alternative but fundamentally compatible analysis of the special properties of mathematical knowledge; see also Kaput, 1987a, 1987b; Nesher, 1989; Ohlsson, 1987.)

Mathematics as Abstract Knowledge

In all domains of knowledge, forming a concept requires abstractions that go beyond individual objects that can be denoted. The concept of a chair or a dog requires children to construct a representation that abstracts over the specific dogs or chairs they may encounter. In most domains that young children deal with, however, there are at least *members* of a class or concept that one can point to, and it is possible to reason about specific cases. Mathematics does not have this property. There are not, strictly speaking, denotatable objects in mathematics. For example, although one can point to a set of three *objects,* one cannot point to a *three.* Number, as such, is a *conceptual* entity (cf. Greeno, 1983), not directly embodied physically. This means that before people can reason in truly mathematical ways they must engage in a process of constructing the conceptual entities about which they will reason.

Mathematics as Formal Knowledge

Although one can reason about some aspects of quantity without using written notation, there are very strict limits on how much reasoning about number one can do without using formalisms. Even counting engages a formalism, for a standard set of labels (the count words) must be used in a standard sequence, and these labels must be paired with objects in accordance with strict constraints (one label to one object, each used once and only once, in a fixed order). The dependence of mathematical reasoning on formalisms becomes more marked as one proceeds to more complex levels of mathematical development. Many concepts in arithmetic—for example, division by a fraction or subtraction of a negative number—can only be understood within a system of formal relationships. Efforts to explain these concepts with respect to physical quantities are cumbersome and limited in their application. The central role of formalism in mathematics becomes particularly evident when one considers algebra, where the formalism allows one to reason about operations on numbers and relations between numbers without reference to any particular numbers.

The Dual Role of Mathematical Language

Throughout mathematics, the terms and expressions in the formal notation have both referential and formal functions. As referential symbols, they refer to objects (e.g., a set of three apples) or cognitive entities (e.g., the number *three*) external to the formalism. As formal symbols, they are elements in a system that obeys rules of its own, and they can function without continuous reference to the physical or mathematical objects they name. For example, when one applies the count words in sequence in the course of counting, one is using the count words as purely symbolic tokens in a formally constrained procedure. The words do not refer to anything; they just keep the procedure running appropriately. However, when the same words are used to name the cardinality of the whole set that has been counted, they are names that have a referent, albeit a more abstract referent than many of the names in natural languages.

The dual role of mathematical symbols is particularly obvious and complicated in the case of algebra. One great power of algebra is that it allows extensive manipulation of relationships among variables within a completely reliable system that does not require continuous attention to the referential meaning of the intermediate expressions generated. The fact that the algebra system can "run on its own," so to speak, is surely a factor in favor of its efficiency. Potentially unbearable demands on processing capacity would be placed on individuals who tried to reason through some of the complex problems for which algebra is used if, at each step, they were considering physical, situational, or specific quantitative referents for the transformations they produced. But algebra is not only a device for reducing capacity demands. Its very abstraction away from the situations, quantities, and relationships that are its referential meaning is part of what permits certain mathematical deductions to be made.

These characteristics of mathematical thinking mean that, to think mathematically, it is necessary to go beyond the kinds of intuitions that can be related directly to physical embodiments of quantity. Mathematical entities must be constructed, and fluency in reasoning about those entities must be developed. This process may be a source of difficulty and at least temporary blockage in mathematics learning. It may be an example in mathematics learning of the kind of epistemological obstacle to which Bachelard (1980) directed our attention in science learning. This suggests that special attention may need to be paid in mathematics education to helping students construct and use the mental entities that constitute mathematical concepts. A group of Soviet psychologists and educators led by Davydov (see Davydov & Markova, 1983) and building on the work of Vygotsky (1978) made this idea the centerpiece of a program of research and curriculum development that made theoretical, as opposed to empirically derived, concepts the heart of instruction even for primary school children. Theoretically oriented teaching did not mean teaching rules for symbol manipulation, but rather finding ways to represent fundamental conceptual ideas of mathematics in ways that allowed children to manipulate and experiment with them. The Davidov group's success in teaching theoretically founded mathematical ideas to children, however, apparently did not produce much ability to reason about practical mathematical problems (Kozulin, 1984).

Mathematical Entities in Elementary School Children's Reasoning

Some of our research has examined the beginnings of reasoning about mathematical entities. Our studies include examples of children at surprisingly young ages who seem to have entered the formal system and are able to reason about relations among abstract entities such as numbers. But they also reveal great difficulties in such reasoning.

Negative Numbers

Considerable attention has been given to trying to develop pedagogical models to help children understand negative numbers (Davis, 1979; Janvier, 1985; Leonard & Sackur-Grisvard, 1987; Murray, 1985). Two basic classes of models have been developed: those that treat negative numbers as a special class of quantities, mirroring the behavior of ordinary quantities but sitting in a special "cancellation" relation to them, and those that treat negative numbers as elements in a formal system defined by a number line with numbers moving outward in both directions from zero. Our research and that of others (e.g., Carraher, 1990) shows that children think quite easily about negative numbers as quantities that stand in a cancellation relation to ordinary quantities. For example, children and unschooled adults reason quite easily about debts. As young as 7 years or so, they understand that debts are created when payments are due that will more than use up an individual's current monetary resources; that debts can accumulate, essentially by addition "on the other side of zero"; that earning money (an action that would seem to imply addition when in the domain of positive quantities) reduces debts and can eventually—by crossing zero—eliminate debts and even create assets (Mukhopadhyay, Resnick, & Schauble, 1990). Children can reason successfully about all of these aspects of negative quantities when these quantities form part of a meaningful story about a character with whose financial problems they identify, even when they are nearly totally incapable of solving simple written addition and subtraction problems involving negative numbers.

Analyzing other "street math" types of reasoning about quantities that the mathematically sophisticated represent with negatively signed numbers, Carraher (1990) has argued that this form of reasoning, although practically powerful, in fact avoids the need for building a truly mathematical conception of signed numbers. An analysis by Peled (1989) implicitly seconds this claim. In it, four levels of understanding of addition and subtraction of signed numbers are laid out. The final level is essentially a formal one. It requires a number line representation of numbers qua numbers—that is, numbers defined in relation to one another rather than as measures of physical quantities. It also requires a definition of the operations of addition and subtraction in terms of arbitrary directions of movement on this nonreferential number line.

In an intermediate stage, when addition always means moving to the right and subtraction always means moving to the left, it is still possible to preserve at least a distant quantity referential meaning for these operations, for subtraction always means moving toward a quantitatively "lesser" quantity and addition always means moving toward a quantitatively "greater" quantity on the line. But in Peled's final stage, even these ordinary meanings of addition and subtraction and of the signs on the numbers are lost. A negative sign now means "flip" or "turn around"; addition means move in the direction you (or the arrow on the line) are facing; and subtraction means move backwards (i.e., in the direction opposite the one you are facing). All of these definitions are perfectly meaningful and "semantic" within the formal system, but to understand them requires accepting the formal system as a self-contained system of relationships with the semantics residing in the relationships among the elements in the system rather than in quantities external to the formal system. In our studies of elementary school children's understanding of negative numbers, we have encountered children as young as third grade who show an intermediate understanding of negative numbers as points on a number line (Peled, Mukhopadhyay, & Resnick, 1988). But prior to formal instruction, we found none with a full formal understanding. Furthermore, many adults continue to be baffled by subtraction of a negative number, which is easily explainable only in the terms of a formal system.

Infinity

Although it is not normally an official part of the school curriculum, children are known to become interested in the concept of infinity at a surprisingly early age (Gelman & Evans, 1981). As young as 6 or 7 years of age, some children recognize that there is no largest number, because it is always possible to add one more. This seems to depend on an appreciation of the formal numeration system, for the Gelman and Evans data also showed that the children who admit that one more can always be added are those who have fully mastered the recursion principle for count words—that is, they understand that when one reaches a boundary (such as 999) one can add a new token ("thousand" in this case) and then cycle through the entire sequence again. In cooperation with Gelman, we conducted a study that used the concept of infinity to explore further children's appreciation of numbers as elements in a strictly formal system (Bee et al., in preparation). We especially wanted to know when children began to recognize the dual function of mathematical notations (as signified and signifier) and the language they used to explain this idea when they did recognize it.

The children in the study were interviewed individually. The portion of the interview relevant to the present question proceeded in the following manner. If a child agreed that there was no largest number (for the ordinary, counting-by-ones sequence of numbers), he or she was then shown a string of even numbers (2, 4, 6, 8 . . .) and asked what the highest number in that string was. Similarly, the child was asked what the highest number in the tens counting string (10, 20, 30 . . .) was. Most children who were firmly convinced that there was no largest ordinary number also concluded that the same thing must be true for the other number strings.[4] These children

---

[4]The interview included several countersuggestions by the experimenter, and it is therefore possible to distinguish reliably between children who strongly believed there was no largest number and those who were not certain or were responding to cues from the experimenter as to what answers were desired.

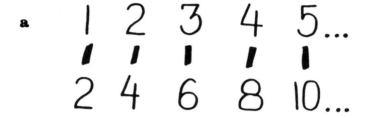

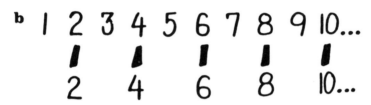

FIG. 7.5.   Panel a. The "Holding Hands" example: Successive numbers in each string are paired. Panel b. Countersuggestion to "Holding Hands" example: Numbers are matched by values. From "The Development of Mathematical Intuition" by L. B. Resnick, 1986, *Perspectives on Intellectual Development: The Minnesota Symposia on Child Psychology* (p. 181) by M. Perlmutter (Ed.), Hillsdale, NJ: Lawrence Erlbaum Associates. Copyright 1986 by Lawrence Erlbaum Associates. Reprinted by permission.

were then asked whether two number sequences (e.g., units and evens) had the same "number of numbers." If a child said that a sequence (usually the units sequence) had more numbers, he or she was shown that the numbers in the two sequences could be made to "hold hands" (as shown in Fig. 7.5a) and was asked whether this kind of pairing could go on forever. If a child said that two number strings were equivalent (either before or after the hand-holding discussion), he or she was shown a different pairing in which the numbers were matched by *values* (as in Fig. 7.5b) and was invited to discuss the implications.

Several classes of responses to the equivalence questions can be distinguished. Some children (most of the younger ones) simply rejected the possibility that there could be just as many even numbers or tens numbers as regular numbers—even though they had observed and agreed to the possibility of the numbers holding hands forever. These children were responding to the number strings as signifiers, symbols referring to cardinalities. On this interpretation there are missing numbers in the twos and tens strings, and if numbers are missing, there must be fewer of them than in the complete set of numbers (the units string). Most sixth and eighth graders, however, recognized that the equivalence question posed a dilemma. They could follow and even accept the hand-holding, one-to-one correspondence argument, but they saw gaps in the twos and tens number strings as well. In the face of this dilemma, many children followed the interviewer's suggestions on both sides of the arguments and shifted their positions several times in the course of the interview. Some resolutely focused on the numerical symbols themselves without reference to the cardinalities to which they referred. That is, they focused on the symbols as signified rather than signifier. Here is an example of such a child:

> *There's the same amount.* Of counting numbers and even numbers? *Yeah.* How do you see that? *Because there's a match with every one of those. There's a two for a one, and a four for a two.* Before you said there was more of these, right? *Yeah.* What changed you mind? *When I see they all have a match so there must be the same.*

This child gave a "correct" answer to the equivalence question but had not really resolved the dilemma. It is by focusing on only one aspect of the number strings that she was able to respond. A few children, however, showed us in their responses what a full and conscious resolution of the dilemma would sound like in children's terms. They explained that both interpretations of the number strings were possible, and that one could arrive at either answer (the same number of evens as units, or fewer evens than units) depending on which interpretation one chose. Here is an example from one of the protocols:

> Why do you say there are just as many? . . . *Because you cannot . . . you could connect the. . . . Like the first even number would be two. . . . First counting number would be one. They would be even, as they're both the first number. Then, the second.* I see, so you make. . . . *You've got the same value of the number* [on the hand-holding model of the Figure, points to a number in the units then to the same number in the evens string]. . . . *But there's still the same number as. . . . You see this little symbol on your paper. There's the same number of little symbols.*

What this child was saying is that, if you ignore the external referential meaning of the written numbers and just connect the first numbers in each string (1 and 2), then the second (2 and 4), then the third (3 and 6), and so on, there will always be another number in each string, so the two are equal. But she noted parenthetically—although she did not complete the sentence—that, if you pay attention to the referential meaning (the value) of the numbers and want to connect 2 with 2, 4 with 4, and so on, the equivalence will not hold (there will be "extra" numbers in the units string).

FORMS OF MATHEMATICAL KNOWLEDGE
AND CONDITIONS FOR THEIR DEVELOPMENT

The preceding discussion has offered many examples of mathematical knowledge and activity and explored some relations among them. It is time to attempt a more systematic account of the different kinds of mathematical knowledge and of how they are learned. In the following subsections of this chapter, I first describe four kinds of mathematical thinking and their apparent sequential relations. Then I show how the mathematical properties discussed earlier might develop across these four kinds of thought. Finally, in preparation for a concluding section on teaching mathematics on the basis of intuitive knowledge, I consider how children might learn each of the four forms of mathematical thinking.

Four Kinds of Mathematical Thinking

The idea that mathematical knowledge develops through a sequence of stages characterized by changes in representational content—that is, the kinds of conceptual entities that are recognized and reasoned about—is shared by a number of theorists (e.g., Fuson, 1988; Steffe, Cobb, & von Glasersfeld, 1988; Steffe, von Glasersfeld, Richards, & Cobb, 1983). Most of these analyses have focused heavily on the representations underlying counting and the transitions from counting objects to reasoning about cardinalities of sets. In an interpretive review of these theories and other research on mathematical concept development by developmental psychologists, cognitive scientists, and mathematics educators, Resnick and Greeno (1990) identified four kinds of mathematical thinking about quantity and number. Our analysis is compatible with other representational development theories but extends them to include a form of reasoning about quantity that precedes the ability to count individual objects or sets and an advanced form of reasoning in which operators and relations are represented as conceptual entities. The four kinds of mathematical thinking Resnick and Greeno identified are summarized in Table 7.2.

In the *mathematics of protoquantities,* reasoning is about amounts of physical material. Comparisons of amounts are made and inferences can be drawn about the effects of various changes and transformations on the amounts; but no numerical quantification is involved. The language of protoquantitative mathematical thinking is a language of descriptive and comparative terms applied directly to the physical objects or amounts: a *big* doll, *many* eggs, *more* milk. In the mathematics of protoquantities, operations are actions that can be performed directly on physical objects

TABLE 7.2
Four Types of Mathematical Thinking

Mathematics of:	Objects of Reasoning	Linguistic Terms	Operations
protoquantities	physical material	much, many, more, less, big, small, etc.	increase, decrease, combine, separate, compare, order
quantities	measured physical material	n objects, n inches, n pounds, etc. Add, take away, divide	increase and decrease quantified sets by specific numbers of objects; increase and decrease measured amounts of material by measured amounts
			combine and partition quantified sets or measured amounts
			divide a set or measured amount into equal shares
numbers	specific numbers	n more than, n times, plus n, minus n, times n, n plus m, n divided by m	actions of adding, subtracting, multiplying, dividing applied to specific numbers
operators	numbers in general, operations, variables	addition, subtraction, multiplication, division, difference, equivalence, times greater than, times less than, 1/nth of	commute, associate, distribute, compose, decompose

or material: increasing and decreasing, combining and separating, comparing, ordering, pairing. The simplest form of protoquantitative reasoning is direct perceptual comparison of objects or sets of different sizes. This permits recognizing the larger of a pair of objects, for example, something infants of 3 months are known to be capable of (Fantz & Fagan, 1975). More advanced protoquantitative reasoning works on a mental representation of amounts of material and allows one to reason about the results of imagined increases and decreases in those amounts. Thus, protoquantitative reasoners can say that there *will be* more apples after mother gives each child some additional ones, or that some mice *must have been removed* if there are now less than before, without being able to look simultaneously at the objects in their *before* and *after* states. Similarly, mental combining and separating operations permit children to reason protoquantitatively about the relations between parts and whole—for example, more fruits in the bowl than either apples or oranges (Fuson, Lyons, Pergament, Hall, & Kwon, 1988; Markman & Siebert, 1976; McGarrigle, described in Donaldson, 1978).

In the *mathematics of quantities,* reasoning is about numerically quantified amounts of material. Numbers are used as measures: *4* dolls, *3 feet* of board, *7 pounds* of potatoes. In the mathematics of quantities, numbers function as adjectives; they describe a property (the measured amount) of a physical quantity. The numbers take their meaning from the physical material they refer to and describe. Terms from formal mathematics, such as *add* or *divide,* may be used, but their reference is to action on physical material. Operations in the mathematics of quantities are actions on measured amounts of material. For this reason it is possible to distinguish several different kinds of addition, subtraction, multiplication, and division. Addition can mean *combining* 4 apples and 3 apples or *increasing by 5* a set of 20 marbles. Subtraction can mean *taking away 20* potatoes from a bin containing 50 potatoes or *partitioning* a set of 15 cakes into 5 for the family and "the rest" to give to friends. Multiplication and division have even more possible referential meanings in the mathematics of quantities, such as *combining* 5 sets of 3 books each, *enlarging by a factor of 3* a 10-inch strip, *sharing* 20 cookies equally among 4 children. Always, in the mathematics of quantities, the reasoning is about specific quantities of material and actions on those quantities; the numbers function as descriptors of the quantities.

By contrast, in the *mathematics of numbers,* numbers function not as adjectives describing something else but as nouns. That is, numbers are conceptual entities that can be manipulated and acted upon. One can now add 3 and 4 (not 3 apples and 4 apples) or multiply 3 (not 3 books) by another number. In the mathematics of numbers, numbers *have* properties rather than being properties *of* physical material. The properties of numbers are defined in terms of other numbers. Numbers have magnitudes in relation to one another: For example, 12 is *8 more than* 4; it is *3 times* 4; it is *⅓ of* 36. Numbers are also compositions of other numbers: thus, 12 is *8 + 4, 7 + 5, 6 + 6,* and so on. Operations in the mathematics of number are actions taken on numbers, resulting in changes in those numbers. Thus, 12 can be changed to 4 by *subtracting 8* or, alternatively, by *dividing by 3.* It can be changed to 36 by *multiplying by 3* or by *adding 24.* The numbers being compared, composed, and changed in these examples are purely *conceptual* entities. Their meaning derives entirely from their relations to one another and their place within a system of numbers. Physical material need not be imagined.

It is not the fact of doing arithmetic mentally that distinguishes the mathematics of numbers from the mathematics of quantities. The mathematics of quantities can be done mentally—in one's head. One can think of splitting 12 apples into two collections, of 8 apples and 4 apples, say, or enlarging a 12-inch square photo to one that is 24 inches square. The calculation can be mental, but it belongs to the mathematics of quantities as long as what is mentally represented is actual physical quantities and actions on them. One is engaged in the mathematics of number only when the mental representation is of numbers as abstract entities, with properties defined relative to the system of numbers themselves, not to physical quantities.

The final type of mathematical thinking we identify is the *mathematics of operators,* in which not only numbers but also operations on numbers are conceptual entities that can be reasoned about. In the mathematics of numbers, operations are like transitive verbs. They describe actions that can be performed on numbers. But they are not themselves objects with properties, objects on which actions can be taken. Similarly, in the mathematics of numbers, one can describe relations *between* numbers, but the relations are essentially adjectives describing properties of the numbers. They are not themselves noun-like objects with properties that can be reasoned about. In the mathematics of operators, operations do behave like nouns. They can be reasoned *about,* not just applied. For example, it can be argued that the operation of *addition by combining* is always commutative, no matter what pair of numbers is composed.

In the mathematics of operators, operations can also be operated *on.* The operation of *adding 4,* for example, can be composed with another operation of *subtracting 3,* and this composition can be recognized as equivalent to an operation of *adding 1.* This equivalence is perfectly general; it holds no matter which particular numbers are operated on. Relations between numbers also are objects to reason about in the mathematics of operators. A *difference of 3,* for example, can be understood as a property of the pair, 11 and 8. Differences can be compared, so that one can recognize that [11 − 8] is less than [24 − 20], or even operated on so that [11 − 8] can be subtracted from [24 − 20]. Similarly, a multiplicative relation, × *4*, can be recognized as equivalent whether one is describing the pair [2,8], [15,60] or [11,44]. This kind of reasoning about relations as mental objects is what it takes to understand functions.

Developmental Relations Among the Forms of Mathematical Thinking

How do these forms of mathematical reasoning develop, and what kind of relations hold between them? A plausible story—one that accords with available evidence on the ages at which each form of mathematical thinking typically appears in highly schooled cultures—is that they are genetically related to one another. Reasoning about quantities—with numbers functioning as adjectives and operations as verbs—is built on a foundation of schemas for reasoning protoquantitatively about the relations between amounts of physical material. Once children become fluent with the mathematics of quantities, that is once they can reason easily about actions on numerically quantified physical material, they can begin to lift the numbers out of the physical quantity relations and treat them as objects in their own right. In this way the mathematics of numbers is developed. Gradually, over time and with extensive practice, numbers can become nouns, and the mathematics of numbers begins—with operators still functioning as verbs but now describing actions on the mental entities of specific numbers. Only after extensive practice in operating on numbers as objects will the mathematics of operators, in which operations and relations themselves become objects, be constructed.

This sequential, genetic account need not imply an all-or-none form of development. There is no reason to suppose that people pass all at once from a protoquantitative way of thinking to the mathematics of quantities or from the mathematics of quantities to the mathematics of numbers. There might be some developmental limits—of the kind developed by Case (1985) and Fischer (1980), for example—on how many chunks of information can be thought about at once, and this would be a brake of sorts on the pace at which new objects and properties can be incorporated into the mental system. But most evidence suggests that mental objects are built up specific bit by specific bit, rather than emerging in discrete stages. So, for example, children may be doing the mathematics of quantity on dimensions such as manyness and length, while still reasoning only protoquantitatively about weight or speed. Further, they may convert small integers (e.g., 1, 2, 3, and 4) into mental entities and perform the mathematics of number on them while still using higher numbers only as descriptors of amounts of physical material. Similarly, operators may be transformed from verbs to nouns one at a time. Children can reason about the commutativity of addition, over all numbers, well before they can reason about multiplicative functions. Furthermore, as each new kind of number—for example, positive integers, negative integers, fractions—is encountered, it is likely that learning will entail passage through the successive layers of the mathematics of protoquantities, quantities, numbers, and operators. Thus, at any given moment, a child can be functioning at several different layers of mathematical thought.

Furthermore, as more advanced forms of mathematical reasoning are developed, the earlier ones are not discarded but remain part of the individual's total knowledge system. People who are able to think abstractly about numbers and operators as conceptual entities can also use numbers to refer to specific measured quantities. This capacity to move back and forth between the mathematics of quantities, numbers, and operators is crucial in enabling people to relate their abstract mathematical knowledge to practical situations. They may reason in a partly formal (mathematics of operators) manner and partly physical (mathematics of quantities) manner on different parts of the same complex problem. Engineers sometimes reason protoquantitatively about physical systems (e.g., deKleer & Brown, 1985; Forbus, 1985), using the conclusions reached about how quantities should change or relate to one another to constrain and check the results of more formal calculations. Schwartz (1988) has argued that, at least as scientists use numbers, they are always fundamentally referential to measured quantities.

The Psychological Origin of Mathematical Properties

This sequential theory of the development of four kinds of mathematical thinking provides new lenses for examining the evidence presented earlier of children's intuitive understanding of arithmetic. It is especially instructive to review the mathematical properties that young children seem to appreciate to determine how they might be rooted in successive levels of mathematical thinking and where difficulty might be encountered in passing to the later levels.

Properties Based on a Part/Whole Schema

Consider first the set of properties that can be viewed as elaborations of a protoquantitative part/whole schema, which is fundamentally a representation of additive composition. Children know from their experience of the physical world how material comes apart and reassembles. Before they can reliably quantify physical material, that is, when they are still functioning in the mathematics of protoquantities, they know that a whole quantity (W) can be cut into two or more parts $(P_1, P_2, P_3. . .)$, that the parts can be recombined to make the whole, and that the order in which the parts are combined does not matter in reconstituting the original amount. This knowledge can be represented as a set of protoquantitative equations:

$$P_1 + P_2 + P_3 = W \tag{1}$$

$$P_1 + P_2 = P_2 + P_1 \tag{2}$$

$$(P_1 + P_2) + P_3 = P_1 + (P_2 + P_3) \tag{3}$$

Equation 2 is a protoquantitative version of the commutativity of addition property; Equation 3 is a protoquantitative version of the associativity of addition property.

As children apply their counting skills in situations that earlier were reasoned about only protoquantitatively, they begin to develop the mathematics of quantities. In the process, the part/whole schema becomes quantified. All of the relationships between whole and parts that were present in the protoquantitative schema are maintained, but now the relations apply to specific, quantified amounts of material. As a result, children can now reason using quantified equations, such as:

$$3 \text{ apples} + 5 \text{ apples} + 4 \text{ apples} = 12 \text{ apples} \tag{4}$$

$$3 \text{ apples} + 5 \text{ apples} = 5 \text{ apples} + 3 \text{ apples} \tag{5}$$

$$(3 \text{ apples} + 5 \text{ apples}) + 4 \text{ apples} = 3 \text{ apples} +$$
$$(5 \text{ apples} + 4 \text{ apples}) \tag{6}$$

Equations 5 and 6 constitute versions of the commutativity and associativity properties within the mathematics of quantities.

As numbers are lifted out of their external referential context and the mathematics of numbers begins, the part/whole schema can organize knowledge about relations among numbers:

$$3 + 5 + 4 = 12 \tag{7}$$

$$3 + 5 = 5 + 3 \tag{8}$$

$$(3 + 5) + 4 = 3 + (5 + 4) \tag{9}$$

Equations 8 and 9 constitute versions of commutativity and associativity in the mathematics of numbers.

Finally, in the mathematics of operators, attention switches from actions on particular numbers to more general relations between numbers. Commutativity and associativity are *always* true for addition, no matter what the numbers. Thus:

$$n + m = m + n \tag{10}$$

$$(n + m) + p = n + (m + p) \tag{11}$$

The important thing to note about this sequence of equations is that the very same *relations* remain in place in each successive form of mathematical thinking, but the *objects* of thinking change: first unquantified amounts, then quantified amounts, then specific numbers, and finally numbers in general. The same rooting of properties in protoquantitative knowledge and reasoning can be seen for more complex properties as well. The property of complementarity of addition and subtraction (additive inverse), for example, also begins with the protoquantitative part/whole schema, as the following set of equations shows:

$$P_1 + P_2 = W \tag{12}$$

$$W - P_1 = P_2 \tag{13}$$

$$W - P_2 = P_1 \tag{14}$$

These equations express the basic logic of part/whole relations: namely, that if a whole is split into two parts, and one part is removed, the other part is what remains. The same logic is maintained under the mathematics of quantities:

$$4 \text{ cakes} + 7 \text{ cakes} = 11 \text{ cakes} \tag{15}$$

$$11 \text{ cakes} - 4 \text{ cakes} = 7 \text{ cakes} \tag{16}$$

$$11 \text{ cakes} - 7 \text{ cakes} = 4 \text{ cakes} \tag{17}$$

and of numbers:

$$4 + 7 = 11 \tag{18}$$

$$11 - 4 = 7 \tag{19}$$

$$11 - 7 = 4 \tag{20}$$

The logic becomes fully general, applying to any numbers, under the mathematics of operators:

$$m + n = q \tag{21}$$

$$q - m = n \tag{22}$$

$$q - n = m \tag{23}$$

Properties Based on an Increase/Decrease Schema

The protoquantitative increase/decrease schema organizes children's knowledge of the effects of growth or shrinkage in a quantity or the results of adding or taking away material from an established amount of that material. On the basis of this schema, children are able to conclude that, when something is added to a starting amount, the new amount is greater than before; when something is taken away from a starting amount, the new amount is less than before; and when nothing is added or taken away, there is the same amount as at the start.

In the mathematics of quantities, a quantified increase/decrease schema plays an important role in early story problem solutions. One of the kinds of problems that have been shown to be easy even for kindergartners to solve is one-step stories about changes in sets. Few primary children have much difficulty even with two-step stories such as: "John had 17 marbles. He lost 11 of them in a first game and 4 in a second game. How many does he have left?" Children solve problems of this kind by physically or mentally representing a set of 17 objects, removing 11 of them, removing another 5, and counting the remainder.

In this problem the numbers 11 and 4 specify the size of decreases, actions on established sets. This can be symbolized as:

$$17 \text{ marbles } (-11 \text{ marbles}) (-4 \text{ marbles}) = 2 \text{ marbles,} \qquad (24)$$

where the parentheses indicate that the numbers quantify the operations of removing marbles. In the mathematics of numbers, the equation would become:

$$17 (-11) (-4) = 2 \qquad (25)$$

But only in the mathematics of operators would it be possible to compose the two transformations as in:

$$(-11) + (-4) = (-15) \qquad (26)$$

Children have a great deal of difficulty for some time in thinking of the transformations as objects that can themselves be combined as in Equation 26. For many years they think of numbers as describing the cardinalities of sets, rather than as quantifications of transformations, increases, or decreases. Evidence of this preference comes from a study by Resnick et al. (1987), who asked 11- through 14-year olds to make up stories that would yield expressions such as $17 - 11 - 4$. Many of the younger students created stories similar to these: "The boy has 17 marbles. His friend would have 11, and another would have 4, just a little batch. . . ." and "There are 17 marbles in the morning, the marbles at noontime, and 4 in the evening. . . ."

Older children usually could successfully create stories that would produce the expression $17 - 11 - 4$, but they often could not combine the two transformations into a total "loss" of 15 marbles, except by doing successive subtractions on the starting set. Thus, they would perform a sequence of operations such as $17 - 11 = 6; 6 - 4 = 2; 17 - 2 = 15$ to find an answer. But they could not solve the problem directly by composing the two transformations, as in Equation 26. Still less could they reason generally about composition of operators as in:

$$(-m) + (-n) = -(m + n). \tag{27}$$

The protoquantitative increase/decrease schema joins with protoquantitative part/whole to provide the early intuitive foundation for another important property: additive equivalence classes. The combination of the two schemas allows children to reason about the effects of changes in parts and wholes on one another. Figure 7.6 shows the kinds of inferences that are possible under a wholly protoquantitative form of reasoning. As the figure shows, children are able to conclude that, if something is added to one of two parts while the other stays constant, the whole must increase. Or, if the whole is decreased, at least one of the parts (perhaps both) must also decrease. The most complex reasoning enabled by the combination of the protoquantitative part/whole and increase/decrease schemas concerns how the whole can be maintained unchanged by compensating changes in the two parts:

$$(P_1 + A) + (P_2 - A) = W \tag{28}$$

That is, if an amount is added to Part 1 and the same amount is removed from Part 2, the whole remains unchanged.

In the mathematics of quantities, the compensation schema takes on specific values. For example, Equation 15 can be modified by addition and subtraction of the same amount of cakes from the two parts without changing the whole:

$$(4 \text{ cakes} + 2 \text{ cakes}) + (7 \text{ cakes} - 2 \text{ cakes}) = 11 \text{ cakes} \tag{29}$$

Eventually, when the mathematics of operators is reached, the role of compensation in maintaining equivalence becomes general, as in,

$$(m + a) + (n - a) = (m + n) + (a - a) = m + n. \tag{30}$$

General relationships of this kind are reflected in the rules for derived fact arithmetic described by Putnam, deBettencourt, and Leinhardt (1990) and are shown in Table 7.1.

A. Changes in the Whole

Change in
One Part

Change in the Other Part

Change in One Part	+	0	–
+	+	+	?
0	+	0	-
-	?	-	-

B. Changes in One Part

Change in
the Whole

Change in the Other Part

Change in the Whole	+	0	–
+	?	+	+
0	-	0	+
0	-	-	?

FIG. 7.6. Inferences from combined protoquantitative increase/decrease and part/whole schemas.

Properties Based on a Compare Schema

The protoquantitative compare schema is, very probably, children's earliest form of mathematical knowledge. It permits even infants to make comparative judgments about amounts of physical material (see Resnick, 1983). The compare schema is called upon in both part/whole and increase/decrease protoquantitative reasoning, permitting judgments about the relative magnitude of parts and wholes and about amounts of material before and after transformations. Almost as soon as they learn to count, children are able to judge the relative magnitudes of numbers, even without referential quantities of material. They can decide, for example, that 7 is more than 4, or 3 is less than 5. But it is some years before most children are able to quantify differences, to say how *much* more 7 is than 4.

Solving comparison story problems, such as "There are 5 worms and 8 birds. How many more birds than worms?", is difficult for most children until the age of 8 or 9 (Riley & Greeno, 1988). This kind of problem requires establishing a *quantified difference relationship* between the two *numbers,* 5 and 8. This can be done only in the mathematics of numbers, for a difference can be quantified only between like objects, and this means forgetting about the worms and birds and thinking only about the 5 and 8. A further development of thinking about differences comes with the mathematics of operators. When differences are mental entities that can be compared with one another, it becomes possible to construct *equivalence classes of differences.* This permits recognition that many different pairs of numbers have the same difference, as in,

$$(2 - 0) = (3 - 1) = (4 - 2) = (20 - 18) = (133 - 131) = \ldots \ldots (31)$$

More generally, this leads to a constraint on transformations of numbers that *conserves differences* by addition or subtraction of the same amount to the minuend and the subtrahend of a subtraction pair:

$$n - m = (n + a) - (m + a) \tag{32}$$

$$n - m = (n - a) - (m - a) \tag{33}$$

This constraint underlies certain subtraction procedures. For example, in many countries children are taught to subtract in the following way:

132		$13^1 2$ (add 10 to minuend)
	is changed to:	
-28		$- 3\ 8$ (add 10 to subtrahend)

Mental arithmetic methods sometimes apply this constraint, as well. For example, to take advantage of a well-known subtraction fact, an individual might convert $[9 - 4]$ to $[10 - 5]$. However, children are far less likely to make this kind of conversion than they are conversions based on additive compensation, as in Equation 30 (Putnam, deBettencourt, & Leinhardt, 1990). Thus, it appears that additive pairs become mental objects earlier than differences.

To this point, my discussion has assumed a developmental sequence in which the different forms of mathematical thinking are both sequentially and genetically related to one another. This sequential account is perfectly compatible with what current data show. However, it cannot be taken as fully established, and it is certainly incomplete, for it contains no clear account of how people learn each successive form of thinking or of exactly how earlier forms of thinking play a role in acquiring later forms. I sketch here a view of learning processes that, although not yet fully developed, may provide the missing theoretical piece. My intent is to unite the genetic account, in which later developing competencies in some sense depend on earlier ones, with recently revived and elaborated theories of contextualized or *situated* cognition (e.g., Brown, Collins, & Duguid, 1989; Suchman, 1987). These theories argue that every cognitive act must be viewed as a specific response to a specific set of circumstances, and that to understand what a person knows we must build an account of the situations of practice that led to the knowledge.

Situated Cognition and Mathematics Learning

Learning, in the particular version of situated cognition that I find promising, is a matter of passing through successive situations in which one becomes a competent actor. The competence that is acquired is quite specific to each situation. However, one does not enter each new situation without a history. As a result of prior situational engagements, each individual has a repertoire of concepts, that is, ways of thinking and ways of behaving that are available as a basis for beginning to act in the new situation. These old ways will be tried out in the new situation to the extent that the new situation evokes them more or less automatically or, in a more reflective process, to the extent that the individual judges them potentially relevant. Thus, although old ways of thinking and behaving play a role in learning, they can never be simply imported into a new situation. Developed as adaptions to a particular situation, concepts or ways of acting borrowed from one's past must now be adapted to the new situation. This process of adaptation is what is meant by situated learning; it is a process that creates, for each successive situation encountered, a new, contextualized form of competence.

This view of learning suggests that we consider each of the four forms of mathematical thought discussed here as a way of thinking suited to a particular range of situations. To account for learning, then, we must ask what kinds of situations would support development of each of the four kinds of thinking. To understand the possible genetic relationship between the forms of thinking, we must further examine how concepts and ways of acting suitable for one kind of situation might be carried into another situation as a basis for forming a new contextualized competence. In the coming sections I describe the kinds of situations that are likely to produce each kind of mathematical thinking, with special attention to how such situations might be deliberately created in the mathematics classroom.

Situations for Learning the Mathematics of Protoquantities

The mathematics of protoquantities is likely to develop in situations of direct engagement with physical material and in situations in which protoquantitive properties of material are named and discussed. Both kinds of situations are frequent in the life of the preschool child, at least in our culture. Very early forms of engagement with physical material have been described in detail by Piaget (1952) in his studies of sensorimotor development. These engagements may be purely visual in the youngest infant but will very soon include manipulative activity. Once the child can talk, situations of physical engagement often include linguistic activity. Children may follow or give commands that involve protoquantitative language ("Get me a big spoon"), may accept or give guidance using such terms ("You need a longer stick to reach that far"), or may simply listen to or produce protoquantitative descriptions of physical material relations. Furthermore, physical and linguistic activity calling for protoquantitative reasoning is often embedded in social problem solving, such as sharing food or making comparisons that have social implications. So children's earliest forms of mathematical thinking are likely to be inseparable from their social as well as their physical reasoning.

Most 5- and 6-year olds come to school with already well developed protoquantitative knowledge for the additive composition aspects of physical material. That is, they already know and can apply the schemas such as those expressed in Equations 1 through 3, 12 through 14, and 28 (see Resnick & Greeno, 1990, for a detailed account of the evidence for this claim). Some children may need special assistance; Case and Griffin (1990), for example, have developed a program that helps preschool and kindergarten children develop some of the basic schemas. For children without these special needs, the first year or two of mathematics schooling will probably not need to teach the basic schemas so much as help children talk about and reflect on them. Practice in talking about the relations embodied in the protoquantitative schemas (e.g., by saying "A whole is always bigger than its parts" or "You always have less if someone takes some away") in the context of well-understood problem situations can provide children's earliest introduction to explicit mathematical reasoning and justification. Children can learn these self-reflective meta abilities the way they learn anything else—by participation in situations in which these activities are a normal way of behaving. Accordingly, the primary school classroom ought to establish itself as a place in which talk about mathematical relations, ideas, and reflection on how one arrives at them is a normal way of behaving. Cobb, Wood, and Yackel (1990) added to this prescription the further suggestion that children should also talk about the very process of talking about mathematics, in order to develop an understanding of the inquiry nature of mathematical discourse. This suggestion is consonant with Margaret Donaldson's (1978) call for explicit attention in earliest schooling to helping children reflect on their own language use and thereby come to treat words and sentences as analyzable objects.

In addition to talk about the additive protoquantitative schemas that most children bring with them to school, the primary grade classroom can be a place for developing protoquantitative schemas that will be the basis for eventual elaboration of multiplication, division, fraction, ratio, and proportion concepts (cf. Resnick & Singer, in press). Schemas of positive and inverse covariation, for example, can be developed through problems involving ordering of physical material. Children's protoquantitative understanding of repetition can also be developed at an early stage; this is a precursor of multiplication (cf. Nesher, this volume). Repetition of a quantity is at the heart of measurement (the blue stick can be stepped along the desk top 10 times). Thus, all kinds of measurement activities (e.g., number of lengths, number of cups of liquid) can serve to develop a repetition schema. Finally, there is the inverse of repetition: partitioning into equal units, which is an early form of division (see also Kieren, this volume). Here, problems of sharing are natural for children: Maintaining equivalent shares is for them a natural way to make things fair.

Situations for Learning the Mathematics of Quantities

The situations in which children develop the mathematics of protoquantities do not demand precise numerical quantification. But children in our culture also participate from an early age in other situations in which there is an explicit demand for exact quantification. Gelman and Gallistel (1978) have shown that preschool children possess a set of principles (perhaps biologically prepared) underlying counting. These principles permit children to learn quickly the specifics of their culture's counting strategies. However, the situations in which the youngest children are likely to apply their counting skills to quantify sets are limited to those in which quantification is directly demanded, usually in the form of a *How many?* question (e.g., Fuson, 1988; Sophian, 1987). In other words, quantification situations are separate, from the very young child's point of view, from the problem-solving situations that give rise to the protoquantitative part/whole, compare, and combine schemas.

To develop the mathematics of quantities, a new kind of situation is needed, one in which the two initially separate streams of knowledge—counting and quantity relations—must be combined (see Lawler, 1981, for an analysis of separately situated knowledge streams and their eventual combination to form new concepts). The most effective situation for this development is one in which exact quantitative answers are expected for comparison, combination, and increase/decrease problems. For some children, this kind of demand begins at home or "on the streets." For many, it may not come until school begins. By engaging children in counting activities in the context of problems they already know how to solve protoquantitatively, teachers can help children invest counting results with all of the meaningful relations inherent in the protoquantitative schemas. Learning to perform in this new situation should produce *quantification of the protoquantitative schemas.* In the quantified schemas, the relations inherent in the original, protoquantitative compare, combine, and increase/decrease schemas are maintained but with numbers attached.

The easiest way to invoke contexts that children understand protoquantitatively is to build earliest school arithmetic activity on story problems. Resnick, Bill, Lesgold, and Leer (1991) and Carpenter et al. (1989) describe successful classroom programs based on story problems. This story-based strategy for beginning arithmetic instruction is explicitly designed to allow children to use concepts and skills developed in earlier nonschool situations. It is a strategy that contrasts quite sharply with traditional methods of arithmetic drill in which practice on number proceeds independently of situations involving quantity. Such drill removes numbers from the referential context that evokes the schemas and is likely to promote fragile knowledge that children are unable to apply in problem solving. Rather than decontextualized drills, what is needed is extensive practice in solving well understood quantity problems. These problems can be presented by the teacher, or brought to school, or made up by the children. Children can also be encouraged to find quantification problems in their everyday lives.

At first, children will need to work problems using manipulative materials so that they can apply their counting skills directly. For children to effectively use counting to solve story problems, their counting skill must be sufficiently developed that they can count objects more or less automatically, without much conscious attention. Otherwise, attention to the goal of counting will drive from memory the protoquantitative relations. This may mean that some children at school entrance will be able to solve by themselves only problems involving very small quantities. However, even these children can benefit by participating "peripherally" (cf. Lave, 1991; Lave & Wenger, 1990) in classroom discussions in which others are solving problems involving larger quantities. Such participation can alert them to the idea that quantitative solutions are possible for large quantities, indeed for any quantities. This is an important form of *scaffolding* (Greenfield, 1984; Wood, Bruner, & Ross, 1976) that provides children with frameworks for using counting skills even before the counting skills are fully developed.

All of the various classes of story problems described in the now extensive literature on addition and subtraction stories can be included in these early steps toward quantification of the protoquantitative schemas. Research establishing a sequence of difficulty for these problems (see Riley & Greeno, 1988, for a summary and theoretical interpretation) can be used to guide the sequence of introduction. However, there has not been enough research on the deliberate introduction of these classes of problems to strictly constrain an instructional sequence. Indeed, the notion of learning through scaffolded situational participation would argue against very much deliberate sequencing in the introduction of problems. In any group of children, there is likely to be wide variation in ability to solve quantified problems. But if problems are chosen for which the children already have the necessary protoquantitative schemas, all children will be able to engage the problem with some form of mathematical thinking. Some will be able to do it on their own only protoquantitatively—that is, in terms of *more* and *less,* but not *how many.* Others will be able to solve it by directly counting the objects or representations (such as fingers, tick marks, or other manipulatives) of objects in the story. Still others will be able to solve the problems mentally, using number facts and relations between numbers that have by now become familiar for them.

In a class discussion of the problem and various solution strategies, the least developed children will observe others solve the problem quantitatively—through counting or even number relationships—and can be coached through counting solutions themselves. For this to work, some method of making different children's solution methods visible to one another is needed. In several programs (e.g., Cobb et al., 1991; Resnick, Bill, Lesgold, & Leer, 1991), this is accomplished by having children solve the problem privately, then share solutions in small groups, then describe and justify their solutions to the whole class. In this way, several different solutions, each a valid option for the situation, are collected. Children can also be asked to record their own and others' solutions. Figure 7.2, presented earlier, gives an example of the range of solutions that can appear in one day's discussion of a single problem. This further heightens children's awareness of the variety of solutions possible.

Situations for Learning the Mathematics of Numbers and Operators

The mathematics of numbers and operators is not likely to develop informally—at least for most children—because situations required for their development are not part of most children's everyday lives (cf. Davydov & Markova, 1983; Vygotsky, 1978). To develop the competencies associated with the mathematics of numbers and operators, one must participate in situations of reasoning and talking about numbers and their relations and about operators *without immediate reference to counted or measured quantities of material.* That is, numbers and operators must, in the discussion, take on the status of conceptual entities. For most children, such discussions are unlikely to occur except in school; but schools do not, in fact, provide many occasions for this kind of talk. The infrequency of situations for practicing the mathematics of numbers and operators may be why the capacity for such reasoning does not seem to come early or easily to most children.

One approach that appears promising for helping children move toward the mathematics of numbers is encouraging children to use formal notations (equations) to record their invented computational procedures. The formal notation, more than other representations, seems to invite and support talk about numbers and their compositions (Resnick, Bill, & Lesgold, in press). By using a standard mathematical notation to record conversations carried out in ordinary language and rooted in well-understood problem situations, the formalisms take on a meaning that is directly linked to children's mathematical intuitions. At the same time, the formal notation serves as a public display that itself can be discussed and analyzed. For this to work well for the youngest children, careful attention to linking the formalism to the "semantics" of the problem situation will be needed. Otherwise, the formal notation risks becoming nothing more than a set of syntactic rules. Figure 7.7 shows how one very effective teacher solves this problem in her teacher-led discussions. In the analyzed episode, the children (second graders) are proposing a solution to a story problem. The teacher carefully links elements of the proposed solution to the actual physical material involved in the story (a tray of cupcakes) and an overhead schematic of the tray. Only after the referential meaning of each number has been carefully established is the number written into the equation. (See Leinhardt, 1987, for another example of a teacher carefully relating different representations of numbers but without the use of the equation formalism.)

As this example illustrates, very special forms of classroom discourse are likely to be necessary to help children move from the mathematics of quantity to the mathematics of number and operators. This requirement does not diminish—indeed, may become more pressing—as children ad-

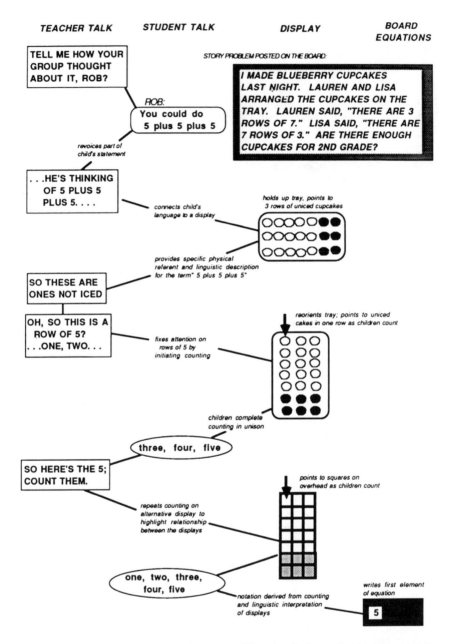

FIG. 7.7. Part of a class discussion of a story problem showing how referents for an equation are developed. From "Thinking in Arithmetic Class" by L. B. Resnick, V. Bill, S. Lesgold, and M. Leer, 1991, in B. Means, C. Chelemer, and M. S. Knapp (Eds.), *Teaching Advanced Skills to At-Risk Students: Views from Research and Practice* (pp. 40–41), San Francisco: Jossey-Bass. Copyright by Jossey-Bass, Inc.

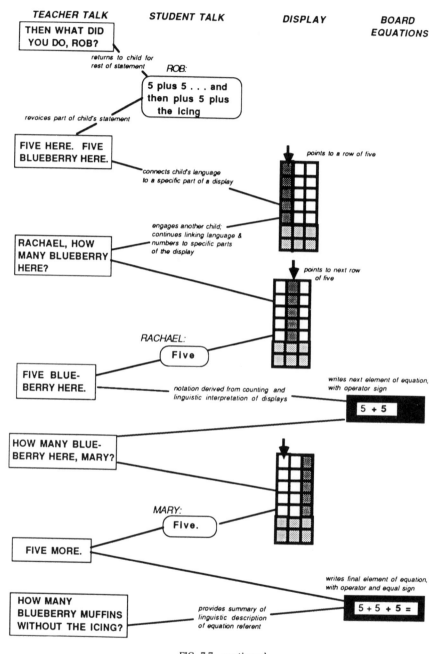

FIG. 7.7., continued

vance through the grades and the mathematical ideas under consideration become more varied and complex. Lampert (e.g., 1986, 1990), whose work is based on detailed analysis of her own teaching, has provided the most detailed accounts of the forms that meaning-centered classroom mathematics discourse can take. She engages children in extended discussions of concepts and computational procedures, such as multidigit multiplication, long division, fractions, and decimals, using multiple representations of the problems under discussion. Her choices of problems and representations, as well as style of questioning and using children's contributions, are designed to bring out children's interpretations of mathematical concepts and nudge them toward more complete and correct ideas while at the same time promoting a general conception of mathematics as a domain in which children themselves can construct reasonable ideas. Schoenfeld (in press) has developed a similar theme but with a focus on older students and the development of more formal mathematical reasoning. He speaks of *enculturation* into the mathematical ways of thinking by virtue of extended participation in certain forms of discourse and reasoning (cf. Collins et al., 1989; Resnick, 1988). In his own teaching (Schoenfeld, 1985), he has developed forms of discourse designed to enculturate students into the forms of reasoning associated with proof. These analyses illustrate the complexity of the instructional task for which, at the moment at least, only general guidelines and no absolute prescriptions can be offered.

The first property of number likely to become accessible to children on the basis of their quantified part/whole schema is the property of numbers as *additive compositions* of other numbers. Knowledge of this property will take substantial time to develop, because in the mathematics of numbers, the composition property applies not to numbers in general but to each individual number. Furthermore, each number has many compositions in which it participates. All of these characteristics of individual numbers must be learned. A strategy likely to help children toward an appreciation of the compositional properties of numbers is to introduce the whole additive "conceptual field" (cf. Vergnaud, 1982) as quickly as possible. This would mean introducing the full range of addition and subtraction problem situations, large numbers treated as compositions of smaller numbers, and regrouping as a special application of the part/whole schema in the first few months of school rather than sequentially over 2 or 3 years. Doing so requires accepting the idea that full mastery (speed, flexibility of procedures, articulate explanations) of elements of the system need not be expected at first but will develop over many months of practice.

A program of this kind constitutes a major challenge to an idea that has been widely accepted in educational research and practice. This is the notion of learning hierarchies, specifically that it is necessary for learners to master simpler components before they try to learn complex skills. According to theories of hierarchical and mastery learning, children should, for example, thoroughly master single-digit addition and subtraction before attempting multidigit procedures, and they should be able to perform multidigit arithmetic without regrouping smoothly before they tackle the complexities of regrouping. The alternative is a *distributed* curriculum in which multiple topics are developed all year long, with increasing levels of sophistication and demand rather than a strictly sequential curriculum. To convey the flavor of the process, Fig. 7.8 shows the range of topics planned for a single month in the second grade program taught by Victoria Bill (Resnick, Bill, & Lesgold, in press). All topics shown are treated at changing levels of sophistication and demand throughout the school year. This distributed curriculum discourages decontextualized teaching of components of arithmetic skill. It encourages children to draw on their existing knowledge framework (the protoquantitative schemas) to interpret advanced material, while gradually building computational fluency and moving from the mathematics of quantities toward the mathematics of numbers and, eventually, the mathematics of operators and relations.

Domain	Specific Content
Reading/Writing Numerals	0-9,999
Set Counting	0-9,999
Addition	2- and 3-digit regrouping, Basic Facts 20
Subtraction	2-digit renaming, Basic Facts 20
Word Problems	Addition, Subtraction, Multiplication
Problem Solving	Work backward, Solve an easier problem, Patterns
Estimation	Quantities, Strategies, Length
Ratio/Proportion	Scaling up, Scaling down
Statistics/Probability	Scaling up, Scaling down, Spinner (1/4), Dice (1/16), 3 graphs
Multiplication	Array (2, 4 tables), Allocation, Equal groupings
Division	Oral problems involving sharing sets equally
Measurement	Arbitrary units
Decimals	Money
Fractions	Parts of whole, Parts of set, Equivalent pieces
Telling Time	To hour, To half hour
Geometry	Rectangle, square (properties)
Negative Integers	Ones, tens

FIG. 7.8. Topic coverage planned for a single month of Grade 2. From "Developing Thinking Abilities in Arithmetic Class" by L. B. Resnick with V. Bill and S. Lesgold, in A. Demetriou, M. Shayer, and A. Efklides (Eds.), *The Modern Theories of Cognitive Development Go to School* (in press), London: Routledge. Copyright by Routledge. Reprinted by permission.

CONCLUDING COMMENTS

The theory of situated learning presented here is emergent and developing. Efforts to apply it systematically to designing instruction are very recent. Thus, only a few examples of instructional programs are available for analysis, and because several of these began with other theoretical perspectives, they are only now being reinterpreted in light of the new theory. I have stressed forms of instruction that rely heavily on teacher-led group discussions as a means of developing particular forms of mathematical discourse. Others (e.g., Gardner, 1991), drawing on a compatible theory of cognitive development embedded in culturally specific forms of knowing and behaving, have suggested a quite different approach to teaching, one based heavily on individual projects and portfolios of work developed by children. Until now, these two forms of instruction—teacher-led discussions aimed at developing forms of disciplinary discourse and extended student-developed projects—have been developed by different groups of researchers who interact little with one another. It is striking that the project approach has not been much explored as a means of teaching fundamental mathematics ideas. Perhaps the two approaches are each uniquely suited to different disciplines. Equally as likely, teaching in all or most disciplines could benefit from some carefully planned mixture of the two. Exploring such possibilities is likely to be one of the most interesting and productive developments of the next several years of instructional research.

ACKNOWLEDGMENT

This paper constitutes a five-year report (1985–1990) on the Formal and Intuitive Knowledge in School Mathematics project of the Center for the Study of Learning, supported by the Office of Educational Research and Improvement at the Learning Research and Development Center, University of Pittsburgh.

REFERENCES

Bachelard, G. (1980). *La formation de l'esprit scientifique*. Paris: Librairie Philosophique J. Vrin.

Brown, J. S., & Burton, R. R. (1978). Diagnostic models for procedural bugs in basic mathematical skills. *Cognitive Science, 2,* 155–192.

424

Brown, J. S., Collins, A., & Duguid, P. (1989). Situated cognition and the culture of learning. *Educational Researcher, 18*(1), 32–42.

Brown, J. S., & VanLehn, K. (1980). Repair theory: A generative theory of bugs in procedural skills. *Cognitive Science, 4,* 379–426.

Brown, J. S., & VanLehn, K. (1982). Towards a generative theory of "bugs." In T. P. Carpenter, J. M. Moser, & T. A. Romberg (Eds.), *Addition and subtraction: A cognitive perspective* (pp. 117–135). Hillsdale, NJ: Lawrence Erlbaum Associates.

Burton, R. R. (1982). Diagnosing bugs in a simple procedural skill. In D. Sleeman & J. S. Brown (Eds.), *Intelligent tutoring systems* (pp. 157–183). New York: Academic Press.

Buswell, G. T. (1926). *Diagnostic studies in arithmetic.* Chicago: University of Chicago Press.

Carpenter, T. P., Fennema, E., & Peterson, P. L. (1987). Cognitively guided instruction: The application of cognitive and instructional science to mathematics curriculum development. In I. Wirszup & R. Streit (Eds.), *Developments in school mathematics education around the world* (pp. 397–417). Reston, VA: National Council of Teachers of Mathematics.

Carpenter, T. P., Fennema, E., Peterson, P. L., Chiang, C. P., & Loef, M. (1989). Using knowledge of children's mathematics thinking in classroom teaching: An experimental study. *American Educational Research Journal, 26*(4), 499–531.

Carpenter, T. P., & Moser, J. M. (1984). The acquisition of addition and subtraction concepts. In R. Lesh & M. Landau (Eds.), *Acquisition of mathematics: Concepts and processes* (pp. 7–44). New York: Academic Press.

Carraher, T. N. (1990). Negative numbers without the minus sign. *Proceedings of the Fourteenth International Group for the Psychology of Mathematics Education Conference, 3,* 223–230.

Carraher, T. N., Carraher, D. W., & Schliemann, A. D. (1985). Mathematics in the streets and in schools. *British Journal of Developmental Psychology, 3,* 21–29.

Case, R. (1985). *Intellectual development: Birth to adulthood.* New York: Academic Press.

Case, R., & Griffin, S. (1990). Child cognitive development: The role of central conceptual structures in the development of scientific and social thought. In C.-A. Hauert (Ed.), *Advances in psychology—Developmental psychology: Cognitive, perceptuo-motor, and neurological perspectives* (pp. 193–230). Amsterdam: Elsevier Science Publishers.

Cobb, P., Wood, T., & Yackel, E. (1990, April). *Coping with the complexity of classroom life.* Paper presented at the meeting of the American Educational Research Association, Boston.

Cobb, P., Wood, T., Yackel, E., Nicholls, J., Wheatley, G., Trigatti, B., & Perlwitz, M. (1991). Assessment of a problem-centered second-grade mathematics project. *Journal for Research in Mathematics Education, 22*(1), 3–29.

Collins, A., Brown, J. S., & Newman, S. E. (1989). Cognitive apprenticeship: Teaching the crafts of reading, writing, and mathematics. In L. B. Resnick (Ed.), *Knowing, learning, and instruction: Essays in honor of Robert Glaser* (pp. 453–494). Hillsdale, NJ: Lawrence Erlbaum Associates.

Cox, L. S. (1975). Systematic errors in the four vertical algorithms in normal and handicapped populations. *Journal for Research in Mathematics Education, 6,* 202–220.

Davis, R. B. (1979). Analysis of student answers to signed numbers arithmetic problems. *Journal of Children's Mathematical Behavior, 2*(2), 114–130.

Davis, R. B. (1984). *Learning mathematics: The cognitive science approach to mathematics education.* Norwood, NJ: Ablex.

Davydov, V. V., & Markova, A. K. (1983). A concept of educational activity for schoolchildren. *Soviet Psychology, 21,* 50–76.

deKleer, J., & Brown, J. S. (1985). A qualitative physics based on confluences. In D. Bobrow

(Ed.), *Qualitative reasoning about physical systems* (pp. 7–84). Amsterdam: Elsevier Science Publishers.

Donaldson, M. (1978). *Children's minds.* New York: Norton.

Fantz, R. L., & Fagan, J. F., III. (1975). Visual attention of size and number of pattern details by term and preterm infants during the first six months. *Child Development, 16,* 3–18.

Fischer, K. W. (1980). A theory of cognitive development: The control and construction of hierarchies of skills. *Psychological Review, 87,* 477–531.

Forbus, K. (1985). Qualitative process theory. In D. Bobrow (Ed.), *Qualitative reasoning about physical systems* (pp. 7–84). Amsterdam: Elsevier Science Publishers.

Fuson, K. C. (1988). *Children's counting and concepts of number.* New York: Springer-Verlag.

Fuson, K. C. (1990). Conceptual structures for multiunit numbers: Implications for learning and teaching multidigit addition, subtraction, and place value. *Cognition and Instruction, 7,* 343–403.

Fuson, K. C., Lyons, B., Pergament, G., Hall, J., & Kwon, Y. (1988). Effects of collection terms on class-inclusion and on number tasks. *Cognitive Psychology, 20,* 96–120.

Gardner, H. (1991). *The unschooled mind: How children think and how schools should teach.* New York: Basic Books.

Gelman, R., & Evans, D. W. (1981, April). *Understanding infinity: A beginning inquiry.* Paper presented at the meeting of the Society for Research in Child Development, Boston.

Gelman, R., & Gallistel, C. R. (1978). *The child's understanding of number.* Cambridge, MA: Harvard University Press.

Ginsburg, H. P. (1977). *Children's arithmetic: The learning process.* New York: Van Nostrand.

Ginsburg, H. P. (1982). The development of addition in the contexts of culture, social class, and race. In T. P. Carpenter, J. M. Moser, & T. A. Romberg (Eds.), *Addition and subtraction: A cognitive perspective* (pp. 191–210). Hillsdale, NJ: Lawrence Erlbaum Associates.

Ginsburg, H. P., & Allardice, B. S. (1984). Children's difficulties with school mathematics. In B. Rogoff & J. Lave (Eds.), *Everyday cognition: Its development in social context* (pp. 194–219). Cambridge, MA: Harvard University Press.

Ginsburg, H. P., Posner, J. K., & Russell, R. L. (1981). The development of mental addition in schooled and unschooled people: A cross-cultural study. *Journal of Cross-cultural Psychology, 12,* 163–178.

Ginsburg, H. P., & Russell, R. L. (1981). Social class and racial influences on early mathematical thinking. *Monographs of the Society for Research in Child Development, 44*(6, serial no. 193).

Greenfield, P. M. (1984). A theory of the teacher in the learning activities of everyday life. In B. Rogoff & J. Lave (Eds.), *Everyday cognition: Its development in social context* (pp. 117–138). Cambridge, MA: Harvard University Press.

Greeno, J. G. (1983). Conceptual entities. In D. Gentner & A. L. Stevens (Eds.), *Mental models* (pp. 227–252). Hillsdale, NJ: Lawrence Erlbaum Associates.

Greeno, J. G., Riley, M. S., & Gelman, R. (1984). Young children's counting and understanding of principles. *Cognitive Psychology, 16,* 94–143.

Groen, G. J., & Resnick, L. B. (1977). Can preschool children invent addition algorithms? *Journal of Educational Psychology, 69*(6), 645–652.

Hiebert, J., & Wearne, D. (1985). A model of students' decimal computation procedures. *Cognition and Instruction, 2,* 175–205.

Janvier, C. (1985). Comparison of models aimed at teaching signed integers. *Proceedings of the Ninth International Conference for the Psychology of Mathematics Education, 1,* 135–140.

Kaput, J. J. (1987a). Representation systems and mathematics. In C. Janvier (Ed.), *Problems of representation in the teaching and learning of mathematics* (pp. 19–32). Hillsdale, NJ: Lawrence Erlbaum Associates.

Kaput, J. J. (1987b). Towards a theory of symbol use in mathematics. In C. Janvier (Ed.), *Problems of representation in the teaching and learning of mathematics* (pp. 159–196). Hillsdale, NJ: Lawrence Erlbaum Associates.

Kozulin, A. (1984). *Psychology in Utopia: Toward a social history of Soviet psychology.* Cambridge, MA: MIT Press.

Lampert, M. (1986). Knowing, doing, and teaching multiplication. *Cognition and Instruction, 3*, 305–342.

Lampert, M. (1989). Choosing and using mathematical tools in classroom discourse. In J. Brophy (Ed.), *Advances in research on learning* (Vol. 1, pp. 223–264). Greenwich, CT: JAI Press.

Lampert, M. (1990). When the problem is not the question and the solution is not the answer: Mathematical knowing and teaching. *American Educational Research Journal, 27*, 29–64.

Lave, J. (1988). *Cognition in practice: Mind, mathematics, and culture in everyday life.* Cambridge: Cambridge University Press.

Lave, J. (1991). Situating learning in communities of practice. In L. B. Resnick, J. Levine, & S. D. Teasley (Eds.), *Perspectives on socially shared cognition* (pp. 63–82). Washington, DC: American Psychological Association.

Lave, J., & Wenger, E. (1990). *Situated learning: Legitimate peripheral participation* (IRL Report No. 90-0013). Palo Alto, CA: Institute for Research on Learning.

Lawler, R. W. (1981). The progressive construction of mind. *Cognitive Science, 5*, 1–30.

Leinhardt, G. (1987). Development of an expert explanation: An analysis of a sequence of subtraction lessons. *Cognition and Instruction, 4*, 225–282.

Leonard, F., & Sackur-Grisvard, C. (1987). Necessity of a triple approach of misconceptions of students: Example of teaching directed numbers. (I) Theoretical analysis. *Proceedings of Psychology of Mathematics Education, 11* (Vol. 2, pp. 444–448).

Markman, E. M., & Siebert, J. (1976). Classes and collections: Internal organization and resulting holistic properties. *Cognitive Psychology, 8*, 516–577.

Matz, M. (1982). Towards a process model for high school algebra errors. In D. Sleeman & J. S. Brown (Eds.), *Intelligent tutoring systems* (pp. 25–50). New York: Academic Press.

Mukhopadhyay, S., Resnick, L. B., & Schauble, L. (1990, July). *Social sense making in mathematics: Children's ideas of negative numbers.* Paper presented at the Psychology of Mathematics Education Conference, Mexico City.

Murray, J. C. (1985). Children's informal conceptions of integer arithmetic. *Proceedings of Psychology of Mathematics Education, 9* (pp. 147–153).

Nesher, P. (1986). Are mathematical understanding and algorithmic performance related? *For the Learning of Mathematics, 6*(3), 2–9.

Nesher, P. (1989). Microworlds in mathematical education: A pedagogical realism. In L. B. Resnick (Ed.), *Knowing, learning, and instruction: Essays in honor of Robert Glaser* (pp. 187–215). Hillsdale, NJ: Lawrence Erlbaum Associates.

Ohlsson, S. (1987). Sense and reference in the design of interactive illustrations for rational numbers. In R. Lawler & M. Yazdani (Eds.), *Artificial intelligence and education* (pp. 307–344). Norwood, NJ: Ablex.

Peled, I. (1989, July). *Signed numbers: Formal and informal knowledge.* Paper presented at the meeting of the Psychology of Mathematics Education, Paris.

Peled, I., Mukhopadhyay, S., & Resnick, L. B. (1988, November). *Formal and informal sources of mental models for negative numbers.* Presented at the 29th Annual Meeting of the Psychonomics Society, Chicago.

Piaget, J. (1952). *The origins of intelligence in children.* New York: International Universities Press.

Putnam, R. T., deBettencourt, L. U., & Leinhardt, G. (1990). Understanding of derived fact strategies in addition and subtraction. *Cognition and Instruction, 7*(3), 245–285.

Putnam, R. T., Lampert, M., & Peterson, P. L. (1990). Alternative perspectives on knowing mathematics in elementary school. *Review of Research in Education, 16,* 57–150.

Resnick, L. B. (1982). Syntax and semantics in learning to subtract. In T. P. Carpenter, J. M. Moser, & T. A. Romberg (Eds.), *Addition and subtraction: A cognitive perspective* (pp. 136–155). Hillsdale, NJ: Lawrence Erlbaum Associates.

Resnick, L. B. (1983). A developmental theory of number understanding. In H. P. Ginsburg (Ed.), *The development of mathematical thinking* (pp. 109–151). New York: Academic Press.

Resnick, L. B. (1986). The development of mathematical intuition. In M. Perlmutter (Ed.), *Perspectives on intellectual development: The Minnesota Symposia on Child Psychology* (Vol. 19, pp. 159–194). Hillsdale, NJ: Lawrence Erlbaum Associates.

Resnick, L. B. (1988). Treating mathematics as an ill-structured discipline. In R. I. Charles & E. A. Silver (Eds.), *The teaching and assessing of mathematical problem solving* (pp. 32–60). Hillsdale, NJ/Reston, VA: Lawrence Erlbaum Associates./National Council of Teachers of Mathematics.

Resnick, L. B., Bill, V., & Lesgold, S. (in press). Developing thinking abilities in arithmetic class. In A. Demetriou, M. Shayer, & A. Efklides (Eds.), *The modern theories of cognitive development go to school.* London: Routledge.

Resnick, L. B., Bill, V., Lesgold, S., & Leer, M. (1991). Thinking in arithmetic class. In B. Means, C. Chelemer, & M. S. Knapp (Eds.), *Teaching advanced skills to at-risk students: Views from research and practice* (pp. 27–53). San Francisco: Jossey Bass.

Resnick, L. B., Cauzinille-Marmeche, E., & Mathieu, J. (1987). Understanding algebra. In J. A. Sloboda & D. Rogers (Eds.), *Cognitive processes in mathematics* (pp. 169–203). New York: Oxford University Press.

Resnick, L. B., & Greeno, J. G. (1990). *Conceptual growth of number and quantity.* Unpublished manuscript, University of Pittsburgh, Learning Research and Development Center.

Resnick, L. B., Nesher, P., Leonard, F., Magone, M., Omanson, S., & Peled, I. (1989). Conceptual bases of arithmetic errors: The case of decimal fractions. *Journal for Research in Mathematics Education, 20*(1), 8–27.

Resnick, L. B., & Omanson, S. F. (1987). Learning to understand arithmetic. In R. Glaser (Ed.), *Advances in instructional psychology* (Vol. 3, pp. 41–95). Hillsdale, NJ: Lawrence Erlbaum Associates.

Resnick, L. B., & Singer, J. (in press). Protoquantitative origins of ratio reasoning. In T. P. Carpenter, E. Fennema, and T. A. Romberg (Eds.), *Rational numbers: An integration of research.* Hillsdale, NJ: Lawrence Erlbaum Associates.

Riley, M. S., & Greeno, J. G. (1988). Developmental analysis of understanding language about quantities and of solving problems. *Cognition and Instruction, 5,* 49–101.

Sackur-Grisvard, C., & Leonard, F. (1985). Intermediate cognitive organization in the process of learning a mathematical concept: The order of positive decimal numbers. *Cognition and Instruction, 2,* 157–174.

Saxe, G. B. (1988). The mathematics of child street vendors. *Child Development, 59,* 1415–1425.

Schliemann, A., & Acioly, N. (1989). Mathematic knowledge developed at work: The contribution of practice versus the contribution of schooling. *Cognition and Instruction, 6,* 185–221.

Schoenfeld, A. H. (1985). *Mathematical problem solving.* New York: Academic Press.

Schoenfeld, A. H. (in press). Learning to think mathematically: Problem solving, metacognition, and sense-making in mathematics. In D. Grouws (Ed.), *Handbook for research in mathematics teaching and learning.* New York: Macmillan.

Schwartz, J. L. (1988). Intensive quantity and referent transforming arithmetic operations. In M. Behr & J. Hiebert (Eds.), *Number concepts and operators in the middle grades* (pp. 41–52). Reston, VA: National Council of Teachers of Mathematics and Hillsdale, NJ: Lawrence Erlbaum Associates.

Scribner, S. (1984). Studying working intelligence. In B. Rogoff & J. Lave (Eds.), *Everyday cognition: Its development in social context* (pp. 9–40). Cambridge, MA: Harvard University Press.

Scribner, S., & Cole, M. (1981). *The psychology of literacy.* Cambridge, MA: Harvard University Press.

Sleeman, D. (1984). An attempt to understand students' understanding of basic algebra. *Cognitive Science, 8,* 387–412.

Sophian, C. (1987). Early developments in children's use of counting to solve quantitative problems. *Cognition and Instruction, 4,* 61–90.

Steffe, L. P., Cobb, P., & von Glasersfeld, E. (1988). *Construction of arithmetical meanings and strategies.* New York: Springer-Verlag.

Steffe, L. P., von Glasersfeld, E., Richards, J., & Cobb, P. (1983). *Children's counting types: Philosophy, theory, and applications.* New York: Praeger.

Suchman, L. A. (1987). *Plans and situated actions: The problem of human-machine communication.* Cambridge: Cambridge University Press.

Svenson, O., & Hedenborg, M. L. (1979). Strategies used by children when solving simple subtractions. *Acta Psychologica, 43,* 1–13.

VanLehn, K. (1990). *Mind Bugs.* Cambridge, MA: MIT Press.

Vergnaud, G. (1982). A classification of cognitive tasks and operators of thought involved in addition and subtraction problems. In T. Carpenter, J. Moser, & T. Romberg (Eds.), *Addition and subtraction: A cognitive perspective* (pp. 39–59). Hillsdale, NJ: Lawrence Erlbaum Associates.

Vygotsky, L. S. (1978). *Mind in society: The development of higher psychological processes.* Cambridge, MA: Harvard University Press.

Wood, D., Bruner, J. S., & Ross, G. (1976). The role of tutoring in problem solving. *Journal of Child Psychology and Psychiatry, 17,* 89–100.

Woods, S. S., Resnick, L. B., & Groen, G. J. (1975). An experimental test of five process models for subtraction. *Journal of Educational Psychology, 67*(1), 17–21.

Young, R. M., & O'Shea, T. (1981). Errors in children's subtraction. *Cognitive Science, 5,* 153–177.

Epilogue

Marilyn Rauth
Lovely Billups
American Federation of Teachers

Contents

A central question now facing the teaching profession is, "What steps are necessary to bring new research and clinical knowledge to life in schools?". Emerging from research are new insights on how children learn mathematics. The implications of such insights for practice, however, are not self-evident. This book represents an important step in bringing researchers and teachers together to work toward improving mathematics learning and instruction in elementary and middle school classrooms.

Although they were written primarily for other researchers, the chapters in this volume were informed by interactions between the chapter authors and teachers. As described in the Preface, these conversations evolved out of a National Science Foundation-funded collaboration between the American Federation of Teachers (AFT) and the Learning Research and Development Center (LRDC). One goal of this collaborative partnership was to bring researchers and teachers together to discuss critical syntheses and disseminate current research on mathematics teaching and learning. The focus was on combining current research and the wisdom of practice. A second goal was to develop and demonstrate a form of communication between researchers in mathematics learning and the teaching profession

431

that would yield both improved practice and stronger programs of research. *Analysis of Arithmetic for Mathematics Teaching* represents one part of the collaboration: the formal research voice. The formal voice of the teachers exists in a collection of teacher training materials entitled *Thinking Mathematics* (Bodenhausen et al., in preparation).

In this epilogue, we discuss the roles that teachers and the AFT have played in this collaborative project to blend current research on learning and teaching mathematics with the clinical wisdom of practicing teachers. We begin with a brief history of the AFT's Educational Research and Dissemination Network (ER&D), which is serving as an important means for sharing with other teachers what has been learned about mathematics teaching from this project. We then consider teachers' roles in the AFT/LRDC collaboration, particularly their development of *Thinking Mathematics,* a synthesis for teachers of key ideas and findings of the research. We also discuss what teachers and researchers have learned and how their beliefs about mathematics research and about mathematics teaching and learning have changed as a result of their participation in this collaborative project. We close with thoughts about the value of collaboration and increased teacher professionalism in efforts to reform mathematics teaching in our schools.

THE AFT'S EDUCATIONAL RESEARCH
AND DISSEMINATION NETWORK

The AFT began concerning itself with educational research and its dissemination over a decade ago when AFT President Albert Shanker cautioned teachers that their claim to professionalism is seriously undermined by the lack of a recognized knowledge base for teaching. He pointed out that, although there is never likely to be one correct approach to teaching, it makes sense that some approaches in given situations are likely to be more effective than others. Formal research on teaching and educational practices provides an important source of knowledge about teaching methods and practices, not to be applied blindly but to be used along with teachers' more local experience-based knowledge of their students and instructional contexts to make educational judgments and decisions. In debates over methods, Shanker asserted, teachers' professional freedom rests on the assumption that each teacher has a repertoire of strategies and is capable of explaining the reasons for choosing one approach over another. As professionals, teachers have a responsibility to understand and explain why they choose particular methods; educational research should provide part of this justification.

The ER&D program grew out of these concerns, first as a small pilot project and subsequently as a national dissemination network with sites in hundreds of school districts throughout the country, including most urban systems. In these local sites, teachers come together to review educational research findings and use them as tools to reflect on their practice. Often, research findings are revealing and open doors to new teaching strategies. Just as often, teachers have found that the process has provided affirmations of effective practice that they have had in place but could not support in documented fashion. By helping teachers take advantage of both research and their own teaching experience, the ER&D program has provided a process for teachers to engage in ongoing inquiry and assessment and to come to think about teaching practice in entirely new ways. Recipient of the American Educational Research Association's Professional Service Award, the ER&D program has received national recognition for bridging the gap between research and practice. Evaluations of the program have documented success in increasing teachers' morale and intellectual stimulation, as well as changes in their classroom practice (Gee, 1985).

Prior to the AFT/LRDC collaboration, the ER&D program focused on research on effective teaching and instructional practices not tied to specific subject matter domains. This research included classroom management, teacher feedback and praise, interactive teaching, cooperative small-group learning, and communications in multicultural classrooms. Research in domains such as these was synthesized and "translated" by visiting practitioners, experienced teachers placed in residence at research-oriented universities for 1 year. These visiting practitioners prepared summaries of research literature along with materials and activities to be used by small groups of teachers throughout the ER&D network. Other teachers were then selected and prepared by the national AFT to become familiar with the materials to share with other teachers. These Local Site Coordinators would try out these new approaches in their classrooms and subsequently train additional teachers to share information formally and informally with teachers and principals in their buildings. The key to this entire effort is that it is voluntary for teachers and conducted in a nonthreatening, nonevaluative atmosphere. The research is treated as a tool of inquiry, not as a set of prescriptions, thus fostering teachers' developing ownership for the ideas, as well as inviting the adoption of them based on the teachers' own clinical knowledge.

THE AFT/LRDC COLLABORATION

The collaboration with LRDC represents the AFT's first attempt to focus on research that deals with the learning and teaching of specific subject-matter content. The project has extended the idea of having teachers visit university settings to a more highly collaborative interaction between teachers and researchers, thus merging insights of research with those of the clinical wisdom of teachers. Researchers (the authors of the chapters in this book) focused on synthesizing current research in the learning and teaching of mathematics. Experienced teachers from across the country who represent different instructional settings—elementary, secondary, self-contained or rotatory classrooms, Chapter 1, urban, and rural—came to Pittsburgh to work with LRDC research staff to investigate the research in the chapters, interact with eminent researchers, including the authors of the chapters in this book, and develop a training process and resources that would be disseminated through the existing ER&D network. The underlying theme of the program that is emerging from this ongoing collaborative relationship is that educators can make substantial changes in the way mathematics is taught by reconsidering some basic assumptions.

A number of basic ideas about teaching mathematics emerged from the teachers' consideration and critiques of the research syntheses and other research. These have been incorporated into the *Thinking Mathematics* approach (Bodenhausen et al., in prep.). These include the need for teachers to:

- build from students' intuitive knowledge;
- establish a strong number sense through counting, estimation, use of benchmarks, and understanding the effects of operations;
- base instruction on situational story problems;
- use manipulatives and other representations to build up meaningful representation of problem situations;
- develop students' capability to describe and support their mathematical thinking;
- accept multiple correct solutions paths;
- use a variety of teaching strategies;
- balance conceptual and procedural learning;
- use ongoing and new types of assessment to guide instruction;
- adjust the curriculum timeline.

The teachers have given substance to these general principles of *Thinking Mathematics* through several resource manuals that include a rationale for rethinking mathematics instruction, a discussion of the principles on which *Thinking Mathematics* is based and their instructional implications, an overview of how children learn mathematics, a glossary of terms, references, appendices, and training activities, and materials to be used by teacher trainers.

The *Thinking Mathematics* materials draw heavily from the research synthesized in this volume, but with direct consideration of how the ideas might influence classroom practice. Thus, the AFT teachers working on the project have brought knowledge from their own teaching to blend with the research perspectives. This idea of teachers contributing substantially to developing a knowledge base for their professional practice is an important one for the AFT, which strives to help strengthen the teaching profession and the school restructuring movement in significant ways. Being in a unique position to help the teaching profession rethink traditional ideas, the union throughout this project has promoted open-mindedness and reconceptualization of traditional school practice and constructs. This has been done in the context of the belief that current practice falls far short of helping students at all levels learn mathematics with sufficient understanding and focus on applying what they learn, but with the understanding that radical change will not happen overnight. Current practices that prove effective in light of new research should be retained, and colleagues sharing the new knowledge must start with teachers where they are to help them rethink their perspectives on teaching and learning.

In addition to a commitment to insuring teachers have a voice in the developing knowledge base of their profession, the AFT has brought to the collaborative project means for reaching teachers with these ideas about mathematics teaching. The existing ER&D network will bring the research perspectives and the *Thinking Mathematics* materials to groups of teachers across the country. The AFT national office recruits local teacher union support for the piloting of *Thinking Mathematics*. Local union presidents then approach their boards of education and administration, requesting that their school systems collaboratively participate as pilot sites. As a result, *Thinking Mathematics* is not an isolated pilot project. Instead, it is linked to the teaching profession nationally through AFT, to the research community through LRDC, and to individual and networked teachers through teacher-prepared professional development materials and procedures.

WHAT THE COLLABORATION
HAS MEANT FOR TEACHERS

An important goal of the AFT/LRDC collaboration has been to facilitate ongoing communication between communities of researchers and practitioners. The sustained interchanges that have been systematically documented between experienced teachers and researchers working together have provided opportunities for researchers to consider their ideas in the context of practice and for teachers to come to think about research in new ways. Having direct contact with researchers greatly affected project teachers' dispositions and beliefs about the value of educational research and the function of the university in contributing to a knowledge base for teaching. Formal presentations of these findings were made at the 1990 annual meeting of the American Educational Research Association (Bickel & Hattrup, 1990; Billups & Rauth, 1990; Gill, 1990; Leinhardt & Grover, 1990).

Project teachers, for example, have related that they were once skeptical, at best, about the value of educational research for informing teaching practice. Teachers have attributed these feelings to the gap they found between the theories espoused in their own teacher education programs and the reality of teaching and learning encountered in schools. The university, in their minds, remained far removed from the classroom. Through close examination of research and interaction with researchers, however, project teachers have modified their views. They have been impressed by the number of hours researchers studying mathematics learning have spent observing students and teachers in classrooms, their grasp of the realities and constraints of schooling, and their efforts to go beyond artificial laboratory settings to study learning in classroom environments. The resulting credibility of the researchers has helped to facilitate communication among teachers and researchers, with the discourse becoming more constructive and useful over time.

An important aspect of developing communication and collaboration among the project teachers, chapter authors, and LRDC researchers has been each group's adapting to the other's language and norms for interacting—learning to interact productively with one another both intellectually and socially. Teachers note that they initially reacted to researchers' interactions with dismay. The persistent questioning and challenging of ideas that pervades researchers' discourse violates accepted norms in the world of teaching. In the typical school culture, such exchanges might be perceived as comparable to personal attacks rather than a means of extending knowledge. The teachers have related that they have come to recognize that questioning and challenging ideas is an important part of establishing a community of inquiry and learning. They are willing to share their ideas and accept challenges to them, coming to view this kind of collaboration in the university setting as a model of discourse among professional teachers.

As the project teachers have become more comfortable expressing and challenging ideas, trying to bring together the findings and insights of researchers with their own clinical wisdom, many of them have questioned and changed their own teaching practice. For example, one participating teacher from an urban setting described the following changes in her teaching and thinking:

> The collaborative's first summer changed my thinking so radically that I put my textbook aside, abandoned long pages of practice, worked to develop patience for a new role as teacher, and made a deliberate effort to listen more carefully to students and try to understand the source and direction of their thoughts. Process became at least as important as the right answer. Students' self-esteem blossomed, and math became fun.
>
> Before being involved in the collaboration, mathematics was a one-track, "memorize the rules" discipline. Computation was the cornerstone and prime goal for every child. When I grew to understand that there are many paths in math, that there was a way children could relate to those cold numbers and that children didn't necessarily think the way adults did, my teaching changed as well as what I valued children being able to do. While both I and my children enjoyed math, there was also evidence of understanding and thinking I hadn't seen before.

Another veteran teacher who has had some experience in working with mathematics research observed a consequence of the collaborative experience. She recalls that, normally, teachers go to inservice workshops to pick up new ideas and activities that relate to the classroom. But because these ideas are filtered through the teacher's experienced-based knowledge and beliefs, they are often incorporated into existing practice, and little change is evident. In general, teachers continue to teach as they were taught. The project also has helped teachers develop skills to synthesize research, to know what to look for, and when, in evaluating research or practice, and to use research to support or challenge their own ideas. In addition to developing increased awareness of the benefits of research, teachers are gaining the confidence to question specific research findings. The collaborative project has brought into focus for teachers the value of research in looking beyond one's own narrow world to make professional decisions that could result in real change in practice.

One teacher came to the project already accustomed to teaching in a collaborative, problem-focused way. Her unique examples of specific lessons and materials enhanced the discussion between the collaborating partners. In turn, she gained a system of language and evidence to empower her with mechanisms of communication that could reach a wider audience.

Another project teacher from an inner-city school district came to LRDC with a record and reputation as a highly successful teacher, with her students scoring well above average on achievement tests. Yet, by her own admission, her traditional thinking about and approaches to teaching mathematics changed dramatically as a result of examining research on children's learning of mathematics. This teacher's experience posed a powerful question to the group: How are people moved to change even though they are perceived as successful? To fail to address this question creates the impression that adjustments to mathematics instruction are remedial in nature and are useful only for unsuccessful teachers. Nothing could be further from the truth.

WHAT NEXT?

We believe that although much remains to be learned, the emerging research on mathematics learning and teaching represented in the chapters of this book is sufficient to warrant radical rethinking of the goals and methods of mathematics instruction. Effecting meaningful change through efforts like *Thinking Mathematics* will be an arduous task, complicated by inappropriate assessment techniques, inflexible schooling structures, inadequate resources, insufficient time for staff development, and deeply entrenched attitudes and beliefs. Evidence of school- and system-wide reform initiatives stemming from the implementation of the *Thinking Mathematics* approach in the classroom is emerging. A primary school teacher, noting improvements in her students' attitudes about mathematics and marvelling at the array of multiple solutions to problems developed by her students, began to worry about what would happen when these students moved on to a traditional classroom setting in the next grade. This single concern has opened discussions on team teaching and teacher-advancing-with-class proposals. As more grades become involved, an element of school restructuring takes form. This development is of specific importance to the AFT, whose organizational imperatives are invested in the school restructuring movement, focusing on the role of the teacher in shaping school change. Because the changes required are massive and extend widely across educational and political arenas, success will depend on increasing collaboration and cooperation among many groups, including researchers, teachers, teacher educators, administrators, and teacher unions. Meaningful mathematics reform is likely to depend not only on establishing more broadly based professional dialogues but on creating an atmosphere of professional activism as well, where a hallmark of this activism is teachers' commitment to working together with others to establish a richer and more systematic knowledge base for their practice.

Teachers, through their integration of research and experience-based knowledge and their increasing contacts with the research community, are moving toward this sort of professionalism. They will be in a position to require researchers, policy makers, administrators, and teacher educators to listen to their thoughts, build on their intuitive beliefs, and ground reforms in their narrative of experiences. The AFT/LRDC collaborative and its products, *Analysis of Arithmetic for Mathematics Teaching* and *Thinking Mathematics* are important examples of this movement.

REFERENCES

Bickel, W. E., & Hattrup, R. A. (1990). Restructuring Practitioner-Researcher Dialogue in Education: A Case Study of Institutional Collaboration to Enhance Knowledge Use. In M. Rauth (Chair), *Restructuring practitioner-researcher collaboration: Changing dissemination to dialog.* Symposium conducted and the annual meeting of the American Educational Research Association, Boston, MA.

Billups, L., & Rauth, M. (1990). The role of the profession in creating, interpreting and disseminating knowledge. In M. Rauth (Chair), *Restructuring practitioner-researcher collaboration: Changing dissemination to dialog.* Symposium conducted at the annual meeting of the American Educational Research Association, Boston, MA.

Bodenhausen, J., Denhart, N., Gill, A., Kaduce, M., Miller, M., Grover, B., Resnick, L., Leinhardt, G., Bill, V., Rauth, M., & Billups, L. (in preparation). *Thinking mathematics: Vol. 1. Foundations.* Washington, DC: American Federation of Teachers.

Bodenhausen, J., Denhart, N., Gill, A., Kaduce, M., Miller, M., Grover, B., Resnick, L., Leinhardt, G., Bill, V., Rauth, M., & Billups, L. (in preparation). *Thinking mathematics: Vol. 1T. Training modules.* Washington, DC: American Federation of Teachers.

Bodenhausen, J., Denhart, N., Gill, A., Kaduce, M., Miller, M., Grover, B., Hojnacki, S., Resnick, L., Leinhardt, G., Bill, V., & Billups, L. (in preparation). *Thinking mathematics: Vol. 2. Extensions.* Washington, DC: American Federation of Teachers.

Bodenhausen, J., Denhart, N., Gill, A., Kaduce, M., Miller, M., Grover, B., Hojnacki, S., Resnick, L., Leinhardt, G., Bill, V., & Billups, L. (in preparation). *Thinking mathematics: Vol. 2T. Training modules.* Washington, DC: American Federation of Teachers.

Gee, E. W. (1985). *Applying effective instruction research findings in elementary teacher education programs: A cross-site analysis of influencing factors.* Paper presented at the annual meeting of the American Educational Research Association, Chicago, IL.

Gill, A. (1990). Teacher-researcher dialog: A basis for knowledge in the classroom. In M. Rauth (Chair), *Restructuring practitioner-researcher collaboration: Changing dissemination to dialog.* Symposium conducted at the annual meeting of the American Educational Research Association, Boston, MA.

Leinhardt, G., & Grover, B. W. (1990). Interpreting research for practice: A case of collaboration. In M. Rauth (Chair), *Restructuring practitioner-researcher collaboration: Changing dissemination to dialog.* Symposium conducted at the annual meeting of the American Educational Research Association, Boston, MA.

Author Index

SUBJECT INDEX

A

Abstract knowledge, mathematics as, *see also* Entities, mathematical, 395
Addition and subtraction, 53–178
  additive inverse, *see* Addition and subtraction, complementarity of
  basic facts, *see* Addition and subtraction, sums and differences
  borrowing, *see* Regrouping
  complementarity of, 100, 386
  instructional research, 77, 118–130, 155–171
  instructional recommendations, 78–89, 116, 130–135, 416–418, 171–177
  multidigit, *see also* Number, multidigit; Regrouping, 135–177
    in current textbooks, 148–151
    embodiments for, *see* Representations, concrete objects as
    students' knowledge of, *see also* Procedures, buggy, 151–155
    subtraction, 375, 390
  number line, 116
  solution strategies, 7
    derived fact, 96, 110, 119–121, 386
    developmental levels of, 81–113
    instructional research on, 118–129
    sums and differences, 70–72, 118–129, 386

  ten-structured methods, 126–129
  word problems, 64–70, 75, 101–113, 418
  situations, *see* Addition and subtraction, word problems
  sums and differences
    in current textbooks, 74, 77, 113–115
    memory of, 71, 96
    solution strategies, *see* Addition and subtraction, solution strategies, sums and differences
    students' knowledge of, 117
    with written symbols, 70–72, 74
  word problems, 7, 64–70, 101–113, 190–193, 410
    change, 64–68, 74, 80, 101–112, 191
    combine, *see* Addition and subtraction, word problems, put together
    compare, 69, 80, 101–112, 191, 412
    in current textbooks, 74–76, 80, 115
    equalize, 101–103, 107, 384
    put together, 66, 80, 191
    solution strategies, *see* Addition and subtraction, solution strategies, word problems
    in Soviet textbooks, 27, 74, 115
    structural variables in, 191
Additive composition, *see* Number, composition and decomposition of
Additive structures, 226, 422

449